Lecture Notes in Computer Science 4753

Commenced Publication in 1973
Founding and Former Series Editors:
Gerhard Goos, Juris Hartmanis, and Jan van Leeuwen

Erik Duval   Ralf Klamma   Martin Wolpers (Eds.)

Creating New Learning Experiences on a Global Scale

Second European Conference
on Technology Enhanced Learning, EC-TEL 2007
Crete, Greece, September 2007
Proceedings

 Springer

Volume Editors

Erik Duval
Katholieke Universiteit Leuven and Ariadne Foundation
Departement Computerwetenschappen
Celestijnenlaan 200A, 3001 Leuven, Belgium
E-mail: erik.duval@cs.kuleuven.be

Ralf Klamma
RWTH Aachen University, Informatik 5
Ahornstr. 55, 52056 Aachen, Germany
E-mail: klamma@informatik.rwth-aachen.de

Martin Wolpers
Katholieke Universiteit Leuven, Departement Computerwetenschappen
Celestijnenlaan 200A, 3001 Leuven, Belgium
E-mail: martin.wolpers@cs.kuleuven.be

Library of Congress Control Number: 2007934980

CR Subject Classification (1998): K.3, I.2.6, H.5, J.1

LNCS Sublibrary: SL 2 – Programming and Software Engineering

ISSN	0302-9743
ISBN-10	3-540-75194-7 Springer Berlin Heidelberg New York
ISBN-13	978-3-540-75194-6 Springer Berlin Heidelberg New York

Springer is a part of Springer Science+Business Media

springer.com

© Springer-Verlag Berlin Heidelberg 2007
Printed in Germany

Typesetting: Camera-ready by author, data conversion by Scientific Publishing Services, Chennai, India
Printed on acid-free paper   SPIN: 12163779   06/3180   5 4 3 2 1 0

Preface

You are holding more than 500 pages of combined wisdom on Technology Enhanced Learning (TEL) in your hands!

With the advance of metadata, standards, learning objects, Web 2.0 approaches to rip, mix and burn learning, wikis, blogs, syndication, user-generated content, Web-based video, games and the ubiquitous availability of computing devices we can and have to offer more flexible learning services on a global scale. As one of the objectives of the 7th Framework Program of the European Commission puts it: We need "responsive environments for technology-enhanced learning that motivate, engage and inspire learners, and which are embedded in the business processes and human resources management systems of organizations." An important challenge is to form a bridge between informal learning strategies of the knowledge society and formal competence development programs of organizations.

After the success of EC-TEL 2006, the 2nd European Conference on Technology Enhanced Learning (EC-TEL 2007) provided a unique forum for all research related to technology enhanced learning, including its interactions with knowledge management, business processes and work environments. This is a competitive and broad forum for technology enhanced learning research in Europe and world-wide through specialized workshops, the doctoral consortium and the main conference. EC-TEL 2007 provided unique networking possibilities for participating researchers throughout the week and included project meetings and discussions for ongoing and new research activities supported by the European Commission.

Again this year, the TEL community was very active sending high-quality contributions on established and new research topics. We received 116 submissions. All of these were reviewed by at least three reviewers – many thanks to both the authors and the reviewers! Really!

After detailed deliberations, we selected 28 submissions as full papers: this means that EC-TEL 2007 had an acceptance rate of less than 25%! That is just one indicator of how this conference has already established itself in its second year as one of the main research venues in the field.

We also selected 18 submissions as short papers. Even though these papers did not pass the most strenuous scientific review process, each one of them included an idea that was certainly relevant to the community and we wanted to make sure that this idea could spread...

The program also included keynote presentations by two sources of inspiration for the field:

- Bruce Sterling, professor at the European Graduate School and "visionary in residence" at the Art Center College of Design in Pasadena, California is one of the early visionaries of the "Internet of Things." His famous speeches introduced new memes (like spime) that continue to be an inspiration for many researchers. Bruce is also a science fiction writer (http://blog.wired.com/sterling)!

- Hermann Maurer is professor of computer science at the Technical University Graz in Austria, with an impressive list of achievements in the form of numerous papers, books, companies and patents. Hermann is one of the pioneers of Technology Enhanced Learning in Europe and a widely acclaimed and sought after speaker. He is also a science fiction writer (http://www.iicm.tugraz.at/maurer)!

Other highlights in the program included:

- Global Experiences: The GLOBE consortium of learning repository networks (http://globe-info.org/) used its panel session to hold a public dialogue on your requirements for share and reuse and how it can address them. This will be a unique opportunity to learn more about this global community of repositories.
- Industry Meets Research: there was almost a full day of industrial sessions, where participants from IMC, BT, EADS, IDS, Synergetics and Giunti presented their experiences and lessons learned.
- Research funding opportunities: Several high-ranking officials from the European Commission presented their views on technology enhanced learning, with a specific focus on research funding, the 7th Framework Program calls and other funding instruments.

Preceding the program, a number of high-profile workshops and a doctoral consortium took place. The workshops focused on specific topics in a more interactive fashion. The doctoral consortium was a unique opportunity for advanced PhD students to present their work in progress in front of experienced and reputable researchers in the field of technology enhanced learning.

In conclusion, it may be useful to remind ourselves how important this work on technology enhanced learning is: if we get better at learning, we "get better at getting better." If we can help people to learn in more effective or efficient ways, then they will be able to deal better with many of the serious and difficult problems of our times.

We feel very privileged to have worked with all of you in making progress in the domain of technology enhanced learning – thank YOU!

And thank you also to our sponsors and media partners, like IMC, L3S, EA-TEL, PRO-LC, Know-Center and elearning Europe!

September 2007

Wolfgang Nejdl
Erik Duval
Ralf Klamma
Barbara Kieslinger
Martin Wolpers

Organization

EC-Tel 2007 was organized by the Professional Learning Cluster (PRO-LC) and the European Association of Technology Enhanced Learning (EA-TEL).

Executive Committee

General Chair	Wolfgang Nejdl (Research Center L3S and University of Hannover, Germany)
Program Chairs	Erik Duval (K.U. Leuven, Belgium and Ariadne Foundation)
	Ralf Klamma (RWTH Aachen University, Germany)
Publicity Chair	Barbara Kieslinger (ZSI, Austria)
Workshop Chair	Frans van Assche (EUN, Belgium)
Local Organization Chair	Constantin Makropoulos (NCSR Demokritos, Greece)
Organizing Chair	Martin Wolpers (K.U. Leuven, Belgium)
Industrial Session Chair	Volker Zimmermann (IMC AG, Germany)
Doctoral Consortium Chairs	Katherine Maillet (INT, France)
	Tomaz Klobucar (IJS, Slovenia)
	Denis Gilet (EPFL, Switzerland)

Supporting Organization Committee

Alberto Moyano Sánchez (RWTH Aachen University, Germany)
Helen Zampaka (NCSR Demokritos, Greece)
Stella Dalamaga (NCSR Demokritos, Greece)

Program Committee

Heidrun Allert, Austria
Lora Aroyo, The Netherlands
Kalina Bontcheva, UK
Peter Brusilovsky, USA
Jean-Pierre David, France
Stefano Ceri, Italy
Alexandra Cristea, UK
Paul De Bra, The Netherlands
Peter Dolog, Denmark
Dieter Euler, Switzerland

Magda Fayek, Egypt
Monique Grandbastien, France
Jim Greer, Canada
Kai Hakkarainen, Finland
Marek Hatala, Canada
Caroline Haythornthwaite, USA
Friedrich Hesse, Germany
Nicola Henze, Germany
Christopher Hoadley, USA
Geert-Jan Houben, Belgium

Matthias Jarke, Germany
Nikos Karacapilidis, Greece
Barbara Kieslinger, Austria
Kinshuk, Canada
Paul Kirschner, The Netherlands
Rob Koper, The Netherlands
Harald Kosch, Germany
Stefanie Lindstaedt, Austria
Peter Loos, Germany
Stephan Lukosch, Germany
Erica Melis, Germany
Riichiro Mizoguchi, Japan
Wolfgang Nejdl, Germany
Gustaf Neumann, Austria
Claus Pahl, Ireland
Gilbert Paquette, Canada
Brigitte de La Passardière, France
Juan Quemada, Spain
Dan Rehak, USA
Christoph Rensing, Germany

Griff Richards, Canada
Jeremy Roschelle, USA
Demetrios Sampson, Greece
Vittorio Scarano, Italy
Mark Schlager, USA
Peter Scott, UK
Marcus Specht, The Netherlands
Pierre Tchounikine, France
Klaus Tochtermann, Austria
Gottfried Vossen, Germany
Vincent Wade, Ireland
Gerhard Weber, Germany
Stephan Weibelzahl, Ireland
David Wiley, USA
Ingo Wolf, Germany
Barbara Wasson, Norway
Martin Wolpers, Belgium
Volker Wulf, Germany
Volker Zimmermann, Germany

Sponsoring Institutions

Platinum Sponsors

Best Paper Award Sponsor

Silver Sponsor

Table of Contents

Full Papers

From a Specific Tracking Framework to an Open and Standardized
Attention Environment Based on Attention.XML 1
    Julien Broisin and Philippe Vidal

Cross-System Validation of Engagement Prediction from Log Files 14
    Mihaela Cocea and Stephan Weibelzahl

Exploiting Policies in an Open Infrastructure for Lifelong Learning 26
    Juri L. De Coi, Philipp Kärger, Arne W. Koesling, and
    Daniel Olmedilla

Proposing the Underlying Causes That Lead to the Trainee's Erroneous
Actions to the Trainer 41
    Naïma El-Kechaï and Christophe Després

Smart Indicators on Learning Interactions 56
    Christian Glahn, Marcus Specht, and Rob Koper

A Qualitative and Quantitative Evaluation of Adaptive Authoring of
Adaptive Hypermedia 71
    Maurice Hendrix and Alexandra Cristea

Making Sense of IMS Learning Design Level B: From Specification to
Intuitive Modeling Software 86
    Susanne Heyer, Petra Oberhuemer, Stefan Zander, and
    Philipp Prenner

Using MotSaRT to Support On-Line Teachers in Student Motivation .. 101
    Teresa Hurley and Stephan Weibelzahl

LOCO-Analyst: A Tool for Raising Teachers' Awareness in Online
Learning Environments 112
    Jelena Jovanović, Dragan Gašević, Christopher Brooks,
    Vladan Devedžić, and Marek Hatala

Supporting Incremental Formalization in Collaborative Learning
Environments 127
    Nikos Karacapilidis and Manolis Tzagarakis

Exploiting Preference Queries for Searching Learning Resources 143
    Fabian Abel, Eelco Herder, Philipp Kärger, Daniel Olmedilla, and
    Wolf Siberski

How Do People Learn at the Workplace? Investigating Four Workplace
Learning Assumptions 158
  Jose Kooken, Tobias Ley, and Robert de Hoog

E-Learning on the Social Semantic Information Sources 172
  Sebastian Ryszard Kruk, Adam Gzella, Jarosław Dobrzański,
  Bill McDaniel, and Tomasz Woroniecki

Capturing, Management and Utilization of Lifecycle Information for
Learning Resources... 187
  Lasse Lehmann, Tomas Hildebrandt, Christoph Rensing, and
  Ralf Steinmetz

Improving the Search for Learning Objects with Keywords and
Ontologies 202
  Lothar Lemnitzer, Cristina Vertan, Alex Killing, Kiril Simov,
  Diane Evans, Dan Cristea, and Paola Monachesi

Exploiting Context Information for Identification of Relevant Experts
in Collaborative Workplace-Embedded E-Learning Environments....... 217
  Robert Lokaiczyk, Eicke Godehardt, Andreas Faatz, Manuel Goertz,
  Andrea Kienle, Martin Wessner, and Armin Ulbrich

Negotiating the Path from Curriculum Design to E-Learning Course
Delivery: A Study of Critical Success Factors for Instructional Systems
Design.. 232
  Maggie McPherson and Miguel Baptista-Nunes

A Game-Based Adaptive Unit of Learning with IMS Learning Design
and <e-Adventure> 247
  Pablo Moreno-Ger, Daniel Burgos, José Luis Sierra, and
  Baltasar Fernández-Manjón

Relevance Ranking Metrics for Learning Objects 262
  Xavier Ochoa and Erik Duval

Supporting Attention in Learning Environments: Attention Support
Services, and Information Management 277
  Claudia Roda and Thierry Nabeth

Personalized Links Recommendation Based on Data Mining in
Adaptive Educational Hypermedia Systems 292
  Cristóbal Romero, Sebastián Ventura, Jose Antonio Delgado, and
  Paul De Bra

A Media Theoretical Approach to Technology Enhanced Learning in
Non-technical Disciplines.. 307
  Marc Spaniol, Yiwei Cao, and Ralf Klamma

MACE – Enriching Architectural Learning Objects for Experience
Multiplication   322
    Moritz Stefaner, Elisa Dalla Vecchia, Massimiliano Condotta,
    Martin Wolpers, Marcus Specht, Stefan Apelt, and Erik Duval

ICT Supported Interorganizational Knowledge-Creation: Application
of Change Laboratory   337
    Seppo Toikka

Theoretical Framework of the iCampFolio – New Approach to
Comparison and Selection of Systems and Tools for Learning
Purposes   349
    Terje Väljataga, Kai Pata, Mart Laanpere, and Mauri Kaipainen

Evaluating the ALOCOM Approach for Scalable Content
Repurposing   364
    Katrien Verbert and Erik Duval

Community Tools for Repurposing Learning Objects   378
    Chu Wang, Kate Dickens, Hugh C. Davis, and Gary Wills

Building Domain Ontologies from Text for Educational Purposes   393
    Amal Zouaq, Roger Nkambou, and Claude Frasson

Short Papers

Organizational Learning at University   408
    Marie-Hélène Abel, Dominique Lenne, and Adeline Leblanc

FAsTA: A Folksonomy-Based Automatic Metadata Generator   414
    Hend S. Al-Khalifa and Hugh C. Davis

The Macro Design as an Own Task in WBT Production: Ideas,
Concepts and a Tool   420
    Abdelhak Aqqal, Christoph Rensing, and Ralf Steinmetz

Reasoning-Based Curriculum Sequencing and Validation: Integration in
a Service-Oriented Architecture   426
    Matteo Baldoni, Cristina Baroglio, Ingo Brunkhorst,
    Elisa Marengo, and Viviana Patti

Curriculum Model Checking: Declarative Representation and
Verification of Properties   432
    Matteo Baldoni and Elisa Marengo

Workplace Learning: How We Keep Track of Relevant Information   438
    Kerstin Bischoff, Eelco Herder, and Wolfgang Nejdl

A Digital Library Framework for Reusing e-Learning Video
Documents   444
   Paolo Bolettieri, Fabrizio Falchi, Claudio Gennaro, and
   Fausto Rabitti

A Situation-Based Delivery of Learning Resources in Pervasive
Learning   450
   Amel Bouzeghoub, Kien Ngoc Do, and Claire Lecocq

Web Services Plug-in to Implement *"Dispositives"* on Web 2.0
Applications   457
   Pierre-André Caron

Flexible Processes in Project-Centred Learning   463
   Stefano Ceri, Maristella Matera, Alessandro Raffio, and
   Howard Spoelstra

A p2p Framework for Interacting with Learning Objects   469
   Andrea Clematis, Paola Forcheri, and Alfonso Quarati

A Framework for the Automatic Generation of Algorithm Animations
Based on Design Techniques   475
   Luis Fernández-Muñoz, Antonio Pérez-Carrasco,
   J. Ángel Velázquez-Iturbide, and Jaime Urquiza-Fuentes

The Development of TE-Cap: An Assistance Environment for Online
Tutors   481
   Elise Garrot, Sébastien George, and Patrick Prévôt

KnowledgeBus – An Architecture to Support Intelligent and Flexible
Knowledge Management   487
   Knut Hinkelmann, Johannes Magenheim, Wolfgang Reinhardt,
   Tobias Nelkner, Kai Holzweißig, and Michael Mlynarski

IKASYS: Using Mobile Devices for Memorization and Training
Activities   493
   Naiara Maya, Ana Urrutia, Oihan Odriozola, Josune Gereka,
   Ana Arruarte, and Jon Ander Elorriaga

Pedagogical Validation of Courseware   499
   Mark Melia and Claus Pahl

Improving Authoring-by-Aggregation and Using Aggregation Context
for Query Expansion   506
   Marek Meyer, Christoph Rensing, and Ralf Steinmetz

Questioning Usability of Visual Instructional Design Languages: The
Case of CPM   511
   Nodenot Thierry

Author Index   517

From a Specific Tracking Framework
to an Open and Standardized Attention Environment
Based on Attention.XML

Julien Broisin and Philippe Vidal

Institut de Recherche en Informatique de Toulouse,
118 route de Narbonne, 31062 Toulouse Cedex 9, France
{broisin,vidal}@irit.fr

Abstract. This paper addresses the challenge of providing users with personalized learning resources by gathering and sharing attention information. Starting from our previous works related to the tracking of learning objects' exploitation within learning systems, we suggest here an extension of this framework based on the Attention.XML standard to offer the opportunity to share attention information between various and heterogeneous applications. An Attention.XML service based on web technologies has been elaborated and integrated within the existing architecture, thus offering standardization and availability to the global environment. This approach makes it easy to integrate existing learning environments and tools, and thus facilitates the generation of attention data specific to these applications.

Keywords: personal learning environment, attention metadata, Attention.XML, information model.

1 Introduction

Providing personalized data or resources currently represents an important challenge, as the number of tools and initiatives dealing with this topic illustrates it. A step towards the achievement of this process consists in collecting, analyzing and exploiting attention information resulting from users' activities. Attention data are bits of information about how users choose to interact with software, be it accessible through the internet or not [4], and make it possible to provide tools and services able to find out what a user is paying attention to. Quality and relevance of attention information are critical. Indeed, the more systems know about users' interests, the more they will deliver relevant and personalized resources to end-users. It is thus necessary to design and deploy open systems able to manage and share attention information with others environments.

The authors set up in [5] and [6] a tracking framework based on a model driven approach together with an object oriented database that provides a means to capture usage information about Learning Objects (LO) from different Learning Management Systems (LMS) and Learning Object Repositories (LOR) in order to analyze the usage patterns of the users through a management application. However, the

E. Duval, R. Klamma, and M. Wolpers (Eds.): EC-TEL 2007, LNCS 4753, pp. 1–13, 2007.

non-standard format of attention information stored into this database limits the possible use of this information by others systems, because existing applications should be reprogrammed to understand and treat information. Moreover, some standardization efforts dealing with attention are being led within the computer community. Among these efforts, is the Attention.XML standard [3] suggested by Steve Gillmor that allows to keep tracking on what users visit, read, download, etc. This standardization will lead to the opportunity to share attention information between various and heterogeneous applications.

To contribute to this objective, this paper shows how our tracking framework can be exploited to generate attention metadata that are compliant with the Attention.XML standard. For readability reasons, the section 2 reminds the model driven approach and points out information available within this framework, whereas section 3 introduces Attention.XML by presenting its organization and properties. The mapping between our information model and Attention.XML elements, together with some extensions that enrich the collection and management of attention metadata are exposed in the section 4. The implementation of this mapping is depicted in section 5 and validates the theoretical proposition. Finally we conclude before exposing some further works.

2 Our Model Driven Approach

In order to offer a mechanism for tracking learning objects' usage and users' activities within heterogeneous systems such as LMS or LOR, we suggested a model driven approach based on the Common Information Model (CIM) suggested by the Domain Management Task Force [13]. This last exploits object concepts like classes, attributes, methods, associations or inheritance for systems, networks and applications management, and is characterized by an extensible approach that allows to build generic models related to a domain more specific to a project or environment.

Therefore, we built an information model according to the CIM specification and describing the systems, resources and users interacting within a learning environment. The model is divided in two generic models collaborating together: the environment model focuses on learning systems and resources, whereas the user model aims at describing users and theirs interactions with these systems and resources. Figure 1 shows the resulting information model.

The aim of this paper is not to precisely describe classes and associations depicted in Figure 1; we invite lecturers to read [5] and [6] for more details about the whole information model. Basically, the user model aims at describing identity, roles and accounts of users, whereas the environment model allows to retrieve:

- Resources stored within a specific learning object repository, or the LOR hosting a given learning object.
- Courseware deployed within a specific learning management system, together with the LMS integrating a given courseware.
- Labels (or comments) and ratings characterizing a specific resource, and learning objects or courseware that are associated with a given label or rate level.

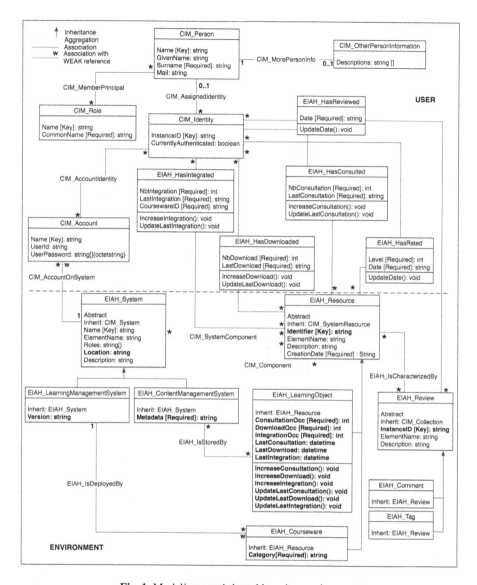

Fig. 1. Modeling a web-based learning environment

The various relations defined between the environment and user models offer the opportunity to get:

- Labels or comments specified by a specific user, and all users having specified a given label or comment.
- Users having consulted metadata related to a specific resource, or the set of resources that have been consulted by a given user.

- Users having downloaded a specific learning object, together with the set of resources that have been downloaded by a given user.
- Users having imported an external learning object (a resource stored within a LOR) into one or several courseware, and learning objects imported by a specific user.
- Rate levels defined by a specific user to learning objects, and the set of users having attributed a rate level to a given resource.

In order to benefit from the information model, we implemented the Web-Based Enterprise Management (WBEM) architecture [15] that supports the CIM concepts (see Figure 2). According to actions executed by users within a LMS or a LOR and involving a learning object (consultation, download, integration within a courseware, indexation), the matching classes and properties are instanciated/updated and stored within a CIM repository through an entity called the CIM Object Manager (CIMOM) and responsible for interactions with this repository. A graphical management application based on web technologies then sends queries to the CIMOM for providing users with tracking information that translates their activities related to learning objects.

CIM is natively dedicated to systems, networks and applications management, but it is not elaborated to share and give access to its management information. Indeed, such information is critical for an organization and does not have to be available to others systems and users. In our context, sharing attention information constitutes the main objective. Therefore, we have to open our tracking framework in order to give access to the CIM repository to others existing applications interested in attention information. This open solution is based on the Attention.XML standard presented in the next section.

3 The Attention.XML Standard

According to the Technorati Developers Wiki [3], Attention.XML is an open standard that helps users keep track of what they have read, what they are spending time on, or what they should be paying attention to. Attention.XML specially focuses on Really Simple Syndication (RSS) feeds and blogs. In Attention.XML all feeds and posts that users read are being tracked. For each post or feed it tracks how much time users spend on it, the last time they checked it and an optional rating of the information. Based on this it should be possible to advice users about information they should read and spend time on.

Table 1 illustrates elements included within the Attention.XML schema. We won't detail each property of this framework here, instead we invite the reader to visit [3] for a full explanation.

The choice of focusing on blogs and feeds is probably due to the huge number of blogs available on the web and resulting from the development of Internet. In addition, more and more web sites offer the opportunity to read news as RSS feeds, and most common email clients such as Thunderbird make it possible for users to subscribe to feeds. However, the need for attention within the e-learning context has already been highlighted by several projects and researchers. If one could log or maintain a history of users' interests and activities, and convey that back to a web based

Table 1. The Attention.XML schema

Group	Blog/Feed/Site	Post/Item/Page
title	title	Title
	url	permalink/guid
	alturls	Type
	etag	etag
	lastupdated	lastupdated
	dateadded	lastread
	dateremoved	duration
	lastread	followedlinks
	readtimes	rev/votelink
	userfeedtitle	tags
	rel/xfn	
	rev/votelink	
	tags	

system that could provide customized learning objects or resources, this might be quite powerful.

AtGentive [2], a project part of the FP6 framework of the European Community, contributes to this objective and investigates the use of artificial agents for supporting the management of the attention of young or adult learners in the context of individual and collaborative learning environments. The Contextualized Attention Metadata framework [10] outlines the need for Attention.XML metadata to collect and manage rich usage data, and to enhance users' models and feed personalization; this work has also been designed to bring the theoretical bases to bridge the gap between the estimated and the real knowledge in companies [16]. Attention.XML has also been exploited in [11] for providing a meaningful and scalable way to rank or recommend learning material.

To benefit from this standard and become interoperable with systems and approaches mentioned above, a mapping between the information model and the Attention.XML schema detailed in the section has been designed.

4   From the Model to Attention.XML

This section demonstrates how the model described in section 2 can be mapped to the Attention.XML standard. We first focus on the Attention.XML schema that can be built from our native information model, before supplying the model with extensions that make it more compliant with the Attention.XML format. Finally we suggest additional elements to include within the Attention.XML schema in order to bring it suitable properties to e-learning.

4.1   Generating an Attention.XML Schema

The first task to achieve consists in identifying the mapping of Attention.XML entities to classes included in our information model. From the Technorati point of view, a Group item is a set of blogs or feeds. In the e-learning context, an Attention.XML

Group can be associated to an e-learning system such as a learning object repository (*EIAH_ContentManagementSystem*) or a learning management system (*EIAH_LearningManagementSystem*). Depending on the nature of this system, Blog/Feed/Site and Post/Item/Page items are represented by various classes of the information model (see Table 2):

- In the case of a LOR, the Attention.XML Blog/Feed/Site and Post/Item/Page entities will both be mapped to a learning object (*EIAH_LearningObject*). Indeed, a LOR stores learning objects, and a learning object may be built on the aggregation of several LO presenting a smaller granularity.
- In the case of a LMS, the Attention.XML Blog/Feed/Site and the Post/Item/Page entities will respectively be associated to a courseware (*EIAH_Courseware*) and a learning object: a learning management system delivers learning services and trainings that integrate at least one learning object.

Table 2. Mapping between the Attention.XLM entities and classes of the information model

		Blog/Feed/Site	Post/Item/Page
Group	EIAH_ContentManagementSystem	EIAH_Learning Object	EIAH_LearningObject
	EIAH_LearningManagementSystem	EIAH_Courseware	EIAH_LearningObject

Starting from the four classes identified above, the next step that allows to map the information model to the Attention.XML format relates on the identification of some attributes of these classes that match with the properties exposed in Table 1. Let us note that a minimal feed syncing application or service must support, for each type of entities, the following subset of the Attention.XML schema [3]:

- For Group: title
- For Blog/Feed/Site: url, lastread
- For Post/Item/Page: permalink/guid, lastread

Table 3 takes into account the above requirements and provides classes and attributes' names that can be mapped to an Attention.XML element. The *title* element matches with the attribute *ElementName* of the *EIAH_System* and *EIAH_Resource* classes and applies for LOR, LMS, LO and courseware: *EIAH_ContentManagement System* and *EIAH_LearningManagementSystem* both inherit from the *EIAH_System* class, whereas *EIAH_LearningObject* and *EIAH_Courseware* inherit from the *EIAH_ Resource* class.

The *url* element is only required for Blog/Feed/Site entities, that is for learning objects and courseware. This property can be generated by associating the URL of the LOR or LMS (identified by the *Location* attribute of the *EIAH_System* class) and the identifier of the learning object or courseware (identified by the *Identifier* attribute of the *EIAH_Resource* class). The unification of these two parameters then allows to build the specific URL of the learning object or courseware. The *permalink/guid* element [9] is only required for Post/item/Page entities; in our context it relates on learning objects, and it can be generated by exploiting the approach described above.

The *lastread* element is applicable to learning object and courseware, and matches with the *LastConsultation* attribute defined within the *EIAH_HasConsulted* class that gives the last consultation date of a specific resource.

The *dateadded* element within the Attention.XML framework gives the date the Blog/Feed/Site entity has been created. It matches with the *CreationDate* attribute of the *EIAH_Resource* class that indicates the date a learning object or a courseware has been created within a learning system.

Finally, the *rev/votelink* and *tags* elements that apply for Blog/Feed/Site and Post/Item/Pages entities within the Attention.XML framework are respectively associated with the *Level* attribute of the *EIAH_HasRated* class, and the *ElementName* attribute of the *EIAH_Tag* class: through the *EIAH_HasReviewed, EIAH_Review, EIAH_IsCharacterizedBy* and *EIAH_Rescource* classes (see Figure 1), the information model allows users to add tags and/or comments to a specific resource in order to offer a personalized classification of learning resources or courseware, whereas the *EIAH_HasRated* class offers users the opportunity to rate a specific resource.

Table 3. Mapping between the Attention.XML elements and classes' attributes of the information model

Attention.XML elements	Classes of the information model			
	LOR	LMS	LO	Courseware
title	EIAH_System.ElementName	EIAH_System.ElementName	EIAH_Resource.ElementName	EIAH_Resource.ElementName
url	None	None	EIAH_System.Location and EIAH_Resource.Identifier	EIAH_System.Location and EIAH_Resource.Identifier
permalink/guid	None	None	EIAH_System.Location and EIAH_Resource.Identifier	None
lastread	None	None	EIAH_HasConsulted.LastConsultation	EIAH_HasConsulted.LastConsultation
dateadded	None	None	EIAH_LearningObject.CreationDate	EIAH_LearningObject.CreationDate
rev/votelink	None	None	EIAH_HasRated.Level	EIAH_HasRated.Level
tags	None	None	EIAH_Tag.ElementName	EIAH_Tag.ElementName

The mapping presented in this section is directly and natively achieved because it does not require modification of neither the Attention.XML standard, nor our information model. However, some additional elements or properties are available within one of these two approaches, but they don't appear within the other. In order to harmonize these two frameworks and to make them more consistent, the next section focuses on extensions specific to our information model whereas section 4.3 suggests additional elements to include within the Attention.XML format that make it more suitable to e-learning.

4.2 Extending the Information Model

On one hand, the Blog/Feed/Site and Post/Item/Page entities defined within the Attention.XML standard may be described by the *lastupdated* element that indicates the last time the entity was updated. On the other hand, the information model defines some association classes (*EIAH_HasConsulted*, *EIAH_HasDownloaded* and *EIAH_HasIntegrated*) that bind a *CIM_Identity* with an *EIAH_Resource* managed classes in order to:

1. indicate the resources consulted, downloaded or integrated by a specific person
2. offer the possibility to retrieve the various users having consulted, downloaded or integrated a specific resource.

These association classes are respectively composed of the *LastConsultation*, *LastDownload*, and *LastIntegration* attributes (see Figure 1) for indicating the last time a user has consulted, downloaded or integrated a specific resource. Therefore, in order to be able to take into account the *lastupdated* element within the information model, the same approach has been exploited and resulted in the creation of a new association class: *EIAH_HasUpdated*. This association binds a *CIM_Identity* with an *EIAH_Resource* classes and is composed of two attributes:

− *UpdateDates* gives the various dates a user has updated a specific resource.
− *LastUpdate* informs about the last date a user has updated a resource.

Two methods, *UpdateUpdateDates()* and *UpdateLastUpdate()*, are associated to these attributes and allow their modifications.

The *readtimes* element that applies to the Blog/Feed/Site entity gives the various dates a user has read such an entity. Until now, our model offered the opportunity to know the number of consultation of a specific resource through the *NbConsultation* attribute of the *EIAH_HasConsulted* class, but did not specify each consultation dates. To tackle this issue and to increase the mapping between our model and the Attention.XML schema, we (1) added the new attribute *ConsultationDates* as an array of string within the *EIAH_HasConsulted* class, and (2) removed the *NbConsultation* property because it matches with the number of elements included within the *ConsultationDates* attribute. Methods associated to these modifications have also been updated, and the same adjustments have been carried on the *EIAH_HasDownloaded* and *EIAH_HasIntegrated* classes so that each date resulting from an action of a user is now recorded within our information model.

The last modification we brought to the information model relates on the *dateremoved* element defined within the Attention.XML standard and applying to Blog/Feed/Site entities, that is learning objects and courseware in our context. In order to take into account this element, the additional property *RemoveDate* has been introduced as a string within the *EIAH_Resource* class, and gives the date the resource has been removed from a learning system.

4.3 Extending the Attention.XML Format

Among associations mentioned in the previous section, are the *EIAH_HasDownloaded* and *EIAH_HasIntegrated* classes that respectively indicates the number of downloads of a resource on a local host and the number of integrations of a learning object within a courseware, together with (last) dates of download/integration. None of the element defined within the Attention.XML format relates on this aspect because a blog or a web page is never downloaded nor integrated within another web site. Therefore, the Attention.XML format should be extended with the following elements to increase concerns with e-learning:

- *lastdownload*: ISO8601 datetime indicating the last time the user has explicitly downloaded a learning object.
- *downloadtimes*: FIFO queue of ISO8601 datetime indicating each date the user has explicitly downloaded a learning object.
- *lastintegration*: ISO8601 datetime indicating the last time the user has explicitly integrated a learning object within a courseware.
- *integrationtimes*: FIFO queue of ISO8601 datetime indicating each date the user has explicitly integrated a learning object within a courseware.

The reason is not explicitly given on the Technorati web site, but the *lastread* element applies for Blog/Feed/Site and Post/Item/Page entities, whereas the *readtimes* element only concerns the Blog/Feed/Site entity. Thus we suggest to include the *readtimes* element within the Post/Item/Page entity in order to know the dates a user has explicitly read a post, and to add the four new elements listed above within both the Blog/Feed/Site and Post/Item/Page entities.

This section has introduced the mapping between classes defined within the information model and elements specified by the Attention.XML schema. This process makes the data representation of attention information understandable by others applications, but a service has to provide these tools with an access to the data. An Attention.XML service based on web technologies has been elaborated and integrated within the existing architecture, thus validating our approach and offering standardization and availability to the global environment.

5 The Attention.XML Service

An Attention.XML application consists in two main operations: storing Attention.XML metadata into a repository, and retrieving this information as an Attention.XML-compliant file. The first process has already been achieved through the tracking architecture (see Figure 2). Indeed, agents located within learning tools (at this time INES, Moodle and SILO - the tool interfacing with the Ariadne Knowledge Pool System [1]) send tracking information to a CIM entity (the CIM Object Provider) that creates/modifies the matching CIM instances before transferring these information to the CIMOM. Finally, this last stores the CIM instances within the CIM repository.

Therefore, we focus here on the generation of Attention.XML files based on the mapping between our information model and the Attention.XML standard. Section

5.1 exposes the global architecture of the framework together with the associated technologies, whereas section 5.2 gives the specification of the Attention.XML service together an example of an Attention.XML file resulting from the information model.

5.1 Architecture and Support Technologies

The global framework is based on the architecture defined in [5] and [6]. Concerning the tracking components, our approach is mainly composed of the WBEM Services [14], a tool developed by SUN providing a CIMOM (with its object repository) and a client API that allows to query the CIMOM.

The service responsible for the model's mapping and the generation of Attention.XML files is based on web services. This web service, accessible through SOAP requests, has been developed using the Java™ programming language and communicates with the CIM Object Manager using both the client API provided by WBEM Services and the XML/HTTP protocol (see Figure 2). The DMTF implements the HTTP protocol to transport CIM information by encapsulating XML descriptions of CIM information in HTTP data units. At this time, our Attention.XML service comprises a unique method, *attentionQuery()*, described in the next section.

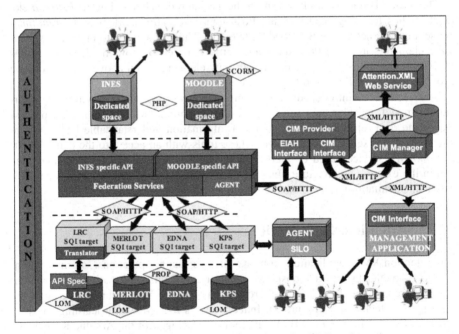

Fig. 2. The tracking architecture and the Attention.XML web service

5.2 The Attention.XML Service: Generating Attention.XML Files

The Technorati web site recommends two main technologies for generating Attention.XML-compliant files:

1. OPML (Outline Processor Markup Language) [12] is an XML-based format that allows exchange of outline-structured information between applications running on different operating systems and environments.
2. XOXO (eXtensible Open XHTML Outlines) [8] is a simple, open outline format written in standard XHTML and suitable for embedding in (X)HTML, Atom, RSS, and arbitrary XML.

For technical, reuse and time-saving objectives, the second technology has been implemented. Indeed, several sample codes are available on the Internet [17] and facilitate the development of Attention.XML frameworks based on XOXO. Thus, starting from the Java™ source code provided in [18], we developed a web service offering the possibility for a user to retrieve its Attention.XML metadata. The specification of the *attentionQuery()* method appears in Table 4: it searches within the CIM repository the identity matching with the *userFirstName* and *userLastName* parameters, then retrieves the various instances this user is involved in, and finally executes the mapping before delivering the matching Attention.XML XOXO file.

Table 4. Specification of the *attentionQuery()* method

Method name	**attentionQuery**	
Return type	String	
Parameters	Name	Type
	userFirstName	String
	userLastName	String
Fault	INVALID_USER_FIRST_NAME	
	INVALID_USER_LAST_NAME	
	METHOD_FAILURE	

The XOXO file bellow illustrates a very simple result of the invocation of the *attentionQuery()* method: the user sending the request has only consulted the metadata of one learning object stored within the Ariadne Knowledge Pool System.

```
<ol class="xoxo">
  <li>
    <a
href="http://ariadne.cs.kuleuven.be/silo2006/">ARIADNE
Knowledge Pool System</a>
    <dl>
      <dt>items</dt>
      <dd>
        <ol>
          <li>
            <a
href="http://ariadne.cs.kuleuven.be/silo2006/ShowDescri
ption.do?ID=CS_LKP_v_3.1_nr_64327">Attention Metadata:
Collection and Management<a>
              <dl>
                <dt>lastread</dt>
                <dd>2007-03-16T00:00:00Z</dd>
```

```
            <dt>dateadded</dt>
            <dd>2006-07-29T00:00:00Z</dd>
            <dt>lastupdated</dt>
            <dd>2006-07-29T00:00:00Z</dd>
            <dt>rev/votelink</dt>
            <dd>agree</dd>
            <dt>readtimes</dt>
            <dd>2006-07-29T00:00:00Z;2007-01-
   14T00:00:00Z;2007-03-16T00:00:00Z</dd>
            <dt>tags</dt>
            <dd>Attention</dd>
         </dl>
      </li>
     </ol>
    </dd>
   </dl>
  </li>
 </ol>
```

The attention service has just been achieved; bugs have been identified and corrected, and we expect to provide a beta version of this service in the next three months. The *attentionQuery()* method currently produces attention data dealing with learning objects, it is not able to generate attention information related to courseware yet. Indeed, this feature requires the development of an additional agent responsible for tracking users' activities within courseware that are most often specific to a given LMS. However, some work is in progress to develop an agent specific to the well-known LMS Moodle.

6 Conclusions and Further Works

We presented in this paper a tracking environment that offers the opportunity to share attention information between various and heterogeneous applications by exploiting the Attention.XML standard. Until now, this tracking framework based on an object oriented approach didn't offer the opportunity to share information because data representations were compliant with a specific model. Now the framework conforms to the Attention.XML standard, thus bringing compatibility and interoperability with a large number of additional applications based on this open standard. It is thus possible to share attention information related to users activities and interests dealing with learning objects, and provide a means to combine information coming from various applications for providing users with more specific and relevant data and resources.

The information model suggested here is extensible and allows to easily integrate existing learning environment. Indeed, in order to build and provide Attention.XML metadata, the model mainly exploits two abstract classes; one for modeling systems, another for representing resources. These classes can thus be specialized to meet the requirements and specifications of any application or tool; at this time, learning object repositories and learning management systems specialize the system class, whereas learning objects and courseware inherit from the resource class. Therefore, if the specifications of a system such as an authoring tool are integrated within the information model, the generation of Attention.XML metadata will be achieved using the approach described in this paper and will not require any additional modification or development; the only work to perform consists in modeling the system that needs to be integrated within the framework.

As future work, we plan to build RSS feeds by exploiting attention information as source of feeds. Edu_RSS [7] suggests such a system and retrieves weblog RSS feeds dealing with educational technology from across the web and stores them into a central database. Starting from attention information recorded within the object oriented database, we want to generate RSS feeds for providing users with a mechanism that allows to automatically be aware of new existing learning material. Users could subscribe to learning objects matching with their preferences, and thus wouldn't need to search for learning objects anymore. This evolution would also reinforce the standardized and open position of the global attention framework.

References

1. Ariadne Foundation (2005), http://www.ariadne-eu.org
2. AtGentive: Attentive Agents for Collaborative Learners, http://www.atgentive.com/
3. Attention.XML, Attention.XML specifications http://developers.technorati.com/wiki/attentionxml
4. Belizki, J., Costache, S., Nejdl, W.: Application Independent Metadata Generation. In: International ACM Workshop on Contextualized Attention Metadata: Collecting, Managing and Exploiting of Rich Usage Information (2006)
5. Broisin, J., Vidal, P., Duval, E.: A Model driven Approach for the Management of Learning Objects' Usage. In: Intelligent, Interactive, Learning Object Repositories Network (2005)
6. Broisin, J., Vidal, P., Sibilla, M.: A Management Framework Based On A Model Driven Approach For Tracking User Activities In A Web-Based Learning Environment. In: World Conference on Educational Multimedia, Hypermedia & Telecommunications (2006)
7. Edu_RSS, http://www.downes.ca/xml/edu_rss.htm
8. eXtensible Open XHTML Outlines, http://microformats.org/wiki/xoxo
9. Identifying Atom, http://www.xml.com/lpt/a/2004/08/18/pilgrim.html
10. Najjar, J., Wolpers, M., Duval, E.: Attention Metadata: Collection and Management. In: WWW2006 workshop on Logging Traces of Web Activity: The Mechanics of Data Collection (2006)
11. Ochoa, X., Duval, E.: Use of Contextualized Attention Metadata for Ranking and Recommending Learning Objects. In: International ACM Workshop on Contextualized Attention Metadata: Collecting, Managing and Exploiting of Rich Usage Information (2006)
12. Outline Processor Markup Language, http://www.opml.org/
13. Systems Management: Common Information Model. Open Group Technical Standard C804, DMTF, ISBN: 1-85912-255-8 (1998)
14. WBEM Services, http://wbemservices.sourceforge.net/
15. Web-Based Enterprise Management (1996), http://www.dmtf.org/standards/wbem
16. Wolpers, M., Martin, G., Najjar, J., Duval, E.: Attention Metadata in Knowledge and Learning Management. In: 6th International Conference on Knowledge Management (2006)
17. XOXO example, http://developers.technorati.com/wiki/AttentionSample
18. XOXO Sample Code, http://microformats.org/wiki/xoxo-sample-code

Cross-System Validation of Engagement Prediction from Log Files

Mihaela Cocea and Stephan Weibelzahl

National College of Ireland, School of Informatics,
Mayor Street, Dublin 1, Ireland
{mcocea,sweibelzahl}@ncirl.ie

Abstract. Engagement is an important aspect of effective learning. Time spent using an e-Learning system is not quality time if the learner is not engaged. Tracking the student disengagement would give the possibility to intervene for motivating the learner at appropriate time. In previous research we showed the possibility to predict engagement from log files using a web-based e-Learning system. In this paper we present the results obtained from another web-based system and compare them to the previous ones. The similarity of results across systems demonstrates that our approach is system-independent and that engagement can be elicited from basic information logged by most e-Learning systems: number of pages read, time spent reading pages, number of tests/ quizzes and time spent on test/ quizzes.

Keywords: e-Learning, engagement prediction, log files analysis, data mining.

1 Introduction

Engagement is an indicator of student's motivation. It is well know that motivation is essential for learning: lack of motivation is correlated to learning rate decrease [2]. E-Learning systems can motivate students through an attractive design, by using multimedia materials or by including game features that have great potential [8] and have been proved successful in a number of cases (e.g. [4]). Despite these efforts, students are not always focused on learning and even try to game the systems ([21], [22]). Thus, motivation needs to be addressed beyond design issues at individual level and motivational diagnosis is required.

There are several models for eliciting motivational knowledge starting from learner's activity. In this paper we are focused only on one aspect of motivation, engagement, and on validating across two different e-Learning systems, HTML Tutor and iHelp, a previously proposed approach for engagement prediction [7]. The paper is structured as follows. In Section 2 previous work related to engagement prediction is presented. Section 3 includes the analysis of the iHelp data. Section 4 compares the results obtained by the two systems and also relates our outcomes with the previous approaches to engagement prediction. Section 5 discusses the results and concludes the paper.

E. Duval, R. Klamma, and M. Wolpers (Eds.): EC-TEL 2007, LNCS 4753, pp. 14–25, 2007.
© Springer-Verlag Berlin Heidelberg 2007

2 Previous Research

Several concepts are used in motivational research [16], besides motivation itself: engagement, interest, effort, focus of attention, self-efficacy, confidence etc. For the results presented in this paper the focus of our research on motivation is on engagement. A student is engaged if he/she is focused on the learning activity.

A number of concepts in motivational research such as interest, effort, focus of attention and motivation are related though not identical to engagement (see e.g., [16]): 1) engagement can be influenced by *interest*, as people tend to be more engaged in activities they are interested in; thus, interest is a determinant of engagement; 2) *effort* is closely related to interest in the same way: more effort is invested if the person has interest in the activity; the relation between engagement and effort can be resumed by: engagement can be present with or without effort; if the activity is pleasant (and/or easy), engagement is possible without effort; in the case of more unpleasant (and/or difficult) activities, effort might be required to stay engaged; 3) the difference between engagement and *focus of attention*, as it is used in research is that focus of attention refers to attention through a specific sensorial channel (e.g. visual focus), while engagement refers to the entire mental activity (involving in the same time perception, attention, reasoning, volition and emotions); 4) in relation to *motivation*, engagement is just one aspect indicating that, for a reason or another, the person is motivated to do the activity he/she is engaged in, or the other way, if the person is disengaged, he/she may not motivated to do the activity; in other words, engagement is an indicator of motivation.

Although there are several approaches to motivational issues in e-Learning, we are going to present only some of them, with a focus on those related to engagement prediction.

2.1 Relevant Literature on Motivation and Engagement Prediction

Several approaches for motivation detection from learner's interactions with the e-Learning system have been proposed. A rule-based approach based on ARCS Model [13] has been developed [9] to infer motivational states from the learners' behavior using a ten questions quiz. 85 inference rules were produced by the participants who had access to replays of the learners' interactions with the system and to the learners' motivational traits.

Another approach [17] based on ARCS Model is used to infer three aspects of motivation: confidence, confusion and effort, from the learner's focus of attention and inputs related to learners' actions: time to perform the task, time to read the paragraph related to the task, the time for the learner to decide how to perform the task, the time when the learner starts/ finishes the task, the number of tasks the learner has finished with respect to the current plan (progress), the number of unexpected tasks performed by the learner which are not included in the current learning plan and the number of questions asking for help.

Engagement tracing [3] is an approach based on Item Response Theory that proposes the estimation of the probability of a correct response given a specific response time for modeling disengagement; two methods of generating responses are assumed: blindly guess when the student is disengaged and an answer with a certain probability of being correct when the student is engaged. The model also takes into account individual differences in reading speed and level of knowledge.

A dynamic mixture model combining a hidden Markov model with Item Response Theory was proposed in [12]. The dynamic mixture model takes into account: student proficiency, motivation, evidence of motivation, and a student's response to a problem. The motivation variable can have three values: a) motivated, b) unmotivated and exhausting all the hints in order to reach the final one that gives the correct answer: unmotivated-hint and c) unmotivated and quickly guessing answers to find the correct answer: unmotivated-guess.

A Bayesian Network has been developed [1] from log-data in order to infer variable related to learning and attitudes toward the tutor and the system. The log-data registered variables like problem-solving time, mistakes and help requests.

A latent response model [2] was proposed for identifying the students that game the system. Using a pretest–posttest approach, the gaming behavior was classified in two categories: a) with no impact on learning and b) with decrease in learning gain. The variables used in the model were: student's actions and probabilistic information about the student's prior skills.

The same problem of gaming behavior was addressed in [21], an approach that combines classroom observations with logged actions in order to detect gaming behavior manifested by guessing and checking or hint/ help abuse. Prevention strategies have been proposed [22]: two active interventions for the two types of gaming behavior and a passive intervention. When a student was detected to manifest one of the two gaming behaviors, a message was displayed to the student encouraging him/her to try harder, ask the teacher for help or pursue other suitable actions. The passive intervention had no triggering mechanism and consisted in providing visual feedback on student's actions and progress that was continuously displayed on screen and available for viewing by the student and teacher.

2.2 Our Approach to Engagement Prediction

In previous research [7] we proposed a different approach to engagement prediction that would cover both the learning and the testing tasks in an e-Learning system. We analyzed log files from HTML Tutor – a web based interactive learning environment. In a preliminary investigation [6] where we used sessions as basis for analysis, we found that we could predict the level of engagement after 45 minutes of activity. As most of disengaged students would log out before that time leaving no possibility for intervention, we decided to split the sessions in sequences of 10 minutes and thus overcome this problem. Using several data mining techniques we showed that the user's level of engagement can be predicted from logged data mainly related to reading pages and taking tests. Similar results obtained using different techniques and different numbers of attributes showed the consistency of prediction and of the attributes used. The best prediction for all levels of engagement (engaged, disengaged and neutral) was 88%, obtained using Classification via Regression and including two more attributes related to hyperlinks and glossary besides the ones related to reading and tests. The best prediction for disengaged students was 93%, obtained using Bayesian Networks.

Our approach is different from the previous ones in the fact that it envisages prediction of engagement from both main activities encountered in e-Learning systems: reading pages and taking tests. The two models based on IRT presented in Section 2.1 may work very well for quizzes, but they have the disadvantage of considering engagement after the learning activity. Tracking engagement when the student is learning (reading pages) allows intervention at appropriate time and before the evaluation of learning (quizzes), when bad performance could be caused by disengagement in answering the questions, but also by disengagement during learning time.

3 Data Analysis

In order to validate our approach for engagement prediction presented above we analyzed data from iHelp, the University of Saskatchewan web-based system. This system includes two web based applications designed to support both learners and instructors throughout the learning process: the iHelp Discussion system and iHelp Learning Content Management System. The latter is designed to deliver online courses to students working at a distance, providing course content (text and multimedia) and quizzes/surveys. The students' interactions with the system are preserved in a machine readable format.

The same type of data about the interactions was selected from the registered information in order to perform the same type of analysis as the one performed with HTML Tutor data. An HTML course was also chosen in order to prevent differences in results caused by differences in subject matter.

We used logged data from 11 users (from a total of 21 students studying the selected course), meaning a total of 108 sessions and 450 sequences (341 of exactly 10 minutes and 109 less than 10 minutes). So far, we have processed the data from only these 11 students; further work includes an analysis of the data from all 21 learners.

3.1 Attributes Description

In the analysis several attributes mainly related to reading pages and quizzes events were used. These attributes are presented in Table 1. The terms tests and quizzes will be used interchangeably; they refer to the same type of assessment, except that in HTML they are called tests and in iHelp they are named quizzes.

Total time of a sequence was included as attribute for the trials that took into account the sequences less than 10 minutes, as well as those of exactly 10 minutes. Compared to the analysis of HTML Tutor logs, for iHelp there are fewer attributes related to tests/ quizzes. Thus, information on number of questions attempted and on time spent on them is included, but information about the correctness or incorrectness of answers given by users was not available at the time of the analysis.

Two new attributes were introduced for this analysis, attributes that were not considered for HTML Tutor: the number of pages above and below a certain time threshold, described in the subsequent section.

Table 1. The attributes used for analysis

Codes (as used in analysis)	Attributes
NoPages	Number of pages read
AvgTimeP	Average time spent reading
NoQuestions	Number of questions from quizzes/ surveys
AvgTimeQ	Average time spent on quizzes/surveys
Total time	Total time of a sequence
NoPpP	Number of pages above the threshold established for maximum time required to read a page
NoPM	Number of pages below the threshold established for minimum time to read a page
Eng	Engagement level: e=engaged; d=disengaged

3.2 Level of Engagement

For each 10 minutes sequence, the level of engagement was rated by an expert using the same approach as in our previous research [7], adding two extra rules related to the two additional attributes regarding number of pages that are above or below a threshold, depending on time spent reading.

At first we intended to use the average time spent on each page across all users, as suggested by [18], but analyzing the data, we have seen that some pages are accessed by a very small number of users, sometimes only one, problem encountered in other research as well [10]. Thus, we decided to use the average reading speed known to be in between 200 and 250 words per minute [19, 20]. Looking at the number of words on each page we found that out of 652 pages accessed by the students, 5 pages need between 300 and 400 seconds to be read at average speed, 41 pages need between 200 and 300 seconds, 145 between 100 and 300 seconds and the 291 need less than 100 seconds. Some pages include images and videos. Only 2 of the 11 students attempted to watch videos, one giving up after 3.47 seconds and the other one watching a video (or being on the page with the link to a video) for 162 seconds (almost 3 minutes).

Taking into account the above mentioned information about iHelp pages, we agreed that less than 5 seconds or more that 420 seconds (7 minutes) spent on a page indicates disengagement.

In our previous research with HTML Tutor logs, the level of engagement was established by human experts that looked at the log files and established the level of engagement for sequences of 10 minutes or less, in a similar way to [9]. The same procedure was applied for iHelp, plus the two rules aforementioned.

Accordingly, the level of engagement was determined for each sequence of 10 minutes or less. If in a sequence the learner spent more that 7 minutes on a page, we considered that he/she was disengaged during that sequence. Related to pages accessed less than 5 seconds, we agreed to consider a user disengaged if 2/3 of the total number of pages were below 5 seconds.

With HTML Tutor, three level of engagement were used: engaged, disengaged and neutral. Neutral was used for situations when raters found it hard to decide whether the user was engaged or disengaged. With iHelp, this difficulty was not encountered.

With HTML Tutor, we verified the rating consistency by measuring inter-coding reliability. A sample of 100 sequences (from a total of 1015) was given to a second rater and results indicated high inter-coder reliability: percentage agreement of 92%, Cohen's kappa measurement of agreement of .83 (p<.01) and Krippendorff's alpha of .84 [14]. With iHelp only one rater classified the level of engagement for all sequences.

3.3 Analysis and Results

Using the attributes described above, an analysis was conducted in order to investigate engagement prediction with iHelp and compare the results with the ones from HTML Tutor.

Waikato Environment for Knowledge Analysis (WEKA) [23] was used to perform the analysis. The same methods as the ones used in our previous research were experimented and four datasets were used: (i) Dataset 1 including all attributes and all sequences, (ii) Dataset 2 obtained from Dataset 1 by eliminating the two additional attributes (NoPgP, NoPgM), (iii) Dataset 3 including all attributes, but only sequences of 10 minutes and (iv) Dataset 4 obtained from Dataset 3 by eliminating the two additional attributes (NoPgP, NoPgM). Dataset 2 and 4 were used in order to compare the results with the ones from HTML Tutor. Table 2 presents the datasets with the corresponding attributes and sequences.

Table 2. Datasets used in the experiment

Dataset	Sequences	Attributes
Dataset1	All sequences	NoPages, AvgTimeP, NoQuestions, AvgTimeQ, Total time, NoPpP, NoPM
Dataset2	All sequences	NoPages, AvgTimeP, NoQuestions, AvgTimeQ, Total time
Dataset3	Only 10 minutes sequences	NoPages, AvgTimeP, NoQuestions, AvgTimeQ, Total time, NoPpP, NoPM
Dataset4	Only 10 minutes sequences	NoPages, AvgTimeP, NoQuestions, AvgTimeQ, Total time

The eight methods [15, 23] used for the analysis are: (a) Bayesian Nets with K2 algorithm and maximum 3 parent nodes (BN); (b) Logistic regression (LR); (c) Simple logistic classification (SL); (d) Instance based classification with IBk algorithm (IBk); (e) Attribute Selected Classification using J48 classifier and Best First search (ASC); (f) Bagging using REP (reduced-error pruning) tree classifier (B); (g) Classification via Regression (CvR) and (h) Decision Trees with J48 classifier based on Quilan's C4.5 algorithm [23] (DT). The experiment was done using 10-fold stratified cross validation iterated 10 times.

Results are displayed in Table 3, which comprises the percentage of correctly classified instances, the true positives rate for disengaged class, the precision indicator (true positives/ (true positives (TP) + false positives)) for disengaged class and the mean absolute error. For us, TP rate is more important than precision because TP rate

Table 3. Experiment results summary

		BN	LR	SL	IBk	ASC	B	CvR	DT
Dataset1	%correct	89.31	95.22	95.13	95.29	95.44	95.22	95.44	95.31
	TP rate	0.90	0.95	0.95	0.94	0.94	0.94	0.95	0.95
	Precision	0.90	0.95	0.95	0.96	0.97	0.97	0.96	0.96
	Error	0.13	0.07	0.10	0.05	0.08	0.08	0.08	0.07
Dataset2	%correct	81.73	83.82	83.58	84.00	84.38	85.11	85.33	84.38
	TP rate	0.78	0.82	0.81	0.79	0.77	0.79	0.80	0.78
	Precision	0.86	0.86	0.86	0.89	0.91	0.91	0.91	0.91
	Error	0.22	0.24	0.26	0.20	0.25	0.23	0.23	0.25
Dataset3	%correct	94.65	98.06	97.91	98.59	97.65	97.65	97.76	97.47
	TP rate	0.95	0.97	0.96	0.98	0.96	0.96	0.96	0.96
	Precision	0.94	0.99	0.99	0.99	0.99	0.99	0.99	0.99
	Error	0.07	0.02	0.04	0.02	0.05	0.04	0.03	0.03
Dataset4	%correct	84.29	85.82	85.47	84.91	84.97	85.38	85.26	85.24
	TP rate	0.78	0.77	0.76	0.77	0.75	0.76	0.75	0.75
	Precision	0.88	0.92	0.92	0.89	0.92	0.92	0.92	0.92
	Error	0.18	0.22	0.23	0.20	0.25	0.23	0.24	0.24

indicates the correct percentage from actual instances of a class and precision indicates the correct percentage from predicted instances in that class.

The results presented in Table 3 show very good levels of prediction for all methods, with a correct prediction varying between approximately 81% and 98%. There are similar results for the disengaged class, the true positives rate and the precision indicator for disengaged class varying between 75% and 98%. The mean absolute error varies between 0.02 and 0.25. As in the results for HTML Tutor, the very similar results obtained from different methods and trials shows consistency of prediction and of the attributes used for prediction. The results for Dataset 1 and 3 are better that the ones from Dataset 2 and 4, suggesting that the two new attributes bring significant information gain.

Table 4. The confusion matrix for instance based classification with IBk algorithm

		Predicted	
		Engaged	Disengaged
Actual	Engaged	180	1
	Disengaged	4	155

The highest percentage of correctly predicted instances was obtained using Instance based classification with IBk algorithm on Dataset 3: 98.59%. The confusion matrix is presented in Table 4. Focusing on the disengaged learners we see that the same method performs best on the same dataset: 98%. The distribution of true positives rate is displayed in Fig 1. The vertical axes in the figure are due to fractional true positive rates of the 340 cases, for example 295/340 is approximately 87%. More common results for the true positive rate of a given trial are visible in the density of the color along the line.

Distribution of True Positives Rate

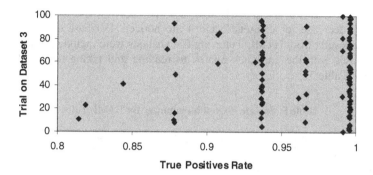

Fig. 1. Distribution of TP rate for disengaged class using instance based classification with IBk algorithm

Looking at the disengaged learners as they are our main interest, the rate of correct classification is similar: 98% of the disengaged students are correctly classified.

Investigating further the information gain brought by the two additional attributes, attribute ranking using information gain ranking filter as attribute evaluator was performed and the following ranking was found: NoPgP, AvgTimeP, NoPages, NoPgM, NoQuestions and AvgTimeQ. Thus the attributes related to an upper and a lower bound for time spent on a page, are more important that the attributes related to quizzes.

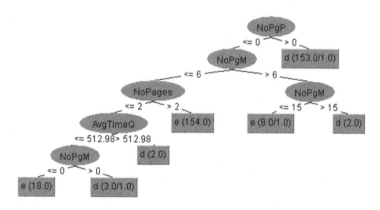

Fig. 2. Decision Tree graph for Dataset 3

The information gain brought by NoPgP is also reflected in the decision tree graph displayed in Fig. 2, where NoPgP is the attribute with the highest information gain, being the root of the tree. Thus one of the rules used for determining the level of engagement is reflected in the results.

4 Results Comparison

Comparing the results of iHelp to HTML Tutor, an improvement for datasets 1 and 3 and a small decrease for datasets 2 and 4 are noticed. For ease of comprehension some of the results from HTML Tutor log file analysis were included. These are only for the dataset with the attributes related to reading and taking tests and they are presented in Table 5.

Table 5. Experiment results summary for HTML Tutor

	BN	LR	SL	IBk	ASC	B	CvR	DT
%correct	87.07	86.52	87.33	85.62	87.24	87.41	87.64	86.58
TP rate	0.93	0.93	0.93	0.92	0.93	0.93	0.92	0.93
Precision	0.91	0.90	0.90	0.91	0.92	0.92	0.92	0.91
Error	0.10	0.12	0.12	0.10	0.10	0.12	0.12	0.11

The decrease observed for Dataset 2 and 4 might be explained by the two missing attributes related to quizzes: number of correct and number of incorrect answers that were available for HTML Tutor. The increase noticed for Datasets 1 and 3 could be accounted by the contribution of the two additional attributes.

The two missing attributes related to correctness or incorrectness of quizzes answers may improve even more the prediction level. Looking at their role in prediction with HTML Tutor, using three attribute evaluation methods with ranking as search method for attribute selection, these two attributes were found to be the last ones. Thus, according to chi-square and information gain ranking the most valuable attribute is average time spent on pages, followed by the number of pages, number of tests, average time spent on tests, number of correctly answered tests and number of incorrectly answered tests. OneR ranking differs only in the position of the last two attributes: number of incorrectly answered tests comes before number of correctly answered tests. The attribute ranking using information gain filter for iHelp attributes, shows similar positions for attributes related to reading and tests, meaning that attributes related to reading come before the ones related to tests. This indicated that the two missing attributes with iHelp are not essential, but, if available, they could improve the prediction level. Table 6 summarizes the similarities and dissimilarities between the findings from iHelp and HTML Tutor.

Even with these differences, the fact that a good level of prediction was obtained from similar attributes on datasets from different systems using the same methods indicate that engagement prediction is possible using information related to reading pages and taking test, information logged by most e-Learning system. Thus, our proposed approach for engagement prediction is system independent and can be generalized for any system. A component for detection of engagement level can be built and attached to e-Learning systems to keep track of the learner's engagement status and thus, be able to intervene when appropriate. In our research, disengagement detection is the first step to motivation elicitation. Thus, after detection of disengagement we plan to have a dialog with the learner in order to find out more about his/her motivation [5], information to be used for intervention [11].

Table 6. Similarities and dissimilarities between iHelp and HTML Tutor

Characteristic	iHelp	HTML Tutor
Prediction based on reading and tests attributes	81% to 85% with no information on correctness /incorrectness of quizzes and no additional attributes 85% to 98% with the two additional attributes	86-87%
Attribute ranking	- NoPgP (Number of pages above a threshold) - AvgTimeP (Average time spent reading) - NoPages (Number of pages read/ accessed) - NoPgM (Number of pages below a threshold) - NoQuestions (Number of questions from quizzes) - AvgTimeQ (Average time spent on quizzes)	- average time spent on pages - number of pages - number of tests - average time spent on tests - number of correctly answered tests - number of incorrectly answered tests

5 Discussion and Conclusions

With both iHelp and HTML Tutor some patterns in the disengaged users' behavior were distinguished: a) the disengaged students that click fast through pages without reading them and b) the disengaged students that spend long time on a page, (far) exceeding the needed time for reading that page. Two of the previous approaches mentioned in Section 2.1 also present some patterns, with the difference that those patterns are related only to learners' behavior when answering quizzes. Thus, we find a similarity between blindly guess in [3] or unmotivated-guess in [12], on one hand, and the fast click through pages, on the other hand, as both reflect students' rush and lack of attention. Knowledge about these two patterns would be useful for a more targeted intervention and in further work the possibility to predict them will be investigated.

Engagement or disengagement prediction in previous research was limited to quiz-type activities, while our approach focuses on the learning time. Learning time usually includes some material to read and/ or watch, and a form of self-assessment for the covered topic. Quizzes could be used in such a form, being actually a learning activity, or they could be used to evaluate the student at the end of a course. In HTML Tutor and iHelp, the tests/ quizzes are learning activities.

Gaming is a type of disengagement, as the learner's focus is not on the activity itself, but on how to complete the activity with the least effort. In previous research, like for engagement, gaming detection [2, 21] is addressed only for quiz-type activities and is based on Item Response Theory. For this approach, like for the other ones as well, information on correctness or incorrectness of answers is very important if not essential. For our approach this information has some importance as mentioned previously, but it is not indispensable.

Thus, our approach on disengagement detection is not limited to quizzes and in our research project, detecting the disengaged students is just a first step towards motivation assessment. We are interested in detecting the disengaged in order to intervene before they give up and when it's still time to improve learning outcomes.

To conclude, in this paper we presented results for engagement prediction from iHelp logged data. The analysis showed a good prediction, e.g. 98% using instance based classification with IBk algorithm, for overall prediction and for disengaged class. These results were compared to the ones obtained using log files from HTML Tutor and the similarity of results suggest that our approach on engagement prediction is system independent. Thus, we validated engagement prediction from logged data related to reading pages and taking tests and we can conclude that a prediction module could be added to educational systems, with the great benefit of finding the appropriate time for intervention.

Further work includes 1) the same analysis with all 21 subjects; 2) an attempt to predict the two distinguished patterns of disengagement, as the information may be valuable for effective intervention.

Acknowledgments. We would like to acknowledge the support of ARIES group from Department of Computer Science, University of Saskatchewan for access to the data from their web-based system.

References

1. Arroyo, I., Woolf, B.P.: Inferring learning and attitudes from a Bayesian Network of log file data. In: Looi, C.K., McCalla, G., Bredeweg, B., Breuker, J. (eds.) Artificial Intelligence in Education, Supporting Learning through Intelligent and Socially Informed Technology, pp. 33–34. IOS Press, Amsterdam (2005)
2. Baker, R., Corbett, A., Koedinger, K.: Detecting Student Misuse of Intelligent Tutoring Systems. In: Proceedings of the Seventh International Conference on Intelligent Tutoring Systems, pp. 531–540 (2004)
3. Beck, J.: Engagement tracing: Using response times to model student disengagement. In: Looi, C., McCalla, G., Bredeweg, B., Breuker, J. (eds.) Artificial Intelligence in Education: Supporting Learning through Intelligent and Socially Informed Technology, pp. 88–95. IOS Press, Amsterdam (2005)
4. Chen, G.D., Shen, G.Y., Ou, K.L., Liu, B.: Promoting motivation and eliminating disorientation for web based courses by a multi-user game. In: Proceedings of the ED-MEDIA/ED-TELECOM 98 World Conference on Educational Multimedia and Hypermedia and World conference on Educational Telecommunications, June 20-25, Germany (1998)
5. Cocea, M.: Assessment of motivation in online learning environments. In: Wade, V., Ashman, H., Smyth, B. (eds.) AH 2006. LNCS, vol. 4018, pp. 414–418. Springer, Heidelberg (2006)
6. Cocea, M., Weibelzahl, S.: Can Log Files Analysis Estimate Learners' Level of Motivation? In: ABIS 2006. Proceedings of ABIS Workshop-14th Workshop on Adaptivity and User Modeling in Interactive Systems, Hildesheim, pp. 32–35 (2006)

7. Cocea, M., Weibelzahl, S.: Eliciting Motivation Knowledge from Log Files towards Motivation Diagnosis for Adaptive Systems. In: Conati, C., McCoy, K., Paliouras, G. (eds.) UM 2007. LNCS (LNAI), vol. 4511, pp. 197–206. Springer, Heidelberg (2007)
8. Connolly, T., Stansfield, M.: Using Games-Based eLearning Technologies in Overcoming Difficulties in Teaching Information Systems. Journal of Information Technology Education 5, 459–476 (2006)
9. De Vicente, A., Pain, H.: Informing the Detection of the Students' Motivational State: an empirical Study. In: Cerri, S.A., Gouarderes, G., Paraguau, F. (eds.) Intelligent Tutoring Systems, 6th International Conference, pp. 933–943. Springer, Berlin (2002)
10. Farzan, R., Brusilovsky, P.: Social navigation support in E-Learning: What are real footprints. In: IJCAI'05 Workshop on Intelligent Techniques for Web Personalization, Edinburgh, U.K. pp. 49–56 (2005)
11. Hurley, T.: Intervention Strategies to Increase Self-efficacy and Self-regulation in Adaptive On-Line Learning. In: Wade, V., Ashman, H., Smyth, B. (eds.) AH 2006. LNCS, vol. 4018, pp. 440–444. Springer, Heidelberg (2006)
12. Johns, J., Woolf, B.: A Dynamic Mixture Model to Detect Student Motivation and Proficiency. In: AAAI 2006. Proceedings of the Twenty-first National Conference on Artificial Intelligence, Boston, MA (2006)
13. Keller, J.M.: Development and use of the ARCS model of instructional design. Journal of Instructional Development 10(3), 2–10 (1987)
14. Lombard, M., Snyder-Duch, J., Campanella Bracken, C.: Practical Resources for Assessing and Reporting Intercoder Reliability in Content Analysis Research (2003) Retrieved on 06/11/06 from http://www.temple.edu/mmc/reliability
15. Mitchell, T.M.: Machine Learning. McGraw-Hill, New York (1997)
16. Pintrich, P.R., Schunk, D.H.: Motivation in education: theory, research and applications. Prentice Hall, Englewood Cliffs (2002)
17. Qu, L., Wang, N., Johnson, W.L.: Detecting the Learner's Motivational States in an Interactive Learning Environment. In: Looi, C.-K., et al. (eds.) Artificial Intelligence in Education, pp. 547–554. IOS Press, Amsterdam (2005)
18. Rafter, R., Smyth, B.: Passive Profiling from Server Logs in an Online Recruitment Environment. In: Proceedings of the IJCAI Workshop on Intelligent Techniques for Web Personalization (ITWP 2001) pp. 35–41, Seattle, Washington, USA (2001)
19. ReadingSoft.com found at HYPERLINK, http://www.readingsoft.com
20. TurboRead Speed Reading found at HYPERLINK, http://www.turboread.com
21. Walonoski, J., Heffernan, N.T.: Detection and Analysis of Off-Task Gaming Behavior in Intelligent Tutoring Systems. In: Ikeda, A., Chan (eds.) Proceedings of the Eight International Conference in Intelligent Tutoring Systems, pp. 382–391. Springer, Berlin (2006)
22. Walonoski, J., Heffernan, N.T.: Prevention of Off-Task Gaming Behaviour within Intelligent Tutoring Systems. In: InIkeda, A., Chan (eds.) Proceedings of the Eight International Conference in Intelligent Tutoring Systems, pp. 722–724. Springer, Berlin (2006)
23. Witten, I.H., Frank, E.: Data mining. Practical Machine Learning Tools and Techniques, 2nd edn. Morgan Kauffman Publishers, Elsevier, Amsterdam (2005)

Exploiting Policies in an Open Infrastructure for Lifelong Learning

Juri L. De Coi, Philipp Kärger, Arne W. Koesling, and Daniel Olmedilla

L3S Research Center and Leibniz University of Hannover, Hannover, Germany
{decoi,kaerger,koesling,olmedilla}@L3S.de

Abstract. Nowadays, people are in need for continuous learning in order to keep up to date or be upgraded in their job. An infrastructure for
lifelong learning requires continuous adaptation to learners needs and
must also provide flexible ways for students to use and personalize them.
Controlling who can access a document, specifying when a student may
be contacted for interactive instant messaging or periodical reminders in
order to increase motivation for collaboration are just some examples of
typical statements that may be specified by e.g., learners and learning
management system administrators. This paper shows how policies can
represent a way of expressing these statements and describes the extra
benefits of its adoption like flexibility, dynamicity and interoperability.

Keywords: Policy, lifelong learning, agent, negotiation, access control.

1   Introduction

Society and current labor market evolves rapidly. Nowadays, a learner is potentially any person in the world, who wants to keep up to date on any specific topic,
be it at work or in any other facet of her life. Therefore, there is a growing need
for more flexible and cost-effective solutions for learners allowing them to study
at different locations (e.g., at home) and at times that are better arranged with
their working hours. In addition, learners do not necessarily work isolated but
may collaborate with or contact other persons, like learners or tutors. Systems
addressing these requirements must allow users to have a big flexibility in the
way they use the system, how they collaborate, how they share their content,
etc. Controlling who can access a document, specifying when a student may be
contacted for interactive instant messaging or periodical reminders in order to
increase motivation for collaboration are just some examples of typical statements that may be specified by e.g., learners and learning management system
administrators. Policies represent an appropriate way for expressing this kind
of statements because of their flexibility and dynamicity as well as their ease of
use (they are typically declarative, that is, users specify "what" to do but not
"how" something is to be done, therefore making its use more accessible to e.g.,
learners). Furthermore, lately there has been extensive research, that provides
not only the ability of specifying these statements but also advanced mechanisms
for reasoning on, exchanging and exploiting them.

E. Duval, R. Klamma, and M. Wolpers (Eds.): EC-TEL 2007, LNCS 4753, pp. 26–40, 2007.

This paper focuses on the use of policies, a well-defined declarative and dynamic approach in order to specify and control the behavior of complex and rapidly evolving infrastructures for lifelong learning. First, Section 2 identifies example situations in which the specification of policies would increase the flexibility of the interactions and collaborations as well as enhance the learners experience. These examples show that dynamicity and ease of use, are a crucial requirement, both being two of the main characteristics of policies. The benefits of the integration of policies into learning management systems and personal learner agents in order to support such situations are described in Section 3, as well as the out-of-the-box benefits of their exploitation. In addition, Section 4 analyzes existing policy languages and frameworks in order to present an overview of available solutions to the reader. It provides a comparison of their main features as well as their advantages and disadvantages from the perspective of their integration into lifelong learning infrastructures. Later, Section 5 exemplifies the formalization of policies using a selected policy language and describes some of the added benefits of its use such as negotiations and advanced explanations. Finally, related work is presented in Section 6 and Section 7 concludes the paper.

2   Motivation Scenario

Alice holds a master degree in computer science and works successfully in a company. Recently, she was assigned the task of managing a new project starting in a couple of months and therefore she would need to learn and refresh her knowledge on project management. Since she has a full time job including many business trips, she uses an on-line learning client that allows her to improve her competences whenever she has some available time. With this learning client she is able to collaborate and to send questions or answers to other learners or tutors, and therefore she is able to chat with other students and even participate in a social network. However, since she uses her chat tool also for her job she restricts her chat facility in a way that during working time only business contacts and other employees of her company can start a conversation therefore allowing other students to contact her only in her leisure time. Of course, students trying to contact her during working time get a brief explanation of why a conversation is not possible at that very moment and which even indicates when Alice can be contacted.

Within the program Alice is following, she accesses different learning activities and objects through her learning client. Some of this material is free of charge but a couple of learning activities she is interested in are offered each one by a different content provider that sells it. Since the material is sold on a good price, she decides to purchase it. Each provider tells Alice that either she has to have an account or she has to provide a credit card for payment of the learning activity. For the first provider she does have an account and provides her username and password. Therefore she retrieves the requested material. However, she does not know the second provider and she must disclose her credit card. Alice protected her credit card in a way that it would only be disclosed to providers she may trust and the learning client provides a mechanism by which a content provider and Alice can trust each other even if they have not had any transaction in common before.

The learning client Alice is using allows her to share exercises and other relevant documents stored in her computer (e.g., using a peer-to-peer network [12,10]) with other students following the same program or within the same learning network. She may even create some new material out of what she learned and her experience at work. She specifies which documents are to be shared and which conditions other student must fulfill in order to be able to retrieve it (e.g., be part of same program or be a tutor). In order to ensure the success of the students, the learning client includes a personalizable agent. Among other uses for this agent, Alice can create some guidelines in a way that the agent reminds her when she has to finish some learning activities or sends her an e-mail when she has been inactive for more than a week. Tutors can also attach these kinds of rules to the learning activities or programs in order to motivate their students or even to define some guidelines for on-line games that will be followed by their students [11]. Thanks to all these flexible facilities and all their personalization and configuration possibilities Alice is able to finish her program successfully.

3   Using Policies for Lifelong Learning

The term policy is generally defined as "statement specifying the behavior of a system" and it is intended to guide decisions and actions. Policies are encountered in many real world situations in our daily life like, for instance, shops may have a non return policy, with an exception for the week after Christmas, when a lot of unwanted items are returned. However, with the digital era, the specification of policies has emerged in many web-related contexts and software systems. E-mail clients filters are a specific kind of policy. One of the main application areas where policies have been lately used is security, privacy and the business domain (business rules). Policies yield many advantages compared to other conventional approaches. To mention some of them, policies are dynamic (and therefore can be easily change without recompiling the system that uses them), declarative (a step from the programmer closer to the user of a system since they state what to be done and not how it is to be done) and they typically have well-defined semantics and therefore they are easily exchangeable and understood by other parties, they usually allow reasoning over them (allowing to infer knowledge and not only explicit knowledge).

Considering the example from above (see also Figure 1), policies can support Alice in the situations described bringing in all the benefits of its use. Alice may formulate her personal preferences as a set of policies, for instance, her working hours or leisure time, as well as whom she considers as business contact or as a friend. Even a more powerful situation arises when Alice communicates with other parties. In our example, Alice uses the learning client to

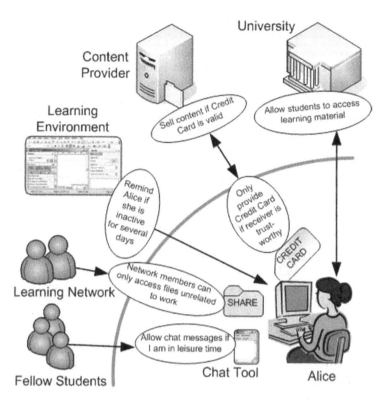

Fig. 1. Example policies in an open and flexible lifelong learning infrastructure

access content providers and receive access information or payment methods in a way her system can understand and process. Or she may easily define sophisticated methods to control who accesses the resources she has locally stored in her computer. In this situation, policies allow users and systems to characterize new users or systems by their properties and not simply by their identity (crucial in an open environment where completely strangers may interact with each other). For example, content providers may provide discount to students of a university (without having to know and update the whole list of students registered at the university) or Alice specifying that any user of a community she is in can access some of the resources in her computer or to whom she would disclose her credit card. Even negotiations can be (semi)automatically performed among entities driven by their policies [16].

Furthermore, policies can be used to control the behavior of software agents in order to send notifications, drive electronic games and simulations for educational purposes or many other approaches in order to increase her motivation while learning. All in all, policies have the potential to enhance the possibilities an open infrastructure offers while increasing its flexibility and ease of use.

4   Comparison of Existing Policy Languages

This section first extracts requirements from our running example and identifies the features a policy framework should meet in order to address them. Then, it compares existing frameworks based on these features. The scenario presented above exploits policies in several ways like for example restrictions stated by Alice for incoming chat connections or conditions under which her locally stored resources (either documents or her credit card number) may be disclosed, content providers specifying whether a resource is free-of-charge or at cost (and the payment methods together with business rules like e.g., discounts) or general statements indicating how some entity (e.g., a software agent) should react to a specific event. An open lifelong learning infrastructure must provide sufficient functionalities in order to support all these situations. The following is a list of the most important features identified:

Positive vs. negative authorization: policies specifying conditions under which resources can be accessed may be of two types: positive or negative. Positive authorization policies specify that if the conditions are satisfied access is granted (e.g., "business contacts may start a conversation at any time") while negative authorization policies specify that if the conditions are satisfied access is denied (e.g., "if it is working time disallow students to contact Alice"). Although one may think that these two kinds of policies retain the natural way people express policies, it can be argued that the specification of negative authorizations complicates the enforcement of access control in a system [4] and adds the extra complexity of having to define metapolicies, that is, in case two policies conflict (one policy grants access and another denies it) a statement should specify which final decision is taken. Furthermore, this situation is scenario dependent. When dealing with security and access control, a typical approach is assuming that access to any resource is denied by default and only positive authorization policies are defined stating which resources are allowed [7,2]. The reason is that if there exists an error in a policy, the cost of disclosing a sensitive resource is much higher than the cost of not disclosing a non-sensitive one.

Evaluation: it is important to allow policies to be private, that is, they are not disclosed unless some conditions are fulfilled. The reason is that policies may be sensitive. Imagine, Alice states that her friends can contact her via chat but not any of her business contacts. Most probably Alice does not want her business contacts to see this policy. Therefore, it is important to distinguish how policy evaluation is performed in different frameworks. Some of them assume that policies from different parties can be collected in a centralized place where a local algorithm is performed while other frameworks allow each entity to keep control of its policies without disclosing them to any other party and the algorithm for policy exchange and evaluation is distributed.

Negotiations: directly related to the previous requirement, the support for negotiations is another desirable feature in lifelong learning. Entities should be able to exchange policies with other entities at runtime. Since some policies may be private it may lead to negotiations like the on-line transaction between Alice and the content provider asking for her credit card[1].

Explanations: It should be possible to generate explanations out of the policies. On the one hand, they help a user to check whether the policies she created are correct and, on the other hand, they inform other users about why a decision was taken (or how the users can change the decision by performing a specific action). For example, if a student tries to contact Alice during her working time, that student would rather appreciate receiving a message like "I am not available from 8:00am to 5:00pm" instead of "I am not available". Or if Alice discloses her credit card number to a content provider and it is not accepted a message like "This credit card is invalid because it is expired" would be more useful than simply "Invalid credit card".

Strong/lightweight evidences: in many cases, entities have to provide information in order to satisfy other entities' policies. In some cases, these properties need to be proved (e.g., Alice's credit card or her student card number should be digitally signed for the content provider to accept it) and sometimes such strong evidence is not needed (e.g., Alice providing her e-mail address to the same content provider). It is important that a policy framework allows for both kinds of evidences.

Ontologies: as stated above, policies will be exchanged among entities within the lifelong learning infrastructure. Although the basic constructs may be defined in the policy language (e.g., rule structure and semantics), policies may be used in different applications and even define new concepts. Ontologies help to provide well-defined semantics for new concepts to be understood by different entities.

To date many policy languages have been developed. Among the most popular ones we can include KAoS [15], PeerTrust [7], Ponder [4], Protune [2], Rei [9], WSPL [1] and XACML [13]. The number and variety of languages is justified by the different requirements they were designed to accomplish. Ponder allows for local security policy specification and the description of security management activities like registration of users or logging and audit events to be used in the context of firewalls, operating systems or databases. WSPL's name itself (namely Web-Services Policy Language) suggests its goal: supporting description and control of various aspects and features of a web service. Web services are addressed by KAoS too, as well as general-purpose grid computing authorization, although it was originally oriented to software agent applications (where dynamic runtime policy changes need to be supported). PeerTrust provided a simple but powerful language for performing negotiations on the Web, in peer-to-peer networks and on the grid, based on distributed query evaluations. Rei's design was primarily concerned with supporting pervasive computing applications in which people and devices are mobile and use wireless networking technologies to discover and access services and devices). Protune's broad notion of policy aims

---

[1] Alice may require the content provider to provide a credential of the "Better Business Bureau" before she discloses her credit card, therefore leading to an iterative disclosure of policies and/or credentials.

Table 1. Policy language comparison (Y = supported)

	KAoS	Ponder	PeerTrust	Protune	Rei	WSPL	XACML
Authorization types	Positive & negative	Positive & negative	Positive	Positive	Positive & negative	Positive & negative	Positive & negative
Negotiations			Y	Y			
Evaluation	Centralized	Centralized	Distributed	Distributed	Centralized	Centralized	Centralized
Explanations				Advanced			Simple text
Kind of Evidences			Strong & lightweight	Strong & lightweight	Strong		
Delegation		Y	Y	Y	Y		
Ontology support	Actions, actors...	Roles, groups...		Actions	Classes, properties...		
Open source implementation			Y	Y			Y

at addressing any general application scenario, including e.g., trust management, security and privacy policies, business rules and quality of service specifications. Finally XACML was meant to be a standard general purpose access control policy language, ideally suitable to the needs of most authorization systems.

As shown in Table 1, Ponder, Rei, PeerTrust and Protune support delegation but only PeerTrust and Protune also allow for negotiations and both strong and lightweight evidences. However, Protune is the only policy language also supporting advanced explanation mechanisms and seems to be one the most complete language (as it is also demonstrated in [5]). On the other hand, Protune assumes by default that resources are private, therefore not allowing for the specification of negative authorizations, which is a feature supported by other frameworks like Rei or KAoS. However, Protune does not only allow for distributed evaluation of policies (therefore allowing policies to be kept private), but also open source implementations are available, making it easily accessible, usable and extendible.

5   Formalizing Policies in an Open Infrastructure

Previous sections describe the benefits obtained from the use of policies in an open system. In addition, they provide a description of some of the most important policy languages defined to date. In this section, we select the Protune policy language and, after a brief introduction to the language, we materialize some of the policies described in natural language in section 2 and present some of the added benefits that they provide, namely explanations and negotiations.

5.1   Protune Language

In this section a brief overview of the Protune language is provided. Only the features which are required in order to support the scenarios we are interested in are described here. For an overall view of the language, as well as for a thorough description of its syntax and semantics see [2].

The Protune policy language is based on normal logic program rules

$$A \leftarrow L_1, \ldots, L_n.$$

where A is a standard logical atom (called the *head* of the rule) and $L_1, \ldots, L_n$ (the *body* of the rule) are literals, that is, L_i equals either B_i or $\neg B_i$, for some logical atom B_i.

In addition to usual Logic Programming-based languages, Protune provides support to actions, evidences and metapredicates.

Actions. Protune allows to specify actions within a policy: typical examples of actions are sending evidences, accessing legacy systems (e.g., a database) or environmental properties (e.g., time). Actions are represented as usual predicates (called *provisional* predicates). Provisional predicates hold if they have been successfully executed

Evidences. Protune allows to refer to evidences (i.e., credentials and declarations) from within a policy. Evidences can be regarded as a set of property-value pairs associated to an identifier. Each property-value pair is represented according to an object oriented-like dot notation *id.property* : *value*

Metapredicates. Protune allows to define predicate properties. A *metapredicate* is a predicate associated with property-value pairs. They are represented through a notation close to the one used for evidences, namely *predicate* → *property* : *value*. Rules containing metapredicates are called *metarules*. Metarules are typically exploited to assert some information about predicates occurring in a policy, e.g., the type of the predicate (property `type`) or some directives for the verbalization of the predicate which are meant to be used by the explanation facility (property `explanation`). Some properties apply only to provisional predicates: the value of the property `ontology` is the identifier of the action associated to the provisional predicate as reported in some ontology, whereas property `actor` (resp. `execution`) specifies which peer should carry out the action (resp. when the action should be performed)

In the rest of this section a policy fragment will be presented and explained. The fragment will be exploited in section 5.2 as well.

(1) *is_colleague(Name)* ←
(1.1)   *credential(C)*,
(1.2)   *C.type* : *employee*,
(1.3)   *C.owner* : *Name*,
(1.4)   *C.issuer* : *companyXYZ*,
(1.5)   *C.public_key* : *K*,
(1.6)   *challenge(K)*.

(2) *is_colleague(_)* → *type* : *abbreviation*.

(3) *credential(_)* → *type* : *provisional*.
(4) *credential(_)* → *actor* : *peer*.

(5) *challenge(_)* → *type* : *provisional*.
(6) *challenge(_)* → *actor* : *self*.
(7) *challenge(K)* → *execution* : *immediate* ←
         ground(K).

This policy fragment contains a rule (1) and six metarules (from (2) to (7)). The rule states that the predicate *is_colleague* holds if each literal in the body of the rule holds.

– Metarules (2), (3) and (5) state that predicates *credential* and *challenge*, but not *is_colleague*, are provisional predicates
– Metarule (4) (resp. (6)) states that the action associated to *credential* (resp. *challenge*) must be performed by the other (resp. current) peer. In the following we assume that provisional predicate *credential* (resp. *challenge(K)*)

is associated to the action of sending a credential to the other peer (resp. checking whether the other peer is the holder of the public key K through a standard challenge procedure)

– Metarule (7) states that $challenge(K)$ can be executed if K is ground, i.e., instantiated

Assuming that we want to check whether Bob is a colleague, the policy fragment will be evaluated against the goal $is\_colleague('Bob')$ as follows

– line (1.1) checks whether a credential $cred$, has been sent by the other peer. If it is the case the evaluation proceeds, otherwise a failure is reported
– lines from (1.2) to (1.5) check whether the values of the properties of $cred$ correspond to the ones listed in the body of the rule. If it is the case the evaluation proceeds, otherwise a failure is reported
– when evaluating line (1.6) the action associated to $challenge(key)$ is executed, where key is the public key of $cred$

5.2   Motivation Scenario (Revisited)

Our running scenario in section 2 contained many policies specified in natural language. In this section, we formalize them using the Protune policy language as a proof of concept of its power. It is important to note that users will not be requested to specify their policies in a rule-based logic language such as Protune. In contrary, end-users will be able to select and instantiate existing policies from a standard library[2] or, for advanced users, appropriate tools for the specification of new policies will be provided. In fact, most of the policy languages presented in section 4 provide management editors that help end-users and administrators to create and manage their policies.

In our running example Alice needs to specify that during work time her chat facility must only accept incoming messages from business contacts and other employees of her company.

Alice:
$allow(access(chat(Requester, init\_conversation))) \leftarrow$
$\quad working\_time(),$
$\quad is\_business\_contact(Requester).$

$allow(access(chat(Requester, init\_conversation))) \leftarrow$
$\quad working\_time(),$
$\quad is\_colleague(Requester).$

$allow(access(chat(Requester, init\_conversation))) \leftarrow$
$\quad leisure\_time().$

---

[2] E.g., similar to the mechanisms used in Microsoft Outlook for the instantiation of filtering rules.

$allow(access(chat(Requester, Action))) \rightarrow explanation :$
      $Requester \ \& \ "\ can\ contact\ Alice\ for\ action\ "\ \&\ Action.$

where *working_time, leisure_time, is_business_contact* and *is_colleague* may be defined as

Alice (contd.):
      $working\_time() \leftarrow$
            $time(T),$
            $T > 8 : 30, T < 17 : 00.$

      $leisure\_time() \leftarrow$
            $not\ working\_time().$
      $is\_business\_contact(Name) \leftarrow$
            $retrieve\_contact(Name),$
            $Name.category :' Business'.$

      $is\_colleague(Name) \leftarrow$
            $credential(C),$
            $C.type : employee,$
            $C.owner : Name,$
            $C.issuer : companyXYZ,$
            $C.public\_key : K,$
            $challenge(K).$

      $working\_time() \rightarrow explanation : "It\ is\ working\ time".$
      $leisure\_time() \rightarrow explanation : "It\ is\ leisure\ time".$
      $time(T) \rightarrow explanation : "Time\ is\ "\ \&\ T.$
      $\cdots$

Specially important in this example is that using Protune, in case Bob, a friend that studies with Alice, tries to contact her during her working time, an explanation will be automatically generated from the specified policy [3]. Such explanation provides natural language statements such as

It can't be proved that
Bob can contact Alice for action init_conversation because
      there is no Requester such that
      Requester is a business contact   [details]
AND
      there is no Requester such that
      Requester is a colleague in companyXYZ   [details]
AND
      it is not true that
      It is leisure time   [details]

In this explanation, statements that are made true and do not depend on the requester are hidden so the explanation is focused on the conditions which are not fulfilled (still full explanations providing such details can be generated too). In addition, clicking on *[details]* in a line provides a new explanation for the concept described in such a line. This way end-users may use hyperlinks in order to explore the proofs generated during the policy evaluation, from a more general description to a focused explanation of the concepts.

In addition, Alice also has the following policy protecting her credit card when trying to access on-line resources at different learning resource providers:

Alice (contd.):
    $allow(access(CC)) \leftarrow$
        $CC.type : credit\_card,$
        $bbbMember(User).$

    $bbbMember(User) \leftarrow$
        $credential(C),$
        $C.issuer :' Better\ Business\ Bureau',$
        $C.name : User,$
        $C.public\_key : K,$
        $challenge(K).$

She finds a course she is interested in and requests access to it. The provider she is contacting has the following policy:

Learning Provider:
    $allow(access(Course)) \leftarrow$
        $price(Course, Price),$
        $paid(User, Course, Price).$

    $paid(User, Resource, Price) \leftarrow$
        $credential(CC),$
        $CC.type : credit\_card,$
        $CC.owner : User,$
        $authenticated(User),$
        $charged(Resource, Price, CC).$

    $allow(release(credential(bbbCredential))).$

When Alice requests access to the course, these two policies raise a dynamic negotiation (as depicted in figure 2) allowing them to satisfy their respective policies in an iterative way and successfully perform such an on-line interaction although they were strangers and had not had any other transaction in common.

6   Related Work

To the best of our knowledge, using policy-based behavior control in technology-enhanced learning environments has not been extensively researched. An

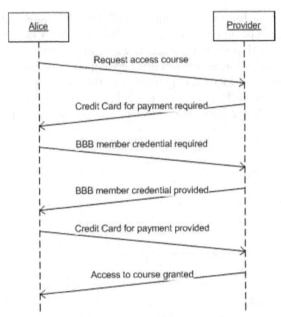

Fig. 2. Example negotiation sequence between Alice and the learning provider

approach aiming at federated access control in web-service based repositories is presented in [8]. In order to allow for an appropriate access control, the policy language XACML and the federated trust framework Shibboleth have been extended and integrated into an ECL middleware. In this framework, policies are based on a simple attribute directory service. In LionShare [10], there is a similar approach exploiting Shibboleth. Security is provided by so-called Access Control Lists expressed in XACML. These lists define which user can access which file depending on the users'properties, such as the membership of a certain faculty. However, none of these approaches allow for expressive access control supporting e.g., action executions, negotiations or explanations and therefore they do not meet the requirements identified in our scenario. Furthermore, using Shibboleth implies the existence of institutions users belong to - which is an assumption that does not apply in an open scenario for lifelong learning. [6] provides an abstract overview on privacy and security issues in advanced learning technologies, suggesting that policies may be used in an educational context. But neither scenarios nor specific details are provided. [17] deals with policies based on the Ponder policy language within the scope of collaborative e-learning systems. The use of policies in such a framework is basically restricted to role-based access control and therefore does not match the need of an open learning environment as described above.

7   Conclusions and Further Work

Open lifelong learning environments require flexible and interoperable approaches which are easy to use and to personalize by learners and tutors. This paper describes an advanced scenario for collaboration, exchange and utilization of learning resources. It also shows how policies can naturally address the requirements extracted from such a scenario providing benefits not only in flexibility and dynamicity but also additional features like reasoning and exchangeability. The paper gives an overview of existing policy frameworks and compares them according to the requirements previously identified. Finally, the paper shows how an existing policy language can be used in order to specify policies that may be used at runtime to e.g., control access to resources, perform negotiations or generate explanations.

As part of the TENCompetence project [14], which aims at supporting individuals, groups and organizations in lifelong competence development, we are currently working toward the exploitation of policies in order to increase and enhance the possibilities the TENCompetence infrastructure provides. According to the features provided by the different frameworks, we investigate the use Protune in order to support, among others, negotiations and advanced explanations, key issues for our open infrastructure.

Acknowledgements

The authors' efforts were (partly) funded by the European Commission in the TENCompetence project (IST-2004-02787) (http://www.tencompetence.org).

References

1. Anderson, A.H.: An introduction to the web services policy language (wspl). In: POLICY '04: Proceedings of the Fifth IEEE International Workshop on Policies for Distributed Systems and Networks (POLICY'04), p. 189. IEEE Computer Society, Washington, DC, USA (2004)
2. Bonatti, P.A., Olmedilla, D.: Driving and monitoring provisional trust negotiation with metapolicies. In: 6th IEEE International Workshop on Policies for Distributed Systems and Networks (POLICY 2005), Stockholm, Sweden, pp. 14–23. IEEE Computer Society, Los Alamitos (2005)
3. Bonatti, P.A., Olmedilla, D., Peer, J.: Advanced policy explanations on the web. In: Piero, A. (ed.) 17th European Conference on Artificial Intelligence (ECAI 2006), Riva del Garda, Italy, pp. 200–204. IOS Press, Amsterdam (2006)
4. Damianou, N., Dulay, N., Lupu, E., Sloman, M.: The ponder policy specification language. In: Sloman, M., Lobo, J., Lupu, E.C. (eds.) POLICY 2001. LNCS, vol. 1995, pp. 18–38. Springer, Heidelberg (2001)
5. Duma, C., Herzog, A., Shahmehri, N.: Privacy in the semantic web: What policy languages have to offer. In: 8th IEEE International Workshop on Policies for Distributed Systems and Networks (POLICY 2007), Bologna, Italy, IEEE Computer Society, Los Alamitos (2007)
6. El-Khatib, Korba, Xu, Yee: Privacy and security in e-learning. International Journal of Distance Education (2003)
7. Gavriloaie, R., Nejdl, W., Olmedilla, D., Seamons, K.E., Winslett, M.: No registration needed: How to use declarative policies and negotiation to access sensitive resources on the semantic web. In: Bussler, C.J., Davies, J., Fensel, D., Studer, R. (eds.) ESWS 2004. LNCS, vol. 3053, pp. 342–356. Springer, Heidelberg (2004)

8. Hatala, M., Eap, T.M.T., Shah, A.: Unlocking repositories: Federated security solution for attribute and policy based access to repositories via web services. In: ARES '06: Proceedings of the First International Conference on Availability, Reliability and Security (ARES'06), pp. 895–903. IEEE Computer Society, Washington, DC, USA (2006)

9. Kagal, L., Finin, T.W., Joshi, A.: A policy language for a pervasive computing environment. In: 4th IEEE International Workshop on Policies for Distributed Systems and Networks (POLICY), Lake Como, Italy, p. 63. IEEE Computer Society, Los Alamitos (2003)

10. The lionshare project, http://lionshare.its.psu.edu/

11. Nabeth, T., Roda, C., Angehrn, A.A., Mittal, P.K.: Using artificial agents to stimulate participation in virtual communities. In: IADIS International Conference CELDA (Cognition and Exploratory Learning in Digital Age) (2005)

12. Nejdl, W., Wolf, B., Qu, C., Decker, S., Sintek, M., Naeve, A., Nilsson, M., Palmer, M., Risch, T., Edutella, A.: P2P networking infrastructure based on RDF. In: 11th International World Wide Web Conference (WWW'02), Hawaii, USA (June 2002)

13. OASIS eXtensible Access Control Markup Language, http://www.oasis-open.org/specs/index.php#xacmlv2.0

14. TENCompetence: building the european network for lifelong competence development. http://www.tencompetence.org/

15. Uszok, A., Bradshaw, J.M., Jeffers, R., Suri, N., Hayes, P.J., Breedy, M.R., Bunch, L., Johnson, M., Kulkarni, S., Lott, J.: Kaos policy and domain services: Toward a description-logic approach to policy representation, deconfliction, and enforcement. In: 4th IEEE International Workshop on Policies for Distributed Systems and Networks (POLICY), Lake Como, Italy, p. 93. IEEE Computer Society, Los Alamitos (2003)

16. Winsborough, W.H., Seamons, K.E., Jones, V.E.: Automated trust negotiation. DARPA Information Survivability Conference and Exposition. IEEE Press, Los Alamitos (2000)

17. Yang, Lin, Lin: Policy-based privacy and security management for collaborative e-education systems. In: 5th IASTED Multi-Conference Computers and Advanced Technology in Education, Cancun, Mexico (2002)

Proposing the Underlying Causes That Lead to the Trainee's Erroneous Actions to the Trainer

Naïma El-Kechaï and Christophe Després

Laboratoire d'Informatique de l'Université du Maine (LIUM)
Avenue Laënnec, 72085 Le Mans Cedex 9, France
{elkechai,despres}@lium.univ-lemans.fr

Abstract. When a trainer aims to provide trainees with appropriate help and assistance, she/he needs to know what errors the trainee is making and furthermore what causes lead to these errors. In this paper, we propose a mechanism which infers the underlying causes that lead to the production of the trainee's erroneous action in order to support the trainer in her/his monitoring activity. This mechanism is based on and uses CREAM, a second-generation method of Human Reliability Analysis (HRA). We implement this mechanism by using Dempster-Shafer's theory.

Keywords: Causal mechanisms of erroneous actions, Safety and emergency procedures, Trainer assistance, CREAM, Dempster-Shafer's Theory.

1 Introduction

The context of this work relates to the design and development of Virtual Environments for Training (VET). We are interested in Learning By Doing (LBD) activities [1] that aim at enabling trainees to develop skills related to procedural tasks in the vocational training area. More precisely, we focus on procedural tasks dealing with issues of safety and risk. These procedures can imply emergency (surgery and intensive care procedures), complexity (diagnostic of breakdowns/failures), risks (handling switches on high speed train tracks) etc.

Because these activities are strongly and highly involving, they require a great attention from the trainer who monitors the trainees and manages the training sessions. We assume that the trainer rely on the trainees' errors to advise, help, and provide the trainees with appropriate and relevant guidance during the task achievement. Nevertheless, the trainer cannot observe and manage several trainees at the same time and in the same way. To support the trainer and assist her/him in her/his monitoring activity, in a previous work [2], we proposed a framework that supports two main issues (i) the detection of the trainee's unforeseen behavior by using Hollnagel's classification of erroneous actions [3-5], and (ii) a recognition process based on a task model METISSE that we proposed. This model which is used to describe the procedures the trainee has to do, allows the trainee's erroneous actions to be detected.

E. Duval, R. Klamma, and M. Wolpers (Eds.): EC-TEL 2007, LNCS 4753, pp. 41–55, 2007.
© Springer-Verlag Berlin Heidelberg 2007

This article is about the continuation of the proposals mentioned above. We propose here to seek the underlying causal mechanisms which lead to the occurrence of the trainee's erroneous actions. We believe that providing the trainer with the causes which may explain the trainee's situation of failure allows her/him to focus on and decide what assistance she/he will provide the trainee with.

This mechanism is based on CREAM [4], a second-generation method of Human reliability Analysis (HRA). CREAM allows us not only to infer the causes of the trainee's erroneous actions but also the explanations about the succession of the causal links leading to these inferences. The results produced by this mechanism (causes and causal links) are then proposed to the trainer. To implement this mechanism we use a probabilistic theory, the Dempster-Shafer theory [6] [7].

We point out that the objective of this work is not to evaluate how the trainers will use the results produced by this mechanism. We aim to address causality about the trainee's erroneous actions by using a human reliability analysis method and to show how we automate this method which remains, as far as we know, a manual method.

2   Related Works

Approaches based on formal models of probability for reasoning under uncertainty have met a growth of interest in plan inference techniques [8] [9]. Nevertheless, they have received little attention in intelligent tutoring systems [10] [11]. Students are by definition incompetent in the domain and such users tend to have very novel ways of erring. This adds a great deal of uncertainty when inferring student' plans. Much effort has been devoted to the student modeling [12] to understand what the student is trying to do. For instance, [13] [14] and [15] use Bayesian networks to make probabilistic cognitive diagnosis, plan recognition, and knowledge assessment. Like these approaches, we use formal models of probability, i.e. causal networks and Dempster-Shafer's theory (cf. §5.2 and 5.4). However, unlike these approaches, we do not attempt to "build" a trainee model or to assess the trainee's knowledge. The focus of our work is to "understand", not exclusively at a "knowledge level", why the trainee's erroneous actions occurred, in order to suggest to the trainer the causes which are likely to explain the production of these erroneous actions. And for doing this diagnosis; we use a human reliability analysis method which fits our context, i.e. the procedures dealing with issues of safety and risk.

3   Previous Work

In a previous work, we proposed an approach which consists of three propositions in order to assess what the trainee is doing and to interpret her/his behavior. The first deals with task modeling, the second with error detection, and the third with plan recognition. We summarize these propositions. For more details, see [2].

For describing the procedures that the trainee has to do according to pedagogical goals, we proposed METISSE a tutoring-oriented task model. METISSE is based on the ergonomics task model MAD* [16] adapted to the training area by integrating the Task/Method paradigm [17] [18]. METISSE describes the procedure in terms of

Tasks and *Methods*, which respectively correspond to declarative (what to do) and procedural (how to do it) characteristics of a task.

To detect the trainee's errors, we proposed to use Hollnagel's classification of erroneous actions [3-5]. This classification, which provides a structured way of modeling a space of possible errors, is adapted to METISSE and allows the trainee's unforeseen behavior to be identified. Hollnagel [3, 4] proposed a clear distinction between manifestations, i.e. observable actions, and causes leading to the production of these actions. He proposes the term *erroneous actions* to describe a certain type of action without implying anything about the cause. To highlight this distinction, Hollnagel uses the terms *phenotype* to refer to patterns of *erroneous action* that are observable, and *genotype* to refer to patterns in the *underlying causal mechanisms* that lead to *phenotypes*. The *phenotypes* also referred to as *error modes* are used to infer the *genotypes*. This aspect, which is the core issue of this work, is developed in the following section.

To assess what the trainee is doing and infer her/his plans, we proposed a plan recognition mechanism based on the task model METISSE. Plans are derived from METISSE *tasks* and *methods*. A plan is simple if it relates to an observable action and composite if it splits a task into sub-tasks. In [2], we showed how the algorithms of simple and composite plans lead to the detection of *erroneous actions* according to Hollnagel's classification.

Now we address the core issue of this work, namely the need to infer the causes which lead to the production of the trainee's erroneous action. In other words, giving the result of the previous work described above, i.e. the *phenotype*, we propose to use a second-generation method of Human Reliability Analysis (HRA) called CREAM [4] to seek the causes, i.e. the *genotypes*. This method is, as far as we know, used manually by human analysts. We propose here a mechanism for implementing it. The results obtained by this mechanism are then proposed to the trainer and consists of (i) the *genotypes* that lead to the occurrence of this *phenotype;* and (ii) explanations about these inferences, i.e. the succession of the causal links from the *phenotype* towards its *genotypes*.

4   From Erroneous Actions Towards Its Underlying Causes

Hollnagel points out that a model of phenotypes of erroneous action is not simply that it can describe all possible behaviours, but the value of a phenotype model is precisely that it can provide pointers or suggestions to the analyst about the genotypical forms or causes that produced the behavior. Therefore, rather than simply constructing a set of patterns of deviation that are sufficient to describe the phenomenon of interest, Hollnagel adopts a more structured approach. This approach, called CREAM, relates to the human reliability analysis (HRA).

Before going further, we point out that although methods of HRA have been mostly applied to task performance in the context of critical systems, they could serve as a framework for monitoring errors during task performance in training situations, especially when these tasks relate to procedures dealing with issues of safety and risk.

4.1 CREAM

CREAM, acronym for Cognitive Reliability and Error Analysis Method, can be used as a stand-alone analysis method for either retrospective (identification of the causes that lead to the observed manifestations) or prospective (prediction of the possible and probable outcomes) analyses, using a consistent taxonomy for *error modes* (or *phenotypes*) and *error causes* (or *genotypes*) [4]. This work lies on the retrospective analysis since we seek the causal mechanisms which underlie the trainee's observed erroneous actions.

CREAM consists of three components: a *method*, a *classification scheme*, and a *model of cognition*. Owing to the lack of space, we will only detail the two first components.

4.2 CREAM Method

The method describes how the analysis of actions can be performed in order to find the possible and probable causes; in particular how the concepts and categories used for explanation can be applied. This method explicitly describes how each step is to be carried out, as well as define the principles to determine when the analysis has come to an end-point, i.e. the stop rule. The *method* refers to the *classification scheme* and is recursive due to its *classification scheme* organization.

Before going further, we make a note on the used terminology. The analysis will contain a number of consecutive steps providing the explanation why the erroneous action occurred. Each step has got a cause, and causes an effect, so it might be confusing using the terms *'cause'* and *'effect'* both for the beginning and end and for describing the steps in between. Thus, in the following the terms 'effect' or *phenotype*, and 'cause' or *genotype*, are used for the start and end points of the analysis; the effects of the steps in between are called *consequents* (happening as a result) and the causes are called *antecedents* (happening before), respectively. A *consequent/antecedent* can be *general* or *specific*.

The analysis is performed by carrying out the following steps. The first step consists in determining and describing the context by using the concept of the *Common Performance Conditions (CPC)*. In short, the *CPC* are proposed as a way of capturing the essential aspects of the situation and the conditions of work which through long experience are known to have consequences for how work is carried out and in particular for how erroneous actions occur [4]. The second step consists in describing the different *error modes* (or *phenotypes*). The third and last step consists in identifying the *genotypes* which may explain the occurrence of the *phenotype* by taking into account the *CPC*.

The starting point of the retrospective analysis is the *phenotype* and from there the analysis is performed in a cyclic way as illustrated in figure1. For the determined *error mode*, or *phenotype*, the general *antecedent*(s) is (are) to be determined by using the relations describing tables. For each *general antecedent* the matching *general consequents* have to be searched, again by using the tables. If there are any, the procedure is repeated for each *general consequent*. The analysis is completed when for a given *general consequent* (1) a *specific antecedent* is found (2) no *general antecedent* and no *specific antecedent* is found or (3) no 'reasonable' *antecedent* is found in the given context.

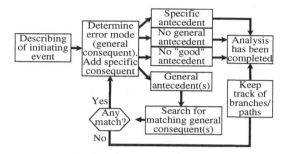

Fig. 1. Detailed method for retrospective analysis [4]

4.3 CREAM Classification Scheme

A number of flexibly connected groups are used in the CREAM *classification scheme*. There are four, one referring to *phenotypes* or *error modes*, and three referring to *genotypes*. We provide here a brief description of all four, a complete list is provided in [3, 4].

The *phenotypes* or *error modes* (Fig. 2) are of four sub-groups: action at wrong time (timing, duration), action of wrong type (distance, speed, direction, force), action at wrong object (neighbour, similar, unrelated object), action in wrong place (omission, jump forward, jump backwards, repetition, reversal, wrong action).

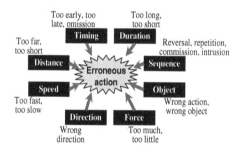

Fig. 2. Dimensions of error modes [3-5]

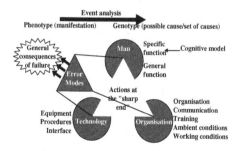

Fig. 3. The four categories of the CREAM classification scheme [4]

The *genotypes* are of three categories (Fig 3): *Person*, *Technology*, and *Organisation related genotypes*.

The first category lies to *the person related genotypes* and consists of three groups of *antecedents*. The first group is about the *specific cognitive functions of a person*. The second and third ones are more general person related functions: *temporary* and *permanent functions*. *The specific cognitive functions* provide explanations about the erroneous action (*phenotype*). Hollnagel makes a distinction between analysis and synthesis. Analysis used to identify the current situation, includes *observation, identification, recognition, diagnosis* etc. Synthesis used to determine what to do and how to do it includes *choice, planning, scheduling* etc. Analysis is described through the sub-groups *observation* and *interpretation*, synthesis through *planning* and *execution*, where *execution* has already been described through the *error modes*. *The temporary person related functions* describe the psychological, physical and emotional states of the person. They may have a limited duration (memory failure, fear, distraction, physiological/psychological stress, fatigue, inattention, and performance variability). *The permanent person related functions* are functional impairment, cognitive style, and cognitive bias. The second category lies to the *technology related genotypes*. It covers technical malfunctions as well as inadequacies of the operational support system and issues of the interface. This category consists of four groups of *antecedents*: *equipment* (equipment failure, software fault); *procedures* (inadequate procedures); *temporary interface problems* (access limitations, ambiguous and/or incomplete information); and *permanent interface problems* (access problems and mislabeling). The last category lies to the *organisation related genotypes*. It covers *genotypes* related to the environment and consists of five groups of *antecedents*: *communication* (communication failure, missing information); *organisation* (maintenance failure, management problem, social pressure etc); *training* (insufficient skills and/or knowledge); *ambient conditions* (temperature, sound etc); and *working conditions* (excessive demand, inadequate team support etc).

5   Using CREAM in Our Context

We use CREAM to infer the causal mechanisms (*genotypes*) which underlie the trainee's erroneous actions (*phenotypes*) in order to propose them to the trainer. CREAM has three advantages: (i) the starting-point of the retrospective analysis of CREAM is the *phenotype* and in our case, the *phenotype* is detected and obtained during the recognition process we proposed in [2]; (ii) CREAM is not a "black box" since it works in an iterative manner and, giving a *phenotype*, produces a *genotype* by providing all the possible causal links. In other words, the different links between *consequents* and *antecedents* are "visible" and clear. Thus, the results suggested to the trainer provide on the one hand, the *genotype(s)* which may explain the trainee's erroneous actions, and on the other hand the different links which explain these results. This allows the trainer to better "understand" the inferences; (iii) the third advantage is that CREAM can be applied for different applications and domains. This is due mainly to the fact that its *classification scheme* is "generic". Nevertheless, Hollnagel points out that the *classification scheme* can be adapted to a domain or a particular application by modifying some categories. In the following section we summarize the main modifications and adaptations we have made.

5.1   Adaptation and Modification of the CREAM Classification Scheme

The *classification scheme* used in CREAM has two criteria. The first one is that the groups of the classification must respect the principle of differentiation or specialization between the three categories of *genotypes*. The second one is that the number of groups must be sufficiently important to recognize all the "reasonable" *antecedents* and *causes*. However, it should not be too important or the analysis would be more difficult.

We adapt the CREAM *classification scheme* by removing the *antecedents* strongly related to industry like *maintenance failure, inadequate quality control, inadequate work place* and *management problem*. We have also modified some terms to fit the training context. We replaced *working conditions* by *training conditions, equipment* by *resource, boss/colleague* by *trainer/other trainees*. Moreover, the use of virtual environments may induce some other difficulties for the trainees in addition to those related to the task requirements and achievement. So we added some (but not exhaustive) *specific antecedents* like *bad manipulation of virtual objects, wrong orientation, bad visual quality, latency time* and *cybersickness*.

To search for the *causes* which underlie the trainee's erroneous actions, we need to know to what category the different *antecedents* (*general* and *specific*) belong to. So the last modification we have made is to dispatch the different *specific antecedents* into the three classification categories: *Person, Technology,* and *Organization* noted respectively *P, T,* and *O*. For example, *cognitive overload* belongs to the *P* category, *parallel tasks* to the *O* category, and *bad visual quality* to the *T* category.

5.2   The Causal Network

As mentioned earlier, the two first steps of the CREAM method are: describing the *CPC,* and describing the different *error modes* or *phenotypes* (cf. §4.2). In our case, the *phenotype* is obtained during the recognition process (cf. §3). The last step consists in identifying the *genotypes* which may explain the occurrence of the *phenotype* by taking into account the *CPC*.

So, we assume that a good way for implementing the method CREAM consists in identifying the categories which seem more relevant to "explain" the occurrence of the trainee's erroneous action. For this, we consider Hollnagel's classification as a *causal network* where nodes represent the different *antecedents* and *consequents,* and the arcs between nodes represent the *causal links* or dependencies. For example, the figure 4 illustrates a small and simplified part of the *network* related to the phenotype *Wrong Object* (the trainee carried out an action on an object different from the expected one). For a purpose of simplification, we give a simplified example; the whole network is illustrated in figure 5.

In this example, *Wrong object* has three *antecedents: Observation missed* which belongs to the *P* category, *access problems* which belongs to the *T* category, and *communication failure* which belongs to the *O* category. In addition, *Observation missed* and *Communication failure* have each one two *antecedents: Faulty diagnosis* and *Inattention* for the first; *Functional impairment* and *Inattention* for the second. The arrow direction represents the link causality: *Inattention* may lead to *Observation missed* which in turn may lead to *Wrong object*. In this network example, there are four leaves representing four *genotypes* which have no *antecedents*: *Faulty diagnosis*, *Inattention*, *Access problems*, and *Functional impairment*. These four genotypes are the possible causes which explain the use of a wrong object. To classify them from the most likely to the least one, we propose to:

- Outweigh the different categories *P*, *T*, and *O* according to the context since each node (*consequent* and *antecedent*) belongs to one of them;
- Spread these weights in the network by using Dempster-Shafer's Theory.

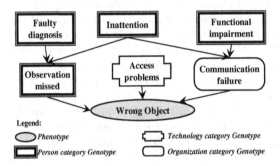

Fig. 4. A simplified causal network for the 'Wrong object' *phenotype*

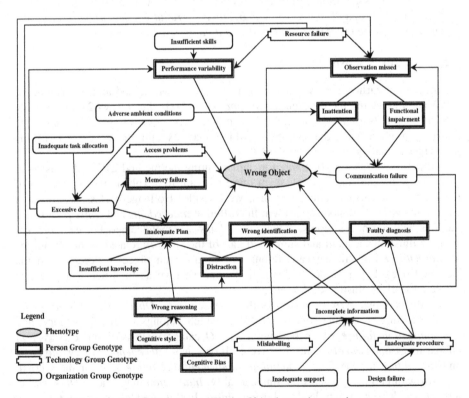

Fig. 5. The whole '*Wrong Object*' causal network

5.3 Weighting the Three Categories

As said before, the purpose of the *CPC* is to provide an adequate description using a limited number of factors or aspects which describe the general determinants of performance. The number of *CPC* is kept relatively small in order to make the analysis manageable [4].

The identification of the *CPC* as proposed in CREAM is manually done by human analysts. In our context, it would require a great involvement from the trainer and this work aims to assist her/him in her/his monitoring activity and not to overload her/him. That is why we propose to automate this identification by asking her/him few specific questions before the training session in order to initialize and set the weights of the three categories of *consequents* and *antecedents*. Currently, this Yes/No questionnaire is relatively simple and consists of six questions, two per category (*P, T,* and *O*). These questions illustrated in the figure 6, are inspired by those proposed by Hollnagel to the human analysts who use CREAM.

The weight of a category *Ci* is obtained thanks to the formula (1). This weight is included in the interval [0,1].

$$Weight(Ci) = \frac{\text{Number of "Yes" to the questions relating to the category } Ci}{\text{Number of "Yes"}} \quad (1)$$

where *Ci* is one of the categories *P, T,* or *O*.

If all the trainer's answers are negatives, or all the trainer's answers are positives, or if she/he ignores the questionnaire, we consider the three categories as equally plausible so the weight of each is 0.33. For example, if thanks to the questionnaire we obtain the following results: *P* 0,5; *T* 0,25; and *O* 0,25; the *P* category *genotypes* are those which are likely to explain the trainee's erroneous actions. In this case, in the figure 4 example, it seems at first sight that the following inferences are the most likely because all the *antecedents* of the causal links relate to the category *P* (*Inattention → Observation missed → Wrong object*), and (*Faulty diagnosis → Observation missed → Wrong object*).

Now, we show how we automate the spreading of the categories weight through the network and how we obtain the intuitively found result by using Dempster-Shafer's Theory (DST) [6] [7].

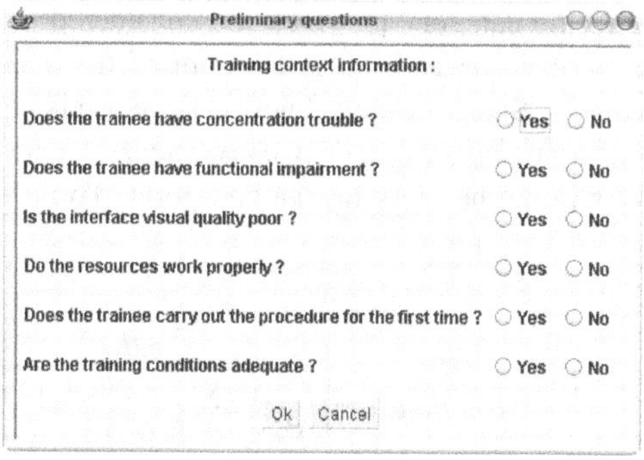

Fig. 6. The questionnaire proposed to the trainer

5.4 Spreading the Masses in the Causal Network by Using the Evidence Theory

The basic idea of Dempster-Shafer's Theory (DST) or *Evidence Theory* is that an observation makes that a certain *degree of confidence* is assigned to various hypotheses. Additional information will cause the *degree of confidence* (or the *evidence mass*) to be concentrated on a smaller number of hypotheses until eventually the correct one remains.

Let Ω denote the set of all possible hypotheses $\{H_1, H_2, \ldots, H_N\}$, called *frame of discernment*. From this *frame of discernment*, a set 2^Ω is defined which corresponds to the 2^N subsets A of Ω: $2^\Omega = \{A | A \subseteq \Omega\} = \{\emptyset, \{H_1\}, \ldots, \{H_N\}, \{H_1, H_2\}, \ldots, \Omega\}$.

2^Ω corresponds to the singleton subsets of Ω (each hypothesis H_i) but also to the non-singleton subsets A of Ω standing for the disjunction of all their members. The DST assigns the *degree of confidence,* also referred to as a *mass* (in the following, we will use the term *mass*) to 2^Ω by using a *belief function* $m_\Omega : 2^\Omega \to [0,1]$ having these two properties $m_\Omega(\emptyset) = 0$ and $\sum m_\Omega(A) = 1$ where $A \subseteq \Omega$.

From our point of view, the main advantage of DST relatively to other probabilistic approaches like Bayesian networks (cf. §2) is the possibility to assign a *mass* to a set A but not to a particular subset of A. In other words, $m_\Omega(A)$ pertains only to the set A and makes no additional claims about any subsets of A, owing to the lack of knowledge. And in our context, the incoming information we have is (1) the causal network representing the CREAM *classification scheme* (2) the trainee's erroneous action, i.e. the *phenotype* obtained during the recognition process, and (3) the weight of each of the three categories P, T, and O. Thus, we can not "transpose" the *classification scheme*, i.e. the causal network, into a probabilistic graph since we cannot valuate its different nodes. The information we have (weights of the three categories P, T, and O) allows us to only give a *mass* to the sets of *consequents/antecedents* belonging to a specific category. In our case, Ω corresponds to the nodes of the causal network, i.e. all possible *consequents/antecedents* of the *classification* which may explain the cause of the trainee's erroneous action. The network leaves represent the *genotypes* and the sum of their mass is equal to 1. The *genotypes* proposed to the trainer are the network leaves classified by descending order according to their *mass*.

To calculate each leaf mass, we spread the *masses* from the *consequents* towards the *antecedents* of the classification. Each *consequent* gives to its *antecedent* a part of its *mass* according to the category to which the considered *antecedent* belongs to (P, T, or O). The *mass* of an *antecedent* is the sum of the *masses* provided by its parents, i.e. its *consequents*. Since the causal network we use is acyclic, an *antecedent* cannot be at the same time *antecedent* and *consequent* of another *antecedent*, the spreading of the *masses* in the network has an end-point. To do this we propose this formula:

$$m(a) = w\big(C(a)\big) \times \sum_{\forall b \in Cons(a)} \left(\frac{m(b)}{\sum_{\forall i \in \{P, T, O\}} \big(w(i) \times n_{ib}\big)} \right) \qquad (2)$$

Where:
- *m(a)* is the mass of the *antecedent* a,
- *C(a)* is the category of *a,*
- *Cons(a)* is the *consequents* set of *a,*

- *w(i)* is the weight of the category *i,*
- n_{ib} is the number of the *antecedents* of *b* belonging to the category *i.*

Let us detail the calculation of the *mass* of *Inattention* of the figure 4 example. For doing this, we need the *masses* of *Observation missed* and *Communication failure* since *Inattention* is the *antecedent* of these two *consequents.*

m(Observation missed)=0,5; m(Communication failure)=0,25.

According to the formula (2), the *mass* of *Inattention* (see fig 7) is thus *m(Inattention)=0,375.* According to these results, the *genotypes* and *causal links* proposed to the trainer are as follows (tab.1), they correspond well to those found intuitively (cf §5.3).

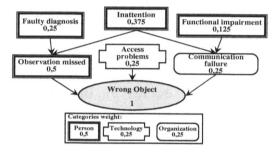

Fig. 7. Spreading of the masses in the causal network

Table 1. The genotypes and causal links proposed to the trainer

Genotype, Mass	Causal Link
1 Inattention, mass=**0,375**	Inattention→Observation missed→Wrong object
2 Faulty diagnosis, mass=0,25	Faulty diagnosis→Observation missed→Wrong object
2 Access problems, mass=**0,25**	Access problems→Wrong object
3 Functional impairment, mass=**0,125**	Functional impairment→Communication failure→ Wrong object

6 Implementation of CREAM

We have implemented CREAM using a rule-based approach for two main reasons. The first is that a rule-based system works in an opportunist way. A rule is triggered only when the associated *phenotype* is concerned, so the analysis and the spreading of the *masses* is not done on the whole classification. There are as many causal networks as *phenotypes* and each phenotype will trigger its causal network. The second reason is that the classification is not "hard-coded", a modification in the classification does not imply major ones. In the section §0, we outlined some modifications we have made in the classification to fit our context. So, if we want to add, modify, or remove some *antecedents/consequents* of a given *genotype*, we only have to add, modify, or remove its corresponding rule and also modify the number of *antecedents* of the considered *genotype* in the formula (2). For example, the table below describes some *general* and *specific antecedents* of the *genotype 'Memory failure'* of *P* category, group *temporary functions.*

Table 2. Some *general* and *specific antecedents* for *Memory failure*

General consequent	General antecedents	Specific antecedents
Memory failure	Excessive demand	Other priority

The rule which adds the genotype *'Memory failure'* and its *antecedents* to the knowledge base is:

```
(defrule Memoryfailure
?f1<-(genotype (name "Memory failure") (category
Person) (mass ?m) (nbchildP ?nbP) (nbchildT ?nbT)
(nbchildO ?nbO) (link $?c))
=>
(assert (genotype (name "Excessive demand") (category
Organization) (mass (calculpoids ?m ?*valO* ?nbP ?nbT
?nbO)) (nbchildP 0) (nbchildT 0) (nbchildO 4) (link
Excessive demand --> ?c)))
(assert (genotype (name "Other priority") (category
Person) (mass (calculpoids ?m ?*valO* ?nbP ?nbT ?nbO))
(nbchildP 0) (nbchildT 0) (nbchildO 0) (link Other
priority --> ?c))))
```

Where:
- mass is the formula (2) which calculates the genotype *mass.*
- nbchildX is the number of the genotype *antecedents* (*specific* and *general*) belonging to the category X (*P*, *T*, or *O*). In this example, *Excessive demand* has 4 *antecedents* which all belong to the *O* category: 2 general (*inadequate task allocation, adverse ambient conditions*) and 2 specific (*unexpected tasks, parallel tasks*)[1]. *Other priority*, which belongs to *Person* category, has no *antecedents* since it is a *specific antecedent.*

7   Some Results and Discussion

We implemented this mechanism for the training of train drivers of the SNCF (the French National Railway Company) to handle the switches on high speed train tracks.

These switches are remotely controlled by a railway signalman. When a technical problem removes this remote control, the railway signalman asks the train driver (the train which is moving towards the defective switch rail) to handle manually the switch rail, i.e. to perform a procedure called MAIL (for Manoeuvre d'AIguiLle désignée, i.e. handling manually the switch rail). This procedure consists of several tasks. Once on the track, the driver, equipped with a post key, must go to the post containing the

---

[1] These antecedents, corresponding to other tables, are added to the knowledge base.

key of the (defective) switch rail engine; open the case using the post key; take the key on right (the post contains two keys similar in appearance but only the key on right can switch off the remote control); find the engine and handle the switch rail manually; and report. The sub-task "take the key on right" is represented with the task model METISSE in Fig. 8. During training sessions; a typical erroneous action (*phenotype*) often occurs. The trainee takes the key on left instead of the one on right. This erroneous action occurs either when the trainee does not know what key to take or when he has difficulties to take the key on right in the VET.

Fig. 8. 'A wrong object' example in the procedure MAIL of the SNCF

When applied to this simple example, our mechanism produced the results given in table 3, and this according to different combinations of the (*P, T, O*) weights. If there are more than five results for a combination, we give only the five first. As shown, most of the results correspond to the expected ones. When the *P* (or *T*) category weight is equal to 1, all the proposed causes belong to the *P* (or *T*) category. But when the *O* category weight is equal to 1, the mechanism gives a single result corresponding to the *specific antecedent Noise* of the *O* category. This single result is unconvincing and this is may be due to the fact that we have not adapted sufficiently the *classification scheme* to our context. In addition, the *masses* of some causes are very closer; this is mainly due to the simplicity of the questionnaire proposed to the trainer. This suggests that our mechanism would gain to be improved by refining both the *classification scheme* and the questionnaire.

Table 3. Some causes and causal links of the 'Wrong object' *phenotype*

(P,T,O) weights	Genotype, mass	Causal links
(1; 0; 0)	1 : Inattention, mass=**0,24**	Inattention → Wrong object
	2 : Cybersickness, mass=**0,10**	Cybersickness → Performance variability → Wrong object
	2 : Illness, mass=**0,10**	Illness → Performance variability → Wrong object
	3 : Information overload, mass=**0,09**	Information overload → Wrong identification → Wrong object

Table 3. (*continued*)

	4 : Distraction, mass=**0,08**	Distraction → Wrong identification → Wrong object
(0; 1; 0)	1 : Inadequate procedure, mass=0,33	Inadequate procedure → Wrong object
	1 : Incorrect label, mass=0,33	Incorrect label → Wrong object
	1 : Problem access, mass=**0,33**	Access problems → Wrong object
(0; 0; 1)	1 : Noise, mass=1,00	Noise→Communication failure→Wrong object
(0,33; 0,33; 0,33)	1 : Adverse ambient conditions, mass=0,16	Adverse ambient conditions → Inattention → Wrong object
	2 : Design failure, mass=0,12	Design failure → Inadequate procedure → Wrong object
	3 : Incorrect label, mass=0,11	Incorrect label → Wrong object
	3 : Problem access, mass=0,11	Access problems → Wrong object
	4 : Functional impairment, mass=0,04	Functional impairment → Communication failure → Wrong object
	4 : Noise, mass=0,04	Noise → Communication failure → Wrong object

8   Summary and Perspectives

The main objective of this work is to support and assist the trainer in her/his monitoring activity by providing her/him with relevant information about (1) the plausible causes that lead to the production of the trainee's erroneous action; and (2) the causal links explaining these inferences. We believe that addressing causality about the trainee's erroneous actions enable the trainer to better understand why the erroneous action occurred, and to react consequently. We did not evaluate how the trainers will use the results produced by this mechanism. The main focus of this work is to show how automating the CREAM method which remains, as far as we know, a manual method

Currently, we propose a questionnaire to the trainer before the training session in order to initialize the nodes *masses* in the causal network. This questionnaire is relatively simplistic and would be improved by additional information. For example, more precise information could be considered such as "classes" of problems, "classes" of procedures, or "classes" of trainnees that the trainer encounter in her/his monitoring activity.

In addition, the causes (with the causal links) are proposed to the trainer according to their *mass*. The trainer can choose among the cause(s) and causal links(s) the one(s) which seem more relevant to her/him. In other words, the trainer's ordering may differ from the one produced by the mechanism. Therefore we have and need to take into account her/his choices and adapt the mechanism to her/his practices. In order to reflect the impact of her/his choices on the valuation of the hypothetic causes and assess new evidences, we intend to improve our mechanism by integrating machine learning techniques, what Dempster-Shafer's Theory enable us to do.

References

1. Schank, R.C., Berman, T.R., Macperson, K.A.: Learning by doing, in Instructional-Design Theories and Models. In: Reigeluth, C.M. (ed.) A New Paradigm of Instructional Theory, pp. 161–181. Lawrence Erlbaum Associates, Mahwah, NJ (1999)
2. El-Kechaï, N., Després., C.: A Plan Recognition Process, Based on a Task Model, for Detecting Learner's Erroneous Actions. In: ITS, Jhongli, Taïwan, pp. 329–338. Springer-Verlag, Berlin Heidelberg (2006)
3. Hollnagel, E.: The phenotype of erroneous actions. International Journal of Man-Machine Studies 39, 1–32 (1993)
4. Hollnagel, E.: Cognitive Reliability and Error Analysis Method. Elsevier Science, Oxford (1998)
5. Hollnagel, E.: Looking for errors of omission and commission or the hunting of the Snark revisited. Reliability Engineering and Systems Safety 68, 135–145 (2000)
6. Shafer, G.: A Mathematical Theory of Evidence. Princeton University Press (1976)
7. Dempster, A.P.: Upper and lower probabilities induced by a multivalued mapping. Annals of Mathematical Statistics, 325–339 (1967)
8. Charniak, E., Goldman, R.P.: A Bayesian model of plan recognition. Artificial Intelligence 64, 53–79 (1992)
9. Bauer, M.: A Dempster-Shafer approach to modeling agents preferences in plan recognition. User Modeling and User-Adapted Interaction 5(3-4), 317–348 (1995)
10. Greer, J., Koehn, G.M.: The Peculiarities of Plan Recognition for Intelligent Tutoring Systems. In: IJCAI Workshop on the Next Generation of Plan Recognition Systems, pp. 54–59 (1995)
11. Carberry, S.: Techniques for Plan Recognition. User Modeling and User-Adapted Interaction 11(1-2), 31–48 (2001)
12. Shute, V.J., Psotka, J.: Intelligent Tutoring Systems: Past, Present and Future. In: Jonassen, D. (ed.) Handbook of Research on Educational Communications and Technology, Scholastic Publications (1996)
13. Conati, C., VanLehn, K.: Probabilistic plan recognition for cognitive apprenticeship. In: 18th Annual Meeting of the Cognitive Science Society, San Diego, CA. USA. pp. 403–408 (1996)
14. Conati, C., Gertner, A., Vanlehn, K.: Using bayesian networks to manage uncertainty in student modeling. User Modeling and User-Adapted Interaction 12(4), 371–417 (2002)
15. Tchétagni, J.M.P., Nkambou, R.: Hierarchical Representation and Evaluation of the Student in an Intelligent Tutoring System. In: ITS, pp. 708–717 (2002)
16. Scapin, D., Bastien, J.M.C.: Analyse des tâches et aide ergonomique à la conception: l'approche MAD*. In: de l'IHM, K. (ed.) Analyse et conception, France, pp. 85–116 (2001)
17. Trichet, F., Tchounikine, P.: DSTM: a Framework to Operationalize and Refine a Problem-Solving Method modeled in terms of Tasks and Methods. Expert Systems With Applications (ESWA) 16, 105–120 (1999)
18. Choquet, C., et al.: Modeling the Knowledge-Based Components of a Learning Environment within the Task/Method Paradigm. In: ITS, pp. 56–65. San Antonio, USA (1998)

Smart Indicators on Learning Interactions

Christian Glahn, Marcus Specht, and Rob Koper

OTEC, Open University of the Netherlands, Valkenburger Weg 177, 6411AT Heerlen,
The Netherlands
{christian.glahn,marcus.specht,rob.koper}@ou.nl

Abstract. Indicators help actors to organise, orientate, and navigate through environments by providing contextual information that is relevant for performing learning tasks. In this article we analyse the requirements, present a model and an initial prototype of a software system that uses smart indicators to support learners to be more engaged into the learning process. We argue that indicators need adaptation as learners develop on their learning paths in order to support interactions throughout the learning process. The learning interaction cycle of Garries, Ahlers and Driskel is used as a model for developing an architecture that supports the interaction between a learner and a learning environment. The technical feasibility of the architecture has been tested by implementing that is critically reflected on technical and educational concepts. This article concludes with an outlook on our future research, in which the model will be evaluated by applying the prototype in a learning community.

Keywords: personal learning environments, adaptive instructions, learner support, context awareness.

1 Introduction

When performing a learning task, people need various types of information in order to monitor the progress of the task. The basis for this information is provided by what we call *indicators*. Indicators provide a simplified representation of the state of a complex system that can be understood without much training. For instance, the fuel needle of a car is an indicator that summarizes how full the tank is and how far one can drive. Without much training people understand that it is necessary to find a filling station if the fuel needle points towards the lower end of the scale. To make the appropriate decision it is not necessary to know the size of the fuel tank, the exact amount of fuel that is left in it, or about the fuel consumption of the motor. Some cars switch on an additional light, if the fuel level falls below a critical level. Such indicators focus the attention to important facts that one could miss or ignore otherwise. The telephone bell is another example for such indicators: It indicates that someone is calling on the phone, of which one would not be aware of, unless the telephone line is checked actively. This leads to another characteristic of indicators: They help to focus on relevant information when it is required, while people don't have to bother about it most of the time.

Actors depend on indicators in order to organise, orientate and navigate through complex environments by utilising contextual information [8, 45]. Contextual

E. Duval, R. Klamma, and M. Wolpers (Eds.): EC-TEL 2007, LNCS 4753, pp. 56–70, 2007.
© Springer-Verlag Berlin Heidelberg 2007

information on the learning process has been proven as important to support. This information stimulates the learners' engagement in and commitment to collaborating processes [4, 31, 39]; it helps to raise awareness of and stimulates reflection about acquired competences [28, 29]; and it supports thoughtful behaviour in navigation and on learning paths [43]. Despite this evidence on the role of indicators, little research has been conducted on the problem of adapting indicators to the changing needs of the learners throughout their learning process.

The research presented in this article investigates how to make non-formal and informal learning more attractive. The main focus is on how to support learners in their engagement in and reflection on the learning process by providing smart indicators. In this article we critically reflect on our work on smart indicators: Based on the concept of context aware systems [16] and the learning interaction cycle of Garries, Ahlers, & Driskel [21] we specify the requirements of smart indicators. These requirements are discussed in the following two sections. In order to meet these requirements, we have developed a model and a system architecture. In section four we explore this architecture and analyse the gaps in current research on indicators related to it. The technical feasibility has been tested of the architecture by implementing a prototype. In the fifth section, we critically reflect on the technical and educational concepts that were implemented into this system. We conclude this article by giving an outlook on our future research, in which we evaluate the model by applying the prototype to support learner engagement in collaborative learning.

2 Defining Indicator Systems

In the previous section we have highlighted some principles of indicators. With regard to learning technology, feedback and recommender systems meet these principles. Therefore, it is necessary to distinguish indicator systems from them. Feedback systems [38, 40] analyze user interactions to inform learners on their performance on a task and to guide the learners through it. Recommender systems analyze interactions in order to recommend suitable follow-up activities [1]. The objective of both system types is to affect a learner's future activities by providing useful information. Both approaches are tightly coupled to goals or processes that are shared within a learning community. In contrast, indicator systems provide information about past actions or the current state of the learning process, without making suggestions for future actions. Having these considerations in mind, we define indicator systems as following.

An indicator system is a system that informs a user on a status, on past activities or on events that have occurred in a context; and helps the user to orientate, organize or navigate in that context without recommending specific actions.

It is a fundamental insight that humans actively search for relations to their previous interactions, in particular for indicators that provide information on the success and the value of their actions. This is especially the case if the actions are based on strategies that require alignment during the interaction process [25, 45]. In other words, people continuously seek for indicators that help them to verify or modify their actions, tactics and strategies.

One can argue that this applies to learning processes as we learn from research on feedback and self-regulated learning [8, 30, 34, 37]. Indicators on learning are important facilitators of these processes and are based on three general principles [15, 28, 30]:

- Indicators rely on monitoring of the learning actions and the learning context.
- Indicators have to adapt according to a learners' goals, actions, performance, outcomes, and history as well as to the context in which the learning takes place.
- Indicators are responses to a learner's actions or to changes in the context of the learning process, where the response is not necessarily immediate.

Most indicators implement a static approach of providing information to learners rather than adapting to the learning process [2, 5, 9, 10, 19, 20, 22, 24, 26, 28, 32, 33, 35, 36]. These approaches are considered as static as they follow a fixed rule-set to collect, to aggregate and to indicate information to learners. In contrast, *smart indicator systems* adapt their approach of information aggregation and indication according to a learner's situation or context.

3   Cycles of Learning Interactions

Indicators are part of the interaction between a learner and a system, which is either a social system, such as a group of learners who are supported by a trainer, or a technical system like software for computer-supported training. A single interaction is defined by two parts: an action performed by an actor and a response to this action from the system. With regard to learning, a learning process is described as a chain of interactions: Garries, Ahlers, & Driskel [21] define the learning interaction cycle by single interactions that are connected by the interpretation of a system's response by the learner. At this level a learning process is a flow of interactions between a learner and a corresponding system. On the level of learning interaction cycles, learning processes are considered from a micro-perspective.

However, this definition of the learning interaction cycle is limited because it focuses on the learner's cognitive processes [8, 21]. Indicators are part of the interface of a system. In order to provide smart indicators "the system" cannot be simplified as a black box. Following concepts of context aware systems [14, 16, 47], interaction appears as a symmetrical process between an actor and a system that is interconnected by the system's interface (see **Fig. 1**): Each action of an actor on the interface is analysed and assessed by the system. Based on this analysis the system provides a response to the action on the interface. The actor analyses and reflects on this response to judge the results of the initial action. Further actions depend on the outcomes of this last phase [3, 21].

For learner support it is necessary to understand that each phase of the process affects the learners' engagement and performance [21, 23, 39] which is guided by reflection on actions and past experiences. Schön's [41] concept of *reflection in action* also highlights the relation of past experiences to the current situation of an actor. Regarding the learning interaction cycle, learners utilise past experiences to judge the results of their actions in the same way as smart indicators rely on the learners' interaction history.

Wexelblat & Maes [46] define *interaction history* as traces of interactions between learners and objects. The authors argue that interaction history is extensively used by learners to guide actions, to make choices, and to find things of importance or interest [46]. Dron, Boyne, & Mitchell [18] use the term *footprint* to indicate the value and meaning of each interaction in creating social spaces, for which the authors introduce the term *stigmergy*. This concept was also applied for social navigation [17]. Recently, Farzan & Brusilovsky [20] use the term *interaction footprint* to refer to different traces that are left during the interaction process. Examples for such traces are notes about accessing a resource in a repository, or the time a learner spent reading a document [20].

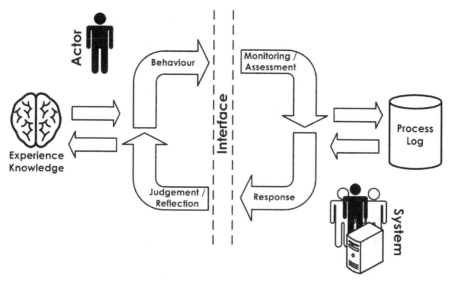

Fig. 1. Learning interaction cycle

4 An Architecture for Smart Indicators

A smart indicator is a component of a context aware system that traces a learner's interactions as well as contextual data in order to provide meaningful information in response to learning actions. In this section we describe a system's architecture for smart indicators.

We applied an architecture for context aware systems as it has been described in Zimmermann, Specht, & Lorenz [47]. The architecture has four layers and specifies operations on the data and information flow through a system from the learner input to the system response (see **Fig. 2**). The layers are the sensor layer, the semantic layer, the control layer, and the indicator layer.

The *sensor layer* is responsible for capturing the interaction footprints. A *sensor* is a simple measuring unit for a single type of data. The objective of sensor layer is to trace learner interactions. It also includes other measures that are relevant for the learning process which are not a direct result of an interaction between the learner and the system. Sensors that do not gather information about a learner's interactions are called *contextual sensors*. Examples for contextual sensors are location tracker, or tagging activities and contributions of peer-learners. In the architecture the sensor layer adds data to process log in order to allow the adaptation to the interaction history.

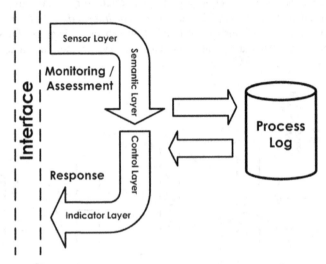

Fig. 2. Layers for context-aware information processing

The *semantic layer* collects the data from the sensors and from the process log and aggregates this data into higher level information. The semantic layer defines operations or rules for processing sensor data [13]. A definition of how the data from one or more sensors has to be transformed is called an *aggregator* [14]. These rules are named according to their meaning, for instance *activity* or *interest*.

The aggregated information is interpreted by the *control layer* according to the history and context of a learner. The specific approach for interpretation is called a *strategy* [13]. It defines the conditions for selecting and combining aggregators as well as their presentation according to the learner's context. A strategy also controls the personalization of aggregators.

Finally, the aggregated information has to get presented to the learner. The *indicator layer* handles this part of the interaction. At this level the actual response is created by translating aggregated values into representations that are not just machine-readable but also accessible to humans. The active strategy of the control layer selects these representations and provides the aggregated information to them.

The first two layers are also considered as *interaction assessment* [7] or *user modelling* [27]. This suggests the integration of the sensor and semantic layer, although they expose different feature sets: The sensor layer is concerned with data collection of "low level information [...] including, for example, key strokes, task initiation and completion, answers of quizzes etc." [7]. Its main objective is to organise incoming interaction footprints for further processing. In contrast, the semantic layer enriches , clusters, or transforms the data.

The last two layers are mentioned in the literature as *adaptation decision making* [7]. The control and indicator layer are commonly integrated as part of the user interface [2, 6, 11, 28, 29]. This is not always desirable because different combinations of strategies and indicators have varying effects on the learning processes and outcomes [42].

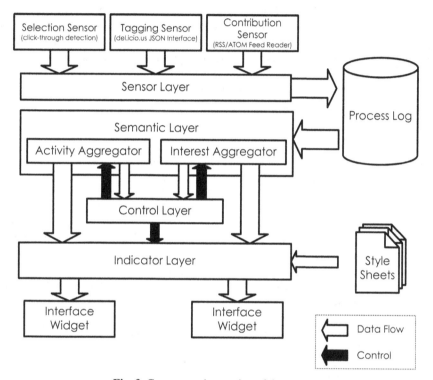

Fig. 3. Component interaction of the prototype

Many approaches in adaptive hypermedia implement adaptation on the level of the semantic layer, while the main strategy at the level of the control layer does not adapt to the learning process [e.g. 2, 5, 9, 10, 11, 20, 44]. In contrast, our approach of smart indicators adapts the strategies on the control layer in order meet the changing needs of a learner. By doing so, the adaptation strategies are adaptable to the different phases of the learning process.

5   A Prototype for Smart Indicators

In order to develop a better understanding of supporting strategies of the learning interaction cycle we implemented a web-based prototype of smart indicators. The prototype integrates smart indicators into a community system. This system combines learner web-logs with del.icio.us[1] link lists and tag clouds of the community members. The indicator provides information on the interest and the activity to the learners. It contains two core components: An interest tag cloud and an overall activity chart. To maintain these indicators the system tracks selection activities, tagging activities, and contributions. The system adapts the presented information according to a learner's activity and interest level: It provides richer information the more a learner contributes to the community. Therefore, new participants will have different information indicated than those who contribute regularly to the community.

According to the architecture the prototype has four functional layers: A sensor layer monitors the learners' activities and collects traces of interest. A semantic layer provides two aggregators to transform the data provided by the sensors. A control layer controls the indicator behaviour according to the results of the aggregators of the semantic layer. The indicator layer transforms the information into widgets that are integrated into the user interface of the system.

5.1 Sensor Layer

The sensor layer captures sensor information on contributions, tagging activities and selections. This layer gathers and organises the interaction footprints of a learner in the community system. The prototype implements this by immediate and delayed interaction tracing. Immediate interaction tracing is implemented only for selections (so-called click-through), through which the system gathers information about requests of web-log entries or links from the link list. Data about contributions is accumulated from RSS2[2] or ATOM[3] feeds independently from a learner's activity on the user interface. Information on the collected links and comments for the community is gathered through del.icio.us' RPC interface[4]. The tagging activities are extracted from the data on tag clouds that is provided from both the link lists and the learner's web-logs. A learner tags a link or a web-log entry if a tag is added to the contribution. The data collected by the different sensors is stored in a central process-log for further processing.

The prototype uses six sensors to monitor the actions and interest of the community members:

1. *Tagging sensor*, which traces the tags that a learner applied either to a link in del.icio.us or to an entry in a web-log.
2. *Tag selection sensor*, which traces those tags that were selected from a tag cloud or a tag list of an entry in a web-log.
3. *Tag tracing sensor*, which traces the tags that are assigned to web-log entries or del.icio.us links when a learner visits this entry.
4. *Entry selection sensor*, which traces the hyperlinks a learner has accessed.
5. *Entry contribution sensor*, which traces the contributions of a learner to the community.
6. *Access time sensor*, which traces the time of an interaction.

---

[1] http://del.icio.us
[2] http://blogs.law.harvard.edu/tech/rss
[3] http://tools.ietf.org/html/rfc4287
[4] http://del.icio.us/help/json/

5.2 Semantic Layer

The semantic layer of the prototype provides two aggregators: an activity aggregator and an interest aggregator. The semantic layer analyses the sensor data according to a definition given by the aggregators. Different to the sensor layer, the semantic layer is not limited to organising incoming sensor data, but it uses the aggregators to *transform* the sensor data into meaningful information.

The activity aggregator selects the data from the *entry contribution sensor, entry selection sensor, tag selection sensor,* the *tagging sensor,* and the *access time sensor.* Activity is defined as the number of actions per time interval. The activity aggregator calculates the activity for a time period and for a learner or for the entire community. Additionally, the activity aggregator provides absolute or relative activity values. The absolute activity value is the total number of a learner's activities per time interval. The relative activity value is defined by the relation of the absolute activity values of a learner or the community and the best performing community member. Both activity values are provided as numbers.

The activity aggregator respects that the sensors do not contribute in the same way to the results with regard to effort, frequency and relevance. The aggregator rates contributions much higher than selections by adding a bias to the contribution activities. For example, selecting a hyperlink requires less effort than tagging some information, which itself requires less effort than contributing a new web-log entry or commenting a link in del.icio.us. It is also less likely that a learner tags a web-page or a web-log entry that has been already tagged by another learner. Thus, selections are likely to occur more frequently than tagging activities or contributions.

The interest aggregator selects data from the *tagging sensor, tag selection sensor, tag tracing sensor*, and e*ntry contribution sensor.* Interest is defined as the number of actions that relate to a tag. In other words, the more actions of a learner that are related to a tag, the higher is the interest in it.

Claypool and colleagues identified that different types of sensors have varying relevance for identifying the learners' interest [12]. They distinguish between explicit and implicit interest sensors. Learners show explicit interest in a topic, if they select a tag from a tag cloud, label a link using a certain tag, or contribute a web-log entry on the topic. Implicit interest is given if learners follow tagged hyperlinks, or visit web-log entries that are related to a topic.

In this context, entry contributions, tagging actions and tag selections are explicit interest sensors while tag tracing sensors and entry selection sensors are implicit interest sensors. For the interest value, explicit sensor data is of higher relevance and has therefore a greater impact on the results of the aggregator. The interest aggregator reflects this by adding a bias to the values of the implicit interest sensors. This aggregator calculates for each tag in the tag cloud the interest value, and provides a data-set of tags and interest values as a result.

The interest value provides information about the kind of interest a learner has in a topic. For the prototype we distinguished between passive and active interest. Learners show passive interest in a topic if they access or tag information. Active interest is given if learners contribute comments on items of the link list and through the web-log entries. The interest aggregator indicates this information by signed interest values. A positive value identifies those topics that are of active interest, while negative values show a learner's passive interest.

5.3 Control Layer

The control layer defines how the indicators adapt to the learner behaviour. The prototype implements two elemental strategies. The first strategy aims at motivating learners to participate to the community activities. The objective of the second strategy is to raise awareness on the personal interest profile and stimulate reflection on the learning process and the acquired competences. The prototype adapts the strategies according to a learner's participation to the community.

The typical activity for learners who are new to a community is to explore the environment in order to develop knowledge about the community's interests, activities and participants. Hence, it is unlikely that learners start contributing actively to the community from the very beginning. During this phase the smart indicator shows only the absolute activity values in an activity chart and the raw tag list of the community (see **Fig. 4**). With each selection of a link or a web-log entry the learner's activity status grows and indicates that each activity has its value. The community's tags are shown as a plain list of tags. This gives the learners the opportunity to explore and to understand the different topics and relate themselves to the community's interests, without receiving suggestions on the most relevant tags in the community so far.

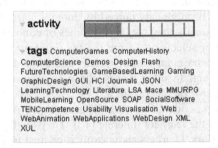

Fig. 4. Sample indicator of the first level strategy

Once a learner starts contributing links or web-log entries to the community, the control strategy selects relative activity values from the activity aggregator (see **Fig. 5**). The information displays the activity of the learner and the community for the last seven days as well as for the previous seven days. This adds a competitive element to the indicator: Learners see their activity in relation to the average community member and the best performing one. Additionally, it allows the learners to assess the changes of their activity levels from one week to another. For motivational reasons, this is not applied before a learner starts contributing, because contributions have a greater impact on the average activity value than selection activities have. Therefore, it is difficult for non-contributing community members to reach the average activity level, whereas the bias on the contributions allows contributing members to reach activity levels above the average level more easily.

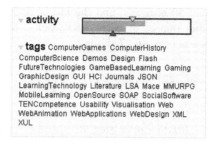

Fig. 5. Indicator of the second level strategy

After ten web-log entries, the tag cloud starts to display the learner's active and passive interests in the tag cloud (see **Fig. 6**). A large number of contributions mark the end of the exploration phase. From this point in time trends of a learner's interest in different topics become assessable. Therefore, the third level control strategy uses the activity aggregator as well as the interest aggregator. By highlighting the interest in the different topics to the learners, the learners are enabled to identify the most beneficial topics of the community for their own learning process. This stimulates the awareness of concepts and their relations to the community activities.

Fig. 6. Indicator of the third level strategy

5.4 Indicator Layer

The main purpose of the indicator layer is to embed the values selected by the control layer into the user interface of the community system. The indicator layer provides different styles of displaying and selects an appropriate style for the incoming information. To display information, the indicator layer of the prototype uses style-sheets to transform the data provided by the control layer into a learner accessible form. Depending on the style sheet the indicator layer generates an image or a widget.

For the prototype two graphical indicators and one widget indicator are defined. One graphical indicator is used during the first level of the control strategy. This indicator shows the amount of activities for the last seven days. The indicator has ten scales. Kreijns [28] suggests using logarithmic scales to give early steps a greater visual impact. We adopted this idea for the last three scales of the activity indicator: The first seven scales represent each three item accesses; the eighth scale represents

21 item accesses, the ninth 50 accesses, and the last scale represents 200 accesses. This assures a high visible impact of early interactions, while the activity bar is difficult to fill by active learners as **Fig. 7** shows.

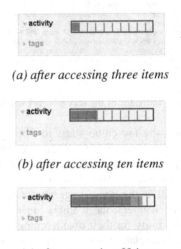

(a) after accessing three items

(b) after accessing ten items

(c) after accessing 60 items

Fig. 7. Different stages of the initial activity indicator

The second control strategy uses a different graphical indicator. It displays the activity in comparison to the average community member. The maximum value of the scale used by this indicator is that of the most active community member (see **Fig. 8** a). The upper bar indicates the relative activity of the learner for the last seven days. The lower bar indicates the activity of the average community member during the same time period. Additionally, the indicator has two arrows. The upper arrow indicates the learner's activity for the previous seven days, whereas the lower arrow indicates the average community activity during that time. If a learner is the most active community member, a star is added to the end of the activity chart (see **Fig. 8** b).

(a) learner is less active than the community and less active than last week

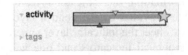

(b) Most active community member

Fig. 8. Different activity visualisations of contributing community members

At the third level of the control strategy, the indicator layer provides a tag cloud widget for displaying the interests of a learner. In principle this widget is a list of hyperlinks. The tag cloud indicates higher interest values for each topic as the bigger font sizes of the related tags. For those tags that were of passive interest, the tag is set in italics. **Fig. 6** shows a tag cloud for an active learner.

6 Conclusions and Further Research

In this article we discussed a first prototype for smart indicators. Its implementation is based the principles of the learning interaction cycle and context aware systems. The prototype showed the feasibility of implementing the architecture for smart indicators in a non-formal learning environment. Currently, we are evaluating the validity of the educational approach and the adaptation strategy as defined on the prototype's control layer. The evaluation is being conducted in a small community of PhD students. Although the research is still in an early phase, we look forward to presenting the concept of smart indicators together with the first results of the evaluation.

Acknowledgements

This paper is (partly) sponsored by the TENCompetence Integrated Project that is funded by the European Commission's 6th Framework Programme, priority IST/Technology Enhanced Learning. Contract 027087 (www.tencompetence.org).

References

1. Adomavicius, G., Tuzhilin, A.: Towards the next generation of recommender systems: a survey of the state-of-the-art and possible extensions. IEEE Transactions on Knowledge and Data Engineering 17, 734–749 (2005)
2. Ahn, J.-w., Brusilovsky, P., Farzan, R.: A Two-Level Adaptive Visualisation for Information Access to Open-Corpus Resources. In: Ardissono, L., Brna, P., Mitrović, A. (eds.) UM 2005. LNCS (LNAI), vol. 3538, pp. 1–12. Springer, Heidelberg (2005)
3. Beck, J.C., Wade, M.: Got Game: how the gamer generation is reshaping business forever. Harvard Business School Press, Boston, MA (2004)
4. Beenen, G., et al.: Using social psychology to motivate contributions to online communities. ACM conference on computer supported cooperative work (CSCW 2004) Chicago, Illinois pp. 212–221 (2004)
5. Bretzke, H., Vassileva, J.: Motivating cooperation on peer to peer networks. In: Brusilovsky, P., Corbett, A.T., de Rosis, F. (eds.) UM 2003. LNCS, vol. 2702, pp. 218–227. Springer, Heidelberg (2003)
6. Brusilovsky, P., Eklund, J.: A Study of User Model Based Link Annotation in Educational Hypermedia. Journal of Universal Computer Science 4, 429–448 (1998)
7. Brusilovsky, P., Karagiannidis, C., Sampson, D.: The benefits of layered evaluation of adaptive application and services. In: Bauer, M., Gmytrasiewicz, P.J., Vassileva, J. (eds.) UM 2001. LNCS (LNAI), vol. 2109, Springer, Heidelberg (2001)
8. Butler, D.L., Winne, P.H.: Feedback and self-regulated learning: a theoretical synthesis. Review of Educational Research 65, 245–281 (1995)

9. Cheng, R., Vassileva, J.: Adaptive rewarding mechanism for sustainable online learning community. In: 12th International Conference on Artificial Intelligence in Education (AIED'05), Amsterdam (2005)

10. Cheng, R., Vassileva, J.: User motivation and persuasion strategy for peer-to-peer communities. In: 38th Hawaii International Conference on System Sciences (HICSS'05), IEEE, Hawaii, United States p. 193a-193a (2005)

11. Cheng, R., Vassileva, J.: Design and evaluation of an adaptive incentive mechanism for sustained educational online communities. User Modelling and User-Adapted Interaction 16, 321–348 (2006)

12. Claypool, M.: Inplicit Interest Indicators. In: ACM Intelligent User Interfaces Conference (IUI 2001), pp. 33–40. ACM, Santa Fe, New Mexico (2001)

13. Cristea, A., Calvi, L.: The three layers of adaptation granularity. In: Brusilovsky, P., Corbett, A.T., de Rosis, F. (eds.) UM 2003. LNCS, vol. 2702, pp. 4–14. Springer, Heidelberg (2003)

14. Dey, A.K.: Enabling the use of context in interactive applications. Computer-Human Interaction de Hague, NL (2000)

15. Dey, A.K., Abowd, G.D.: Towards a Better Understanding of Context and Context-Awareness. In: CHI 2000 Workshop on the What, Who, Where, When, and How of Context-Awareness (2000)

16. Dey, A.K., Abowd, G.D., Salber, D.: A Context-based Infrastructure for Smart Environments. In: 1st International Workshop on Managing Interactions in Smart Environments (MANSE '99), Dublin, Ireland, pp. 114–128 (1999)

17. Dieberger, A.: Supporting social navigation on the world wide web. International Journal of Human-Computer Studies 46, 805–825 (1997)

18. Dron, J., Boyne, C., Mitchell, R.: Footpaths in the the stuff swamp. In: World Conferences on the WWW and Internet, Orlando, Florida, United States (2001)

19. Ellis, G., Dix, A.: Visualising web visitations: a probabilistic approach. In: 8th International Conference on Information Visualisation (IV'04), pp. 599–604. IEEE Computer Society Press, Los Alamitos (2004)

20. Farzan, R., Brusilovsky, P.: Social navigation support in e-learning: what are the real footprints? In: Mobasher, B., Anand, S.S. (eds.) Intelligent Techniques for Web Personalisation (ITWP'05), Edinburgh, Scotland (2005)

21. Garries, R., Ahlers, R., Driskel, J.E.: Games, motivation, and learning: a research and practice model. Simulation & Gaming 33, 441–467 (2002)

22. Gatalsky, P., Andrienko, N., Andrienko, G.: Interactive analysis of event data using space-time cube. In: 8th International Conference on Information visualisation (IV'04), pp. 145–152. IEEE Computer Society Press, Los Alamitos (2004)

23. Gee, J.P.: What video games have to teach us about learning and literacy. Palgrave Macmillian, New York (2003)

24. Greer, J., et al.: Supporting peer help and collaboration in distributed workplace environments. International Journal of Artificial Intelligence in Education (IJAIED) 9, 159–177 (1998)

25. Jamieson-Noel, D., Chu, S.T.L., Winne, P.H.: The effect of feedback on calibration of study tactics and performance. American Educational Research Association (AERA), San Diego, CA (2004)

26. Klerkx, J., Duval, E., Meire, M.: Using information visualisation for accessing learning object repositories. In: Eighth International Conference on Information Visualisation (IV'04), pp. 465–470. IEEE Computer Society Press, Los Alamitos (2004)

27. Kobsa, A.: Generic User Modeling Systems. User Modeling and User-Adapted Interaction 11, 49–63 (2001)
28. Kreijns, K.: Sociable CSCL Environments; Social Affordances, Sociability, and Social Presence, Open University of the Netherlands (2004)
29. Kreijns, K., Kirschner, P.A.: Group Awareness Widgets for Enhancing Social Interaction in Computer-supported Collaborative Learning Environments: Design and Implementation. 32nd ASEE/IEEE Frontiers in Education Conference, Boston, MA (2002)
30. Ley, K., Young, D.B.: Instructional principles for self-regulation. Educational Technology Research and Development 49, 93–103 (2001)
31. Ling, K., et al.: Using social psychology to motivate contributions to online communities. Journal of Computer-Mediated Communication 10, article 10 (2005)
32. Marcos, J.A., Martinez, A., Dimitriadis, Y., Anguita, R.: Adapting interaction analysis to support evaluation and regulation: a case study. In: Sixth International Conference on Advanced Learning Technologies (ICALT), pp. 125–129. IEEE Computer Society, Kerkrade (2006)
33. Mealha, Ó., Sousa Santos, B., Nunes, J., Zamfir, F.: Integrated visualisation schemes for an information and communication web log based management system. In: Nunes, J., Zamfir, F. (eds.) 8th International Conference on Information Visualisation, pp. 295–301. IEEE Computer Society Press, Los Alamitos (2004)
34. Mory, E.H.: Feedback Research Revisited. In: Jonassen, D.H. (ed.) Handbook of research for educational communications and technology: A Project of the Association for Educational Communications and Technology, pp. 745–784. Macmillan, New York (2003)
35. Ng, C.U., Martin, G.R.: Automatic selection of attributes by importance in relevance feedback visualisation. In: 8th International Conference on Information Visualisation (IV'04), pp. 588–595. IEEE Computer Society Press, Los Alamitos (2004)
36. Nguyen, Q.V., Huang, M.L., Hawryszkiewycz, I.: A New Visualization Approach for Supporting Knowledge Management and Collaboration in E-Learning. In: 8th International Conference on Information Visualisation (IV'04), pp. 693–700. IEEE Computer Society Press, Los Alamitos (2004)
37. Orange, C.: Using peer modelling to teach self-regulation. Journal of Experimental Education 68, 21–40 (1999)
38. Passier, H., Jeuring, J.: Ontology based feedback generation in design oriented e-learning systems. IADIS e-Society 2004 (2004)
39. Rashid, A.M., et al.: Motivating participation by displaying the value of contribution. In: Conference on human factors in computing systems (CHI 2006) Montreal, Quebeq, Canada pp. 955–958 (2006)
40. Rieber, L.P., Tzeng, S.-C., Tribble, K., Chu, G.: Feedback and elaboration within a computer-based simulation: a dual coding perspective. In: 18th National Convention of the Association for Educational Communications and Technology, Indianapolis, IN (1996)
41. Schön, D.A.: The Reflective Practitioner: How Professionals think in Action. Maurice Temple Smith, London (1983),
42. Specht, M., Kobsa, A.: Interaction of domain expertise and interface design in adaptive educational hypermedia. In: 7-th International Conference on User Modeling (UM99), Banff, Canada (1999)
43. Van Nimwegen, C., Van Oostendorp, H., Burgos, D., Koper, R.: Does an interface with less assistance provoke more thoughtful behaviour? In: Seventh International Conference of the Learning Sciences, Erlbaum, Bloomington, IN (2006)

44. Vassileva, J.: Harnessing p2p power in the classroom. In: Lester, J.C., Vicari, R.M., Paraguaçu, F. (eds.) ITS 2004. LNCS, vol. 3220, pp. 305–314. Springer, Heidelberg (2004)
45. Weber, R.A.: Learning and Transfer of Learning with No Feedback: An Experimental Test Across Games, Carnegie Mellon Social & Decision Sciences Behavioral Decision Research Paper (2003)
46. Wexelblat, A., Maes, P.: Footprints: history-rich tools for information foraging. In: Conference on Human Factors in Computing Systems. ÀCM, Pittsburgh, Pennsylvania, United States, pp. 270–277 (1999)
47. Zimmermann, A., Specht, M., Lorenz, A.: Personalisation and context management. User Modeling and User-Adapted Interaction 15, 275–302 (2005)

A Qualitative and Quantitative Evaluation of Adaptive Authoring of Adaptive Hypermedia

Maurice Hendrix and Alexandra Cristea

Department of Computer Science, The University of Warwick, Coventry CV4 7AL,
United Kingdom
{maurice,acristea}@dcs.warwick.ac.uk

Abstract. Currently, large amounts of research exist into the design and implementation of adaptive systems. The complex task of authoring of such systems, or their evaluation, is addressed less. We have looked into the causes of this complexity. Manual annotation is a serious bottleneck for authoring of adaptive hypermedia. All means for supporting this authoring process by reusing automatically generated metadata would therefore be helpful. Previously, we proposed the integration of a generic Adaptive Hypermedia authoring environment, MOT, into a semantic desktop environment, indexed by Beagle++. Based upon this approach, a prototype was constructed. The approach in general, as well as the prototype in particular, where evaluated through both qualitative and quantitative experiments. This paper is a synthesis of our work so far, describing theoretical findings and hypotheses, their implementation in short, and finally, the combined results of the evaluations.

Keywords: Authoring; Adaptive Educational Hypermedia, CAF; Evaluation, Metadata, RDF, Semantic Desktop, Semi-automatic adding, MOT, Beagle++.

1 Introduction

Authoring Adaptive Hypermedia can generate valuable personalized (learning) experiences [6], but it is known to be a difficult and time-consuming task [7]. A possible solution to this problem is to use automatically generated authoring as much as possible, and there has already been research into how to automatize authoring in different ways [3, 13]. A good basis is to use already annotated resources (such as provided by the Semantic Desktop [9,22]), which can be automatically retrieved when necessary, as dictated by the authoring process. In a Semantic Desktop, resources are categorized by rich ontologies, and semantic links can express various kinds of semantic relationships between the resources. For a file representing a paper, for example, the Semantic Desktop stores not only a filename, but also information about where it was published, when, by whom, etc. These metadata are generated automatically, and stored in the user's personal data store in RDF format. This rich set of metadata makes it easier for the user to semi-automatically retrieve appropriate material for different contexts, for example, when a teacher wants to select materials that fit a certain lecture. In this context, an author has to create some basic lesson material, which then serves as a framework for the final lesson to be created.

E. Duval, R. Klamma, and M. Wolpers (Eds.): EC-TEL 2007, LNCS 4753, pp. 71–85, 2007.
© Springer-Verlag Berlin Heidelberg 2007

In [17] and [16] and [18] we previously described the interaction and exchange of data between the adaptive hypermedia authoring environment MOT [10,19], and the Beagle++ environment [1,2,8]. Here we are going to review only the essential parts allowing comprehension of the evaluation work.

MOT [10] is a *concept*-based adaptive educational hypermedia authoring environment with adaptive authoring support. It is an advanced system for authoring personalized e-courses based upon the LAOS [11] authoring framework and offers a web forms interface for the authoring process. The main parts of the LAOS framework it offers are the Goal & Constraints Model and the Domain Model. Elementary blocks of content are represented in the Domain Map, and in the Goal & Constraints Map blocks from domain maps are brought together. This forms an initial version of what end-users (students taking a course) will see before any adaptation is applied to it.

Currently, there are two versions of MOT. Fig. 1 shows a snapshot of the interface for authoring Domain Maps in the new MOT version.

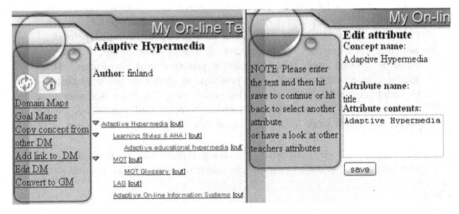

Fig. 1. Domain authoring in the new MOT

Beagle++ is an advanced search and indexing engine for the semantic desktop. It is an extension to the Beagle [1,8] search tool which generates and utilizes metadata information, and keeps a metadata index of all files. Initially, extraction tools are used to populate this metadata index.

Our approach uses a standalone Java application called the *Enricher* (or *Sesame2MOT conversion*) to implement the link between the MOT and Beagle++ systems described above. As is introduced in more detail in section 3, the Sesame2MOT conversion works by reading current courses from MOT in an XML format called CAF (Common Adaptation Format) and querying the Metadata index kept by Beagle++.

In this paper we evaluate our approach to conversion in general, and the Enricher prototype [18], which has been constructed, in particular. As MOT has a new version, we also evaluate whether this new version is indeed preferable, and whether we should base development of our prototype on this version of MOT.

The remainder of this paper is organized as follows. Based on [18], section 2 and 3 give a short illustrative scenario and a brief introduction of the system setup. The evaluation consists of both quantitative experiments [18], and qualitative experiments. The quantitative experiments consist of a SUS-questionnaire [5] testing the system usability [15], and of a focussed questionnaire [14]. The evaluation methodology used for these experiments is described in section 4, and in section 5 the results of the evaluation are presented. Finally, in section 6 we discuss what these results mean for our approach in general and for the prototype in particular.

2 Motivational Scenario

We use a scenario for adaptive authoring that builds upon a combination of automatically and manually generated metadata, as introduced in [18].
Prof. Jones is a hypothetical lecturer who is preparing a new course. His university allocates a limited amount of time to this. He uses MOT,

- because he considers it useful to be able to extend the course in the future with more alternative paths guided by adaptivity, and
- because he wants to benefit from automatic help during authoring.

This takes slightly more time than static course creation, as the course has to be divided into conceptual entities with explicit, independent semantics and semantic labelling.

The advantage is that the adaptive authoring system can afterwards automatically enrich the course based on pedagogical strategies. For example, the version created by Jones can be considered as the version for beginner students. For advanced students, such as those wishing to pass the course with high marks, the adaptive authoring system can use the Semantic Desktop search to automatically find on Jones' desktop any existing scientific papers that are relevant to the current course. These papers could then be used as alternative or additional material to the main storyline of the static course. This mechanism builds upon the following assumptions.

- Since Jones is a specialist in the subject he is teaching, he both publishes and reads papers of interest on the subject, which are likely to be stored on his computer.
- His collection of papers can be considered as useful extra resources for the current course, and can therefore be reused in this context.
- The storing process has taken place over time, and Jones may not know exactly where on his computer each article relevant to the current course is.
- Jones has been using the Beagle++ Semantic Desktop System to store both papers and all relevant metadata automatically in RDF format.

This situation can be exploited by the authoring tool; a search will find some of Jones' own papers on the course topic, as well as some papers written by his colleagues on the same topic. He may have saved these papers by himself, received them by e-mail from a colleague, or may have bookmarked them using his browser. In order for these retrieved resources to be relevant to the course, two conditions have to be fulfilled:

- the domain concept in the course where each resource is most relevant has to be found (*the right information*), and next,
- the resource must be bound to that particular concept (*in the right place*).

How can Jones find the right resource and store it in the right place? The automatic search can take place via the keywords labelling both the course components created by Jones and the matching keywords labelling the papers and resources on his desktop. How Jones can enrich his course automatically, without much extra work, as well as keep at all times overall control and a coherent overview, is described in more detail in [18]. The following sections evaluate this specific approach, as well as a prototype for it which has been implemented, and discuss possible improvements.

3   The Approach and System Setup

In this section we shortly review our method and system setup. As can be seen in Fig. 2, Beagle++, the Semantic Desktop Environment used in our prototype, stores all metadata in the Sesame RDF database [21]. All Beagle++ components that generate metadata (for example, the email, publication, web cache and file metadata generators) add the metadata to this database. All Beagle++ components which use metadata (for example, the search and indexing module, the ranking module or the browsing modules) retrieve their data from this repository, and, in some cases, write back new data (such as the PageRank [8] value for documents or other resources).

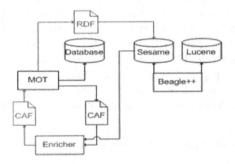

Fig. 2. System overview

It is easy to accommodate additional modules in this environment by writing appropriate interface components, which read and write from this repository. This is what we have done for MOT [10,19]. We have focused on the semi-automatic addition of articles stored on the user's desktop to a MOT lesson [10]). This represents an instantiation of the concept of adaptive authoring: authoring that adapts to the author's needs. In MOT, the addition is done to an existing lesson. Based on pedagogic goals, the author can then process the data, by adding more information on the article after the conversion. These additions can then be fed back into the RDF store, if necessary. We use CAF [12], a system-independent XML exchange format, to simplify the transformation process from RDF to the MOT MySQL storage format.

3.1   Enrichment of the Lesson and Domain Model

MOT is mainly a tool for authoring educational (adaptive) material, thus the internal information structures are based on strict hierarchies. When enriching the domain maps and lessons, we therefore aim at getting the right information in the right place in this hierarchy. To achieve this, the program first queries the Sesame database, using as search terms *title* and *keywords* of each domain concept found in the current existing lesson. The basic RDF query in the SeRQL [4] language looks as follows:

```
SELECT x FROM x {p} y WHERE y LIKE "*keyword*" IGNORE CASE
```

Some alternative retrieval methods have been studied, implemented and evaluated, as follows.

3.1.1   Concept-Oriented Versus Article-Oriented

For computing the mutual relevance between an article and a concept, in order to decide the appropriate place of articles in the concept hierarchy, we previously [16], [17] have developed two slightly different theoretical alternatives, as follows.

3.1.2   Concept-Oriented Relevance Ranking Method

This method computes relevance of an article for a given concept as follows:

$$rank(a,c) = \frac{|k(c) \cap k(a)|}{|k(a)|}$$

where:
$rank(a,c)$ is the rank of article a with respect to the current domain concept c;   (1)
$k(c)$ is the set of keywords belonging to the current domain concept c;
$k(a)$ is the set of keywords belonging to the current article a;
$|S|$ = the cardinality of the set S, for a given set S.

This formula is *concept-oriented*, in the sense that articles 'battle' for the same concept: a given article is placed in the appropriate place in the hierarchy by it.

3.1.3   Article-Oriented Relevance Ranking Method

This method computes the relevance of a concept to a given article as follows (notations same as above):

$$rank(a,c) = \frac{|k(c) \cap k(a)|}{|k(c)|}$$

(2)

The equation shows how many of the keywords (shared by the article and the concept) are present in the concept, relative to the number of keywords present in the concept. As an extreme example, if two concepts share the same number of keywords with a given article, but one concept has less keywords than the other, ,the former concept will have a higher rank and 'win' the article, as it is more focussed on the shared keywords than the latter one.

3.1.4   Sets Versus Multisets

Next, once the formula is chosen, there is another possible distinction to be made: the cardinality of the intersection can take two forms; one set-based (with intersection operation on sets, as defined above), and one with *multisets* or bags (and the respective intersection operation on bags). The reason to use sometimes bags instead of sets is that the number of times keywords appear in certain texts can be relevant in itself (not just which keywords). A text containing a greater number of occurrences of a specific keyword could be a better match for that keyword than a text with only one occurrence of the respective keyword. The author can choose between the two.

3.1.5 Duplicates Handling for Sibling Concepts
The same resource may be relevant in more then one place within the hierarchy. In that case, the resource will be added to the place where it has the highest relevance, by default. If there are more places in the hierarchy with a value equal to the highest relevance, the current implementation yields the one with the higher position in the tree to win. For siblings with the same position in the tree, and with the same (highest) relevance, a decision has to be made: either to allow duplicates, or to select randomly one of the candidate sibling concepts and allocate the resource to it. This decision depends on how the option of concepts pointing to the same resources looks like from the point of view of the current pedagogic strategy. Therefore, the current implementation allows the author to decide, via a switch called '*allow duplicates*'.

3.1.6 Adding Meta-Data as Separate Concepts or as Attributes
The retrieved metadata also has a structure. For example, a retrieved paper might have a location it was presented at and a year it was presented in. This metadata can be added either as attributes of the new article-concept in MOT, or as a set of new sub-concepts, with their own attributes. The author can switch between these two possibilities in the Enricher program.

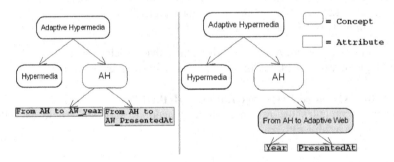

Fig. 3. result without; right, result with the 'add medatada as separate concepts' option

4 Evaluation

The evaluation of the conversion process, Enricher, and new MOT system has taken place in two steps so far.

4.1 First Evaluation Step

The first step was a small-scale qualitative experiment with 4 PhD students of the IMPDET course organized by the University of Joensuu in Finland, based on the think-aloud method [20]. As can be found in [18], the system was mainly *understood*, but respondents were unable to provide feedback on the method itself. Some *shortcomings of the user interface* of the prototype were identified and corrected as a result of this first evaluation step [18].

4.2 Second Evaluation Step

The second evaluation was of a much larger scale and conducted at the Politehnica University of Bucharest in January of 2007, and took place within an intensive two-week course on "Adaptive Hypermedia and The Semantic Web", which was delivered as an alternative track to the regular "Intelligent Systems" course. The students were 4th year undergraduates in Engineering studies and 2nd year Masters Students in Computer Science, all from the English-language stream. Firstly, basic knowledge on Adaptive Hypermedia and Semantic Web was addressed – the first course week was dedicated to theory, and finished with a theoretical exam. Out of the initial 61 students, only the students with a satisfactory knowledge of the theory were selected to continue with the practical part. The 33 students that passed the theory exam worked with the two versions of MOT (*old* versus *new*) and the Sesame2MOT (Enricher) conversion, the prototype constructed for the automatic authoring approach [16]. After these experiments, they were requested to submit questionnaires, to answer both generic and specific issues regarding the automatic generation of adaptivity and personalization. The questionnaires consisted of five parts; first a *SUS* [5] questionnaire for each of the three systems, and then two more specific questionnaires, for the *Sesame2MOT conversion* and for the *comparison of the new version of MOT with the previous version*. Here, we mainly focus on the *usability aspect* targeted in the evaluation process.

4.3 Hypotheses

We based our evaluation firstly on a number of generic, high level hypotheses, as follows:

1. The respondents *enjoyed* working as authors in the system.
2. The respondents *understood* the system.
3. The respondents considered that *theory and practice match* (for Sesame2MOT).
4. The respondents considered the *general idea of Adaptive Authoring useful*
5. The respondents have acquired *more knowledge* than they initially had with the help of the theoretical course (explanation) part.
6. The *new MOT has a better usability then the old version*; hence we should base further developments on this version of MOT.
7. The respondents' overall *preference* (from a usability perspective) is as follows, in increasing order: old MOT, new MOT, Sesame2MOT.
8. The *user interface* of both version of MOT is *sufficient*.
9. The *upload functionality* in the new version of MOT is a *necessary* improvement.

We refined these into more specific, lower granularity hypotheses (see Table 1), which ultimately generated our questions for the questionnaires. To explain the construction of the sub-hypotheses, let's take, for instance, hypothesis 3. There, we check the matching between theory and practice, i.e., between theory and the implementation. For the Enricher application, from a theoretical point of view, we have defined different ranking methods and other options, such as allowing duplicates or not between the imported articles, etc. These have been implemented as options for the user to select, and therefore, in this particular case, matching theory and practice means that these methods render *different results*, firstly, and secondly, that *these different results should be as the theory has predicted*. Therefore, sub-hypothesis 3.4, and its sub-hypotheses, 3.4.1, 3.4.2 and 3.4.3 emerged. As said, the hypotheses and sub-hypotheses feed into and determine the question.

Respondents where given the option to comment on their preferences, in order to also gain qualitative feedback. We also directly asked for comments on all three systems, as well as the approach in general.

4.4   The Questionnaires and Their Rationale

As said, we used two main types of questionnaires to estimate the truth value of our hypotheses. One type is standard questionnaires, such as SUS (System Usability questionnaire, [5]), and the other type is questionnaires built by ourselves, targeting specific aspects of the main hypotheses.

Moreover, we used two types of questions: one was numerical or multiple choice question (the latter also mapable on a numerical scale), and the other one was open-ended questions trying to extract respondents' opinions as well as possible aspects we have missed in the numerical questions.

Finally, out of the questionnaires we built ourselves, questions targeted two main issues: the *theory* behind the system and separately, the *system* itself.

4.4.1   SUS
As we were in fact evaluating three systems (old MOT, new MOT and the Sesame2MOT conversion) we applied the SUS questionnaire three times, once for each of them. SUS stands for System Usability scale [5] and gives a measure for comparing the usability of different systems. A SUS questionnaire consists of 10 questions with a 1 to 5 scale of agreement. By alternating positive and negative questions, respondents are forced to think about their agreement to each question. For the positive questions the score is the *agreement level-1*, for the negative questions the score is *1-the agreement level*. This now yields the *SUS score*, which is ideal for comparing the generic usability of different systems. This scores give us however little insight into where exactly the problems lie; therefore it is advisable to design more specific, targeted questions to extract these answers.

4.4.2   Sesame2MOT
We therefore also constructed a more specific questionnaire for the Sesame2MOT conversion. Here, we directly asked respondents whether they consider the general idea of semi-automatic authoring useful, as well as enjoyable. We also asked whether they understood each of the ranking methods and selection options, whether these did what was expected and whether their selection choice had any visible influence on the conversion process.

4.4.3 OLD Versus NEW MOT

For the comparison of the OLD and NEW MOT we constructed a more specific questionnaire as well. To gain more insight into specific issues than a SUS questionnaire can provide, we asked respondents directly:

- whether they consider the general idea of authoring support of adaptive hypermedia useful, and enjoyable;
- whether they enjoyed working with both MOT versions;
- whether they understood how both MOT versions work;
- whether they thought the user interfaces were sufficient;
- whether they thought both MOT versions where easy to use;
- whether they thought both MOT versions make Adaptive Hypermedia creation easier.

We also directly asked them their overall preference and their preference for Domain Model and Goal Model editing [11].

5 Evaluation Results and Discussion

As said in section 4, for testing our hypotheses we used two different types of questionnaires for all three systems, a SUS questionnaire to gain insight in the systems' usability and more specific questionnaires, to target our hypotheses more directly. In this section we will discuss the results obtained from both types of questionnaires, as well as discuss the qualitative feedback obtained both from the IMPDET experiment as well as from the experiment in Bucharest.

For testing our hypotheses against the quantitative feedback obtained, we used numerical averages, and tested their significances with the help of a T-test. We have used the parametric test based on the assumption of equidistant points of measurement of the interval scale. We assumed a confidence of 95% would be reasonable. The T-test establishes whether the difference between a value and the average of a sample or the averages of two samples is significant. For a hypothesis to be confirmed the difference needs to be significant and be in the direction the hypothesis suggests. For example, if we test the difference between pre-test and post-test exam and have as hypothesis that respondents did better in the post exam, the average from the post exam must be higher and the difference between pre- and post exam needs to be significant. The difference between two samples or a sample and a value is considered *significant* if the probability P that the difference arose by chance is $P<0.05$.

5.1 Questionnaire Feedback

In order to obtain numerical averages for testing our hypotheses, we mapped the multiple-choice answers of the questionnaires as follows: '*Yes*' was mapped to 1, '*no*' to -1 and '*mostly*' to 0. Hence the average was always 0 and the T-test was applied by comparing against the neutral result of 0. Below we present a table with each hypothesis, T-test results (T value, degrees of freedom Df, Mean M, probability P) and whether the results show that it was confirmed or not. The main hypotheses are shown in bold. Their result is obtained by combining the results of the sub-hypotheses.

Table 1. Sesame2MOT Conversion hypotheses results

Nr.	Hypotheses	T	Df	M	P	Confirmed (M>0; P<0.05)
1	**The respondents enjoyed working as authors in all systems**					**Not confirmed**
	Sesame2MOT	2.709	31	0.438	0.011	Confirmed
	OLD MOT	1.161	32	0.121	0.254	*Not confirmed*
	NEW MOT	3.546	32	0.333	0.001	Confirmed
2	**The respondents understood all systems.**					**Confirmed**
	Respondents understood Sesame2MOT					Confirmed
	Respondents understand the option: Concept oriented	4.458	31	0.625	0.000	Confirmed
	Article oriented	3.788	31	0.563	0.001	Confirmed
	Allow duplicates	10.063	31	0.875	0.000	Confirmed
	Compute resources as set	5.271	31	0.688	0.000	Confirmed
	Add meta-data as separate concepts	6.313	31	0.750	0.000	Confirmed
	Respondents understood OLD MOT	5.899	32	0.576	0.000	Confirmed
	Respondents understood NEW MOT	6.197	32	0.546	0.000	Confirmed
3	**The respondents considered that theory and practice match (for Sesame2MOT).**					**Confirmed**
	The two ranking methods (concept-, article-oriented) do deliver different results.					Confirmed
	Concept Oriented	6.313	31	0.750	0.508	Confirmed
	Article Oriented	6.313	31	0.750	0.508	Confirmed
	Ranking methods (concept-, article-oriented) in line with the theory.		31			Confirmed
	Concept Oriented	2.252	31	0.375	0.032	Confirmed
	Article Oriented	2.709	31	0.438	0.011	Confirmed
	The different options influence the result		31			Confirmed
	Allow duplicates	7.760	31	0.813	0.000	Confirmed
	Compute resources as set	3.215	31	0.500	0.032	Confirmed
	Add meta-data as separate concepts	6.313	31	0.750	0.000	Confirmed
	The results of the conversion are in line with the theory					Confirmed
	The two ranking methods					Confirmed (see above)
	Allow duplicates	7.760	31	0.813	0.000	Confirmed
	Compute resources as set	2.252	31	0.375	0.032	Confirmed
	Add meta-data as separate concepts	4.458	31	0.625	0.000	Confirmed
4	**General idea useful**	**15.000**	**31**	**0.938**	**0.000**	**Confirmed**
5	**The respondents have acquired more knowledge than they initially had**	**25.59**	**57**	**5.75[1]**	**0.000**	**5.75 out of 10; p=0.00<0.05; t=25.59),**

[1] An average increase in grades occurred of 5.75, out of a possible 1-10 with 10 being the best.

Table 1. (*continued*)

6	**The new MOT is more usable then the old version; we should base further developments on this version of MOT.**					**Confirmed**
	Respondents preferred NEW MOT (over OLD MOT) for authoring	5.600	32	0.636	0.000	Confirmed
	Respondents would choose NEW MOT (over OLD MOT) for DM authoring in general	9.339	32	0.788	0.000	Confirmed
	Respondents would choose NEW MOT (over OLD MOT) for GM authoring in general	9.238	32	0.727	0.000	Confirmed
	Respondents prefer all editing sub functions of NEW MOT (over OLD MOT) for DM authoring					Confirmed
	Adding/modifying DM sub-concepts	3.213	32	0.394	0.003	Confirmed
	Deleting DM sub-concepts	5.555	32	0.545	0.000	Confirmed
	Adding/modifying DM attributes	3.922	32	0.455	0.000	Confirmed
	Deleting DM attributes	5.899	32	0.576	0.000	Confirmed
	Respondents prefer all editing sub functions of NEW MOT (over OLD MOT) for GM authoring					Confirmed
	Conversion from GM	10.902	32	0.788	0.000	Confirmed
	Adding/modifying GM labels	10.000	32	0.758	0.000	Confirmed
	Deleting GM labels	8.579	32	0.697	0.000	Confirmed
	Adding/modifying GM weights	9.238	32	0.728	0.000	Confirmed
7	**The user interface of both version of MOT is sufficient.**					**Not confirmed**
	OLD MOT user interface is sufficient	-1.715	32	- 0.152	0.096	Not confirmed
	NEW MOT user interface is sufficient	1.971	32	0.057	0.057	Not confirmed
8	**The upload functionality in the new version of MOT is a necessary improvement.**	9.339	32	0.788	0.000	**Confirmed**

As we have seen, most hypotheses have been confirmed based on the current data. The Sesame2MOT conversion is indeed considered useful and in line with the theory. Its options are understood. Respondents agreed strongly with most of our hypotheses, with all means above zero. Looking at the ones with lower scores, such as concept-oriented and article-oriented method, as well as computation of resource as set, they were less sure in their statements. This is probably due to the fact that they did not work with these options enough. This shows that more targeted evaluations may be necessary to establish without a doubt the acceptance rate of these features. Also respondents where not clear about enjoying working with the old version of MOT. This might be related to either the formal setting of the course or to the difference in user interface.

5.2 SUS Usability Feedback

With a SUS score the usability of systems can be compared. The average score can be contrasted and visual graphs can be constructed to identify specific problem points. The questions (which are alternately positive and negative) are plotted on a circle using a scale from 1 (strongly disagree) to 5(strongly agree), with 1 in the centre and 5 at the border. If the results for the questions are placed on the scale, the ideal system should show a perfect star shape, as positive and negative questions alternate. In Fig. 4 below, the SUS scores for the different systems are shown in such a SUS graph. The figure shows that the systems have relatively similar scores. Visible differences are that Sesame2MOT seems to have a higher perceived learning threshold, whereas the old MOT is considered more inconsistent and more cumbersome.

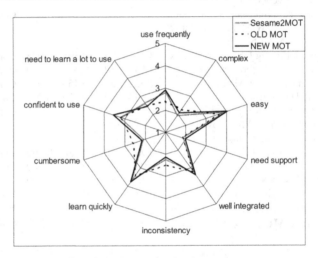

Fig. 4. SUS score for the three systems

Normalized responses range from 0 to 4, see [5]. Thus we applied a T-test comparing the normalized results against the average neutral value of 2. A paired T-test was used, since we compared answers of the same sample (group of students). Moreover, the main hypotheses were further broken into sub-hypotheses.

5.2.1 General Hypotheses
Below we list some of the main hypotheses, which are related to the SUS questionnaires, and comment on how much they are supported by the SUS results.

1. *The respondents enjoyed working as authors in the three systems from a usability perspective.*
   The results for the old MOT (mean 2.39 (expected >2); p=0.519>0.05; t=0.65) and Sesame2MOT (mean 2.78 (exp >2); p=0.095>0.05; t=1.72) on enjoyment were not significant. The respondents did significantly enjoy working with the new MOT (mean 2.97 (exp >2); p=0.01<0.05; t=2.66). The

hypothesis as a whole cannot be supported. This is possibly due to the formal setting of the course.

5. *The respondents' overall preference, from a usability perspective, is as follows, in increasing order: old MOT, new MOT, Sesame2MOT.*

   The results on learning preferences, and the preference for Sesame2MOT over the new MOT (difference -0.07 (>0 exp.); p=0.18<0.05; t=-1.44) were not significant. The hypothesis cannot be supported. Preference for the new over the old MOT (diff 0.26 (>0 expected); p=0.00<0.05; t=4.16) was confirmed.

6. *The new MOT is more usable, hence we should base further developments on this version of MOT.*

   For all different parts, as well as overall SUS score (see hypothesis 3), the new version of MOT is preferred over the old version. Thus we should indeed focus further development on the new version. The hypothesis is supported.

In general SUS questionnaires cover more issues than just the main hypotheses. For instance, none of the hypotheses related to learning threshold showed any significant difference between the three systems. This is possibly due to the fact that systems respondents had to learn all the theory before working with the three systems, or that both MOTs are very similar from a theoretical point of view.

We computed the correlation between the SUS scores for the 3 different systems. This showed that the respondents' answers to all three systems' SUS questionnaires are significantly correlated. This seems to be due to one of the following two reasons:

- respondents were not quite aware for which systems they were filling in the SUS questionnaire (suspicion based on some questions from students)
- or the students perceived the three systems as variants or parts of the same system.

Moreover, we also found that the correlation between the scores for the new MOT and for the Sesame2MOT conversion is highest. This could indicate that a substantial number of respondents viewed the Sesame2MOT conversion and the new MOT as one system, since Sesame2MOT is currently integrated into the new MOT.

5.3 Qualitative Feedback

As discussed in section 4, the prototype was also qualitatively evaluated both in a small scale experiment in cooperation with the University of Joensuu as well as in the larger scale experiment in Bucharest. The IMPDET experiment showed that the system was mainly understood, but respondents were unable to provide feedback on the method itself. Some shortcomings of the user interface of the prototype were identified. The qualitative feedback gathered from the Bucharest experiment showed a few issues. First of all, the user interface needs to be improved. Tool tip help functionality, a better interface for weight/label setting that allows changing of individual weights/labels and extra information, like ranking of the article is needed.

6 Conclusions

In this paper we have reviewed an authoring environment for personalized courses, as well as an Enricher mechanism and prototype based on Semantic Desktop technology. The paper briefly sketches the theoretical considerations for the implementation of the Enricher, and then, in parallel, the evaluation of these considerations, as well as of the prototype. From the two evaluation steps performed, the general result is that, to the extent it was understood, the theoretical concept of Adaptive Authoring of Adaptive Hypermedia was perceived as useful. We have also gained some important feedback into possible improvements to the Enricher application itself. Respondents in our experiments pointed out that the integration is currently not optimal and the user interface has to be improved. We plan to integrate the Enricher further into MOT by making a web based version and enhance the usability of the selection options. As especially the qualitative feedback showed the user interface of Sesame2MOT clearly needs to be improved.

Beside the hypotheses analysed here, we are also looked into the correlation between the students' responses and their comprehension of the theory on adaptive hypermedia and authoring thereof; students with higher grades in general responded more positively to the direct questions about liking the systems. For the SUS questionnaire we couldn't find any correlation. We performed comparisons of the students' preferences, however we didn't find any significant results.

Concluding, these tests have shown us that automatic generation and linking of material for adaptive presentation is possible, and that students with only one week of introduction into the whole concept of adaptive hypermedia as well as to the systems implementing it were able to work with our prototypes. For educational researchers, such as in the Joensuu test, this was possible after only one session. These tests however point to the fact that preliminary schooling is necessary for authors to be able to correctly use these concepts and apply personalization to their content presentation.

Acknowledgments. We acknowledge the Socrates mobilities exchange program, the ALS Minerva Socrates Project and Prof. Dr. Paul Cristea for giving us the opportunity to conduct our evaluation experiments.

References

1. Beagle website, viewed 21 March 21, 2007, http://beagle-project.org/Main_Page
2. Beagle++ website, viewed March 21, 2007, http://beagle.kbs.uni-hannover.de/
3. Brailsford, T.J., Ashman, H.L., Stewart, C.D., Zakaria, M.R., Moore, A.: User Control of Adaptation in an Automated Web-Based Learning Environment. In: First International Conference on Information Technology & Applications (ICITA 2002). Bathurst, Australia (2002)
4. Broekstra, J., Kampman, A.: SeRQL: An RDF Query and Transformation, viewed March 21, 2007, http://wwwis.win.tue.nl/ jbroekst/papers/SeRQL.pdf

5. Brooke, J.: SUS: a quick and dirty usability scale. In: Jordan, P.W., Thomas, B., Weerdmeester, B.A., McClelland, A.L. (eds.) Usability Evaluation in Industry, Taylor and Francis, London (1996)
6. Brusilovsky, P.: Adaptive hypermedia, User Modelling and User Adapted Interaction. In: Kobsa, A. (ed.) Ten Year Anniversary vol. 11 (1/2), pp. 87–110 (2001)
7. Celik, I., Stewart, C., Ashman, H.: Interoperability as an Aid to Authoring: Accessing User Models in Multiple AEH Systems. In: Proceedings of A3H: 1st International Workshop on Authoring of Adaptive and Adaptable Hypermedia (2006)
8. Chirita, P.-A., Costache, S., Nejdl, W., Paiu, R.: Beagle++ Semantically Enhanced Searching and Ranking on the Desktop. In: Proceedings of the 3rd European Semantic Web Conference, Budva, Montenegro (2006)
9. Chirita, P.-A., Gavriloaie, R., Ghita, S., Nejdl, W., Paiu, R.: Activity-Based Metadata for Semantic Desktop Search. In: Proceedings of the 2nd European Semantic Web Conference, Heraklion, Crete (2005)
10. Cristea, A.I., De Mooij, A.: Adaptive Course Authoring: My Online Teacher. In: Proceedings of ICT'03, Papeete, French Polynesia (2003)
11. Cristea, A.I., De Mooij, A.: LAOS: Layered WWW AHS Authoring Model and their corresponding Algebraic Operators. In: WWW03 (The Twelfth International World Wide Web Conference), Alternate Track on Education,Budapest,Hungary (2003)
12. Cristea, A.I., Smits, D., De Bra, P.: Writing MOT, Reading AHA! - converting between an authoring and a delivery system for adaptive educational hypermedia. In: A3EH Workshop, AIED'05, The Netherlands, Amsterdam (2005)
13. Cristea, A.I., Stewart, C.: Automatic Authoring of Adaptive Educational Hypermedia. In: Web-Based Intelligent e-Learning Systems: Technologies and Applications, IDEA Publishing group, Zongmin Ma (2005)
14. Hendrix, M., Cristea, A.I.: Evaluating Adaptive authoring of Adaptive Hypermedia. In: A3EH: 5th International Workshop on Authoring of Adaptive & Adaptable Educational Hypermedia, the 11th Internat. Conf. on User Modeling, Corfu Greece (2007)
15. Hendrix, M., Cristea, A.I., Joy, M.S.: Evaluating the automatic and manual creation process of adaptive lessons. In: The 7th IEEE International Conference on Advanced Learning Technologies (ICALT), Niigata, Japan (2007)
16. Hendrix, M., Cristea, A.I., Nejdl, W.: Authoring Adaptive Learning Material on the Semantic Desktop. In: 1st International Workshop on Authoring of Adaptive and Adaptable Hypermedia, Adaptive Hypermedia Dublin Ireland (2006)
17. Hendrix, M., Cristea, A.I., Nejdl, W.: Automatic and Manual Annotation Using Flexible Schemas for Adaptation on the Semantic Desktop. In: Nejdl, W., Tochtermann, K. (eds.) EC-TEL 2006. LNCS, vol. 4227, Springer, Heidelberg (2006)
18. Hendrix, M., Cristea, A.I., Nejdl, W.: Authoring Adaptive Educational Hypermedia on the Semantic Desktop. International Journal of Learning Technologies (IJLT) (to appear, 2007)
19. MOT homepage, viewed March 21, 2007, http://prolearn.dcs.warwick.ac.uk/mot.html
20. Nielsen, J.: Usability Engineering. Academic Press, Boston (1993)
21. Schlieder, T., Naumann, F.: Approximate tree embedding for querying cml data. In: ACM SIGIR Workshop on CML and Information Retrieval
22. Semantic Desktop, viewed March 21, 2007, http://www.semanticdesktop.org/

Making Sense of IMS Learning Design Level B: From Specification to Intuitive Modeling Software

Susanne Heyer[1], Petra Oberhuemer[1], Stefan Zander[2], and Philipp Prenner[2]

University of Vienna
[1] Center for Teaching and Learning, Porzellangasse 33a, 1090 Wien, Austria
[2] Department of Distributed and Multimedia Systems, Liebiggasse 4/3-4, 1010 Wien, Austria
{susanne.heyer,petra.oberhuemer,stefan.zander}@univie.ac.at,
philipp.prenner@fh-vie.ac.at

Abstract. The IMS Learning Design (IMS LD) specification offers a language for modeling teaching and learning situations and flows. The specification contains great complexity, which represents a high entrance barrier to its use. To lower this entrance barrier to Learning Design, easy-to-handle software is needed that translates from the language used by instructional practitioners to IMS LD. This paper describes an approach for performing this translation. First, an analysis is described that was used for deriving typical uses of IMS LD Level B properties and conditions. Second, the resulting cases and translation transactions are presented. It is hypothesized that a wizard allows practitioners access to Level B functionalities even though the wizard reduces the complexity of the specification.

Keywords: IMS Learning Design, Level B, analysis, complexity reduction, Graphical Learning Modeler.

1 The Specification IMS Learning Design

The IMS LD specification [1] prescribes a standardized modeling language for representing learning designs as a description of teaching and learning processes able to be executed by a software system that coordinates all involved people, resources and services. The specification hence supports the interoperability of learning designs aiming at enhancing sharing and re-usability of didactic settings.

The concept of the *learning activity* is central to the modeling language; IMS LD can thus be seen as an answer to the shortcomings of existing learning technology specifications focusing mainly on the sequencing of learning objects. Each learning activity is associated with learning objectives, prerequisites, a description and an environment. *Activities* and *environments* (consisting of resources and services) together with *roles* (e.g. learner) constitute the core *components* of IMS LD being managed by a *method*. The method uses the concepts of a theatrical play to orchestrate the activities. Within the method, the *role-part* connects roles to activities. Sequential *acts* containing the role-parts describe the teaching and learning flow, whereas the transition from one act to the next serves as a point of synchronization.

E. Duval, R. Klamma, and M. Wolpers (Eds.): EC-TEL 2007, LNCS 4753, pp. 86–100, 2007.

Acts finally constitute the *play*, which ends on completion of the last act. Refer to Fig. 1 for a visualization of components and method.

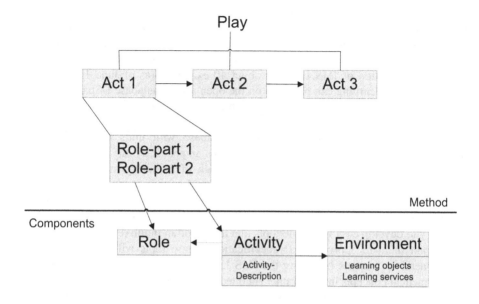

Fig. 1. IMS Learning Design model [8]

In this paper, we are using the differentiation introduced by Britain [2] between the general concept of learning design, which refers to the design of learning activities and learning environments, using small 'l', small 'd', and the concepts in the IMS specification instantiated as units of learning[1] using capital 'L' and 'D' (Learning Design).

The specification has put forth three levels in order to enable phasing the software implementation efforts: Levels A, B, and C. Each of these levels offers an increasingly higher amount of detail and complexity for designing teaching and learning scenarios. Level A provides all basic elements for linearly sequencing activities and linking learning objects as well as services to activities. Although Level A leaves grey areas of interpretation [3], its principles can be well conceived. The more advanced mechanisms of IMS LD lie at Level B. While Level A mainly looks at the sequencing of activities, Level B allows for the structuring of individualized learning paths using *properties* to store data and *conditions* to act upon them. This means that learning objects and activities in a unit of learning can be adapted during runtime based on personal preferences or situational circumstances like assessment scores of learners. Last but not least, Level C adds the possibility to automatically send notifications, i.e. messages, upon events that take place within the

---

[1] A unit of learning refers to a complete, self-contained unit of education or training, such as a course, a module, a lesson etc. [8]. From a technical point of view, a unit of learning is defined as an IMS content package that includes an IMS Learning Design [1].

Learning Design. These notifications can be sent within the Learning Design or to external receivers.

Many researchers have proven that the IMS LD specification is indeed able to express a wide range of pedagogical approaches (e.g. [4]) showing that the specification is coherent and workable. The downside of the specification is, however, that only specialists, who have spent tremendous time working with the specification, are able to use it properly and to its full extent. For example, more than four years after the introduction of IMS LD only about 40 examples (as of June 13, 2007) of runnable units of learning can be found on the open access database DSpace [W001]. Most of these units of learning were added in 2005; only two units of learning were added in all of 2006[2].

While LD specialists feed the DSpace database with units of learning, the application of IMS LD by practitioners remains impeded by the complexity and technical nature of the specification [5]. The lack of authoring tools and runtime environments supporting the creation and delivery of Learning Designs represents yet another hindrance to a broad adoption of LD. As it cannot be expected from practitioners to familiarize themselves with the details of the specification, it is necessary to develop easy-to-handle tools that allow for an intuitive modeling process if we want them to apply the LD specification. These tools will have to support practitioners' approaches by hiding the IMS LD terminology and by translating the varied practical concepts into the rather rigid technical language of IMS LD.

In this article, we focus on describing the translation work to build a bridge from the IMS LD specification to intuitive modeling software in relation to Level B.

2 Tool Perspectives and Preparation of Analysis

For capturing and sharing learning designs electronically, a functional and technical architecture is required allowing for the visual representation and interpretation of teaching and learning activities. Tools like the Reload Editor [W002] are not suitable for practitioners, since they require that learning designers know the specification and its functional concepts in detail. However, as the Reload software allows the use of *all* elements that the IMS LD specification defines, it provides a suitable basis for building a graphical modeling tool.

We thus developed the Graphical Learning Modeler (GLM) based on the Reload Editor, where the GLM provides an intuitive graphical user interface (GUI). The GLM encapsulates part of the complexity of IMS LD, its main functions being the interpretation of graphical Learning Designs and the translation to IMS LD code at Level A and partially at Level B including the identification of role-parts, concurrent activities, acts, activity structures, and dependencies among activities that require conditions. Learning designers are thus enabled to build Learning-Design-compliant units of learning without pre-knowledge of the specification.

The problem we faced was how to best present the more complex options at Level B of the IMS LD specification in a graphical modeling tool. Just looking at the

---

[2] There was a third addition to the DSpace database in 2006; however, it contained presentation slides by David Griffiths and not an actual unit of learning.

IMS LD Information Model [1], it is next to impossible to immediately perceive the potential applications at Level B. Koper & Burgos [6] recognized this lack of perception and wrote about sample use instances of Level B functionalities. Practitioners are better referred to these concrete descriptions of uses, since a more common language and less IMS LD specific terminology is employed.

Increasing the perception by describing concrete applications of IMS LD at Level B as Koper & Burgos [6] have done serves two purposes: first, we are thus able to create a bridge between the language most practitioners use and the IMS LD specification, and second, we are thus able to derive rules for translating from typical applications to IMS LD code. In this regard, we answer the question of best representation by constructing software in wizard-structure, which will be integrated in the GLM and which guides the learning designers in creating interactive and individualized learning experiences. The wizard then represents the connection between practitioner-oriented language and the formal vocabulary offered by IMS LD.

As a first step of defining the wizard set up, we analyze Level B Learning Designs in order to describe typical uses of properties and conditions. As a second step, we make the correlations between typical uses and the setup of Level B's core concepts, namely properties, explicit. Based on these data, we are looking for translation mechanisms for the Graphical Learning Modeler wizard.

3 Analysis

In this section, we describe the analysis of units of learning to derive typical uses for properties. We see the property as the main component of Level B that is acted upon by conditions and monitor services. Within the analysis, we are thus focusing on properties in the first place, and put secondary foci on conditions and monitoring.

3.1 Set Up

First, we took all publicly available units of learning – eighteen in number – that were conform to at least Level B of the IMS LD specification. These included units of learning from the DSpace database [W001], examples from the Best Practice and Implementation Guide [7], and the Learning Design Book [8]. We looked at the imsmanifest.xml[3] of these units of learning and, if available, at the source code of the accompanied resources of type imsld content[4]. From these files, we collected data regarding the contained properties including their property-type, datatype, place of use, and function. The data was recorded in a spreadsheet application and then analyzed. The following questions guided our data analysis:

- What uses exist for properties?
- How does the type of property and its datatype relate to its use?

---

[3] The imsmanifest.xml is the part of the unit of learning content package containing the Learning Design.

[4] The IMS LD Information Model [1] states that objectives, prerequisites, learning objects, and activities are bound to be of type imsld content (XML files). Just like other resources (e.g. web content) imsld content can be referenced from a Learning Design but is not explicitly part of the IMS LD Information Model.

The total number of data sets collected approximated 800. This number does not equal the number of properties in the units of learning but the number of use instances of the properties, since one property defined in the components section (refer to Fig. 1) of the imsmanifest.xml could be used more than once within the Learning Design itself or in resources of type imsld content. For instance, the same property could be used in an eXtensible Markup Language (XML) file, where the user of the unit of learning will select a value for the property, and then be used in a comparison inside a condition to detect whether the choice the user made was correct. Each usage of a property, when possible to determine, was documented.

From the nearly 800 use instances for properties, we looked at a sample of 331 use instances more closely to draw correlations and to obtain a distribution for property functions. This sample was made up of property uses we could clearly describe and which could be included in the detailed analysis in a timely manner.

Problematic regarding the data recording were properties that were used within resources of type imsld content, which were not accessible to us. For instance, in the example units of learning of the Best Practice and Implementation Guide, resources of type imsld content were sometimes referenced in the imsmanifest.xml but not listed with their code. Accordingly, we were not able to determine the exact usages of the respective properties. Furthermore, some of the properties were essentially listed twice in our data set, since some units of learning received their structure from another, almost identical, unit of learning. For instance, the units of learning Quo Builder[5] and Quo Builder 2[6] are almost identical in terms of their property structures.

3.2 Results

The results of the analysis showed that almost all property-types defined in the IMS LD specification could be found in the sample units of learning. In part, strong correlations between certain property-types and datatypes could be identified. Yet, not all datatypes specified in the Learning Design specification [1] were represented in the sample units of learning. Also, not all functions provided by conditions had been applied in the sample units of learning.

3.2.1 Categorization of Property Functions

We found that from the property data sets we could derive six main categories of use instances:

- calculation
- change the value of a property
- manually determine the end of activities
- notifications
- show or hide components of the Learning Design
- view the value of a property.

Refer to Table 1 for a list of these main property functions including their subcategories, and descriptions.

---

[5] http://dspace.ou.nl/handle/1820/427
[6] http://dspace.ou.nl/handle/1820/428

Table 1. Categories including subcategories of property functions

Main Category	Subcategory	Description
Calculation	none	Properties containing numerical values are used as operands in summation, subtraction, multiplication or division, or preparations thereof, for instance, counting points.
Change Value	in a resource of type imsld content	A property's value is changed through an according setup in a resource of type imsld content, inside a condition, or along with the end of an activity.
	on completion of activities	
	via condition	
Determine End	learning activity	A certain value of a property determines when a learning or support activity is over.
	support activity	
Notification	none	Used to send notifications to users taking part in the unit of learning to inform them of certain happenings in the unit of learning such as the ending of an activity.
Show or Hide	activity structure	Used in a condition, this function checks if properties have reached a certain value. Upon that value, components of the Learning Design such as activities or environments can be shown or hidden.
	class[7]	
	environment	
	learning activity	
View Value	none	The value of a property is made visible by placing it in a resource of type imsld content that is used in the unit of learning.

The categories introduced in Table 1 are interrelated. For instance, for a property to be viewed, its value was usually changed in advance. The change, however, could take place through a calculation inside a condition or through an input that a user of the unit of learning provides during runtime. Also, the Show function and the Hide function often appear together in the imsmanifest.xml, meaning that an activity will be hidden until a certain property value has been reached and only then is the activity being shown to the learner.

Fig. 2 shows the distribution of the 331 sample property use instances according to the main functions described in Table 1. For the identified functions Change Value, Show/Hide, and Determine End, their corresponding subcategories have been listed separately as a portion of the total count.

Looking at Fig. 2, Change Value is the most frequently used function with properties among the sample we took. This is not surprising since it can be regarded as the primary function of properties: the intention of properties is that values are input and stored. Change value thus represents the possibility to provide input and have this input stored. All other functions except for Notification are usually consequences of the Change Value function of a property.

---

[7] The attribute class is a global attribute, which was defined by the World Wide Web Consortium initially for XHTML use in cascading style sheets [W005].

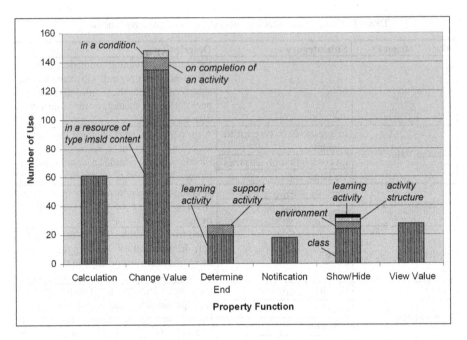

Fig. 2. Distribution of main property functions including subcategories

The values of properties are most often changed inside resources of type imsld content. This is apparent when looking at the subcategory "in a resource of type imsld content" of the Change Value function in Fig. 2. Properties set inside imsld content resources allow learners to provide own input and interact with the system. For instance, learners can only provide feedback or give answers through interaction with a property that is placed inside a resource of type imsld content. Only through properties is this type of interaction and personalization in Learning Designs possible.

For a change of a property value inside a resource, the global element set-property is used. Implementing the set-property element requires that the learning designer knows XML-coding, since the set-property element is included in the XML content schema using XML namespaces. This means that even if we use the Reload Editor, which takes over the part of coding the LD conforming XML, learning designers would still need XML-coding skills to write the accompanying imsld content.

The same is true for the Show or Hide function (refer to Fig. 2): most of the time, the class attribute was used to show or hide portions of text (e.g. differing feedback depending on a result or choice made by the learner). Thus, only if the learning designer knows XML, s/he is able to employ such personalized elements in the Learning Design. This is a major demand of the LD users from our point of view.

The View Value function is possibly underrepresented in the distribution of our sample in Fig. 2. We explain this misrepresentation since in some units of learning a property's value may only have been changed once but was made visible in different resources of type imsld content or in several classes. Furthermore, a *change* of a property's value inside a resource may be inferred and thus the data recorded if the property has no other defined purpose within the imsmanifest.xml, even if the resource's source code is not accessible. *Viewing* a property's value, on the other hand, may not as easily be concluded, since the property could just be carrying needed information in the background of the Learning Design. Determining if a property will in fact be *viewed*, i.e. shown to a role, can only be achieved by looking at the source code of imsld content. We thus attribute this potential misrepresentation in Fig. 2 to time constraints in checking all imsld content and the non-accessible codes of imsld content resources that were merely referenced in the imsmanifest.xml.

We are aware that the distribution shown in Fig. 2 is not representative of all the properties in the Learning Design example units of learning. The units of learning differ highly in the number and type of properties they employ. For instance, the unit of learning "Learning to Listen to Jazz" [9] makes use of 108 properties, 23 property groups and one property-type. On the other hand, the unit of learning "Programmed Instruction" from the Best Practice and Implementation Guide [7] only uses two properties, no property groups and one property-type. Thus, including one unit of learning and excluding another may dramatically change the distribution.

3.2.2 Correlations Between Property-Type and Datatype

Of the five types of properties that IMS LD allows (local, local-personal, local-role, global-personal, global), the examples we analyzed used all of these but the global property-type. The most commonly used datatypes were boolean[8], integer[9], string[10] and uri[11]. The datatypes text and file were also used, but considerably less often than the formerly named datatypes. We couldn't find usages of the datatypes datetime[12], duration[13], other[14], and real[15] within our sample of the example units of learning.

The analysis of the properties showed that there are typical correlations between the type of property being used, its datatype and the concrete application. An example for this is that all properties used for the category Calculation (cp. Table 1) were of property-type local-personal, and had the datatype integer. Their concrete use was, for example, to calculate points of achievement. Another example is that the end of an activity is often determined by a property of type local-personal with datatype boolean. Local-personal property is here used so that each learner can individually determine the end of the activity, while the boolean datatype is used because the activity can only have two status: finished or not finished.

Notifications, which are only of concern at Level C, are not in our immediate focus since we first aim at implementing Level B in the Graphical Learning Modeler. Nevertheless, properties that are used with notifications are always of type global-personal and use the datatype uri (in our analysis usually the email address of the tutor). Among all units of learning, global-personal properties were always 'existing href' (due to their conceptual nature of working across units of learning).

---

[8] Represents binary logic, e.g. on/off, true/false.
[9] Represents whole positive and negative numbers.
[10] Represents legal character strings, no longer than 2000 characters.
[11] uri is short for Uniform Resource Identifier.
[12] Specifies a date and time in a specific format.
[13] Specifies an amount of time in a specific format.
[14] Random datatype without specification.
[15] Represents arbitrary precision decimal numbers.

Information collected from such correlations between uses of properties, property-type and datatype, builds the basis for our wizard design to be integrated in the Graphical Learning Modeler. The wizard design will be further described in section 4.

3.3 Limitations of Property Use

Within the results of the analysis, we pointed out a few limitations of both the example units of learning and technical setup of the IMS LD specification. Regarding the latter, the fact that the value of properties is most often changed inside resources of type imsld content (XML-files) and that the attribute class is mainly used for showing and hiding text surprised us. Consequentially, the learning designer must possess the ability to construct valid XML-files in order to implement personalized or interactive elements in a Learning Design. To work around this, we have to develop new use concepts that are still able to provide these functionalities, yet, at the same time, hide the XML-specific terminology. These particular requirements have not yet been considered in the design of the wizard-structure for the Graphical Learning Modeler described herein but will be subject to further developments.

In addition to the limited use of datatypes for properties, only a portion of the possible condition operations was used in the sample units of learning. Examples for expressions that were not used in any of the units of learning are users-in-role, complete-an-act reference, time-unit-of-learning-started, and current-datetime. Therefore, we were not yet able to identify typical uses for these expressions.

When deriving the set of rules guiding the development of the Graphical Learning Modeler wizard, we focused primarily on those functionalities we were able to detect in the analyzed applications. More concrete descriptions of these translation efforts are described in the following section.

4   Projecting Analysis Results onto Development of Level B Wizard

In order to derive useful input for designing a wizard to be used in the GLM for Learning Design, we are correlating three types of data:

1. the concrete applications of properties described in the sample units of learning (like "students place a written comment on a controversial topic into a text box")
2. the categorization we established in the analysis (cp. Table 1, for instance, Change Value, Calculate etc.), and
3. the correlation between property-type and datatype.

For each application that we identified in a unit of learning (1.), we related the property-type and its datatype (3.) as well as the place of use of the property (2.) to the application in order to find typical uses and to derive rules where appropriate.

From the first data, we can derive what the learning designer might expect to see, since the specific examples comprise activities or procedures that teaching practitioners can relate to in their own terminology. The second data in relation to the first will inspire the user interface setup (for instance, showing and hiding are displayed together in the GUI since they are conceptually and technically related).

Using the third data and relating it to the first two, we are able to determine what code must be written upon the choice that the user makes inside the wizard. These interrelations will be described in the following sections.

4.1 Combining Property Applications and Property Functions

Taking the example units of learning, we found different applications of properties. Examples of uses are "writing a comment regarding a controversial statement", and "writing an answer to a short essay question". Even though practitioners are best able to understand this type of concrete description, for the design of a wizard it would not be advantageous to create lengthy lists of descriptions with very specific use instances.

Instead of providing each concrete use its own place in the wizard, we are attempting to group the uses sensibly and create a name for that group on a first abstraction level. For instance, the two examples given above (writing a comment and writing an answer to a question) are highly related from a technical point of view within IMS LD. Conceptually on a teaching practice level, they are related as well. Although these uses represent two different cases, we are able to group them on a first abstraction level to "writing a short text". Even one more abstraction level above, we would call this "giving textual input during runtime". "Giving textual input during runtime" would then be a subgroup of "giving input during runtime". Via inductions like this, we are able to construct a decision tree that starts at more abstract levels and as you go into the tree, become more specific.

In a next step, we have to combine the so developed decision tree with the technical functions that IMS LD allows. For this, we mesh the decision tree with the categorization of property functions (cp. Table 1) and again draw correlations. Using this technique, we were able to derive four main categories that represent the entrance level for our Graphical Learning Modeler wizard. In combining the conceptual uses with the functions of properties as listed in Table 1, we created the following functional entrances:

1. Show/Hide (subsumes View Value and Show/Hide functionalities)
2. Providing Input Possibilities (subsumes Change Value functionalities)
3. Points (subsumes Calculation functionalities)
4. Administration and Control (subsumes Determine End of Activities, and grouping of Input Possibilities)

Each of these four main choices contains several substeps that get more and more specific. For instance, the second menu option "Providing input possibilities" opens the options of choosing either a "Choice from predefined values" (opening a drop-down box at runtime to select, and therefore input, values) or "Free input" (a space is provided at runtime for the learner to enter any text or numbers). Upon choice of the former, there is an option of differentiating between "multiple choice" (which in the background of the GLM employs the datatype "string" as well as the restriction type "enumeration" for properties) or "vote" (which in the background uses the datatype "boolean"). Providing these choices at the time of design, the learning designer is thus able to include interactive elements and individualized learning paths in the unit of learning. Whenever there is additional input needed, for instance, if the learning designer specifies the values that are to be chosen among like answers to a multiple choice question, the GLM provides a dialog that will ask for this information in common language.

4.2 Wizard Setup for Determining Property-Type and Datatype from Use

As we have shown in the analysis, the type of property (local, local-personal etc.) often had strong correlations with the application and datatype being used. Because of this, we felt reassured that developing a wizard-like structure is a manageable approach, since we are able to either directly derive the required information from the correlations or to limit the questions we need to ask the learning designer. The wizard's main function is to guide the learning designer through a set of decision steps, which produces IMS LD conformant code in the background. This way, the learning designer will not be faced with IMS LD specific terminology.

For example, if the learning designer picks from the wizard (via several steps) the option to "show this activity only when the learner has reached a certain number of points", then we know that we have to construct (if it is a new property) or refer to (if the learning designer already established a property for counting points) a property of type local-personal with datatype integer. We then have to refer to this property within a condition, which will observe whether the property has reached the specified value (which we ask the learning designer to determine in a dialog; e.g. five points must be reached). The condition will then have the following setup (only relevant portions of the code are being shown):

```
<if>
    <is>
            <property-ref ref="points">
            <property-value>5
<then>
    <show>
            <learning-activity-ref ref="activity-name">
<else>
    <hide>
            <learning-activity-ref ref="activity-name">
```

As the learner, who will go through the described learning path, collects points, s/he will only see the specified activity once s/he has collected the necessary points. Since for every learner the system detects individually whether they have reached the five points, we are using the property type local-personal for this purpose. Since points are usually whole numbers that are to be added or calculated, we are using the datatype integer.

For every path that can be selected within the wizard, we have developed functionalities that follow the herein presented schema. Thus, we derived rules how to set up the imsmanifest.xml from the choices that the learning designer makes using the wizard.

At this point, we are at the conceptual stage of this development. However, we are implementing this wizard into our existing Graphical Learning Modeler.

4.3 Challenges for the Graphical Learning Modeler

We are aware that a wizard designed in the way we just described allows the construction of *typical* uses for properties and conditions. For application of a greater number of Level B functions beyond these typical use instances, the learning designer would have to be able to use the LD terminology. In further developments, we strive to reduce this gap between the available functions of the wizard and the potential functions offered in the LD specification.

Despite the restrictions that the wizard possesses on the one hand, on the other hand, it finally offers practitioners access to IMS LD and places them in a position to design Learning Designs including functions of properties without any knowledge of XML or IMS LD: Just as users of wysiwyg[16]-HTML-editors do not need to know coding procedures in HTML, so do users of a Graphical Learning Modeler not need to know Learning Design specific coding procedures. This is the advantage that we see in developing the GLM.

Suppose that the provision of a Graphical Learning Modeler leads in turn to a higher adoption rate of the IMS LD specification – only then would the learning design community be able to judge whether the specification truly fulfils its promise of supporting the exchange and re-use of Learning Designs [1].

5 Technical Setting

The GLM makes substantial use of functionalities implemented in the Reload Learning Design Editor and extends them with additional information and business logic necessary for visually representing IMS LD elements such as learning activities and their dependencies among each other.

Our decision to use the Graphical Editing Framework (GEF) as the graphical toolkit and framework for modeling teaching and learning workflows on top of the rich client platform Eclipse [W003] was driven by the results from a previously conducted evaluation of existing modeling frameworks. In this evaluation phase, considerations had also been given to the Graphical Modeling Framework (GMF), which provides suitable functions for building graphical modeling tools. The main difference between GEF and GMF lies in the conceptual orientation of GMF, which is more suitable for building Unified Modeling Language (UML) models. GMF also requires the underlying data model to be conform with the Eclipse Modeling Framework (EMF) data model specification. The Eclipse platform and GEF [W004] are both open source technologies and are ideally suited to provide the technical basis on which the Graphical Learning Modeler is built.

The Graphical Editing Framework provides capabilities to easily develop rich and adaptable visual representations of existing data models. These editing capabilities allow for the creation of graphical editors for almost any arbitrarily complex model as well as user interactions on this model. Modifications on the underlying data model based on user interactions, such as changing element properties or changing the model structure, are supported as well as performed by using common functions such as drag and drop, copy and paste, and actions invoked from menus and toolbars [10]. The underlying model will be updated accordingly.

To display graphical elements called widgets, GEF makes use of the Standard Widget Toolkit (SWT), which acts as a bridge for accessing and presenting GUI

---

[16] wysiwyg is short for What You See Is What You Get.

elements from the underlying operating system. The main advantage of SWT over existing and related technologies such as the Advanced Window Toolkit (AWT) or Swing is its seamless integration into the existing working environment since SWT – in contrast to other technologies – does not emulate the graphical interface. It rather acts as an adapter or bridge to the GUI-Elements and Services of the operating system.

The use of SWT as a mechanism for representing graphical elements also provides enhanced interaction with the prevailing working system components while making better use of existing system resources. The disadvantage resulting from the usage of SWT is the loss of platform neutrality and independency, since the application needs to be compiled for any target operation system separately.

Due to the fact that GEF is fully compliant with the Model-View-Controller principle[17], it provides a basis for extending and improving the existing functionality while leaving the domain models untouched. The separation of business logic, visual presentation, and the domain model allows a great form of flexibility in extending the functional range of the Graphical Learning Modeler where additional functions can be added without much effort.

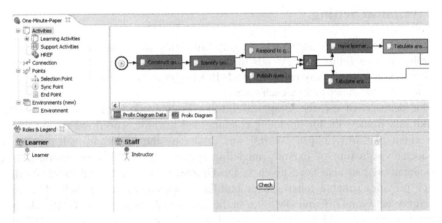

Fig. 3. Screenshot of the Graphical Learning Modeler

Fig. 3 depicts the Graphical Learning Modeler: activity and environment lists as well as design functions are seen in the upper left, learner and staff roles in the lower left, the graphical workspace holding the activity sequence in the upper right, and a provisional "check" window in the lower right. The check window is used during development to quickly verify that the GLM interprets the graphical layout in terms of IMS LD correctly. The Level B wizard for the more complex functions as presented in the analysis will be integrated as part of the design functions in the upper left among operations like selection point or deliberate synchronization. Level B functionalities,

---

[17] Interactive applications, which follow the Model-View-Controller architectural approach, are divided into three layers (model, view, and controller) and decouple their respective responsibilities. Each layer handles specific tasks as well as has specific responsibilities and interdependences to other layers and their respective components. This form of separation among model, view, and controller objects reduces code duplication and eases the maintenance of applications.

which the GLM is able to interpret directly from the graphical layout, will be automatically translated without input from the learning designer.

The GLM encapsulates the actual data components implemented in the Reload Editor and complements them with additional information to build its own model on which the visual representations are generated. Reload data components and business logic is extended with GLM-specific data and logic to provide the desired functionality. The Graphical Learning Modeler therefore acts as an additional functional layer on top of Reload incorporating its own business logic and data model for generating visual representations of IMS LD elements. The use of the graphical framework GEF allows for the uncomplicated extension and customization of this functional layer with additional functionalities.

6 Conclusion

In this article, we introduced a system for providing Level B properties in a translated form to users of a Graphical Learning Modeler. We used publicly available samples of units of learning to derive typical uses of properties. The analysis showed that only part of the potential that Level B holds has been expressed in publicly available units of learning. This fraction, however, can be translated into typical uses and placed into a structure, which gives practitioners of IMS LD access to the functions of Level B properties and conditions.

Acknowledgments. This article was written in the context of the research and development integrated project PROLIX, which is co-funded by the European Commission under the Sixth Framework Programme "Information Society Technologies". The Graphical Learning Modeler that is being discussed in this paper is a development of the University of Vienna with main contributions from Maia Zaharieva at the Multimedia Information Systems Group headed by Wolfgang Klas.

References

1. Koper, R., Olivier, B., Anderson, T. (eds.): IMS Learning Design Information Model. IMS Global Learning Consortium (2003)
2. Britain, S.: A Review of Learning Design: Concept, Specifications and Tools. A report for the JISC E-learning Pedagogy Programme (2004)
3. Oberhuemer, P., Heyer, S.: Probleme bei der Umsetzung didaktischer Modelle in IMS Learning Design: eine Anwenderperspektive. Zeitschrift für e-Learning, Lernkultur und Bildungstechnologie, in press (2007)
4. van Es, R., Koper, R.: Testing the pedagogical expressiveness of IMS LD. Journal of Educational Technology & Society 9(1), 229–249 (2006)
5. Beetham, H.: Review: developing e-Learning Models for the JISC Practitioner Communities. Version 2.1. Joint Information Systems Committee e-learning and Pedagogy Programme (2004)
6. Koper, R., Burgos, D.: Developing Advanced Units of Learning Using IMS Learning Design Level B. International Journal on Advanced Technology for Learning 2(4), 252–259 (2005)

7. Koper, R., Olivier, B., Anderson, T. (eds.): IMS Learning Design Best Practice and Implementation Guide. IMS Global Learning Consortium (2003)
8. Koper, R., Tattersall, C. (eds.): Learning Design: A Handbook on Modelling and Delivering Networked Education and Training. Springer, Heidelberg (2005)
9. Tattersall, C., Burgos, D.: Learning to Listen to Jazz, Retrieved March 26, 2007 (2005), from http://dspace.ou.nl/handle/1820/371
10. Moore, B., Dean, D., Gerber, A., Wagenknecht, G., Vanderheyden, P.: Eclipse Development Using the Graphical Editing Framework and the Eclipse Modelling Framework. IBM Red Book: ibm.com/redbooks (2004)

[W001] http://dspace.learningnetworks.org/handle/1820/16/browse-title
[W002] http://www.reload.ac.uk/ldeditor.html
[W003] http://www.eclipse.org/
[W004] http://www.eclipse.org/gef/
[W005] http://www.w3.org/TR/REC-html40/struct/global.html#h-7.5.2

Using MotSaRT to Support On-Line Teachers in Student Motivation

Teresa Hurley and Stephan Weibelzahl

National College of Ireland, School of Informatics,
Mayor Street,
Dublin 1, Ireland
{thurley,sweibelzahl}@ncirl.ie

Abstract. In classrooms teachers know how to motivate their students and exploit this knowledge to adapt or optimize their instruction when a student shows signs of demotivation. In on-line learning environments it is much more difficult to assess the motivation of the student and to have adaptive intervention strategies and rules of application to help prevent attrition. We developed MotSaRT – a motivational strategies recommender tool – to support on-line teachers in motivating learners. The design is informed by Social Cognitive Theory and a survey on motivation intervention strategies carried out with sixty on-line teachers. The survey results were analysed using a data mining algorithm (J48 decision trees) which resulted in a set of decision rules for recommending motivational strategies. MotSaRT has been developed based on these decision rules. Its functionality enables the teacher to specify the learner's motivation profile. MotSaRT then recommends the most likely intervention strategies to increase motivation.

Keywords: on-line learning, motivation, intervention strategies, on-line teachers, self-efficacy, goal orientation, locus of control, perceived task difficulty, recommender tool.

1 Introduction

On-line learning is a dynamic and potentially enriching form of learning but attrition remains a serious problem, resulting in personal, occupational and financial implications for both students and academic institutions [5]. Motivation to learn is affected by the learner's self-efficacy, goal orientation, locus of control and perceived task difficulty. In the traditional classroom, teachers infer learners' levels of motivation from several cues, including speech, behaviour, attendance, body language or feedback, and offer interventional strategies aimed at increasing motivation. Intelligent Tutoring Systems (ITS) need to be able to recognize when the learner is becoming demotivated and to intervene with effective motivational strategies. Such an ITS would comprise two main components, an assessment mechanism that infers the learner's level of motivation from observing the learner's behaviour, and an adaptation component that selects the most appropriate intervention strategy to increase motivation. This paper presents the results of a survey of on-line teachers on how they motivate their learners. These results

E. Duval, R. Klamma, and M. Wolpers (Eds.): EC-TEL 2007, LNCS 4753, pp. 101–111, 2007.

informed the development of the adaptation component by extracting and validating selection rules for strategies to increase motivation. The recommender tool, MotSaRT, has been developed based on these rules. Its functionality enables the teacher to specify the learner's motivation profile. MotSaRT then recommends the most likely intervention strategies to increase motivation.

2 Background

The focus of this research is intervention strategies which can be implemented and validated in an Intelligent Tutoring System to increase motivation and reduce attrition. Previous approaches in this field were mainly based on the ARCS model - attention, relevance, confidence, and satisfaction, which is an instructional design model ([4][14][18]). These states are inferred from behavioural cues in the interaction such as time taken, effort, confidence, and focus of attention.

2.1 Learner Modelling

We argue that a model of motivational states of learners should build upon a well established theory of motivation in learning. The approach being taken in this research is based on Social Cognitive Theory (SCT) [1], particularly on self-efficacy, locus of control, perceived task difficulty and goal orientation. As learners differ widely in these constructs, intervention strategies must be adapted to suit the individual and the task. The interventions may take the form of verbal persuasion, vicarious experience (someone else models a skill), mastery experience (repetitive successes instill a strong sense of self efficacy which becomes quite resistant to occasional failures), and scaffolding (help from a more able peer or mentor).. Such interventions therefore focus the attention on the learner rather than on instructional design.

2.2 Motivation

Motivation in general is defined as "the magnitude and direction of behaviour and the choices people make as to what experiences or goals they will approach or avoid and to the degree of effort they will exert in that respect" [6]. Students with higher levels of intrinsic motivation and self-efficacy achieve better learning outcomes [11]. Intrinsic motivation is created by three qualities: challenge, fantasy and curiosity [8].

Social cognitive theory provides a framework for understanding, predicting, and changing human behaviour. The theory identifies human behaviour as an interaction of personal factors, behaviour, and the environment.

2.3 Self-efficacy

Self-efficacy is an "individuals' confidence in their ability to control their thoughts, feelings, and actions, and therefore influence an outcome" [1]. Individuals acquire information to help them assess self-efficacy from (a) actual experiences, where the individual's own performance, especially past successes and failures, are the most reliable indicator of efficacy; (b) vicarious experiences, where observation of others performing a task conveys to the observer that they too are capable of accomplishing that task; (c) verbal persuasion, where individuals are encouraged to believe that they possess the capabilities to perform a task; and (d) physiological indicators, where individuals may interpret bodily symptoms, such as increased heart rate or sweating, as anxiety or fear indicating a lack of skill. Perceptions of self-efficacy influence actual performance [7], and the amount of effort and perseverance expended on an activity [3].

2.4 Attribution Theory

Attribution Theory [16] has been used to explain the difference in motivation between high and low achievers. Ability, effort, task difficulty, and luck have been identified as the most important factors affecting attributions for achievement. High achievers approach rather than avoid tasks relating to achievement as they believe success is due to ability and effort. Failure is attributed to external causes such as bad luck or a poor exam. Thus, failure does not affect self-esteem but success builds pride and confidence. Low achievers avoid success-related tasks because they doubt their ability and believe success is due to luck or other factors beyond their control. Success is not rewarding to a low achiever because he/she does not feel responsible, i.e. it does not increase his/her pride or confidence.

2.5 Locus of Control

Locus of control [15] is a relatively stable trait and is a belief about the extent to which behaviours influence successes or failures. Individuals with an internal locus of control believe that success or failure is due to their own efforts or abilities. Individuals with an external locus of control believe that factors such as luck, task difficulty, or other people's actions, cause success or failure.

2.6 Perceived Task Difficulty

Perception of task difficulty will affect the expectancy for success, and strongly influences both instigation of a learning activity as well as persistence [10]. The learner's sense of accomplishment, as well as their reaction to failure, if often tied to their subject beliefs about the difficulty of the goal they have undertaken.

2.7 Goal Orientation

One classification of motivation differentiates among achievement, power, and social factors [9]. Goals enhance self-regulation through their effects on motivation, learning, self-efficacy and self-evaluations of progress [1]. According to self-regulated learning (SRL) theorists, self-regulated learners are "metacognitively, motivationally, and behaviourally active participants in their own learning process" [19]. Individuals with a learning goal orientation strive to master the task and are likely to engage in self-regulatory activities such as monitoring, planning, and deep-level cognitive strategies. Individuals orientated towards performance approach goals are concerned with positive evaluations of their abilities in comparison to others and focus on how they are judged by parents, teachers or peers. Individuals with performance avoidance goals want to look smart, not appear incompetent and so may avoid challenging tasks, or exhibit low persistence, when encountering difficulties [13]. Individuals may have both mastery and performance goals [12]. Disengaged orientation is displayed by students who "do not really care about doing well in school or learning the material; their goal is simply to get through the activity" [2].

3 Eliciting Intervention Strategies from On-Line Teachers

In order to find out about the intervention strategies used by on-line teachers we designed questionnaires that would systematically elicit recommended strategies for given learner profiles.

A learner model was created based on the SCT constructs of Self-Efficacy, Goal Orientation, Locus of Control and Perceived Task Difficulty, as these are the four most important factors contributing to self-regulation. Research has shown that self regulatory behaviour can account for academic achievement [10]. The model contained 21 learner profiles. These were systematically developed using the above constructs (see Table 1). The profiles were selected from a possible 48 as the most likely to experience demotivation. For example, a person with the profile of Persona 1 is likely to become demotivated when not sufficiently challenged.

Table 1. Profile of personas

Persona	1	2	3	4	5	6	7	8	9	10	11	12	13	14	15	16	17	18	19	20	21
SE	H	H	M	M	M	M	L	L	M	H	L	L	M	M	M	M	H	L	L	M	M
GO	M	M	M	M	M	M	M	Pa	Pa	Pa	PA	PA	PA	PA	PA	PA	PA	D	D	D	D
LOC	I	E	I	I	E	E	E	E	E	E	I	E	I	E	I	E	I	I	E	E	I
PTD	L	L	L	H	L	H	H	H	H	H	H	H	L	L	H	H	L	H	H	H	H

Key: Self Efficacy (SE) [High (H)/Medium (M)/Low (L)]; Goal Orientation (GO) [Mastery (M)/Performance Avoidance (Pa)/Performance Approach (PA)/Disengagement (D)]; Locus of Control (LOC) [Internal (I)/External (E)]; Perceived Task Difficulty (PTD)[Low (L)/High (H)]

Based on the model, personas (i.e., short textual descriptions) were then developed, e.g. Persona 1: "Chris is an intelligent student who enjoys learning for its own sake. She is motivated to learn new things and enjoys being challenged (*GO: Mastery*). She believes she can do very well in her studies as she has a very good understanding of her subject (*SE: High*). Chris believes hard work will conquer almost any problem and lead to success (*LOC: Internal*). However, she finds that she becomes bored when she has to work on a concept which she already understands well (*PTD: Low*)." Note that the italic profile labels were inserted here for illustration, but were not part of the instruction given to the participants.

From the literature on motivation and an initial pilot questionnaire, completed by classroom teachers, a list of intervention strategies was compiled (see Table 2). In order to identify rules to determine which intervention strategy is the most appropriate for each learner's persona, on-line teachers were surveyed. If, for example, a learner had low self-efficacy and external locus of control, teachers might indicate that reviewing progress with the student at regular intervals would be a strategy to adopt. In this way the relationship between motivational states and intervention strategies was elicited with the assistance of the on-line teachers.

Table 2. Intervention strategies

1	Review progress with student at regular intervals
2	Provide regular positive and specific feedback to student
3	Encourage student to clearly define his/her academic goals
4	Encourage the student to use on-line quizzes
5	Remind student of the student support services
6	Encourage student to use the chat room/discussion forums
7	Help student to develop a study plan/timetable
8	Explain importance of and encourage student to maintain contact with tutor
9	Encourage peer to peer contact
10	Encourage student to base self-evaluation on personal improvement/mastery when possible, rather than grades
11	Encourage the student to reflect on and evaluate his/her learning
12	Explain why learning a particular content is important
13	Provide guidance to extra learning resources
14	No intervention required

As there were twenty-one personas to be considered, the on-line survey was divided into six parts with three or four personas in each. The personas were similar to the example above, but without the references to the theoretical constructs. Every effort was made to ensure that the personas in each of the surveys were based on different constructs. For example, in Survey No. 1, each persona had either high, medium or low self-efficacy and had different goal orientations. Participant teachers were randomly assigned to one of the six surveys. The same 14 intervention strategies were presented in the same order under each persona. The teachers were asked to select the strategies they would *Highly Recommend, Recommend* or considered *Not Applicable* for each persona. They were also asked to suggest any further strategies that they find particularly useful in the case of each persona type. The teachers were required to have at least two years experience teaching on-line. The survey could be completed anonymously or the participants could enter their email address if they wished to get feedback on the results. Sixty participants completed the surveys which resulted in each persona getting a minimum of six and a maximum of fourteen responses.

4   Survey Results

The participants varied widely in the number of years of experience they had as on-line teachers. The least experienced participants had tutored on-line for two years, and the most experienced had tutored for eighteen years. The average was five years.

For the purpose of this paper, we merged Highly Recommended and Recommended strategies into one category "Recommended".

Using the Weka data mining tool set [11], five different algorithms were applied to predict whether a strategy was marked as recommended by the teachers or not. These algorithms included the following classifiers: 1) Bayesian Networks; 2) IBk, an instance-based k-nearest neighbours classifier; 3) J48, generating pruned C4.5 decision trees; 4) PART, a classifier based on partial C4.5 decision trees and rules;

and 5) Naïve Bayes as a standard baseline. All experiments were run with a 10-fold stratified cross validation. J48 decision trees turned out to provide the best predictions (see Table 3).

Table 3. Correct predictions (%) of the J48 decision tree algorithm separated by the 13 intervention strategies

Strategy 1	89.86
Strategy 2	93.26
Strategy 3	84.55
Strategy 4	66.58
Strategy 5	77.31
Strategy 6	86.50
Strategy 7	68.83
Strategy 8	83.60
Strategy 9	88.90
Strategy 10	82.64
Strategy 11	88.90
Strategy 12	79.24
Strategy 13	80.67

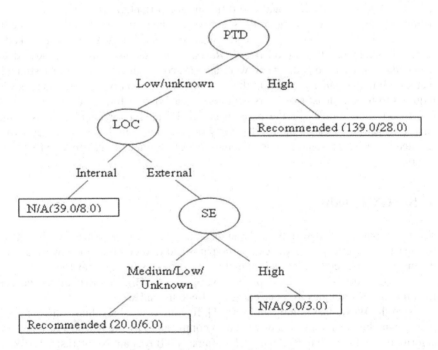

Fig. 1. Decision Tree for Strategy 5

The J48 analysis results in one decision tree per strategy predicting under which circumstances a certain strategy would be recommended or not. Figure 1 gives an example of such a decision tree: Strategy 5 – Remind students of the student support services. If Perceived Task Difficulty (PTD) is high, then Strategy 5 is recommended If PTD is low or unknown and Locus of Control (LOC) is internal, then Strategy 5 is not recommended. If PTD is low or unknown and LOC is external and Self-Efficacy (SE) is high, then Strategy is not recommended. If PTD is low or unknown and LOC is external and SE is medium, low or unknown, then Strategy 5 is recommended.

5   MotSaRT – Motivational Strategies: A Recommender Tool for On-Line Teachers

Using the recommendation rules derived from the questionnaire study, we have developed a recommender tool, MotSaRT, to support on-line teachers in motivating learners (see Figure 2). Its functionality enables the facilitator to specify the learner's motivation profile. MotSaRT then recommends the most likely intervention strategies to increase motivation for any particular profile.

Technically, MotSaRT is a Java Applet and can thus be integrated into most L[C]MS fairly easily. Observing the activities of learners in the learning environment and possibly interacting with them synchronously or asynchronously through instant messaging, email or fora, teachers would assess learners in terms of their self-efficacy, goal-orientation, locus of control and perceived task difficulty. MotSaRT would then classify this case and sort the strategies in terms of their applicability. Teachers could then plan their interventions according to these recommendations.

5.1 MotSaRT Functionality

By observing the progress of the students and interacting with them either synchronously or asynchronously, an on-line teacher will become aware if a student is falling behind and not submitting assignments or making sufficient progress in the coursework. At this stage the teacher can contact the student and through dialogue and/or the use of a reliable and validated motivation survey instrument assess the motivation level of the student. If it becomes obvious that the student is demotivated and thus possibly exit from the course, the teacher can utilize the functionality of MotSaRT to select suitable intervention strategies to attempt to motivate the student and thus prevent attrition. From the dialogue and the motivation survey the teacher will be able to access the student's level of self-efficacy, goal orientation, locus of control and perceived task difficulty. With this information the teacher would use MotSaRT as follows:

In the Learner Profile area, the teacher would select the student profile:
Self-Efficacy – High, Medium, Low or Unknown
Goal Orientation – Performance Approach, Performance Avoidance, Mastery, Disengagement or Unknown
Locus of Control – Internal, External or Unknown
Perceived Task Difficulty – Low, Medium, High or Unknown

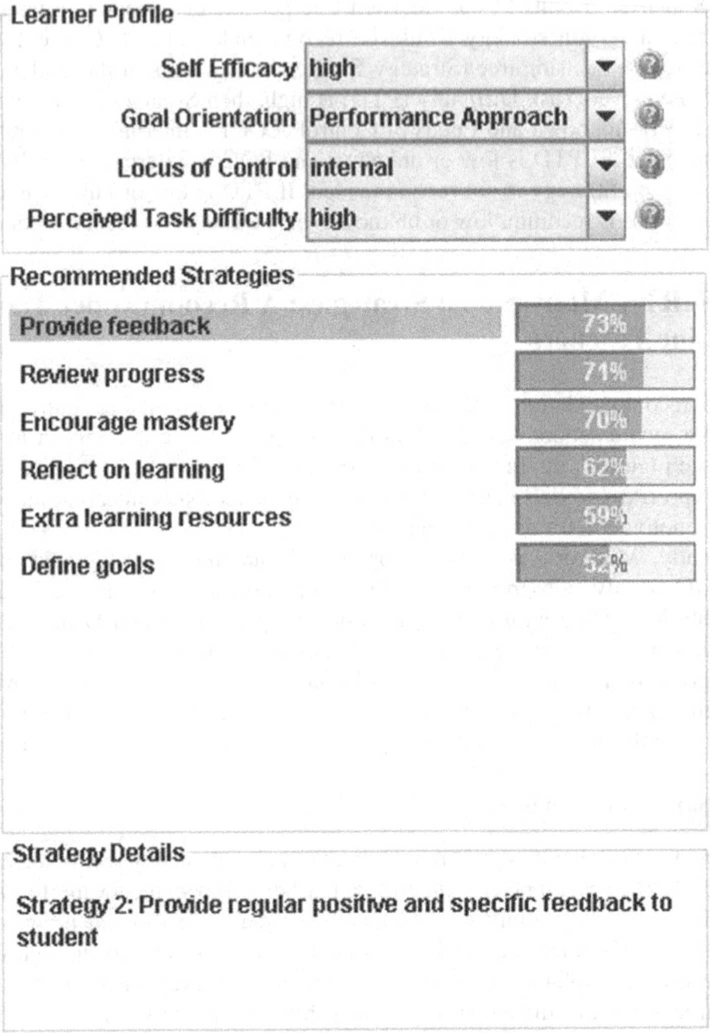

Learner Profile

Self Efficacy	high ▼ ⑦
Goal Orientation	Performance Approach ▼ ⑦
Locus of Control	internal ▼ ⑦
Perceived Task Difficulty	high ▼ ⑦

Recommended Strategies

Provide feedback	73%
Review progress	71%
Encourage mastery	70%
Reflect on learning	62%
Extra learning resources	59%
Define goals	52%

Strategy Details

Strategy 2: Provide regular positive and specific feedback to student

Fig. 2. Screenshot of MotSaRT

A question mark located beside each of the constructs enables the teacher to find out more about the construct if desired.

In the Recommended Strategies area, depending on the profile entered by the teacher, a list of strategies will appear showing the percentage recommendation according to the J48 decision tree algorithm.

By clicking on a strategy, an elaboration of the strategy will appear in the Strategy Details area.

From the suggested strategies the teacher selects the strategy that they believe is the most suitable for intervention with the particular student. The teacher can then monitor the student's progress to see if the motivation level of the student increases and the student begins to make progress in the coursework again.

5.2 Testing MotSaRT

Approximately half of the on-line teachers who took part in the survey on the intervention strategies requested feedback. It is planned to make MotSaRT available to these teachers. They will be asked to comment on the usability and usefulness of the tool. They will also be asked for suggestions for improvement and recommended changes. If they actually use the tool as outlined in Section 5.1 above, they will also be asked to report on any perceived increase in the student's motivation level. In this way it is intended also to get feedback on both the quality and appropriateness of the recommendations. Preliminary results are expected soon on this part of the research.

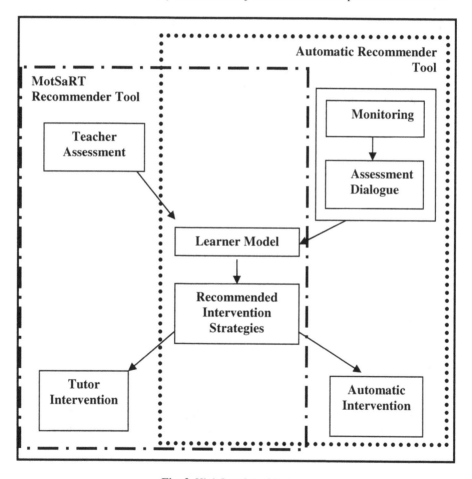

Fig. 3. High Level Architecture

6 Future Perspectives

Informed by a study with on-line teachers, we developed MotSaRT, a tool that shows appropriate intervention strategies for motivational profiles. Prompting on-line teachers with personas we were able to elicit their knowledge about suitable interventions and modelled these decisions using a decision tree algorithm. Predictions are accurate. Future work will focus on an empirical validation of the predictions in a real e-Learning environment to see if the intervention strategies adopted actually increase the motivation of the learner.

Our vision is to develop an automated tool which can be used in a fully automatic system, a semi-automatic system or in a manual system (Fig 2), to recommend motivational intervention strategies to students who are diagnosed as becoming demotivated during the course of their studies. This diagnosis may be made either by a teacher or by automatic assessment. The diagnosis will be fed into the learner model. MotSaRT can then be used to either make recommendations to the teachers or to make an automatic intervention.

As this stage MotSaRT will be used to implement the path on left hand side of Figure 3 (dashed outline). However, it is envisaged that eventually other possible uses will include either the teacher or the ITS identifying the preferred intervention strategy using MotSaRT and the selected strategy being implemented automatically by the ITS.

References

1. Bandura, A.: Social foundations of thought and action: A social cognitive theory. Prentice-Hall, Englewood Cliffs, NJ (1986)
2. Beal, C.R., Lee, H.: Creating a pedagogical model that uses student self reports of motivation and mood to adapt ITS instruction. Workshop on motivation and affect in educational software, July 18-22, Amsterdam, Netherlands. Retrieved on March 23, 2006 from http://www.wayangoutpost.net/paper/Beal&LeeCRC.pdf
3. Brown Jr., I., Inouye, D.K.: Learned helplessness through modeling: The role of perceived similarity in competence. Journal of Personality and Social Psychology 36, 900–908 (1978)
4. De Vicente, A., Pain, H.: Validating the Detection of a student's Motivational State. In: Mendez Vilas, A., Mesa Gonzalez, J.A., Mesa Gonzalez, J. (eds.) Proceedings of the Second International Conference on Multimedia Information & Communication Technologies in Education (m-ICTE2003) (2003)
5. Dille, B., Mezack, M.: Identifying predictors of high risk among community college telecourse students. The American Journal of Distance Education 5(1), 24–35 (1991)
6. Keller, J.M.: Motivational design of instruction. In: Reigeluth, C.M. (ed.) Instructional design theories and models: An overview of their current status, Erlbaum, Hillsdale, NJ (1993)
7. Locke, E.A., Frederick, E., Lee, C., Bobko, P.: Effect of self-efficacy, goals, and task strategies on task performance. Journal of Applied Psychology 69, 241–251 (1984)
8. Malone, T.: Towards a theory of instrinsically motivating instruction. Cognitive Science 4, 333–369 (1981)

9. McClelland, D.: Human motivation. Scott, Foresman, New York (1985)
10. Pajares, F., Schunk, D.H.: Self-Beliefs and School Success: Self-Efficacy, Self-Concept, and School Achievement. In: Riding, R., Rayner, S. (eds.) Perception, pp. 239–266. Ablex Publishing, London (2001)
11. Pintrich, P.R., De Groot, E.V.: Motivational and self-regulated learning components of classroom academic performance. Journal of Educational Psychology 82(1), 33–40 (1990)
12. Pintrich, P.R., Garcia, T.: Student goal orientation and self-regulation in the college classroom. In: Maehr, M.L., Pintrich, P.R. (eds.) Advances in motivation and achievement: Goals and self-regulatory processes, vol. 7, pp. 371–402. JAI Press, Greenwich, CT (1991)
13. Pintrich, P.R., Schunk, D.H.: Motivation in education: Theory, research, and practice. Prentice Hall, Englewood Cliffs, NJ (1996)
14. Qu, L., Wang, N., Johnson, W.L.: Detecting the Learner's Motivational States in an Interactive Learning Environment. In: Looi, C.-K., et al. (eds.) Artificial Intelligence in Education, pp. 547–554. IOS Press, Amsterdam (2005)
15. Rotter, J.B.: Generalized expectancies for internal versus external control of reinforcement. Psychological Monographs, 80 (Whole No. 609) (1966)
16. Weiner, B.: Achievement motivation and attribution theory. General Learning Press, Morristown, N.J (1974)
17. Witten, I.H., Frank, E., Trigg, L.E., Hall, M., Holmes, G., Cunningham, S.J: Weka: Practical machine learning tools and techniques with Java implementations. In: Proc ICONIP/ ANZIIS/ANNES99 Future Directions for Intelligent Systems and Information Sciences, Dunedin, New Zealand, pp. 192–196 (November 1999)
18. Zhang, G., Cheng, Z., He, A., Huang, T.: A WWW-based Learner's Learning Motivation Detecting System. Proceedings of International Workshop on Research Directions and Challenge Problems in Advanced Information Systems Engineering, Honjo City, Japan, September 16–19, 2003, http://www.akita-pu.ac.jp/system/KEST2003/
19. Zimmerman, B.J.: Theories of self-regulated learning and academic achievement: An overview and analysis. In: Zimmerman, B.J., Schunk, D.H. (eds.) Self-regulated learning and academic achievement: Theoretical perspectives, 2nd edn. vol. 4(1), pp. 1–37. Lawrence Erlbaum Associates, Mahwah, NJ (2007)

LOCO-Analyst: A Tool for Raising Teachers' Awareness in Online Learning Environments

Jelena Jovanović[1], Dragan Gašević[2,3], Christopher Brooks[4],
Vladan Devedžić[1], and Marek Hatala[3]

[1] FON-School of Business Administration, University of Belgrade, Belgrade, Serbia
jeljov@gmail.com, devedzic@fon.bg.ac.yu
[2] School of Computing and Information System, Athabasca University, Canada
dgasevic@acm.org
[3] School of Interactive Arts and Technology, Simon Fraser University, Surrey, Canada
mhatala@sfu.ca
[4] Department of Computer Science, University of Saskatchewan, Saskatoon, Canada
cab938@mail.usask.ca

Abstract. The paper presents LOCO-Analyst, an educational tool for providing teachers with feedback on the relevant aspects of the learning process taking place in a web-based learning environment. The feedback provision is based on the learning context, which we dubbed Learning Object Context and consider as a complex interplay of learning activities, learning objects, and learners. Here we present a usage scenario based on the real data obtained from the Web-based iHelp Courses Learning Content Management System, in order to illustrate some of the functionalities that LOCO-Analyst provides. We also briefly overview Semantic Web technologies that lay beneath LOCO-Analyst and make it a generic feedback provision tool. Related work is presented as well. The paper concludes with a sketch of our current and planned future efforts for further improving LOCO-Analyst.

Keywords: Ontologies, Semantic Annotation, Learning Context, Educational Feedback.

1 Introduction

Most distant educators would agree that online teaching necessarily involves (but is not limited to):

- preparation of online learning materials;
- structuring and organization of the prepared materials in order to offer and deliver instruction through online courses;
- tracking the students' activities and interacting with them online;
- adapting the courses (both the included materials and the applied instructional design) constantly, in order to improve the students' performance and their learning efficiency, as well as to meet the educational institution's business goals.

The first three of the above group of activities are nowadays largely supported by Learning Content Management Systems (LCMSs) – a widely adopted technology that

E. Duval, R. Klamma, and M. Wolpers (Eds.): EC-TEL 2007, LNCS 4753, pp. 112–126, 2007.

enables setting up online courses and managing the students and their activities. The learning content provided by a LCMS is typically organized as a collection of learning objects. LCMSs support the use of standards for describing the learning objects, packaging them into larger content and learning units (such as lessons and courses), and applying various instructional design strategies and techniques. It is up to a teacher and/or instructional designer to prepare and upload their learning objects and structure them into a coherent online course. LCMSs support all of these activities in a rather straightforward way.

However, support for adaptation of e-learning materials is much trickier and less straightforward, hence widely used LCMSs (such as Moodle[1] and Blackboard & WebCT[2]) enable only simple content editing features for this purpose. The main problem regarding adaptation of e-learning content stems from the teachers need for an appropriate and reliable feedback about the students' usage of the learning materials. Unlike traditional learning situations where a teacher has consequential awareness of what students are working on and how satisfied they are with the content, most LCMSs provide only simple statistics about the technology the students have used, and only high level view on their interactions (e.g. page views) with the learning content.

Our goal is to augment the e-learning process with more semantic awareness information. For example, why good students who took a quiz performed poorly? Did some students maybe take a wrong sequence of steps while studying the materials online? If so, can we identify automatically some patterns in their erroneous learning behavior and use them to improve the instructional design? Are there reliable mechanisms for discovering automatically the topics that the students have difficulties with?

We have developed a number of heuristics that enable intelligent analysis of LCMS log data and automatic creation of useful feedback for online teachers. We implemented these heuristics within LOCO-Analyst, our tool that helps teachers figure out what is really going on in online classrooms and how to improve the content and/or instructional design of their courses accordingly.

2   What Is LOCO-Analyst?

LOCO-Analyst is an educational tool aimed at providing teachers with feedback on the relevant aspects of the learning process taking place in a web-based learning environment, and thus helps them improve the content and the structure of their web-based courses. It provides teachers with feedback regarding:

- all kinds of activities their students performed and/or took part in during the learning process,
- the usage and the comprehensibility of the learning content they had prepared and deployed in the LCMS,
- contextualized social interactions among students (i.e., social networking) in the virtual learning environment.

The generation of feedback in LOCO-Analyst is based on analysis of the user tracking data. These analyses are based on the notion of Learning Object Context

---

[1] http://moodle.org
[2] http://www.blackboard.com

which is about a student (or a group of students) interacting with a learning content by performing certain activity (e.g. reading, quizzing, chatting) with a particular purpose in mind. The purpose of learning object context is to facilitate abstraction of relevant concepts from user-tracking data of various e-learning systems and tools.

LOCO-Analyst is a Semantic Web application. It is built on top of the LOCO (Learning Object Context Ontologies) ontological framework [2], which we developed to enable formal representation of the learning object context data (see Section 5.1). Furthermore, it exploits semantic annotation (see Section 5.2) to interrelate diverse learning artifacts such as lessons, tests, messages exchanged during online interactions. Finally, it employs reasoning to derive meaningful information from the learning object context data. Contrary to the majority of approaches based on the Semantic Web which are technology driven, when developing LOCO-Analyst we have used Semantic Web technologies as a toolset, but have put focus on the actual people involved in the learning process (learners and teachers) and the advantages they get from the technology.

Note that LOCO-Analyst is implemented as an extension of Reload Content Packaging Editor[3], an open-source tool for creating courses compliant with the IMS Content Packaging[4] (IMS CP) specification. By extending this tool with the functionalities of LOCO-Analyst, we have ensured that teachers effectively use the same tool for creating e-learning courses, receiving and viewing automatically generated feedback about their use, and modifying the courses accordingly.

In the following section we briefly present different kinds of feedback that LOCO-Analyst can generate and explain how we have identified these as being relevant for online educators.

3 Feedback

In order to determine how learning context data can address the unsatisfied requirements of teachers of Web-based courses, we conducted a survey from Mid July to Mid August, 2006. Specifically, the goal of the survey was to elicit teachers' opinions on what would help them improve the learning experience of their students. The participants in this survey were teachers and instructional designers of Web-based courses working at Simon Fraser University, the University of Saskatchewan, and the University of British Columbia. We also contacted members of the International Forum of Educational Technology & Society[5] mailing list which is well-known among on-line educators around the world. We received responses from 15 experts in Web-based education. Among other important findings, a particularly interesting one was that all survey participants reported a lack of feedback about the learning process, which if available would be highly beneficial for them. Accordingly, our next step was to further analyze the collected responses in order to identify the kinds of feedback our teachers would appreciate. We distilled the following kinds of feedback as the most relevant:

---

[3] http://www.reload.ac.uk/editor.html
[4] http://www.imsglobal.org/content/packaging/
[5] http://ifets.ieee.org

- Recognition of problems at coarse grain level (e.g. learning modules);
- Recognition of differences between successful and unsuccessful learning trajectories;
- Detection of content (i.e. lessons) that was hard for students to comprehend;
- Identification of students' difficulties at a topic level;
- Identification of frequently discussed topics;
- Identification of the students' level of engagement in online communication and collaboration activities.

The correctness of these findings were confirmed by making a comparison with the findings of two recent empirical studies that investigated the instructors' needs when teaching at distance using course management systems [7], [13]. In addition, our findings are in accordance with the study conducted in the scope of Kaleidoscope European Network of Excellence, with the aim of defining design patterns for recording and analyzing usage in online learning environments[6].

The aforementioned types of feedback are implemented in LOCO-Analyst. Therefore, LOCO-Analyst provides feedback on diverse levels of content granularity (starting from the level of a single lesson to the entire learning module), as well as feedback about different types of learning content (e.g., lessons and tests). In that way, a teacher is provided with more relevant information that can help him better distinguish what is wrong (if something is wrong) in his course. Furthermore, LOCO-Analyst provides teachers with feedback about each individual student – the student's interactions with the learning content as well as interactions with other students.

LOCO-Analyst is tested with the user tracking data of the iHelp Courses[7], an open-source standards-compliant LCMS [1]. This LCMS captures fine-grained interactions between learners and content (e.g., time and duration of visit to a piece of content, links clicked on, and videos watched) and between learners (e.g., the content and time of messages sent in chat rooms along with the participant list, and the times learners read one another's discussion messages). LOCO-Analyst transforms this user tracking data into ontological representation compliant with the ontologies of the LOCO framework (see Section 5.1).

LOCO-Analyst is not coupled to any specific LCMS. Despite differences in the format of the tracking data provided by various LCMSs, there are commonalties in the content and the structure (e.g., history of pages visited, marks students received on quizzes, and messages posted in online discussions). These commonalties can be captured in the form of learning object context data and formally represented in accordance with the ontologies of the LOCO framework. Since LOCO-Analyst works with ontological representation of learning object context data, it is fully decoupled from any specific e-learning system/tool and can be considered as a generic feedback generation tool applicable to diverse distance learning environments. The only thing that needs to be adjusted is the mapping between the tracking data format and the LOCO-Cite ontology (see Section 5.1 for more details about the ontologies of the LOCO framework).

---

[6] http://lp.noe-kaleidoscope.org/
[7] http://ihelp.usask.ca/

4 LOCO-Analyst – A Usage Scenario

To illustrate some of the functionalities that LOCO-Analyst provides, in this section, we present a usage scenario of inspecting feedback regarding the students' performance on a quiz. The usage scenario is based on the "CMPT100: Introduction to Computer Science for Non-Majors" course deployed on the iHelp Courses LCMS at the University of Saskatchewan, Canada.

Fig. 1 presents feedback for the quiz of the "Programming Process" learning module. To be more precise, the feedback is given in the right half of the screen (after the user selects 'Quiz' item from the tree), whereas the left half (Fig. 1M) hosts the manifest tree of the IMS CP specification and some general content packaging data. In other words, the left part of the screen is 'inherited' from Reload Editor, whereas the right part is intrinsic to LOCO-Analyst. One can notice that the feedback panel is divided into three sub-panels, each providing a specific type of feedback.

The top panel (Fig. 1A) shows some basic statistical data regarding the time students spent doing the quiz. In particular, the average time spent and the standard deviation are given. Since the quiz consists of no more than 10-15 multiple choice questions, it is not surprising that students have spent on average 5 minutes doing the quiz.

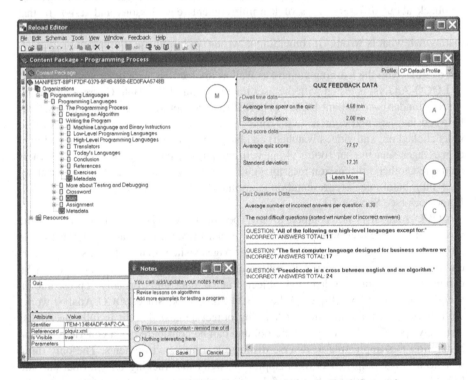

Fig. 1. A screenshot of LOCO-Analyst, presenting feedback for a quiz

The middle panel (Fig. 1B) presents some statistical data regarding the students' performance on the quiz: the average score on the quiz and standard deviation from the average value. In addition, the teacher is enabled to learn more about the students' scores. In particular, a click on the 'Learn More' button brings up a new dialog (Fig. 2) which provides the teacher with more information about the students' performance.

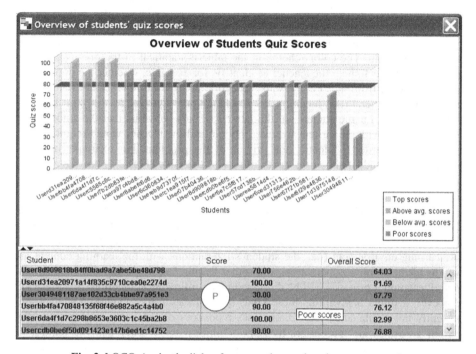

Fig. 2. LOCO-Analyst's dialog for presenting students' scores on a quiz

The 3D bar graph, in the upper half of the dialog, presents the students' quiz scores (students ids[8] are on the X axis, whereas the Y axis measures the quiz score). As Fig. 2 indicates, the students are classified according to their quiz score into the following 4 categories:

- The *Top-scores* category gathers the students whose quiz score exceeds the average score by more than one standard deviation; in the given example (Fig. 2), the students belonging to this category have the quiz score above 94.88 points; this category is represented with the blue color;
- The *Above avg. score* category comprises students with quiz scores above the average, but not exceeding the standard deviation; the violet color is used for representing this category;
- The *Below avg. score* category includes students with quiz score lower than the average value, but not less than one standard deviation; this category is represented with the yellow color, since yellow is typically used for warnings;
- The Poor scores category groups the students with the lowest quiz results, that is, with results that are below the average value for more than one deviation; in the

---

[8] Please note that for the sake of privacy issues, unique identifiers are used instead of the students' real names.

given example, those are the students with less than 60.26 points and they are colored in red – the color often used to indicate problems.

In the bottom half of the dialog (Fig. 2P), there is a table that provides a comparative overview of the students' results on the given quiz and their average scores on all other previously taken quizzes (i.e. quizzes from other learning modules). Note that rows of the table are colored differently. These colors indicate the category each student belongs to. The color scheme in the table is identical to the one used in the graph. The idea is to help the teacher to identify, for example, whether the poor result of some student from the 'Poor results' category stems from him/her not being very industrious in general (i.e., having weak results on other quizzes as well), or that low score is atypical for the student. In the latter case, it is obvious that the student has some problems with the current learning module and the teacher would require more information in order to identify the origins of the problem. For example, one can notice that the student shown in the third row of the table (Fig. 2P), has the average score on other quizzes more than two times greater than the score on the current quiz, thus it is an obvious signal for conducting further analysis.

By making a double click on the row of the table holding data about the student that the teacher is interested in, the teacher brings up a new dialog aimed at presenting diverse information about all kinds of interactions between the selected student and the learning environment (i.e., the student's interactions with the learning content as well as his/her (online) interactions with other learning participants). This dialog and the information it provides will be discussed in the following subsection (Section 4.1). However, it might happen that these kinds of information for the chosen student are presently not available in LOCO-Analyst's repository of feedback. In that case, the system generates an appropriate message to inform the teacher that the requested information is missing and gives him an opportunity to initiate the process of analysis that will eventually result in the requested info. Due to the nature of the analyses that LOCO-Analyst performs when generating feedback, it cannot instantly respond to the teacher's request. However, the teacher can proceed with inspection of the available feedback data, and the system will notify him as soon as the requested feedback becomes available.

The last panel on Fig. 1 (mark C) presents information about the students' performance on the questions level. In particular, the teacher is provided with the average number of incorrect answers per question, as well as a list of questions that were the most difficult for students (i.e. those that received the highest number of incorrect answers). The list is sorted in ascending order of the questions difficulty (i.e. the number of incorrect answers). For each 'difficult' question, the question text and the number of students who answered it incorrectly are given. In addition, each question is related to the lesson(s) discussing the domain topic(s) covered by the question. The linkage between quiz questions and lessons was made possible thanks to the semantic annotation of the learning content (see Section 5.2). Hence, when the teacher selects a question from the list, the lesson(s) discussing concept(s) included in the question are highlighted in the manifest tree (Fig. 1M). Furthermore, by making a double click on any 'difficult' question (Fig. 1C), the teacher is presented with a new dialog listing students' messages (exchanged via online communication tools) related to that question, i.e., messages mentioning the domain topics covered by the question. This functionality is enabled by semantic annotation of students' messages, as explained in Section 5.2. The teacher can make a double-click on any of these messages to see its content. The content of each message is semantically annotated, that is, the terms that represent domain concepts are highlighted using different colors (i.e., one color for each concept). In this way teacher can easily spot which topic(s) the message discusses and in which manner/tone (i.e., is it a student's complaint for not being able to understand the respective topic, an inquiry or something else). In the given example (Fig. 1C), it is obvious that the students are struggling with the concept of pseudocode. That is, the number of students who gave an incorrect answer to this question is three times higher than the average number of incorrect answers per question. Accordingly, the teacher has to find a better way to explain this concept to his students.

Using similarly organized panels (Fig. 1 A, B, C), LOCO-Analyst provides teachers with feedback on the level of a single lesson, a composite lesson (i.e., a lesson composed of two or more content items) and a learning module as a whole.

Note that, while reviewing a feedback, a teacher can write down some notes such as an interesting observation and a reminder that something needs to be re-checked, or changed. In addition, the teacher can set the importance level of the feedback, i.e., mark it as either important or irrelevant. To do this, he uses the Notes dialog (Fig. 1D) which becomes available by clicking on the Notes toolbar button (the last one in the row).

4.1 Learning More About the Selected Student

The dialog aimed at presenting feedback about a selected student (Fig. 3) can be accessed in different ways, but in the context of this usage scenario (i.e. inspecting students' performance on a quiz) it appears after a teacher selects a student that he is interested in from the table in Fig. 2P. The dialog is implemented through three tab panels, each one presenting a specific kind of information that LOCO-Analyst possesses about the student (i.e., the information it managed to generate from the available data on the student's interaction with the LCMS). In particular, the dialog comprises three overlapping panels, named 'Forums', 'Chats', and 'Learning'. Whereas the first two panels are aimed at informing teachers about the student's online interactions (in discussion forums and chat rooms, respectively) with other participants in the learning process, the third panel is intended for presenting information regarding the student's interaction with the learning content. Due to the space limit for this paper, here we present only the 'Learning' panel.

Fig. 3 shows the student's interaction with the learning content of the 'JavaScript Concepts' learning module. The available information is presented in a chart and a table. The chart presents the student's interactions with the learning content in chronological order. Accordingly, the horizontal axis is the time axis, whereas the Y axis measures the amount of time that the student spent on the lessons (dwell time) of the selected learning module (i.e. 'JavaScript Concepts' in this example). Different lessons are represented with graphical symbols of different shapes and/or colors – the legend is given to enable identification of lessons. However, this graph is not intended for gaining insight into dwell time for any specific lesson, but to gain an overall impression of the student's learning behavior – to recognize some general pattern and/or trend in his/her behavior, as well as some deviations from that pattern/trend. In the given example (Fig. 3), it is easy to detect that the student was 'active' from the end of February till the beginning of March. It is also obvious that (s)he typically did not spend much time on the module's content (approximately 2.5 minutes and less). Furthermore, one can notice some deviations from the general pattern – for example, the student spent considerably more time on the content item named 'Tutorial' (represented with a blue square), as well as on 'Assignment' (yellow triangle). The teacher can have a closer view on this data by changing the time scale of the X axis. This can be done via a dialog that pops up after clicking on the 'Time Focus' button (Fig. 3T). In addition, via the options 'Horizontal Mouse Zooming' and 'Vertical Mouse Zooming' (Fig. 3Z), the teacher can switch on and off the horizontal and vertical lines that can be moved (using the mouse) along both axis. These lines are intended to facilitate precise identification of the position of each symbol (i.e. content item) on the chart. The table given in the bottom of the dialog provides some basic statistical data regarding the student's interaction with the content of the selected module. The teacher can get access to this kind of data for any module of the course – it suffices to select the desired module from the 'For Module' combo box (Fig. 3M).

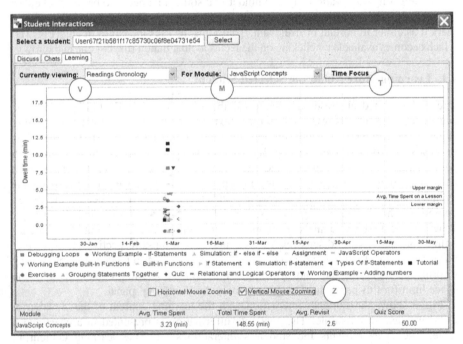

Fig. 3. LOCO-Analyst's dialog presenting feedback regarding a student's interactions with the learning content

Note that Fig. 3 shows just one view (i.e. version) on the 'Learning' panel, dubbed 'Readings Chronology'. The other view, named 'Statistical Overview' provides information about the average time and the total time that a student spent on each content item of the learning module, as well as the number of revisits for each item. This information is given in the form of a double 3D bar graph with a common X axis (holding content items of the module). Switching from one view to the other can be accomplished via the 'Currently viewing' combo box (Fig. 3V).

5 LOCO-Analyst's Semantic Web Groundings

In this section, we explain the ontological foundation of LOCO-Analyst and present how we use semantic annotation to enable integration of diverse learning artifacts. An example of a query over the (ontological) repository of learning object context data is given as well.

5.1 LOCO Framework

LOCO-Analyst is developed on top of the LOCO ontological framework. The framework was initially aimed at facilitating reusability of learning objects and learning designs [5], and later extended to also provide support for personalized learning [2]. The LOCO-Cite ontology is the central component of the framework and serves as an integration point of other types of learning related ontologies such as user model ontology, an ontology of learning design, and a content structure ontology [2].

   The focal point of the LOCO-Cite ontology is the *LearningObjectContext* class (Fig. 4a) which is, in accordance with the given definition of learning object context (see Section 2), related to the activity (*Activity*) that a learner or a teacher (*um:User*[9]) undertook while interacting with a learning content (*ContentUnit*). An instance of *LearningObjectContext* is always related to exactly one *Activity* instance as well as one *ContentUnit* instance. However, it can be related to more than one *um:User* instances in case of a collaborative activity engaging more users (e.g., various forms of online discussions).

   The *Activity* class represents any kind of activity typically occurring in a virtual learning environment (e.g., LCMS). A few basic kinds of learning activities are recognized and modeled as subclasses of the *Activity* class – for example, students are either reading some learning content (*Reading*), or doing an assessment (*Quizzing*), or interacting with other participants in the learning process (*Discussing*). Each recognized kind of activity is further formally described through a number of classes and properties. Of course, the *Activity* class can further be extended if an e-learning system has some specific types of activities. In what follows, we describe in more details the part of the ontology related to the quizzing activity, since it is relevant for the usage scenario presented in the previous section.

   The class *Quizzing* and its related classes are introduced in the LOCO-Cite ontology to enable modeling the activity of students' knowledge assessment (Fig. 4b). Since the same assessment instrument (e.g. a quiz) can be used to verify students' knowledge in different courses, the quizzing activity is related (via the *courseRef* property) with the course in the context of which it took place. In order to keep track not only of a student's final score on a quiz, but also his/her answers to each quiz question, the quiz result is modeled as a separate concept (*QuizResult*). It keeps the value of the quiz's final score (via the *score* property). In addition, it is made 'aware' of the student's response to each single quiz question (*QuestionResult*). An instance of the *QuizResult* is connected (via the *questionResultRef* property) with as many

---

[9] The *um* prefix indicates that the *User* class comes from the User Model ontology.

instances of the *QuestionResult* class as there are questions on the respective quiz. An instance of *QuestionResult* holds a reference (*questionRef*) to the respective question (*quiz:QuestionItem*), as well as a reference (*selectedAnswer*) to the answer the student has chosen (*quiz:Answer*). Finally, the *isCorrect* property indicates whether the chosen answer is correct. The prefix *quiz* identifies *QuestionItem* and *Answer* as classes from a tiny ontology that we developed to formally represent an assessment instrument (i.e. a quiz).

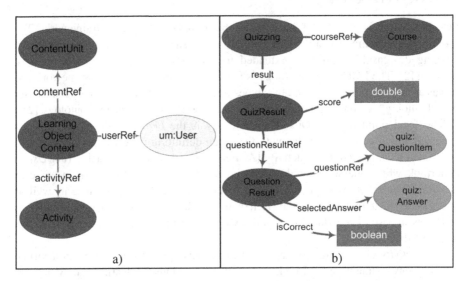

Fig. 4. The LOCO-Cite ontology: the basic concepts (a); the quizzing activity (b)

Besides the LOCO-Cite ontology, LOCO-Analyst also makes use of the user model ontology and domain ontologies of the LOCO framework.

Having decided to use tools of the Knowledge & Information Management (KIM) platform [9] to annotate semantically (see the next subsection) the learning content, we implicitly made decision regarding the format of domain ontologies (i.e. ontologies that formally describe the subject matter of learning content). In particular, we modeled domain concepts and their relations by instantiating appropriate classes and properties of the PROTON upper-level ontology[10], as KIM requires.

To describe formally a participant in the learning process, we use the class *User* which originates from the user model ontology that we had developed in our previous work, in the scope of the TANGRAM project[11]. The ontology is described in detail in [3]. However, to make the ontology fully applicable for the purposes of LOCO-Analyst, we needed to slightly extend it with a few classes and properties that enable tracking of some additional teachers' data, such as teachers' feedback requests.

---

[10] http://proton.semanticweb.org/
[11] http://iis.fon.bg.ac.yu/TANGRAM/

All ontologies can be inspected from the following URL: http://iis.fon.bg.ac.yu/LOCO-Analyst/loco.html.

5.2 Semantic Annotation in LOCO-Analyst

Semantic annotation of learning artifacts is about annotating (i.e. describing) their content with semantic information from domain ontologies [11]. Semantic annotation of learning content proved as highly beneficiary for feedback provision since it enabled establishing semantic relations among all learning artifacts – lessons, quizzes, forum postings and chat messages. For example, as we explained in Section 4, semantic annotation of quiz questions and lessons enabled linkage of semantically related questions and lessons (i.e., questions and lessons discussing the same or similar domain concepts). Furthermore, semantic annotation of students' messages exchanged via online communication tools (chat rooms and discussion forums) made it possible to identify whether and how often the students have been discussing different domain topics.

In LOCO-Analyst, semantic annotation is performed using the annotation capabilities of the KIM platform [9]. In order to apply KIM's annotation facilities on content from a specific subject domain, KIM has to be extended with knowledge about that domain[12].

During the annotation process each learning artifact (e.g., lesson, quiz, forum posting or chat message) is assigned zero or more semantic annotations (i.e., concepts from the domain ontology). In terms of ontological representation, each instance of the *ContentUnit* class is assigned (via the *hasSemAnnotation* property) zero or more instances of the *SemAnnotation* class (Fig. 5). The later class has two properties: the *dc:subject*[13] property and the *rdfs:label* property. The value of the former property is a domain concept, i.e., the URI of a concept from the domain ontology. The latter property is a human readable label of the domain topic given in the *dc:subject* property.

5.3 Searching the Semantic Repository

LOCO-Analyst integrates *Repository of LOCs* which holds learning object context (LOC) data represented as instances of the LOCO-Cite ontology. The repository relies on Sesame[14], an open source Java framework for storing and querying ontological data.

For querying the repository we use SeRQL (Sesame RDF Query Language) query language. Fig. 6 shows a SeRQL query which we use to retrieve LOC data required for generating feedback regarding students' performance on a specific quiz (illustrated in the previous section). Specifically, this query is relevant for informing teachers about the students' performance on the question level (see Fig. 1C).

---

[12] Detailed instructions how to extend the KIM platform to cover a new domain can be found in KIM's online documentation: http://www.ontotext.com/kim/doc/sys-doc/index.html

[13] *dc* stands for the Dublin Core metadata schema (http://purl.org/metadata/dublin-core)

[14] http://www.openrdf.org/

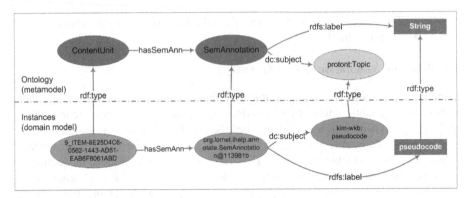

Fig. 5. A content unit annotated with the domain concept of pseudocode which is integrated into the KIM's knowledge base[15]

```
SELECT question, questionTxt, correct
FROM {lc} rdf:type {lococite:LearningContext},
    {lc} lococite:contentRef {quiz},
    {lc} lococite:activityRef {q},
    {q} lococite:result {quizRes},
    {quizRes} lococite:questionResultRef {questionRes},
    {questionRes} lococite:questionRef {question},
    {question} quiz:questionItem {questionItem},
    {questionItem} quiz:content {questionTxt},
    {questionRes} lococite:isCorrect {correct}
WHERE localname(quiz) LIKE quizID
USING NAMESPACE lococite = <http://www.lornet.org/loco-cite.owl#>,
    quiz = <http://www.lornet.org/loco/quiz.owl>
```

Fig. 6. SeRQL query for retrieving data about students' performance on a specific quiz (identified with quizID), on the level of individual questions

6 Related Work

Classroom Sentinel is a Web service aimed at improving day-to-day instructional decision-making by providing teachers with timely and fine grained patterns of students' behavior in classrooms [10]. In particular, it mines electronic sources of students' data to detect critical teaching/learning patterns. As a pattern is detected, the teacher is informed about it in the form of an alert which consists of the observed pattern, a set of possible explanations, and a set of possible reactions. In that way, the teacher is enabled to take a timely corrective action. Unlike this system that targets learning in traditional classrooms, our approach focuses on Web-based learning environments where student-teacher and student-student interactions are more complex to correctly detect, follow and analyze.

---

[15] *kim-wkb* stands for the namespace of the KIM's 'working knowledge base', i.e. repository of ontological instances (http://www.ontotext.com/kim/2005/04/wkb)

Kosba and his associates have developed the *Teacher ADVisor* (TADV) framework which uses LCMS tracking data to elicit student, group, and class models, and using these models help teachers gain a better understanding of their distance students [6]. It uses a set of predefined conditions to recognize situations that require teachers' intervention, and when such a condition is met, TADV generates an advice for the teacher, as well as a recommendation for what is to be sent to students. Whereas TADV is focused on the teachers' day-to-day activities, LOCO-Analyst aims at helping them rethink the quality of the employed learning content and learning design.

Zinn & Scheuer are developing *Teacher Tool*, a tool which analyzes and visualizes usage-tracking data in order to help teachers learn more about their students in distance learning environments. The development of the tool was preceded by a user study aimed at identifying the information that, on one hand, is valuable for teachers, and on the other hand, can be generated from user-tracking data. However, unlike Teacher Tool which is bounded to ActiveMath[16] (a Web-based, user-adaptive learning environment for mathematics) and iClass[17] (an intelligent cognitive-based open learning system), our solution, thanks to its ontological foundation, is tool-independent.

Our work is also related to the research done in the area of Web usage mining which is about nontrivial extraction of potentially useful patterns and trends from large web access logs. For example, Zaine & Luo (2001) applied advanced data mining techniques on access logs of an LMCS in order to extract patterns useful for evaluating and interpreting on-line course activities [12]. Teachers can tailor the data mining process to their needs by expressing them as constraints on the mining process (e.g., they can select desired student or study group, the desired time period, etc). The discovered patterns are presented in the form of charts and tables. *TADA-Ed* (Tool for Advanced Data Analysis in Education) is another data mining platform which integrates various visualization and data mining facilities to help teachers discover pedagogically relevant patterns in students' online exercises [8]. Unlike these and similar systems that focus on a single learning activity (reading and exercises, respectively, in the aforementioned systems), LOCO-Analyst analyzes diverse kinds of learning activities typically occurring in today's LCMSs. In addition, it is easy to use (as our user study has demonstrated [4]), which is not the case with data mining based tools.

7 Conclusion

The paper presents LOCO-Analyst, the tool aimed at raising teachers' awareness in online learning settings and thus helping them improve the content and/or instructional design of their courses. We have already conducted an evaluation study of LOCO-Analyst and the results were generally very positive [4]. Besides confirming the usefulness of our work, this study also helped us identify directions for further work. In particular, the majority of freeform comments suggested better visualizations of feedback data. We have already started addressing this issue – for example, the charts presented on Fig. 2 and Fig. 3, are a part of our efforts to improve the visualization of feedback. In addition, we are working on detection of learning patterns from usage data,

---

[16] http://www.activemath.org
[17] http://www.iclass.info

which we intend to offer to teachers as higher level learning designs that might help them to define/improve the course structure. We also intend to formalize the extracted learning patterns (e.g., in the form of the IMS Learning Design[18] specification) in order to make them reusable and hence enable exchange of best pedagogical practices. Finally, we are planning another evaluation study to verify the latest developments.

References

1. Brooks, C., Kettel, L., Hansen, C.: Building a Learning Object Content Management System. In: Proc. of the 10th World Conf. on E-Learning in Corporate, Government, Healthcare, and Higher Education (E-Learn2005), Vancouver, Canada, pp. 2836–2843 (2005)
2. Jovanović, J., Knight, C., Gašević, D., Richards, G.: Learning Object Context on the Se mantic Web. In: Proc. of the 6th IEEE Int'l Conference on Advanced Learning Technologies (ICALT 2006), Kerkrade, The Netherlands, pp. 669–673 (2006)
3. Jovanović, J., Gašević, D., Devedžić, V.: Dynamic Assembly of Personalized Learning Content on the Semantic Web. In: Proc. of the 3th European Semantic Web Conference, Budva, Montenegro, pp. 545–559 (2006)
4. Jovanović, et al.: LOCO-Analyst: Semantic Web Technologies in Learning Content Usage Analysis. Int'l Journal of Continuing Engineering Education and Life-Long Learning (forthcoming, 2007)
5. Knight, C., Gašević, D., Richards, G.: Ontologies to integrate learning design and learning content. Journal of Interactive Media in Education (2005/7)
6. Kosba, E., Dimitrova, V., Boyle, R.: Using Student and Group Models to Support Teachers in Web-Based Distance Education. In: Proc. of the 10th International Conference on User Modeling, Edinburgh, UK, pp. 124–133 (2005)
7. Mazza, R., Dimitrova, V.: Informing the Design of a Course Data Visualisator: an Empirical Study. In: the Proc. of the 5th International Conference on New Educational Environments (ICNEE 2003) Lucerne, May 2003, pp. 215–220 (2003)
8. Merceron, A., Yacef, K.: TADA-Ed for Educational Data Mining. Interactive Multimedia Electronic Journal of Computer-Enhanced Learning 7(1) (2005), [Online] Available http://imej.wfu.edu/articles/2005/1/03/index.asp
9. Popov, B., Kiryakov, A., Kirilov, A., Manov, D., Ognyanoff, D., Goranov, M.: KIM – Semantic Annotation Platform. In: Fensel, D., Sycara, K.P., Mylopoulos, J. (eds.) ISWC 2003. LNCS, vol. 2870, pp. 834–849. Springer, Heidelberg (2003)
10. Singley, M.K., Lam, R.B.: The Classroom Sentinel: Supporting Data-Driven Decision-Making in the Classroom. In: Proc. of the 13th World Wide Web Conference, Chiba, Japan, pp. 315–322 (2005)
11. Uren, V., Cimiano, P., Iria, J., Handschuh, S., Vargas-Vera, M., Motta, E., Ciravegna, F.: Semantic annotation for knowledge management: Requirements and a survey of the state of the art. Journal of Web Semantics 4(1), 14–28 (2006)
12. Zaiane, O.R., Luo, J.: Towards Evaluating Learners' Behaviour in a Web-Based Distance Learning Environment. In: Proc. of the IEEE Int'l Conference on Advanced Learning Technologies, Madison, USA, pp. 357–360. IEEE, Los Alamitos (2001)
13. Zinn, C., Scheuer, O.: Getting to Know your Student in Distance-Learning Contexts, Innovative Approaches for Learning and Knowledge Sharing. In: Proc. of the 1st European Conference on Technology Enhanced Learning, pp. 437–451 (2006)

---

[18] http://www.imsglobal.org/learningdesign/index.html

Supporting Incremental Formalization in Collaborative Learning Environments

Nikos Karacapilidis[1,2] and Manolis Tzagarakis[2]

[1] IMIS Lab, MEAD, University of Patras, 26500 Rio Patras, Greece
[2] Research Academic Computer Technology Institute, 26500 Rio Patras, Greece

Abstract. Arguing that a varying level of formality needs to be offered in systems supporting collaborative learning, this paper proposes an incremental formalization approach that has been adopted in the development of CoPe_it!, a web-based tool that complies with collaborative principles and practices to provide members of communities with the appropriate means to manage individual and collective knowledge, and collaborate towards the solution of diverse issues. According to the proposed approach, incremental formalization can be achieved through the consideration of alternative projections of a collaborative workspace, as well as through mechanisms supporting the switching from one projection to another. Related features and functionalities are presented through an illustrative example.

Keywords: Collaborative Knowledge Building and Sharing, Incremental Formalization, Services for Technology Enhanced Learning, Problem Solving Support, Learning Communities and Distributed Teams.

1 Introduction

Argumentative collaboration, conducted by a group of people working towards solving a problem, can admittedly facilitate and augment learning in many ways, such as in explicating and sharing individual representations of the problem, maintaining focus on the overall process, maintaining consistency, increasing plausibility and accuracy, as well as in enhancing the group's collective knowledge [1-3]. Designing software systems that can adequately address users' needs to express, share, interpret and reason about knowledge during an argumentative collaboration session has been a major research and development activity for more than twenty years. Technologies supporting argumentative collaboration usually provide the means for discussion structuring and visualization, sharing of documents, and user administration. They support argumentative collaboration at various levels and have been tested through diverse user groups and contexts. Furthermore, they aim at exploring argumentation as a means to establish a common ground between diverse stakeholders, to understand positions on issues, to surface assumptions and criteria, and to collectively construct consensus [4].

However, when engaged in the use of these technologies through a software system supporting argumentative collaboration, users have to follow a specific formalism. More specifically, their interaction is regulated by procedures that

E. Duval, R. Klamma, and M. Wolpers (Eds.): EC-TEL 2007, LNCS 4753, pp. 127–142, 2007.

prescribe and - at the same time - constrain their work. This may refer to both the system-supported actions a user may perform (e.g. types of discourse or collaboration acts), and the system-supported types of argumentative collaboration objects (e.g. one has to strictly characterize a collaboration object as an idea or a position). In many cases, users have also to fine-tune, align, amend or even fully change their usual way of collaborating in order to be able to exploit the system's features and functionalities. Such formalisms are necessary towards making the system interpret and reason about human actions (and the associated resources), thus offering advanced computational services. However, there is much evidence that sophisticated approaches and techniques often resulted in failures (see, for instance, [5, 6]). This is often due to the extra time and effort that users need to spend in order to get acquainted with the system, the associated disruption of the users' usual workflow [7], as well as to the "error prone and difficult to correct when done wrong" character and the prematurely imposing structure of formal approaches [8].

As a consequence, we argue that a varying level of formality should be considered. This variation may either be imposed by the nature of the task at hand (e.g. decision making, joint deliberation, persuasion, inquiry, negotiation, conflict resolution), the particular context of the collaboration (e.g. legal reasoning, medical decision making, public policy making), or the group of people who collaborate each time (i.e. how comfortable people feel with the use of a certain technology or formalism). The above advocate an incremental formalization approach, which has been adopted in the development of CoPe_it![1], a web-based tool that is able to support argumentative collaboration at various levels of formality. CoPe_it! complies with collaborative learning principles and practices, and provides members of communities engaged in argumentative discussions and decision making processes with the appropriate means to collaborate towards the solution of diverse issues. According to the proposed approach, incremental formalization can be achieved through the consideration of alternative projections (i.e. particular representations) of a collaborative workspace, as well as through mechanisms supporting the switching from one projection to another.

This paper focuses on the presentation of the above approach. More specifically, Section 2 comments on a series of background issues related to reasoning and visualization, as well as on related work. Section 3 presents our overall approach, illustrates the features and functionalities of CoPe_it! through a representative example and sketches the procedure of switching among alternative projections of a particular workspace. Finally, Section 4 discusses advantages and limitations of the proposed approach and outlines future work directions.

2 Background Issues

The representation and facilitation of argumentative collaboration being held in diverse settings has been a subject of research interest for quite a long time. Many software systems have been developed so far, based on alternative models of argumentation structuring, aiming to capture the key issues and ideas during meetings, and create a shared understanding by placing all messages, documents and reference material for a project on a "whiteboard" [9]. More recent approaches pay

---

[1] http://copeit.cti.gr

particular attention to the visualization of argumentation [10]. Generally speaking, existing approaches provide a cognitive argumentation environment that stimulates reflection and discussion among participants (a comprehensive consideration of such approaches can be found in [11]). However, they receive criticism related to their adequacy to clearly display each collaboration instance to all parties involved (usability and ease-of-use issues), as well as to the formal structure used for the representation of collaboration. In most cases, they merely provide threaded discussion forums, where messages are linked passively. This usually leads to an unsorted collection of vaguely associated positions, which is extremely difficult to be exploited in future collaboration settings. As argued in [12], "packages in the current generation of argument visualization software are fairly basic, and still have numerous usability problems". Also important, they do not integrate, in most cases, any reasoning mechanisms to (semi)automate the underlying decision making processes required in a collaboration setting². Thus, there is a lack of alternative formalization, consensus seeking and decision-making support abilities.

Various surveys of Computer-Supported Collaborative Learning (CSCL) environments also reveal much criticism on the solutions offered. For instance, it has been admitted that these solutions often require that users carry out activities that do not naturally belong to their work, or they support activities which are infrequent in normal work and do not help users to carry out their most frequent activities [15]; thus, such activities are often considered artificial or insignificant by users. The exploration of the possibilities to enrich CSCL environments with tools to support collaborative interaction, as reported in [16], led to the development of a collaboration management cycle from a systems perspective; the related reviewing of CSCL systems that instantiate the three stages of this cycle, namely mirroring, monitoring and advising, identified the fact that these systems address only a single stage (even partially, in most cases). In other words, the evolution of the collaboration management cycle is not appropriately supported. Other works reveal the necessity of CSCL systems to provide alternative representational features in order to demonstrate a significant effect on the learners' collaborative knowledge building process and on learning outcomes [17].

Taking the above into account, we claim that an integrated consideration of various *visualization* and *reasoning* issues is needed in an argumentation-based collaborative learning context. Such an integrated consideration should be in line with *incremental formalization* principles. More specifically, it should efficiently and effectively address problems related to formality. As stressed in [6], "users want systems be more of an active aid to their work - to do more for them; yet they already resist the low level of formalization required for passive hypertext". According to the proposed incremental formalization approach, problems related to formality have to be solved by approaches that (i) do not necessarily require formalization to be done at the time of input of information, and (ii) support (not enable or automate) formalization by the appropriate software.

---

² Recently developed systems such as *Araucaria* [13] and *ArguMed* [14] address the issues of argument diagramming and formalization of argumentation. However, they do not comply with incremental formalization principles, while they were built to serve a particular context.

At the same time, the abovementioned integrated consideration should be also in line with the *information triage process* [18], i.e. the process of sorting and organizing through numerous relevant materials and organizing them to meet the task at hand. During such a process, users must effortlessly scan, locate, browse, update and structure knowledge resources that may be incomplete, while the resulting structures may be subject to rapid and numerous changes.

3 An Incremental Formalization Approach

The research method adopted for the development of the proposed solution follows the Design Science Paradigm, which has been extensively used in information systems research [19]. Moreover, the proposed solution is the result of action research studies [20] concerning the improvement of practices, strategies and knowledge of diverse collaborative learning environments. Building on the above, our main contribution lies in the formulation of an incremental formalization approach, and the corresponding development of a web-based tool for supporting argumentative collaboration as well as the underlying creation, leveraging and utilization of the relevant knowledge. Generally speaking, our approach allows for distributed (synchronous or asynchronous) collaboration and aims at aiding the involved parties by providing them with a series of argumentation, knowledge management and decision making features. Moreover, it exploits and builds on issues and concepts discussed in the previous section.

3.1 Analysis of Requirements

A series of interviews with members of diverse communities (from the engineering, management and education domains) has been performed in order to identify the major issues they face during their argumentative collaboration practices. These issues actually constituted a set of challenges for our approach, in that the proposed collaboration model and infrastructure must provide the necessary means to appropriately address them. Major issues identified were:

- *Management of information overload:* This is primarily due to the extensive and uncontrolled exchange of comments, documents and, in general, any type of information/knowledge resource, that occurs in the settings under consideration. For instance, such a situation may appear during the exchange of ideas, positions and arguments; individuals usually have to spend much effort to keep track and conceptualize the current state of the collaboration. Such situations may ultimately harm a community's objectives.
- *Diversity of collaboration modes as far the protocols followed and the tools used are concerned:* Interviews indicated that the evolution of the collaboration proceeds incrementally; ideas, comments, or any other type of collaboration object (i.e. knowledge items) are exchanged and elaborated, and new knowledge emerges slowly. When a community's members collaboratively organize information, enforced formality may require specifying their knowledge before it is fully formed. Such emergence cannot be attained when the collaborative environment enforces a formal model (i.e.

predefined types of knowledge items and relationships) from the beginning. On the other hand, formalization is required in order to ensure the environment's capability to support and aid the collaboration efforts. In particular, the abilities to support decision making, estimation of present state or summary reports benefit greatly from formal representations of the information units and relationships.

- *Expression of tacit knowledge:* A community of people is actually an environment where tacit knowledge (i.e. knowledge that the members do not know they possess or knowledge that members cannot express with the means provided) predominantly exists and dynamically evolves. Such knowledge must be able to be efficiently and effectively represented in order to be further exploited in a collaborative learning environment.
- *Integration and sharing of diverse information and knowledge:* Many resources required during a collaborative session have either been used in previous sessions or reside outside the members' working environment (e.g. in e-mailing lists or web forums). Moreover, outcomes of past collaboration activities should be able to be reused as a resource in subsequent collaborative sessions.
- *Decision making support:* Many communities require support to reach a decision. This means that their environment (i.e. the tool used) needs to interpret the knowledge item types and their interrelationships in order to proactively suggest trends or even calculate the outcome of a collaborative session (e.g. as is the case in voting systems).

3.2 Conceptual Approach

To address the above issues, our approach builds on a conceptual framework where formality and the level of knowledge structuring during argumentative collaboration is not considered as a predefined and rigid property, but rather as an adaptable aspect that can be modified to meet the needs of the tasks at hand. By the term formality, we refer to the rules enforced by the system, with which all user actions must comply. Allowing formality to vary within the collaboration space, *incremental formalization*, i.e. a stepwise and controlled evolution from a mere collection of individual ideas and resources to the production of highly contextualized and interrelated knowledge artifacts, can be achieved. As shown in Figure 1 (bottom part), this evolution is associated with a set of functionalities (namely, collection and sharing of knowledge items, exploitation of legacy resources, interrelation and evolution of knowledge items, informal / semiformal argumentation, informal / semiformal aggregation of knowledge items, semantic annotation of knowledge items, formal exploitation of knowledge items patterns, and formal argumentation and reasoning), which are ordered (from left to right) in terms of formality level.

In our approach, *projections* constitute the "vehicle" that permits incremental formalization of argumentative collaboration (see Figure 1). A projection can be defined as a particular representation of the collaboration space, in which a consistent set of abstractions able to solve a particular organizational problem during argumentative collaboration is available. With the term abstraction, we refer to the particular knowledge items, relationships and actions that are supported through a particular projection, and with which a particular problem can be represented, elaborated and - ultimately - be solved. Our approach enables the switching from a projection to another, during which abstractions of a certain formality level are transformed to the appropriate abstractions of another formality level. This transformation is rule-based; such rules can be defined by users and/or the facilitator of the collaboration and reflect the evolution of a community's collaboration needs. According to our approach, it is up to the community to exploit one or more projections of a collaboration space (upon users' needs and expertise, as well as the overall collaboration context).

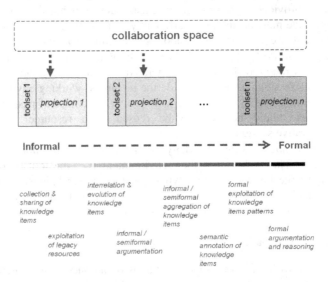

Fig. 1. The proposed incremental formalization approach[3]

Each projection of the collaboration space provides the necessary mechanisms to support a particular level of formality (e.g. `projection_1` may cover only needs concerning collection / sharing of knowledge items and exploitation of legacy resources, whereas `projection_n` may cover the full spectrum of the functionalities shown at the bottom part of Figure 1). The more informal a projection is, the more easiness-of-use is implied; at the same time, the actions that users may perform are intuitive and not time consuming (e.g. drag-and-drop a document to a shared collaboration space). Informality is associated with generic types of actions and resources, as well as implicit relationships between them. However, the overall context is human (and not system) interpretable. On the other hand, the more formal a projection is, easiness-of-use is reduced (users may have to go through training or reading of long manuals in order to comprehend and get familiar with sophisticated system features); actions permitted are less and less intuitive and more time consuming. Formality is associated with fixed types of actions, as well as explicit relationships between them. The overall context in this case is both human and system interpretable.

---

[3] Please visit http://tel.cti.gr/tzag/EC-TEL2007/ for a high-resolution version of all figures included in this paper.

As derives from the above, the aim of an informal projection of the collaboration space is to provide users the means to structure and organize knowledge items easily, and in a way that conveys semantics to them. Generally speaking, informal projections may support an unbound number of knowledge item types (e.g. comment, idea, note, resource). Moreover, users may create any relationship among these items (there are no fixed relationship types); hence, relationship types may express agreement, disagreement, support, request for refinement, contradiction etc. Informal projections may also provide abstraction mechanisms that allow the creation of new abstractions out of existing ones. Abstraction mechanisms include: (i) *annotation and metadata* (i.e. the ability to annotate instances of various knowledge items and add or modify metadata); (ii) *aggregation* (i.e. the ability to group a set of instances of knowledge items so as to be handled as a single conceptual entity; this may lead to cases where a set of knowledge items can be considered separately, but still in relation to the context of a particular collaboration); (iii) *generalization/specialization* (i.e. the ability to create semantically coarse or more detailed knowledge items in order to help users manage information pollution of the collaboration space); (iv) *patterns* (i.e. the ability to specify instances of interconnections between knowledge items of the same or a different type, and accordingly define "collaboration templates").

An informal projection also aims at supporting *information triage*. It is the informal nature of this projection that permits such an ordinary and unconditioned evolution of knowledge structures. While such a way of dealing with knowledge resources is conceptually close to practices that humans use in their everyday environment (e.g. their desk), it is inconvenient in situations where support for advanced decision making processes must be provided. Such capabilities require knowledge resources and structuring facilities with fixed semantics, which should be understandable and interpretable not only by the users but also by the tool. Hence, decision making processes can be better supported in environments that exhibit a high level of formality. The more formal projections of a collaboration space come to serve such needs.

3.3 Example

As mentioned in the introductory section, CoPe_it! is the tool enabling the proposed incremental formalization approach. It is a web-based tool that allows for both asynchronous and synchronous collaboration. The layout of the tool's main user interface is shown in Figures 2 and 3. Upon having the appropriate permissions, users may either create a new workspace for the needs of their community or collaborate with their peers in existing ones (there is also the option of maintaining private or public workspaces). The left hand side bar of the interface enables users to open a new browser, quickly search for related information (through Google and Wikipedia, or in the local repository), subscribe to RSS feeds, maintain a list of bookmarks, and be aware of other online members of their community.

Users may easily create and upload various types of knowledge items; these can be either existing multimedia resources (the content of which can be displayed upon request or can be directly embedded in the workspace) or dedicated item types such as *ideas*, *notes* and *comments*. Ideas stand for items that deserve further exploitation; they may correspond to an alternative solution to the issue under consideration and they usually trigger the evolution of the collaboration. Notes are generally considered as items expressing one's knowledge about the overall issue, an already asserted idea or note. Finally, comments are items that usually express less strong statements and are uploaded to express some explanatory text or point to some potentially useful information. Knowledge item types may change upon the evolution of the collaboration (e.g. a user that has asserted a particular comment may – at some point of the collaboration – elaborate it further and change its type to an idea).

All the above items can be interrelated by trouble-free user actions (as in the case of their creation and uploading, such actions are performed through the mouse). When interrelating items, users may select the color of the connecting arrow and provide (if they wish) a legend describing the interrelationship they conceive. These legends are intentionally arbitrary. An interesting feature of the tool is that it enables users to spatially arrange the uploaded items and cluster them in a meaningful way. Examples of such actions are given below; the spatial arrangement of items is also an easy task (users have just to click on an item and drag it to the desired position).

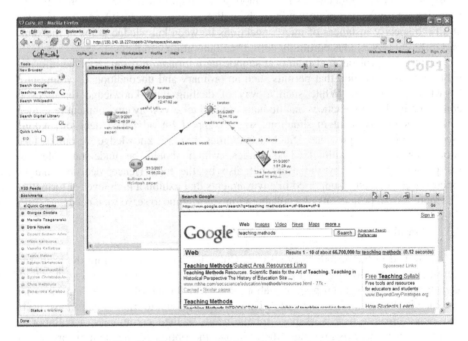

Fig. 2. A first instance of the collaborative workspace

To better present the features and functionalities of our approach, this subsection presents an illustrative example concerning real collaboration between members of a community of educators, aiming on considering *alternative teaching modes* to (potentially) reach a decision on which is the most appropriate one. Figure 2 illustrates an early instance of the collaborative workspace created for the needs of the above community (for the particular issue under consideration). As shown, only one user has contributed so far (nickname: karakap) by: (i) uploading on the workspace some useful resources (a "very interesting paper" and a "useful URL"), (ii) proposing the idea "traditional lecture" (as an alternative of teaching modes), and (iii) interrelating his idea with two additional items, one that clearly (according to him) argues in favor of the abovementioned proposal (to do so, he has uploaded the argument "The lecture can be used in any size class and is often the only option in large classes", and has related it - with a green arrow - to the idea "traditional lecture"), and a second one corresponding to related work ("Sullivan and McIntosh paper", which has been also related to his proposal).

Figure 3 illustrates a second instance of the collaborative workspace under consideration (the screenshot depicts only the workspace area). As shown, two more users (nicknames: dora and tzagara) have been contributed to the collaboration by: (i) proposing a second idea ("project work", asserted by dora), (ii) uploading additional related resources (e.g. a comment pointing to a "forum about motivation of students", a comment stating that "The instructor can spend more time with those students or groups who need attention", a note stating that "Because student participation is minimal, lecturing promotes passivity in students"), (iii) interrelating knowledge items (e.g. the note "By working together, students learn from one another and become less dependent on the instructor" to the idea about "project work", declaring that the former is an item that "argues in favor" of the latter, or the note "Because the lecture is teacher-centered, it tends to promote one-way communication and the notion that truth resides in the instructor" to the previously asserted idea about "traditional learning", also declaring that the former is

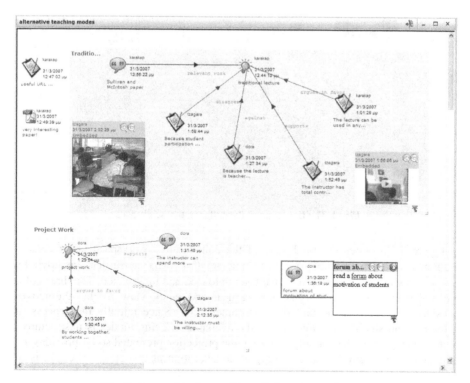

Fig. 3. A second instance of the collaborative workspace

"against" the latter), and (iv) uploading multimedia resources that are relevant to some knowledge items (in the instance shown, a video and an image have been embedded and placed intentionally close to the related items).

Beyond coloring of the arrows that interrelate knowledge items (in the example given, green arrows declare support whereas red ones declare opposition for the specific community), another visual cue that appears in Figure 3 concerns the colored rectangles that have been created by users to cluster related items (the two rectangles shown correspond to the two alternative ideas proposed so far). Although - at this instance - these rectangles are simply visual conveniences, they may play an important role during the switch to a more formal projection, enabling the implementation of appropriate abstraction mechanisms. Other visual cues supported in this projection may bear additional semantics (e.g. the thickness of an edge may express how strong a resource/idea may object or approve a teaching mode).

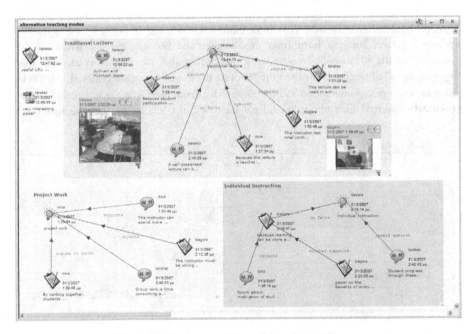

Fig. 4. The final state of the collaborative workspace

Figure 4 illustrates the final state of the collaborative workspace under consideration. As shown, a third idea has come up ("individual instruction", asserted by tzagara), while additional items have been uploaded and interrelated. The three color rectangles constructed aid users have a neat and quick view of the alternatives considered as well as the underlying argumentation. Since initially the process of gathering and sharing resources about the available teaching modes is unstructured, highly dynamic and thus rapidly evolving, the projection presented so far provides the most appropriate environment to support collaboration at this stage. The aim is to bring the session to a point where main trends crystallize, thus enabling the switch to a more formal projection (upon the participants' wish).

3.4 Switching Projections

The collaboration instances discussed above correspond to a projection that complies with the abovementioned information triage principles and allows incremental formalization (from a mere collection and sharing of knowledge items to exploitation of legacy resources, interrelation and evolution of knowledge items, and informal/ semiformal argumentation and aggregation of knowledge items)[4]. Such a projection could perfectly serve the needs of a particular community (for a specific context). However, some communities may have the need to further elaborate the knowledge items considered so far, and exploit additional functionalities to advance their argumentative collaboration. Such functionalities can be provided by other (more formal) projections that may enable the semantic annotation of knowledge items, the formal exploitation of collaboration items patterns, and the deployment of appropriate formal argumentation and reasoning mechanisms. As highlighted above, while an informal projection of the collaboration space aids the exploitation of information by users (user-interpretable view), a formal projection aims mainly at the exploitation of information by the machine (machine-interpretable view). Formal projections provide a fixed set of discourse element and relationship types, with predetermined, system-interpretable semantics.

Further elaborating the example of the previous subsection, let us assume that, at some point of the collaboration, an increase of the formality level is decided (e.g. by an individual user or the session's facilitator). In this case, there is the need to switch to a more formal projection, where knowledge items' and relationships' types have to be transformed, filtered out, or kept "as-is". The above are determined by the underlying visualization and reasoning model of the formal projection (consequently, this process can be partially automated and partially semi-automated). An instance of a projection enabling formal argumentation and group decision making is shown in Figure 5 (the screenshot depicts only the formal projection, which now appears in a separate window; the previous projection is still accessible). This formal projection adopts an IBIS-like formalism [21] and exploits functionalities of a previously developed argumentation support system [22]. It provides a structured language for argumentative discourse and a mechanism for the evaluation of alternatives. Taking into account the input provided by users, this projection constructs an illustrative discourse-based knowledge graph.

The knowledge items allowed in this projection are *issues, alternatives, positions,* and *preferences.* Issues correspond to problems to be solved, decisions to be made, or goals to be achieved. For each issue, users may propose alternatives (i.e. solutions to the problem under consideration) that correspond to potential choices. Positions are asserted in order to support the selection of a specific course of action (alternative), or avert the users' interest from it by expressing some objection. A position may also refer to another (previously asserted) position, thus arguing in favor or against it. Finally, preferences provide individuals with a qualitative way to weigh reasons for and against the selection of a certain course of action. A preference is a tuple of the form *[position, relation, position]*, where the relation can be "more important than" or

---

[4] The projection presented also allows for easy exploitation of existing web forums (items of a forum can be inserted in the workspace and further manipulated by users); this functionality is not shown due to space limitations.

"of equal importance to" or "less important than". The use of preferences results in the assignment of various levels of importance to the alternatives in hand. Like the other discourse elements, they are subject to further argumentative discourse. The above four types of items enable users to contribute their knowledge on the particular problem or need (by entering issues, alternatives and positions) and also to express their relevant values, interests and expectations (by entering positions and preferences). Moreover, the projection continuously processes the elements entered by the users (by triggering its reasoning mechanisms each time a new element is entered in the graph), thus facilitating users to become aware of the elements for which there is (or there is not) sufficient (positive or negative) evidence, and accordingly conduct the discussion in order to reach consensus.

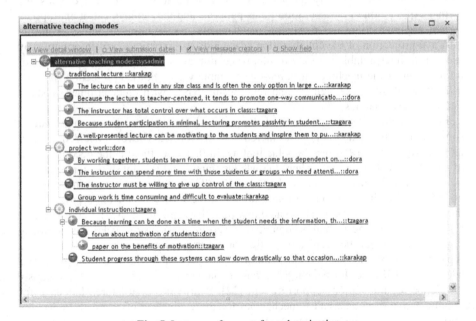

Fig. 5. Instance of a more formal projection

The instance shown in Figure 5 has been automatically built by transforming the projection instance of Figure 4 (the switching to this, more formal, projection has been initiated by the session's facilitator by requesting the related service from the tool). More specifically, the colored rectangles appearing in Figure 4 have been transformed to the alternatives of Figure 5 (each alternative is expressed by the related idea existed in the previous projection). Other knowledge items have been transformed to positions in favor or against (exploiting the coloring and the legends of the interrelating arrows)[5].

---

[5] A detailed explanation of the related transformation and graph structuring procedures, which may also take into account the semantic annotation of knowledge items, goes out of the scope of this paper.

It is noted that, after the above transformation, the collaboration may continue at this projection, where users are able to exploit a richer set of features and functionalities that is associated to a higher formality level. For instance, further to the argumentation-based structuring of a collaborative session, this projection integrates a reasoning mechanism that determines the status of each discourse entry, the ultimate aim being to keep users aware of the discourse outcome. More specifically, alternatives, positions and preferences of a graph have an activation label (it can be "active" or "inactive") indicating their current status. This label is calculated according to the argumentation underneath and the type of evidence specified for them ("burden of proof"). Activation in this projection is a recursive procedure; a change of the activation label of an element is propagated upwards in the discussion graph. Depending on the status of positions and preferences, the mechanism goes through a scoring procedure for the alternatives of the issue (for a detailed description of the projection's reasoning mechanisms, see [22]). At each discussion instance, users are informed about what is the most prominent (according to the underlying argumentation) alternative solution.

Alternative projections of a particular workspace should be considered (and exploited) jointly, in that a switch from one to the other can better facilitate the argumentative collaboration process. One may also consider a particular collaboration case, where decrease of formality is desirable. For instance, while collaboration proceeds through a formal projection, some discourse elements need to be further justified, refined and elucidated. It is at this point that the collaboration session could switch to a more informal view in order to provide participants with the appropriate environment to better shape their minds (before possibly switching back to the formal projection). Switching from a formal to an informal projection is also supported by our approach.

3.5 Other Issues

In addition to the above, our approach permits users to create one or more private spaces, where they can organize and elaborate the resources of a collaboration space according to their understanding (and their pace). Although private in nature, users are able to share such spaces with their peers. Moreover, each projection is associated with a set of tools that better suit to its purposes. These tools enable the population, manipulation and evolution of the knowledge item types allowed in that particular projection. There can be tools allowing the reuse of information residing in legacy systems, tools permitting authoring of multimedia content, annotation tools, as well as communication and management tools.

A first release of CoPe_it!, supporting various levels of formality using projections as the ones described above, has been already implemented. The tool makes use of Web 2.0 technologies, such as AJAX (Asynchronous JavaScript and XML), to deliver the functionalities of the different projections to end users. Based on these technologies, concurrent and synchronous collaboration in every projection is provided. Individual collaboration sessions are stored in XML format.

4 Discussion and Conclusion

Referring to [5], we first draw remarks concerning the advantages and limitations of the proposed approach against issues such as cognitive overhead and management of information overload, management of tacit knowledge, premature structure, and situational differences. Speaking about the first issue, we argue that our approach mirrors working practices with which users are well acquainted (they are part of their ordinary tasks), thus exhibiting low "barriers to entry". Moreover, it reduces the overhead of entering information by allowing the reuse of existing documents (mechanisms for reusing existing knowledge sources, such as e-mail messages and entries or topics of web-based forums, have been also integrated). In addition, our approach is able to defer the formalization of information until later in the task. This may be achieved by the use of the appropriate annotation and ontology management tools. In any case, however, users may be averted from the use of such (usually sophisticated) tools, thus losing the benefits of a more formal representation of the asserted knowledge resources. A remedy to that could be that such processing is performed by experienced users. One should also argue here that, due to the collaborative approach supported, the total overhead associated with formalizing information can be divided among users.

Speaking about management of tacit knowledge, we argue that the alternative projections offered, as well as the mechanisms for switching among them, may enhance its acquisition, capturing and representation. Limitations are certainly there; nevertheless, claiming that our approach promotes active participation in knowledge sharing activities (which, in turn, enhances knowledge flow), we expect that all four phases (i.e., internalization, socialization, combination and externalization) of the Nonaka's and Takeuchi's famous knowledge transformation spiral [23] can be leveraged. Reuse of past collaboration spaces also contributes to bringing previously tacit knowledge to consciousness.

Our approach does not impose (or even advocate) premature structure; upon their wish, participants may select the projection they want to work with, as well as the tasks they want to perform when working at this projection (e.g. a document can be tagged or labeled whenever a participant wants; moreover, this process has not to be done in one attempt). Decision making support issues are also addressed in a stepwise manner. Finally, considering situational differences, we argue that our approach is generic enough to address diverse collaboration modes and paradigms. This is achieved through the proposed projection-oriented approach (each projection having its own structure and rationale), as well as the mechanisms for switching projections (such mechanisms incorporate the rationale of structures' evolution).

As mentioned above, the proposed framework is the result of action research studies for collaborative learning improvement. It has been already introduced in various settings for a series of pilot applications. Preliminary results show that it fully covers the user requirements analyzed in Section 3.1; also, it stimulates interaction, makes users more accountable for their contributions, while it aids them to conceive, document and analyze the overall collaboration context in a holistic manner.

Concluding, we argue that the proposed approach is able to fully support the evolution of the collaboration management cycle (see Section 2) and provides the means for addressing the issues related to the formality needed in collaborative knowledge building and learning support systems. It aims at contributing to the field of social software, by supporting argumentative interaction between people and groups, enabling social feedback, and facilitating the building and maintenance of social networks. Future work directions include the extensive evaluation of CoPe_it! in diverse contexts and collaboration paradigms, which is expected to shape our mind towards the development of additional projections, as well as the experimentation with and integration of additional visualization cues, aiming at further facilitating and augmenting the information triage process.

Acknowledgments. Research carried out in the context of this paper has been partially funded by the EU PALETTE (Pedagogically Sustained Adaptive Learning through the Exploitation of Tacit and Explicit Knowledge) Integrated Project (IST FP6-2004, Contract No. 028038). The authors would also like to thank the CTI's development team of CoPe_it! for their valuable help in implementing the proposed approach.

References

1. Koschmann, T.D.: Toward a dialogic theory of learning: Bakhtin's contribution to understanding learning in settings of collaboration. In: Hoadley, C.M., Roschelle, J. (eds.) Proc. of the CSCL'99 Conference, pp. 308–313. Lawrence Erlbaum, Mahwah, NJ (1999)
2. Andriessen, J., Baker, M., Suthers, D.: Argumentation, computer support, and the educational context of confronting cognitions. In: Andriessen, J., Baker, M., Suthers, D. (eds.) Arguing to learn: confronting cognitions in computer-supported collaborative learning environments, pp. 1–25. Kluwer Academic Publishers, Dordrecht (2003)
3. Ravenscroft, A., McAlister, S.: Designing interaction as a dialogue game: Linking social and conceptual dimensions of the learning process. In: Juwah, C. (ed.) Interactions in Online Education: implications for theory and practice. Routledge, pp. 73–90 (2006)
4. Jonassen, D.H., Carr, C.S.: Mindtools: Affording multiple representations for learning. In: Lajoiem, S.P. (ed.) Computers as cognitive tools II: Theory change, paradigm shifts and their influence on the use of computers for instructional purposes, pp. 165–196. Erlbaum, Mawah, NJ (2000)
5. Shipman, F.M., Marshall, C.C.: Formality Considered Harmful: Issues, Experiences, Emerging Themes, and Directions. Tech. Rep. ISTL-CSA-94-08-02, Xerox Palo Alto Research Center (1994)
6. Shipman, F.M., McCall, R.: Supporting knowledge-base evolution with incremental formalization. In: Proceedings of CHI'94 Conference, Boston, MA, April 24-28, 1994, pp. 285–291 (1994)
7. Fischer, G., Lemke, A.C., McCall, R., Morch, A.: Making Argumentation Serve Design. Human Computer Interaction 6(3-4), 393–419 (1991)
8. Halasz, F.: Reflections on NoteCards: Seven Issues for the Next Generation of Hypermedia Systems. Communications of the ACM 31(7), 836–852 (1988)
9. de Moor, A., Aakhus, M.: Argumentation support: from technologies to tools. Communications of ACM 49(3), 93–98 (2006)
10. Kirschner, P., Buckingham Shum, S., Carr, C.: Visualizing argumentation: software tools for collaborative and educational sense-making. Springer, London, UK (2003)

11. Karacapilidis, N., Loukis, E., Dimopoulos, S.: Computer-supported G2G collaboration for public policy and decision making. Journal of Enterprise Information Management 18(5), 602–624 (2005)
12. van Gelder, T.: Enhancing Deliberation through Computer Supported Argument Visualization. In: Kirschner, P., Buckingham Shum, S., Carr, C. (eds.) Visualizing Argumentation: Software Tools for Collaborative and Educational Sense-Making, pp. 97–115. Springer, London (2003)
13. Reed, C.A., Rowe, G.W.A.: Araucaria: Software for Argument Analysis, Diagramming and Representation. International Journal of AI Tools 14(3-4), 961–980 (2004)
14. Verheij, B.: Artificial argument assistants for defeasible argumentation. Artificial Intelligence 150(1-2), 291–324 (2003)
15. Lehtinen, E., Hakkarainen, K., Lipponen, L., Rahikainen, M., Muukkonen, H.: Computer Supported Collaborative Learning: A Review. In: Meijden, H., Simons, R., de Jong, F. (eds.) Computer supported collaborative learning in primary and secondary education. Final report for the EC Project 2017, pp. 1–46. Univ. of Nijmegen (2000), http://etu.utu.fi/papers/clnet/clnetreport.html
16. Soller, A., Martinez, A., Jermann, P., Muehlenbrock, M.: From Mirroring to Guiding: A Review of State of the Art Technology for Supporting Collaborative Learning. International Journal of Artificial Intelligence in Education 15, 261–290 (2005)
17. Suthers, D.: Representational Guidance for Collaborative Learning. In: Hoppe, H.U., Verdejo, F., Kay, J. (eds.) Artificial Intelligence in Education, pp. 3–10. IOS Press, Amsterdam (2003)
18. Marshall, C., Shipman, F.: Spatial Hypertext and the Practice of Information Triage. In: Proceedings of the 8th ACM Conference on Hypertext, Southampton UK, pp. 124–133. ACM Press, New York (1997)
19. Hevner, A.R., March, S.T., Park, J., Ram, S.: Design Science in Information Systems Research. MIS Quarterly 28(1), 75–105 (2004)
20. Checkland, P., Holwell, S.: Action Research: Its Nature and Validity. Systemic Practice and Action Research 11(1), 9–21 (1998)
21. Conklin, J., Begeman, M.: gIBIS: A tool for all reasons. Journal of the American Society for Information Science 40(3), 200–213 (1989)
22. Karacapilidis, N., Papadias, D.: Computer Supported Argumentation and Collaborative Decision Making: The HERMES system. Information Systems 26(4), 259–277 (2001)
23. Nonaka, I., Takeuchi, H.: The Knowledge-Creating Company. Oxford University Press, Oxford (1995)

Exploiting Preference Queries for Searching Learning Resources

Fabian Abel, Eelco Herder, Philipp Kärger, Daniel Olmedilla,
and Wolf Siberski

L3S Research Center and Leibniz University of Hannover, Hannover,
Germany
{abel,herder,kaerger,olmedilla,siberski}@L3S.de

Abstract. While the growing number of learning resources increases the choice for learners, it also makes it more and more difficult to find suitable courses. Thus, improved search capabilities on learning resource repositories are required. We propose an approach for learning resource search based on preference queries. A preference query does not only allow for hard constraints (like 'return lectures about Mathematics') but also for soft constraints (such as 'I prefer a course on Monday, but Tuesday is also fine'). Such queries always return the set of optimal items with respect to the given preferences. We show how to exploit this technique for the learning domain, and present the Personal Preference Search Service (PPSS) which offers significantly enhanced search capabilities compared to usual search facilities for learning resources.

1 Introduction

Search capabilities in educational repositories and networks have been improved in recent years by the introduction of personalization and semantic-based queries. These techniques are typically realized by adding into the query hard constraints representing the user wishes (e.g., from the user profile), that is, conditions that must be fulfilled. Examples of these hard constraints are "results must be either in English or German and must provide a certification". There are two choices how to incorporate these additional constraints into a given query, both leading to suboptimal answer sets. Either, we use a conjunctive query, i.e., the additional constraints are connected with an 'and'. In this case, the danger is high that we end up with an empty result set because of the query becomes too specific. Or, we add the constraints disjunctively, i.e., all constraints connected with an 'or'. But then, the size of such a result set grows significantly, and will contain many scarcely relevant results.

In order to solve the problem of large number of returned results, ranking mechanisms try to sort the results showing to the user the best matches first, but this notion of relevancy is typically a score computed out of i.e. number of occurrences of a keyword, TF/IDF[1], proximity of keywords, popularity of the resource, etc., elements that do not necessarily represent the user wishes.

---

[1] Term frequency / inverse document frequency.

E. Duval, R. Klamma, and M. Wolpers (Eds.): EC-TEL 2007, LNCS 4753, pp. 143–157, 2007.

A closer look reveals that in most cases additional constraints are not hard constraints. Typically a user may want to express that she wants "courses preferably in English but if there are not, also in German would suffice and which take place on Mondays better than Tuesday or Fridays". These "preferably" and "better-than" indicate soft constraints in which a user specifies *what she prefers*, that is, her wishes as preferences. These preferences can then be used in order to filter out non-relevant results. For example, if two courses are found, both on Mondays and one is in English and the other one in German, intuitively the latter can be discarded since given the same (or worse) conditions, the user prefers English over German. This way, only optimal results according to preferences are returned. This improves the satisfaction of the users and reduces the time they must spend in order to scan large query result sets.

It is important to note that the term *user preferences* has been extensively used in the field of user modeling [1] and adaptive hypermedia [2,3]. Typically, these user preferences are a set of properties for which learners express interest (and which are added in the queries as hard constraints). By contrast, our method is more expressive since it does not only allow such interests to be modelled but also allows users to indicate which properties they prefer to another by allowing for a *preference order*.

This paper describes how preference-based queries can be used in order to a) increase the expressivity of queries, helping users describing more accurately their wishes and interests and b) retrieve efficiently optimal matches according to the user preferences discarded the rest. The paper is organized as follows: in Section 2 our approach is motivated with a running scenario. Theoretical background about preferences and its use in query processing is provided in Section 3. Section 4 applies this theory to our running example in order to show how preferences may be applied to search of learning resources. Section 5 describes our prototype implementation and presents some experiments. Finally, Section 6 compares our approach with existing initiatives, Section 7 discusses some important issues regarding to user interface and Section 8 concludes the paper.

2   Motivation Scenario

In the following, we picture a scenario to demonstrate how preference-based search supports learners in finding suitable courses. We will use this example throughout the paper to illustrate our approach.

Bob has just bought his first digital camera and now he is looking for a course about photography. He is not sure what different kinds of courses are available, but he has certain ideas of his likes and dislikes. For instance, Bob prefers a class-room course in which he can learn with and get inspired by fellow learners above a rather solitary distance learning course. Bob is not a professional in photography: so he does not insist on gaining a certificate. But should there be a course with a certificate at the same or better conditions (price, etc.), he would prefer to take the one with the certificate. However, he does not want to pass an exam for gaining the certificate. Bob believes that he will like doing image processing with his computer. Hence, he also wants a course comprising some kind of homework.

Bob would prefer a course offered in the evening on working days, except on Monday; then he has a weekly appointment with a friend for jogging. If needed, he could reschedule this appointment, though. He also likes to keep the Friday evening free for meeting with his chess club. If there are no courses available during the week, he might consider a course on Saturday or Sunday. Bob would like to have the course taking place once a week, in a period of about three months. A course with two meetings per week, or one meeting every two weeks, would be fine as well. But he absolutely dislikes weekend block courses, as he is not willing to stay away from home for a longer time over the weekend. However, since he just got his new camera he wants the course to start as soon as possible as not to lose any time.

As Bob is an avid cyclist, he does not mind riding up to 10 km to the course, provided that he can follow a scenic track with cycle lanes. If the course takes place in the south of the city center he can take the way through the park, otherwise he has to struggle with cars. Concerning financial issues, Bob also has some constraints: he is not willing to pay more than 100 euros for the course.

With current search interfaces, it is not possible to specify such a complex search request. A platform providing extended search capabilities to take into account all given hard and soft constraints is desirable. With such a platform, Bob would be able to specify some of his ideas of the desired course: it should deal with digital photography, it does not need to provide a certificate, it should start immediately, etc. Additionally, the system exploits its knowledge about Bob, such as his age, which languages he prefers beyond his mother language. It also uses Bob's preferences gained from his past interactions, such as his fondness for meeting people, the location where he lives, his regular meeting on Fridays. By taking all these constraints into account, the system is able to perform a query comprising most of the particularities in Bob's idea of a course. Probably there will be no course matching all the constraints, but the system will provide Bob with a small result set, containing the courses with - according to his preferences - the lowest deviation from the given preferences.

3   Preferences and Preference-Based Queries

In order to model the kinds of hard and soft constraints Bob is able to specify his preferences with, we will now introduce the notion of Preferences and Preference-based Queries. As we have seen in the scenario, advanced search for suitable courses is needed. Searching is not well supported with a query model where users can only specify hard constraints on course characteristics. To provide more effective search capabilities in such cases, query languages like SQL over relational databases and, recently, SPARQL over RDF graphs have been extended to facilitate preference-based retrieval algorithms [4,5].

These approaches assign a degree of match with respect to user-specified soft constraints to each object and then aggregate this degree to compute the set of *best matching answers*. Under the common exact match paradigm too specific query predicates often lead to empty result sets, while too unspecific hard constraints may yield huge numbers of results. The notion of best matches fits much better to typical user's search requests, because it automatically adapts query specificity to the available objects. Our proposed solution to achieve best matches is exploiting preference orders for querying.

The notion of preference-based querying in the context of databases has been formalized independently by Kießling [6] and Chomicki [7]. To describe user's preferences in a way exploitable for querying, we rely on the preference query formalization proposed by Chomicki in [7]. In this extension to relational algebra, preferences are expressed as binary relations over a set of objects R.

Definition 1. *Let $A = \{a_1, \ldots, a_n\}$ be the set of available attributes of the elements in R, and U_i, $1 \leq i \leq n$ the respective set of possible values of a_i. Then any binary relation $\succ$ which is a subset of $(U_1 \times \ldots \times U_n) \times (U_1 \times \ldots \times U_n)$ is a preference relation over R.*

For combining several preference relations, *uni- or multidimensional composition* of the preference relations is needed. Unidimensional composition is applicable if the relations are defined over the same attribute subset. If the relations are imposed over different sets of attributes, we need a multidimensional composition imposing a new preference relation over the Cartesian product of the sets of attributes. For a composed preference, the combined preference relations are called *dimensions of the composed preference relation*. According to [7], two multidimensional compositions are common:

- *lexicographic composition* combines two dimensions by considering one as more important than the other.
- *pareto composition* allows to combine two preference relations without imposing a hierarchy on the dimensions - all dimensions are considered to be equal.

In most of the cases, imposing a priority to the dimensions is difficult for a user. For example, in our given scenario it is difficult for the user to decide what is more important, the schedule of a photography course or its location. It is best to consider them as equally important, and then let the user do the final choice given on the found courses. Therefore, we use pareto composition as default to combine preference relations.

Pareto composition yields a new preference relation following the principle of pareto domination. An object X is said to *pareto-dominate* an object Y iff X is better than Y in terms of at least one of the preference relations and equal or better in terms of all other preference relations. Or, more formally:

Definition 2. *Given the preference relations $\succ_1, \ldots, \succ_n$ over the sets of attributes $A_1, \ldots, A_n$, the pareto composition $\succ_P$ of $\succ_1 \ldots \succ_n$ is defined as:*

$$x \succ_P y \Leftrightarrow (\forall i : x \succ_i y \lor x =_i y) \land \exists j : x \succ_j y.$$

For instance, in our scenario a low-cost course X dominates an expensive course Y only iff in terms of all other preference relations (e.g., imposed on the attributes location, duration, etc.) X is at least equally good as Y.

This principle has been exploited in the area of database systems for the so-called *skylining* [8,9,10]. In skyline queries, each single attribute is viewed as an *independent*, non-weighted query dimension. Best matches for skyline queries are determined according to the principle of pareto optimality: each object which is not dominated by any other object is considered as optimal and as a best match. All these non-dominated objects are called the *skyline of the query*.

Pareto composition can be combined with lexicographic composition in the following way: on some of the pareto-combined dimensions a hierarchy can be imposed such that only if two objects are equal in terms of the first preference relation, the second one will be considered. We call the resulting preference expression a *cascaded preference*.

In the next section, we show how these preference expressions are applied to effectively search for learning resources.

4   Preferences on Metadata of Learning Resources

With the preferences at hand, we are now able to specify the constraints in the scenario in Section 2 in a formal way. For each preference Bob provides, a preference relation is imposed upon the corresponding attribute. Preference relations can be expressed over a single attribute (such as Bob's preferences concerning the weekday of the course) or over several attributes (such as Bob's preference relation about the venue of the course: it depends on two attributes, the location (north or south) and the distance from his home). According to that, we can formally define Bobs preferences. For example the preference relation over the attribute *weekday* can be represented as:

$$\succ_{weekday} = \{(Tuesday, Monday), (Wednesday, Monday), (Thursday, Monday), \ldots\}$$

And his multi-attribute preference over the venue can be defined as follows:

$$\succ_{venue} = \{$$
$$(location = south \wedge dist. = 10km, location = south \wedge dist. < 10km),$$
$$\ldots$$
$$(location = north \wedge dist. = 10km, location = north \wedge dist. < 10km)\}$$

In a similar way we can define $\succ_{type\_of\_learning}$, $\succ_{is\_homework}$, $\succ_{cycle}$, $\succ_{price}$, etc.

Preference relations build partial orders on the values of the attributes they are imposed on. In some cases, a preference correspond to a total order (such as Bob's preference on price), but usually a total order is too restrictive and do not allow for indifferences (such as Bob's indifference concerning Tuesday, Wednesday, or Thursday). Figure 1 shows the partial orders representing Bob's preference relations.

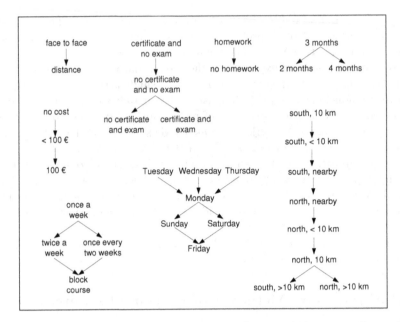

Fig. 1. Partially Ordered Sets representing the preference relations according to Bob's preferences

These single preferences build up a pareto-composed preference relation $\succ_{Bob}$. Given two courses C_1 and C_2, $C_1 \succ_{Bob} C_2$ holds if all attributes of C_1 are equal or better according to the attributes preference relations to C_2 and in at least one attribute C_1 is better than (and not equal to) C_2.

Considering the relation $\succ_{Bob}$, the optimal course would be the one fulfilling all the values of Bob's preferences, since all others would be dominated by this relation. And obviously, he would be really happy with a regular 3 month course happening once a week on Tuesday, Wednesday, or Thursday without an exam but with a certificate and all the desired features. Unfortunately, in most of the cases this course does not exist, and it is a challenge to find out which of the courses available provide an optimal trade-off between desired and existing features. We will now show by the hand of the dataset depicted in Figure 2 that the pareto composition $\succ_{Bob}$ provides exactly the intended best match result, i.e., the courses in the skyline, or, more precisely, the courses which are not dominated by any other course.

As stated above, a course C is considered a best match according to Bob preferences if there is no course C' such that $C' \succ_{Bob} C$, i.e. there is no other course that dominates C. Given this, we can conclude, that course B in Figure 2 is irrelevant since it is dominated by A: A is equal to B according to the dimensions price, distance, and location; but A is better than B according to $\succ_{weekday}$ (Bob prefers a course on Tuesday to a course on Monday) which lets A dominate B. So Bob will not be interested in B since A provides a better alternative. Let us have a look at A and C: A is better than C concerning $\succ_{weekday}$ but otherwise C

$\succ_{venue}$ A holds. Given the pareto composition of these preferences, A and C are not comparable since none of them dominates the other. Hence, Bob is probably interested in both since they are orthogonal alternatives.

For attending course D, Bob has to ride to the north of the city what he really dislikes. But D is for free, so he may accept to drive to the north because he saves money. $\succ_{Bob}$ ensures that also this alternative will be included into the result set since it is not dominated (although it is the last option in terms of $\succ_{venue}$).

Course	Weekday	Price	Distance	Location
A	Tuesday	44 Euro	2 km	south
B	Monday	44 Euro	2 km	south
C	Wednesday	72 Euro	2 km	south
D	Wednesday	no cost	10 km	north
E	Wednesday	32 Euro	10 km	north

Fig. 2. Some available courses for Bob

From the courses depicted in Figure 2, the preference based search with the query described in the scenario presents the courses A, C, and D. It prunes the courses B and E. B is dominated by A because on Monday Bob prefers to attend the jogging with his friend, and A is equally good in all other dimensions. E is dominated by D, because it is more expensive and not better in any other dimensions.

5   Preference Search Prototype

To show that preference-based search is a promising approach for managing huge data sets of learning resources, we implemented a Web Service for preference-based queries over the whole database for lectures currently held at the University of Hannover. The data set comprises about 10,000 lectures each with about 10 attributes. This yields an RDF graph of over 100,000 triples.

In order to realize the preference-enhanced search facilities, we implemented a Service called *Personal Preference Search Service (PPSS)*[2] integrated as a Web Service into the Personal Reader Framework [11].

5.1   The Personal Reader Framework

The *Personal Reader Framework* [11] enables developers to create web service based Semantic Web applications. Such applications are composed of different kinds of services as illustrated in Figure 3: *Syndication Services* implement the application logic and utilize RDF data that is provided by the *Personalization Services* which themselves are called via a *Connector Service* by specifying a goal.

---

[2] Available at `http://semweb.kbs.uni-hannover.de:8081/PreferenceQueryGUI`

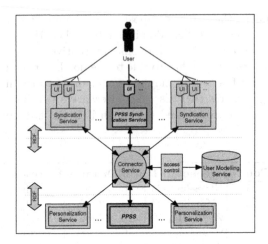

Fig. 3. The PPSS integrated into the Personal Reader Framework

Based on this goal the Connector Service detects the best suiting Personalization Services. Both Syndication and Personalization Services are able to access user data managed by a central *User Modelling Service*.

As shown in Figure 3 the Personal Preference Search Service is integrated into the Personal Reader Architecture as a Personalized Service including the following components:

1. User Interface which enables the user to formulate preference queries and visualizes the results of a search
2. Syndication Service which preprocesses the preferences, initiates the search, and processes the results
3. Personalization Service called *Personal Preference Search Service* offering the core search engine for Learning Resources

Given this setting, the PPSS is able to benefit from the shared user model while other services of the Personal Reader Framework will benefit from the functionality of the PPSS for their part. For example the *Personalization Service for Curriculum Planning* [12] and the *MyEar Music Recommender* [13] can utilize the PPSS to offer an improved search for adequate courses and music files respectively. The *Personal Publication Reader* [14], which allows users to browse publications within an embedded context, would be able to provide suggestions on publications that suit the user's preferences by integrating the PPSS. Such integration issues are current research topics.

5.2   The Personal Preference Search Service

Querying with preferences in the context of the Semantic Web is a relatively new field. In [5], we made a first contribution by establishing an extension for the RDF query language SPARQL empowered with an implementation based on the ARQ SPARQL Processor [15] part of the Jena Framework.

To specify preferences, the SPARQL language has been extended by the PREFERRING-construct, two atomic preference expressions, and two facilities for combining preference dimensions. For atomic preferences, the following expression types are offered:

- *Boolean preferences* are specified by a boolean condition. Results satisfying that condition are preferred over results which do not satisfy it.
- *Scoring preferences* are specified by a HIGHEST (resp. LOWEST) followed by a numeric expression. Results for which this expression leads to a higher value are preferred over results with a lower value (resp. vice versa).

These atomic preference expressions can be composed to two types of multidimensional preferences (c.f. Section 3):

- A *pareto composed preference* consists of two preference expressions connected by an AND. Both expressions are evaluated independently. An object is preferred if it is better in one of both preferences, and at least equally good in the second one.
- In a *cascading preference*, two preference expressions are connected by a CASCADE; the first preference is evaluated first; only for objects which are equally good with respect to the first preference, the second preference is considered.

The PPSS operates on top of the extended ARQ engine. If the PPSS receives an RDF description of preference definitions, it creates a SPARQL query, passes it to the engine, collects the result set, and returns an RDF description of that result set. The separation of functionalities in the PPSS (i.e., the separation of SPARQL query generation, the query processing, and the assembly of the result set) as well as the architecture of the Personal Reader enables the system to query each RDF-based data set of learning resources.

The current user interface (shown in Figure 4) allows the user to define his preferences. Currently we provide total ordered single-attribute preferences (c.f. Section 3). Due to the complexity of a user interface allowing the definition of partial orders and dependend dimensions, we currently do not allow for these kinds of preference structure, although our implementation is able to handle them. Considerations concerning the user interface are discussed in Section 7.

5.3   Experiments

We have performed experiments with the lecture database of the learning management system of the University of Hannover. That system currently comprises 9829 lectures. As an example, given the following preference query, we show how preference queries optimize the result set and provides the desired learning resources without pruning relevant results or returning non-relevant objects:

> *Return courses about mathematics. I am interested in readings rather than in tutorials and seminars. If possible, I would like to attend a 90 minutes lecture. 60 minutes are also fine, but 120 minutes are too long.*

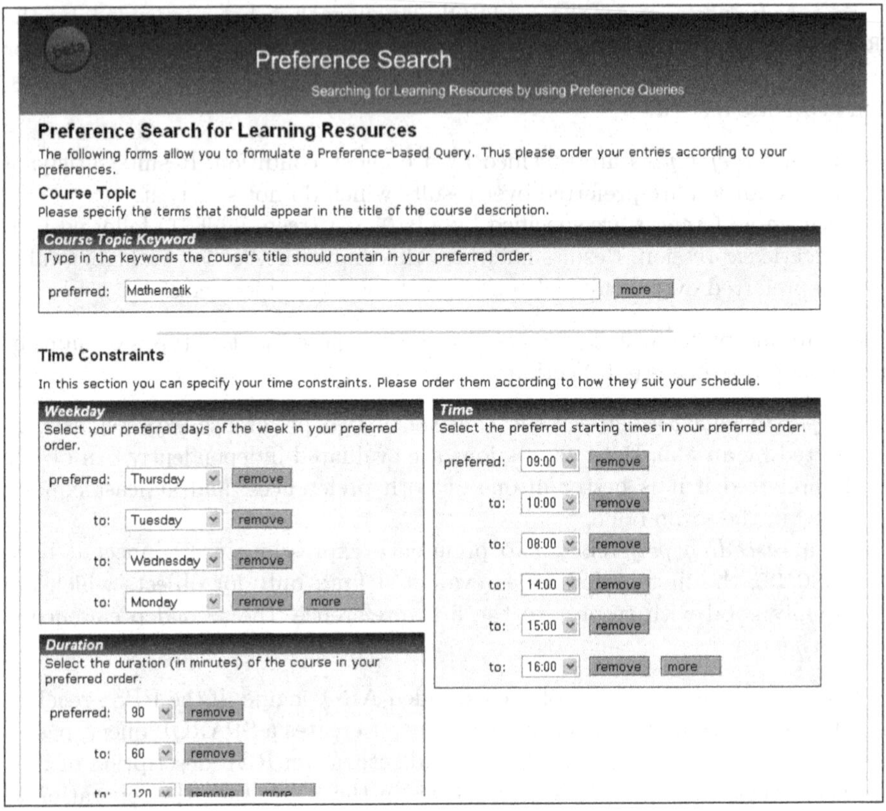

Fig. 4. The user interface of the Personal Preference Search Service

I like to have the lecture in the morning rather than in the afternoon. Due to the lunch break, noon is not possible for me. I don't want to have a lecture on Friday. Thursday would be my first choice, then Tuesday. Wednesday would also be acceptable and is preferred to Monday, where I am usually still at my parents.

The SPARQL query according to this desired course is shown in Figure 5. Its corresponding result set is shown in the table in Figure 6. Obviously, none of the returned courses matches all the desired attributes: the first lecture is held too late, on Tuesday, and it is not a reading; the second is too long, and so on. (Mind that the order in the table does not correspond to a ranking: all six results are equally relevant.) However, concerning all the 64 courses about Mathematics, these 6 results are optimal: the remaining 58 courses are worse in terms of at least one preference relation.

Without the possibility to define preference orders, there are two alternative approaches in classic, i.e., best match search interfaces: The first is to conjunctively connect all preferred attributes and do several queries by going step by step down according to the preference order. This manner of querying returns

```
PREFIX xsd: <http://www.w3.org/2001/XMLSchema#>
PREFIX rdf: <http://www.w3.org/1999/02/22-rdf-syntax-ns#>
PREFIX j.0: <http://www.13s.de/studip#>
PREFIX fn: <java:com.hp.hpl.jena.query.function.library.>

SELECT ?name ?starttime ?type1 ?weekday ?duration ?faculty
WHERE {
        ?x j.0:name ?name.
        ?x j.0:type1 ?type1.
        ?x j.0:weekday ?weekday.
        ?x j.0:start_time ?starttime.
        ?x j.0:duration ?duration.
        ?x j.0:faculty ?faculty.
        FILTER (fn:contains(?name,"Mathematik")).
}
PREFERRING
        ?type1 ='Vorlesung'
            CASCADE ?type1 ='Uebung'
            CASCADE ?type1 ='Seminar'
AND
        ?weekday='Thursday'
            CASCADE ?weekday ='Tuesday'
            CASCADE ?weekday ='Wednesday'
            CASCADE ?weekday ='Monday'
AND
        ?starttime='09:00'
            CASCADE ?starttime ='10:00'
            CASCADE ?starttime ='08:00'
            CASCADE ?starttime ='14:00'
            CASCADE ?starttime ='15:00'
            CASCADE ?starttime ='16:00'
AND
        ?duration ='90'
            CASCADE ?duration ='60'
            CASCADE ?duration ='120'
```

Fig. 5. Preference-extended SPARQL query

to few and - in most of the cases - no results. After some queries with no results the user gets frustrated, and even if some results are returned, the user needs to create queries with all different alternatives in order to be able to select the best match. In our current example the conjunctive query yields an empty result since non of the courses in Figure 6 bear each of the most preferred properties.

The second approach is to disjunctively put all the possible desired outcomes into a single query. This query usually returns a huge result set containing the desired optimal courses but also a lot of non optimal results which are dominated by better ones. In our example, this querying yields to 25 courses (see an excerpt

Course	Start time	Type	Weekday	Duration	Faculty
Mathematics Exercises	10:00	Tutorial	Tuesday	120	Applied Math.
Mathematics (Economics)	09:00	Reading	Thursday	120	Algebra
Mathematics (Geography)	08:00	Reading	Thursday	90	Analysis
Mathematics (Engineers)	10:00	Reading	Tuesday	60	Applied Math.
Mathematics (Chemistry)	09:00	Reading	Thursday	120	Chemistry
Mathematics and Physics	10:00	Reading	Tuesday	90	Chemistry

Fig. 6. Optimal courses at University Hannover

of the results in Figure 7), including courses with suboptimal attribute combinations. For instance the lecture "Mathematics (Engineers)" held at the Faculty for Algebra is suitable but obviously worse than "Mathematics (Geography)" held by the Faculty for Analysis (third item in Fig. 6) because the latter dominates the former since it is a 90 minutes lecture which is preferred to a 120 minutes one. For that reason, the longer lecture is not worth to be included into the result set. By doing that the PPSS reduces the number of results from 25 to 6.

Both, the conjunctive as well as the disjunctive approach are not satisfactory: the first one comes up with no results whereas the second alternative bothers the user with many non relevant courses.

Course	Start time	Type	Weekday	Duration	Faculty
Math. in Physics	14:00	Seminar	Wednesday	120	Theor. Physics
Math. in Assurances	08:00	Reading	Monday	90	Mathematics
⋮	⋮	⋮	⋮	⋮	⋮
Mathematics (Engineers)	10:00	Reading	Thursday	120	Algebra
Math. for Beginners	08:00	Tutorial	Wednesday	120	Algebra

Fig. 7. Courses at University Hannover matching the disjunctive query

6 Related Work

Beyond the theoretical achievements in preferences (as summarized in [7,6]), several applications of this theory have been realized to support search. In [16], preference-enhanced search engines for e-shopping are presented. In any of these systems, preferences are hard-wired into the search mask and cannot be easily specified or refined by the user. Preference-based search in a digital library is provided in [17]. There, preferences are defined for one single dimension, i.e., over keywords of the desired object. Due to that fact, the preferences are used to sort the results and can not be exploited to filter irrelevant objects. [18] compares different approaches for catalog search and shows that the preference-based alternative is the most promising. However, the opportunities for defining preferences in the search form of the compared preference approach are limited to the identification and prioritization of dimensions but do not allow for preferences between the values of the dimensions. This is crucial for complex domains such as learning resources where most of the dimensions are discrete.

7 Discussion

In the previous sections we have seen that preference queries provide a powerful means for accessing large e-learning repositories, allowing the users to specify their preferences without having to give priority to one preference or another. As only optimal results are returned, all recommended items may be considered equally relevant. However, some user interface issues should be considered to maximize the benefits for the users.

It is a well-known phenomenon that 'first things' are perceived as being most important. As an example, Web users almost never look beyond the first page of search results [19]. This implies that the further from the start of a result list, the less likely it is that an item will be selected - even if they are as relevant as the results shown first. The same yields for the order in which preferences are elicited. Ideally, preferences should be elicited in such a way that any preference can be given in any order, with immediate and preferably visible feedback [20].

The closed-world assumption of skylining - that only those preferences explicitly stated by the user are relevant - is not always correct. When planning ahead, users typically have an idea of what they want, but are unable to directly express their needs. Only after having seen the first result set and inspecting its contents, they are able to communicate more advanced preferences. Such a process of *orienteering* [21] helps the users in finding what they want rather than what they ask for. As skylining only returns the results that are deemed the perfect solution, this process of orienteering might become disrupted: the user will not be aware of results that are initially second-best, but that might turn out to be better, based on preferences not yet expressed. For this reason, a careful combination of preference eliciting and critiquing [22] should be chosen.

8   Conclusions and Further Work

Search capabilities in existing educational repositories typically allow users to specify hard constraints a query must fulfill. However, users typically do not think on hard constraints but rather soft constraints such as "Monday is better but Tuesday would also be fine". Preferences allow users to specify their wishes in a way that can be processed by engines in order to return only the best matches based on such wishes, that is, those results that *dominate* the rest of potentially relevant ones. In this paper, we describe how such preferences and preference-based queries can be used in the context of search of learning resources. We show how our approach is more expressive than existing ones and returns optimal result sets. In addition, we present our implementation as a web service in the Personal Reader Framework and demonstrate its value via some experiments in the Hannover University learning management system.

Our future work focuses on the improvement of our current prototype with optimized algorithms based on latest results on skylining research and investigate an enhancement to our user interface in order to allow the more expressive preferences that our implemented engine already support. In addition, preferences can also be used for automatic course generation (e.g., curriculum planning) and for recommendation algorithms [23], directions that we are currently exploring.

Acknowledgements

The authors would like to thank Mohammad Alrifai and Ingo Brunkhorst who provided the data set and helped to preprocess it. The authors' efforts were (partly) funded by the European Commission in the TENCompetence project (IST-2004-02787) (www.tencompetence.org).

References

1. Kobsa, A.: Generic User Modelling Systems. In: Brusilovsky, P., Kobsa, A., Nejdl, W. (eds.) The Adaptive Web: Methods and Strategies of Web Personalization. LNCS, vol. 4321, Springer, Heidelberg (2007)
2. Brusilovsky, P.: Adaptive hypermedia. User Modeling and User-Adapted Interaction. In: Kobsa, A. (ed.) Ten Year Anniversary Issue 11, pp. 87–110 (2001)
3. Peylo, P.B.C.: Adaptive and intelligent web-based educational systems. International Journal of Artificial Intelligence in Education, Special Issue on Adaptive and Intelligent Web-based Educational Systems 13, 159–172 (2003)
4. Kießling, W., Köstler, G.: Preference sql - design, implementation, experiences. In: Proceedings of 28th International Conference on Very Large Data Bases (VLDB), pp. 990–1001 (2002)
5. Siberski, W., Pan, J.Z., Thaden, U.: Querying the semantic web with preferences. In: Cruz, I., Decker, S., Allemang, D., Preist, C., Schwabe, D., Mika, P., Uschold, M., Aroyo, L. (eds.) ISWC 2006. LNCS, vol. 4273, pp. 612–624. Springer, Heidelberg (2006)
6. Kießling, W.: Foundations of preferences in database systems. In: Proceedings of the 28th International Conference on Very Large Data Bases, Hong Kong, China, pp. 311–322 (2002)
7. Chomicki, J.: Preference formulas in relational queries. ACM Trans. Database Syst. 28(4), 427–466 (2003)
8. Borzsonyi, S., Kossmann, D., Stocker, K.: The skyline operator. In: Proceedings of the 17th International Conference on Data Engineering (ICDE), Heidelberg, Germany (2001)
9. Tan, K.L., Eng, P.K., Ooi, B.C.: Efficient progressive skyline computation. In: Proceedings of the 27th International Conference on Very Large Databases (VLDB), Rome, Italy (2001)
10. Papadias, D., Tao, Y., Fu, G., Seeger, B.: An optimal and progressive algorithm for skyline queries. In: Proceedings of the ACM SIGMOD International Conference on Management of Data, San Diego, CA, USA, pp. 467–478. ACM Press, New York (2003)
11. Henze, N., Kriesell, M.: Personalization functionality for the semantic web: Architectural outline and first sample implementations, semantic web challenge 2005. In: De Bra, P., Nejdl, W. (eds.) AH 2004. LNCS, vol. 3137, Springer, Heidelberg (2004)
12. Baldoni, M., Baroglio, C., Brunkhorst, I., Marengo, E., Patti, V.: A personalization service for curriculum planning. In: ABIS 2006. 14th Workshop on Adaptivity and User Modeling in Interactive Systems (October 2006)
13. Henze, N., Krause, D.: Personalized access to web services in the semantic web. In: SWUI 2006 - 3rd International Semantic Web User Interaction Workshop, Athens, Georgia, USA (November 2006)

14. Abel, F., Baumgartner, R., Brooks, A., Enzi, C., Gottlob, G., Henze, N., Herzog, M., Kriesell, M., Nejdl, W., Tomaschewski, K.: The personal publication reader, semantic web challenge 2005. In: 4th International Semantic Web Conference (November 2005)
15. Seaborne, A.: An open source implementation of sparql. In: WWW 2006 Developers track presentation (2006), http://www2006.org/programme/item.php?id=d18
16. Kießling, W., Köstler, G.: Preference SQL - design, implementation, experiences. In: 28th International Conference on Very Large Data Bases (VLDB 2002), Hong Kong, China (2002)
17. Spyratos, N., Christophides, V.: Querying with preferences in a digital library. In: Jantke, K.P., Lunzer, A., Spyratos, N., Tanaka, Y. (eds.) Federation over the Web. LNCS (LNAI), vol. 3847, Springer, Heidelberg (2006)
18. Dring, S., Fischer, S., Kießling, W., Preisinger, T.: Optimizing the catalog search process for e-procurement platforms. deec 0, 39–48 (2005)
19. Spink, A., Wolfram, D., Jansen, B.J., Saracevic, T.: Searching the web: The public and their queries. Journal of the American Society for Information Science and Technology 52(3), 226–234 (2001)
20. Pu, P., Faltings, B., Torrens, M.: User-involved preference elicitation. In: Proc. IJCAI 2003 Workshop on Configuration (2003)
21. Teevan, J., Alvarado, C., Ackerman, M.S., Karger, D.R.: The perfect search engine is not enough: a study of orienteering behavior in directed search. In: CHI '04: Proceedings of the SIGCHI conference on Human factors in computing systems, pp. 415–422. ACM Press, New York (2004)
22. Viappiani, P., Faltings, B., Pu, P.: Evaluating preference-based search tools: A tale of two approaches. In: Proceedings of The Twenty-First National Conference on Artificial Intelligence, Boston, Massachusetts, USA, July 16-20, 2006 (2006)
23. Satzger, B., Endres, M., Kießling, W.: A Preference-Based Recommender System. In: E-Commerce and Web Technologies, Springer, Berlin (2006)

How Do People Learn at the Workplace?
Investigating Four Workplace Learning Assumptions

Jose Kooken[1], Tobias Ley[2], and Robert de Hoog[1]

[1] Faculty of Behavioral Sciences, University of Twente
P.O. Box 217, 7500 AE Enschede, The Netherlands
[2] Know-Center[1]
Inffeldgasse 21a, 8010 Graz, Austria
j.p.kooken@utwente.nl, tley@know-center.at,
r.dehoog@utwente.nl

Abstract. Any software development project is based on assumptions about the state of the world that probably will hold when it is fielded. Investigating whether they are true can be seen as an important task. This paper describes how an empirical investigation was designed and conducted for the EU funded APOSDLE project. This project aims at supporting informal learning during work. Four basic assumptions are derived from the project plan and subsequently investigated in a two-phase study using several methods, including workplace observations and a survey. The results show that most of the assumptions are valid in the current work context of knowledge workers. In addition more specific suggestions for the design of the prospective APOSDLE application could be derived. Though requiring a substantial effort, carrying out studies like this can be seen as important for longer term software development projects.

Keywords: workplace learning, multi-method approach, informal learning, learning bottlenecks, task driven learning.

1 Introduction

Any software development project starts from certain assumptions about the state of the world that are thought to be valid. Most EU funded project are no exception to this rule. However, checking the truth of these assumptions is often hard to do and most projects proceed as if they are true. From the many failures in software development (see for example, [1], [2], [3], [4]) we know that a mismatch between assumptions and reality is one of the main causes why things don't turn out as expected. In the context of the APOSDLE project[2], about supporting workplace learning, we decided to investigate the assumptions behind the project plan and goals, by carrying out a

---

[1] The Know-Center is funded by the Austrian Competence Center program Kplus under the auspices of the Austrian Ministry of Transport, Innovation and Technology (http://www.ffg.at), by the State of Styria and by the City of Graz.
[2] APOSDLE (http://www.aposdle.org) is partially funded under grant 027023 in the IST work program of the European Community.

E. Duval, R. Klamma, and M. Wolpers (Eds.): EC-TEL 2007, LNCS 4753, pp. 158–171, 2007.

workplace learning study in participating, organizations, followed by a more general questionnaire distributed over several other companies and organizations. This paper starts with describing the context of the APOSDLE project focusing on the assumptions about reality underlying the project. In order to place the project in the wider context of workplace learning a brief overview of this research domain is given with the aim to clarify some terminological issues. Next we will turn to the design of the empirical investigation. The research questions are answered in the results section. Finally results are compared with the assumptions and consequences for the future design and implementation of the APOSDLE system are discussed. Attention will also be paid to lessons learned that could be relevant for other projects.

2 The APOSDLE Project

The goal of the APOSDLE project is to enhance knowledge worker productivity by supporting informal learning activities in the context of knowledge workers' everyday work processes and work environments. This is to be achieved by building and testing a comprehensive and integrated computer based set of work, learn and communication tools. The key distinction of the APOSDLE approach, compared to more traditional (e)Learning approaches, is that it will provide integrated ICT support for the three roles a knowledge worker fills at the professional workplace: the learner, the expert and the worker. Chiefly the support will be provided within the working environment and not in a separate learning environment. It will utilize contextualized communication for knowledge transfer. Finally, it will be based on personal and digital knowledge sources available in an organization and does not require the switch to a new system [5].

The following assumptions about the state of the world underlie the APOSDLE project:

- People do learn during work quite frequently
- Learning during work is mainly driven by the work people are doing
- While learning during work, bottlenecks occur that must be overcome
- Interpersonal communication is important when learning during work

The major thrust of this paper is to report the results of empirical research into the validity of these assumptions and the consequences for the APOSDLE approach. More in general, it addresses the following research questions derived from the assumptions:

- How frequently do people learn during work?
- What drivers/triggers learning during work?
- Are there bottlenecks when people learn during work?
- Which solutions do people use to satisfy a learning/knowledge need during work?

3 Workplace Learning: A Brief State of the Art

Workplace learning is a complex and challenging research area: there is still a lack of standardized research and appropriate conceptual and methodological tools [6].

Nevertheless, some characteristics of workplace learning are agreed upon, like the influence of work tasks and contexts on what and how people can learn at work [6]. Learning at work can also occur in many forms, varying from formal learning in training courses to informal learning like 'over the shoulder learning' [7]. According to [8], most adults prefer to have some responsibility for their own learning. To stay competent, knowledge workers have to take responsibility for their learning. They learn autonomously by exploring and using knowledge in their daily work. This type of learning is defined as self-directed learning. In [9] self-directed informal learning is described as ' [...] intentional job-specific and general employment-related learning done on your own, collective learning with colleagues of other employment-related knowledge and skills, and tacit learning by doing'. Self-directed learning includes using one or more learning strategies, which are defined as thoughts and behaviours engaged in by the learner in order to achieve certain goals or purposes [10].

Several psychological and educational scientists have studied self-directed learning and learning strategies. The first empirical studies of informal learning activities of adults date back to the 1960s (U.S. national survey, see [9]), although first significant empirical research concerning adults' self-directed learning projects started in the 1970s, inspired by Knowles and pioneered by Tough (see [9]). Still, it was only since the 1990s that this subject attracted more attention. In 1996, [11] stated that 'the explosion of knowledge, research, literature, and interest related to self-directed learning has been phenomenal during the past decade'. Currently, self-directed learning is still a prominent focus of research [12]. Up till now, most research about self-directed learning is conducted in educational settings, from preschool till postgraduate levels. Learning strategies have also almost never been systematically measured in work-related research either [13]. Therefore, more needs to be known about current workplace learning practices.

In terms of [14] APOSDLE is directed towards non-formal learning. Non-formal learning can be distinguished from formal learning by lacking key characteristics of formal learning:

- A prescribed learning framework
- An organised learning event or package
- The presence of a designated teacher or trainer
- The award of a qualification or credit
- The external specification of the outcomes

Non-formal learning is classified by [14] using two dimensions:

1. Time of local event or stimulus: past episodes, current experience, future behaviour
2. Level of intention: implicit learning, reactive learning, deliberative learning

The type of non-formal learning addressed in APOSDLE can be characterized, using these terms, as based on current experiences (work), reactive (near spontaneous and unplanned) and deliberative (time set aside specifically for this purpose). More in general it is about *incidental* noting of facts, opinions, impressions ideas and *recognition* of learning opportunities (**reactive**) and *engagement* in decision-making, problem-solving and planned informal learning (**deliberative**).

Based on these theoretical considerations we decided to use the following operational definitions of the main concepts:

- **Workplace.** *'A physical location, a time and the nature of the workplace (computational or not). It is in fact a micro world in which an employee works'.* In the context of APOSDLE a workplace is described as a *computer based work environment.*
- **Learning.** The focus of the study is mainly on actual behaviour: what people do. As one cannot mostly observe learning directly without administering some kind of test, which is clearly not feasible in actual work contexts, an operational definition is needed that relies on other cues. The use of information or knowledge is considered as learning *if the information or knowledge is stored consciously or subconsciously for future use.* This is in line with the conceptual model of knowledge work as proposes by [15] which states that the outcome of performing knowledge work can either be *learning* (a change in the state of an organization's knowledge resources) and/or *projection* (the embedding of knowledge in an organization's product and service outputs). If only the latter occurs, no learning takes place.
- **Knowledge Worker.** A knowledge worker is described as someone who has been schooled to develop, use, and/or transfer knowledge[3], rather than using mainly physical force or manual skills.

4 Design of the Investigation

The study consisted of two successive phases. Collecting detailed data about workplace learning, as it currently occurs for knowledge workers in the four organizations participating in the project, was performed in Phase 1. The findings from this phase provide an in depth insight into current workplace learning practices in a *limited* number of organizations. In order to obtain a *more general* insight, the objective of Phase 2 was to verify and generalize important outcomes of Phase 1. To investigate this, knowledge workers of a larger sample of European organizations were involved.

In general, the study was focused on obtaining data concerning *actual behaviour of knowledge workers at their workplaces,* as it is this actual behaviour that provides the context for the future fielding of APOSDLE. From previous research (see for example [16]) it became clear that investigating workplace learning in terms of actual behaviour requires a variety of data collection methods that allow for data collected at different times and places in order to prevent a blinkered view on what actually happens.

Our multi-method data collection approach consisted of four methods:

1. *Workplace observations*: collecting objective data about actual self-directed learning behaviour in a limited time span;
2. *Interviews*: collecting opinions and self reports about self-directed learning behaviour based on recollection of memories;
3. *Online diaries*: self recording of self-directed learning behaviour over a longer time span than can be achieved with observations by using an online diary;

---

[3] This division in these three different activities of knowledge workers is based on how the Dutch Central Bureau of Statistics divides the knowledge worker population.

4. *(Online) Questionnaire based survey*: an online questionnaire containing the most important outcomes of the first four methods and aiming to collect data to verify these results.

The first three methods were used in Phase 1. The fourth one, the online survey, is used in Phase 2. As organizations from the private, as well as from the public sector were involved and because the methods were sampled over time, work and people, generalization of the results to a wider range of contexts is possible.

4.1   Phase 1: Data Collection in the APOSDLE Application Partners' Organizations

In this phase use was made of workplace observations, interviews and online diaries.

For the observations and interviews 2-3 day visits to each application partner were organized. The purpose of the visit was deliberately not told, to avoid an effect (a bias) on the usual behavior of the employees. As they know their organisations best, partners were asked to select locations, times and of participating employees that fit best the requirements of the study. In the selection of employees there should also be as much variation as possible in tasks, functions and levels of experience.

The data collection consisted of sessions that lasted approximately 60 to 105 minutes. Observations at the workplace lasted 60 minutes and were followed by an interview, which took 45 minutes. During an observation, the participant had to maintain his normal work activities and pretend there was no observer, while the observer sat nearby the employee and made notes about the behaviour. The results of these observations were short descriptions of the observed behaviour of the participants, especially workplace learning behaviour. For the interview a schema was used which contained questions about reported learning events.

In the diary part, participants were asked to report successful and unsuccessful personal learning moments that took place in their work context during six weeks. It was stressed that unsuccessful learning moments could also be reported, because the amount of time that people spend in learning processes is not necessarily positively correlated with successful learning outcomes [9]. A participant could report about three types of learning moments: successful and intended, successful and coincidental, and unsuccessful learning moments. To report learning moments, Eureka Reports, a type of diary study that focuses on recording learning in everyday work, were used as a starting point for the design of the diary [17]. The APOSDLE partners decided on suitable participants from their organizations, based on the request to find knowledge workers that spend at least 60% of their working time at a computer based workplace. The Eureka Report was accessible through a webpage. To reduce the burden for the participants, they were asked to fill in the Eureka Reports only a few (work) days a week.

4.2   Phase 2: Workplace Learning Survey

The data collection for Phase 2 made used a of questionnaire accessible through Internet. The goal of the Work Place Learning Survey was to verify which findings of Phase 1 could be generalized. This was a crucial question since Phase 1 was conducted at four partner organizations and for APOSDLE to succeed, a broader scope is required.

4.2.1 Sampling

As it is next to impossible to draw a random sample from the target users of APOSDLE, and mass mailings of questionnaires to organizations yield very low response rates, we decided to opt for a kind of "snow balling" sample procedure that intends to maximize responses from target users. This approach entailed that each APOSDLE partner got in touch with some of their contacts in different organizations (first step) and asked them to find some suitable respondents (second step). As it was not possible to influence the precise number of people who received a request to participate, it was not possible to calculate a response rate. The contacts could come from organizations like current or former customers, associations, daughter companies, and so on. Some of the participants could come from the partners' own organization, as long as they were not directly involved in APOSDLE or had participated in Phase 1. However, the maximum proportion of participants from the partners' own organization shouldn't be more than 33%. The contact organizations received an instruction which explained the type of participant looked for. Suitable respondents were described as knowledge workers who spend at least 60% of their working time at a computer based workplace.

4.2.2 Procedure

The survey was based on insights from the first results of the study. Also, relevant literature about learning strategies at work was used in the design process of the survey. Although at the start of the survey the analysis of the data from Phase 1 of the study wasn't yet completed, it was clear that several factors of the model of [16] partly matched the first insights about used learning strategies. Therefore several statements were used in the survey to identify and validate used learning strategies from Phase 1. Overall the focus was again on identifying behaviour rather than attitudes.

For this paper the questions in which 100 points have to be allocated to several answer categories, the constant sum scale questions, are the most relevant. An example of this kind of question is:

> *When you consult colleagues, there are different ways to do it. If you had 100 points, how would you distribute them over the 4 ways listed below?*
> *Please base your distribution on the degree you actually use these ways to consult colleagues in your daily work. The way you use most frequently in these situations should receive most points. It is not necessary to distribute all 100 points.*
> *When I consult colleagues, I do that*
>   *by asking them face-to-face....... points*
>   *by using e-mail....... points*
>   *by calling them...... points*
>   *by writing a message on paper....... points*

In the second part of the survey, some general questions concerning personal information and general information about the organization had to be answered.

5 Results

In this section we present the results of the two phases for the research questions based. As they are based on different types of data, we start with an elaboration of the data collected.

5.1 Characteristics of the Sample

The unit of analysis for the data collected in Phase 1 is a *learning event,* which is defined as a situation during work when new information or knowledge is acquired that has a high likelihood to be (re)used in the future. These learning events were extracted from observations, interviews and diaries using a predefined coding scheme. To examine the reliability of the coding, a second coder coded a subset of 50 (see [18]) of all collected learning moments. Cohen's Kappa, which is suitable measure for nominal data, was obtained (.807). It turned out that 93% of the collected learning moments could be classified as learning events. Altogether 135 learning events were recorded.

The unit of analysis in Phase 2 is a *person* reporting in general terms about his/her learning experiences during work. We received 104 filled in questionnaires. Seven were not filled in completely for unknown reasons and were removed from the sample, leaving 97 questionnaires for the analysis. The goal of sampling was to obtain a reasonable distribution over several characteristics that extend the range of observations we made during Phase 1. The first, and probably most important factor, is the nature of the work of the respondents. We asked them to distribute 100 points over three different types of work related activities: developing new knowledge (for example, working in a research environment), pass on knowledge to others (for example, teaching), use obtained knowledge (for example, applying knowledge in engineering). Table 1 shows that the distribution over the three types is almost equal. This means that our survey covers respondents who are active in every type, excluding a bias to one of the types.

Table 1. Average number of points (out of 100) allocated to three types of knowledge work[4]

Types of knowledge work	Average number of points
Developing new knowledge	32
Passing on knowledge to others	32
Using obtained knowledge	38

As APOSDLE is focused on working and learning at a computer based workplace we asked the percentage of their time the respondents worked at such a workplace. Of the respondents, 91% spend 50% or more of their time at a computer based workplace. This makes the sample fit the target users of APOSDLE.

---

[4] Tables 1, 3, 5, 6 and 8 give the average number of points allocated out of 100 by the respondents. Respondents were not forced to allocate all 100 points.

Phase 1 of the study was mainly conducted at relatively small organizations. Our intention was to broaden the organizational scope of the study in the survey, so we asked for the size of the organization (see Table 2). From this table it is very clear that we succeeded: 66% of the respondents came from large organizations. This enables us to investigate whether the results of Phase 1 can be generalised to larger organizations.

Table 2. Size of the company

Company size	Percentage of answers
Small (<50 employees)	21 %
Medium (50-250 employees)	13 %
Large (>250 employees)	66 %

The three variables presented above are the key ones for assessing the nature of the sample. Based on this we can say that the sample to a very large extent satisfies our initial ideas about how it should look like for making a comparison with findings from Phase 1.

When making a comparison between results from Phase 1 and Phase 2, two issues must be taken into account. The most important caveat has to do with the nature of the data. In Phase 1 the unit of analysis is a reported or observed learning event. The unit of analysis in Phase 2 is a person, who does not report about one specific learning event but about general experiences during learning at the workplace. The second reason has to do with different ways of data collection. In the survey we used self-report questions, while in Phase 1 observations, interviews and diary reports were used which subsequently were coded. Though we tried to measure the same concepts in both Phases, we can't be sure that different ways of measuring the same concepts yield comparable outcomes.

5.2 Do People Learn Quite Frequently During Work?

In terms of collected data we cannot answer this question precisely as we did not keep a tally of "not learning at work". An indication can be found in the Phase 1 observation and diary data. Of the 138 learning events, 48 were observed during 62 observation sessions, each lasting 1 hour, which is an 0.77 hourly occurrence rate. In the diaries 71 learning events were reported in the submitted reports of 17 people over a time period of 6 weeks, though not covering all days in that period: about 11 learning events per week, or two a day. This indicates a lower incidence of learning events compared with the observations. Taking the observational data as the upper bound and the diary data as the lower bound, we can safely state that within this interval learning during work is a quite frequent.

5.3 Is Learning During Work Mainly Driven by the Work People Are Doing?

In the Phase 1 data we made a distinction between two "triggers" for a learning event: intentional (driven by the work the person is doing) and unintentional (driven by curiosity or coincidence). Of the recorded learning events, 75% were intentional and 25% unintentional, clearly indicating a preponderance of work(task) driven learning.

In the survey we asked people to distribute 100 points over three types of learning triggers. The results are shown in Table 3. Task driven learning dominates, but curiosity driven learning is more prevalent than in Phase 1. An explanation for this difference may be due to the presence of a larger number of people from large organizations.

Table 3. Average number of points (out of 100) allocated to three types of learning triggers (constant sum scale)

Learning triggers	Average number of points received
Driven by the task(s) I'm carrying out	50
Driven by my curiosity	34
Driven by coincidence	15

5.4 Do Bottlenecks Occur While Learning During Work?

From the data in Phase 1 we can first derive whether learning events were successful or not. Of the recorded learning events 72% were successful, 7% failed, 15% were not yet finished and 6% postponed. This indicates a reasonable success rate[5]. However, being successful does not imply that everything went smoothly. Of the recorded learning events 48% did not encounter any bottlenecks, but 52% did. Overall 104 bottlenecks were reported. Table 4 gives an overview of the most frequently reported bottlenecks.

Table 4. Bottlenecks participants experienced during learning events

Bottleneck category	Description	Frequencies
Interpersonal help seeking	Can't reach colleagues to help.	5
	Colleagues can't help (e.g. because of the specific nature of the question(s)	6
Information problems	The information is too specific for immediate use.	5
	Too much information (for example: needs to filter it to find the information looked-for, which costs time.)	7

---

[5] Though comparable data are hard to come by, this percentage is higher than the 50% reported by [19] whose data are about information search in general.

Table 4. (*continued*)

	The information is not sufficient to solve the problem.	8
	No information is available.	7
Search problems	Don't knowing exactly what it is you're looking for.	7
	Don't knowing exactly what it is important to know.	4
	Don't knowing exactly where to look for the information.	6
"Opportunity" problems	Not having enough time to learn.	7
	Not having access to all information.	5

Most problems seem to be related to information: there is too much information, the information is not sufficient to solve the problem or no information is available. Problems also occur often when people search information: it is unclear what has to be found, what is important to know or where the information can be found. Not having sufficient time to learn is also a problem that is mentioned frequently.

In the survey in Phase 2 we made a distinction between bottlenecks experienced when trying to find help from persons (Table 5) and when trying to find help in written material (Table 6).

Table 5. Average number of points (out of 100) allocated to three bottlenecks experienced in personal help seeking (constant sum scale)

Bottlenecks interpersonal help seeking	Average number of points received
I often don't know who knows what in our organization	23
Colleagues I consult are often too busy to help me	21
Colleagues often can't help me, question too specific	27

The differences between the three bottlenecks are small, indicating that the respondents experienced these bottlenecks almost equally. From Table 6 one can derive a strong need for more specific information that is delivered relatively fast. At the same time, either the sources in the own organization are insufficient or not well accessible.

5.5 Which Solutions Do People Use to Satisfy a Learning/Knowledge Need During Work?

In Phase 1 we recorded what kind of solutions people use to satisfy a learning/knowledge need during work. During one learning event several solutions could

Table 6. Average number of points (out of 100) allocated to four bottlenecks experienced in seeking help from written material (constant sum scale)

Bottlenecks seeking help from written material	Average number of points received
The information I find is often too general for immediate use	26
I often don't find helpful information in sources from my own organization	22
I often don't find helpful information in sources from outside my own organization	15
Trying to find something in written material often costs me too much time	29

be attempted. We found four solution categories: interpersonal help seeking, seeking help from paper based written material, seeking help from digital written material and practical application ("trial and error"). Interpersonal help seeking is used most frequently (70%). Digital written material, like PDF-articles, follows (63%). Paper based written material, like books or magazines, play a less important role (17%). Practical application, trying things out, is less used (16%). Clearly contacting people for helping is quite frequent. Which communication medium people use when contacting other people for help is shown in Table 7. It is not surprising that face-to-face communication is used most, followed by e-mail. The use of the phone is almost equal to the use of e-mail. Paper based media (for example written notes) are used rarely.

Table 7. Types of communication media used in learning events (N=194)

Types of communication media used	Frequency	Percentage
Face-to-face (like colleagues, a meeting)	119	61 %
E-mail	36	19 %
Phone call colleague	35	18 %
Paper based medium	4	2 %

For the survey data we cannot directly compare the used solution types. For technical reasons we asked the question for interpersonal help seeking using a constant sum scale, while for turning to digital material and practical application we used a 4-point rating scale asking whether the described situation is not similar or completely similar to what a respondent usually does. For interpersonal help seeking the option "I ask a colleague for assistance" received on average 73 points out of 100. This shows a substantial preference for contacting people close by. The similarity of turning to written material is 75% (very similar (42%) and completely similar (33%)).

The results for practical application are different. The "somewhat similar" category receives 44% of the responses, against 42% for "very similar" (34%) and "completely similar" (8%). Clearly interpersonal help seeking and turning to written material also dominate in the survey[6].

Table 8 shows how survey respondents distribute 100 points over different communication media to contact other people for interpersonal help seeking. As can be seen from Table 9 face-to-face contact is used most frequently, followed by E-mail and calling.

Table 8. Average number of points (out of 100) allocated to four types of communication media used in interpersonal help seeking (fixed sum scale)

Types of communication media used	Average number of points received
Face-to-face	45
E-mail	27
Phone call colleague	23
Paper based medium	3

6 Summary and Discussion

The research reported in this paper was arranged around four questions related to the assumptions behind the APOSDLE project. The data allow us to answer these questions and spell out the consequences for APOSDLE.

- **How frequently do people learn during work?** At computer based workplaces learning is ubiquitous. *Consequence for APOSDLE*: APOSDLE addresses a phenomenon that is widespread in many different organizations.
- **Are there bottlenecks when people learn during work?** Learning is currently overall reasonably successful, though bottlenecks are present. *Consequence for APOSDLE*: There is room for improvement, in particular in solving specific bottlenecks

- **What drives/triggers learning during work?** Workplace learning is strongly driven by work tasks, but learning driven by curiosity is also present. *Consequence for APOSDLE*: With the task related approach to learning support, APOSDLE fits into current practice. In addition, room must be present for not directly task related learning.

- **Which solutions do people use to satisfy a learning/knowledge need during work?** When seeking help, interpersonal help seeking using face-to-face contact is used most often. When seeking help from written material, digital sources are used most. *Consequence for APOSDLE*: APOSDLE needs to replicate, replace or supplement face-to-face contact. It should either have its own facilities for

---

[6] These results are overall in line with the ones reported by [20].

interpersonal help seeking or fit seamlessly and effortless into current tools and practices. Providing easy and tailored access to digital sources is important.

Overall we can say that the findings corroborate the four key assumptions behind the APOSDLE approach. Apart from the results reported in this paper, other results from the investigation will influence the design of subsequent APOSDLE prototypes.

As for similar system development projects which depend on a tight integration into organizational settings, this investigation can be seen as a very valuable addition to more common requirements elicitation procedures, which have the tendency to drift into wish lists for which not much empirical evidence can be mustered. Furthermore, a more detailed investigation using observations, interviews and diaries which can only be done in a limited number of organisations, can be fruitfully combined with a more survey oriented approach covering a wide range of organisations. However, there is a cost involved. Doing and reporting the research requires the investment of several person months of effort. Nonetheless, when planning projects, considering including a more detailed study into the empirical validity of its underlying assumptions about the state of the world should not be overlooked.

References

1. Grudin, J.: Why CSCW applications fail: Problems in the design and evaluation of organizational interfaces. In: Proceedings of the Conference on Computer-Supported Cooperative Work (CSCW '88), pp. 85–93. ACM, New York (1988)
2. Grudin, J.: Groupware and social dynamics: eight challenges for developers. Communications of the ACM 37(1), 93–105 (1994)
3. Vassileva, J., Deters, R., Greer, J., McCalla, G., Bull, S., Kettel, L.: Lessons from Deploying I-Help. In: Proceedings of the Workshop Multi-Agent Architectures for Distributed Learning Environments (AIED '2001), San Antonio, TX, USA, pp. 3–11 (2001)
4. Plowman, L., Rogers, Y., Ramage, M.: What are workplace studies for? In: Marmolin, H., Sunblad, Y., Schmidt, K. (eds.) Proceedings of the Fourth European Conference on Computer Supported Cooperative Work (ECSCW'95), pp. 309–324. Kluwer Academic Publishers, Dordrecht (1995)
5. Lindstaedt, S.N., Mayer, H.: A Storyboard of the APOSDLE Vision. In: Nejdl, W., Tochtermann, K. (eds.) EC-TEL 2006. LNCS, vol. 4227, pp. 628–633. Springer, Heidelberg (2006)
6. Collin, K.: Connecting work and learning: design engineers' learning at work. Journal of Workplace Learning 18(7/8), 403–413 (2006)
7. Twidale, M.B.: Over the shoulder learning: supporting brief informal learning. Computer Supported Cooperative Work 14(6), 505–547 (2005)
8. Hiemstra, R.: Self-directed learning. In: Husen, T., Postlethwaite, T.N. (eds.) The International Encyclopedia of Education, 2nd edn. Pergamon Press, Oxford (1994)
9. Livingstone, D.W.: Adults' Informal Learning: Definitions, Findings, Gaps and Future Research. Position paper for the Advisory Panel of Experts on Adult Learning, Applied Research Branch, Human Resources Development Canada (2001)

10. Olgren, C.: Learning Strategies for Learning Technologies. In The Strategic Use of Learning Technologies. New Directions for Adult and Continuing Education, no. 88, edited by E. J. Burge, pp. 7–16. San Francisco: Jossey-Bass (2000)
11. Hiemstra, R.: Self-directed adult learning. In: de Corte, E., Weinert, F.E. (eds.) International Encyclopedia of developmental and instructional psychology, pp. 771–777. Pergamon, Oxford/New York (1996)
12. Montalvo, F.T., Torres, M.C.G.: Self-regulated learning: current and future directions. Electronic Journal of Research in Educational Psychology 2(1), 1–34 (2004)
13. Warr, Allan, Bidi: Predicting three levels of training outcome. Journal of Occupational and Organizational Psychology 72(3), 351–375 (1999)
14. Eraut, M.: Non-formal learning and tacit knowledge in professional work. British Journal of Educational Psychology 70, 113–136 (2000)
15. Holsapple, C.W., Joshi, K.D.: A Knowledge Management Ontology. In: Holsapple, C.W. (ed.) Handbook on Knowledge Management, vol. 1, pp. 89–124. Springer, Heidelberg (2003)
16. Holman, D., Epitropaki, O., Fernie, S.: Short research note. Understanding learning strategies in the workplace: A factor analytic investigation. Journal of Occupational and Organizational Psychology 74, 675–681 (2001)
17. Rieman, J.: A field study of exploratory learning strategies. ACM Transactions on Computer-Human Interaction 3(3), 189–218 (1996)
18. Skalski, P.D.: Resource C: Computer content analysis. In: Neuendorf, K. (ed.) The content analysis guidebook, Sage Publications, Thousand Oaks, CA (2002)
19. Feldman, S.: The high cost of not finding information. KMWorld 13(3) (2004)
20. Bartlett, J.: Knowing people. Knowledge management (2000)

E-Learning on the Social Semantic Information Sources

Sebastian Ryszard Kruk, Adam Gzella, Jarosław Dobrzański,
Bill McDaniel, and Tomasz Woroniecki

Digital Enterprise Research Institute
National University of Ireland, Galway
IDA Business Park, Galway, Ireland
firstname.lastname@deri.org

Abstract. E-Learning grows on the fertile soil of the Internet technologies; it fails, however, to reach their full potential. With new, emerging technologies of the second generation Internet there is even more to be captured and adopted: knowledge sharing with blogs, wikis, and social bookmarking services. In this article we argue that those technologies can be adapted to improve user experience in e-Learning; we present an online social bookmarking system called Social Semantic Collaborative Filtering (SSCF). SSCF supports SIOC (Semantically-Interlinked Online Communities) metadata which ultimately transforms it in to a browser of blogs, fora, and other community sites. We show how a digital library system, such as JeromeDL, utilising this technology can be used in the e-Learning process, which takes advantage of recent research in the Internet.

1 Introduction

The Internet brings many changes to our lives; it helps to build an information society; it is sought to be a remedy for various problems, a new way of delivering various services. One of the services, however, which has not been facilitated by the Internet is e-Learning [20]; even though one can learn over the Internet, the style does not usually suit this new communication medium. The new, better Internet emerges through technologies, such as Semantic Web [2] or Web 2.0 [21]; the divergence with e-Learning, however, can become even more perceptible, unless the new technologies will be adopted to support e-Learning [26].

The new internet technologies, Semantic Web and Web 2.0, could be seen as competing solutions; the former focuses on delivering machine-processable content; the latter one defines collaborative computing services, such as wikis or blogs. Those technologies can be, however, combined [17] into a one, dynamic social semantic information source [7,15]; e-Learning needs to leap-frog to using these new technologies in the most productive way.

In this article we present one possible e-Learning solution based on the social semantic information sources; we do not, however, claim that our solution is complete, but we expect it to be complemented with a number of other solutions, such as dynamic learning material assembling [26].

E. Duval, R. Klamma, and M. Wolpers (Eds.): EC-TEL 2007, LNCS 4753, pp. 172–186, 2007.

1.1 Use Case Scenario

Our motivation scenario finds John (see Fig. 1), a high school teacher, preparing a new course on biology for his class; his students, however, live in a number of small villages across the county; they attend classes over the Internet and they only meet twice a year for the exams.

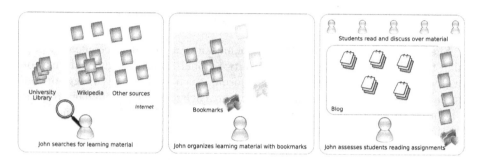

Fig. 1. Use Case Scenario - John, a lecturer, prepares lessons for his students

John's course on biology consists of 15 lectures; each lecture is assisted with reading material. John would like to easily distribute the reading material related to each lesson a week in advance, no sooner, no later; he would like to make sure his students will read and understand delivered information. Furthermore he would like to pre-assess students based on their reading assignments and their comprehension of given material; additionally, he would like to pass the knowledge gathered by the current students to the next year's students.

John finds that most of the materials he would like to deliver to the students comes either from university library, Wikipedia, and other online sources. He also discovers that some bookmark sharing systems can help him with material delivering process. John decides to use a blogging platform to gather students opinions and references on the read material; he will assess his students' reading assignments based on their activity. The blog will also gather students' knowledge, which will be passed to next year's students.

John is quite pleased with his solution; he understands the potential of informal sources of knowledge, such as digital libraries, Wikipedia, bookmarks sharing, and blogs. He noticed, however, that using so many different services is time-consuming: he needs to discover the resources with different search features, and to bookmark them locally; than he copies bookmarks to shared space on the Internet bookmarking service; finally, he has to create a blog entry for each reading material item. John wishes there was an easier and more productive way.

1.2 Related Work

Blogs [3,1] has recently become a major mean of the free publishing; they are used by many people to tell about their everyday life. Blogs are being applied to the commercial and political world [23]; companies use blogs to inform their clients about new product releases; politicians communicate through blogs with their electors. Blogs are also considered as one of the additional sources of e-Learning material [12]. Since blogs can be rich sources of information a number of research activities has been initiated to enrich blogs with semantic technologies. SemiBlog [19] allows users to link other resources related to the blog post, and semantically annotate the blog and the references. Cayzer [6] presents how blogs can be used to create a collective knowledge space. Finally, initiatives, such as the SIOC project [5], allow to export blogging metadata for further processing in semantic applications.

Sharing knowledge through social bookmarking services has become very popular; their implementations adapt one of two models: sharing tagged information or sharing folders with bookmarks. The former, such as del.icio.us[1], digg[2] or connotea[3], allow users to assign keywords (*tags*) to each resource they find interesting. The latter enables users to collaboratively filter information [8] by transcluding eachothers' folders [15]. A number of scenarios have been discussed for using online social bookmarking in enterprises [18]. Intriguing social aspects of sharing knowledge through social bookmarking have initiated research on the folksonomies [17] and data mining on social relations between bookmarks and users [25].

Social networks and semantic technologies are starting to be adopted by the e-Learning solutions [11]. Collaborative learning [22] is presented as a low cost model. The Didaskon project [26] delivers a course composition solution based on semantic annotations and social interactions. E-Learning has also gained focus from the digital libraries community; by adapting semantic web and social networking technologies digital libraries, such as JeromeDL [16], are becoming rich sources of e-Learning material [24,26].

1.3 Contribution

This paper contributes to the subject of e-Learning and research on the online social networks:

- it presents how a digital library can be combined with services providing access to social semantic information sources;
- it exemplifies how modern e-Learning can benefit from a digital library system using semantic web and social technologies.

1.4 Outline

This article is structured as follows. The next section presents how knowledge can be created using online community portals, such as blogs or fora. Section 3 describes how knowledge can be shared among members of the social network; followed by section 4 which presents how a knowledge repository can be extended to utilize social semantic information sources. Finally, section 6 describes

---

[1] Del.icio.us: http://del.icio.us/

[2] Digg: http://digg.com

[3] Connotea: http://www.connotea.org/

future research planned by the authors of this paper; followed by conclusions in section 7.

2 Creating Knowledge in Online Communities

Online services, such as blogs, boards, or fora are based on collaborative contributions and interactions between the members of the online community. Users create a social network where they feel free to band together: share ideas and opinions, publish links and works, and comment them. Everything can be annotated and shared; therefore, a lot of relevant data are passed around. In fact, online communities live by virtue of users working together. Members can, based on given opinions, read a better article, watch a better movies, or bake an even more tasty cake by using a proven recipe. An online community becomes a powerful source of informal knowledge; this knowledge, harvested from the online communities, play a great role in the learning process.

It is easy to get lost among all information gathered. Users, however, can easily get lost, while navigating through this vast information space; without dedicated solutions they are presented with a garbage information. Online communities are also scattered in the Internet, and isolated from each other; it may be difficult to effectively harness relevant information [5].

SIOC[4] [5] is a framework for interconnecting online communities. SIOC can be used in publish or subscribe mechanisms; it stores community metadata, such as information about the post's author, enclosed links, the creation time, and connections with other posts. The core of SIOC framework is the SIOC ontology which is based on RDF [13]. The most essential concepts, defined in the SIOC ontology, are *Site, Forum, Post, Usergroup, User* [19]. A site, represented with a *Site* concept, is the location of an online community or a set of communities. *Forum* is a discussion area, housed on a site, where *posts* are published. A post can be an article, a message or an audio- or videoclip. Each post has an author, a member of an online community, represented by a *User* concept. Then, *Usergroup* is a set of accounts of users interested in a common subject matter.

After the success of the first version of the ontology, the SIOC community decided to expand the ontology with support for other collaborative services; it is now possible express data from services, such as wikis, image galleries, event calendars, address books, audio and video channels.

SIOC allows to exchange communit data by importing and exporting information to/from different native vocabularies. SIOC-enabled sites take advantage of exchanging relevant information with other SIOC-enabled services. SIOC allows perform cross-site queries, topic related searches and importing SIOC data from other sites. SIOC can also provide statistics mechanism, e.g., to find the most active user. Finally, SIOC metadata can be detected by using crawlers or using browser plugins [4].

In the world of classic literature and classic teaching methods brick and mortal libraries were always perceived as the source of high quality information; this

---

[4] Semantically-Interlinked Online Communities: http://sioc-project.org/

situation did not change much in the era of the Internet, digital libraries and e-Learning. The next generation Internet, however, is a convergence between social communication and semantically-rich information; therefore, it is pushing the goal posts for libraries even further. Digital libraries can no longer be *only* libraries; in order to serve the next generations of users they need to become isomorphic with other Internet services; they need to adapt both semantic web and social networking technologies, to continue their mission.

Digital libraries boast high quality information; their content, however, remains virtually immune to the knowledge acquired by readers; they are unable to pass the knowledge to other readers in forms other than "word of mouth". One of possible solutions is to allow users to extend the information space related to each resource with their own comments and thoughts; a blog or a forum platform can be integrated with a digital library system for that purpose. Users' comments, on library resources, in a form of blog responses can be integrated with other social semantic information sources, by exposing information using SIOC metadata, or similar. As a result, current readers can easily deliver new knowledge for future readers; this contribution, however, does not have to be constrained library world only; other users can facilitate this knowledge using SIOC aggregation services like PingSemanticWeb.com.

3   Sharing Knowledge in Social Networks

A social network is a set of people, with some pattern of interactions or "ties" between them [10]. A social network is modelled by a digraph, where nodes represent individuals; a directed edge between nodes indicates a direct relationship between two individuals.

In our scenario, John and his students are connected in one social network. Each individual has different interests, very often has more knowledge on one subject then the others. John can be seen as an expert in the subject (biology) he teaches. The main aim of the Social Semantic Collaborative Filtering (SSCF) [15] is to allow users to save the knowledge and share it with others.

Users maintain their private collections of bookmarks to the interesting, valuable resources. In other words, each user gathers, filters, and organises a small part of knowledge. What is important, SSCF allows a user to share this knowledge with others within a social network; one could easily import friends' bookmarks and utilise their expertise and experience in specific domains of knowledge.

In SSCF users collect the bookmarks and store them in special directories; each directory is semantically annotated using a popular taxonomies, such as WordNet [9], DMoz[5] or DDC. They can be used to determine the content of the directory or to find the correct one. A student is able to easily find the subject or the topic, which she or he is interested in, related to the course that she or he attends to.

Another important aspect is the security in the SSCF. Very often users collect information that should be shared only within specific group of people: closest

---

[5] http://dmoz.org/

friends, class mates, students, etc. SSCF allows users to set fine grained access rights for every directory; access control is based on the distance and the friendship level between friends in the social network. For example, a resource can be shared only with friends with distance not bigger than two and at least 50% friendship level. *Distance not bigger than two* refers to maximal two degrees of separation between the owner and the requester. Friendship level is an extension to the FOAF model introduced with FOAFRealm [14] which allows users to express how well one person knows, or trusts, another. For example 0% can be interpreted as *Never met*, and 100% as *the best friend*. A user could freely set this value, according to her/his feelings. Friendship level between indirect friends is computed by multiplying the values on the path.

In our scenario John is able to share resources concerning the specific part of the course just after this part was introduced. With SSCF it is possible to have all bookmarks ready before starting the course. Initially all directories, one for each part of a course, have a strict access policy, so none of the students can access them. During the course John changes the access rights on the directories; students can easily find and import interesting bookmarks. They are able to broaden their knowledge in the topic that is currently taught at John's course.

4 Knowledge Repository on Social Semantic Information Sources

We have introduced the SIOC standard for knowledge creation (see Sec 2); we have presented possible ways of using it in online communities. We have presented SSCF (see Sec. 3) and explained how it can be used for knowledge sharing. In this section, we will show how we incorporate SIOC into SSCF and into the Social Semantic Digital Library - JeromeDL.

4.1 Problem Solution

The goal of Social Semantic Collaborative Filtering (SSCF) is to enhance individual bookmarks with shared knowledge within a community.

A user is given a chance to annotate directories of bookmarks with semantic information. Resources stored in one's bookshelf (collections of directories and bookmarks) can be browsed by his or her friends, who are interested in a particular subject and are allowed to access it. Furthermore, contents of directories one has access to can be easily imported to his or her own bookshelf. Users can include information from different friends by importing their directories into her/his own.

The knowledge is based on the bookmarks of interesting and valuable books, articles or other materials. SSCF can be used to bookmark various types of resources, e.g., those provided by digital libraries; a digital library with SSCF can act as a knowledge repository. We can share bibliographic resources through the social network; this information can be enhanced with knowledge from other community portals, which also use SSCF service.

4.2   Bookmarking Community-Based Content

In the current Web, blogs become more and more popular. There are many different types of blogs; sometimes, they are published by a person with a good expertise in a certain domain. A lot of knowledge is also delivered through the Web fora; the discussions are topic-oriented. They, very often, contain solutions to problems, or point to other interesting posts, which add valuable views in to the debate. Such sources are rich in knowledge; therefore, it is crucial to use their potential. So far SSCF had no mean for utilising information sources like blogs or fora.

We have delivered such features by incorporating SIOC into SSCF model and SSCF bookmarks interface (see Fig. 2). There is a special directory dedicated for storing SIOC data in a private bookshelf. This catalogue can maintain three types of SIOC concepts (see Sec. 2); users can bookmark posts, or whole fora or sites. For each resource, it is possible to browse the content. The SIOC-specific resources behave just like classic SSCF ones; a user can copy a SIOC entry and paste it into another SSCF directory. This way, a standard knowledge repository is enriched with community based content.

In our scenario John was using a separate bookmarking tool for saving the links to the resources from the digital library and links to community sources (blogs). SSCF used in a digital library and enriched with SIOC creates the

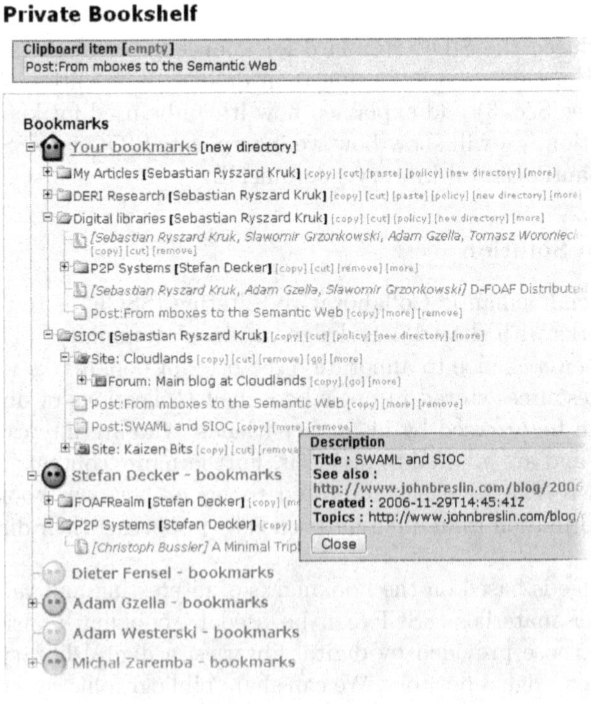

Fig. 2. SSCF Bookmarks interface with SIOC resource browsing

first step to the better knowledge repository. John can browse resources, then bookmark them, and finally incorporate knowledge from other interesting sources from the Internet in one place.

4.3 Resources Annotations

In our scenario John has shared with students some material from a digital library; for each material he had to create a blog entry, where he was gathering the comments from students. With SSCF annotations and evaluations component, each library resource becomes blog post; users can comment on the resource directly in the digital library.

This solution brings a lot of opportunities for John; he can now track the progress of assimilating the material by the students; he knows their opinion on a specific resource. Furthermore, every student's comment enriches the learning material with additional knowledge. This knowledge can be utilised by the next year's students. Year by year this will bring a broader and more complete view of a specific resource or topic.

SSCF annotations and evaluations component uses SIOC vocabulary. Every comment is saved as a SIOC resource (*sioc:Post*) and can be exported with semantic description. This can be reused later on in other pages or services. We can also display the comments on the resources in the SSCF bookmarks interface. It is an easy way to explore in one place the comments for many different and interesting, bookmarked by a member of the social network, resources.

4.4 Knowledge Repository

Our solution allows John to incorporate in one place the digital library, social semantic bookmarking service and the semantic blog. John can store the resources required in his course, find and bookmark links to other interesting resources. These resources can be then shared with students in the correct order. Students are able to comment the resources in a blog-style discussion; the students are able to share and import the bookmarks to the bibliographic or community based resources, and browse all the bookmarks and resource comments with one interface.

5   JeromeDL - Social Semantic Digital Library

JeromeDL [16] is a Digital Library with semantics; it uses the SSCF component (see Sec. 4) for knowledge aggregation and sharing. Every library user can bookmark interesting books, articles or other materials in semantically annotated directories. Users can share them with others within a social network. We enriched the standard SSCF browser with the ability to bookmark and browse community based data. JeromeDL also has a feature which allows it to treat a single library resource as a blog. With SIOC based annotations users can to comment the content of the resource and in this way create a new knowledge.

5.1   Integration Process

The application and technologies mentioned in the paper are based on the Semantic Web technology. JeromeDL and SSCF are built upon the Semantic Web standards, they store and exchange RDF data. JeromeDL and SSCF define an ontology which describes how the information is organised and how resources are related to each other.

The role of SIOC is slightly different; the SIOC project defines an ontology that can be used to describe the community-based content on the Web. Information on blogs and fora described with SIOC is easier to find and connects with other sources. Applying SIOC to the Web resources increases their interoperability.

To achieve our goals and build the social semantic digital library we had to:

1. Support the SIOC ontology in both JeromeDL and SSCF – since both applications use RDF, for storing and exchanging information, SIOC information is handled on the data (RDF) level.
2. Align the SIOC ontology with existing ontologies – the knowledge added by the users of digital library is saved with SIOC concepts.

SIOC ontology support. In our social semantic digital library users can bookmark an interesting post, forum or site by giving its URL. We use SIOC Browser[6], which takes the URL of the post, forum or site, to access RDF with SIOC metadata about the given URL. The description is filtered out from unnecessary information which could make the bookshelf unclear and difficult to browse. All relevant data is saved in the SSCF RDF repository.

The SSCF module which generates the bookmarks tree was enhanced to be able to display SIOC information. As we already mentioned (see Sec. 4.2) the SIOC-based items are saved in a special directory and can be browsed just like the standard SSCF resources; they can be freely pasted into the bookmarks directories. The interface is based on AJAX technology, so all actions on bookmarks or directories are performed in a real time, without reloading the browser window.

In JeromeDL users can annotate and evaluate the resources. Our implementation is based on the integration with SIOC ontology (see Sec 4.3). Annotations and Evaluations are stored as a SIOC:Posts (with limited number of properties, see Tab. 1) in an RDF repository. JeromeDL displays this information in the resource description page. Therefore, each resource can be treated as a blog post. A registered user can comment on a resource or others notes the same way he used to annotate a generic post on a blog or a forum. Consequently, relying on the community opinions, a user filter out a proper resource out of many.

The annotation mechanism was implemented in the AJAX technology. When user reads a resource, she/he can read summarises of the discussion threads as well. The thread could be expanded to show the full content of the comment and all the possible replies. A user can write her/his own annotation or reply to the existing one. It is also possible to export the annotations in SIOC RDF.

---

[6] http://sparql.captsolo.net/browser/browser.py?url=URL

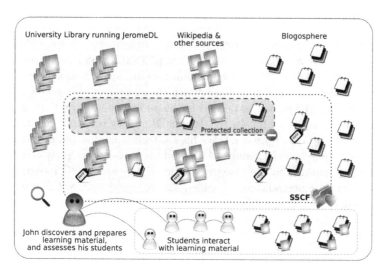

Fig. 3. John prepares lectures with SSCF and JeromeDL

Table 1. Aligning SIOC:Post concepts with the information about the annotations in JeromeDL

Class or property name	Description
sioc:Post	Annotation of the resource
dc:title	Title of the post
sioc:related_to	Points to the annotated resource
dc:description	Body of the annotation
dcterms:created	When the annotation was created
sioc:has_creator	Author of the annotation
sioc:has_reply	Represents a reply for that annotation

Ontology alignment To fully utilise the benefits of JeromeDL and SSCF integration with SIOC we needed a compliance of the used ontologies. The main reason for doing this would be the ability to expose the information gathered in JeromeDL (especially in resources blogs) in an understandable SIOC format. We achieve that by creating some content using SIOC metadata and delivery mediation mechanism for other SSCF/JeromeDL content (see Fig. 4).

A module for annotating and evaluating the content in JeromeDL uses the SIOC:Post class for representing the information in RDF. There is no need to map or translate this resources; they are ready to be exported.

The rest of the classes in SSCF and JeromeDL ontologies required mapping to the SIOC ontology. A JeromeDL instance is presented as a site containing the fora; a forum represents the resource in the digital library - JeromeDL's book concept. Directory, the SSCF class, can also be seen as a Forum or as a Site (a root directory). A user (Person) is translated to SIOC:User; the Resource is simply mapped into SIOC:Post concept.

5.2   Evaluation

We have created a complete answer to the problem stated in the scenario (see Fig. 3). Based on JeromeDL we have built a platform that joins three separate applications: digital library, blog and bookmarking application. Eventually we created a social semantic digital library, which answers John's needs; is a place where he can keep the resources needed for his biology course and any additional materials which can help him. In the JeromeDL, every resource becomes a blog (with SIOC support), so John can track his students opinions and progress. SSCF incorporated into JeromeDL, allows John and his students to freely create, share and import bookmarks to the resources. With SSCF and SIOC integration also community based materials can be added and browsed with SSCF interface.

Integration of services provided by JeromeDL platform clearly decreases effort needed for completing the described scenario. We present a simplified comparison of times (see Fig. 5) required to perform a sequence of activities done by John in order to prepare the course. Using JeromeDL with SSCF component, it takes roughly half the time, to perform all necessary actions, than by using standard, separate solutions.

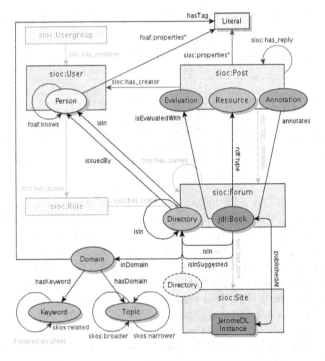

Fig. 4. Alignment of SSCF and SIOC ontology

John finds out that working with an integrated platform such as JeromeDL is less time consuming. He spends less time on logging-in to different systems and searching through them. John can immediately bookmark resources and start a blog about them, without copying or linking to other systems.

To summarise, JeromeDL became a service that allows users to keep old and create new knowledge. It is a tool that can be very helpful in many domains, especially in e-Learning. JeromeDL is a place where a community meets and individuals influence each other.

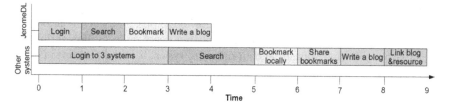

Fig. 5. Comparison of time required for performing a task with JeromeDL and other systems

6 Future Work

Currently, we are developing SSCF into a few directions. One of them is turning SSCF, enriched with SIOC, into a universal bookmarking tool for the Internet.

SSCF will offer many interesting features that are currently not part of Web bookmarking applications. One of these is a fine grained access rights control to the bookmarks. For instance, a user can share a directory only with her/his closest friends, other directories with co-workers, or the family. In almost all current bookmarking services it is not possible as they allow a user to only say that some of bookmarks are private or public.

Another interesting SSCF feature is connected to the SIOC integration. A user is able to take advantage of semantically enabled blogs and easily, with one click, insert them into the bookmarks structure with all related information. The blog can then be browsed from the bookmarks interface level and blogs, fora and posts can be freely mixed with standard Internet bookmarks.

In the further stream of development, SSCF is separated from the FOAFRealm project and moved into the new project called Social Semantic Search and Browsing (S3B). S3B will consist of SSCF, multifaceted browsing and query expansion modules. It will play a service role to other applications in which developers would like to use advanced methods of search and retrieval. It will be based on SOA (Service-Oriented Architecture) layer and will use REST Web Services approach. It will expose the features of SSCF to other applications in a simple and clear way, based on the HTTP protocol and unique identifiers of resources.

7 Conclusions

The integration of social semantic information services into an e-Learning architecture provides capabilities that have not existed to date. e-Learning needs new models of interaction and knowledge sharing to move beyond the existing page turner style of systems. A more collaborative architecture is needed to provide tomorrow's students with learning environments that mirror the data rich, virtual community driven world they live in.

Social semantic information services provide this collaborative architecture. They support the complex interactions which learners can use to trade information, express knowledge, achieve consensus and synthesise knowledge from e-Learning environments.

An example of this is the synthesis of knowledge possible when collaboration is supported in a semantic fashion. As multiple users collect information on a subject, from differing sources and in differing types, a social semantic network can be enabled which aids in the correlation and validation efforts of the users. For example, video clips being harvested from the web on a topic such as procedures in a bio lab can be correlated with another user's collection of bookmarks to Wikipedia articles, university class notes, and online e-books. Another user collects still images of related techniques. The semantic nature of their collaboration environment then aids them in associating the This supports validation or usefulness of materials by illuminating the relationships between the learning objects and by isolating those which do not pertain or which cannot be confirmed through a resolution with other elements

In a business context, a task team in an organisation would use such a semantically powered community environment to interrelate policy documents to historical operations. For example, one user collects invoices and accounts payable documents while another researches corporate policy documents on compliance and governance. The semantic nature of the collaboration environment (SIOC, SSCF, and JeromeDL) provides the ability to interrelate the policy documents (large, unstructured, and with the knowledge deeply encoded in language) with the business documents (small, structured, and with more precise records of events).

This works if both types of documents are tagged with semantic information either as they are being reviewed or, more preferably, when they are being stored. The best way for this tagging to be accomplished remains an open problem, but SIOC and SSCF provide ways forward.

Both examples (and the story of John elsewhere in this paper) result in synthesis of knowledge. At the outset, the community has a rather scattered and disconnected set of knowledge. At the completion, it has been correlated and what has emerged is not only the better organised dataset, but new knowledge about the relationships between the components, a consensus view from the community as to what elements are important and which are valid and which are in-valid. From that view, the entire community is better aware of the knowledge that was, before the effort, hidden not just in the documents and images and videos, but hidden in their lack of connectedness.

If this approach is applied to an e-Learning task, one sees formal learning objects distributed in a learning space. Instructors posed with the task of creating a course about the specifics of a topic (business compliance policy for example)

can collaborate to build examples and exercises, reusing resources and being better assured that the results are both accurate and relevant. Students can form collaborative communities to study the formal source material thus created, followed by dynamic exercises using the same original objects from the semantic digital library. Finally, the now trained personnel can use the same collaborative environment to research and extract knowledge from the live data and documents. The semantically powered environments for collaboration extends from the trainer to the trainee to the professional.

Acknowledgments

This material is based upon works supported by Enterprise Ireland under Grant No. ILP/05/203. Authors would like to thank Uldis Bojars, John Breslin and Stefan Decker for help and fruitful discussions.

References

1. Bausch, P., Haughey, M., Hourihan, M.: We Blog: Publishing Online with Weblogs. John Wiley & Sons, Inc. Chichester (2002)
2. Berners-Lee, T., Hendler, J., Lassila, O.: The semantic web. Scientific American Magazine (2001)
3. Blood, R.: The Weblog Handbook: Practical Advice on Creating and Maintaining Your Blog. Perseus Books Group (2002)
4. Bojars, U., Breslin, J., Passant, A.: Sioc browser - towards a richer blog browsing experience. In: Accepted for the 4th Blogtalk Conference (Blogtalk Reloaded), Vienna, Austria (2006)
5. Breslin, J.G., Harth, A., Bojars, U., Decker, S.: Towards semantically-interlinked online communities. In: 2nd European Semantic Web Conference 2005 (2005)
6. Cayzer, S.: Semantic blogging and decentralized knowledge management. Commun. ACM 47(12), 47–52 (2004)
7. Decker, S., Frank, M.R.: The networked semantic desktop. In: Proc. WWW Workshop on Application Design, Development and Implementation Issues in the Semantic Web, New York City (2004)
8. Fanjiang, T., Congrong, L., Wang, D.: Evolving information filtering for personalized information service. J. Comput. Sci. Technol. 16(2), 168–175 (2001)
9. Fellbaum, C.: WordNet An Electronic Lexical Database. MIT Press, Cambridge (1998)
10. Fukui, H.O.: SocialPathFinder: Computer Supported Exploration of Social Networks on WWW (2003)
11. Harden, R.: E-learning and all that jazz. Medical Teacher 24(1), 120–120 (2002)
12. Should all learning professionals be blogging?
http://learningcircuits.blogspot.com/
13. Resource Description Framework (RDF). W3C Recommendation (1999),
http://www.w3.org/TR/rdf
14. Kruk, S.R.: FOAF-Realm - control your friends access to the resource. In: FOAF Workshop proceedings (2004)

15. Kruk, S.R., Decker, S., Gzella, A., Grzonkowski, S., McDaniel, B.: Social semantic collaborative filtering for digital libraries. Journal of Digital Information. Special Issue on Personalization (2006)

16. Kruk, S.R., Decker, S., Zieborak, L.: JeromeDL - Adding Semantic Web Technologies to Digital Libraries. In: Andersen, K.V., Debenham, J., Wagner, R. (eds.) DEXA 2005. LNCS, vol. 3588, Springer, Heidelberg (2005)

17. Mika, P.: Ontologies are us: A unified model of social networks and semantics. In: Gil, Y., Motta, E., Benjamins, V.R., Musen, M.A. (eds.) ISWC 2005. LNCS, vol. 3729, pp. 522–536. Springer, Heidelberg (2005)

18. Millen, D.R., Feinberg, J., Kerr, B.: Dogear: Social bookmarking in the enterprise. In: CHI '06: Proceedings of the SIGCHI conference on Human Factors in computing systems, pp. 111–120. ACM Press, New York (2006)

19. Moeller, K., Bojars, U., Breslin, J.G.: Using semantics to enhance the blogging experience. In: Sure, Y., Domingue, J. (eds.) ESWC 2006. LNCS, vol. 4011, pp. 679–696. Springer, Heidelberg (2006)

20. O'Nuallain, C., Grzonkowski, S.: Collaboration. In: Proceedings of the poster session of IADIS International Conference WWW/Internet 2006 (2006)

21. O'Reilly, T.: O'reilly network: What is web 2.0 (September 2005)

22. Rick, J., Guzdial, M., Holloway-Attaway, K.C.L., Walker, B.: Collaborative learning at low cost: Coweb use in english composition. In: Proceedings of CSCL 2002, Boulder, CO (2002)

23. Rogers, R.: Poignancy in the us political blogsphere. Aslib Proceedings 57(4), 356–368 (2005)

24. Shum, S.B., Motta, E., Domingue, J.: Scholonto: an ontology-based digital library server for research documents and discourse. Int. J. on Digital Libraries 3(3), 237–248 (2000)

25. Stoilova, L., Holloway, T., Markines, B., Maguitman, A.G., Menczer, F.: Givealink: mining a semantic network of bookmarks for web search and recommendation. In: LinkKDD '05: Proceedings of the 3rd international workshop on Link discovery, pp. 66–73. ACM Press, New York (2005)

26. Westerski, A., Kruk, S.R., Samp, K., Woroniecki, T., Czaja, F., O'Nuallain, C.: E-learning based on the social semantic information sources. In: Proceedings to LACLO 2006 (2006)

Capturing, Management and Utilization of Lifecycle Information for Learning Resources

Lasse Lehmann, Tomas Hildebrandt, Christoph Rensing, and Ralf Steinmetz

KOM - Multimedia Communications Lab, Technische Universität Darmstadt,
Merckstrasse 25, 64283 Darmstadt

Abstract. During their lifecycle, Learning Resources undergo a multitude of processes while being created, used, provided or re-used. However, in order to be reusable, a Learning Resource often has to be adapted to a new context of use. This in turn implies multiple Re-Authoring processes being performed on the Learning Resource. During all these processes different types of information emerge. When captured, this information can be helpful for a later on retrieval, use or re-use of the Learning Resources. In this work, the lifecycle of Learning Resources along with the information being generated herein is analyzed and a distributed architecture is proposed, that allows the capturing, processing, management and utilization of the named information in a generic way.

1 Introduction and Motivation

During their lifecycle, Learning Resources undergo a multitude of processes while being created, used, provided or re-used. All these processes generate information about the Learning Resource that is not taken into account in most systems. Besides, it is a widely accepted fact, that Learning Resources should be re-used in order to be efficient. However, a re-use of Learning Resources "as is", i.e. in an unchanged and not adapted shape is seldom possible. Learning Resources are mostly created in a specific context and with a high granularity. From a didactic point of view this surely makes sense [1]. However, the re-use of these resources is quite difficult. Usually it is inevitable to edit the Learning Resources, change or remove parts of them, add parts of other Learning Resources, update them or adapt the Learning Resources to new facts in order to re-use them [4] [13]. All these actions are subsumed by the concept of Re-Authoring and defined, described and classified in [13]. In the course of Re-Authoring processes a multitude of information about the resources taking part in these processes emerges and can be captured. Especially the relations that result from Re-Authoring processes are not considered by most existing approaches. Often, an adaptation or Re-Authoring of a Learning Resource is seen as the starting point of a new lifecycle of a new Learning Resource without taking the relations that connect both instances into account. Nevertheless, there is a multitude of situations where this additional information can be helpful. However, the captured information has to be organized and stored in order to be processible. Most existing systems do not support the capturing and storage of lifecycle information in a sufficient way and if so, the

E. Duval, R. Klamma, and M. Wolpers (Eds.): EC-TEL 2007, LNCS 4753, pp. 187–201, 2007.

information gets stuck at system borders. This paper proposes a system for the capturing, management and utilization of lifecycle information beyond system borders.

In section 2 of this paper our definition of a Learning Resource's lifecycle is presented and the information that is generated when a Learning Resource proceeds through this lifecycle is analysed. Additionally, possibilities for the utilization of lifecycle information are depicted. Section 3 addresses the storage of lifecycle information and proposes an extension for the well known LOM standard [8]. In section 4, a comprehensive architecture for the capturing, management and utilization of lifecycle information is described while section 5 covers the implementation of the proposed system in the course of the Content Sharing project [3]. Section 6 handles related work in this area and section 7 concludes this paper and gives an outlook on ongoing and future work on this topic.

2 Lifecycle Information

In this section the lifecycle of Learning Resources is analysed. Starting there from we identify two general types of lifecycle information that occur in the different stages of the lifecycle: *Relation* information and *context* information. After taking a closer look on both types, we close this section with an analysis of methods and approaches to utilize both kinds of information.

2.1 The Lifecycle of Learning Resources

In Figure 1 the lifecycle of a Learning Resource following our definition is shown. Learning Resources are created with authoring tools (*Authoring Phase*), before they are provided to customers, teachers or learners, e.g. in a learning object repository (*Provision Phase*). Finally they are used and utilized, which typically takes places in a learning management system (*Learning Phase*). However, in the majority of cases, the Learning Resources available in a repository do not fit the special needs of most customers or users who search for Learning Resources in repositories. In order to be reusable the Learning Resources have to be adapted to a new context of use. To cover this, the *Re-Authoring Phase* is introduced to the lifecycle model. By using Re-Authoring tools, existing Learning Resources can be unitized, adapted, updated and re-aggregated. Parts can be added to or removed from a Learning Resource or parts of different Learning Resources can be joined to form a new one. In Figure 2 an example for this whole process is depicted. At first, the existing Learning Resource E is disassembled. Thus, four new Learning Resources are generated (A, B, C and D). In this scenario, two of the newly generated resources are adapted to a new context (Adaptation), before the parts are put into a new order (Permutation) and, together with a new Learning Resource (H), put together to form the Learning Resource E' (Aggregation). This process is called Re-Purposing, because the original Learning Resource is changed to suit a new purpose. Re-Purposing is a special kind of Re-Authoring [7]. We distinguish two kinds of information being generated during the lifecycle of a Learning Resource: *Relation* and *Context* information. In the following we will discuss both concepts and analyse in which phases of the lifecycle which kinds of information occur.

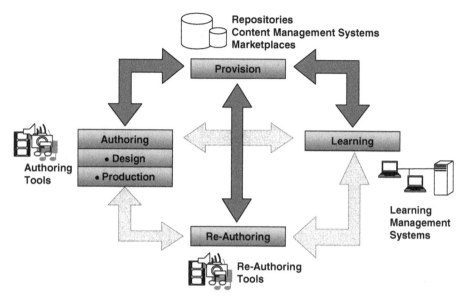

Fig. 1. The Lifecycle of Learning Resources

2.2 Relation Information

Relation information emerges in consequence to specific authoring or Re-Authoring actions performed by a user. A relation always connects two instances of a Learning Resource to each other. Regarding the lifecycle shown in Figure 1, relation information is mostly generated in the Authoring and the Re-Authoring phase, since these are the two phases where the content of the Learning Resources is actually changed. In some cases relations are build in other phases, too, e.g. when a Learning Resource is downloaded from a repository and thus a new version or instance of this Learning Resource is created. We have identified a set of relation types, being generated during the Authoring and Re-Authoring phase of the lifecycle model. These relation types are described in the following, before they are correlated to certain (Re-) Authoring actions.

Aggregation Relations or 'part of' relations result from the composition of several Learning Resources in order to get a new Learning Resource. Each of the composed Resources has than a 'part of' relation to the latter.

Sequence Relations exist between Learning Resources with a certain sequential order. Two consecutive Learning Resources are connected by a predecessor or successor relation respectively.

Permutation Relations connect two Learning Resources who consist of the same modules, while these modules have a different sequential order.

A Reduction / Extension Relationships occurs, when parts are removed from a Learning Resource. In that case the two versions of the Learning Resource are connected by an isReductionOf or rather isExtensionOf relation.

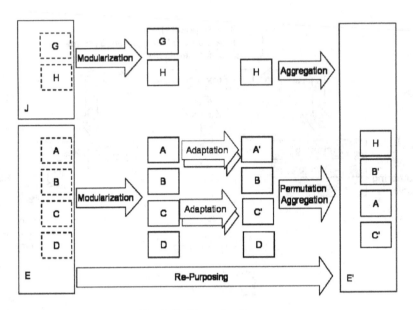

Fig. 2. Re-Purposing Process

Requirement Relations are created, when the processing of a Learning Resource requires the processing of a second Learning Resource.

Version Relations relate two instances of a Learning Resource in the same version history to each other. These relations occur, if a Learning Resource is only slightly changed, for example in order to correct errors or to update facts.

Variant Relations persist between different variants of a Learning Resource. Variants are branches in the version history of a Learning Resource. They mostly result from adaptation processes, like translations, layout adaptations or changes in the design of a Learning Resource, which transfer the Learning Resource to a different context of use.

In [11] and [16] Re-Authoring processes in general, as well as adaptation processes in particular, are defined. This encompasses 15 different adaptation processes used most often in practice. Each of these Re-Authoring and adaptation processes implies a certain type of relation information being generated. Table 1 gives an overview of these processes along with the information that occurs.

Updates and *Corrections* are Re-Authoring processes often performed, which implicate the creation of version relations. Examples for user actions inflicting these relations are the adaptation of the content to new circumstances like the introduction of the Euro currency or the correction of errors.

The *Modularization* of a Learning Resource implies that it is decomposed into a certain number of modules. Modules are, by definition, Learning Resources by themselves. The decomposition accounts for the generation of relation information like aggregation relations between the decomposed Learning Resource and each of the modules and sequential relations between consecutive modules.

Table 1. Re-Authoring Processes and implicated relation types

Re-Authoring	User Action	Generated Relation Types
Update	Update Learning Resource	Version
Correction	Correct errors	Version
Modularization	Decomposition	Aggregation / Sequence
Adaptation	e.g. Translation, provide Printability, provide Accessibility, Layout etc. see [16]	Variant, Reduction
Aggregation	Aggregation	Reduction / Extension / Permutation / Aggregation / Sequence

The *Adaptation* of a Learning Resource implies – as mentioned above – a Variant relationship between the source and the target Learning Resource of the adaptation process. A variant relation implies a heavier change of the Learning Resource than a version relationship does. A variant has its own version history that goes parallel to the other one. Version and Variant relationships are a little bit fuzzy by nature and very generic. Therefore the kind of adaptation that led to the generation of a variant or version should be taken into account, too. Thus the variant relation needs to by typed. The actual type of adaptation can easily be captured during the Re-Authoring process. It just has to be stored in a proper way.

Finally, the *Aggregation* process implies different types of relation information, like aggregation, permutation, reduction, sequence or permutation relations. In fact most of these relations occur during the whole Re-Authoring process, but since the Aggregation is often the last step of the whole process, the named relations can not be captured until the final aggregation has been performed.

2.3 Context Information

While relation information always connects two or more Learning Resources, context information is restricted to one Learning Resource and thus represents the context of one specific Learning Resource. It is generated implicitly, mainly during the usage or retrieval of a Learning Resource. Thus, it is mostly generated during the *Provision* and *Learning Phase*. An example for context information is the number of views a Learning Resource got in a repository or market place. Accordingly, the number of downloads or the number of times a Learning Resource was sold could represent valuable information. In a community based scenario ratings, comments or feedback messages are context information, too. In the Learning Phase several kinds of context information can be collected. The learning duration a learner took to learn a Learning Resource, the assessment statistics or the number of students who viewed or even failed the assessment of a certain Learning Resource are only few of the many different types of information that can be collected. Naturally even in the authoring or Re-Authoring phase there is context information to capture, e.g. the time a Learning Resource has been edited, which editor was used or by whom it was edited. Even feedback from learners or other authors related to a Learning Resource is context information in our opinion. The concept "Attention Metadata", sometimes called "Contextualized Attention Metadata", is comparable to what we call context information (see section 6).

2.4   Utilization of Lifecycle Information

There are several possibilities for the utilization auf lifecycle information. The identification of new ways to support authors, learners, providers or just plain users of Learning Resources is an ongoing process. We implemented capturing mechanisms for lifecycle information in our combined repository / authoring tool ResourceCenter [7]. In [9] we present several utilization approaches, including the ranking of Learning Resources and the provision of links to related Resources. There are several approaches trying to help in finding resources that are somehow structurally or semantically related to a target resource. This can be made a lot easier, if the relations between Learning Resources are actually captured when they emerge. Figure 3 shows an example for the utilization of relation information we implemented in the ResourceCenter. Here, related Learning Resources and instances are linked on the overview page of a Learning Resource.

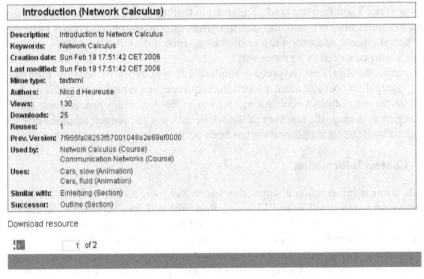

Fig. 3. Utilization of Relation Information in the ResourceCenter

A few examples and ongoing work regarding the utilization of lifecycle information in general is given in the following:

- Ranking search results for Learning Resources [9], [12]
- Recommendations for Learning Resources [12]
- Browsing along relations for better search results [9]
- Searching 'without' search terms [9]

- Finding structurally and semantically related Learning Resources (ongoing work)
- Extending information about learner behaviour for efficient learner modelling [10], [11]
- Support authors in authoring by aggregation by recommending Learning Resources with the help of the aggregation context (ongoing work)
- Collecting and providing feedback from learners and other authors to the authors of Learning Resources [14]
- Notification of authors about interesting updates or new Learning Resources through relation and context information (ongoing work)
- Update and consolidate metadata with context information (ongoing work)

3 Storage of Lifecycle Information

When lifecycle information is captured, it needs to be stored somewhere. This section describes a concept for the storage of both lifecycle and context information.

Since the Learning Object Metadata (LOM) Standard [8] is a widely used standard for metadata, we decided to use it as basis for the storage of relation based lifecycle information. LOM metadata consist of 9 categories with about 60 fields. The category that matches our interests best is category 7: Relation. In this category the storage of relation information is intended. It may consist of an arbitrary number of relation fields containing the ID of the resource the relationship exists to and the type of relation. However, the vocabulary, taken from the Dublin Core standard [15], that is intended to express the relationships in the LOM relation category is not sufficient to fulfil our needs specified in section 2. Therefore we developed our own vocabulary, which enables us to express our types of relations. Table 2 shows how the different kinds of relations are named.

Table 2. Relation types and their vocabulary

Relation Type	Vocabulary of the LOM Extension
Aggregation	haspart / ispartof
Sequence	ispredecessorof / issuccessorof
Permutation	ispermutationof
Reduction/Extension	isreductionof / isextensionof
Requirement	requires / isrequiredby
Version	hasversion / isversionof
Variante	hasvariant / isvariantof

As shown in section 2.2, variant and version relations need to be typed. Therefore we need to figure out a unique mapping to a certain aspect of change without changing the underlying LOM standard too much. The LOM standard itself is very rich and covers many aspects in respect of content. Therefore we can relate to these aspects and thus stay independent from the content of the Learning Resource itself. For this purpose, the relation category was extended by one field named *Changes*. This field exists for every relation and consists of a pointer and a value. The pointer points to the LOM metadata field that was changed by the process that led to the existence of the relation and the value depicts the old value of that field.

Thus, when a Learning Resource is translated from German to English, the value of the LOM field *General.Language* would change from '*de*' to '*en*'. The Changes field would then hold the pointer to *General.Language* as well as the old value: 'de'. Thus it is possible to reconstruct which relation implied which changes. In turn it is also possible to include the changes in the original Learning Resource in order to determine, which changes have been done to it, too. While it is especially helpful to type variant relations, other kinds of relations can be typed, too. The following figure shows an excerpt of a relation element depicting a reduction relation resulting from a change of the semantic density and learning duration of a Learning Resource.

```
<relation>
    <kind>
        <source>http://www.contentsharing.com/relation</source>
        <value>isreductionof</value>
    </kind>
    <resource>
        <identifier>
            <catalog>content_sharing</catalog>
            <entry>"modul1-uuid"</entry>
        </identifier>
    </resource>
    <changes>
        <date/>
        <categorie>educational</category>
        <dataelement>educational/typicalLearningTime</dataelement>
        <oldvalue>PT30M</oldvalue>
    </changes>
    <changes>
        <date/>
        <categorie>educational</category>
        <dataelement>educational/semanticalDensity</dataelement>
        <oldvalue>medium</oldvalue>
    </changes>
</relation>
```

Fig. 4. LOM Extension Excerpt

While relation information is independent from the application or context it was generated in and therefore it makes sense to store it within the metadata close to the Learning Resource itself, *context information* is highly dependent on the system it emerges in. That means that for example the number of views or queries for a Learning Resource in one marketplace might have a different meaning than in another marketplace or repository, due to the number of users, the number of Learning Resources provided or the target group. Therefore context information is stored in an independent format in a central instance. The schema for the storage of context information includes the identifier of the Learning Resource, the type of information - like sold, bought, downloaded, viewed, ... - and finally an identifier for the system the information was captured in. Thus it is possible to weight the captured context information accordingly.

4 Architecture

Form the different types of systems covering the different phases of a Learning Resource's lifecycle, like authoring tools, repositories or learning management systems, there are few, where lifecycle information is captured at all; and if it is captured, the captured information remains in these systems and gets stuck at system borders. Examples for information already being captured by some systems are usage and assessment information in learning management systems or the number of downloads or purchases in repositories or marketplaces. However, if the Learning Resources are transported via system borders, this information gets lost. This is due to the lack of a standardized format for the storage and management of this kind of information. The goal of the proposed architecture is therefore to enable the storage, capturing and utilization of lifecycle information beyond system borders. To achieve this, we propose an architecture with a central component called *Lifecycle Information System* and distributed *Capturing* and *Accessing Components*. The different components are described in detail in the following sections.

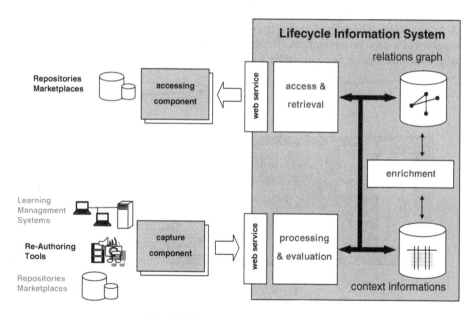

Fig. 5. Lifecycle Information System

4.1 Lifecycle Information System

The components of the LIS are shown in Figure 5. The LIS is designed as an online central application and is interconnected to the capture and accessing components via web services, i.e. the components use web services running on the LIS to send the information collected for a certain set of Learning Resource to the LIS or to retrieve it from there respectively. We decided to have the LIS centralized, because this allows us to easily connect to it and have the information being updated. The LIS is the one central system, which integrates all the data sources and manages the incoming data. In the LIS the gathered information is processed, evaluated and stored in a database. The separately stored context and relation information is enriched by making use of a special rule set (e.g. if A isPartOf B and B isPartOf C then A isPartOf C etc.). The enriched information about a Learning Resource can be retrieved by the accessing components as an XML document.

4.2 Capture Components

The distributed Capture Components are integrated into the tools that are used for creation, usage and modification of Learning Resources. A capture component monitors the creation, change and usage processes and extracts the necessary information generated during these processes on an event handling basis. One feature of the capture component is that it does not require a persistent connection to the LIS. It may work in an offline mode, in which it caches the captured lifecycle information. When a connection is established again, the cached information is transmitted to the LIS. As a fallback solution – in case an online connection can never be established – the lifecycle information may be attached as metadata to the Learning Resource; the Resource itself then serves as the transfer medium. Figure 6 shows the component diagram of a capture component. The core component is connected to the application where the information is captured by a generic interface.

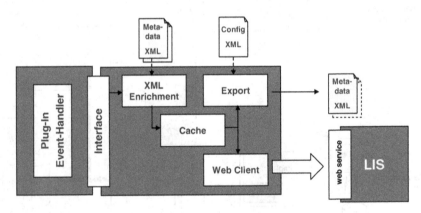

Fig. 6. Capture Component

The captured information of a certain Learning Resource is merged with already existing lifecycle information about it received from the LIS to enrich its existing metadata. The cache is used for caching the gathered information on the local computer, where the application is in use, while the web client connects to a web service of the LIS to send the information there, if a connection is available. If this is not the case, the information is cached until a connection is available and can be utilized by the applications on the local computer. Besides that, there is also the possibility to export the information to a local serialized metadata representation (usually XML), which can be configured during runtime by an external configuration file. The capturing itself is realised by plug-ins which connect to the generic interface of the core component and collect the usage or modification data on an event-handling basis. The LIS collects all information that is related to any version of a Learning Resource. From these individual facts, a lifecycle record, for that Learning Resource is built. This lifecycle record contains a representation of all instances (versions and variants) of the Learning Resource, relations between the instances and context information for each instance.

4.3 Accessing Components

Accessing components are plugged into applications where the gathered lifecycle information can be of particular use. This applies for example to applications used for the retrieval of Learning Resources, where context and relation information can be combined to provide better search results. The accessing components retrieve the information about the Learning Resources via a web service interface from the LIS and present it in a helpful way. That might for example be by means of providing links to closely related Learning Resources or ranking a search result on the basis of the collected context information (see section 2.4). Accessing components, as well as capture components, are designed as plug-ins for applications being used. However, for most applications it makes sense to have not exclusively an accessing or capture component plugged in, but both of them. While searching in a repository, the captured information about the Learning Resources contained in the repository is especially helpful, so that an accessing component for the utilization is mandatory. Additionally there is information being generated while using the repository as well: The selection and access of Learning Resources will increase the selection and access counters and provide additionally information on the relative significance of certain Learning Resource instances. On top of that it is possible to use lifecycle information even, when no internet connection is available. A local accessing component can make use of the local cache of the capture component as a data source.

5 Implementation

We have implemented the above architecture as a proof of concept in the course of the Content Sharing project [3]. Figure 7 shows which components are implemented at the moment and how. Capture components are integrated in the developed Module Editor as well as in the Content Sharing Repository. An Accessing Component in the repository helps users in finding, searching and retrieving the Learning Resources they want. And finally the Lifecycle Information System is implemented, too. For this implementation the local caching features of the Capture Components are used to transfer the captured data via the Content Sharing Repository to the Lifecycle Information System. The Module Editor is a combination of modularization, aggregation and adaptation component. Currently the adaptation processes shown in Figure 8 are supported. Hence the Capture Component theoretically captures all the relation information described in section 2.2. Although this is only possible if the according processes are actually performed. At the moment this Capture Component captures relation information only.

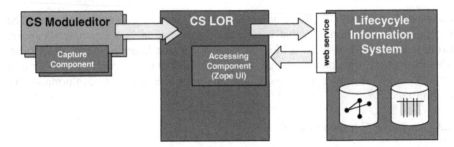

Fig. 7. Implemented Components

The Capture Component integrated into the Content Sharing Repository captures context information like the views or purchases of the Learning Resources in the repository, while the Accessing Component processes all the captured relations and provides links to related Learning Resources. For the sake of the utilization of lifecycle information, this implementation is far from complete, but serves as a proof of concept.

An example **usage scenario** with this system looks as follows: A Learning Resource is downloaded from the Content Sharing Repository, while the Capture Component of the repository counts the view and the download towards the context information of this resource. It is opened in the Module Editor and modularized into smaller Learning Resources. The Capture Component in the Module Editor captures the aggregation and sequence relations between the existent resources and stores it with the metadata of the Learning Resources in the local cache (or sends it to the LIS).

Some of the sub modules are adapted, which inflicts relation information being captured as well, and even newly created Learning Resources are added. Finally the Learning Resources are aggregated and the corresponding information captured. The

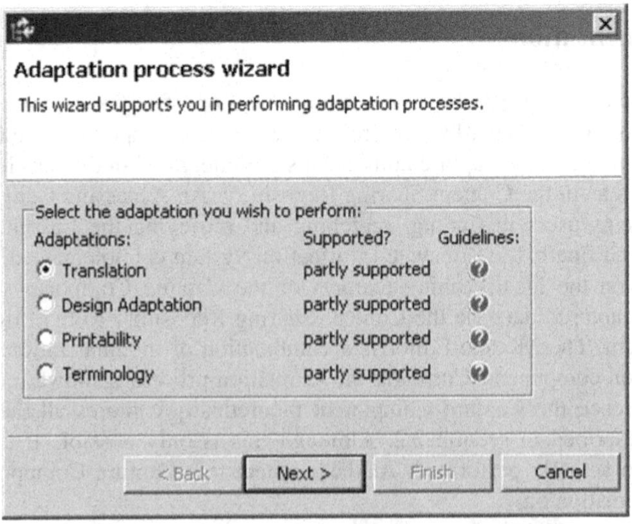

Fig. 8. Adaptations of the CS Module Editor

author can decide which of the created Learning Resources he wants to upload to the repository. He may upload any created or adapted Learning Resource or he may choose to upload the final Learning Resource only. The relation information is transported to the repository either via the metadata of the Learning Resources or via the central LIS. In the current implementation the former is the case. In the repository, the Accessing Component gets the information from the metadata or the LIS respectively and processes it to generate links or recommendations. Before this is done, the information is filtered to show links to resources only, which truly exist in the repository.

6 Related Work

Regarding the capturing of information during the lifecycle of a Learning Resource there is a similar approach called *Ecological Approach* [2], [10]. This work also constitutes that information should be gathered during the actual use of a Learning Resource and not during explicit labelling phases. However, the authors focus mainly on one phase of the lifecycle to gather information about the learner to support their approach to learner modelling. Relations between Learning Resources or other phases of the lifecycle than the actual learning phase are not taken into account.

The utilization of *context* information in a wider sense is conducted for several years now in known applications like eBay or Amazon as well as in many works in the information retrieval research area [6], though there are hardly any works that concentrate on the capturing of information during its creation.

Attention Metadata is a kind of context information about the attention a user pays to different Learning Resources via different applications. It can be gathered and utilized to receive information about the user's experience [11], or actually be used for the retrieval of Learning Resources [12]. For the capturing of Attention Metadata a similar approach involving plug-ins and a central instance is used. While at first only the actual usage of an object was considered by the approach the authors propose in [10] that the creation phase as well as re-used components should be taken into account, too. Therefore the CAMS system is very closely related to our work. However, they do not consider relations between different Learning Resources and instances of Learning Resources.

A system where *relation* information is used is the *HyLOS* system [5]. HyLOS is a Learning Management System in the first place and the user or semi automatic generated relations are used to provide additional links to learners in order to enable a constructivist learning style. The method to store the relation information is mainly based on the named Dublin Core extension for the LOM relation category. The relations used in HyLOS are on a semantically higher level than the relations taken into account by our approach, although it would be nice to have the approaches merged. One of the core features the HyLOS system provides is the relation enrichment. An existing set of relation is processed involving a certain rule set to generate new relations. This is a quite the same what the enrichment component in the here proposed LIS does.

7 Conclusion and Future Work

In this paper we have shown that lifecycle information of Learning Resources can be helpful in many ways. The information generated in the different phases of a Learning Resource's lifecycle was analysed and structured. We proposed a system that supports the capturing, management and utilization of lifecycle information and enables us to collect and use the information in all phases of the lifecycle. The implementation shows that this system is possible and practical. To proof its efficiency, evaluations with user groups still have to be conducted. The generic, plug-in based architecture enables us and other developers to extend the number of supported applications easily. In future one major step, besides the evaluation, will be the development of further plug-ins for capture and accessing components for different types of applications. Additionally, with the growing availability of information about Learning Resources new ways of utilization will emerge that have to be implemented to support learners, authors, providers or just plain users of Learning Resources in different ways. We are currently trying to widen the focus of this approach and not consider Learning Resources only but knowledge documents in general, as well.

References

1. Baumgartner, P.: The ROI Paradox. Keynote Presentation at the Gesellschaft für Medien in den Wissenschaften Conference held in Graz, Austria (2004), HYPERLINK, http://www.c3-initiative.info/peter/2004/09/12
2. Brooks, C., McCalla, G.: Towards Flexible Learning Object Metadata. In: Proceedings of Int. J. Cont. Engineering Education and Lifelong Learning, vol. 16(1/2) (2006)
3. Content Sharing Project (2007), HYPERLINK, http://contentsharing.com
4. Duval, E., Hodgins, W.: A LOM Research Agenda. In: Hencsey, G., White, B., Chen, Y., Kovacs, L., Lawrence, S.H. (eds.) Proceedings of the twelfth international conference on World Wide Web, Seite, pp. 1–9 (2003)
5. Engelhardt, M., Hildebrand, A., Lange, D., Schmidt, T.C.: Semantic Overlays in Educational Content Networks. In: Proceedings of TERENA Networking Conference (2006)
6. Good, N., Schafer, J.B., Konstan, J.A., Borchers, A., Sarwar, B., Herlocker, J., Riedl, J.: Combining Collaborative Filtering with Personal Agents for Better Recommendations. In: Proceedings of the 'AAAI/IAAIEcological Approach (1999)
7. Hoermann, S., Hildebrandt, T., Rensing, C., Steinmetz, R.: ResourceCenter - A Digital Learning Object Repository with an Integrated Authoring Tool. In: Proceedings of the Edmedia (2005)
8. IEEE Learning Technology Standards Committee: IEEE Standard for Learning Object Metadata 1484.12.1 (2002)
9. Lehmann, L., Rensing, C., Steinmetz, R.: Lifecycle Information Management and Utilization in an Authoring by Aggregation Environment, Accepted at Edmedia (2007)
10. McCalla, G.: The Ecological Approach to the Design of E-Learning Environments: Purpose-based Capture and Use of Information About Learners. Journal of Interactive Media in Education 7 (2004)
11. Najjar, J., Wolpers, M., Duval, E.: Towards Effective Usage-Based Learning Applications: Track and Learn from Users Experience(s). In: Proceedings of the IEEE ICALT (2006)

12. Ochoa, X., Duval, E.: Use of Contextualized Attention Metadata for Ranking and Recommending Learning Objects. In: Proceedings of the CAMA (2006)
13. Rensing, C., Bergsträßer, S., Hildebrandt, T., Meyer, M., Zimmermann, B., Faatz, A., Lehmann, L., Steinmetz, R.: Re-Use, Re-Authoring, and Re-Purposing of Learning Resources - Definitions and Examples. Technical Report, Technische Universität Darmstadt (2005)
14. Rensing, C., Tittel, S., Lehmann, L., Steinmetz, R.: Ein System zur Realisierung expliziten Lerner-Autor Feedbacks im E-Learning. In: Proceedings of the Workshop Effiziente Erstellung von E-Learning Content at the DeLFI (2006)
15. Request for Comment (RFC) 2413 Relation Element Working Draft (1997) HYPERLINK http://dublincore.org/documents/1997/12/19/relation-element/
16. Zimmermann, B., Rensing, C., Steinmetz, R.: Format-übergreifende Anpassungen von elektronischen Lerninhalten. In: Proceedings of the DeLFI 2006 - die 4. e-Learning Fachtagung Informatik (2006)

Improving the Search for Learning Objects with Keywords and Ontologies

Lothar Lemnitzer[1], Cristina Vertan[2], Alex Killing[3], Kiril Simov[4],
Diane Evans[5], Dan Cristea[6], and Paola Monachesi[7]

[1] Seminar für Sprachwissenchaft, Universität Tübingen, Germany
[2] Natural Language Systems Divison, Institute or Informatics, University Hamburg, Germany
[3] Center for Security Studies, ETH Zrich, Switzerland
[4] LML, IPP, Bulgarian Academy of Sciences, Sofia, Bulgaria
[5] The Open University, Milton Keynes, UK
[6] University of Iasi, Romania
[7] Utrecht University, Uil-OTS, Utrecht, The Netherlands

Abstract. We report on an ongoing project which aims at improving the effectiveness of retrieval and accessibility of learning object within learning management systems and learning object repositories. The project *Language Technology for eLearning* approaches this task by providing Language Technology based functionalities and by integrating semantic knowledge through domain-specific ontologies. We will report about the development of a keyword extractor and a domain-specific ontology, the integration of these modules into the learning management system ILIAS and the validation of these tools which assesses their added value in the scenario of searching learning objects across different languages.

Keywords: learning object, metadata, keyword extraction, ontology, multilinguality.

1 Introduction

Significant research has been carried out in the area of Language Technology and within the Semantic Web. Several initiatives have been launched in the last years both at the national and international level aiming at the development of resources and tools in the areas of NLP, Corpus Linguistics and Ontology development. However, their integration in enhancing eLearning systems has not been fully exploited yet.

The aim of the *Language Technology for eLearning project* (LT4eL, www.lt4el.eu) is to improve eLearning with language technologies and resources in order to provide new functionalities which will enhance the adaptability and the personalization of the learning process through the software which mediates it. In our project, we show how language resources and tools can be employed to

E. Duval, R. Klamma, and M. Wolpers (Eds.): EC-TEL 2007, LNCS 4753, pp. 202–216, 2007.

facilitate tasks which are typically performed in an LMS such as the search for learning material in a (multilingual) domain, semi-automatic metadata development based on keywords and generating glossaries on the basis of definitions of key terms.

However, the main objective of the LT4eL project is to improve on the retrieval of the learning material and we tackle this problem from two different but related angles: from the content end and from the retrieval end.

On the content side, a steadily growing amount of content cannot be easily identified in the absence of systematic metadata annotation. Providing metadata is a tedious activity and the solution we offer is to provide a Language Technology based functionality, that is a key word extractor which allows for semi-automatic metadata annotation on the basis of a linguistic analysis of the learning material. While keyword extractors have been provided mainly for English [11], the innovative aspect of our project is that we provide this functionality for all the eight languages represented in our project, that is Bulgarian, Czech, Dutch, English, German, Polish, Portuguese and Romanian and that we embed such a tool within the eLearning context.

On the retrieval side, the standard retrieval systems, based on keyword matching, only consider the query terms. They do not really take into account the systematic relationships between the concepts denoted by the queries and other concepts that might be relevant for the user. In the LT4eL project, we use an ontology as an instrument to express and exploit such relationships, which should improve the search results and allow for more sophisticated ways to navigate through the learning objects. Furthermore, by linking the ontology to language specific lexica, multilingual retrieval will be possible. We believe that the potential of ontologies in the area of multilingual retrieval is not sufficiently exploited yet and with our project we intend to make a contribution in this direction.

In this paper, we focus on how retrieval of learning objects within a Learning Management System can be improved on the basis of semi-automatically generated metadata as well as a domain ontology. As basis for the extraction of the keywords and the development of the ontology, we use linguistically annotated learning material which has been converted into XML. This process is described in section 2. Our approach on the extraction of keywords is presented in section 3 while the ontology developed to support the search process is introduced in section 4. The developed functionalities (i.e. keyword extraction and ontology) are integrated in the ILIAS Learning Management System and the integration process is discussed in section 5. Validation is briefly addressed in section 6 while section 7 contains some concluding remarks on future work.

2   Preparing the Data

The development and testing of the keyword extractor and ontology are based on domain specific corpora for the various languages. It was decided to collect corpora of learning objects of at least 200.000 running words per language. The topics of these learning objects are information technology for the non-expert, mainly introductory texts and tutorials for word processing, HTML etc., texts which convey basic academic skills, and texts about eLearning. Around one third of the corpora is truly parallel in the sense that we used translations of the same basic text into the various languages. To this end, we chose the CALIMERA document (`http://www.calimera.org/`) because it is close to our domains.

The documents we collected with an opportunistic method vary considerably in size – from a few sentences to more than 50 pages. Wrt to the information extraction and search functionalities, the size of the documents has the following impacts:

- The statistical measures of the keyword extractor all rely, as we will show later on, on document frequency of a term. Therefore, the smaller the document and larger the number of documents in a collection, the more precise the statistics can capture the distributional behaviour of terms. So smaller documents are preferable from this point of view. On the other hand, the selection of keywords implies that the documents are not too small, though it is hard to determine where the limit is.
- With regard to searching, smaller documents are also preferable because the search can thus be more easily narrowed down the content which the user really needs, which might not always be the case with documents which are long and multi-thematic.

Therefore, the techniques we describe here are more well-suited for small to medium documents, which is realistic for the document type of a learning object, even if this is not reflected in all of our collections. We are aware of the fact that the individual corpora are rather small and cannot be considered to be representative for the text sort of instructive texts. But we assume that the corpora are large enough to build and test the extraction tools upon them. The evaluation results, about wich we report in section 3.6, prove this assumption.

The texts which we were able to acquire come also in different formats, namely PDF, DOC and HTML. Part of the work was to transform these texts into structurally and linguistically annotated documents. These documents serve as input to the information extraction tools and as resource for the ontology building. Some preprocessing was necessary to unify the different formats. We used third party tools[1], some auxiliary scripts and modest manual intervention. As result, the text together with some basic structural and layout features is preserved in a project-specific format called BaseXML. This format serves as input to the individual linguistic annotation chains (LAC). In principle, the LAC for each language consists of a sentence and a word segmenter and a linguistic annotator

---

[1] Those were in particular conversion tools which convert the DOC format to text, tools, available under Linux, which convert PDF to text, and online tools on the ADOBE website, cf. `http://www.adobe.com/products/acrobat/ access_onlinetools.html` .

which determines the base form (e.g. *derive* for the word *derives*) and the part of speech (e.g. VERB for the word *derives*), and its morphosyntactic features (e.g. 3RD PERSON SINGULAR PRESENT for the word *derives*). The latter is particularly important for the many morphologically rich languages in the project. For some languages, also noun phrases were detected and marked, as they play a central role as keyword and defined terms[2].

Figure 1 presents an example of a fully annotated sentence from the German corpus, in the LT4el annotation format (LT4ELAna), which translates to *Write an e-mail!*.

```
<par id="p63" name="p"><s id="s114">
  <tok base="schreiben" ctag="VVFIN" id="t1091"
    msd="pl,0,0,third,0,present,0,0" rend="ol,li">Schreiben</tok>
  <tok base="Sie" ctag="PPER" id="t1092"
    msd="pl,bot,nom,third,0,0,0,0" rend="ol,li">Sie</tok>
  <chunk category="NP" id="c247">
    <tok base="eine" ctag="ART" id="t1093"
      msd="sg,fem,acc,0,0,0,0,0" rend="ol,li">eine</tok>
    <tok base="E-Mail" ctag="NN" id="t1094"
      msd="sg,fem,bot,third,0,0,0,0" rend="ol,li,b">E-Mail</tok>
  </chunk>
  ...
</s>
...
</par>
```

Fig. 1. LT4eLAna example. Legend: par = paragraph; s = sentence, tok = token; base = lemma; ctag = part of speech; msd = morpho-syntactic description of the word, in the form of a feature vector; rend = layout information.

In the project, we provide a Document Type Definition (DTD) which defines the structural, the layout and the linguistic information of these documents. This DTD, called *Lt4ELAna*, is derived from the widely used XCESAna DTD for linguistic corpus annotation. This guarantees that our annotated corpora will be re-usable in other research projects.

On top of the linguistic annotation, the DTD allows for the markup of keywords and definitions. This has been done manually in the first project phase. At least 1000 keywords and 450 definitions have been identified and marked in the texts. These pieces of information are used for the training of the information extraction tools as well as for their testing and evaluation[3].

---

[2] We provide more details of the conversion and annotation process in [9], with the German corpus as an example.

[3] The annotated corpora will be made available towards the end of the project, which is May 2008 – at least those documents for which the IPR issues can be cleared.

3 Keyword Extraction

3.1 Purpose of the Tool

As has been said above, one of the aims of the LT4eL project is to improve the retrieval and accessibility of eLearning content through the identification of the learning material by means of descriptive metadata. Since it is not yet current practice for authors to provide keywords, but, on the other hand, effective retrieval of learning objects relies on them, we want to assist authors with the extraction of keyword candidates from their texts. The keyword extractor draws on qualitative and quantitative, in particular distributional, characteristics of good keywords.

3.2 Measuring Keywordiness

Good keywords are supposed to represent the topic(s) of a text. They therefore tend to appear more often in that text than could be expected if all words were distributed randomly over a corpus.

A well-established way to measure the distribution of terms over a collection documents is *tf*idf*, cf. equation 1.

$$tf * idf \quad \text{where} \quad IDF = \log_2 \frac{N}{df} \tag{1}$$

Another quite useful statistics used to model the expected distribution of words in texts is Poisson distribution or a mixture of Poisson distributions (cf. [4] and equation 2).

$$\pi(k; \theta) = \frac{e^{-\theta}\theta^k}{k!} \tag{2}$$

While the distribution of e.g. function words like *of, the, it* is close to the expected distribution under the Poisson distribution model, good keyword candidates deviate significantly from the expectation. The score of this deviation can be used as a statistics by which the lexical units are ranked ([5]). The deviation of the observed distribution of a word from the expected distribution under the Poission model, i.e predicted IDF (cf. equation 3) is called Residual RIDF (short: RIDF).

$$-log_2(1 - e^{-\theta}) \quad \text{where} \quad \theta = \frac{cf}{N} \tag{3}$$

During our experimenting with these metrics we recognized that RIDF does not take the term frequency in the analysed document into account. Since this is the most important factor in our statistics, we added it and arrived at a statistics which we call Adjusted Residual IDF (short: ADRIDF. cf. equation 4).

$$(IDF - PredictedIDF)\sqrt{tf} \tag{4}$$

The evaluation of the keyword extractor for all languages is described in the section 3.6.

3.3   Using Linguistic Information

The linguistically annotated text provides us with the base form, the part of speech and morphosyntactic features for each word. This information is used to remove words of those categories which are unlikely to be keywords. For most languages, only nouns, some verbs and words marked as unknown are taken into account as keyword candidates. These restrictions are defined in the so-called language models of the keyword extractor. These models can easily be adjusted to new domains or languages.

3.4   Multiword Keywords

Lexical items which span more than one word, e.g. *learning management system, font selection menu*, play an important role as keywords and should therefore be treated as such by the extractor. The manually annotated keywords in our reference texts showed that while for languages like Dutch and German the single word keywords make for more than 90 % of all keywords, the share of multi-word keywords is nearly two-thirds for Polish. We therefore put some effort to properly deal with these items. The implementation of the keyword extractor can be parameterized to take multi-word sequences up to a certain length into account, which is useful for e.g. Polish, or to ignore them, which might be good for Dutch and German.

3.5   Structural and Layout Information

Good keyword candidates tend to appear in certain salient regions of a text. These are the headings and the first paragraphs after the headings as well as an abstract or summary. Salient terms might also be highlighted or emphasised by the author, e.g. by using italics. We give an extra weight to terms which show this behaviour.

3.6   Evaluation

The quantitative evalutation of the keyword extractor comprised three parts: a) assessing the response time(s) of the tool, b) comparing the output of the tool to the human annotation, and c) an experiment in inter-annotator agreement.

The response times of the tool. i.e. the time it takes to analyse the document and return the keyword candidates, is good enough to use the tool in real time. Once the language model, i.e. information extracted from all analysed documents is loaded into memory, which is done only once, the time needed to extract keywords from one document ranges from 25ms up to 1.5 seconds, depending on the document size. That has been measured on a 1.5GHz Pentium machine with 512MB RAM, with a language model of around 400000 tokens.

In the second part of the evaluation, we compared the automatically extracted and ranked keywords (according to either of the three statistics mentioned above) with the manually marked keywords. For a document where n keywords have been marked manually (with $n > 5$), we selected the n best keywords according the ranking of the keywords and recorded the overlap. From this evaluation across all languages, the three statistics, and different maximum lengths of keywords it could be observed that:

- Results varied significantly from slightly more than 40 % overlap at average for the German documents to more than 60 % overlap for the Czech documents;
- In general, tf*idf and ADRIDF nearly produced the same results, with one outperforming the other on one language, and vice versa for another language, while RIDF performed worst for almost all settings;
- Results improved for all languages if multi-word keywords up to a length of 3 words were included. Using keywords of even higher length improved the results slightly for few languages (e.g. Bulgarian) and decreased results for most other languages. Therefore, including keywords up to a length of three words seems to be the best decision.

This part of the evaluation, however, relies completely on the quality of the manual keyword selection which seems to be good for some and less good for other languages. In order to control this experiment, an evaluation of inter-anntotator agreement (IAA) on the keyword selection task has been performed. For each language, a group of at least 12 persons selected keywords from the same document, a document of modest size. We used kappa statistics to measure IAA, following the approach of Bruce and Wiebe ([3]), which seems to be appropriate for our type of data.

Table 1 presents the results of the inter-annotator agreement for each language:

Table 1. Inter-annotator agreement for human annotators and for the Keyword Extractor compared to the human annotators

Language	average human annotators	Keyword Extractor
Bulgarian	0.2008	0.0683
Dutch	0.2150	0.1373
English	0.1318	0.08964
German	0.2636	0.13208
Polish	0.1996	0.1651
Portuguese	0.1811	0.0893
Romanian	0.2102	0.215784

Results of these experiments reveal that the inter-annotator agreement for this task is low for all languages, indicating that the task of selecting keywords cannot be well defined. The average IAA for the annotators ranged between 0,1 and 0,4. Neither is there a significant difference between languages, nor between unexperienced and experienced annotators. The keyword extractor was at the lower end of this scale for all languages except for Romanian, so there is space for improvement. The generally low IAA might have consequences for our search scenarios though. Documents which are assigned keywords of a wide variety might also be searched by such a wide variety of search terms.

4   Ontological Support of Searching

Current eLearning systems offer only full-text or keyword-based search facilities. We will outline in this section the steps we took in order to implement an ontology search facility and also describe planned extensions for crosslingual search. We will explain the methodology for ontology creation, the semantic annotation of learning objects with concepts from the ontology, and show how lexical items of various languages have been mapped onto the concepts of the ontology.

4.1   Ontology Creation

The domain chosen for our ontology is computer science for non-computer scientists. Details about the choice of the domain and the related documents are given in section 2. Since we were not able to find any ontology which covers our domain in a satisfactory way we proceeded with the creation of our own.

During the creation of the ontology we made sure that the ontology covers (most of) the topics of our learning objects well and in great detail. We used the keywords which have been manually annotated, as well as the results of the keyword extractor which has been described above. A fine granularity of the concepts is required in order to ensure better text annotation. In addition to this, the ontology was aligned with an upper ontology in order to ensure consistency with respect to a general ontology development methodology.

The creation of the ontology can be summarized in the following steps: Processing of keywords and formalisation. On a later stage of ontology development new concepts (not related to the keywords) were added in order to improve the coverage of the domain.

Processing of keywords. In order to ensure a relatively wide coverage with respect to the learning objects we based the construction of the ontology on the keywords which have been annotated in these documents. The ontology is therefore based on lexical items from all the languages of the project. English translation equivalents were provided for these lexical items. This reduced the complexity of mapping the concepts of the ontology to lexical entries of all languages.The processing itself was done in the following way. First of all, the keywords were classified into the conceptual space of the domain. Only those keywords which are connected to the subject of information technology for non-experts were selected.

Secondly, definitions for the concepts were collected. The WWW was searched for definitions of the selected keywords. The rationale behind this step was to define in human readable way the concepts connected to the keywords. We collected a set of multiple definitions for most of the keywords because different definitions highlight different features of the related concept.

Thirdly, the terms were disambiguated and a canonical definition chosen for each meaning. These definitions are the human-readable meaning explications of the concepts which are included in the ontology. When necessary, two or more meaning explications were given for a concept. For instance, the terms *header* and *word* have more than one meaning in our domain. Other keywords show regular polysemy. For example, *MPEG* might signify an organization as well as a standard. Our rule of thumb was to prefer the more general meaning to the more specific ones. For example, we skipped the meanings indicating programming terms because we considered them to be too specific.

Formalisation. In this step formal definitions of the extracted concepts and relations have been defined using OWL-DL (cf. [2]). OWL-DL was chosen due to the availability of reasoners for that language subset. The concepts were formalised in two separate steps. First, for each meaning, an appropriate class in the domain ontology was created. The result of this step is an initial formal version of the ontology. In order to ensure appropriate taxonomic relations between the concepts in the ontology and to facilitate the mapping to an upper ontology, each concept was mapped to synsets in the OntoWordNet version of Princeton WordNet ([6], [7]), which is a version of WordNet which is mapped to the DOLCE ontology. The mapping was performed via the two main relations *equality* and *hypernymy*. The first relation is between a class in the ontology and a synset in WordNet which (lexically) represents the same concept, while the second is a relation between a class in the ontology and a synset denoting a more general concept. Thus, the taxonomic part of the ontology was created. The connection of OntoWordNet to DOLCE allows an evaluation of the defined concepts with respect to meta-ontological properties as they are defined in the OntoClean approach (cf [8]).

4.2   Annotation of Learning Objects with Concepts

From the perspective of the Learning Management System, the ontological annotation concerns only the metadata section of the learning objects. In the metadata, according the the Learning Object Metadata (LOM, [1]) standard, some ontological information can be stored and used later on to index the learning objects for retrieval. The annotation needs not be anchored to the content of the learning object. The annotator of the learning object can include in the annotation all concepts and relations she considers to be important for the classification of the learning object. In order to accurately link a learning object and/or its parts to the proper places in the conceptual space of the ontology, an inline annotation of the content of learning objects is an obligatory intermediate step in the annotation of the learning objects with ontological information. The inline annotation is done by regular grammar rules attached to each concept in the ontology reflecting the realizations of the concept in texts of the corresponding languages. Additionally rules for disambiguation between several concepts are applied when a text realization is ambiguous between several concepts.

Within the project we performed both types of annotation, inline and through metadata. The metadata annotation is used during the retrieval of learning objects from the repository. The inline annotation will be used in two ways: (1) as a step to metadata annotation of the learning objects; and (2) as a mechanism to validate the coverage of the ontology. Additionally we have implemented a ontology-oriented search engine based on the full-text search engine Lucene[4]. It allows searches for documents, paragraphs or sentences that contains annotations of some concepts from the ontology. These searches provide a basis for detailed requests by the users in order to find the appropriate learning object for their needs.

4.3 Mapping Lexicons onto the Ontology

Terminological lexicons represent the main interface between the user's query and the ontological search engine. The terminological lexicons were constructed on the basis of the formal definitions of the concepts within the ontology. In this approach of construction of the terminological lexicon we escaped from the hard task of mapping different lexicons in several languages as it was done in EuroWordNet Project [10]. The main problems with this approach of construction of terminological lexicons are that (1) for some concepts there is no lexicalized term in a given language, and (2) some important term in a given language has no appropriate concept in the ontology which to represent its meaning. In order to solve these problems we, first, allow the lexicons to contains also non-lexicalized phrases which have the meaning of the concepts without lexicalization in a given language. Even more, we encourage the lexicon builders to add more terms and phrases to the lexicons for a given concept in order to represent as many ways of expressing the concept in the language as possible. These different phrases or terms for a given concept are used as a basis for construction of the regular grammar rules for annotation of the concept in the text. Having them, we could capture in the text different wordings of the same meaning. In order to solve the second problem we modify the ontology in such a way that it contains all the concepts that are important for the domain.

We could summarize the connection between the ontology and the lexicons in the following way: the ontology represents the semantic knowledge in form of concepts and relations with appropriate axioms; and the lexicons represent the ways in which these concepts can be realized in texts in the corresponding languages. Of course the ways in which a concept could be represented in text are potentially infinite in number, thus, we could hope to represent in our lexicons only the most frequent and important terms and phrases.

Here is an example of an entry from the Dutch lexcion:

```
<entry id="id60">
    <owl:Class rdf:about="http://www.lt4el.eu/CSnCS#BarWithButtons">
        <rdfs:subClassOf>
            <owl:Class rdf:about="http://www.lt4el.eu/CSnCS#Window"/>
        </rdfs:subClassOf>
    </owl:Class>
    <def>A horizontal or vertical bar as a part of a window,
         that contains buttons, icons.</def>
    <termg lang="nl">
        <term shead="1">werkbalk</term>
```

---

[4] Apache Lucene is a full-featured text search engine: http://lucene.apache.org/

```
      <term>balk</term>
      <term type="nonlex">balk met knoppen</term>
      <term>menubalk</term>
    </termg>
  </entry>
```

Each entry of the lexicons contains three type of information: (1) information about the concept from the ontology which represent the meaning for the terms in the entry; (2) explanation of the concept meaning in English; and (3) a set of terms in a given language that have the meaning expressed by the concept. The concept part of the entry provides minimum information for formal definition of the concept. The English explanation of the concept meaning facilitates the human understanding. The set of terms stands for different wordings of the concept in the corresponding language. One of the terms is the representative for the term set. This representative term will be used where just one of the terms from the set is necessary to be used, for example as an item of a menu. In the example above we present the set of Dutch terms for the concept http://www.lt4el.eu/CSnCS#BarWithButtons. One of the term is non-lexicalized - attribute type with value nonlex. The first term is representative for the term set and it is marked-up with attribute shead with value 1.

5   Integration into the ILIAS Learning Management System

5.1   Purpose and Method of Integration

The primary focus of the integration of the LT functionalities into ILIAS is to build a running prototype of a learning management system that provides extended functionalities supported by the use of the language technology tools. The basis for the integration process are use cases which have been defined for the keyword extractor and the ontology enhanced searching and browsing capabilities. The use cases have been the major input for the specification of a web service interface between the language technology tools and the learning management system. It is a major goal of the project to make the language technology based functionalities re-usable for other learning management systems. To make the integration of the tools as easy as possible, the interface of the tools will be well-documented and standards-based. The implementation of the interface as web services should ensure that these goals are met.

5.2   Integration Setup

Figure 2 shows the major components of the integration setup. The language technology server on the left provides the keyword extractor, definitory context finder and ontology management system functionalities. The tools are developed using the Java programming language and are hosted on a Java web server. The functionalities can be accessed directly on the webserver for test purposes or

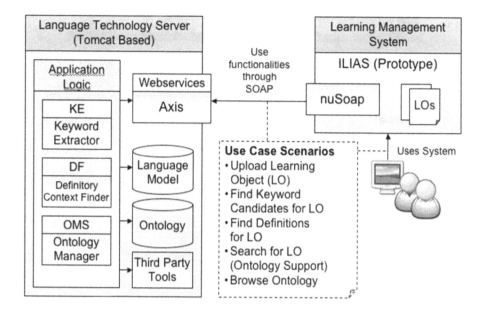

Fig. 2. Architecture of the Language Technology enhanced LMS

they can be used by the learning management system through the web service interface.

The fact that multiple developers are working on different parts of the overall structure has led to the decision to setup a Subversion server as a central code repository. The project partners have also decided to make the results immediately available to the general public and to give everyone the opportunity to join and collaborate with the project. The source code is available under an open source licence and it is hosted on the SourceForge portal for open source projects at `https://sourceforge.net/projects/lt4el/`. Figure 3 shows the first integration of the keyword extractor into the ILIAS learning management system. The function is embedded into the existing LOM metadata handling of ILIAS to enable a semi-automatic generation of keywords. In the future the definitory context finder operations will be used to provide the new functionality of semi-automatic glossary generation within the ILIAS authoring environment. The web service operations of the ontology management system will extend the functionalities of the ILIAS search function by enabling semantic and multilingual retrieval of learning objects[5].

6   Validation of the Tools and Value Added

The tools described in this paper are currently tested and validated with real users. For this purpose we designed validation scenarios. According to the

---

[5] A demonstration of these functionalities will be given during the talk.

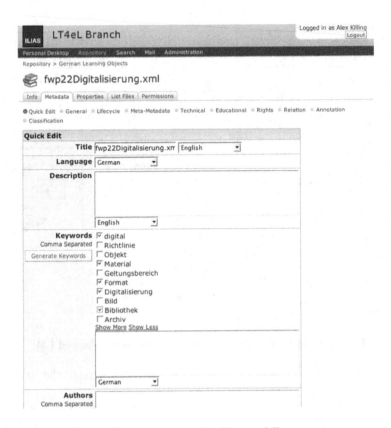

Fig. 3. User interface to the Keyword Extractor

different functionalities of the system the validation scenarios can be classified as either being monolingual or bilingual.

monolingual scenario. From the teacher's perspective, the keyword extractor will be used to select and add keywords to a new document. The ontology can be used to find related keywords which might not have been appeared in the document. From the student's perspective, the ontology and keyword based searching will be used to elicit infomation from a set of learning objects, e.g. for answering a quiz.

bilingual scenario. Teachers as well as students will use the ontology to retrieve contents and terms in other languages than their own native language. Texts of different languages can be combined from multilingual learning packages.

These very general, high-level scenarios will be detailed further to get exact instructions for the test persons to follow. We will measure the added value of the language technology by comparing the outcome of the tasks with and without them as well as by evaluating the satisfaction of users with the new functionalities.

7   Further Work and Perspectives

The main objective of the LT4eL project is the Integration of Language Technology resources and tools in eLearning which should enhance the search and retrieval of (multilingual) learning material. In order to reach this objectives, we have:

- created a corpus of 200.000 words (1000 pages) of learning objects for all languages of the consortium;
- normalized and converted the corpus in XML;
- annotated the corpus with PoS for all languages;
- developed a keyword extractor based on different statistical measures;
- carried out a preliminary quantitative evaluation of the keywords extracted;
- developed an ontology of about 1000 concepts in an upper ontology and domain ontology in Computer Science for non experts);
- linked the ontology to OntoWordNet;
- semantically annotated learning objects in various languages on the basis of the ontology;
- developed lexica for all the languages to be mapped to the ontology.

One of the major challenges for the future is to make the Linguistic Annotation Chain available for each new document which is submitted. Currently the tools and search can only be applied to our corpora. Intellectual property rights on the annotation tools have to be solved for some languages before we can offer this service.

In parallel with the validation of the monolingual ontological search we are currently working on multilingual search. The main assumption is that users are able to read documents in languages other than their native language (usually at least in English), but traditional search engines will not find them. In the first phase of the project domain-related lexicons were created in all eight languages represented in the project. The lexicons were mapped on the ontology and they provide the interface between the users's query and the search engine. Further work consists in implementing the multilingual engine and validating the multilingual scenarios, as described in the previous section. The extension from monolingual search to multilingual search raises additional issues like:

- Ranking of documents over the various languages, as the user may be less interested in receiving one separate list of documents for each language. Another option is to display the complete list according to the same ranking criteria, and for each document indicate its language. In this way, the user can compare the relevance of two documents even if they are in a different language. A further refinement could be to include the language as a ranking criterion by giving a bonus which differs per language.
- Introducing parameters like possible languages of search query, retrieval languages, etc. to the search functionality.
- The inclusion of other ontologies is also still an issue. We are curerently investigating the possibility of introducing relations corresponding to some pedagogical criteria.

In short, there is much room for improvement in the keyword and ontology driven annotation and search once the basic resources and tools are in place. Currently, we can provide these resources and employ the new functions. Other researchers and developers in the field of technology-enhanced learning are invited to join these efforts and to profit from our achievements.

References

1. Standard for Learning Object Metadata, Final Draft, IEEE P1484.12.1 (2002)
2. OWL. Web Ontology Language (Overview),
   http://www.w3.org/TR/owl-features/
3. Bruce, R., Wiebe, J.: Recognizing subjectivity: A case study of manual tagging. Natural Language Engineering 5(2), 187–205 (1999)
4. Church, K., Gale, W.: Poisson mixtures. Natural Language Engineering 1(2), 163–190 (1995)
5. Church, K., Kenneth, W., Gale, W.: Inverse Document Frequency (IDF): A Measure of Deviations from Poisson. In: Proc. of Third Workshop on Very Large Corpora (1995)
6. Fellbaum, C.: WORDNET: an electronic lexical database. MIT Press, Cambridge (1998)
7. Gangemi, A., Navigli, R., Velardi, P.: The OntoWordNet Project: extension and axiomatisation of conceptual relations in WordNet. In: Meersman, R., Tari, Z., Schmidt, D.C. (eds.) CoopIS 2003, DOA 2003, and ODBASE 2003. LNCS, vol. 2888, Springer, Heidelberg (2003)
8. Guarino, N., Welty, C.: Evaluating Ontological Decisions with OntoClean. Communications of the ACM 45(2), 61–65 (2002)
9. Mossel, E., Lemnitzer, L., Vertan, C.: Language Technology for eLearning – A Multilingual Approach from the German Perspective. In: Proc. GLDV-2007 Spring Conference, Tübingen, pp. 125–134 (2007)
10. Piek, V. (ed.): EuroWordNet General Document. Version 3, Final, July 19, 1998 (1999), http://www.hum.uva.nl/~ewn
11. Sclano, F., Velardi, P.: TermExtractor: a Web Application to Learn the Shared Terminology of Emergent Web Communities. In: Proc. of the 3rd International Conference on Interoperability for Enterprise Software and Applications I-ESA 2007, Funchal, Madeira Island, Portugal, March 28-30, (to appear, 2007)

Exploiting Context Information for Identification of Relevant Experts in Collaborative Workplace-Embedded E-Learning Environments

Robert Lokaiczyk[1], Eicke Godehardt[2], Andreas Faatz[1], Manuel Goertz[1],
Andrea Kienle[3], Martin Wessner[4], and Armin Ulbrich[5]

[1] SAP Research CEC Darmstadt
Bleichstr. 8, 64283 Darmstadt, Germany
{robert.lokaiczyk,andreas.faatz,manuel.goertz}@sap.com
[2] Fraunhofer IGD
Fraunhoferstr. 5, 64283 Darmstadt, Germany
eicke.godehardt@igd.fraunhofer.com
[3] Fraunhofer IPSI
Dolivostr. 15, 64293 Darmstadt, Germany
andrea.kienle@ipsi.fraunhofer.com
[4] Ludwig-Maximilian-University
Leopoldstr. 13, 80802 Munich, Germany
martin.wessner@psy.lmu.de
[5] Know-Center
Inffeldgasse 21a, 8010 Graz, Austria
aulbrich@know-center.at

Abstract. This work introduces an approach to discover collaboration partners and adequate advising experts in a workplace-embedded collaborative e-learning environment. Based on existing papers dealing with work task and user context modelling, we propose the following steps towards a successful collaboration initiation. In the beginning, the user's current process task needs to be identified (1). Taking into account the knowledge about the current process, availability of experts as well as organizational and social distance, relevant experts regarding the actual work task of the learner are pre-selected by the environment (2). Depending on the pre-selection and users' preferences, the potential collaboration partners are displayed in an expert list (3). That way, the learner is able to initiate beneficial collaborations, whose transcripts are used to enhance the existing knowledge base of learning documents (4).

1   Introduction

Frequently changing work contexts, transient processes, short product life-cycles and a rapidly changing world in a dynamic knowledge economy create the need for continuing and lifelong employees' training. Companies believe in workplace-embedded learning solutions to cope with the increasing complexity. Different from the traditional 'learn first, apply later'-approach, the required knowledge

E. Duval, R. Klamma, and M. Wolpers (Eds.): EC-TEL 2007, LNCS 4753, pp. 217–231, 2007.

for solving the current work task is needed right in time during the work process. The user can immediately profit from the learning content that is provided by an embedded e-learning environment. Besides presenting learning resources, potential experts of the work task will be pre-selected by the environment for possible collaboration and discussion. Learning on the fly while performing a task can occur when collaborating, e.g. when users conjointly deal with a specific work task. Within this process, a user might play different roles (c.f. [14]). In a general role of a knowledge worker, the user is working in a knowledge and information intensive work process. As a learner, s/he acquires further know-how by reading documents or collaborating with experts. Last, as an expert, the user shares know-how with others and acts as a teacher. [12] points out that the borders between the mentioned roles are blurred. Depending on the current business process, users dynamically transfer between the different roles. As soon as a knowledge worker has to solve a subtask without having the necessary knowledge, s/he becomes a learner. Having knowledge in some further area, s/he supports others in performing a task as a teaching expert. In the following, we address the identification and selection problem of potential experts for a specific task. The example was added for illustration of our problem:

Example: It is the first time that Anna performs a specific business process. Until now, she did not gain necessary knowledge how to deal with the problem. Indeed, the existing knowledge database provides documents related to the problem. Nevertheless, this information is not sufficient to perform the task in an effective way. She depends on experts and teachers directing her through the process. But who are those experts and how can she find them in the company?

Both the current business process and the learner (Anna) influence the categorization of teachers' expertise within a specific topic. In our paper, two approaches for business process and context modelling will be introduced. Section 3 describes the contextualized initiation of cooperation between learners and teachers by means of the example above. More detailed, subsection 3.1 points out how the current process step (task) can be determined. The process of identification and ranking of potential experts is illustrated in 3.2 and 3.3. Subsection 3.4 introduces a way to integrate and reuse the identified collaboration knowledge into the learning solution. An implementation of the approach will be described in section 4. The paper ends with a short summary and future work in section 5.

2   Related Work

Recently, several approaches for knowledge and business process integration have been developed. Additionally to the processes, business-process oriented knowledge management has to consider and model the users of the knowledge system plus the context of use. Below, several works dealing with process and context models will be mentioned and described in a brief way. Hardly any of the authors in this area raises the issue of collaborative and workplace-embedded e-learning. Furthermore, there is a lack of concepts how to integrate the arising knowledge during collaborations into the knowledge solutions.

2.1   Process Modelling

Process modelling provides background information for determining in which working step experts and learners currently are and which tasks they have already worked on. Moreover, businesses applied process modelling as part of their workflow management systems over the last decade. This means that workplace-embedded learning has to consider process modelling as an essential part of a realistic application scenario. Van Welie defines a "task" as a necessary activity to achieve a specific goal [25]. Existing works in task modelling can be assigned either to event-based or state-based models. In the following, we will deepen one representative for each class.

The Business Process Modelling Notation (BPMN) [17] is a standardized graphical notation for drawing business processes in a workflow. BPMN is highly related to UML-modelling. Beyond a coverage of activities and their temporal and logical constraints, the language allows to group activities which are logically related to each other by swim lanes. Artefacts are mainly data objects. Data objects are typed and represent the input and output of activities. BPMN is a representative for event-based modelling languages defining events and activities as continuous elements.

A Petri net is one of several mathematical representations of discrete distributed systems. As a modelling language, it graphically depicts the structure of a distributed system as a directed bipartite graph with annotations. As such, a Petri net has place nodes, transition nodes, and directed arcs connecting places with transitions. Places may contain a number of tokens. Transitions act on input tokens by a process known as firing. A transition is enabled if it can fire, i.e., there is the defined number of tokens in every input place and the output places are able to store the new tokens. Typed events can be expressed by multi-coloured tokens. Van der Aalst discusses Petri nets for work process modelling in [1]. In contrast to BPMNs, Petri nets are state based. Beyond events and activities, the current state is modelled in form of token assignment.

2.2   Work and User Context

Besides the formalized work process model, there are more indicators of the working users' context, which can be exploited for searching experts. The following paragraph presents related work in two different areas regarding context dependant expert identification for workplace-oriented collaborative learning. On the one hand, the task context of the learner has to be recognized since it highly influences the pre-selection of experts. On the other hand, the users' context is considered in a broader scope to show how it can influence the identification of suitable resources and experts.

Task Context. CALVIN [2] is a system considering the task context. Bauer and Leake define the task context as a term-vector-description of the current document. Using a difference analysis, the Wordsieve system analyses sets of terms over time. Task switches can thus be recognized by considering a difference threshold over the term sets. The system exclusively performs document based information retrieval using the content of a web browser window. [9] expands the definition of task context by the factors complexity, challenges and dependencies. Bayesian belief models indicate suitable moments for disruption of the work process. The structuring and categorization of the process into sub-tasks is done manually by experts. The Pinpoint system [3] provides task-specific document recommendations. Task recognition in an automated way is not intended. The task is manually selected in a list created by domain experts. In a nutshell, existing systems deal with user support in recommendation environments usually without automatic task recognition.

User Context. Apparently, the user's context usually reaches far beyond the current task context. Regarding the context driven expert identification, facts like existing qualifications, experiences with the system and available tools or preferences influence the selection process. Certainly, those facts will be included during the expert selection beyond the common task context.

Existing systems designed for expert recommendations are currently based on application and domain specific heuristics. They compare personal profiles and discover similarities [15]. In the area of cooperative learning, [27] specifies context independent of the user in a first step. Here, the authors basically consider and define a didactic model, the goal, performance instructions, existing input materials and tools, learning methods for the group, time frame, and finally benchmarks. Subsequently, this definition will in case of an upcoming cooperation be extended with user dependant conditions and additional information. Those conditions include, amongst others, previous knowledge, personal preferences for cooperation partners, times and tools. Based on all those attributes, the best fitting partners for cooperation will be selected.

[15] motivates a flexible system architecture to benefit from application and domain specific heuristics while developing expert-recommender systems. Such systems require a profiling supervisor, an identification supervisor and a selection supervisor. The profiling supervisor creates and administers user profiles using configurable modules and diverse data sources. An identification supervisor selects applicable resources and persons consulting configurable heuristics. A selection supervisor filters the list according to dynamic strategies and preferences.

We take up this architecture in an adapted way to fulfil the specific requirements of expert identification in workplace-embedded collaborative e-learning environments.

3   Approach

The following approach for business-process oriented expert selection was designed and developed in the context of the APOSDLE[1] project. APOSDLE is an

---

[1] APOSDLE (**A**dvanced **P**rocess-**O**riented **S**elf-**D**irected **L**earning **E**nvironment) is partially funded under the 6th framework programme (FP6) for R&D of the European Commission within the Information Society Technologies (IST) work program 2004 under contract no. IST-027023. See *http://www.aposdle.org*.

integrated project (IP) in the area of Technology Enhanced Learning (TEL) aiming at a conceptual and technical integration of the three roles knowledge worker, learner and teacher into a model of work-integrated learning. Here, the APOS-DLE platform provides a fusion of learning solutions with the computer-based work environment of the users. The overview below is part of the project and was mainly developed in cooperation and discussions among project partners. Main design focus is the seamless fusion between performing a skill-intensive work process as a knowledge worker and a situation where the knowledge worker as a learner needs to consults one or more experts.

Figure 1 illustrates the approach taking up the example scenario mentioned in section 1. In the upper left corner, the user Anna has already performed some sub-tasks of the overall process. The subsequent tasks require knowledge that she has not learned until now. Anna has to acquire the necessary knowledge. To fasten the learning process, an expert guiding her through the learning process has to be selected. The APOSDLE platform is aware of Anna's current task context (1). Including the task context as well as Anna's and the experts' user context, the platform identifies (2) and displays (3) adequate teachers. In this example, the displayed experts are Michael and John. Michael is working in Anna's department. Since he has performed the process several times before and also edited a related learning document, he can easily guide her through the process. John and his colleagues have defined and established the process in the enterprise. Therefore, he is a well-known expert in this area.

Finally, the learner (Anna) makes a final decision about adequate cooperation partners in the list. In the example, Anna initiates collaboration with Michael. Ideally, relevant information of the cooperation will be extracted for re-use and stored in the APOSDLE platform. Later expert searches will consider this information in the selection process.

Following sections deepen the mentioned steps in detail. The numeration of the subsections relates to the numbering in figure 1.

3.1 Elicitation of Context

The goal of our research project is to enhance the productivity of knowledge workers by integrating learning, teaching, and working. In order to support this and many other aspects of an interweaved learning paradigm, the e-learning system needs to be aware of a user's current working task. This information can be seen as a prerequisite for finding suitable experts or resources and is to be retrieved automatically and unobtrusively using low-level context information as indicators. The applicability of traditional machine learning (ML) algorithms to this problem is the subject of this section.

The goal of task prediction is to know the active task of the user at any point in time. Whereby task is a defined unit of work consisting of activities to reach a certain goal. The problem of task prediction is perceived as a machine learning task. When first using the system, it is untrained and the user needs to specify the task s/he works on from a predefined list of business tasks (manual selection). During the work process a context monitoring component logs

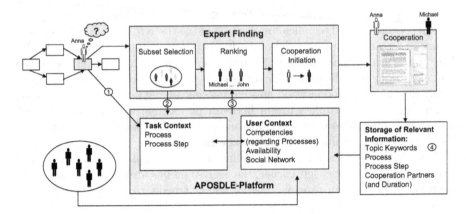

Fig. 1. Sidebar for displaying learning events and initiating collaborations

any desktop events reflecting the user's actions. These include keyboard presses, application launches, document full texts, etc. That way, tagged training material of user's work streams with the task name as class label are collected and as soon as enough material is gathered the system trains a ML model of the user's work task in this business process. The optimal result is achieved when the user continues to work and s/he does not need to manually notify the system of task switches anymore. The task predictor automatically classifies the active tasks using continuously recorded event streams (automated selection). Whenever classification detects a change in tasks, our e-learning environment displays a new list of associated learning resources and suitable experts regarding to the detected work task. The whole scenario is depicted in figure 2.

The machine learning algorithms we implemented and tested are of the types decision tree learning, rule learning, Naïve Bayes, and Support Vector Machines. Naïve Bayes (NB) was chosen due to its good overall performance [8,6], even despite its assumption of class condition independence. Support Vector Machines (SVM) are machine learners that have been reported to perform well on text categorization problems [10]. One efficient training algorithm is *Sequential Minimal Optimization* (SMO) by Platt [18], which was implemented with a modification [23]. SVMs in general are assumed to find a good trade-off between overfitting und over-generalisation [4]. The well-known ID3 implementation by Ross Quinlan [21,19] was chosen as concrete instance of decision tree learners, since it avoids over fitting by a pruning strategy [20]. One of the first successful learning techniques was rule learning [5]. Since it also generates human-readable classification rules and the efficiency and competitiveness was proven by its authors, the incremental reduced error pruning [7] (IREP) algorithm was also chosen for implementation.

In order to evaluate the task prediction in general and the four learning algorithms in particular, a scenario was created that resembles the real use cases well. As evaluation scenario for task prediction we used a modelled business process

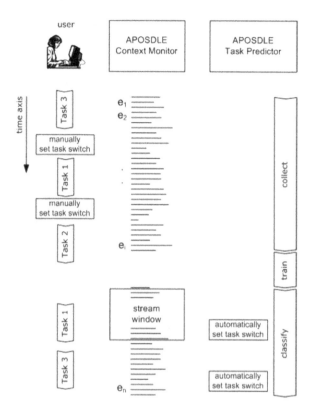

Fig. 2. Task Context Elicitation

of a sample application domain. We decided to model business tasks like *market analysis, product design and specification, find and contact suppliers, contract placement* and *triggering production* in a sequential process model formulated in the process description language YAWL[1], which is based on Petri nets. [2]

An important requirement to our task prediction system is its suitability to situations where labelled training material is sparse. Therefore, the dependence of the implemented algorithms on data availability has been evaluated. Figure 3 shows the preliminary results of a first evaluation of prediction accuracy.

The highest gain of accuracy can be observed for Naïve Bayes. Euclid and IREP are influenced to the smallest degree by the training material availability. Starting at 200 samples, the relations between all algorithms are rather stable. SMO performs best in all scenarios. For the analyzed domain, the trade-off between classification accuracy and cost of collecting labelled data can be maximized with SMO and 300 training samples. This amount is as low as 20 minutes of recording per task (i.e. target label) and yields classification accuracies of 83%.

---

[2] Yet Another Workflow Language. See *http://yawlfoundation.org.*

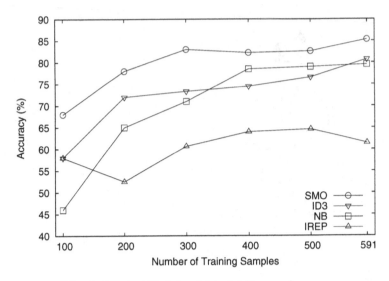

Fig. 3. Effect of Training Material Size on Accuracy

In spite of this positive preliminary evaluation conducted here, the task prediction still has to prove its performance in a larger field study, since the training data this evaluation relied on is just a few hours of recorded desktop work of a student. Several application domains with users of different computer experience and varying numbers of work process tasks need to be considered. Since these data are not yet available from ongoing user studies, the evaluation in this paper was limited to one scenario. Consequently, one of the next tasks is evaluating whether varying application domains with their text domains yield performance differences in context-dependant task prediction. The next section shows how the detected task is used in our approach for finding recommendations of suitable experts.

3.2   Identification of Relevant Experts

Based on the task context (and other information about the user contained in the user profile) we can recommend appropriate tools and resources (i.e. templates, documents and learning material) and collaboration partners (i.e. peers and experts). In this section we will describe how to identify relevant experts. Due to space limitations we can only sketch our approach and go into more detail for some facets. Whether a user A is suitable as a collaboration partner for user B or not is determined by the contexts of users A and B. Note that the various parts of a context are of different importance depending on a user's role (seeking advice or being a potential expert). For example, the current task of the person seeking advice is important for identifying relevant experts, the current task of the potential expert is less important. In order to decide whether or not a user A is a potential expert for a user B who is seeking advice we consider the parameters, which are outlined hereinafter.

Competency. A user's expertise with respect to a given task is inferred from the user's past behaviour. The inference used bases on the APOSDLE's meta-model ([24]). Following the approach outlined in detail in e.g. [13] the meta-model relates (among others) tasks to competencies necessary for performing the task successfully. A user's expertise is inferred from his successful task execution. If for instance user A has performed a given task successfully, then A has shown evidence for possessing the competencies related to this task. The more often user A has performed different tasks, which require a certain competency C, the higher A's expertise regarding competency C is considered.

In order to present user B with a list of experts two steps need to be executed: first user B's current task-specific competency need is concluded from the user's current task (1) and the user's manual selection of the competency he needs to learn (2). In a second step those experts are computed, who have shown highest expertise with respect to the user's current competency need. Hence, for the calculation of most suitable experts regarding a certain competency, the task and competency histories for each user need to be stored permanently and a preceding process modelling becomes crucial.

Availability. This criterion is of special importance in cases where advice is needed urgently. Information about availability originates from different sources:

- Similar to other synchronous communication tools (e.g. Instant Messaging) availability is inferred from the login status of a user. If a user is not logged in, s/he is not available as a potential expert.
- For various reasons a user might not want to be seen as available even if s/he is logged in the system. Reasons include for example high workload or a high amount of advice requests. Therefore, the user needs a way to manually set his status to not available.
- In future versions other sources for detecting availability might be included. For example, the system might use a calendar to check whether there is an imminent upcoming meeting involving the potential expert. In that case the expert is probably not willing to start a collaborative session at the moment.

Organizational distance. Organizational distance can be derived for instance from current or past department or project affiliations of A and B. An organizational model, such as *organizational charts*, can be used to compute this distance. The smaller the organizational distance the higher the suitability of a potential cooperation partner is considered. For the time being shortest paths in hierarchical graph-like organisation charts are used for determining the organizational distance. In future versions further criteria (job role, position etc.) may additionally be considered. That way we can guarantee that a student assistant will not bother the CEO of a company.

Social Distance. Social distance can be derived among others from preferences or dislikes towards users and topics and from extent of and satisfaction with previous collaborations. A social network representing groups and their interaction patterns can be used to compute the social distance. Such social networks visualise users as nodes and sender-receiver relations as edges between nodes. One example of a sender-receiver relation is joint participation in a collaborative session in the APOSDLE environment. Consequently, it is possible to define the social distance between two users A and B as being *small* (and therefore *good*) if A and B have in the past often collaborated with each other.

On principle several different sources, which can be evaluated automatically (e.g. e-mail, Instant Messaging), can be used, to compute social distances. For the time being we consider collaborations, which have taken place in APOSDLE-specific dedicated collaboration rooms (see Figure 5). Methods and algorithms from social network analysis ([26]) are very important in the context of APOSDLE as previous studies have already shown that knowledge about and familiarity with the collaboration partner play a decisive role for knowledge sharing [11].

3.3   Prioritization of the List of Potential Experts

For each of the criteria outlined above (competency, availability, organizational distance, social distance) a ranked list of criterion-specific experts is computed. In a next step the different rankings are merged and a single list of *overall experts* is computed. The aim of this step is to come to a list of potential cooperation partners, which is ordered by descending appropriateness. From this list the learner can choose manually a collaboration partner. The prioritisation of the list of potential experts is determined by the above mentioned criteria as well as by the preferences of the learner. The preferences of the learner specify the *individual* importance of a criterion (scale 0 to 1), where the sum of all weights of the criteria must be 1. They are for example defined by the user as part of his user profile. Furthermore they could be specified interactively in the APOSDLE environment by competing sliders. For the sorting of the list of potential experts a user can for example define that the criterion social distance is absolutely important (scale: 1) and the criterion organisational distance is absolutely unimportant (scale: 0). The final expert suitability as a potential collaboration partner is computed using the following heuristic:

$$suitability(expert) = \frac{\sum_{i=1..n} suitability_i(expert) * weight_i}{n}$$

Here $suitability_i(expert)$ denotes the suitability value of a user with respect to the criterion with number i. $weight_i$ denotes the weighting value, which the user has assigned to criterion i. The experts are presented to the user as a list ordered by descending *suitability* of experts. Please note that for the first implementation all values for $weight_i$ are equal and by that all criteria are considered equally important.

3.4 Return of Relevant Information

After finding and presenting a sorted list of context-related experts by the technical system the learner chooses one or more experts from the presented list. With these experts the learner wants to initiate a cooperation step. The APOS-DLE platform offers a tool that integrates synchronous cooperation, e.g. on a whiteboard, and text-based communication in form of a chat [16]. For this paper the cooperation step itself is not relevant; relevant for this paper is the question which data of such a cooperation step should return to the knowledge base and be available for further queries. Concerning the content of the cooperation situation a transcript can be stored that contains amongst others the communicative contributions. This transcript can be linked to other context information concerning the task or the user in order to find it during a later (expert-)search. Further items of context information concerning the task are:

- **Task/Process:** If the cooperation was initiated with respect to an identified task context (see Figure 1) the information about the concrete task/process should be stored on the platform. A user which has a problem with the same task or process later on could maybe solve his problem by reading the corresponding cooperation transcript. That way, no further cooperation with experts is necessary.
- **Topic of the cooperation artefacts:** In order to relate a cooperation artefact on a content level we follow two paths: The platform offers an automatism to relate the cooperation transcript to topics of an existing list of keywords [22]. Additionally, the participants can add further, manually defined keywords after finishing the cooperation.

Further items concerning the context of the user are:

- **Participants:** The storage of participants has two functions. On the one hand it relates persons and tasks as well as persons and dedicated competencies. For further searches of expert concerning the corresponding task these persons are more probably experts. On the other hand a social network can be built on joint participation in the cooperation. This social network has influence on the choice and presentation of appropriate experts for the person (see "social distance" as described above).
- **Length of a cooperation:** From the length of a cooperation one can derive the intensity of knowledge exchange (at least in some cases). Especially very short cooperations are often less helpful for further situations because they are less detailed or explicit and therefore not comprehensible for others.

4 Realization

During the first year of the project an integrated prototype was created, which supports workplace-embedded, individual and cooperative learning. This prototype was realized in a client/server architecture and developed in the programming languages Java and C# . The user interacts with a sidebar on the client

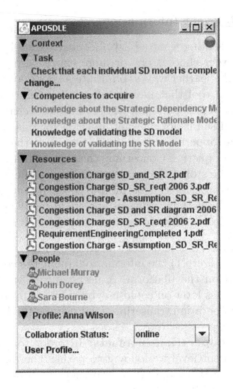

Fig. 4. Sidebar for displaying learning events and initiating collaborations

part of the prototype (see Figure 4). This sidebar displays learning resources and experts suitable to the actual task and necessary competencies. The sidebar additionally holds responsible for merging experts' suitabilities into one list of *overall experts* (see section 3.3).

The computation of criterion-specific expert ranks is executed on the server (i.e. the APOSDLE platform). The platform is used to store extensive user profiles, which contain among others users' task histories, competencies acquired and the availability of potential experts. The platform can identify criterion-specific experts (see section 3.2) using the user profiles stored and inferring information from them by applying the APOSDLE meta-model and diverse heuristics (from e.g. social network analysis and others).

Directly from the sidebar, the user is able to initiate a collaboration with the desired expert. Both collaboration partners join a common collaboration room, where they can exchange text messages und collaboratively work on or discuss about certain documents and presentations. In Figure 5 a collaboration room is depicted, which additionally shares a defined context of the collaboration initiator. Consequently, the invited expert is able to quickly get an idea of the learner's problem and can provide help uncomplicatedly.

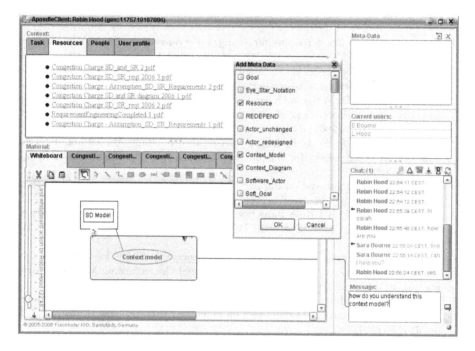

Fig. 5. Collaboration tool with shared context and referenced knowledge artefacts

5   Summary and Outlook

This work introduces a context-aware approach to discover collaboration partners and adequate experts in a workplace-embedded e-learning environment. The
approach fuses the area of process integrated e-learning with on the fly knowledge
transfer. In a first step, Business Process Modelling Notation (BPMN) and Petri
Nets are introduced as promising ways for process modelling. Then, a machine-
learning-approach for task context elicitation is introduced and its preliminary
results are presented. Particularly, this step is a foundation for the main section of identification and prioritization of experts. Whereas, the identification of
relevant experts here is mainly based on competency regarding a certain task,
availability and organizational and social distance between learner and teacher.
Within a list of potential experts, the user finally selects adequate collaboration
partners herself. At the end, the learning process completes with the extraction
and storage of emerging collaboration information in the knowledge platform.
This information both includes the task context like process, topic and the user
context (collaboration partners, competencies, session length). The whole approach is illustrated following an example scenario. Based on this approach, the
APOSDLE prototype was designed and developed. Currently, the system is evaluated in the field in cooperation with project partners. The evaluation will in
principal analyze the capability of the approach under realistic circumstances.
Future work will include a detailed analysis of the study results.

References

1. Aalst, W.: Three Good reasons for Using a Petri-net-based Workflow Management System. In: Navathe, S., Wakayama, T. (eds.) Proceedings of the International Working Conference on Information and Process Integration in Enterprises (IPIC'96), Camebridge, Massachusetts, pp. 179–201 (1996)
2. Bauer, T., Leake, D.: A Research Agent Architecture for Real Time Data Collection and Analysis. In: Proceedings of the Workshop on Infrastructure for Agents, MAS, and Scalable MAS (2001)
3. Birnbaum, L., Hopp, W.J., Iravani, S., Livingston, K., Shou, B., Tirpak, T.: Task aware information access for diagnosis of manufacturing problems. In: IUI, pp. 308–310 (2005)
4. Burges, C.J.C.: A Tutorial on Support Vector Machines for Pattern Recognition. Data Mining and Knowledge Discovery 2(2), 121–167 (1998)
5. Clark, P., Boswell, R.: Rule Induction with CN2: Some Recent Improvements. Proceedings of the Fifth European Working Session on Learning 482, 151–163 (1991)
6. Domingos, P., Pazzani, M.J.: Beyond Independence: Conditions for the Optimality of the Simple Bayesian Classifier. In: International Conference on Machine Learning, pp. 105–112 (1996)
7. Fürnkranz, J., Widmer, G.: Incremental Reduced Error Pruning. In: Proceedings the Eleventh International Conference on Machine Learning, New Brunswick, NJ, pp. 70–77 (1994)
8. Han, J., Kamber, M.: Data Mining. Concepts and Techniques. Morgan Kaufmann Publishers, San Francisco (2001)
9. Horvitz, E., Breese, J., Heckerman, D., Hovel, D., Rommelse, K.: The Lumiere project: Bayesian user modeling for inferring the goals and needs of software users. In: Proceedings of the Fourteenth Conference on Uncertainty in Artificial Intelligence, Madison, WI, pp. 256–265 (1998)
10. Joachims, T.: Text Categorization with Support Vector Machines: Learning with Many Relevant Features. Proceedings of the 10th European Conference on Machine Learning, pp. 137–142 (1998)
11. Kienle, A., Menold, N., Herrmann, T.: Wissensgenese, Wissensverteilung und Wissensorganisation der der Arbeitspraxis, chapter Technische und organisatorische gestaltungsoptionen für unternehmensinterne Wissensmanagementprojekte, pp. 109–153. Westdeutscher Verlag (2003)
12. Lave, J., Wenger, E.: Situated Learning: Legitimate Peripheral Participation. Cambridge University Press, Cambridge (1991)
13. Ley, T., Lindstaedt, S.N., Albert, D.: Competency Management Using the Competence Performance Approach: Modelling, Assessment, Validation and Use. In: Sicilia, M.A. (ed.) Competencies in Organizational E-Learning, pp. 83–119. Information Science Publishing, Hershey, PA (2006)
14. Lindstaedt, S.N., Ley, T., Mayer, H.: Integrating Working and Learning with APOSDLE. In: Proceedings of the 11th Business Meeting of Forum Neue Medien, Graz, Verlag Forum Neue Medien (2005)
15. Mcdonald, D.W.: Supporting nuance in groupware design: moving from naturalistic expertise location to expertise recommendation. PhD thesis, Chair-Mark S. Ackerman (2000)
16. Mühlpfordt, M.: Dual Interaction Spaces: Integration synchroner Kommunikation und Kooperation. In: Mühlhäuser, M., Rößling, G., Steinmetz, R. (eds.) LNI, GI, vol. 87, pp. 99–110 (2006)

17. Object Management Group. OMG BPMN Final Adopted Specification (2006), http://www.omg.org/docs/dtc/06-02-01.pdf
18. Platt, J.: Fast Training of Support Vector Machines using Sequential Minimal Optimization. MIT Press, Cambridge (1998)
19. Quinlan, J.R.: Induction of Decision Trees. Machine Learning 1(1), 81–106 (1986)
20. Quinlan, J.R.: Simplifying Decision Trees. International Journal of Man-Machine Studies 27(3), 221–234 (1987)
21. Quinlan, J.R.: Learning decision tree classifiers. ACM Computing Surveys (CSUR) 28(1), 71–72 (1996)
22. Scheir, P., Hofmair, P., Granitzer, M., Lindstaedt, S.: The OntologyMapper plug-in: Supporting Semantic Annotation of Text-Documents by Classification. In: Semantic Systems From Vision to Applications - Proceedings of the SEMANTICS 2006, pp. 291–301. Österreichische Computer Gesellschaft (2006)
23. Schölkopf, B., Smola, A.J.: Learning with Kernels. MIT Press, Cambridge (2002)
24. Ulbrich, A., Scheir, P., Lindstaedt, S.N., Görtz, M.: A Context-Model for Supporting Work-Integrated Learning. In: Nejdl, W., Tochtermann, K. (eds.) EC-TEL 2006. LNCS, vol. 4227, pp. 525–530. Springer, Heidelberg (2006)
25. van Welie, M., van der Veer, G.C., Eliëns, A.: An Ontology for Task World Models. In: Markopoulos, P., Johnson, P. (eds.) Design, Specification and Verification of Interactive Systems '98, Wien, pp. 57–70. Springer, Heidelberg (1998)
26. Wasserman, S., Faust, K., Iacobucci, D.: Social Network Analysis: Methods and Applications. Structural Analysis in the Social Sciences. Cambridge University Press, Cambridge (1994)
27. Wessner, M.: Kontextuelle Kooperation in virtuellen Lernumgebungen. Eul, Lohmar (2005)

Negotiating the Path from Curriculum Design to E-Learning Course Delivery: A Study of Critical Success Factors for Instructional Systems Design

Maggie McPherson and Miguel Baptista Nunes

School of Education, University of Leeds
E.C.Stoner 7.65, Leeds LS2 9JT, United Kingdom
m.mcpherson@leeds.ac.uk
Department of Information Studies
University of Sheffield
Regent Court, Sheffield, S1 4DP
j.m.nunes@sheffield.ac.uk

Abstract. E-learning has been said to offer many benefits to learners, but to be effective, it requires the combination of a complex set of technological, pedagogical and organizational components. Integrating these very different aspects of e-learning can be challenging and may at times require the resolution of contradictory demands and conflicting needs. Yet, at this point, many universities are still trying to redesign their courses, professional practice and administrative procedures in order to address the emerging demands of this new approach. One matter of crucial importance to any e-learning initiative is the appropriate design and development of its learning environment. Instructional Systems Design (ISD) is the framework whereby the technological, pedagogical and organizational components are considered and brought together to create viable learning environments and programmes. This paper reports on research that identifies and assesses Critical Success Factors (CSFs) for ISD in order to develop coherent and consistent environments that can underpin the successful implementation of e-learning courses and programmes, thus providing an explicit theoretical foundation upon which decision-making and strategic thinking about the design and development of e-learning can be based.

1 Introduction

Just as is the case for face-to-face (f2f) learning, e-learning environments must in actual fact support interactions between the tutor, the learner and her/his peers, subject matter specialists and the learning materials. However, it should be acknowledged that not all of these interactions are necessarily computer mediated and there are occasions where for pedagogical reasons it is desirable to retain some f2f elements. However, within the context of this research, an e-learning environment is an application specifically produced for a particular learning purpose or learning need, built using a particular pedagogical philosophy and a specific delivery technological platform [1]. Thus, these environments have clearly established boundaries, despite being linked with other learning applications, software applications, databases,

E. Duval, R. Klamma, and M. Wolpers (Eds.): EC-TEL 2007, LNCS 4753, pp. 232–246, 2007.
© Springer-Verlag Berlin Heidelberg 2007

computer mediated communication facilities, web pages and portals, or even social software such as that provided through Web 2.0, etc.

As a matter of fact, an e-learning environment can be regarded as an educational system that comprises sets of interacting, interrelated, structured experiences that are designed to achieve specific learning objectives, but organised into a unified dynamic whole [2]. Hence, the design of such a system should result from the specifications emerging from the process of analysing curricular problems and needs. These systems should be seen as open, that is, as a system that is subject to influences from student needs, adopted pedagogical models, technological constraints, institutional norms and societal demands. In effect, the design and implementation of such complex systems requires a systematic process of design, usually known as instructional systems design (ISD) [3]. This process may not necessarily be linear or step-by-step and requires a holistic view of e-learning to be successful [op cit].

This paper reports on a research project that was designed to take a critical research approach aiming at identifying *Critical Success Factors* (CSFs) related to e-learning strategies, implementation, design and delivery from the perspective of e-learning researchers and practitioners. The CSFs discussed in this paper specifically relate to ISD and its influence and impact on the design and development of e-learning. These CSFs were derived from a holistic, consultative and emancipatory perspective. Bearing this perspective in mind, and the necessity of doing research in a complex organisational setting, it was decided to draw inspiration from generic management theory that suggests that the identification of sets of factors that are critical to successful change management is fundamental [4].

2   The Research Design

The general aims and design of this research are defined by the research question, which has been formulated as follows: "*What are the underlying Critical Success Factors required to support the design, development, implementation and management of e-learning within Higher Education (HE) institutions?*" In fact, the notion of isolating critical factors as a guide for business success was first explored as long ago as 1961, but in generic terms, Critical Success Factors (CSFs) can be defined the fundamental factors that practitioners and managers should keep a firm eye on [5]. However, in the case of this research, the CSFs in question have emerged from the evaluation of factors in the limited sphere of e-learning, rather than placing a wider focus on the key performance indicators of HE programme provision in its entirety.

2.1   CSF Analysis in E-Learning

CSF analysis is a widely used top-down methodology [6]. This type of analysis has been very often used in examining factors influenced by technological change and this research methodology is thought to be ideally suited as a means to establish management information requirements, to define information to be managed; and above all to identify the crucial factors that must be addressed for an organisation to do well [op cit]. In this particular investigation, however, the CSF analysis was based on a characterisation of e-learning, comprising a framework with five fundamental

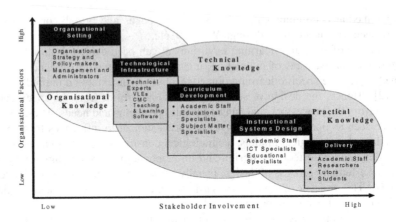

Fig. 1. A framework for the study of e-learning

aspects: organisational; technological; curriculum design; instructional systems design (ISD); and finally e-learning course delivery. The paper presented here focuses explicitly on the ISD component of the framework presented in Fig. 1.

3   Eliciting E-Learning CSFs Through Critical Research

During the initial planning of this study, and in response to the question of the research approach for data collection, survey methods or in-loco individual interview approaches (e.g. grounded theory) were considered, but eliminated because it was felt that these would not allow for cognitive conflict, i.e. breaking with principles of current daily practice and freedom from individual institutional policies considered necessary for a truly liberating process. For a truly productive result to be achieved, it was felt a broad-based consultative approach was needed, i.e., one that would bring together different e-learning stakeholders and enthusiasts from a variety of different HE institutions and backgrounds. Consequently, it was felt that neither interviews conducted within an institutional context nor a case-study approach centring on one HE institution would make it easy for respondents to really break away from their own particular organisational culture, policies and ideologies. Conversely, in order to bring about this transformative knowledge, it was deemed vital to bring together practitioners, researchers, administrators and technologists in a neutral environment in order to enable the discussion and social negotiation of CSFs. Thus, since it would provide the necessary holistic, consultative and emancipatory perspective that was being sought [5], critical research was chosen as the approach for this study.

3.1   Methodological Rationale

After reviewing the options, co-operative inquiry was selected as a suitable methodology to achieve this transformative knowledge and the data collection itself was based on focus group interviews, because this offered a unique and comprehensive form of participative research in which e-learning stakeholders could use the full range of their sensibilities, knowledge and experiences to discuss different aspects and reflect on understandings of this relatively new approach to learning.

A focus group study is a typical co-operative data collection method. In fact, these are thought to be ideal when the research is trying to understand diverse perspectives held by different groups engaged in a particular process [7]. Given that e-learning initiatives involve a number of individuals in distinctive educational roles (i.e., management, IT staff, academics and instructional designers), it was felt that focus groups would provide good support to elicit CSFs. Group forces or dynamics become an integral part of the procedure with participants engaged in discussion with each other rather than directing their comments solely to the moderator. Thus, a focus group is, in essence, a semi-structured interview in which a moderator keeps the direction of discussions under control by utilising a preset list of questions or script.

3.2   A Critical Research Methodology Using Focus Group Interviews

Since a critical research approach had been adopted, it was necessary to ensure that the setting of these group interviews was conducive to socially negotiated, transformative and emancipatory outcomes. Thus, a neutral environment that was both informal and unconstrained by institutional values had to be found. Therefore, the initial thought of conducting focus group interviews in selected HE institutions was rejected. Such group discussions would necessarily be biased and constrained by the organisational structure, culture and policies. After all, "organizational questions are not primary things" [8] and a more holistic view of e-learning within HE was being sought. After much consideration and debate, it was decided to conduct these focus group interviews in research workshops at a number of conferences in the field of educational technology and e-learning.

Although the study was initiated within an English HE institution, it was decided not to limit data collection to UK-based conferences. This decision aimed at allowing the collection of a wider set of opinions and expertise so that the findings could be more emancipatory and less influenced by a respondent's institutional setting. Furthermore, cohesion and consistency of the sample is not paramount in critical research. In fact, in a study that aims at obtaining emancipatory and transformative knowledge, such homogeneity is not advantageous.

Since the main stakeholders in e-learning are educational practitioners, researchers, administrators and technologists, after much consideration and debate, it was decided to conduct these focus group interviews with approximately 15-20 participants in four separate workshops at e-learning/educational technology conferences (AUA 2002, E-Learn 2002, ICALT 2002 and ICCE 2002).

However, although one of the pre-requisites for attending these workshops was that all participants should have a good level of expertise in the field of e-learning, it was not considered possible to have a meaningful discussion or to confer on a complex phenomenon like this unless a reasonable level of pre-understanding could be reached. To achieve this pre-understanding, participants were provided with short position papers that had emerged from an exhaustive critical literature review on each of the five aspects of the e-learning framework. This initial conception was supplemented at each research workshop with short presentations based on the position papers and group discussions which, coupled with the systematic processes of facilitated group dynamics and negotiation of meanings, enabled a deeper understanding of the data [9]. This then represented the theoretical foundation for the understanding and proposal of the e-learning CSFs by the each of the participants.

The strategy for data collection and exploration of participants' views through group discussions around the issues relating to each of the e-learning CSF areas outlined in Fig.1. At the end of each of the focus group sessions, participants were given time to consider the group discussions and to form their own views of CSFs related to each aspect of e-learning conceptual framework. Participants were then asked to draw up, in a tabular form provided, their own top five preferred CSFs in each category. To conclude the workshop sessions, plenary discussions, moderated by the researchers, invited and encouraged any additional debate and the gathering of any final comments.

3.3 Analysis of Focus Group Interview Responses

The questions posed to focus group interviewees were totally open-ended, aiming at enabling total freedom of expression and individual formulation of opinion of their principal CSFs, within each category of the conceptual e-learning framework. The results from participants at all the research workshops (AUA 2002=15, E-Learn 2002=17, ICALT 2002=22, and ICCE 2002=20, i.e. 75 respondents in total) were gathered through an open-ended structured questionnaire which had been filled in by each individual participant at the end of one of the focus group interview sessions as outlined above. In this paper, the category of the e-learning framework (Fig.1) being discussed is that of ISD. Since this research is essentially qualitative and exploratory, the method used to identify the principal e-learning CSF categories in this category was initially identified through a form of thematic analysis [10].

Using this approach, sets of related CSFs, brought together by the interviewees from across organizational boundaries into a grouping that makes sense to them as practitioners, were regarded as core ISD issues. The identification and formulation of the individual CSFs within these themes was made by coding similar terms and ideas in the responses of interviewees. This involved merging responses from the various group sessions and then, due to the choice of using open-ended responses, using a process of selective coding to analyse and synthesise findings as well as to establish relationships between the different codes identified in order to interpret the data. In the case of this analysis, iterative selective coding was being used to identify and present CSFs that could be of use for both academics and practitioners when devising strategies for e-learning.

The concept of selective coding used in this research was adapted from Grounded Theory as proposed by [11]. This does not imply that this is a Grounded Theory study which involves concurrent data collection and analysis; it simply means that the concept of selective coding was used in order to interpret and understand data collected in the open-ended responses. Selective coding involves the *integration* of categories that have been developed to form the initial theoretical framework [12]. In this study, the coding was used to identify the properties, conditions, and relationships between the emerging concepts and categories at each stage of data collection [13]. This process of selective coding implies first the choice of one category to be the core category, and then to relate all other concepts to that category. Once the ISD CSFs were identified, they were then grouped in clusters related to this main category. In this context, in the core e-learning CSFs of ISD, a cluster is a subset of CSFs, within the overall universe of e-learning, which are closely related to one another and relatively far and separated from other CSFs.

Occasionally, many interviewees referred to the same issue, and on other occasions, the same interviewee referred to the same CSF more than once in his/her response by rearranging words with different emphases. Therefore, in implementing the selective coding, it was necessary to apply the following rules:

1. *CSFs that had a frequency of at least two were retained.*
2. *CSFs that were very similar (i.e. with slight variations in wording) were merged.*
3. *CSFs that were mentioned only once, but were nonetheless thought to be important to the domain of e-Learning, were retained.*
4. *Single CSF statements that contained multiple and independent CSFs were separated.*
5. *CSFs that were exact duplicates were eliminated.*
6. *CSFs that were completely unrelated to e-Learning were eliminated.*

For example, although there were ten references to "money" as an issue (rule 5), this was included as one statement. Therefore, the process of clustering in this study is not quantitative, but can be described as having resulted from a qualitative coding approach built through an inductive process, with no particular relevance being given to either frequency of terms or to the repetition of ideas and concepts. Therefore, in this sense, to cluster a set of CSFs was intended to identify similarities within the professional practice that emerges from e-learning [14].

In fact, after merging the data from all workshops, initial analysis clearly showed that CSFs are not neatly bounded by the five aspects of e-learning listed in Fig.1., and it became increasingly apparent that the results of the selective coding process of CSFs for ISD would be best represented using an ontology that "... *defines a common vocabulary for researchers who need to share information in a domain. It includes [...] interpretable definitions of basic concepts in the domain and relations among them.*" [15]. Moreover, ontologies are often developed in order to allow for sharing common understanding, enabling reuse of domain knowledge, making domain assumptions explicit, separating the general domain knowledge from operational knowledge and analyzing domain knowledge [16].

Thus, the ISD CSFs as presented in Appendix 1 were initially characterized through thematic analysis, and then related clusters of CSFs emerging from this process were identified and finally represented in ontology.

4 Research Findings

Four main CSFs were identified within the resultant ISD ontology relating to staffing, pedagogy, design for learning and process issues and the sub-themes identified have been rephrased as questions. This CSF ontology for the category of 'ISD', intended to help researchers understand how individual educationalists and developers construe approaches for transforming curriculum design into a format that would be suitable for e-learning delivery, is presented in Table 1 below:

Table 1. e-Learning CSF Ontology for ISD

Ensure effective collaboration between all staff involved

- Establish which specialist staff need to be involved in the ISD process
- *Which experts in particular need to have a role?*
  - Academic, educational specialists, educational technology/ instructional design specialists, technical staff / ICT (Information Communication Technology) specialists
- Determine profile of staff involvement
- *Does everyone involved have the necessary skills and knowledge?*
  - Is there a system of recognition/reward in place to ensure motivation?
  - Does a culture of collaborative work exist?
  - Is there respect for educational specialists?
- Make certain that it is an effective collaborative process involving all specialists
- *Will the ISD process involve cross-functional teams?*
  - Domain experts, educational specialists, academic staff, faculty, teachers, librarians, IT developers, instructional designer, coach, and former students
- Create a co-evolutionary ethos
- *Can staff be encouraged to share and collaborate in good practice?*
  - Is there a common understanding between educational experts and developers
  - Can this further develop a shared process and understanding: integrating team effort

Ascertain suitability of pedagogical approach

- Consider the various pedagogical strategies (active learning, student learning, metaphors)
- *Is there a clear awareness of the profile of learners?*
  - Is this based on knowledge of student-centered strategies?
  - Is this rooted in constructivist principles?
  - Is it founded on knowledge of continuous learning?
  - Has learning been developed for deep understanding?
  - Has missing knowledge and skills been attended to?
- *Is it appropriate to adopt a blended learning approach?*
  - Should e-learning consist of stand-alone units, i.e. as an extension to existing work?
  - What sort of tasks should be incorporated?
- *Has it been ensured that pedagogy drives technical use, i.e. not teaching just what is on the web?*
  - Have approaches that are not technologically driven been adopted?
  - Is pedagogy correct for technology to work, e.g. e-books used differently to DVD or CMC?

Table 1. (*continued*)

•	Base the pedagogical model on faculty's philosophy of learning
•	*Is this an appropriate pedagogical model with a strong philosophy of learning?*
·	Does this pedagogy fit in with current statues and institutional ordinances?
·	Are there clear learning outcomes?
•	Address testing and assessment processes
•	*Has a suitable testing and assessment framework been devised?*
·	Will assessment be in incremental blocks - end of phase/year etc.?
·	Can it be ensured that assessment is based on the application of knowledge rather than on simple recall tests?
·	How will feedback be provided?
·	What is the way to give feedback?
•	*Deadline for exercises*
·	Take into account timetable, exercises for students

Address the challenge of designing for learning

•	Decide on an appropriate strategy to ensure appropriate learning can take place
•	*Is the ISD strategy grounded on research evidence of what works?*
·	Is it purposeful use rather than just for sake of keeping up with trends?
•	*Which instruction and delivery model should be chosen: online; i.e. web-based / web-delivered; partially online; i.e. web-enhanced (blended); not online; i.e. CD, f2f.*
·	Should the ISD include newer and better methods and models for new technologies (old ones may not work)?
·	What context of use / what is appropriate?
·	Will it be used in various situations (homework, in school, in others' school)?
·	Can the design of learning content be as close as possible for "all" learning styles?
•	*Is the ISD strategy appropriate to the subject domain?*
·	Has the appropriate "ISD" process been identified?
·	Do academics in content area have the appropriate qualifications and experience?
•	Think carefully about the possibilities for personalisation of learning
•	*Will the design be learner-centred?*
·	Are there different paths to learning for students?
·	Does the approach incorporate student learning style?
·	Have users' desires been considered?
·	Will it be possible to develop different layouts for different learners?
•	*Is there sufficient interactivity?*
·	Are the students are able to 'discover' by themselves?
·	Has the individual interaction been put in the forefront line?
·	Is interaction between student-teacher / student-student being built in?

Table 1. (*continued*)

·	Can the learning process allow more dynamic implication from student, less passive action?
·	Have students' motivation been well thought-out?
•	*Can different ways to learn the same content / matters can be offered?*
·	Is it possible to provide a "rich learning environment"?
·	What structure will the learning environment take?
·	Highly structured?
·	What methodology is required?
·	Single method or mixed methods?
•	Decide what level of quality of materials is required so that no lowering of standards occurs
•	*Will it be possible to offer good media presentation (HCI)*
·	Is it possible to convert the subject matter into electronic material, taking into account the functionality the technology provides?
·	Are hyperlinks to outside resources needed?
·	Will the technology include tools which enable the learner to express his/her ideas (like concept maps)?
·	Has readability been taken into consideration; font, spacing, margins?
•	Consider the functionality of the resource
•	*Will it be:*
·	user-friendly?
·	Accessible?
·	Adaptable?
·	consistent?
·	simple and easy-to-use?
·	robust?
•	*Has consideration been given to how the material will be presented?*
·	Will the presentation be informative?
·	Will it make learning fun?
Attend to process issues	
•	Ascertain that the design process will be academic led, with admin input rather than the other way round
•	*Has an appropriate instructional design process been identified?*
·	Can the technology leveraged to turn constraint into opportunity?
·	Will the process be supported rather than constrained by the tools, i.e. no technology driven?
·	Has the full armoury of techniques been contemplated, e.g. the possibility of integrating AI technology?

Table 1. (*continued*)

Attend to process issues (cont.)
• Ensure appropriate change management procedures are in place
• *Can academic staff be assured that eLearning adds value to the traditional lecture?*
· Assure the academic staff that eLearning is reasonably open-ended;
· Will the change bring new possibilities?
• *Can academic staff – ICT – specialists – educational specialists be helped to talk a common language?*
· Have good communication lines been established between domain experts and developers and education experts?
• *Will all aspects of process be formalised?*
· Can this be connected to best practices?
• Pay sufficient attention to suitable staff development, particularly with regard to authoring techniques
• *Have faculty been included/enabled?*
· Can teachers be encouraged to participate?
· Are staff; academic, teachers, designers, properly prepared?
· Do all concerned have a apposite understanding the virtual environment?
• *If teachers are required to create the material, has good support been provided?*
· Has consideration been given as to how to best provide assistance?
· Is the training of academics and all other staff in technology and ICT adequate and appropriate?
· Is online help in the form of eManuals sufficient?
· What backup support systems are in place?
• Decide on an appropriate evaluation process
• *What formative evaluation processes have been put in place?*
· Has evaluation in form of piloting and testing been set up? [i.e. media first: 1st evaluation with small group; 2nd feedback for real learning]
• *Have all suitable evaluation process been established?*
· What pedagogical evaluation processes have been decided upon?
· How will evaluation of design for constant improvement be carried out?
· Should the course be evaluated for continuous improvement?
· Will the use of student feedback be adopted to change and improve?

A visual representation of the main themes emerging from this ontology can be seen in the diagram shown in Fig.2 below. This provides a synopsis of the key ISD CSFs and their associated sub-themes.

Each of these main CSF themes will now be discussed in further detail.

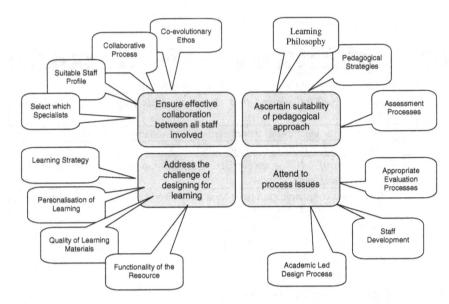

Fig. 2. Synopsis of e-learning CSFs for ISD

4.1 Ensure Effective Collaboration Between All Staff Involved

Since the aim of ISD is to produce effective educational environments, educationalists, subject matter experts and technologists must interact and understand each other, in an integrated and systematic manner, making use of appropriate frameworks. Hence, ISD must integrate the contributions of the *educationalists* that will be primarily responsible for the curriculum design, learning activity specification and learning material creation, *subject matter experts* who are responsible for the primary source materials and *technologists*, who will be responsible for the learning environment design, development and implementation. Therefore ISD methodologies and frameworks must, in a first stage, establish the educational requirements for the particular subject matter and then, in a second stage, develop the environment where learning is to occur. Participants emphasised the importance of collaboration, team work and complementarity of skills and specific sets of knowledge, and these are therefore deemed crucial to the success of e-learning. The sustainability of such cross-functional teams is considered dependent on mutual respect, good communication channels and the creation of common understandings and languages. It is anticipated that the result of these interdisciplinary efforts will be a co-evolution of theories, models, strategies and even frameworks.

4.2 Ascertain Suitability of Pedagogical Approach

The importance of ISD rests in assuring that the whole learning environment is implemented using the same pedagogical approach and is compatible with module, programmes and institutional expected learning outcomes. In fact, if not carefully planned, the e-learning environments could result in a mix of eventually conflicting delivery approaches and theoretical perspectives. Accordingly, there is a proposal that effective ISD and development is only possible if it emerges from deliberate application of a particular theory of learning.

Furthermore, the developers must have acquired reflexive awareness of the theoretical basis underlying the design. This will ensure that pedagogical approaches and ICT conceptual models selected are compatible and all coherently use the same learning philosophy within a particular module. Moreover, participants believe that *"pedagogy should drive technical use"* (13/ICALT 2002) in ISD. Thus, ISD *"must not be technologically driven"* (20/E-Learn 2002), i.e. ISD should be driven by curriculum design and clear learning outcomes, and not driven, as it often has in the past, by technology concerns and fads.

Finally, but not least, it was proposed that ISD needs to conform with organizational *"statutes and ordinances"*. That is, ISD needs to carefully take into consideration organizational constraints and facilities, as well as technological infrastructures and their inherent limitations.

4.3   Address the Challenge of Designing for Learning

The aim of ISD methodologies is to build learning environments that are robust, reliable, efficient, portable, modifiable and maintainable. This is a more traditional view of CSFs in ISD. As expected, participants have identified issues such as usability, accessibility, quality and appropriateness of the learning materials, rich multimedia use, personalization of learning, good computer mediated communication (CMC) and appropriate help and information facilities.

4.4   Attend to Process Issues

Following the argument proposed for pedagogical CSFs, the design of online learning environments usually involves a complex technical component and requires a systematic design and development methodology to translate those pedagogical models into the reality of practice. CSFs associated with this process were sub-divided into four categories: the design process itself, academic acceptance, staff development and evaluation.

The design process must not be technologically driven and needs an *"armoury of techniques"* (14/ICCE 2002), both technological and educational. These need to be integrated by ISD methodologies that enable the dialogue between the different groups. Such a methodology, that consists of a collection of procedures, techniques, tools, and documentation aids that help developers in their efforts to implement a new learning environment.

Learning environments implemented in traditional HE settings usually require processes of change management. These processes, although not necessarily always within the remit of ISD processes, need nonetheless to be considered both at implementation and delivery stages.

Academic acceptance has long been recognized as one of the fundamental CSFs for successful e-learning. Participants proposed that this acceptance is dependant on guaranteeing good communication between educationalists and technologists, creating formalized processes for collaboration, cooperation and evaluation and connecting best practices both within the institution and from other institution's experiences. This will enable co-ownership of design solutions and delivery strategies, the emergence of e-learning champions and therefore allow for better rates of acceptance within the institution.

The transition for a traditional face-to-face learning process to one based on technology enhanced environments, poses serious challenges and cognitive conflicts on both academic staff and students. Consequently, participants have focused heavily on the need for training and support in the use of the e-leaning environments and corresponding affordances.

Finally, evaluation was seen as a crucial component in ISD. Participants propose that this should be a process of *"continuous improvement"* (12/ICCE 2002) that should consider both pedagogical and technical aspects of the design.

5 Conclusions

ISDs could be considered as specialised methodologies which assist and support the activities necessary to produce e-learning environments and include management procedures to control the *process* of deployment of resources and the communication between all the agents actively involved. This methodological approach is of paramount importance in learning environment design and development, since it ensures integration of all *staff* and stakeholders involved in the process: educationalists, content matter specialists, designers and programmers, graphical designers and audio-visual production teams, and even students themselves.

However, as they include concepts and beliefs that define the content and behaviour of the intended systems, as well as values that state which properties of the systems are good and desirable, ISD methodologies are not mere recipes. Thus, these conceptual models have become the vehicle for designers to show the educationalists and subject matter experts involved in the project how to conceive the intended system and thus *design for learning*. Additionally, in learning settings, these models may also be provided to the learners in order to improve conceptual retention, reduce verbatim recall, and improve problem solving transfer. Finally, the philosophical foundations and underlying *pedagogy* determine much of the final structure of the development methodology and even the architecture of the application itself. Although it may seem from these findings that stakeholders (participants) have a very programme-centered-perspective on eLearning, it needs to be pointed out that this paper reports on just one category (ISD) and other CSF sets, such as institutional, technological and curriculum issues have been reported elsewhere [14, 16, 17,18].

It may appear that many of the issues identified in this research are really obvious, but the strength of these findings is that they were elicited from a wide range of seasoned veteran e-learning researchers and practitioners from across the world. It is clear that using ICT to support learning and teaching is complex, and it is felt that if the funding was to be forthcoming, future research might focus on longitutdal implementation studies within a number of institutions to verify whether these CSFs continue to apply over time.

References

[1] Nunes, J.M., Fowell, S.P.: Hypermedia as an Experiential Learning Tool: A Theoretical Model. Information Research 2(1) (1996a) [last accessed 26/01/07] Available online at: http://informationr.net/ir/2-1/paper12.html

[2] Nervig, N.: Instructional Systems Development: A Reconstructed ISD Model. Educational Technology, pp. 40–46 (1990)

[3] Rothwell, W.J., Kazanas, H.C.: What is Instructional Design? In: Rothwell, W.J., Kazanas, H.C. (eds.) Mastering the Instructional Design Process with CD-ROM: A Systematic Approach, 3rd edn. p. 12. Pfeiffer, San Francisco (2003)

[4] Huotari, M.L., Wilson, T.D.: Determining Organizational Information Needs: the Critical Success Factors Approach. Information Research 6(3) (2001), [last accesed: 30/12/2006] E-journal available online at: HYPERLINK http://InformationR.net/ir/6-3/paper108.html

[5] McPherson, M.A., Nunes, J.M.: Critical Research using Focus Group Interviews: An Approach to Elicit Critical Success Factors in eLearning. In: Brown, A., Remenyi, D. (eds.) Proceedings of the 3rd European Conference on Research Methodology for Business and Management Studies, April 29-30, 2004, pp. 263–272. Reading University, UK (2004)

[6] Rockhart, J.F.: Chief Executives Define their own Data Needs. Harvard Business Review 57(2), 238–241 (1979)

[7] Merton, R.K., Fiske, M., Kendall, P.L.: The Focused Interview: A Manual of Problems and Procedures, 2nd edn. Collier MacMillan, London (1990)

[8] Habermas, J.: Theory and Practice (Translated by Viertel, J.), p. 37. Beacon Press, Boston (1973)

[9] Franklin, J., Bloor, M.: Some Issues arising in the Systematic Analysis of Focus Group Materials. In: Barbour, R.S., Kitzinger, J. (eds.) Developing Focus Group Research, pp. 144–155. Thousand Oaks, CA: Sage (1999)

[10] Onwuegbuzie, A.: Effect Sizes in Qualitative Research: A Prolegomenon. Quality and Quantity 37(4), 393–409 (2003)

[11] Strauss, A., Corbin, J.: Basics of Qualitative Research: Grounded Theory Procedures and Techniques. London: Sage (1990)

[12] Pandit, N.: The Creation of Theory: A Recent Application of the Grounded Theory Method. The Qualitative Report, 2(4). Available online at: HYPERLINK [last accessed 3/1/07] (1996), http://www.nova.edu/ssss/QR/QR2-4/pandit.html

[13] Dearnley, C.: Student Support in Open Learning: Sustaining the process. International Review of Research in Open and Distance Learning 4(1), 1492–3831 (2003)

[14] McPherson, M.A., Nunes, J.M.: Organisational Issues for e-Learning: Critical Success Factors as Identified by HE Practitioners. International Journal of Educational Management 20(7), 542–558 (2006a)

[15] Noy, N.F., McGuinness, D.L.: Ontology Development 101: A Guide to Creating Your First Ontology. Web Report, Stanford. [last accessed 26/01/07] (2001) Available online at: HYPERLINK , http://smi.stanford.edu/smi-web/reports/SMI-2001-0880.pdf

[16] McPherson, M.A., Nunes, J.M.: Topped by cross-winds, tugged at by sinuous undercurrents: e-learning organizational critical success factors as identified by HE practitioners. In: Whitelock, D., Wheeler, S. (eds.) Proceedings of the ALT-C 2006 Conference: The Next Generation, September 5-7, 2006, pp. 70–81. Heriot-Watt University, Edinburgh, UK [last accessed 03/02/2007] (2006b), http://www.alt.ac.uk/altc2006/%0baltc2006_documents/research_proceedings_altc2006.pdf

[17] McPherson, M.A., Nunes, J.M.: Flying High or Crash Landing? Technological Critical Success Factors for e-Learning. In: Schofield, M. (ed.) Proceedings of the 1st Conference on Supported Online Learning for Students using Technology for Information and Communication in their Education (SOLSTICE 2006), May 3, 2006 [last accessed 11/06/07] (2006), Available on line at http://www.edgehill.ac.uk/SOLSTICE/Conference 2006/documents/40.pdf

[18] McPherson, M.A., Nunes, J.M.: Kindling a Passion for Acquiring New Knowledge: Critical Success Factors for Creating Appropriate Curricula for e-Learning. In: Proceedings of the ED-MEDIA 2007-World Conference on Educational Multimedia, Hypermedia & Telecommunications, June 25- June 29, Vancouver, Canada (2007)

A Game-Based Adaptive Unit of Learning with IMS Learning Design and <e-Adventure>

Pablo Moreno-Ger[1], Daniel Burgos[2], José Luis Sierra[1],
and Baltasar Fernández-Manjón[1]

[1] Dpto. Ingeniería del Software e Inteligencia Artificial. Fac. Informática. Universidad Complutense. 28040, Madrid. Spain
{pablom,jlsierra,balta}@fdi.ucm.es
[2] Educational Technology Expertise Centre (OTEC). The Open University of the Netherlands. Heerlen. The Netherlands
daniel.burgos@ou.nl

Abstract. In this paper we illustrate how to conceive, implement and play adaptive Units of Learning (UoLs) that embed educational videogames. For this purpose we describe *The Art & Craft of chocolate* UoL, with the game *Paniel and the chocolate-based sauce adventure* as a key feature. The UoL includes a pre-test whose outcome is used to adapt the game. The UoL also assesses the learning process using an in-game exam. This UoL has been modeled using IMS Learning Design (LD), and the embedded game has been developed using the <e-Adventure> educational game engine. This UoL may be deployed in any LD-compliant environment, although some of the features like the adaptation of the game or automatic assessment require special plug-ins that enable the communication between the environment and the <e-Adventure> engine. These plug-ins have been developed as an open-source modification of the SLeD player.

Keywords: edutainment, adaptive e-learning, <e-Adventure>, IMS Learning Design.

1 Introduction

There is a growing interest for the introduction of computer and videogames in educational environments. Games have become one of the biggest entertainment industries, rivalling cinema and surpassing literature [8], mostly because modern games are attractive, engaging and immersive. Additionally, the research about the nature of fun and motivation in videogames highlights a number of elements such as short feedback cycles, high interactivity, or embodiment, which can have a significant impact in educational environments [9,17,18]. The pedagogical benefits of game-based approaches, as well as some of their shortcomings, have been thoroughly studied in the literature [2,10,13,20,29]. Typical problems include social rejection, excessively high development costs, and poor results when the resulting products include very precise and detailed content but fail completely when it comes to

E. Duval, R. Klamma, and M. Wolpers (Eds.): EC-TEL 2007, LNCS 4753, pp. 247–261, 2007.
© Springer-Verlag Berlin Heidelberg 2007

providing entertainment (thus missing the appeal of videogames and its associated pedagogical benefits) [27,28].

Remarkably, educational videogames are complex software artefacts that are executed on the student's computer. This fact makes them very interesting from the perspective of adaptive learning because the videogame can behave differently every time it is run. Indeed, the possibility of choosing different levels of difficulty has been present in videogames since the very beginning. Most games become increasingly difficult as the user progresses (i.e. each level is more challenging than the previous one) and, additionally, it is usually possible to select a base level of difficulty so that the experience is neither too challenging nor too easy. The objective is to keep the player in *the zone* where he or she is forced to perform at the limit of his/her competence but without exceeding it.

The key idea is that videogames and adaptation are synergic fields and we should leverage this when creating adaptive contents and courses.

On the other hand, a field that could benefit most from adaptive learning (and that invests a lot of effort and research in the matter) is online learning. The so-called Learning Management Systems (LMS) facilitate and monitor the learning experiences of large groups of students. Even though these environments are sometimes targeted at a very specific group of users, it is also common to find systems targeted at broad audiences that have different learning styles, differences in their previous background and different learning objectives.

For this reason, there is a lot of research into providing adaptive learning experiences [4,24] in which the adaptation optimizes the focus of the content (by fitting different levels of previous knowledge or different objectives) and the overall learning experience (by fitting different learning styles). In this arena, the IMS Learning Design specification is one of the key elements because it facilitates a formal modelling of the intricacies of adaptive learning paths.

In this paper, we analyze the potential synergies between adaptive games and learning environments based on the IMS Learning Design specification [11]. For this purpose, we have conceived an adaptive Unit of Learning (UoL) built around an educational game. This UoL has been modelled with IMS Learning Design. For the implementation of the adaptive videogame we have used the <e-Adventure> educational game engine [21], leveraging its built-in adaptation and assessment features. The <e-Adventure> engine can be deployed to the student's computer from an LMS and, should the LMS support it, establish a bidirectional communication with the server that can be used to alter the behaviour of the game and to inform the LMS of the activities of the student within the game [19]. The result is an adaptive process with a complete feedback loop in which previous knowledge about the student and his/her performance is used to modify the game and in which the activity of the student within game is used to improve that knowledge and adapt the rest of the learning experience.

The structure of this work is as follows: section 2 describes the adaptive UoL. Section 3 introduces the supporting technologies used in its implementation: IMS Learning Design and <e-Adventure>. In section 4 we outline the technical details regarding the execution environment. Finally, in section 5 we present the conclusions and some lines of future work.

2 The *Art and Craft of Chocolate* UoL

Learning Management Systems in online education are often targeted at broad audiences with varying demographics. The students have different backgrounds, different levels of initial knowledge, different ambitions in terms of learning objectives and even different learning styles.

The inclusion of adaptation techniques to fit the needs of different students is thus pedagogically and commercially sound. In particular, we are mainly interested in studying adaptation in the context of educational games and their use in complex UoLs.

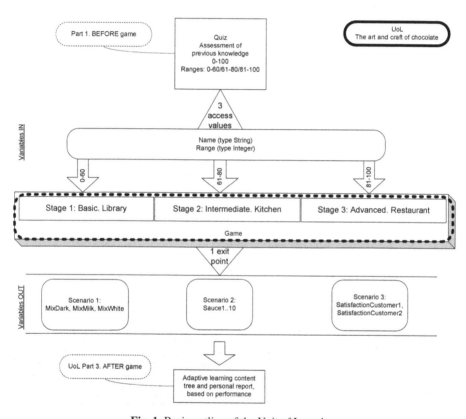

Fig. 1. Basic outline of the Unit of Learning

In order to show how an adaptive UoL involving educational games can be effectively achieved, we have conceived a sample UoL that includes a sample adaptive game. The UoL is entitled *The Art and Craft of Chocolate* and deals with advanced uses of cocoa and chocolate in cooking. The educational goal is to let learners learn how to prepare chocolate sauces by mixing different chocolate types and how to use these sauces to prepare a variety of sophisticated dishes.

The technical goal, however, is to provide a proof-of-concept implementation of the different mechanisms required in order to achieve adaptive UoLs embedding educational videogames. In particular, we focus on two different issues: (i) letting the UoL modify the game's state and, (ii) letting the game modify the UoL's state. For this purpose, we structure the UoL as follows (see Fig. 1):

- The first step of the instructional design includes some traditional content and some basic tests to capture the student's initial level of knowledge.
- Then the game is launched and adapted according to that information.
- The game itself includes an in-game exam. The results of that exam are used to grade the student. Additionally, this assessment can also be used to decide the flow of the rest of the learning experience.

The following subsections describe these phases in greater detail.

Fig. 2. Screenshot of the *Paniel and the Chocolate-based Sauce Adventure* game

2.1 The Game

The main part of the UoL is an educational *point and click* adventure game entitled *Paniel and the Chocolate-based Sauce Adventure* (Fig. 2). The game covers the two chapters of the syllabus (creation of basic chocolate masses and their use to create sauces for different recipes) and includes a final in-game exam in which the student is required to apply the knowledge acquired by finding out about their tastes and preparing the right sauces to accompany the right dishes.

2.2 The script

A key aspect when writing games is to achieve the right balance between the elements that make games engaging (a good story, interesting situations, self-guided exploration, etc.) and the content itself [25]. A simple presentation of the content in a linear fashion with some graphics will not attract the student as much as a more elaborate story.

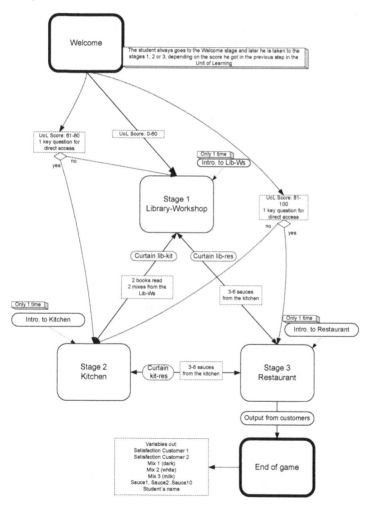

Fig. 3. High-level design of the *Paniel and the Chocolate-based Sauce Adventure* videogame

In this game, Paniel is a young cook enrolled in a course about chocolate. After arriving at the site and engaging in conversation with the beautiful secretary, Paniel is instructed to go to the workshop where the Master Cook is waiting with his first instructions: to browse through the library and prepare some basic chocolate masses with the ingredients available there (black chocolate, milk chocolate, white chocolate, etc). It is up to the player to find the right recipes by consulting the books or by experimentation.

In the second level, the player is asked to prepare a number of chocolate-based sauces in preparation for the final exam. This part of the game is very open as far as the recipes for the sauces are concerned, and information on how to marry sauces with dishes is scattered. Some information can be found in books at the library, the Master Cook provides many recipes and useful information, and some of the recipes can only be obtained by talking the secretary into giving the player some of her personal secret recipes.

Finally, when the player considers that the number of sauces and the knowledge about how to use them is enough, he or she can start the exam. In the exam, the player finds Paniel in the school's restaurant with the tasks of getting information about the customers' tastes and preparing the dishes that will fit those tastes with the available sauces and without the possibility of crafting more sauces or going back to the library for more information.

2.3 Different Paths Through the Game

As sketched in Fig. 3, the high-level design of the game structure is not conceived to be played entirely by every player every time it is run. Indeed:

- Students with previous experience in confectionery will probably already be familiar with the recipes of plain chocolate masses and should be able to skip the first part of the educational game.
- On the other hand, some other students may already have a deep knowledge of the subject. In this case, they can skip the entire learning section in the game and proceed directly to the in-game exam.

Notice that the student is always forced to play the game because it includes the in-game exam that is used as the main grading tool.

2.4 Profiling the Student

In order to exploit the game's adaptive capabilities, the first part of the UoL focuses on capturing information about the students. In full implementations of the system, this step would not need to be as detailed since some of the information would be available in the student's profile.

Apart from basic questions querying the user about his/her name and other preferences, the UoL includes a questionnaire in which we assess the student's initial level in order to skip those parts of the course with which he or she is already familiar. Thus, the questionnaire reflects this information by assigning a score to the student. Then the game is executed and, depending on the initial score, some of its levels are skipped. More precisely, as depicted in Fig. 3:

- If the result is below 60% the game will start from the beginning.
- If the result is between 61% and 80% the first level will be skipped.
- Should the result be above 80%, the game would proceed directly to the final exam with a default set of recipes initially available.

2.5 Built-in Assessment and Reporting

The final in-game exam is used to assess the student's proficiency when it comes to marrying the sauces with their corresponding dishes in order to suit the tastes of the two customers.

After the customers are served, each of them will be satisfied to a certain degree. Their respective satisfaction are the numbers reported back to the UoL, which, in this instance, simply calculates their average and uses it as the new value for the student's grade.

In this simple case, it would be perfectly possible to have the game report simply a final grade. However, the example illustrates the point that turning game data into grades is essentially part of the pedagogical model behind the course and, therefore, the overall instructional design is the most suitable place to tackle these dependencies and calculations.

Depending on the grade obtained in the exam, the learning flow may be altered. A very low mark would result in the learner having to play the game again, overwriting the results of the initial questionnaire so that the game is adapted again, taking into account this new and more refined information. In some cases this may mean playing the game with a lower ranking (the result of the initial questionnaire was not precise enough) or higher (the previous run of the game improved the level of the student).

On the other hand, with an average or high mark the learning process moves forward, displaying two respective pieces of content that would represent different learning paths in a longer UoL.

3 Implementing the *Art and Craft of Chocolate* UoL

The design of rich and complex learning experiences incurs high development costs, which can be alleviated by modelling mechanisms that enable the interoperability of the educational designs. This is precisely one of the objectives of the IMS Learning Design specification [16]: to provide a standardized formalization and modelling tool that enables the interoperability of complex UoLs.

In addition, the inclusion of educational games in these UoLs demands an affordable and cost-effective approach to producing such games. We can meet these requirements by using the <e-Adventure> engine, with the additional advantage of being able to produce games that can be delivered as adaptable and assessable learning objects [19]. Therefore, we have implemented the *Art & Craft of Chocolate* UoL using these technologies, as described in the following sections. The marriage of IMS LD and <e-Adventure> is also addressed in [6].

3.1 IMS Learning Design

The IMS Learning Design specification can be used to model complex instructional designs (or UoLs) in a standardized way, which allows the interchange of those designs and their processing across different learning environments.

Instead of supporting a specific set of pedagogical approaches, specification provides basic syntactic constructs in order to define learning flows consisting of plays, acts, activities, activity structures and environments.

According to [15] a "learning design" specifies the teaching-learning process; that is to say, under which conditions, what activities have to be performed by learners and teachers in order to attain the desired learning objectives.

As stated in the specification, the design of personalization in IMS LD is supported through a mechanism of conditions, properties and global elements. Personal characteristics and information about the state of the learning experience are stored in "properties". Conditions can be defined to adapt the learning design to learner characteristics in runtime.

On the other hand, the specification does not cover (as a design decision, not as a limitation) what a learning activity truly is. The approach taken in [32] envisions service-oriented architectures in which the LD environment uses the Unit of Learning as a map to guide the learning experience, requesting the different services from the available service providers when demanded by the UoL.

Given the relevance of the IMS LD specification, we used it to model our proof-of-concept UoL. The preliminary test, the adaptive game and the alternative learning paths after the game are all *Activities* in the UoL, and we define *Properties* to store the information that should be sent to the game as well as the information that the game should transmit to the UoL.

In our instructional design, the previous test sets the *initial-knowledge* property according to the requirements described in section 2.2. When the game is launched, it should have access to the value of that property in order to modify the behaviour of the game accordingly.

Similarly, the levels of satisfaction of the virtual customers in the in-game test should be stored in the *satisfaction-customer-1* and *satisfaction-customer-2* properties. As mentioned below, deciding what to do to obtain the final grade from the values reported by the games is an issue that belongs to the definition of the instructional design. In our case, the definition of the UoL simply calculates the average of these values and stores it in the *final-grade* property.

It is important to note that the concepts "having access to the value of some properties from the game" and "letting the game store some values in properties" mentioned here pose a significant technological challenge not covered by IMS LD. The rest of this section deals with this issue.

3.2 <e-Adventure>

<e-Adventure> (formerly known as <e-Game>) is a game engine designed to facilitate the creation of educational games, focusing on pedagogical aspects such as adaptation and assessment.

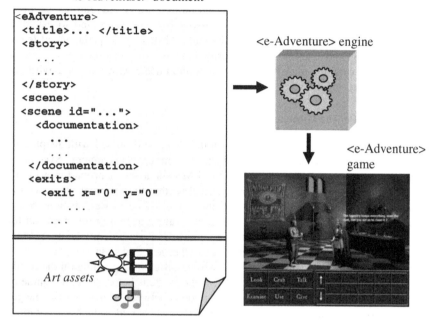

Fig. 4. The <e-Adventure> engine produces executable videogames from their descriptions as XML documents

One of the main shortcomings in the development of educational games is the excessive development cost. Additionally, game development is very demanding in terms of programming skills and game developers are not usually experts in education. Thus, one of the main objectives of <e-Adventure> is the simplification of this process to the point of allowing instructors or educational institutions to develop educational games without requiring a broad team of expert game developers.

To achieve this purpose, <e-Adventure> extends our previous work in a *document-oriented* approach to the production and maintenance of content-intensive applications [26]. For this purpose, <e-Adventure> draws from the existing expertise in the field of Domain-Specific Languages [30] and Descriptive Markup Languages [7], and it provides an XML syntax [3] for the definition of the games. With the objective of keeping the language simple, it only supports a very specific game genre: *point and click* adventure games. Previous research experience suggests that this genre is especially appropriate for education, given its bias for content rather than action [1,14].

When using <e-Adventure>, game *writers* describe the games using the XML syntax and package them along with the necessary art assets (graphics, animations, music, etc.). The engine can read these packages and execute the games (Fig. 4).

The script for the *Paniel and the Chocolate-based Sauce Adventure* game was written as a *point and click* adventure game following the conventions and structure proposed by <e-Adventure> [22]. Then the <e-Adventure> markup was added and the art assets were gathered.

Nevertheless, in addition to facilitating the development process, <e-Adventure> is focused on the field of online education. Even though the <e-Adventure> engine can run on its own, it was designed to be deployed from an LMS and to establish a communication link that would enhance the value of its built-in pedagogical features such as adaptation and assessment, as described in the rest of this section.

In its current version, <e-Adventure> can communicate with our test environment as described in section 4.

3.3 Adaptation of the Games

Educational games developed for <e-Adventure> can be designed with adaptation in mind. When deployed from a compliant Learning Management System, the implementation of the engine can query the LMS for a set of properties which are used to adapt the game. The games are defined so that the different values of those properties will change the initial state of the game. Since in <e-Adventure> every action can be conditioned to that initial state, the values of those properties can force the game to skip some levels, to include new parts of increased complexity or to steer the student to alternative paths more suited to his/her learning style.

In this case, the initial state of the game will be different depending on the result of the initial questionnaire. As we said earlier, if the grade is below 60%, the game runs from its default initial state. However, if the grade is between 61% and 80%, the game will be set to an initial state in which the first level has already been completed. Finally, a grade above 80% sets the game in the state in which the student is ready to face the exam.

3.4 Assessment and Feedback

The <e-Adventure> engine also includes built-in assessment and feedback mechanisms. While the game is being run, the engine monitors the student's activity. The definition of the games includes information about which game states are relevant from a pedagogical perspective and, whenever the game enters one of these states, the engine notifies it in order to let the learning environment update its state.

In our case, the relevant states are those related to the completion of the exam. When the exam ends, the variables that define each customer's satisfaction are identified as relevant and the engine reports their value to the learning environment.

3.5 Integration of <e-Adventure> and IMS Learning Design

The integration of <e-Adventure> and IMS Learning Design addresses two different issues:

-   On the one hand, <e-Adventure> should infer several adaptation properties from the UoL execution state. The best results can be achieved when the games are defined along with the UoL and these game properties are aligned with properties in the UoL. However, it is possible to develop these elements separately and then provide a set of rules that translate properties in the UoL into game states as depicted in Fig. 5.

- On the other hand, the assessment and feedback provided by <e-Adventure> should be communicated to the IMS LD's execution environment. Again, the easiest approach is to directly align some properties from the definition of the state of the game with properties present in the UoL and again it is possible to supply a document with rules that translate game states to properties in the UoL.

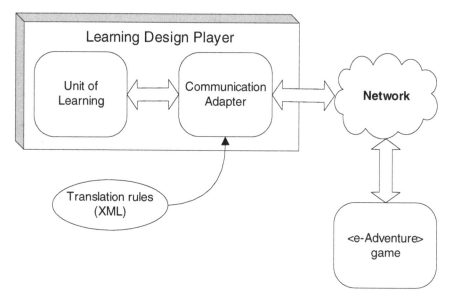

Fig. 5. Communication between the game and the UoL. The communication adapter may use an XML file with translation rules to match game states with IMS LD properties.

4 Executing the *Art and Craft of Chocolate* UoL

IMS Learning Design is simply the formalization mechanism that allows a computer to interpret the design of the UoL. To provide the learning experience modelled by the UoL we need an environment that can understand the IMS Learning Design specification and *play* the UoL. Playing a UoL implies managing the interactions of the users, providing the services required by the UoL, maintaining the values of the properties for different users in different runs of the UoL, and guiding the execution flow of the activities.

There are several systems capable of this, although in our case we have used a modified version of the SLeD environment [23]. Next sections give the details.

4.1 SLeD

SLeD (*Service-based Learning Design Player*) [23] is a front-end for a CopperCore Run-Time (CCRT) environment, which is the reference implementation of the IMS Learning Design specification [31].

One of the key elements in the CCRT is the CopperCore Service Integration (CCSI) layer [32], which enables the integration of different service providers in a CopperCore environment. Examples of services supported by CCSI include forums, web search mechanisms or assessment mechanisms based on the IMS Question & Test Interoperability specification [12].

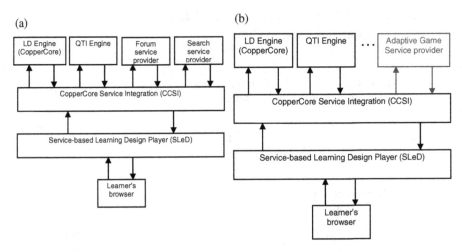

Fig. 6. (a) Architecture of a SLeD environment. The student interacts with the SLeD layer which, in turn, uses the CCSI layer to communicate with the different service providers; (b) the test environment with the new service provider. It supports the execution of UoLs such as *The Art & Craft of Chocolate.*

The CCSI layer manages the communication between the service providers so that they can exchange information and the different services can be triggered when required by the current state of the UoL. Thus, when in a CopperCore environment the UoL requests an assessment or a search operation, the request is passed to the appropriate service through the CCSI layer as in Fig. 6a. This process is detailed in depth in [32].

4.2 Adding Support for Adaptive Games

Neither the IMS Learning Design specification nor the SLeD player were designed with adaptive games in mind. However, the Learning Design specification allows a certain degree of freedom when defining the services required by the different activities and the CCSI layer was specifically designed to facilitate the definition, implementation and connection of these services.

Furthermore, in order to set up our test environment for adaptive games integrated with IMS Learning Design, such as our *Art & Craft of Chocolate* case study, we modified the CCSI layer to include a new type of service called *Adaptive Game Service* (Fig. 6b). This service supports launching an adaptive game and it also establishes bidirectional communication with the game that can be used both to adapt the game and to allow whatever happens inside the game to adapt the rest of the UoL.

The other necessary step was to slightly modify the SLeD front-end so that whenever it identifies a game resource, the appropriate service will be invoked through the CCSI layer.

The result is an IMS Learning Design player enhanced to support adaptive games. When the games are launched the service sends them information that can be used to modify the game's behaviour. Additionally, the service expects the games to report back about what the learner does within the game. Besides, this protocol is understood by the <e-Adventure> educational game engine. The resulting environment allows for the execution of adaptive UoLs that, like our *Art & Craft of Chocolate*, integrate adaptive games compliant with <e-Adventure>.

5   Conclusions and Future work

While the IMS Learning Design specification is a powerful tool when it comes to modelling adaptive learning experiences, educational videogames are an ideal medium to deliver adaptive content.

Previous experiences regarding the combination of IMS Learning Design and educational games have been either based on creating UoLs that behave like games [5] or on embedding games into them and treating the games as immutable elements just like a PDF file would be treated.

The combination of these technologies is an interesting line of research. For this reason, the proof-of-concept UoL *The Art & Craft of Chocolate* was designed as presented in this work. Its design requires, at least at a basic level, the same key elements that a more complex adaptive learning experience would require.

Even if the UoL itself does not cover a lot of content or a broad and complex subject, its main objective is to eliminate the technical barriers to the joint use of IMS LD and educational games in an integrated fashion in order to provide a rich adaptive learning experience.

The implementation and the execution environment described here (using the <e-Adventure> engine and a modified version of the SLeD player and CopperCore) successfully proves this point and opens the gates to the development of more complex UoLs in which the overall learning experience and the events inside the educational games can influence each other.

Future lines of work include the design of more complex UoLs including complex games covering different subjects. Additionally, the communication mechanism and the *Adaptive Game Service Provider* developed for CopperCore were designed generically in order to allow them to work with different game implementations other than the <e-Adventure> engine.

Acknowledgements

This paper is partially supported by the European projects TENCompetence (IST-TEL/2004-2.4.10, www.tencompetence.org) and ProLearn (IST Contract number 507310, www.prolearn-project.org), and the research group <e-Ucm> (www.e-ucm.es). The Spanish Committee of Education and Science (Projects TIN2004-08367-C02-02 and TIN2005-08788-C04-01) and the Regional Government / Complutense University of Madrid (research group 910494 and grant 4155/2005) have partially supported this work.

References

1. Amory, A., Naicker, K., Vincent, J., Adams, C.: The Use of Computer Games as an Educational Tool: Identification of Appropriate Game Types and Game Elements. British Journal of Educational Technology 30(4), 311–321 (1999)
2. Betz, J.A.: Computer Games: Increase Learning in an Interactive Multidisciplinary Environment. Journal of Educational Technology Systems 24(2), 195–205 (1996)
3. Birbeck, M., et al.: Professional XML, 2nd edn. Wrox Press (2001)
4. Brusilovsky, P.: Adaptive Educational Systems on the World-Wide-Web: A Review of Available Technologies. In: WWW-Based Tutoring Wprkshop at 4th International Conference on Intelligent Tutoring Systems, San Antonio, USA (1998)
5. Burgos, D., Tattersall, C., Koper, R.: Can IMS Learning Design be used to model computer-based educational games? Binaria, 5 (2006)
6. Burgos, D., Moreno-Ger, P., Sierra, J.L., Fernández-Manjón, B., Koper, R.: Authoring Game-Based Adaptive Units of Learning with IMS Learning Design and <e-Adventure>. International Journal of Learning Technology (Special Issue on Authoring Adaptive and Adaptable Hypermedia) (In Press)
7. Coombs, J.H., Renear, A.H., DeRose, S.J.: Markup Systems and the Future of Scholarly Text Processing. Communications of the ACM 30(11), 933–947 (1987)
8. ESA, E.S.A. Essential Facts about the Computer and Videogame Industry (cited April 8th, 2007) 2005 Available from: http://www.theesa.com/files/2005EssentialFacts.pdf
9. Garris, R., Ahlers, R., Driskell, J.E.: Games, Motivation and Learning: A Research and Practice Model. Simulation & Gaming 33(4), 441–467 (2002)
10. Gee, J.P.: What video games have to teach us about learning and literacy, p. 225. Palgrave Macmillan, New York, Basingstoke (2003)
11. IMS Global Consortium. IMS Learning Design Specification (2005) (cited April 8th, 2007) Available from: http://www.imsproject.org/learningdesign/index.html
12. IMS Global Consortium. IMS Question & Test Interoperablity Specification (cited April 8th, 2007) (2005) Available from: http://www.imsglobal.org/question/index.html
13. Jenkins, H., Klopfer, E., Squire, K., Tan, P.: Entering the Education Arcade. ACM Computers in Entertainment 1(1) (2003)
14. Ju, E., Wagner, C.: Personal computer adventure games: Their structure, principles and applicability for training. The Database for Advances in Information Systems 28(2), 78–92 (1997)
15. Koper, R., Olivier, B.: Representing the Learning Design of Units of Learning. Educational Technology & Society 7(3), 97–111 (2004)
16. Koper, R., Tattersall, C.: Learning Design - A Handbook on Modelling and Delivering Networked Education and Training. Springer, Heidelberg (2005)
17. Malone, T.: What makes computer games fun? SIGSOC Bulletin 13(2-3), 143 (1982)
18. Malone, T.W., Lepper, M.R.: Making learning fun: A taxonomy of intrinsic motivations for learning. In: Snow, R.E., Farr, M.J. (eds.) Aptitude, learning and instruction III: Cognitive and affective process analysis, pp. 223–253. Lawrence Erlbaum, Hillsdale, NJ (1987)

19. Martinez-Ortiz, I., Moreno-Ger, P., Sierra, J.L., Fernández-Manjón, B.: Production and Deployment of Educational Videogames as Assessable Learning Objects. In: Nejdl, W., Tochtermann, K. (eds.) EC-TEL 2006. LNCS, vol. 4227, Springer, Heidelberg (2006)
20. Mitchell, A., Savill-Smith, C.: The Use of Computer and Videogames for Learning: A Review of the Literature. m-Learning, Trowbridge, Wiltshire: Learning and Skills Development Agency (2004)
21. Moreno-Ger, P., Martínez-Ortiz, I., Sierra, J.L., Fernández-Manjón, B.: Language-Driven Development of Videogames: The <e-Game> Experience. In: Harper, R., Rauterberg, M., Combetto, M. (eds.) ICEC 2006. LNCS, vol. 4161, Springer, Heidelberg (2006)
22. Moreno-Ger, P., Sierra, J.L., Martínez-Ortiz, I., Fernández-Manjón, B.: A Documental Approach to Adventure Game Development. Science of Computer Programming 67, 3–31 (2007)
23. OUUK. Sled player (2005) (cited April 8th, 2007) Available from: http://sled.open.ac.uk
24. Paramythis, A., Loidl-Reisinger, S.: Adaptive Learning Environments and eLearning Standards. Electronic Journal of eLearning 2(1), 181–194 (2004)
25. Prensky, M.: Digital Game Based Learning. McGraw-Hill, New York (2001)
26. Sierra, J.L., Fernández-Valmayor, A., Fernández-Manjón, B.: A document-oriented paradigm for the construction of content-intensive applications. The Computer Journal 49(5), 562–584 (2006)
27. Sim, G., MacFarlane, S., Read, J.: All work and no play: Measuring fun, usability, and learning in software for children. Computers & Education 46(3), 235–248 (2006)
28. Squire, K.: Game-Based Learning: An X-Learn Perspective Paper. MASIE center: e-Learning Consortium (2005)
29. Squire, K.: Video games in education. International Journal of Intelligent Simulations and Gaming 2(1), 49–62 (2003)
30. Van Deursen, A., Klint, P., Visser, J.: Domain-Specific Languages: An Annotated Bibliography. ACM SIGPLAN Notices 35(6), 26–36 (2000)
31. Vogten, H.,, Martens, H.: CopperCore 3.0. 2005 (cited April 8th 2007) Available from, http://www.coppercore.org
32. Vogten, H., Nadolski, M.H.R., Tattersall, C.: CopperCore Service Integration, Integrating IMS Learning Design and IMS Question and Test Interoperability. In: 6th IEEE International Conference on Advanced Learning Technologies, IEEE Computer Society Press, Kerkrade, The Netherlands (2006)

Relevance Ranking Metrics for Learning Objects

Xavier Ochoa[1] and Erik Duval[2]

[1] Information Technology Center, Escuela Superior Politcnica del Litoral,
Va Perimetral Km. 30.5, Guayaquil - Ecuador
xavier@cti.espol.edu.ec
[2] Dept. Computerwetenschappen, Katholieke Universiteit Leuven,
Celestijnenlaan 200A, B-3001, Heverlee, Belgium
Erik.Duval@cs.kuleuven.be

Abstract. Technologies that solve the scarce availability of learning objects have created the opposite problem: abundance of choice. The solution to that problem is relevance ranking. Unfortunately current techniques used to rank learning objects are not able to present the user with a meaningful ordering of the result list. This work interpret the Information Retrieval concept of Relevance in the context of learning object search and use that interpretation to propose a set of metrics to estimate the Topical, Personal and Situational relevance. These metrics are calculated mainly from usage and contextual information. An exploratory evaluation of the metrics shows that even the simplest ones provide statistically significant improvement in the ranking order over the most common algorithmic relevance metric.

Keywords: Learning Objects, Relevance Ranking, Topical Relevance, Personal Relevance, Situational Relevance.

1 Introduction

In a broad definition, learning objects are any digital document with an educational objective. Learning Object Repositories (LOR) exist to enable sharing of such resources. To be included in a repository, learning objects are described by a metadata record provided at publishing time. This metadata can be manually or automatically generated [1]. Most LORs use the metadata information to implement keyword or field search functionality to allow the user to query the collection and retrieve relevant objects. Being any digital document, learning objects could be in any medium (text, pictures, audio, video, etc) and could be stored in any format. The metadata record helps to uniformly identify and describe the object and it is used as an object subrogate. The majority of learning object retrieval implementations is based on queries against the metadata fields stored into some form of database. On the other hand, Information Retrieval techniques based on the content of the object are rarer because of the diversity of the objects' medium and format. That is the reason why all initial LORs

E. Duval, R. Klamma, and M. Wolpers (Eds.): EC-TEL 2007, LNCS 4753, pp. 262–276, 2007.

presented searchers with some kind of electronic form in which they were expected to translate their information need into search criteria for different fields. The LOR compares those values against the stored metadata records and return all the objects that satisfy the query. There was no specific order in which the objects were returned as it was expected that each would fulfill the information need of the user.

The approach based on the original metadata has been moderately successful for isolated repositories where the number of objects is small (in the order of thousands). A detailed query produces few results that the user could easily browse. But working with small, isolated repositories also meant that an important percentage of users did not find what they were looking for [2]. Current research in the Learning Object community has produced technologies and tools that solve the scarcity problem. Technologies as SQI [3] and OAI-PMH [4], enables to search several repositories simultaneously. Another technology, ALO-COM [5], decomposes complex learning objects into smaller components that are easier to reuse. Finally, automatic generation of metadata based on contextual information [6] allows the conversion of the learning content of Learning Management Systems (LMS), into metadata-annotated Learning Objects ready to be stored into a LOR. Although these technologies are solving the scarcity problem, they are creating an inverse problem, namely, abundance of choice.

Traditional retrieval mechanisms of LORs are no longer viable due to the abundance of learning objects. Even very detailed queries based on metadata fields will produce more results than the user is willing or able to browse. A proven solution for this problem is ranking or ordering the result list based on its relevance. To help the user to find relevant learning objects, Duval in [7] proposed the creation of LearnRank, an imaginary ranking function to access the relevance of learning objects similarly to how PageRank[8] access the relevance of web pages. Also, in a previous paper [9] the authors explore how Contextualized Attention Metadata [10] could be mined to obtain meaningful information about the relevance of a specific learning object for a specific user and context. The present work goes a step forward, proposing and testing a set of multi-dimensional relevance ranking metrics. This metrics will use external sources of information in addition to what is explicitly stated in the user query to provide a more meaningful relevance ranking than current query-matching implementations.

The structure of this paper is the following: Section 2 analyzes the different dimensions of the Information Retrieval's Relevance concept and their implications for Learning Object relevance ranking. These relevance dimensions are used as guidelines in Section 3 to propose a set of metrics that can be implemented to rank a list of learning objects based on usage and contextual information. To obtain a rough estimate of the benefit that these metrics could have in a real implementation, an exploratory study, where the metrics are compared against human relevance rankings, is performed in Section 4. The paper concludes with additional details about related and further work.

2   Relevance Ranking of Learning Objects

The first step to build metrics to rank learning objects by their relevance is to understand what "relevance" means in the context of a Learning Object search. Borlund [11], after an extensive review of previous research on the definition of relevance for Information Retrieval, concludes that relevance is a multidimensional concept with no single measurement mechanism. Borlund defines four independent types of relevance: 'System' or 'Algorithmic' relevance which represents how well the query and the object match. Topical relevance that represents the relation between an object and the real-world topic of which the query is just a representation. 'Pertinence', 'Cognitive' or 'Personal' relevance which represents the relation between the information object and the information need that generate the query as perceived by the user. And 'Situational' relevance that represents the relation between the object and the work task that generated the information need.

These abstract relevance types need to be interpreted for the process and context of the learning object search:

- *Algorithmic Relevance.* In learning object search, the most common way to establish the algorithmic (or systemic) relevance is to compare the query parameters with the learning object metadata record. For example if the user searches for "inheritance", the algorithmic relevance of an object in the result list can be calculated as the frequency of times that the word "inheritance" appears in the title and description fields of the metadata record.
- *Topical Relevance.* In the context of learning objects the topic is strongly related to the Course / Lesson / Activity for which the learning objects will be used. For example if the user is searching for learning objects inside a course about Object Oriented Programming, the topical relevance of a learning object can be calculated as the number of times that the object has been used in similar courses.
- *Personal Relevance.* The personal (or cognitive or pertinance) relevance is directly derived from the information need as perceived by the user. In the context of learning, the perception of the information need is based on the teaching or learning style of the user. For example, a personal relevance ranking for a user that prefers highly interactive material should rank higher simulations and animations over text documents and slide presentations, even if all the presented objects have been used to learn the subject at hand.
- *Situational Relevance.* The task (and the task's context) that generates the user's information need determines the situational relevance of a result. Any task is normally aimed at reaching a specific learning objective, that is, to acquire a given knowledge, ability or competence. For example, a learning object with a very detailed explanation of how compilers work, should have different situational relevance ranking scores, depending on the specific public it is aimed towards. This holds true even if courses on the same subject are taught by the same professor to differnt student focus gruops.

The information to estimate these relevance rankings is not only contained in the query parameters and the learning object metadata, but also in records of historical usage and the context where the query takes place. It is assumed that this information is available to the relevance ranker. This could seem unrealistic for classical Learning Object search, where the users, usually anonymous, perform their queries directly to the LOR through a web interface and the only information available are the query parameters. On the other hand, new implementations of LMSs, or plugins for old implementations such as Moodle [12] and BlackBoard [13], enable the capture of information by providing logged-in users with learning objects search capabilities as part of teacher workflow during the creation of courses and lessons.

While this interpretation of the relevance concept is exemplified with traditional or academic learning environment, it is at least as valid in less structured or informal settings such as corporate training or in-situ learning given that the environments used to assist such learning also store information about the topic searched by the user. This information takes te form of personal profiles, preferences, problem descriptions, previous and required competence.

A Ranking mechanism that could apply some combination of the abovementioned four types of relevance should provide the user with meaningfully ordered learning objects in the result list. The next section will propose pragmatic metrics that adjust to these different types of relevance in order to create a set of multidimensional relevance ranking metrics for learning objects.

3 Ranking Metrics for Learning Objects

To enable learning object search tools to exploit the different relevant ranking strategies described above, those strategies should be operationalized as ranking metrics. These metrics can be calculated automatically from existing or easily acquirable information. The metrics proposed here are inspired on methods currently used to rank other types of objects, for example ranking web pages, scientific papers, songs, and so forth. Different metrics for the same type of relevance will account for different levels of computational complexity and availability of usage and contextual information. Each metric is described by the raw data it requires and the algorithm to convert that data into concrete ranking values. These metrics, while not proposed as a complete or optimal way to compute the real relevance of learning object for a given user and task, are a clear first step to set a strong base-line implementation against which the effectiveness of more learning-specific metrics can be compared.

3.1 Topical Relevance Ranking Metrics

Basic Topical Relevance Metric (BT). This metric makes two naïve assumptions. The first assumption is that each object in the result list is on-topic. Consequently, there is no need to explicitly define the topic of the query. The second assumption is that each object is relevant to just one topic. Accordingly, the degree of relevance of the object to the topic can be easily calculated by counting the number of times the object has been reused. Defining NC as the total number of courses of which the system keeps record, BT relevance metric is the sum of the times that the object is present in any of those courses (Equation 2). This metric is an adaptation of the Impact Factor metric [14] in which the relevance of a journal in a field is calculated simply counting the number of reference to papers in that journal during a given period of time.

$$present(object, course) = \begin{cases} 1; if\ object\ is\ published\ in\ course \\ 0; otherwise \end{cases} \qquad (1)$$

$$BT(object) = \sum_{i=1}^{NC} present(object, course_i) \qquad (2)$$

Course-Similarity Topical Relevance Ranking (CST). In the context of learning object technologies, the course in which the learning object will be reused can be directly used as the topic of the query. Objects that are used in similar courses should be ranked higher in the list. In this metric, two courses are considered similar if they have a predefined percentage of learning objects in common. This relationship can be calculated constructing a 2-partite graph where courses are linked to objects published in them. This graph is folded over the object partition leaving a graph representing the existing relationships and strenghts between courses. The number of objects shared between two courses, represented in this new graph as the number of links between two coruses, determines the strenght of the relationship. The edges in the graph are then pruned according to the minimal strenght of relationship desired. The resulting connected sub-graph containing the course where the object will be inserted is taken as the new universe of courses (Figure 1). The ranking metric is calculated counting the number of times that a learning object in the list has been used in this new universe of courses of size NC (Equation 3). This metric is similar to the calculation made by e-commerce sites such as Amazon [15] where additionally to the current item, other items are recommended based on their probability of being bought together.

$$CST(object) = \sum_{i=1}^{NC} present(object, SimilarCourse_i) \qquad (3)$$

Internal Topical Relevance Ranking (IT). This is a refinement of the Basic Topical Relevance Rank based on the HITS algorithm [16] proposed to rank web pages. This algorithm states the existence of hubs, pages that point to other useful pages, and authorities, pages with information about a subject. The algorithm presumes that a good hub is a document that points to many good authorities, and a good authority is a document that many good hubs point to. In the context of learning objects, courses can be considered as hubs and learning

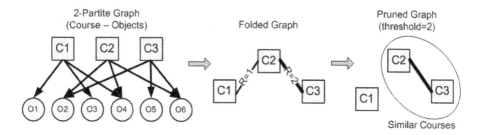

Fig. 1. Calculation of the Course-Similarity Topical Relevance Ranking (CST)

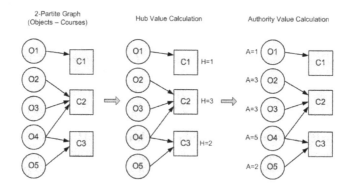

Fig. 2. Calculation of Internal Topical Relevance Ranking (IT)

objects as authorities. To calculate the metric, a 2-partite graph is created with each object in the list linked to its containing courses. The hub value of each course is then calculated as the number of in-bound links that it has. Finally, the rank of each object is calculated as the sum of the hub value of the courses where it has been used (Equation 4).

$$IT(object) = \sum_{i=1}^{N} \deg ree(LinkedCourse_i) = authority(object) \qquad (4)$$

3.2   Personal Relevance Ranking Metrics

Basic Personal Relevance Ranking (BP). The easiest and least intrusive way to generate preference information is for users to analyze the objects they has used previously. First, for a given user, a set of the relative frequencies for the different metadata fields' values present in their objects is calculated (Equation 6). The number of these objects is defined by N. These frequencies are then compared with the metadata values of the objects in the result list. Finally, the relative frequency of the value present in the object is added to the personal relevance ranking value. This procedure is repeated for the NF selected fields the metadata standard (Equation 7). This methodology is especially useful for metadata fields' values based in a finite vocabulary. This metric is similar to that used for automatically recording TV programs in Personal Video Recorders [17]. The metadata of the programs watched by the user, such genre, actors, director and so forth, is averaged and compared against the metadata of new programs to select which ones will be recorded.

$$contains(object, field, value) = \begin{cases} 1; \text{if object's metadata field} = value \\ 0; \text{otherwise} \end{cases} \quad (5)$$

$$freq(user, field, value) = \frac{1}{N} \sum_{i=1}^{N} contains(object(user, i), field, value) \quad (6)$$

$$BP(object, user) = \sum_{i=1}^{NF} (freq(user, field_i, value(field_i)) *$$
$$contains(object, field_i, value(field_i))) \quad (7)$$

User-Similarity Personal Relevance Ranking (USP). Basic Personal Relevance Metric relies heavily on the metadata of the learning object in order to be effective. A more robust strategy to rank objects according to personal educational preferences is to find the number of times similar users have reused the objects in the result list. To find similar users, a process presented above to calculate the CST metric is followed. A 2-partite graph contains the objects linked to the users who have reused them. The graph is folded over the object partition and a relationship between the users is obtained. The graph can be pruned to obtain different levels of similarity. The remaining connected sub-graph, with NU nodes, which include the current user, is used to calculate the USP metric, as in Equation 9. The latter calculation is performed adding the number of times in which similar users have reused the object. This kind of metric is used, for example, by Last.fm and other music recommenders [18] who present new songs based on what similar users are listening to; similarity seen as the number of shared songs in their playlists.

$$hasReused(object, user) = \begin{cases} 1; if object has been reused by user \\ 0; otherwise \end{cases} \quad (8)$$

$$UST(object) = \sum_{i=1}^{NU} hasUsed(object, SimilarUsers_i) \quad (9)$$

3.3   Situational Relevance Ranking Metrics

Basic Situational Relevance Ranking (BS). Both the title and description of the course, lesson or activity in which the object will be inserted are sources of contextual information. Such information is usually written by the instructor to indicate to the students what the course, lesson or activity will be about. Keywords can be extracted from these texts and used to calculate a ranking metric based on the similarity between the keyword list and the content of the textual fields of the metadata record. To perform this calculation, a well known vector space retrieval algorithm [19] is used, which measures the distance between the M-dimensional vectors of the keyphrases extracted from the context and the terms present in the different text fields of the metadata record (Equation 10). One experimental version of this type of metric has been developed by Yahoo for the Y!Q service [20], that can perform contextualized searches based on the content of a web page in which the search box is located.

$$BS(object, context) = \frac{\sum_{i=1}^{M} contextvector_i * objectvector_i}{\sqrt{\sum_{i=1}^{M} contextvector_i^2 \cdot \sum_{i=1}^{M} objectvector_i^2}} \qquad (10)$$

Course-Content Situational Relevance Ranking (CSS). To calculate this metric, other objects present in the course in which the object will be inserted are considered the contextual information. As with that proposed for the BP metric, the N objects contained in the course are "averaged" to create a set of relative frequencies for different fields of the learning object metadata record (Equation 11). This set of frequencies is then compared with the objects in the result list. The relative frequencies of the values present in the object's metadata are added to compute the final rank value (Equation 12).

$$freq(cour, field, value) = \frac{1}{N} \sum_{i=1}^{N} contains(object(cour, i), field, value) \qquad (11)$$

$$CCS(object, course) = \sum_{i=1}^{NF} freq(course, field_i, value(field_i)) * \qquad (12)$$
$$contains(object, field_i, value(field_i))$$

4   Exploratory Experimentation

In order to evaluate the potential impact the proposed metrics could have in the relevance ranking of learning object searches, an exploratory study has been performed, consisting of a small experiment in which subjects were asked to simulate the creation of a lesson inside a LMS. The subjects were required to rank the relevance of a list of learning objects, ranked using a algorithmic relevance metric, and to select from the list objects they consider appropriate for the lesson. The algorithmic relevance metric is compared with the subject's ranking to create a base line performance score. The proposed basic metrics for each one of the subjective relevance types are then used to reorder the list. Finally, the ranking scores are also compared against the subject's relevance score.

4.1   Experimental Setup

Ten users, eight professors and two research assistants from the Computer Science field, were required to create ten lessons related to different computer science concepts presented in Table 1. In each lesson, the subjects were required to write a brief description of the lesson for hypothetical students. The subject was then presented with a list of ten objects. These objects were obtained from a LOR containing all PDF learning objects currently available in the MIT OCW website [21] (34,640 objects). This LOR was queried with a different query phrase for each lesson, as listed in Table 1. The title, description and keyword fields were text-matched with the query terms. The top-10 objects of each result list were used in the experiment. The subject then graded the relevance of each object to the lesson, to which end they used a 7-value scale, from "Not relevant at all" to "Extremely Relevant". Moreover, subject's were required to select the objects they would include in the lesson. The data recollection was conducted using a Web application available at [22].

The initial rank of the objects was performed by the Lucene ranking algorithm, which is based on vector space retrieval [23]. This algorithm can be considered a good representation of current algorithmic relevance ranking. The basic topical relevance metric (BT) was calculated counting the number of times each object was selected to be included in the lesson. The selection of each subject was left out when compared against individual relevance evaluation. The basic personal relevance metric (BP) was calculated using historical information about the objects which subjects had published in their LMS courses. Three fields were captured: classification , document type and context level. These fields were selected on the basis of information available in the LOM record of the MIT OCW learning objects. The basic situational relevance ranking (BS) captured the text fed by the subjects into the description of the lesson. Any stopwords were eliminated and the resulting keywords were used to expand the query made to Lucene. The revised of the 10 objects was extracted then from the new result list.

Once all the metrics were calculated they were compared against the manual rank performed by the subjects. In order to measure the difference between the

Table 1. Task performed during the experiment and their correspondent query phrase

#	Lesson to Create	Query Phrase
1	Inheritance in object oriented languages	inheritance
2	Algorithmic complexity	complexity
3	Introduce the concept of computer networks	networks
4	Introduce Human Computer Interaction concept	human computer interaction
5	Explain tree structures	trees
6	Xml markup	xml
7	Introduce the concept of operating system	operating system
8	Explain the artifical neural networks	neural networks
9	How to normalize database tables	normalization
10	Explain routing of packages in computer networks	routing

manual rank and each of the automated ranks, a variation of the Kendall tau metric [24] which deal with ties in the rank was used. This metric measure the distance between two permutations and is proportional to the number of swaps needed to convert one list into the other using bubble sort. If two ranks are identical, the Kendall tau is equal to 0, if they are in inverse order, Kendall tau is equal to 1.

4.2   Results

Only 12% of the objects presented to the users were manually ranked "Very Relevant"(5), "Highly Relevant"(6) or "Extremely Relevant"(7). This implies that pure algorithmic relevance ranking does a very bad job at providing relevant results to the user in the top-10 positions of the result list, especially if the repository contains a large amount of objects in different topics. Some searches, for example "human computer interaction" return almost "Not Relevant at All" results, even if in the repositories there were material for courses about Interface Design and Human Centered Computing.

The Kendall tau distance between the Base Rank (based on the Lucene algorithmic relevance metric) and the human has a mean value of 0.4 for all the searchers. For general query terms such as "trees"(5) and "human computer interaction"(6) it borders the 0.5 (meaning that there is no relation between both ranks). However, for very specific query terms such as "xml"(6) and "operating systems"(7) it provides a lower value, 0.3 implying a slight correlation between manual and automatic ranks. This is consistent with the low quality of the retrieval.

Table 2. Average distances between the manual ranking and the calculated metrics and the average improvement over the Base Rank

Ranking Metric	Kendal tau	Improvement	Paired T-Test
Lucene score	0.4046	–	
Basic Topical	0.2790	12.56%	t=9.50, df=99, Sig=0.000
Basic Personal	0.3392	6.53%	t=2.93, df=99, Sig=0.004
Basic Situational	0.3183	8.62%	t=6,424, df=99, Sig=0.000
Linear Combination	0.3139	9,07%	t=7.877, df=99, Sig=0.000

If the top-10 results provided by Lucene search engine are reordered using the basic topic relevance metric (BT), the Kendall tau distance is reduced by 12.6% on average compared with the Base Rank. When reordered with the basic personal relevance ranking (BP), the average Kendall tau distance reduction is 6.5%. When the basic situational relevance ranking (BS) is uded, Kendall tau distance is reduced by 8.6%. Finally, the simple linear combination of the metrics (topical, personal and situational) decrease the distance to 9% compared with the Base Rank. For more details on the results and their statistical significance, see Table 2.

4.3   Discussion of Results

Basic topic relevance metric (BT) provides the best correlation with manual ranking. This result was expected because all the subjects participating in the experiment belong to the same field and were performing similar tasks. It fared better than the original ranking in all searches. It was the metric most directly related to human choice, as normally highly relevant items were selected for inclusion in the lessons.

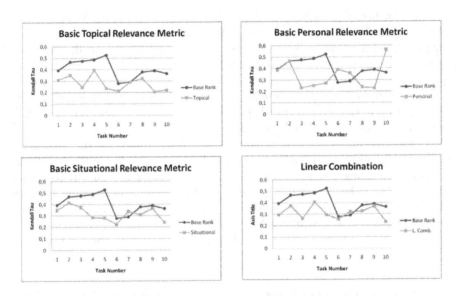

Fig. 3. Results of the Kendall tau distance from the manual ranking of the different metrics and their combination

Basic personal relevance metric (BP) presented some problems in certain queries. This can be explained as errors or unexpected values in the metadata records of the objects. While the object was relevant for a given lesson, metadata values do not always matched user preferences. For example, in search number 10 ("routing"), the topical classification of the objects were "Electrical Engineering", different from the "Computer Science" value that all the subjects had in their profile. Another case which exemplifies this problem was present in search number 1 ("inheritance"). The objects found more relevant came from a Programming course of the Civil Engineering department. This value was completely different from the value present in subject's profile.

Basic situational relevance metric (BS) provided an improvement in all but one search. It performed better for ambiguous query terms (note search number 4 and 5) while almost not affecting the performance of very specific query terms (searches 6 and 7). This result was expected given similar studies on query expansion using contextual descriptions.

To be useful in a comprehensive relevance ranking implementation, the ranks given by different metrics must be (linearly) combined and their estimating power should not be affected. The value obtained between the topical and contextual metrics results show that the combined rank behave well even if no weighting factors are included into the linear combination.

In conclusion, the basic ranking metrics always provide an average increase in the performance of the ranking compared with the Base Rank (Lucene text-based ranking). These results suggest that a full-fledge implementation of these metrics in a real environment will lead to a net benefit for final users searching for relevant learning objects.

5 Related Work

There are few published works on relevance ranking of learning objects, maybe because it was not seen as a critical problem in a world of small and isolated LORs. The work of Chellappa [25] represents the methodology followed by several repositories: adapting full-text search approaches to rank the learning objects based only on the similarity between the query terms and the text fields of the metadata record. This type of calculation only captures the Algorithmic relevance and does not provide the user with a real measurement of the object's Topical relevance, much less adapt the ranking for personal preferences or task. In contrast, the present work uses text similarity measurements only as a component of a more holistic approach to relevance estimation. Dolog et al. [26] propose a rule-based personalization based on the semantic description of both the user profile and the learning object. The main disadvantage of this approach is that it requires very rich metadata annotation of both the user and the object in order to work. Most of our metrics work with automatically created usage information and contextual information manually created as part of th original user workflow.

Taking another approach, Vargo et al propose [27] the use of data generated by user evaluation of the quality of the learning object to sort them into the result list. Users measure the LO quality using the Learning Object Review Instrument, a set of 9 quality parameters which the learning object should meet. The main drawback of this ranking approach is the well documented problem of the lack of scalability of user review. The authors of the present paper believe that this approach, while able to capture Topical relevance, could not be used to estimate Pertinence and Situational relevance. It is very difficult for reviewers to rate an object based in a different set of preferences or conditions than their own. While the Topical relevance estimation proposed in the present paper is not as reliable as a user review, nonetheless, it is scalable. Moreover, the use of personal and contextual information generates an adaptive ranking.

6 Conclusion

The main contribution of this work is the creation of a set of implementable ranking metrics which provide a comprehensive estimation of the multidimensional relevance of a learning object in realation to the user's information need. Usage and contextual information complement the information explicitly stated in both the query and the learning object metadata, in order to provide a more meaningful and robust ordering of the result list. This exploratory study confirmed that the application of even the simplest of these metrics leads to a statistically significant increase in performance compared to the currently most popular ranking method. While these metrics are not proposed as an optimal approach to the relevance ranking of learning objects they can be used to improve current learning objects search engines and set a strong baseline against which future learning-specific metrics could be tested.

7   Further Work

One of the purposes of this work is furtheer the discussion of better ways to help the user find relevant learning objects. In this line, more questions are raised than answered. Valid research topics unaddressed in this work include:

– *Large Scale Implementation* Which architectural compromises should be made to provide an acceptable computation time versus interoperability with current LMSs and LORs?.
– *Federated Search.* How should the metric calculation be adapted to environments in which only the top-k objects of each repository are known? Moreover, how shold the ranking made by different LORs be aggregated?
– *Underlying theory.* Are there deeper pedagogical or cognitive reasons which explain the success or failure of different metrics?
– *Metric combination and Tuning.* Is there an optimal relevance ranking function and if so, how should existing metrics be combined? Do different users prefer different combination of metrics?

The main task left for further work is to execute an empirical study with both a full implementation of the metrics and real users performing within their normal workflow. Once there is enough data collected, the user interaction with the system and the progress of the different metrics could be analyzed to shed light on these questions. We also hope that other researchers start proposing improvements to this initial approach.

References

1. Cardinaels, K., Meire, M., Duval, E.: Automating metadata generation: the simple indexing interface. In: WWW '05: Proceedings of the 14th international conference on World Wide Web, pp. 548–556. ACM Press, New York (2005)
2. Najjar, J., Klerkx, J., Vuorikari, R., Duval, E.: Finding appropriate learning objects: An empirical evaluation. In: Rauber, A., Christodoulakis, S., Tjoa, A.M. (eds.) ECDL 2005. LNCS, vol. 3652, pp. 323–335. Springer, Heidelberg (2005)

3. Simon, B., Massart, D., van Assche, F., Ternier, S., Duval, E., Brantner, S., Olmedilla, D., Miklos, Z.: A simple query interface for interoperable learning repositories. In: Simon, B., Olmedilla, D., Saito, N. (eds.) Proceedings of the 1st Workshop on Interoperability of Web-based Educational Systems, Chiba, Japan, CEUR, pp. 11–18 (2005)
4. Herbert, M.L.N.: Resource harvesting within the oai-pmh framework. D-Lib Magazine (10)
5. Verbert, K., Jovanovic, J., Gasevic, D., Duval, E.: Repurposing learning object components. In: Meersman, R., Tari, Z., Herrero, P. (eds.) On the Move to Meaningful Internet Systems 2005: OTM 2005 Workshops. LNCS, vol. 3762, pp. 1169–1178. Springer, Heidelberg (2005)
6. Ochoa, X., Cardinaels, K., Meire, M., Duval, E.: Frameworks for the automatic indexation of learning management systems content into learning object repositories. In: Kommers, P., Richards, G. (eds.) Proceedings of the ED-MEDIA 2005 World Conference on Educational Multimedia, Hypermedia and Telecommunications (2005)
7. Duval, E.: Learnrank: the real quality measure for learning materials (2005)
8. Page, L., Brin, S., Motwani, R., Winograd, T.: The pagerank citation ranking: Bringing order to the web. Technical report, Stanford Digital Library Technologies Project (1998)
9. Ochoa, X., Duval, E.: Use of contextualized attention metadata for ranking and recommending learning objects. In: CAMA '06: Proceedings of the 1st international workshop on Contextualized attention metadata, pp. 9–16. ACM Press, New York (2006)
10. Najjar, J., Duval, E.: Attention metadata: Collection and management. In: IEEE, WWW 2006, Edinburgh, Scotland (2006)
11. Borlund, P.: The concept of relevance in ir. Journal of the American Society for Information Science and Technology 54, 913–925 (2003)
12. Broisin, J., Vidal, P., Meire, M., Duval, E.: Bridging the gap between learning management systems and learning object repositories: Exploiting learning context information. In: AICT-SAPIR-ELETE '05 (AICT/SAPIR/ELETE'05), pp. 478–483. IEEE Computer Society Press, Washington, DC, USA (2005)
13. Vandepitte, P., Van Rentergem, L., Duval, E., Ternier, S., Neven, F.: Bridging an lcms and an lms: a blackboard building block for the ariadne knowledge pool system. In: Proceedings of ED-MEDIA 2003 World Conference on Educational Multimedia, Hypermedia, and Telecommunications, AACE, AACE, pp. 423–424 (2003), http://go.editlib.org/p/13794.
14. Dong, P., Loh, M., Mondry, A.: The "impact factor" revisited. Biomedical Digital Libraries 2, 7 (2005)
15. Linden, G., Smith, B., York, J.: Amazon.com recommendations: Item-to-item collaborative filtering. IEEE Internet Computing 7, 76–80 (2003)
16. Kleinberg, J.M.: Authoritative sources in a hyperlinked environment. Journal of the ACM 46, 604–632 (1999)
17. Pigeau, A., Raschia, G., Gelgon, M., Mouaddib, N., Saint-Paul, R.: A fuzzy linguistic summarization technique for tv recommender systems. In: IEEE Int. Conf. of Fuzzy Systems (FUZZ-IEEE'2003), St-Louis, USA, pp. 743–748. IEEE Computer Society Press, Los Alamitos (2003)
18. Upendra, S.: Social information filtering for music recommendation (1994)
19. Aizawa, A.: An information-theoretic perspective of tf-idf measures. Information Processing & Management 39, 45–65 (2003)

20. Kraft, R., Maghoul, F., Chang, C.C.: Y!q: contextual search at the point of inspiration. In: CIKM '05: Proceedings of the 14th ACM international conference on Information and knowledge management, pp. 816–823. ACM Press, New York (2005)
21. MIT: (Opencourseware — ocw home, http://ocw.mit.edu/index.html
22. Ochoa, X.: On-line experiment application. user:test, password:test. http://ariadne.cti.espol.edu.ec/ranking
23. Hatcher, E., Gospodnetic, O.: Lucene in Action (In Action series). Manning Publications, Greenwich, CT, USA (2004)
24. Fagin, R., Kumar, R., Mahdian, M., Sivakumar, D., Vee, E.: Comparing and aggregating rankings with ties. In: PODS '04: Proceedings of the twenty-third ACM SIGMOD-SIGACT-SIGART symposium on Principles of database systems, pp. 47–58. ACM Press, New York (2004)
25. Chellappa, V.: Content-based searching with relevance ranking for learning objects (2004)
26. Dolog, P., Henze, N., Nejdl, W., Sintek, M.: Personalization in distributed e-learning environments. In: WWW Alt. '04: Proceedings of the 13th international World Wide Web conference on Alternate track papers & posters, pp. 170–179. ACM Press, New York (2004)
27. Vargo, J., Nesbit, J.C.B.K.A.A.: Learning object evaluation: Computer-mediated collaboration and inter-rater reliability. Iternational Journal of Computers and Applications 25, 198–205 (2003)

Supporting Attention in Learning Environments: Attention Support Services, and Information Management

Claudia Roda[1] and Thierry Nabeth[2]

[1] Computer Science Department, American University of Paris 147, rue de Grenelle 75007 Paris France
croda@aup.fr
http://ac.aup.fr/roda
[2] INSEAD CALT, Boulevard de Constance, 77305 Fontaineableau Cedex, France
thierry.nabeth@insead.edu

Abstract. Learners and knowledge workers are increasingly facing environments where frequent interruptions, multi-tasking, information overload, and insufficient community awareness are the norm rather than the exception. It has been demonstrated that this situation hinders learning in several manners. This paper, after introducing two approaches aimed at supporting attentional processes, analyses the services needed to support learners in environments presenting the above characteristics. It also discusses the conceptual and technical problems related to the collection, modelling, protection, and distribution of attention-related information.

Keywords: Attention Aware Systems, Learning Environments.

1 Introduction

The advent of networked information technology has radically changed the way we value and access information, and communicate. *Information* which used to be a scarce and difficult to access resource, is now readily available, *human attention* instead has become the new "valuable currency" [15]. Taking into account this new condition when designing digital learning environments would provide learners not only access to information and people, but also the means to better manage their attention, reducing extraneous cognitive load and therefore facilitating learning [38].

In previous papers [33, 35] , we have discussed findings in cognitive psychology, information science, and other disciplines that may supply an initial ground for the development of *attention aware* learning environments and we have identified the four stages necessary to support attentional processes: (1) Detecting current user's attentional state, (2) Determining possible alternative foci, (3) Evaluating cost/benefits of possible attentional shifts, (4) Establishing modalities for interventions. Continuing in this research, in this paper we first introduce two approaches that have emerged for attention support in recent years: user-centred and resource-centred (section 2). We then analyse, in section 3, the services that should be

E. Duval, R. Klamma, and M. Wolpers (Eds.): EC-TEL 2007, LNCS 4753, pp. 277–291, 2007.

provided to learners in order to help them coping with several attention-challenging characteristics of modern learning environments (e.g. interruptions, multi-tasking, information overload). In section 4 we discuss the challenges related to collecting, enriching, modelling, and distributing attention-relevant information.

2 Attention Support: User-Centred Versus Resource-Centred

For the purpose of attention management it is essential to model the *interactions* between people and the environment (physical environment, applications, resources, and people). Modelling such interactions requires integrating information that historically has been collected in *user* models, and *resource* models. Attention-related information may include elements such as *how, when, to which end, for how long* a learner has interacted with an application, resource, or his/her environment in general.

Two different approaches have been so far adopted to capture these interactions and provide automatic support to attentional processes: user-centred and resource-centred.

The user-centred approach is the one we have implemented in the Atgentive project [4, 34]. We model attention mainly according to a user perspective. We track and describe user activity in terms of *events* taking place in the environment (e.g. the user starting some process in an application, the user looking at the computer, the user accepting a system suggestion); based on these events a model of the user is created and system's decision are based on this user model. Within the Atgentive system we generate suggestions about possible courses of action, and provide supporting information for the current user activity (e.g. re-starting an interrupted task; interrupting the current task to perform another more urgent, or more relevant one; pursuing the current task in a different manner).

Resource-centred approaches [28, 40] model the interactions of the learner with the environment in terms of the different resources that are accessed during a learning activity. The history of resources' usage (e.g. creation, access, search, repurposing, tagging) is collected as attention-related metadata associated to individual resources; such metadata is then used to guide learners to the most appropriate resources.

Whilst the user-centred approach aims at offering a wider range of services, it has the disadvantage of requiring detailed knowledge of the user activity, which often can be gained only at the price of loss in generality. The resource-centred approach whilst aiming mainly at optimizing resource access, has the advantage of being exploitable in all the applications requiring some form of user access to resources.

In general, the information collected with a user-centred approach will also include the information that resource-centred approaches aim at collecting. For example, the fact that a user U starts reading a document D, in a user-centred approach may be represented as:

```
Event(start, task(read, U, D, …), …)
```

The same information, in a resource-centred approach may be represented by the following metadata associated to resource D.

```
<user=U, action=READ, …>
```

Attention-relevant information about the user activity such as the user being inactive for a certain length of time can be represented in an user-centred approach, whilst such information has no meaning in a resource-centred approach (i.e. user inactivity is a property of the interaction between the user and the whole observed environment, not a property of the interaction between the user and a specific resource). Also the user-centred approach naturally represents user tasks that may "bundle" resources in meaningful associations to users' activities. For example, the fact that, user U has started writing Report1 and in order to do this he needs a certain number of resources R1, ..., Rn can be represented as:

```
Event(start, task(write, U, Report1, resources(R1, …, Rn)))
```

On the other hand, attention-relevant relationships amongst resources are better represented in a resource-centred approach. This information can provide insights on how resources are used by individuals and by the community.

These approaches are complementary in two senses. First, both information about user activity, and resource usage is necessary to supply meaningful and dynamic attention-support services (see discussion in section 3). Second, the largest set of information collected with a user-centred approach can be used to enrich resource models (e.g. by associating task related information to resources one can provide the task context in which the resource is used).

3   Services for the Support of Attention in Learning

In this section we introduce four types of services that may be provided by attention aware digital learning environments (see [31] for a complete description of the services considered within the Atgentive project) and we discuss how integrating user-centred and resource-centred approaches would greatly benefit those services' accuracy and flexibility. The services presented here illustrate various aspects of attention support in modern, community-based, and information-rich learning environments. In such environments the learners' activity is characterized by frequent interruption and multi-tasking, requiring that learners explicitly evaluate their attention allocation strategies. Interruption management is probably the service that has been most discussed in the literature and it aims at minimizing the disruption caused by the inevitable interruptions of modern learning and working environments. Support to task switching and task reminders services endeavour to help learners in managing multiple, often interleaved, tasks. Services for resources searching, ranking, and tracking aim at helping users orienteering within information-reach environments whilst minimizing information overload. Self and community awareness services provide the support necessary for the learner to assess and reflect upon his own and the community's attention allocation strategies.

3.1 Interruptions Management

Interruption management relates to the asynchronous presentation of information. For example the learner may have launched a search agent that responds asynchronously to a query, or he/she may receive an email, or a new entry may be added in a Blog that the learner is tracking. Communicating this information to the user normally results in interrupting his/her current activity. Although interruptions may bring to one's attention information possibly useful for the primary (current) task, or even, in the case of simple primary tasks, facilitate task performance [36]; it has been widely reported that interruptions increase the load on attention and memory [19], may generate stress [7, 42], and compromise the performance of the primary task [18, 26, 27, 36] especially when the user is working on handheld devices in mobile environments [27]. Therefore, in order to minimize disruption whilst ensuring that relevant content is appropriately attended-to, the system must make a decision about the *relevance* to the user of the newly available information in the current context, and consequently select notification *timing* and *modality*.

Assessing the Relevance of newly available information. Research on interruption management is quite extensive (see for example [2]), however the strategies for relevance evaluation proposed so far model data in a static manner that does not allow, for example, the generation of new categories of information to take a role in this evaluation. Although interesting results have been obtained using Bayesian models to evaluate relevance over a static structure [20], the components intervening in such evaluation should be dynamically learned by the system as it observes the user's interactions within a certain context. In [32] we propose that the relevance assigned to sources of interruption by a user varies with time and context, and it is subject to a learning process based on the user's previous interaction with similar resources. This suggests that by integrating resource-centred and user-centred approaches, both events describing the users' activity, and metadata associated to resources can be seen as *traces* [39] of the users' learning about relevance.

Timing of interruptions. The solutions proposed so far for the selection of interruption timing are either based on task-knowledge or on sensory-input.

Task-knowledge based timing relies on the analysis of the structure of the task being performed. Bailey and his colleagues [5, 6] represent tasks as two level hierarchies composed of coarse events further split into fine events and demonstrate that interruptions are less disruptive when presented at coarse breakpoints, corresponding to the completion of coarse events. Alternative task decompositions have also been proposed to select interruption timing, e.g. planning, execution, and evaluation [13].

Sensory-input based timing relies on sensors' input about the user activity to detect best times for interruption. On the basis of the observation that human beings can very efficiently, and in presence of a very small number of cues, evaluate other's interruptibility, Hudson et al. [22] propose that interruptibility evaluation is attainable from simple sensors and that speech detectors are the most promising sensors. Chen and Vertegaal [10] instead use more sophisticated physiological cues (Heart Rate Variability – HRV, and electroencephalogram - EEG) to distinguish between four attentional states of the user: at rest, moving, thinking, and busy. From these, user's states of interruptibility can be derived.

The integration of task-knowledge-based and sensory-input-based approaches would allow the system to rely on both types of cue for the selection of the most appropriate interruption time. Consequently, in the Atgentive project we combine knowledge of a detailed task structure [24] with simple sensory-input to evaluate the strength of breakpoints for possible interruptions.

Further integration of this user-centred approach with a resource-centred one, would enable the evaluation of the level of interruptibility necessary for the learner to cope with the complexity of the resource being proposed.

Interruptions and Collaboration. Most of the work on the evaluation of cost/ benefits of interruptions has been done taking the point of view of the user being interrupted, only a few studies take into account also the cost/benefit to the interrupter, and the joint costs/benefits [21, 29]. In order to support group costs/ benefits evaluation for interruptions, information about both resources use and user activity (respectively collected by resource and user centred approaches) are necessary. For example the state of development of a resource, its relevance to the community, and the deadline of the associated task, may contribute to such analysis.

3.2 Support to Task Switching

Current virtual (as well as physical) learning environments are characterized by an increasing number of resources (e.g. tools, information, communication channels) that cause learners to switch between tasks very frequently. Attention aware digital learning environments may support users in situations of frequent task switching by helping them in restoring the context of resumed tasks and by aiding them in recalling tasks that they should attend to. These two services are briefly discussed below.

Restoring Task Context. Learners frequently use resources as a bundle rather than individually, this is because in order to complete a task they often must access, create, and edit several different resources. When a task is interrupted and subsequently restarted, a large amount of cognitive effort is spent in restoring its contexts, e.g. reassembling all the resources needed for its completion. Experimental studies have demonstrated that simple reminders about the objective of the interrupted task may be quite useful under certain conditions [12], however since returned-to tasks require significantly more documents, on average, than other tasks [14] supporting the user in recovering the resources used in performing the task would significantly lower cognitive load. In order to provide such service, user-centred approach and resource-centred approach must be combined so that the digital learning environment recognises which resources a user associates to a task at a given time of its execution.

We found that providing context restorations for resumed tasks presents a number of conceptual and technical challenges. First of all, it is necessary to establish which resources, amongst the ones originally used by the learner when attending the task, are significant enough to be restored (e.g. a learner may have accessed several web pages but probably only a subset of those pages are relevant at restoration time). Second, it is necessary to establish the level of accuracy at which resources should be restored (e.g. should a text document that the learner was writing/reading when the task was interrupted be restored at the point where the activity was interrupted or at the beginning?) Third, given that resources are accessed through a number of different applications, how can an attention aware learning environment communicate with all other applications in order to know which resources were used, so to restore them in the appropriate manner? In order to address some of these issues, we have explored the possibility of providing the learner with a multi-screen environment that supports user-guided separation of tasks context in order to facilitate resumption after task switching [11]. We are currently in the process of evaluating the effectiveness and usability of this system.

Task Reminders. Experimental studies report that prospective memory failures (failure to remember tasks that need to be performed in the future) may account for up to 70% of memory failures [23] and that 40% of interrupted tasks are not resumed [29]. Services that help learners overcoming these problems may include simple task reminders services such as those associated to many electronic calendars. These services allow users to set alarms that display a text message entered by the user at the time when the reminder was set up. Slightly more complex reminder services are provided by shared calendars (in this case the reminder is associated to an event that has been scheduled amongst a group of people), and by calendars embedded into applications such as Microsoft Office Notification where reminders may be associated to resources, and user-created tasks. The ideal reminder service would provide the user with an environment where task reminders may be associated to user-tasks, group-tasks, as well as various types of resources. By integrating user-centred and resource-centred approaches task reminder could be automatically generated when, for example, a task has been completed, a resource becomes available, a document should be edited, etc. Further, attention-related information would allow inferring task urgency and priority making it possible to deal with the problem of task-reminders overload, which occurs when the number of reminders exceeds the capacity of the learner to attend the reminded tasks. Accurate tasks models associated with attention-related user models would result in services that better help learners in allocating resources to pending tasks. For example, current task reminder systems do not allow to distinguish (neither automatically, nor manually) between tasks that must be completed by a given date (e.g. a required assignment, an article that needs to go to print), tasks that should be completed by a given date but may be delayed if necessary, and tasks that "expire" after a certain date (e.g. go to a meeting). Furthermore, current systems only support stand-alone tasks, however tasks dependencies/sequences, and resources availability are obviously essential elements for intelligent task reminder services. For example, current systems don't allow expressing the fact that a task represents a bottleneck for other personal or community tasks, it is not possible to visualise the consequences of not completing a certain task within a certain date, and reminders are issued at pre-set times even if the conditions for the execution of a task are not met (e.g. prerequisite tasks have not been completed, or resources are not available). Intelligent task reminder services, implementing the above requirements, would lower the load on prospective memory allowing the learner to concentrate on the task currently selected.

3.3 Orienteering in Information Rich Environments

Attentional processes allow us to select, amongst incoming stimuli, those that should be further processes. These processes are obviously put under more strain as the input grows. At a low level, support to input selection in learning environments may be given by visualization tools that allow faster selection amongst several possible input (e.g. graphic display may enable much faster selection than textual ones). At a higher level, filtering mechanisms, such as those guiding search engines, and ranking tools, may also help the user orienteering amongst large amounts of available resources. Visualisation services are not discussed in this paper that instead briefly examines searching, ranking, and tracking of resources.

Resources Searching and Ranking. In order to help learners to find resources relevant to their needs one must have sufficient knowledge of the user, his current activity, and the available resources. For example, assume that two students in your introductory programming course formulate the same request: they want to know more about graphical user interfaces. The first student is doing very well in the course and is well on his way in the development of the assigned Java project. The second student is struggling through the course and still having problems with the analysis stage of the project. You are likely to address the first student directly to the API of some graphic library, and the second one perhaps to the tutorial of the same library.

This type of adaptive search response can be achieved only on the basis of a matching of knowledge about the students (e.g. their abilities, their current activity) and knowledge about the available resources (e.g. the original objective for their creation, the audience they are directed to, the manner how they may be, or have been, used). Similarly, a system may display adaptive search abilities only on the basis of a detailed learner model, which can be built on the basis of the information collected by user-centred approaches, and a detailed resource model, which can be collected by resource-centred approaches. These latter approaches are in fact aimed at collecting the use-history of resources. Such history provides very important insights on the context in which resources have been previously created, accessed, and modified. Erik Duval, for example, proposes *"Objects that have been used in many contexts [...] that are relevant to a specific learner, should have a higher [rank] for that learner. [...] Suppose that we track (as we can!) the correlation between the objects that learners work with and their performance on a post-test that assesses whether they have actually mastered a specific law of thermodynamics. Would that correlation not give a good indication of '[resource] quality'?"* [17].

The matching process between learner models and resource models requires dynamically extracting from the two models relevant information. For example, one may derive from the learner model the fact that a learner has already gained a certain level of knowledge (e.g. he is a good programmer) that would allow him to make efficient use of a complex resource (e.g. the API).

Whilst these types of matching have been experimented with, they are usually based on fixed categories (e.g. fast learner versus slow learner). This presents two disadvantages: First, it isn't possible to statically define all categories that may become necessary in a wide range of learning domains (e.g. good programmer versus bad programmer). Second, current solutions often require that some form of "artificial tagging" be associated to resources and learners (e.g. the resource must be defined as being suitable for beginners, or the student must be tagged as a fast-learner). A much more effective behaviour could be obtained if instead categories were dynamically inferred from the observation of the learners, and of the resource uses in various contexts by several learners.

These types of matching may be done using data mining techniques or, in the case of smaller data sets, using heuristic based artificial intelligence techniques (see section 4.2).

Tracking Resources. Once a resource has been created, tracking services may be provided. For example, a learner may want to know when certain members of the community, notably the instructor (perhaps with a grade), have reacted to the resource. An instructor may want to know whether students have read and reacted to certain learning objects. A knowledge worker may need to know when all the members of a given group have replied to an email. Resource tracking services may provide essential input to task sequencing (e.g. one may need to wait for a set of replies to an email in order to be able to schedule a meeting). They may also provide the resource creator with knowledge about the usefulness of the resource (e.g. many accesses to the resource may indicate that the resource is useful) and therefore may guide users in the decision of whether pursuing a certain goal (e.g. keeping the resource up to date). Some of these tracking services have been implemented before (e.g. Technorati's *watchlist*) but they are not integrated in a more general environment providing attention support services and therefore they require manual user input, and the information they provide cannot automatically be reused by other services. Resource-centred approaches provide a natural information structure for resource-tracking services which can then be exploited using user-centred approaches to support task continuation and task scheduling services (these two services, not described in this paper, are part of Atgentive's conceptual framework [31] and aim at supporting learners in selecting appropriate sequences of actions when pursuing learning goals).

3.4 Self and Community Awareness Tools

The increasing solicitations of modern learning and working environments require that students and knowledge workers gain a much greater awareness about the manner in which they allocate attentional resources. Although performance of several tasks concurrently may be improved with practice [25], limiting multi-tasking, when applicable, is a much more efficient strategy to improve performance. This requires that learners have the tools and ability to plan their activity and to reason and make decisions about their cognitive resources allocation. Awareness services informing learners about their current attention allocation choices may support such reflection. Relevant information may include details about the (type of) resources and/or tasks the user has allocated his time to, and a description of activity fragmentation (how often has a user interrupted a task, how long did it take for him to return to it?). This information may help learners in making attention-allocation decisions, for example, one may decide to block frequent sources of interruption in order to complete a task that has been frequently interrupted. Along with awareness services targeting the individual user, important insights may be gathered through community-awareness services. Notification services supporting awareness may be establish to provide learners with a list of very popular resources within their community. This type of awareness tools is not limited to resource access but it may be based on a variety of community actions such as resources repurposing, bookmarking, downloading, etc.

Awareness services may be based on resource models as well as on task models derived from user-centred approaches.

4 Managing Attention-Related Information

Managing attention-related information presents several challenges associated to its collection, modelling, protection, distribution, and development. This section discusses each one of these challenges highlighting the issues that need to be addresses in order to develop learning environments that support attention in an efficient, un-intrusive, and secure manner.

4.1 Collecting Attention-Related Information

Although any information collection methodology in digital learning environments aims at being accurate and un-intrusive these two objectives are often difficult to achieve when dealing with attention-related information. The collection of *factual* attention-related information (e.g. the learner has accessed a certain resource three times in the last few seconds), which presents challenges in its own, often is not sufficient to guide services supporting attentional processes. It is often necessary to infer more abstract attention information (e.g. the resource accessed by the learner is related to his/her current task). Such inferred information is in general uncertain, and dynamic inference models may be necessary to derive all the interesting aspects of the learner's attentional processes.

This section concentrates on the collection of factual attention-related information, the next section briefly discusses how further information may be inferred.

Factual attention-related information may be collected in at least four manners:

- *Physical observation* collects information about the physical interaction of the user with the environment (e.g. the learner has typed 100 characters in the last minute). At the physical level, attention information is detectable by observing keyboard strikes, mouse movements, eye tracking [41], speech detectors [22], etc. Not all these methodologies are equally un-intrusive: whilst the tracking of keyboard strikes and mouse movements may be completely transparent to the user, eye-tracking devices are only recently becoming less cumbersome and require simpler setting-up procedures.
- *Psycho-physiological observation* allows collecting data about the user's psycho-physiological state (e.g. the learner's heart rate is of 160). This data can then be used to evaluate the learner's involvement with the current task or resource. Psycho-physiological information is detectable through measurements such as Heart Rate Variability – HRV, and electroencephalogram – EEG [10]. Psycho-physiological measurements are problematic because the tools necessary to take such measurements may be very intrusive; further the inferences that the system may make about the user's affective and cognitive state, on the basis of such measurements, are intrinsically uncertain.
- *Application observation* collects information about how an application is used to interact with the environment (e.g. the learner has accessed resource R using application A). Application level information is detectable by observing

application software such as browsers, office applications, and learning management systems (e.g. a tool observing interaction at the application level is the Attention Recorder [3] which captures browsing history in a web browser application). Capturing attention-related information at the application level may be problematic because it requires that the application be extended to make such information available. Although this information is increasingly captured in digital environment, and even starts to be exported (c.f. the work done around APML - attention profiling mark-up language) to be exploited by external applications, asynchronous export of high level events, may not be sufficient to cover the needs of all attention related services. For example, in a text editing application, information about the position within the document where the learner pauses during a composition task may be important for establishing whether the learner is interruptible or not. Capturing this information however requires that the text editing application be capable of synchronously communicating detailed information about the current user activity with a specific resource.

- *User direct input* allows learners to provide the system with information about their states, needs, and desires (e.g. the learner has declared that he is working at assignment 1). While the above three methods of information collection are automatic and may be completely transparent to the learner, user direct input has the disadvantage of being intrinsically intrusive, and it may, in itself, be a cause of distraction from the primary task. In general however, just observing the user may not be sufficient to gain all possible types of information necessary to supply the services described in section 3. Enabling the user to augment the system observations may provide a much richer set of information. For example the learners can easily indicate their motivations and goals, whilst uncertain and complex inferences are generally necessary for the system to automatically infer such goals and motivations.

Information captured using non-intrusive automatic observations may be represented within an appropriate model and used to guide user direct input of manual annotations (e.g. resource tagging or rating) and augmentation (e.g. definition of new tasks structures). Using automatically collected information to guide manual collection has the advantages of: (1) simplifying the learner's task (for example by providing lists of already entered resource tags, and standard structures that the learner augments rather than creating) and (2) enabling consistency checks aimed at reducing error rates.

Information on task-resource association is a good example of attention related information that may significantly gain from this mixed approach; physical level and application level interactions can be captured and used to generate hypothesis on task-resources associations, these hypothesis can be later verified with the user. Another type of data that historically has been collected manually is resource rating. Resource rating however often fails because people do not see the advantage of spending time in entering ratings. Manual ratings also have the disadvantage of easy voluntary or involuntary misuse. Resource ratings may be instead automatically derived by observation of learners' actions (e.g. bookmarks, downloads) similarly to classic social navigation techniques [9, 16, 39]. The automatically derived ratings may then be used to weight manually entered ratings.

4.2 Inferring and Enriching Attention-Related Information

In order to gain enough operable attention-related information, several types of factual information may have to be integrated. For example, methods based solely on gaze-tracking [8] are not sufficient for acquiring information about users' attention. The phenomena of inattentional blindness and inattentional amnesia [30] demonstrate that the current task acts as a filter on visual attention. Experimental studies [37] show that the same gaze pattern may be associated to different attentional foci. Attempts to address this issues include Horvitz and his colleagues' system [20] that associates gaze tracking data with information about application level activity to obtain more precise description of user foci.

In general, on the basis of factual data it is possible to derive further information about the learners' interaction with the system, their states and motivations at the time of the interaction, and about the state of the environment. Two techniques are best suited for these types of derivations: data mining, and rule based inferential reasoning. The former mechanism is necessary whenever the inference is based on a very large amount of data. The latter is applicable only when inferences are based on a small set of data. The main advantage of rule-based inference mechanisms is that rules can easily be created and modified by learners or instructors to suit their needs. On the other hand, as the number of data/facts required for the inference increases, or the set of rules increases, it is possible to assist to complexity explosion producing results that are difficult to control (e.g. rules may have conflicting effects).

Repeated inferences on factual data allow the system to enrich the attention information model with mechanisms such as:

- *Automatic tagging* (e.g. if a learner has stored a document under a folder with a certain name, the document can probably be tagged with that name).
- *Automatic resources associations* (e.g. if a learner has been copying content from a window to another, or flicking a lot between two windows, then the resources contained in the two windows are probably related; and they are probably related to the learner's current task).
- *Automatic community detection* (e.g. if two learners have directly shared – e.g. by email – many resources, they are probably close collaborators; if two learners often access the same resources, they probably share interests)
- *Default access rights definition* (e.g. if learner L1 is a close collaborator of learner L2, then L1 has visibility of all of L2's attention information and vice-versa). Rules of this type allow leveraging organizational charts and social network in order to minimise user effort in access right definition.
- *User model enrichment* (e.g. if a learner repeatedly accesses a resource, then he is probably interested in the subjects associated to it; if a learner creates several resources related to a certain subject, then he is probably an expert in – i.e. has acquired a good level of knowledge about - that subject).

4.3 Modelling Attention-Related Information

Modelling attention related information requires structures that can be dynamically augmented to consistently describe the evolution in time of the activity, needs, and interests of several learners, within several applications. In designing these models a number of constraints must be taken into account, three of the most pressing ones are briefly discussed below.

Temporal Dimension of Attention-Related Information. There is an intrinsic temporal dimension in attention-related information (e.g. interactions happen at a given time, they have a certain duration) that provides important information about attention. For example: (1) more frequently or recently accessed resources may be more relevant than those accessed less frequently or recently; (2) returning to a recently interrupted task may require less system support than resuming a task that was interrupted a long time ago.

Temporal information may also guide the integration of physical, application, and psycho-physiological observations. For example, if application P reports activity A on resource R during the time interval t-t', and psycho-physiologic measurements report high levels of arousal during the same interval, one may derive that activity P on resource R (or resource R itself) is particularly important for the user.

A model of attention-related information must therefore be capable of representing time and temporal relations.

Uncertainty Management. Frequently, data mining and rule-based inferences produce results that are uncertain, this requires that sharable models of attention-related information represent uncertainty. Whilst in some situations it is possible to resolve uncertainty (e.g. by consulting the user), in others situations the uncertainty will need to be dealt-on by the systems providing services using these models.

Assessing and Modelling Tasks. One of the most relevant attention-related information about user's interaction with the environment is the task/goal of the user at the time of the interaction. Representing tasks has been however problematic due to the fact that people may have different definitions of what a task is, and how it could be decomposed. The level of granularity at which tasks should be defined depends on the tasks themselves, the user, and the type of attentional support that one may want to provide. One of the few studies on how knowledge workers may define *tasks* [14] reports great variations in how people define tasks, that people "tended to use generic terms" (ibid p. 177) for their description, and that the granularity at which tasks were defined also varied to a great extent. Given this variability, predefined structures seem ill adapted for task description and an emergent data definition should be sought.

Whilst it is possible, under certain circumstances, to automatically capture information about users' tasks and goals, in general a much more accurate description of this type of data is obtainable if the user inputs this information manually. Users may be motivated to enter such information by the fact that they will receive high value services such as task reminders and context restoration described in section 3.

4.4 Controlling Access to Attention-Related Information, and Privacy Issues

Attention-related information may disclose significant details about people's activity. As a consequence, people may be willing to allow access to *their* attentional information only in a controlled manner. A significant challenge is the definition of tools enabling users to (possibly automatically) identify who will be allowed access to which attention-related information. In between the two easy choices "everyone can see all my data", and "none has access to my data" there is a possibly very large number of alternatives that, if not appropriately supported, may require a significant effort on the side of the user for their specification (e.g. user1 can access information x but not information y, user2 can access information y but not information t and z, etc.). Default access rights may be defined by using simple inferences as briefly hinted in section 4.2. The importance of protecting attention information is quite well recognised [1], and identity management systems (such as OpenID) could provide some additional insights on how to protect learner's attentional data.

5 Conclusions

Although in very recent years the importance of automatic support for attentional processes in learning environments has been increasingly recognised, a great number of both conceptual and technical challenges remain unresolved. Unfortunately, it also appears that partial solutions to attention support provide little benefit and they risk being disruptive, with the result of increasing, rather than decreasing the cognitive load on the learner. While evidence continues being collected on the negative effects of information overload, interruptions, and frequent task switching in learning environments, the knowledge provided by research in neuropsychology and cognitive psychology about attentional processes remains very hard to operationalise within the context of digital learning environments. It is still unclear exactly what information about the learners' activity is relevant for attention support and how it should be collected. Two approaches have so far been proposed to aid learners in their attention allocation: user-centred and resource-centred. However, in this paper we argue that only an integration of the two approaches may lead to the effective implementation of the complete range of services required to deal with information overload, interruptions, and frequent task switching. The wide range of learners activities, applications used in learning environments, resources and learners types, requires models that whilst capable of representing time-related and uncertain knowledge, are open and dynamic so that a shared understanding of attention-related information can be achieved, in time, across users and applications.

Acknowledgments. The work described in this paper was partially sponsored by the EC under the FP6 framework project Atgentive IST-4-027529-STP. We would like to acknowledge the contribution of all project partners.

References

1. Attention Trust (accessed 16.1.2007) www.attentiontrust.org
2. Interruptions in Human Computer Interaction, (accessed 4.1.2005) http://interruptions.net/
3. Attention Recorder, (accessed 13.4.2007) http://attentiontrust.org/users/atx
4. Atgentive, ist-4-027529-stp. 2005-2007
5. Bailey, B.P., Adamczyk, P., Chang, T.Y., Chilson, N.A.: A Framework for Specifying and Monitoring User Tasks. Computers in Human Behavior 22(4), 709–732 (2006)

6. Bailey, B.P., Konstan, J.A.: On the Need for Attention Aware Systems: Measuring the Effects of Interruption on Task - Performance, Error Rate, and Affective State. Computers in Human Behavior 22(4), 685–708 (2006)

7. Bailey, B.P., Konstan, J.A., Carlis, J.V.: The effects of interruptions on task performance, annoyance, and anxiety in the user interface. In: INTERACT '01 (2001)

8. Baudisch, P., DeCarlo, A.: Focusing on the Essential: Considering Attention in Display Design. CACM 46(3), 60–66 (2003)

9. Brusilovsky, P.: Adaptive Educational Systems on the World-Wide-Web: A Review of Available Technologies. In: Workshop WWW-Based Tutoring, 4th International Conference on Intelligent Tutoring Systems (ITS'98), San Antonio, TX (1998)

10. Chen, D., Vertegaal, R.: Using mental load for managing interruptions in physiologically attentive user interfaces. In: xtended abstracts of the 2004 conference on Human factors and computing systems, pp. 1513–1516. ACM Press, Vienna, Austria (2004)

11. Clauzel, D., Roda, C., Stojanov, G.: Tracking task context to support resumption. In: Position paper for 2006 Workshop on Computer Assisted Recording, Pre-Processing, and Analysis of User Interaction Data. in HCI 2006 - Engage, London, UK (2006)

12. Cutrell, E., Czerwinski, M., Horvitz, E.: Notification, disruption, and memory: Effects of messaging interruptions on memory and performance. In: Interact, IFIP Conference on Human-Computer Interaction. 2001. Tokyo, Japan (2001)

13. Czerwinski, M., Cutrell, E., Horvitz, E.: Instant messaging: Effects of relevance and time. In: 14th British HCI group Annual Conference, Univ. of Sunderland, UK (2000)

14. Czerwinski, M., Horvitz, E., Wilhite, S.: A diary study of task switching and interruptions. In: Proceedings of the SIGCHI conference on Human factors in computing systems, ACM Press, Vienna, Austria (2004)

15. Davenport, T.H., Beck, J.: The Attention Economy. Harvard Business School (2001)

16. Dieberger, A., Dourish, P., Hššk, K., Resnick, P., Wexelblat, A.: Social Navigation: Techniques for Building More Usable Systems. interactions 7(6), 36–45 (2000)

17. Duval, E.: LearnRank: the Real Quality Measure for Learning Materials (Tematic Dossier 06, Insight - Oservatory for New Technologies and Education (December 2005)

18. Franke, J.L., Daniels, J.J., McFarlane, D.C.: Recovering context after interruption. In: 24th Annual Meeting of the Cognitive Science Society CogSci. (2002)

19. Gillie, T.,, Broadbent, D.E.: What makes interruptions disruptive? A study of length, similarity and complexity. Psychological Research Policy 50, 243–250 (1989)

20. Horvitz, E., Kadie, C., Paek, T., Hovel, D.: Models of attention in computing and communication: from principles to applications. CACM 46(3), 52–59 (2003)

21. Hudson, J.M., Christensen, J., Kellogg, W.A., Erickson, T.: I'd be overwhelmed, but it's just one more thing to do: availability and interruption in research management. In: SIGCHI conference on Human factors in computing systems, ACM press, Minneapolis, USA (2002)

22. Hudson, S.E., Fogarty, J., Atkeson, C.G., Avrahami, D., Forlizzi, J., Kiesler, S., Lee, J.C., Yang, J.: Predicting Human Interruptibility with Sensors: A Wizard of Oz Feasibility Study. In: CHI 2003, Ft. Lauderdale, Florida, USA, ACM Press, New York (2003)

23. Kvavilashvili, L., Messer, D.J., Ebdon, P.: Prospective memory in children: The effects of age and task interruption. Developmental Psychology 37(3), 418–430 (2001)

24. Laukkanen, J., Roda, C., Molenaar, I.: Modelling tasks: a requirements analysis based on attention support services. In: Workshop on Contextualized Attention Metadata: CAMA 2007 at the ACM IEEE Joint Conference on Digital Libraries, Vancouver, Canada, ACM, New York (2007)

25. Marois, R., Ivanoff, J.: Capacity limits of information processing in the brain. Trends in Cognitive Sciences 9(6), 296 (2005)
26. McFarlane, D.C., Latorella, K.A.: The Scope and Importance of Human Interruption in Human-Computer Interaction Design. Human-Computer Interaction 17(1), 1–62 (2002)
27. Nagata, S.F.: Multitasking and interruptions during mobile web tasks. In: 47th Annual Meeting of the Human Factors and Ergonomics Society (2003)
28. Najjar, J., Wolpers, M., Duval, E.: Attention Metadata: Collection and Management. In: WWW, workshop on Logging Traces of Web Activity: The Mechanics of Data Collection. 2006. Edinburgh, Scotland (2006)
29. O'Conaill, B., Frohlich, D.: Timespace in the Workplace: Dealing with Interruptions. In: CHI '95 Conference Companion, Denver, Colorado, United States, ACM press, New York (1995)
30. Rensink, R.A.: Seeing, sensing, and scrutinizing. Vision Research 40(10-12), 1469–1487 (2000)
31. Roda, C., (ed.): Atgentive (IST-4-027529-STP) Deliverable D1.3 - Atgentive conceptual framework and application scenarios (2006)
32. Roda, C.: Supporting attention with dynamic user models (Extended abstract). in Interactivist Summer Institute, Paris (2007)
33. Roda, C., Nabeth, T.: The role of attention in the design of Learning Management Systems. In: IADIS International Conference CELDA (Cognition and Exploratory Learning in Digital Age, IADIS Press, Lisbon, Portugal (2005)
34. Roda, C., Nabeth, T.: The AtGentive project: Attentive Agents for Collaborative Learners. In: Nejdl, W., Tochtermann, K. (eds.) EC-TEL 2006. LNCS, vol. 4227, Springer, Heidelberg (2006)
35. Roda, C.,,, Thomas, J.: Attention Aware Systems: Theories, Applications, and Research Agenda. Computers in Human Behavior 22(4), 557–587 (2006)
36. Speier, C., Vessey, I., Valacich, J.S.: The effects of interruptions, task complexity, and information presentation on computer-supported decision-making performance. Decision Sciences 34(4), 771–797 (2003)
37. Triesch, J., Ballard, D.H., Hayhoe, M.M., Sullivan, B.T.: What you see is what you need. Journal of Vision 3, 86–94 (2003)
38. van Merrienboer, J.J.G., Kirschner, P.A., Kester, L.: Taking the load of a learners' mind: Instructional design for complex learning. Educational Psychologist, 38(1), 5–13 (2003)
39. Wexelblat, A., Mayes, P.: Footprints: History rich Web browsing. In: Conference on Computer-Assisted Information Retrieval (1997)
40. Wolpers, M., Martin, G., Najjar, J., Duval, E.: Attention Metadata in Knowledge and Learning Management. In: 6th Intern. Conf. on Knowledge Management, Graz, Austria (2006)
41. Zhai, S.: What's in the eyes for attentive input. CACM 46(3), 34–39 (2003)
42. Zijlstra, F.R.H., Roe, R.A., Leonova, A.B., Krediet, I.: Temporal factors in mental work: Effects of interrupted activities. Journal of Occupational and Organizational Psychology 72, 163–185 (1999)

Personalized Links Recommendation Based on Data Mining in Adaptive Educational Hypermedia Systems

Cristóbal Romero[1], Sebastián Ventura[1], Jose Antonio Delgado[1], and Paul De Bra[2]

[1] Córdoba University, Campus Universitario de Rabanales, 14071, Córdoba, Spain
{cromero,sventura,i92deosj}@uco.es
[2] Eindhoven University of Technology (TU/e), PO Box 513, Eindhoven, The Netherlands
debra@win.tue.nl

Abstract. In this paper, we describe a personalized recommender system that uses web mining techniques for recommending a student which (next) links to visit within an adaptable educational hypermedia system. We present a specific mining tool and a recommender engine that we have integrated in the AHA! system in order to help the teacher to carry out the whole web mining process. We report on several experiments with real data in order to show the suitability of using both clustering and sequential pattern mining algorithms together for discovering personalized recommendation links.

1 Introduction

Adaptive and intelligent web-based educational systems (AIWBES) provide an alternative to the traditional just-put-it-on-the-web approach in the development of web-based educational courseware [4]. Their main objective is to adapt and personalize learning to the needs of each student. The task of delivering personalized content is often framed in terms of a recommendation task in which the system recommends items to an active user [17]. Recommender systems help users find and evaluate items of interest. Such systems have become powerful tools in many domains from electronic commerce to digital libraries and knowledge management [23]. Some recommender systems have also been applied to AIWBES for recommending lessons (learning objects or concepts) that students should study next [19] or for providing course recommendation about courses offered that contribute to the student's progress towards career goals [8].

Recommender systems can use data mining techniques for making recommendations using knowledge learnt from the action and attributes of users [23]. The objective of data mining is to discover new, interesting and useful knowledge using a variety of techniques such as prediction, classification, clustering, association rule mining and sequential pattern discovery. Currently, there is an increasing interest in data mining and educational systems, making educational data mining a new and growing research community [20][21]. The data mining approach to personalization uses all the available information about users/students on the web site (in the web course) in order to learn user models and to use these models for personalization. These systems can use different recommendation techniques in order to suggest online learning activities or optimal browsing pathways to students, based on their

E. Duval, R. Klamma, and M. Wolpers (Eds.): EC-TEL 2007, LNCS 4753, pp. 292–306, 2007.

preferences, knowledge and the browsing history of other students with similar characteristics.

In this work, we are going to describe the use of data mining techniques for links recommendation in AIWBES. The task of links recommendation in web-based education can be seen as a special type of adaptive navigation support due to the fact that they share the same goal of helping students to find an optimal path through the learning material [4]. Adaptive educational hypermedia systems can adaptively sort, annotate, or partly hide the links to make it easier to choose or to recommend to the students where they should go from a certain point. This technology is one of the most popular in AIWBES and there are a lot of systems that use it, such as ELM-ART [28] (and its descendents), AHA! [7], KBS-Hyperbook [11], etc. The originality of our personalized recommender system consists in the use of data mining together with hyperlink adaptation. Only a few other recommender systems use data mining for recommending links [8].

This paper is arranged in the following way: first we describe the related background and two architectures for personalization based on-web usage mining. Then, we describe the data mining tool and links recommender engine that we have developed and integrated into the AHA! system. Finally, we describe the experiments that we have carried out, conclusions and future work.

2 Background

Recommendation and personalization techniques can be classified into three different categories [17]: rule-based filtering systems, content-filtering systems and collaborative filtering systems. Rule-based filtering systems rely on manually or automatically generated decision rules that are used to recommend items to users. Content-based filtering systems recommend items that are considered sufficiently similar to the content descriptions in the user profile. Collaborative filtering systems, also referred to as social filtering, match the rating of a current user for items with those of similar users in order to produce recommendations for items not yet rated or seen. Some recent techniques used in collaborative filtering are based on data mining in order to infer recommendation rules or build recommendation models from large data sets [23]. Some of the most common data mining techniques in these recommender applications are clustering, sequence and association mining.

- Clustering is a process of grouping objects into classes of similar objects [13]. It is an unsupervised classification or partitioning of patterns (observations, data items, or feature vectors) into groups or subsets (clusters). This technique groups records together based on their location and connectivity within an n-dimensional space. The principle of clustering is maximizing the similarity inside an object group and minimizing the similarity between the object groups. There are many clustering methods [13], including hierarchical and function-based algorithms. One of the most well-known and commonly used is the k-means algorithm [16] that tries to minimize the distance of the objects to the centroid or mean point of each cluster.

- Sequential modeling or sequential pattern mining [10] discovers inter-session patterns. It is a more restrictive form of association rule [1] in which the accessed items' order is taken into account (the association rule discovers all the relationships without restrictions). Sequential pattern mining was first introduced into the study of customer purchase sequences, as follows [2]: Given a set of sequences, where each sequence consists of a list of elements and each element consists of items, and given a user-specified minimum support threshold, sequential pattern mining tries to find all frequent subsequences, i.e., the subsequences whose occurrence frequency in the set of sequences is no less than the minimum support. Normally, a web server log file is used to discover sequences of resource requests. The problem of mining sequences in web navigational patterns refers to the identification of those web document references which are shared through time by a large number of user sequences, where a user sequence is a time-ordered set of visits. There are several popular pattern discovery algorithms [10] such as AprioriAll, GSP, SPADE, PrefixSpan, CloSpan and FreSpan.

Although personalized recommendation approaches that use data mining techniques are first proposed and applied in E-commerce for product purchase, there are also several works about the application of different data mining techniques within recommender systems in E-learning. The extraction of sequential patterns has been used to find patterns that are used in the process of recommending relevant concepts to students [19]. Sequential rules can also guide a learning resource recommendation service based on simple sequencing specification [24]. Clustering can be used to find clusters of students with similar learning characteristics and to promote group-based collaborative learning in a research paper recommender system [26]. Association rules and clustering methods have been used for recommending a list of web pages on an e-learning web site [27]. A recommender agent which uses association rules has been used to recommend online learning activities or shortcuts on a course web site based on a learner's access history [14][30]. Fuzzy association rules have been used in a personalized e-learning material recommender system [15]. Finally, association rules have been used to provide feedback to the courseware author and to recommend how to improve the courses [9][22].

3 Architectures for Personalized Recommendation Systems

The overall process of Web personalization based on Web usage mining generally consists of three phases: data preparation, pattern discovery and recommendation. The first two phases are performed off-line and the last phase on-line [17]. Data preparation transforms web log files and profiles into data with the appropriate format. Pattern discovery uses a data mining technique, such as clustering, sequential pattern and association rule mining. Finally, recommendation uses the discovered patterns to provide personalized links or contents.

In this work, we distinguish between two different architectures of recommender systems based on web usage mining (see Figure 1).

Basic
Architecture

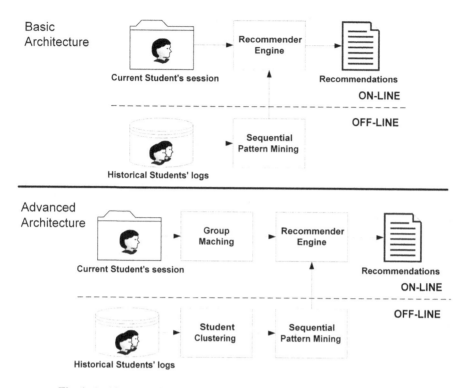

Advanced
Architecture

Fig. 1. Architectures for recommender systems based on web usage mining

- **Basic Architecture of Web-based Recommender Systems.** This is a simple architecture of a recommender system that only uses the student's information stored in web log files. These systems use only one mining algorithm, usually a sequential mining algorithm (see Figure 1 above), over all user navigation sessions to discover the most frequent navigational pattern that can predict the student's navigation and next page request. One problem of this type of system is that the new student obtains the same recommendations based solely on his current navigation.
- **Advanced Architecture of Web-based Recommender Systems.** This is a more advanced architecture of recommender systems that also uses additional information about the students (such as profiles). These systems use several mining algorithms (see Figure 1 down), for example, clustering and sequential pattern mining. In this way they can discover clusters of students showing common behavior and/or knowledge and then they can discover the sequential patterns of each cluster. This type of recommender can personalize the recommendations. First, it classifies the new students in one of the groups of students (clusters). Then, it only uses the sequential patterns of the corresponding group to personalize the recommendations based on other similar students and his current navigation.

4 The AHA!-Based Mining and Recommender System

Most of the current data mining tools such as DBMiner [6], SPSS Clementine [5] and Weka [29] can be too complex for educators to use and their features go well beyond the scope of what an educator may want to do. These tools should have more easy-to-use interfaces to simplify the algorithm configuration and execution, and they have provided specialized visualization facilities to make their results meaningful to educators and courseware designers [20]. For this reason, we have developed a specific data mining tool in order to help the teacher to carry out the web mining process. We have integrated this tool and its corresponding recommendation engine into the well known AHA! [7] (Adaptive Hypermedia Architecture). In this way the whole process can be carried out in a same e-learning system, and the feedback and results obtained can be directly applied to the courses (see Figure 2).

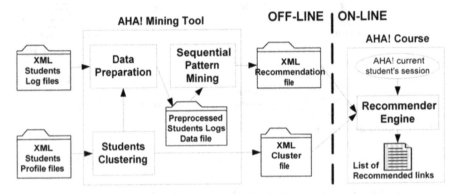

Fig. 2. Data mining tool and recommender engine integrated into AHA! system

As we can see in Figure 2, both the user's data (student log and profile files) and the learning model data (recommendation and cluster files) are stored in XML files in the AHA! server file system. This system can work as both the basic architecture and advanced architecture described in the previous section. And there are two main modules; the off-line module (mining tool) and the on-line module (recommender links engine) that we are going to describe in detail in the next two sub-sections.

4.1 Mining Tool

The mining tool is a Java Applet, just like other AHA! authoring tools [7] such as Concept Editor, Test Editor, etc. The author of the course can execute it when enough information from new students has been collected. The user interface of the mining tool is simple, easy to use and specifically oriented to discover sequential patterns and to recommend personalized links. Its main window consists of a menu and two information areas (see Figure 3). At the top, we can see the information panel that

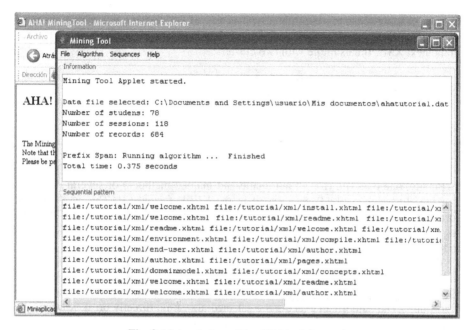

Fig. 3. Main window of the AHA! mining tool

shows general information about the program and algorithms execution. At the bottom, we can see the sequential pattern panel, where the discovered sequences are shown.

First, the author has to create a new data file starting from the student's log files. We have to preprocess the AHA! log files in order to group them into a single data file with the most appropriate format to be mined. In our case, it is not necessary to do user and session identification since all users must log in using their unique ID, and AHA! also stores the session information in log files. AHA! stores all log information for each student in one XML file (the date and time at which the page was accessed, the session identification and the name of the web page). The author only has to select one of his/her courses in AHA! and one method for selecting students (all automatically, manual and clustering) in order to create a data file. The totally automatic method selects all the students in the course. The manual method shows a list with all the students in the courses so that the author can select a group of specific students. The clustering method automatically creates several data files instead of only one data file. We have used the k-means algorithm [16], which is the most popular clustering algorithm and where the user only has to specify the number of clusters (k) to find. In order to do clustering, we have used two of the students' variables: the number of pages visited and the average knowledge obtained from these pages. This information has been obtained from the AHA! XML user profile files (also one per student, containing *visited* and *knowledge* attributes for each concept of the course). It is important to note that in the used AHA! courses each concept has an associated XHTML web page. Each of the clusters obtained corresponds to a specific student's model and is stored in an XML file. In this file we store the centroid of each cluster (in some sense representing a *typical* user of the cluster). In our case we store the number of pages visited and the average knowledge of the centroid, as we can see in the next XML file example with two clusters:

```
<?xml version="1.0" encoding="UTF-8"?>
<ListOfClusters NumberOfClusters="2">
   <cluster NumberOfPagesVisited="2"
      AverageLevelOfKnowledge="45">0</cluster>
   <cluster NumberOfPagesVisited="16"
      AverageLevelOfKnowledge="99">1</cluster>
</ListOfClusters>
```

Finally, one data file (for all automatic and manual methods) or several data files (for the clustering method) are created in the KEEL format [3]. This is a text file format that is similar to and compatible with the well-known Weka format [29]. The log information of each student is grouped together in this file or these files according to the clusters in which they have been classified.

Then, the author can select one data file in order to execute sequential pattern mining algorithms. There are several algorithms available such as AprioriAll [2], GSP [25] and PrefixSpan [18], which are some of the most popular pattern discovering algorithms. The author can execute the selected algorithm directly or, if he wants, he can change its default parameters values. AprioriAll and PrefixSpan algorithms only have one parameter (minimum support threshold that is the minimum number of sessions in which the rule has to appear). The GSP algorithm has a second parameter (maximum number of gaps that is the maximum number of gaps between two links to be considered in the same sequence). When the algorithm finishes its execution, the sequences discovered are shown in the sequential pattern panel of the main tool window (see Figure 3). These sequences can be saved into a text file and they can also be visualized better using the sequence view window. Analyzing these sequences, the teacher can have an idea about what the most general students' browsing behavior during their learning process is.

Finally, the author can recommend links starting from the sequences obtained. In order to do so, we have first split all the sequences with lengths over two in 2-length sub-sequences or rules using two different methods: path recommendation or shortcut recommendation [12]. Path recommendation splits the sequences in all the possible rules (every two pages directly connected in the sequence) and the shortcut recommendation splits the sequence in only one rule (the first and the last page in the sequence). So, a recommendation link is composed of a 2-length sequence considered as a rule with only one element in the antecedent and one in the consequent (the antecedent represents the page in which the recommendation will be shown and the consequent is the link recommended to the student). All the generated recommendation links are shown to the author so that he/she can validate them and select which recommendations will be used by the recommender engine (see Figure 4). The author has to select links/rules (all, none or a specific group) in order to filter the most appropriate recommendations depending on the antecedent and consequent concepts, and the confidence and support values. The confidence of the rules indicates how strong the rules are, whereas the support of the rules indicates their coverage.

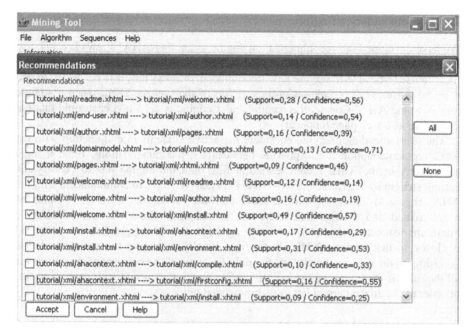

Fig. 4. Recommendation links window

Finally, the selected recommendations are saved into the AHA! system in a XML file as in the following example file:

```
<?xml version="1.0" encoding="UTF-8"?>
<RecommendedLinks>
  <Concept name="tutorial.welcome">
    <Recommendation text="installation"
      autogenerated="true" group="all" color="blue"
      interst="57">tutorial.installation</Recommendation>
    <Recommendation text="readme"
      autogenerated="true" group="all" color="blue"
      interest="14">tutorial.readme</Recommendation>
  </Concept>
</RecommendedLinks>
```

We can see in the previous example file that there two recommended links to the concept/page "welcome" of the course "tutorial". The value of the "recommendation" label indicates the name of the destination web page/concept ("installation" and "readme" respectively). And the meaning of the attributes are: "text" (text of the hyperlink, by default is the concept of the rule consequent), "autogenerated" (boolean value that indicates if the recommendation has been generated by data mining or not), "group" (indicates if the recommendation is for all students or for a specific cluster), "color" (color used by the a triangular image, for example: blue color for all students and red color for clusters), "interest" (the confidence value of the rule).

4.2 Recommendation Engine

We have developed our recommendation engine as another AHA! View class [7], just like the other Views such as MainView, TOCView, ConceptbarView, etc. So, in order for a course to be able to use the new RecommendedLinksView, it is necessary to add it in the corresponding LayoutConfig.xml file of the course. Then, when a student logs in to the AHA! Course, the recommender engine is activated each time that the student visits a web page (concept).

The recommendation engine considers the active students in conjunction with the XML recommendation file to provide personalized recommendations. First, if there are clusters in the XML recommendation file, then the engine has to classify the current student to determine the most likely cluster. We have to communicate with the AHA! engine to obtain the current student Profile (to know the current number of pages visited and average knowledge of the student). Then, we use the centroid minimum distance method [16] for assigning the student to the cluster whose centroid is closest to that student (XML cluster file). Finally, we make the recommendation according to the rules in the cluster. So, only the rules of the corresponding cluster (or all the rules if there aren't clusters) are used to match the current web page (concept) in order to obtain the current list of recommended links.

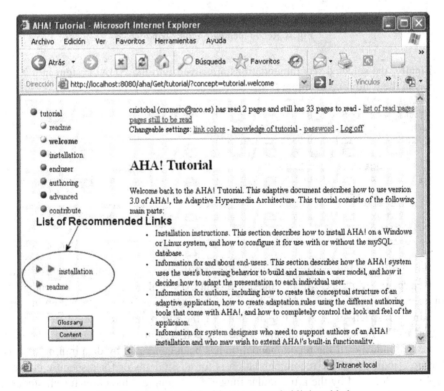

Fig. 5. AHA! Tutorial with recommended links added

In Figure 5 we can see the interface of the AHA! tutorial with a list of recommended links in which the student "cristobal" is located on the "welcome" page and the recommender engine recommends going to the "installation" page (strong recommenddation) and to the "readme" page (normal recommendation). We can see that we have adaptively sorted, annotated and partly hidden [4] the list of recommended links. First, we only show the links that the current student matches on the current page. Next, the links are sorted depending on their confidence value (on a decreasing scale). Then, we annotate the links with triangular icons that can vary in color depending on what data have been used to obtain them (blue for all the data, green to a specific data cluster) and can vary their number depending on the value of the confidence (1 triangle or normal recommendation to values lower than 0.33, 2 triangles or strong recommendation to values higher than 0.33 and lower than 0.66, and 3 triangles or very strong recommendation to values over 0.66).

5 Experimental Results

The data used in this study are real data collected from the on-line AHA! Tutorial (http://aha.win.tue.nl/tutorial/) that consists of 34 web pages or concepts. Although we have the usage data of about two hundred users available, we have selected only a group of good users (users who read a significant part of the tutorial). We have used a total number of 78 students with 118 sessions and 684 records in total. These students are mainly TU/E (Eindhoven University of Technology) students taking a course in adaptive hypermedia and some other Internet users interested in the AHA! system. So, all students used in this work are familiar with adaptive hypermedia.

We have carried out three experiments that we describe in the following section.

In the first experiment, we have executed the three available sequential mining algorithms (AprioriAll [2], GSP [24] and PrefixSpan [17]), using all the data in order to find out which is the best for our problem. We have compared the shortcut recommendation rules discovered (number of rules discovered and the average value of the support and confidence of the rules) by the three algorithms varying the minimum support threshold (from 0.3 to 0.03).

Table 1. Number/average support/average confidence of rules discovered using all data

	Min.Sup.=0.3	Min.Sup.=0.15	Min.Sup.=0.07	Min.Sup.=0.03
AprioriAll	3/0.35/0.55	7/0.24/0.43	22/0.13/0.40	70/0.07/0.32
GSP(gap=1)	2/0.39/0.55	6/0.24/0.43	20/0.16/0.43	62/0.11/0.40
PrefixSpan	2/0.39/0.55	6/0.24/0.43	14/0.18/0.43	61/0.12/0.41

As we can see in Table 1, there are not many differences between the three algorithms (specifically with higher minimum support values). However, GSP and PrefixSpan discover a lower number of rules with higher support and confidence values. In our problem of links recommendation, it is important to show the students only good links (a small number of rules with a higher value of support and confidence). So, although the three algorithms show similar results, the GSP and

PrefixSpan are a bit better than the AprioriAll algorithm. And as far as the minimum support threshold is concerned, we can see that in order not to obtain a lot of rules, a good range is between 0.3 and 0.1.

In the second experiment, we have executed the clustering algorithm in order to find the best number of clusters with our data. We have executed the k-means algorithm [14] varying the k value (number of clusters) from 2 to 5. Table 2 shows the number of students, sessions and records that are obtained in each one of the clusters.

Table 2. Number of students/sessions/records in each data cluster

No clusters	All data				
Number of st./se./r.	78/118/684				
Cluster K = 2	**Cluster 1**	**Cluster 2**			
Number of st./se./r.	48/60/383	30/58/301			
Cluster K = 3	**Cluster 1**	**Cluster 2**	**Cluster 3**		
Number of st./se./r.	18/34/120	32/45/299	28/39/265		
Cluster K = 4	**Cluster 1**	**Cluster 2**	**Cluster 3**	**Cluster 4**	
Number of st./se./r.	23/38/233	12/16/99	11/21/87	32/43/265	
Cluster K = 5	**Cluster 1**	**Cluster 2**	**Cluster 3**	**Cluster 4**	**Cluster 5**
Number of st./se./r.	14/30/106	12/25/81	6/14/40	4/12/26	42/47/449

In our problem of grouping students in different clusters, it is important for the obtained data to be balanced (equal number in each cluster). That is, the number of students, sessions and records must be uniform in all the clusters. In this way, we can later obtain a similar number of sequence rules for each data cluster. We can see in Table 2 that the data are more balanced when we use a low number of clusters (2 and 3 clusters). But when we increase the number of clusters (4, 5 and more) then there are more differences between clusters (some clusters have a lot of data and others very few data). So, two or three clusters give us well balanced data .

In the third experiment, we have done a comparison study between the basic architecture (only sequential mining) and the advanced architecture (clustering and sequential mining). We have compared the shortcut recommendation rules discovered (number of rules discovered and the average value of the support and confidence of the rules) by the PrefixSpan algorithm varying the minimum support threshold (from 0.3 to 0.1),on one hand using all data, and on the other hand the same algorithm using the data obtained from k-means algorithm for 2 and 3 clusters.

We can see in Table 3 that the number of rules discovered using each data cluster is not always less (sometimes even more) than using all the data, as we might have expected. However, their support and confidence values are always higher and this is very important in our problem. So, the advanced architecture can discover a similar number of rules to basic architecture but with higher values of confidence and support. Finally, in order to see if there are differences in the rules obtained from data clusters we are going to show and describe some examples of rules discovered using two data clusters (k=2) and the PrefixSpan algorithm (Min.Sup.=0.15).

Table 3. Number/Average Support/ Average Confidence of rules discovered using PrefixSpan over all data and over different number of clusters

	Min.Sup.=0.3	Min.Sup.=0.15	Min.Sup.=0.1
No Clusters (All data)	2/0.39/0.55	6/0.22/0.43	12/0.20/0.39
K = 2 (Cluster 1)	1/0.40/0.57	6/0.28/0.46	10/0.24/0.47
K = 2 (Cluster 2)	1/0.40/0.63	8/0.23/0.48	14/0.26/0.45
K = 3 (Cluster 1)	2/0.39/0.64	7/0.31/0.53	16/0.21/0.51
K = 3 (Cluster 2)	1/0.39/0.55	6/0.32/0.55	11/0.26/0.53
K = 3 (Cluster 3)	2/0.40/0.62	8/0.32/0.56	13/0.25/0.49

Table 4. Examples of rules discovered

Num	Antecedent =>	Consequence	Support	Confidence	Cluster
1	readme	install	0.23	0.41	1
2	domainmodel	concept	0.25	0.60	2
3	author	pages	0.27	0.32	1
	author	pages	0.21	0.42	2
4	welcome	install	0.48	0.63	1
	welcome	install	0.40	0.52	2

We can see in Table 4 that there are some rules that only appear in one cluster (rule 1 and 2), and there are other rules that appear in both clusters (rule 3 and 4) but with different support and confidence values. Cluster number 1 represents sporadic students who only want to sort out one question about AHA! (its centroid has NumberOfPagesVisited=2 and AverageLevelOfKnowledge=45) and cluster number 2 represents active students really interested in reading all the AHA! Tutorial (its centroid has NumberOfPagesVisited=16 and AverageLevelOfKnowledge=99). Rule number 1 shows that sporadic students go from "readme" web page to "install" web page (these students are looking for some specific question about the AHA! installation). Rule number 2 shows that active students go from the "domainmodel" web page to the "concept" web page (these students are reading/learning about the AHA! core). Rule number 3 shows that both type of students go from the "author" web page to the "pages" web page, but it is a higher number for the active students and the confidence is higher too (these students are reading/learning about the AHA! page format) than for sporadic students. Rule number 4 shows that both types of students go from the "welcome" web page to the "install" web page, but a higher number of sporadic students do so and with higher confidence (they are looking for some specific question about the AHA! installation) than active students.

6   Conclusions and Future Work

In this paper, we have described a personalized recommender system that uses web mining to recommend the next links to visit in an AIWBES. We have developed a specific mining tool and a recommender engine in order to help the teacher to carry out the web mining process. Although we have integrated the tools in the AHA! system [7] with minor modifications (mainly to handle the file and data format and to communicate with the engine of the system), it can in principle also be used in other web-based educational systems. We have carried out several experiments with real user data from the on-line AHA! tutorial in order to show the performance of the implemented algorithms. And we have shown the suitability of an advanced recommender system that uses the clustering and sequential pattern mining algorithms together to discover personalized recommendation links.

In the future, we want to carry out more experiments with a still larger number of students and using more information about the students' profiles for doing clustering. We can also integrate other sequence mining algorithms [10] such as SPADE, FreeSpan, CloSpan and PSP, and other clustering algorithm without requiring the user to specify any parameter. We plan to evaluate the quality of the recommendations based on feedback from students as well as on results using a testing set of data. Finally, it would be very useful to develop a real-time feedback loop between data mining and the recommendation system. We can use, for example, intelligent agents for doing on-line data mining automatically and for communicating with the recommender systems. In this way the system could work completely autonomously. The agents can mine data only when they detect enough volume of new data. And the authors do not have to preprocess and apply mining algorithms; they only have to supervise the new recommender links if they want.

Acknowledgments. The authors[1] gratefully acknowledge the financial subsidy provided by the Spanish Department of Research under TIN2005-08386-C05-02 Project.

References

1. Agrawal, R., Imielinski, T., Swami, A.N.: Mining Association Rules between Sets of Items in Large Databases. In: Proceeding SIGMOD, pp. 207–216 (1993)
2. Agrawal, R., Srikant, R.: Mining Sequential Patterns. In: Proceedings of the Eleventh International Conference on Data Engineering, pp. 3–14 (1995)
3. Alcalá, J., del Jesús, M.J., Garrell, J.M., Herrera, F., Hervás, C., Sánchez, L.: Proyecto KEEL: Desarrollo de una Herramienta para el Análisis e Implementación de Algoritmos de Extracción de Conocimiento Evolutivos. Tendencias de la Minería de Datos en España, Eds. J. Giraldez, J.C. Riquelme, J.S. Aguilar, pp. 413–423 (2004)
4. Brusilovsky, P., Peylo, C.: Adaptive and Intelligent Web-based Educational Systems. International Journal of Artificial Intelligence in Education. 13, 156–169 (2003)
5. Clementine (2007), http://www.spss.com/clementine/
6. DBMiner (2007), http://www.dbminer.com
7. De Bra, P., Calvi, L.: AHA! An open Adaptive Hypermedia Architecture. The New Review of Hypermedia and Multimedia 4, 115–139 (1998)
8. Farzan, R., Brusilovsky, P.: Social Navigation Support in a Course Recommendation System. In: proceedings of 4th International Conference on Adaptive Hypermedia and Adaptive Web-based Systems. Dublin, pp. 91–100 (2006)

9. García, E., Romero, C., Ventura, S., Castro, C.: Using rules discovery for the continuous improvement of e-learning courses. In: International Conference Intellligent Data Engineering and Automated Learning. Burgos, Spain, pp. 887–895 (2006)

10. Han, J., Pei, J., Yan, X.: Sequential Pattern Mining by Pattern-Growth: Principles and Extensions. StudFuzz 180, 183–220 (2005)

11. Henze, N., Nejdl, W.: Adaptation in open corpus hypermedia. International Journal of Artificial Intelligence in Education 12(4), 325–350 (2001)

12. Ishikawa, H., Ohta, M., Yokoyama, S., Nakayama, J., Katayama, K.: On the Effectiveness of Web Usage Mining for Page Recommendation and Restructuring. In: Proceeding of Web, Web-Services, and Database Systems, pp. 253–267 (2002)

13. Jain, A.K., Murty, M.N., Flynn, P.J.: Data Clustering: A Review. ACM Computing Surveys 31(3), 264–323 (1999)

14. Li, J., Zaïane, O.: Combining Usage, Content, and Structure Data to Improve Web Site Recommendation. In: Proceedings of International Conference on e-commerce and Web Technologies, pp. 305–315 (2004)

15. Lu, J.: Personalized E-learning Material Recommender System. In: Proceedings of International Conference on Information Technology for Application, pp. 374–379 (2004)

16. MacQueen, J.B.: Some Methods for classification and Analysis of Multivariate Observations. In: Proceedings of of 5-th Berkeley Symposium on Mathematical Statistics and Probability, pp. 281–297 (1967)

17. Mobasher, B.: Data Mining for Personalization. In: Brusilovsky, P., Kobsa, A., Nejdl, W. (eds.) The Adaptive Web: Methods and Strategies of Web Personalization, pp. 1–46. Springer, Heidelberg (2007)

18. Pei, J., Han, J., Mortazavi-Asl, B., Pinto, H., Chen, Q., Dayal, U., Hsu, M.: PrefixSpan: Mining Sequential Patterns Efficiently by Prefix-Projected Pattern Growth. In: Proceedings of the Seventeenth International Conference on Data Engineering, pp. 2215–2224 (2001)

19. Ksristofic, A.: Recommender System for Adaptive Hypermedia Applications. In: Proceeding of Informatics and Information Technology Student Research Conference, Bratislava, pp. 229–234 (2005)

20. Romero, C., Ventura, S.: Educational Data Mining: a Survey from 1995 to 2005. Expert Systems with Applications 1(33), 135–146 (2007)

21. Romero, C., Ventura, S.: Data mining in e-learning. Wit Press (2006)

22. Romero, C., Ventura, S., Bra, P.D.: Knowledge discovery with genetic programming for providing feedback to courseware author. The Journal of Personalization Research 14(5), 425–464 (2004)

23. Schafer, J.B.: The application of data-mining to recommender systems. In: Wang, J. (ed.) Encyclopedia of data warehousing and mining, pp. 44–48. Idea Group, Hershey, PA (2005)

24. Shen, L.P., Shen, R.M.: Learning Content Recommendation Service Based-on Simple Sequencing Specification. In: Proceedings of Advanced in Web-based Learning, pp. 363–370 (2004)

25. Srikant, R., Agrawal, R.: Mining Sequential Patterns: Generalizations and Performance Improvements. In: Proceedings International Conference on Extending Database Technology, pp. 3–17 (1996)

26. Tiffany, Y.T., Gordon, M.: Smart Recommendation for an Evolving E-Learning System. In: Workshop on Technologies for Electronic Documents for Supporting Learning Australia, pp. 699–710 (2003)

27. Wang, F.H., Shao, H.M.: Effective personalized recommendation based on time-framed navigation clustering and association mining. Expert System with Applications. Elsevier 27, 365–377 (2004)
28. Weber, G., Brusilovsky, P.: ELM-ART: An adaptive versatile system for Web-based instruction. International Journal of Artificial Intelligence in Education 12(4), 351–384 (2001)
29. Witten, I.H., Frank, E.: Data Mining: Practical Machine Learning Tools and Techniques. Morgan Kaufmann, San Francisco (2005)
30. Zaïane, O.: Building A Recommender Agent for e-Learning Systems. In: Proceedings of the International Conference in Education, New Zealand, pp. 55–59 (2002)

A Media Theoretical Approach to Technology Enhanced Learning in Non-technical Disciplines

Marc Spaniol, Yiwei Cao, and Ralf Klamma

Informatik 5, RWTH Aachen University, Ahornstr. 55, D-52056 Aachen, Germany
{mspaniol,cao,klamma}@cs.rwth-aachen.de

Abstract. The success of technology enhanced learning (*TEL*) depends on the careful design of digital media and related communication/collaboration features. Particulary when designing learning environments for professionals and scientists in non-technical disciplines it is crucial that the system is capable of reflecting the nature of learning discourses in these domains. For that purpose, it is necessary to fully understand the occuring digital media operations and knowledge sharing aspects involved in the learning process. *TEL* environments therefore need to reflect the nature of the underlying community processes and their discourses. This paper describes a media theroretical approach to *TEL*, which is capable of synthesizing media operations <u>and</u> knowledge sharing aspects involved in *TEL*. On top of this theoretical framing we introduce our *Virtual Campfire* system as a platform for *TEL* in non-technical disciplines. As a proof of concept, the system is being presented in two different non-technical disciplines: Cultural heritage management and entrepreneurial training.

Keywords: Technology Enhanced Learning, Multimedia, Media Theory, Non-Technical Disciplines.

1 Introduction

Independent of its area of application, Technology Enhanced Learning (*TEL*) requires to provide learners with the most suitable contents at any time and in any context. While the design and implementation of e-learning environments is a challenging issue, in general, certain application domains are more difficult to handle than others. While in technical and pedagogical disciplinies *TEL* is quite common as a means of knowledge management and knowledge sharing and has become an integral part of higher education in recent years, *TEL* in non-technical disciplines (such as the humanities, the cultural sciences or entrepreneurial training) is not that widespread. For that reason, the development of *TEL* environments in non-technical domains – and the cultural sciences in particular – requires a particularly sensitive design process in order to produce rich value-adding learning experiences within the *TEL* environment.

E. Duval, R. Klamma, and M. Wolpers (Eds.): EC-TEL 2007, LNCS 4753, pp. 307–321, 2007.

Within the interdisciplinary collaborative research center "Media and Cultural Communication"[1] (www.fk-427.de) founded in 1999 researchers from various disciplines study the nature and impact of media in cultural communication. From a *TEL* point of view knowledge management and knowledge sharing are special cases of cultural communication, too. In accordance with the basic distinction of scientific communities into two disjoint cultures (humanistic and engineering disciplines) undertaken by Snow [19], studies in the collaborative research center have underpinned these fundamental differences. Even more, previous assumptions about the differences between the ongoing learning processes were transferred to *TEL*. Here, studies have figured out that in *TEL* the basic distinction can be extended to technical and non-technical disciplines in general [8,10]. It means in concrete, that contrary to scholarly education in technical disciplines which aims (more or less) at the processing of factual knowledge, learning processes in the non-technical disciplines tend to be discourse oriented.

As a result, *TEL* cannot be "reduced" to the design and implementation of factual knowledge tests, but requires a consideration of the overall context and the media used that lead to a certain position. Consequently, the success of a learning process can not be simply measured based on the evaluation of answers according to a "simple" true/false scheme, but is coined by a hermeneutical process of insight and mediation. For that reason, the traceability of the complete discourse linked with any multimedia artefact is required at any time as it depends on the context whether a statement can be considered as correctly understood. Thus, scholarly communication in the non-technical disciplines heavily depends on the discursive nature of knowledge creation and the versatile media in use.

A naive understanding of *TEL* – e.g. that multimedia artefacts might stand alone and serve as learning objects – isn't sufficient. Complex interrelations exist between media and complex cultural interfaces to these media [12]. For all the many facets of *TEL* the hypothesis therefore is: Learning – particularly in non-technical disciplines – is the result of knowledge sharing processes and media settings intertwined with each other. For *TEL* this implies that is not sufficient to provide efficient learning support without considering the media operations going on. The research question therefore is: How can we as computer scientists support learners in non-technical disciplines by custom-tailored *TEL* environments? This paper presents a media theoretical approach to *TEL* in order to bridge the gap between the media specific needs inherent in learning processes in non-technical disciplines (and the cultural sciences in particular) and research undertaken in the field of knowledge management. The result is a novel approach to synthesizing both theories in a media theoretical approach for *TEL*.

The rest of the paper is organized as follows. In the next section the underlying theories from media and knowledge management studies are being introduced and compared. Based on the differences and similarities figured out between those approaches, a synthesis of these approaches is undertaken in Section 3.

---

[1] Supported by the German Research Foundation (DFG) and the Ministry for Science and Research of North Rhine Westphalia.

Following, Section 4 describes the newly introduced media theoretical approach utilized in our *TEL* environment called *Virtual Campfire*. We will present the application of *Virtual Campfire* in two different non-technical disciplines namely cultural heritage management and entrepreneurial training. The paper closes with conlusions and gives an outlook on further research.

2   Media Theories and Knowledge Management Theories Compared

Knowledge sharing in the non-technical disciplines is primarily a social process [1,6,25]. In order to get a deeper insight into the hermeneutical learning processes in these disciplines both, media operations <u>and</u> steps in the knowledge sharing process, need to be understood. For that purpose, we now take a closer look at the underlying theories. Particularly, we will point out that for *TEL* it is insufficient to consider them separately, but an intertwined approach is being required. Therefore, we introduce the *Theory of Transcriptivity* at first, which will help us to understand the media operations being performed in the non-technical domain of cultural sciences. After that, we describe a refinement of the renowned *SECI* model. By doing so, the model becomes more feasible and easier to transfer into non-technical disciplines.

2.1   The *Theory of Transcriptivity* by Jäger

Within the collaborative research center on "Media and Cultural Communication" the German philologist Ludwig Jäger developed the so-called *"Theory of Transcriptivity"* [7]. This theory describes a medial practice in creating and further developing of a cultural semantic by symbolic means. Thus, transcriptivity describes the underlying basic relation between knowledge organization and communication in the cultural sciences and other non-technical disciplines. It is based on the following three media operations [4,5]:

- *Transcription* is a media dependent operation in order to make media collections more readable.
- *Localization* means an operation that transfers global media into local practices of communities.
- The term of *(re-) addressing* describes an operation that stabilizes and optimizes the accessibility in communication.

The processes described in the *Theory of Transcriptivity* are shown schematically in Figure 1. While the **transcription** operation can be identified as a distinct procedure constituting a transcript out of previously existing pre-texts (either real texts or undergone experiences), the media operations of **localization** and **addressing** are not visible as separate entities. The reason is, that both processes are to some extent specializations of (and consequently dependent on) the **transcription** and help constituting the feedback loop of "Understanding and Critique" within the overall process. In this aspect, **addressing** can be

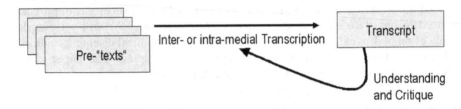

Fig. 1. The *Theory of Transcriptivity* (adopted from [7])

seen as technical means in order to improve distributing and presenting contents (and thus the transcripts). Similarly, **localization** is a procedure that refines the adaptation and presentation of medial artefacts (the transcripts) given a dedicated context.

Altogether, the *Theory of Transcriptivity* represents a model that describes the process of knowledge sharing in the cultural sciences from a media theoretic perspective. However, the implications of the media operations described here are not considered from a technical point of view. Regarding *TEL* the *Theory of Transcriptivity* does not contain any references to the underlying learning processes within the media operations described. Unescorted, the *Theory of Transcriptivity* is not suitable to serve as a model for *TEL* in non-technical disciplines without taking into consideration the learning processes from a knowledge management perspective.

2.2   The *SECI* Model (by Nonaka & Takeuchi) and Beyond

The knowledge creation theory, especially the *SECI* model, by Nonaka and Takeuchi [14] is widely acknowledged in management theory and practice. Also, in CSCL and *TEL* the most prominent knowledge management theories are those of Bereiter, Engeström and Nonaka & Takeuchi [15]. The *SECI* model makes a basic distinction between **tacit** or *procedural* and **explicit** or *declarative* knowledge [13,14,16].

In *TEL* the learning process according to the *SECI* model starts with an individual who has some media-specific knowledge. This individual has basically two alternatives to share his expertise. On the one hand, there is an option to present this information to others by human-human interaction (**Socialization**), which is equivalent to the development of a shared history. On the other hand, individuals may also create new medial artifacts (**Externalization**). These contents may now be further processed within a learning environement (**Combination**). The cycle is closed, when contents are accessed by others (**Internalization**). The overall process might then be initiated and repeated again for many times.

From the viewpoint of non-technical disciplines (such as the cultural sciences and entrepreneurial training) this distinction is quite coarse. Particularly a plain classification of knowledge into just two categories (**tacit** and **explicit**) neglects the fact, that in non-technical siciplines the overall context and the media used have to be taken into account in order to understand a certain position. Thus,

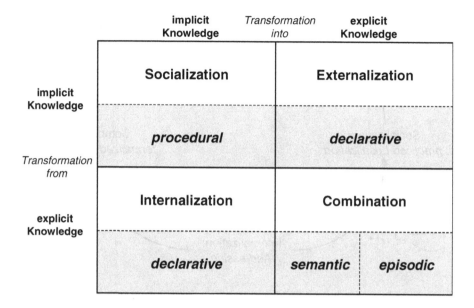

Fig. 2. The *SECI* model of knowledge processing [14] with refinements (in grey) by Ullman [24]

the *SECI* model needs to be refined at the level of **Combination** by the concepts of *semantic* and *episodic* knowledge introduced by Tulving and Ullmann [23,24]. The key point is that only by a combination of *semantic* and *episodic* knowledge the context of media settings (and thus a certain viewpoint) can be correctly understood (cf. Figure 2).

While *semantic* knowledge is kind of semiotic and conceptual like documentation in organizational charts, business process definitions and so forth, *episodic* knowledge are undergone experiences such as episodes and narratives. Thus, documentation is a means of *semantic* knowledge, which can again be refined as *verbal* (linguistic data) and *non-verbal* (e.g. video or visual) contents. However, the situational context leading to a certain document might be lost. Here, *episodic* knowledge comes into play as it covers the situational context of a certain media setting.

In this aspect, the non-technical disciplines require a fine-grained distinction of both is of great importance in order to ensure the success of a learning process. Particularly, as a multimedia artefact (*semantic* knowledge) has to be considered from various viewpoints and can be interpreted in different ways (*episodic* knowledge). Thus, in non-technical disciplines it is crucial to consider the situational context as a distinct concept within the overall learning process.

An approach to developing learning histories [17] is story-telling. It intertwines *semantic* knowledge, i.e. already reified concepts of communities stored as documents, by linking it with the narrative experiences gained from *episodic* knowledge. Consequently, story-telling is an important aspect for knowledge sharing.

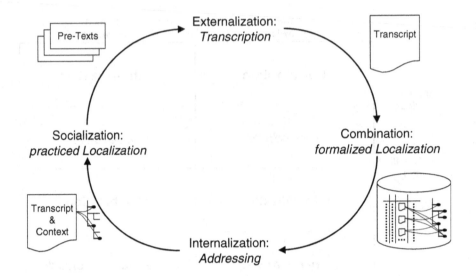

Fig. 3. A Media Theoretical Approach to *TEL*

Here, the aspects of telling, sharing and experiencing stories are a problem-oriented way to learn from the experiences of others.

However, the extended *SECI* model still does not help to gain a deeper insight into the media operations involved in the hermeneutical learning processes in non-technical disciplines. Thus, the next chapter describes a media theoretical approach to *TEL* that synthesizes the previously introduced theories.

3   A Media Theoretical Approach to *TEL*

In order to systematize the learning processes taking place in non-technical disciplines, the media operations taking place need to be linked with a knowledge management theory. Thus, the following section describes the synthesis of the media specific operations extracted from the *Theory of Transcriptivity* with the extended *SECI* model. The result is a media theoretical approach to *TEL* based on the previously introduced media operations in the cultural sciences [5] and social learning and knowledge creation processes adopted from Nonaka & Takeuchi [14] and Wenger [25]. For the sake of clarity, we focus on the media theoretical aspects of the previously named theories without starting an in-depth discussion on communities of practice.

Figure 3 brings together both approaches in a media centric theory of learning for *TEL* in non-technical disciplines. It combines the two types of knowledge (**tacit** resp. ***procedural*** and **explicit** resp. ***declarative*** [13,14,16]) as part of a knowledge creation and learning process with the media specific operations introduced in the *Theory of Transcriptivity*. On the left side, operations dealing with **tacit** (***procedural***) knowledge are visualized. Starting point is an individual having gained some media-specific knowledge. In *TEL* the first step of a learner is a *transcription* by creating a new medial artifact as part of an **externalization** process. This operation leads to the right side of the drawing where the digital learning contents are processed and **explicit** (*declarative*) knowledge is being visualized. The so created contents are now further processed within the *TEL* environment. That means, the contents might not only be **(re-) combined** in an arbitrary fashion, but also a processing of *semantic* and *episodic* knowledge happens. From a media theoretical point of view, this operation describes a *formalized localization* process. Following, *addressing* of contents occurs. In this procedure the contents are **internalized** by a learner bringing us again to the left side of Figure 3. In a final step, the contents might be discussed with others (either within the learning environment or directly among the learners) and such **socialized**. From a media theoretical point of view, this can be best described as *practiced localization*. From then on, the process might be repeated infinitely oscillating between **tacit** and **explicit** knowledge on the epistemological axis and between individuals and the learning community on the ontological axis.

4 Applied Media Theory: *TEL* in Non-technical Disciplines

In this section, we demonstrate the applicability of the previously introduced media theory in the *Virtual Campfire* system. *Virtual Campfire* serves as a platform for *TEL* in non-technical disciplines. Thereby, the community management of *Virtual Campfire* has central importance as the system provides a unique cross-media and cross-community support [9]. Thus, *Virtual Campfire* offers dedicated community management features in order to maintain users and communities as well as their general and community-specific access rights modelled as roles. In addition, an embedded object manager provides access to the contents in *Virtual Campfire* by so-called security objects. For each user there is a list of roles that can be assigned to him either as global permissions or prohibitions. These roles define the dedicated features of services which a user is allowed or forbidden to invoke in *Virtual Campfire*. For that purpose, access control list (ACL) for each security object are maintained. Similar to the UNIX filesystem an ACL defines access rights on three different levels: Users, groups and all others. Within any ACL an arbitrary number of permissions resp. prohibitions to a security object in a specific service method context are being stored (cf. [21] for a detailed overview on the technical details of community management in *Virtual Campfire*).

   In the following, we present – as a proof-of-concept – the application of *Virtual Campfire* in two different non-technical domains. In our first case study, the system is used in cultural heritage management in order to assist researchers and preservationists in preserving the cultural heritage of Afghanistan. Here, the system serves as a learning platform to re-unite a cultural heritage community that has been spread all over the world due to the times of war and isolation. The aim is to transfer the knowledge from the old generation to a new generation grown up and living in Afghanistan. Our second case study deals with

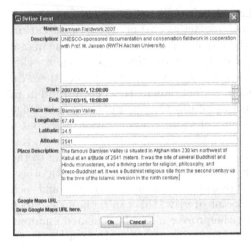

Fig. 4. Creation of MPEG-7 compliant typed media descriptions in Virtual Campfire: Events (left) and states (right)

entrepreneurial training. Since entrepreneurial knowledge is extremely hard to formalize and teach, our *TEL* environment persues a problem based approach where entrepreneurs describe the challenges of starting a company.

4.1   *Transcription* – Collaborative Content Creation

The collaborative approach of content creation in *Virtual Campfire* tries to bridge the gap between folksonomy-style high-level semantic knowledge about multimedia and purely technical low-level content descriptions. The services provided intend to support collaboration in learning communities by the exchange of multimedia content and their low-level and high-level semantic descriptions. Hence, users can **externalize** their knowledge about a certain issue by *transcribing* the multimedia artefact. Thus, the content becomes more understandable to others as these data contain additional information about the context of an artefact.

In order to ensure interoperability among the contents description multimedia metadata standards are being incorporated. The Dublin Core (DC) metadata standard [3] is advantageous, since it is an easily understandable and concise method for media annotations. Nevertheless, DC still has the limitations that it is not suitable for temporal and media specific annotations of multimedia contents. We try to surmount these limitations by combining the loose classifications in DC with more sophisticated description elements for time based media in MPEG-7. We make use of an excerpt of the extensive MPEG-7 multimedia metadata standard and provide typed media descriptions according to the standard (cf. Figure 4). Even more, we provide services for a semi-automatic conversion from DC to MPEG-7 [20] while an affiliated FTP server is used for an automated upload and download of multimedia artifacts by the community to the common

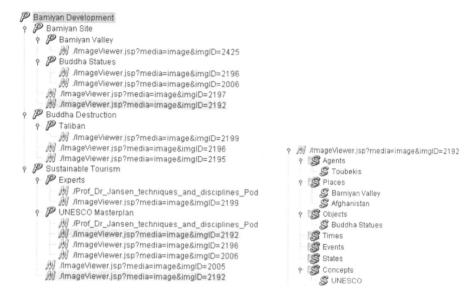

Fig. 5. Decomposition of problems (left) and typed media annotations (right)

repository. The collaborative content creation in *Virtual Campfire* allows the community members to search and browse for multimedia contents described by MPEG-7 for professional learning purposes.

4.2 *Formal Localization* – Episodic Knowledge in Non-linear Multimedia Stories

The **combination** of contents in *Virtual Campfire* is primarily based on non-linear multimedia stories. The reason is simple: Non-linear multimedia stories are an ideal medium to intertwine the ***semantic*** and ***episodic*** knowledge of a multimedia artefact. For that purpose *Virtual Campfire* provides *formal* methods that help to focus on the *local* meaning of multimedia artefacts in a globally accessible *TEL* environment.

Hence, *Virtual Campfire* provides dedicated features to capture the ***semantic*** and ***episodic*** knowledge within non-linear multimedia stories. In order to help learning content designers in creating useful stories (from a structural point of view), the MOD paradigm [18] is being applied as a theoretical basis. For the sake of brevity, we only briefly discuss the major principles here. Details can be found in [22]. Two dedicated user interfaces are available for story-telling support in *Virtual Campfire*, an editor and a player. The editor allows users to create new or to edit already existing non-linear multimedia stories. The player is used to subsequently consume and interact with existing non-linear multimedia stories. Besides the **explicit** knowledge contained in the multimedia contents and their high-level semantic tags are also accessible here (cf. right hand side

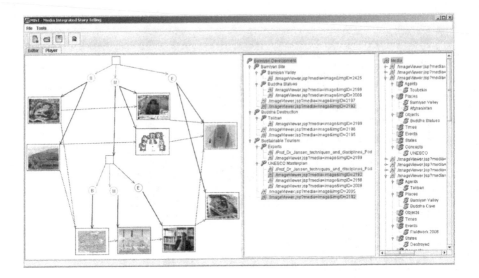

Fig. 6. Creation of a non-linear multimedia story in *Virtual Campfire*

of Figure 5). These multimedia contents can be thereafter temporally arranged in the way that they depend on a certain context. At story creation authors can define paths covering different problematic aspects along the contents. The problems specified depend on the path selected and lead to different endings of a story (cf. left hand side of Figure 5).

Figure 6 shows the editor consisting of three main elements (from left to right): storyboard, plot, and semantic annotations. The plot in the middle represents the declarative knowledge captured in a story. It is rendered by a tree hierarchy, which allows the further decomposition into sub-problems. In addition, problems addressed in a multimedia story can be linked to related multimedia content. The storyboard on the left panel illustrates a visualization of episodic knowledge as paths between content elements. The story decomposition accords to the MOD paradigm with its designated begin (B), middle (M), and end (E) elements. Finally, on the right panel additional semantic annotations can be added to any multimedia element. Users may express verbal-knowledge being associated with non-verbal knowledge.

4.3 *Addressing* – Contextualized Multimedia Presentations

The **internalization** of previously encoded knowledge in *Virtual Campfire* is supported by contextualized multimedia presentations and the consumption of multimedia stories. Here, the *addressing* of multimedia contents contained in the learning environment takes place. *Virtual Campfire* offers two types of learning content presentations: Contextualized multimedia presentations and the consumption of multimedia stories.

Fig. 7. Presentation of multimedia in the context of "Buddha & Bamiyan & Painting"

Contextualized multimedia presentations are used in order to help the learner in searching and exploring the content. Here, plain keyword search and typed semantic retrieval are applied in order to guide the learner to the most relevant contents (cf. Figure 7). Keyword tags enable the learners to search for multimedia artefacts based on a set of plain keywords like it can be done in Flickr (www.flickr.com). Semantic tags search go a step further by allowing users to define semantic entities and to assign semantic entity references to an image or a video. They are more expressive than plain keywords because they carry additional semantics. For example in the domain of cultural heritage management, one could not derive from a plaintext keyword `Buddha`, that it describes an agent. By contrast, for semantic tags, `Buddha` might have been modeled as a semantic entity of type agent. All these high-level content descriptions can be cross-walked with any learning standard by fixed mappings or even dynamically by mapping services [2]. Even more, for retrieval learners can formulate keyword search expressions as propositional logic formulae using keywords as atomic propositions. For example, the keyword search expression "`Buddha and Bamiyan and Painting`" retrieves images and videos having been assigned with all those keywords (cf. Figure 7).

Similarly, the presentation of multimedia stories can be be applied to **internalize** the knowledge contained in the learning contents of *Virtual Campfire*. The

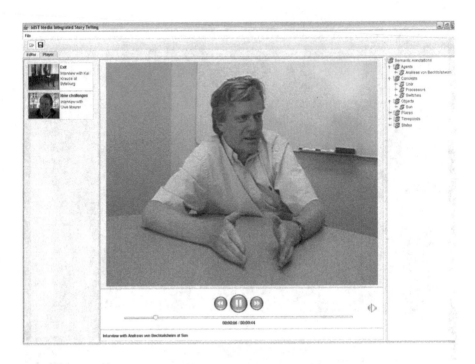

Fig. 8. The mediaplayer for non-linear multimedia stories

multimedia story player of *Virtual Campfire* applied in entrepreneurial training is shown in Figure 8 (cf. [11] for details). It consists – like the story editor – of three tabs. The player located in the middle allows rendering of arbitrary multimedia content such as video, audio, text or image. The entrepreneurial problems addressed by the plot are presented as multimedia content. The tab on the right contains additional semantic annotations related to the medium. In the tab on the left possibly succeeding media are shown in a thumbnail preview. According to the media transitions defined in the editor's storyboard the user can select a medial artefact in order to navigate through one possible path of a non-linear multimedia story.

The final step in **socializing** the learning contents is based on direct human-human communication where the *practices* are discussed *locally*. Thus, it can not be supported "naturally" within a *TEL* environment. However, *Virtual Campfire* at least provides additional forum features where learners can discuss about the contents previously consumed.

5   Conclusions and Outlook

More than in any other technical discipline the success of *TEL* in non-technical disciplines depends on a careful design of the digital media and the related communication/collaboration features. Thus, the occurring media operations and knowledge sharing aspects involved in the learning process need to be fully understood. Only combined it becomes possible to design *TEL* environments for professionals and scientists in non-technical disciplines that reflect the nature of discourses in these domains. In this paper, we therefore presented a media theroretical approach to *TEL*. By doing so, we were able to synthesize media operations <u>and</u> knowledge sharing aspects involved in *TEL*.

The result of the media theoretical considerations has led to a novel learning environment called *Virtual Campfire* providing custom-tailored services for learning communities in non-technical disciplines. In order to achieve this, a key feature of *Virtual Campfire* is the traceability of the complete discourse linked with any multimedia artefact. Thus, it is possible at any time to comprehend the context of multimedia artefact and to decide whether a statement can be considered as correctly understood. Scholarly communication in the cultural sciences heavily depends on the discursive nature of knowledge creation and the versatile media in use. *Virtual Campfire* was then presented in two case studies that have proven the validity of our approach.

Within *Virtual Campfire* we also demonstrated the usefulness of MPEG-7 for the processing of multimedia learning contents by capturing ***episodic*** knowledge inherent in multimedia stories and ***semantic*** knowledge of multimedia content. Due to its easy to use user interfaces, users can now collaborate, exchange knowledge and thus learn anytime and anywhere by exchanging multimedia stories via a common repository.

Current research aims at measuring the learning success of multimedia learning contents created with *Virtual Campfire*. Therefore, we plan to embed user models based on standards like IMS LIP or IEEE PAPI. By doing so, we can investigate the multimedia reception process and identify success factors. Hence, we intend to use pattern based approaches to detect frequently occuring learning behaviour. We will conduct a comprehensive cross-media analysis that might give us a deeper insight to understand media related impacts in learning processes.

Acknowledgements

This work was supported by the German National Science Foundation (DFG) within the collaborative research centers SFB/FK 427 "Media and Cultural Communication", within the research cluster established under the excellence initiative of the German government "Ultra High-Speed Mobile Information and Communication (UMIC)" and by the 6th Framework IST programme of the EC through the NoE on Professional Learning (PROLEARN) IST-2003-507310. We thank our colleagues N. Sharda and G. Toubekis for the inspiring discussions. In addition, we thank our students D. Renzel, H. Janßen, P. M. Cuong, D. Andrikopoulos and A. Hahne for implementing the *Virtual Campfire* services.

References

1. Brown, J.S., Duguid, P.: The Social Life of Information. Harvard Business Press (2000)
2. Chatti, M.A., Klamma, R., Quix, C., Kensche, D.: LM-DTM: An Environment for XML-Based, LIP/PAPI-Compliant Deployment, Transformation and Matching of Learner Models. In: Goodyear, P., Sampson, D.G., Yang, D.J.-T. (eds.) Proceedings of the 5th International Conference on Advanced Learning Technologies (ICALT 2005), Kaohsiung, Taiwan, July 5-8, pp. 567–569 (2005)
3. Dublin Core Metadata Initiative. Dublin core metadata element set, version 1.1: Reference description. Technical report, Dublin Core Metadata Initiative [1.6.2007] (1999), http://dublincore.org/documents/dces/
4. Fohrmann, J., Schüttpelz, E.: Die Kommunikation der Medien. Niemeyer, Tübingen (in German) (2004)
5. Jäger, L.: Die Verfahren der Medien: Transkribieren – Adressieren – Lokalisieren. In: Fohrmann, J., Schüttpelz, E. (eds.) Die Kommunikation der Medien, Niemeyer, Tübingen, pp. 69–79 (2004) (in German)
6. Jarke, M., Klamma, R.: Metadata and cooperative knowledge management. In: Proceedings of the 14th Intl. Conf. on Advanced Information Systems Engineering, Toronto, Ontario, Canada, May 27-31, 2002, pp. 27–31. Springer, Berlin (2002)
7. Jäger, L., Stanitzek, G. (eds.): Transkribieren – Medien/Lektüre. Wilhelm Fink Verlag, Munich (in German) (2002)
8. Klamma, R., Spaniol, M.: Supporting communication and knowledge creation in digitally networked communities in the humanities. In: ACM SIGGROUP Bulletin Special issue on community-based learning: explorations into theoretical groundings, empirical findings and computer support, vol. 24(3), pp. 55–59. ACM Press, New York (2003)
9. Klamma, R., Spaniol, M., Cao, Y.: MPEG-7 Compliant Community Hosting. In: Lux, M., Jarke, M., Kosch, H., MPEG (eds.) MPEG and Multimedia Metadata Community Workshop Results 2005, J.UKM Special Issue (Journal of Universal Knowledge Management), vol. 1(1), pp. 36–44. Springer, Heidelberg (2006)
10. Klamma, R., Spaniol, M., Jarke, M.: Do you know a similar project I can learn from? Self-monitoring of Communities of Practice in the Cultural Sciences. In: He, X., Hintz, T., Piccardi, M., Wu, Q., Huang, M., Tien, D. (eds.) Proceedings of the Third International Conference on Information Technology and Applications ICITA'05, Sydney, Australia, vol. II, pp. 608–613 (2005)
11. Klamma, R., Spaniol, M., Renzel, D.: Virtual Entrepreneurship Lab 2.0: Sharing Entrepreneurial Knowledge by Non-Linear Story-Telling. In: Tochtermann, K., Maurer, H. (eds.) Proceedings of I-KNOW '06, 6th International Conference on Knowledge Management, Graz, Austria, September 6 - 8, J.UCS (Journal of Universal Computer Science) Proceedings, pp. 26–34. Springer, Heidelberg (2006)
12. Manovich, L.: The Language of New Media. MIT Press, Cambridge, MA (2001)
13. Nelson, R.R., Winter, S.G.: An Evolutionary Theory of Economic Change. Harvard University Press, Cambridge, MA (1982)
14. Nonaka, I., Takeuchi, H.: The Knowledge-Creating Company. Oxford University Press, Oxford (1995)
15. Paavola, S., Lipponen, L., Hakkarainen, K.: Epistemological foundations for CSCL: A comparison of three models of innovative knowledge communities. In: Stahl, G. (ed.) Computer Support for Collaborative Learning: Foundations for a CSCL Community. Proceedings of CSCL 2002, pp. 24–32. Lawrence Erlbaum, Mahwah (2002)

16. Polanyi, M.: The tacit dimension. Anchor Books, Doubleday & Co. NY (1966)
17. Roth, G., Kleiner, A.: Car Launch, The Human Side of Managing Change. Oxford University Press, New York (1999)
18. Sharda, N.: Movement Oriented Design: A New Paradigm for Multimedia Design. International Journal of Lateral Computing (IJLC) 1(1), 7–14 (2005)
19. Snow, C.P.: The Two Cultures. Cambridge University Press, Cambridge, UK (1959)
20. Spaniol, M., Klamma, R.: MEDINA: A Semi-Automatic Dublin Core to MPEG-7 Converter for Collaboration and Knowledge Management in Multimedia Repositories. In: Tochtermann, K., Maurer, H. (eds.) Proceedings of I-KNOW '05, 5th Intl. Conf. on Knowledge Management, Graz, Austria, June 29 - July 1, 2005, J.UCS (Journal of Universal Computer Science), pp. 136–144. Springer, Heidelberg (2005)
21. Spaniol, M., Klamma, R., Janßen, H., Renzel, D.: LAS: A Lightweight Application Server for MPEG-7 Services in Community Engines. In: Tochtermann, K., Maurer, H. (eds.) Proceedings of I-KNOW '06, 6th International Conference on Knowledge Management, Graz, Austria, September 6 - 8, 2006, J.UCS (Journal of Universal Computer Science) Proceedings, pp. 592–599. Springer, Heidelberg (2006)
22. Spaniol, M., Klamma, R., Sharda, N., Jarke, M.: Web-Based Learning with Nonlinear Multimedia Stories. In: Liu, W., Li, Q., Lau, R.W.H. (eds.) ICWL 2006. LNCS, vol. 4181, pp. 249–263. Springer, Heidelberg (2006)
23. Tulving, E.: Episodic and semantic memory. In: Organization of Memory, pp. 381–403. Academic Press, New York (1972)
24. Ullman, M.T.: Contributions of memory circuits to language: the declarative/procedural model. Cognition 92(1-2), 231–270 (2004)
25. Wenger, E.: Communities of Practice: Learning, Meaning, and Identity. Cambridge University Press, Cambridge, UK (1998)

MACE – Enriching Architectural Learning Objects for Experience Multiplication

Moritz Stefaner[1], Elisa Dalla Vecchia[2], Massimiliano Condotta[2], Martin Wolpers[3], Marcus Specht[4], Stefan Apelt[5], and Erik Duval[3]

[1] University of Applied Sciences Potsdam, Interaction Design Lab. Pappelallee 8-9, 14469 Potsdam, Germany
moritz.stefaner@fh-potsdam.de

[2] University IUAV of Venice, Faculty of Architecture, Department of Construction Building Terese – Dorsoduro 2206 I-30123 Venezia, Italy
{edallave,massimiliano.condotta}@iuav.it

[3] Katholieke Universiteit Leuven, Celestijnenlaan 200A, BE3001 Leuven, Belgium
{martin.wolpers,erik.duval}@cs.kuleuven.be

[4] Educational Technology Expertise Centre, Open University of the Netherlands, Valkenburgerweg 177, 6419 AT Heerlen, Netherlands
marcus.specht@ou.nl

[5] Fraunhofer Institut FIT, Schloss Birlinghoven, 53754 Sankt Augustin, Germany
stefan.apelt@fit.fraunhofer.de

Abstract. Education in architecture requires access to a broad range of learning materials to develop flexibility and creativity in design. The learning material is compromised of textual and visual media including images, videos, description of architectural concepts or projects, i.e. digital artifacts on different aggregation levels. The repositories storing such information are not interrelated and do not provide unified access so that retrieval of architectural learning objects is cumbersome and time consuming. In this paper, we describe how an infrastructure of federated architectural learning repositories will provide unique, integrated access facilities for high quality architectural content. The integration of various types of content, usage, social and contextual metadata enables users to develop multiple perspectives and navigation paths that support experience multiplication for the user. A standards–based, service–oriented software architecture, and flexible user interface design solutions, based on embeddable widgets, ensure easy integration and re-combinability of contents, metadata and functionalities.

Keywords: Metadata, learning objects, experience multiplication, architectural design, content enrichment, technology enhanced learning.

1 Introduction

Architecture is a complex discipline, where technical and artistic knowledge blend, and influence each other. Due to this double influence, it happens that there is not an "exact" and "unique" solution to architectural design problems. Therefore the architect, while developing a project, will remember, compare, choose and re-elaborate

E. Duval, R. Klamma, and M. Wolpers (Eds.): EC-TEL 2007, LNCS 4753, pp. 322–336, 2007.

a large stock of possible solutions, moving towards the final outcome step by step. The background of this process is the architect's self personal stock of erudition and culture, which mainly consists of images and visual inputs, stored through years in his memory in a life-long process. These visual memories can be about the most different aspects of the subject: from architectonic solutions and shapes to examples of applied theory, suggestions, or personal experiences...

The design solutions produced by an architect therefore are, most of the time, the outcome of a process of images recalling and reworking: the aim of achieving new solutions and shapes is reached through the designer's personal contribution in the interpretation of something already seen and known [1] – [2]. In fact, the mnemonic process which leads the design activity is based on "the repeated view of the same objects",: this condition "entails the setting up, in the nervous system, of experiences (or better, of habits) by virtue of elements (notions, images, ...) that are repeatedly near in space and time" [3]; so, while an architect is working on his personal stock of erudition and culture, his mind will mostly return back only the notions that are perceived as more familiar: in this way, a first selection, and therefore a limitation, is operated on the architect's personal knowledge set.

Evidently, when we focus on architecture education, the case-based aspects of these mental processes are amplified and carried to extremes: when the students are little experienced, they will need a very wide range of possible suggestion providers, and a higher number of examples to look at. This not only entails a broad information need during architectural design; moreover, the same piece of information might be interesting for several reasons, depending on the actual state of the design process.

It should finally be considered that in architecture, as in other disciplines, a large amount of information is held in visual media (images, photos, sketches...), which are in general hard to index and find. Most currently available search tools do not offer the multiple perspectives and exploratory search needed to support effective and seamless interaction within the domain of architecture and engineering.

For these reasons, non-expert designers and students spend a lot of time in libraries, searching for a large number of cases similar to their actual situation, to get cues and suggestions on how to proceed, thus carrying out this activity in a very inefficient and time-wasting way. This happens because of the great variety of information that can be inferred from a single volume, despite its title or general subject (i.e. a technical solution for a window frame detail may often be deduced observing a picture in a monograph on a great architect, and not from a technology manual).

It would probably be of great help to architecture students to spread around all the pages from their books, like the tesserae of a muddle up mosaic of images, drawings, sketches, graphic schemes, to be able to walk through them - ready to catch those contents that can solve the problem.

Given the fact that a considerable part of the knowledge which was once ink-written in architecture books is being moved to digital media, we can get closer to enabling this vision: We can use an enormous mass of factored notions (the single Learning Objects and Assets), which at the moment is spread in a cloud-like shape of notions, but may be re-structured for multiple experiences.

One of MACE project aims is to create the core of a possible future common indexing strategy to structure all these actually rambling "pieces" of architectural information. The final goal is to allow learners to have, through strengthening and optimizing the on–going knowledge digitalization process, a new way of exploring notions and knowledge: a multiplication of the learning opportunity held using the web as a *collective external memory*.

1.1 Digital Media for Experience Multiplication in Architectural Design Process

In the field of computer aided architectural design (CAD), the computer can be useful in the generative process of a project [4] - [5]. Through 3D-modelling software (and other kinds of graphic and technical software), a computer can assist the designer to create sharable, storable and visible representations of personal ideas and suggestions. By proposing an infinite range of new and unexpected shapes, diagrams, or colours or by applying different clustering, ordering, or indexing strategies, computer systems can extend the limit of obtaining and getting solutions from a finite cluster of elements (the personal background of the designer).

This multiplication of perspectives and experiences is important for digital media to allow architects and students to have a new way of exploring notions and knowledge.

One consequence of the ongoing data digitalization process is the so-called "micro-chunking" of information. This is not only an effect of the technologies used to search, publish and communicate information (such as search engines, blogging software, or federated learning object repositories) but also the changing consumption behavior of the users and the according social practices [6]. Providing the right tools for exploration and recombination of these information chunks can lead to novel and rich experiences: the revising of the project's formative elements (context, suggestions, ideas, diagrams, functions, shapes, images, etc.) as factored digital data, as a re-mix of dynamic collections, recombination and juxtapositions, can lead to previously unavailable insights and discoveries.

A second consequence is the availability of a large amount of meta-information for a given piece of notion: who links to that page, how did others like this book, etc. — all these kinds of contextual information are already accessible on the web, however, still distributed over different services and not yet specific for the architectural domain.

In the domain of architectural design, (but also in various sectors of the discipline like history research, representation techniques, urban studies, etc…), we can regard digital media and the web as *experience multipliers*: a digitally assisted design process can have a more complex recombination of multi-facetted, mosaic-like agglomerate of loosely connected information and meta-information. In particular, these additional information can be used not only as raw data, but they can trigger new mental processes.

The tasks of the MACE project is to support the shaping and reorganization this already existing cloud of floating, unorganized information by making it navigable, usable and accessible to an architectural learner. The goal will be reached by creating a system which allows the end user both to enlarge his set of visual memories and to enrich the existing online *"collective external memory"* by recognizing, catching and linking the contents through an interactive navigation system, which has to reflect the typical logical behaviour of an architectural learner.

1.2 Architectural Digital Media Characteristics: Strategies for Mosaic Recomposition

This kind of access to the contents is not yet enabled, for both the architectural discipline and visual media peculiar features. It is necessary to find new indexing strategies, capable to structure a high number of Learning Objects (LO), with the aim of reaching the maximum utility for the final user. Obviously, indexing strategies have to be suitable to the treated discipline; they will have to follow the logic pattern of the user navigating through this contents cloud, and they will have to support his choice criteria.

Choice criteria are many, but can refer to four main typical features of the signifier/signified binomial composing a LO. At first, obviously, the *content* and the *domain* meta-information of the LO will drive the choice of the user, even if this choice is very often influenced or led by *usage* experiences made by others and by the comprehension of their exploration and learning paths. In other situations, the user's and content's *levels of competence*, or the *context*, in which the LO is inserted, might be key to accessing the right kind of information.

2 MACE—Metadata for Architectural Contents in Europe

MACE sets out to integrate architectural learning contents from Learning Object Repositories (LORs) spread around Europe, and enrich them with different types of metadata and classification structures in order to enable improved access and experience multiplication for students, teachers and professionals. Enrichment here includes both the manual and automatic provision of metadata about the learning object itself, its contents or the context of their usage (including social metadata, competence metadata and contextual metadata).

An overview of currently integrated content repositories can be seen in Table 1. The available contents range from multimedia resources about architectural projects over technology enhanced learning courses to literature references and regulations. Our open, standards–based infrastructure allows an integration of further content databases in the future.

Figure 1 gives an overview of the different layers in the MACE approach. Based on a shared technical infrastructure for federated access to the repositories, metadata harvesting and content enrichment, we provide web services for metadata manipulation and retrieval and metadata-based content access. These are the basis for both automatic as well as manual content enrichment. As user interfaces, we develop compact, modular components with rich visualization and interaction possibilities — so–called widgets. These can be used standalone, combined in a search portal or embedded into existing applications. This framework allows usage of our solutions in a variety of scenarios relevant to learning and work situations in the architectural world.

Table 1. MACE core content repositories

Content source	# Objects	# Metadata	Metadata level
WINDS	5529 compound objects, 10542 single content blocks (text, image, multi-media)	1744 index terms (text)	3521 of 5529 objects enriched with content metadata
ARIADNE	5000+ objects, of which several hundreds can be used for MACE	Technical and educational metadata, keywords	Almost all objects have mandatory technical and educational metadata, some content metadata, no context and a few social metadata
DYNAMO	544 architecture projects, 7351 files (text, image)	1944 index terms (text)	High level of content metadata
MONUDOC	15,000 Facts and Literature Reference covering preservation of monuments and historic buildings	bibliographic description, Index terms, classification	All units with classification, bibliographic data and index terms
BAUFO	13000 descriptions of building research projects	Index terms, classifications	All units with classifications and index terms

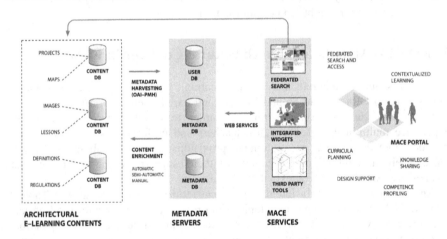

Fig. 1. MACE infrastructure overview

3 Connecting LORs for Architecture

The MACE infrastructure strives to open up the existing Learning Object Repositories (LORs) to enable the access to Learning Objects (LOs) through MACE tools. Therefore, we rely on a hybrid combination of harvesting metadata from and federating searches to existing content repositories. Additionally, the infrastructure enables the enrichment of LO's descriptions with metadata about their usage including contexts of use, necessary competencies, etc. The approach aims to make the learning objects in all repositories jointly searchable and retrievable.

The technical infrastructure allows searching over the contents of all content repositories based on metadata. In order to enable "semantic interoperability" among LORs, the LOs are described through the MACE application profile of the Learning Object Metadata standard (LOM) [7].

Existing metadata from the connected repositories are collected via metadata harvesting, based on the Open Archive Initiative Protocol for Managing Harvesting OAI-PMH (OAI, 2002). Harvesting in this context means the transfer of the content metadata from the providing repository into the central content metadata repository on a regular basis. Note that only the metadata describing the learning objects is transferred; the learning objects themselves will remain in the repository, and thus in control of their owner, without changing the access conditions. In turn, the central content metadata repository also offers an OAI-PMH interface so that interested content metadata providers can retrieve enriched metadata suitable for their learning objects.

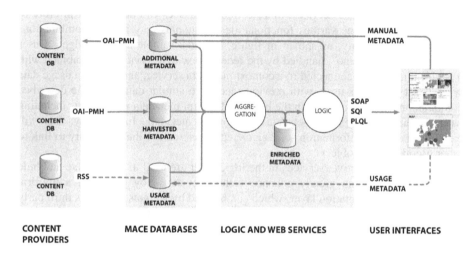

Fig. 2. MACE technical infrastructure

Figure 2 shows how harvesting works in MACE: existing metadata, describing the learning resources, are harvested through the OAI-PMH protocol into the MACE central metadata store. The metadata store supports a search facility that provides references to available and suitable learning objects. In order to access the learning object, the user accesses the learning resource directly at the provider.

Within the database layer, OAI-PMH is used for harvesting content and domain metadata. Data describing the usage (usage metadata) will be collected using the RSS (Rich site summary) protocol [8]. While OAI-PMH is suited to collect changing metadata, we suggest to use RSS when only new metadata instances (like in log files) are added. Usage metadata is obtained from the providers, as well as the MACE tools and bases on the access logs provided by the different applications. In the case of usage metadata captured from front-end tools and widgets, contextual data like the position of the user, or date and time, can be captured to complement the user profile. Exchanged with RSS, the usage data is unified relying on the contextualized attention metadata schema (CAMs) to enable deriving new knowledge about the usage of LOs by correlating usage data from different sources [9].

3.1 MACE Services

Services in MACE connect the presentation layer – in the form of widgets[1] – with data sources. They process user queries and return results, handle user management and provide means for gathering and manipulating metadata. Some services provide simple functions while others are more complex and can even aggregate functionality.

Besides metadata and content retrieval, MACE services will allow users to annotate contents with own metadata, track activities and generate metadata from user actions. Examples for basic services are: "Searching" which takes in a request, queries the appropriate metadata databases and returns the results; "UserHandling" which provides authentication and user management functions; "ServiceRegistry", a directory for discovery and use of services; and so on.

Based on these basic services, more complex services can be realized in order to aggregate and combine various functionalities. Examples may include combinations of widget functionality, as shown in figure 4. In the sample search widget, a user search for "Renzo Piano", handled by the federated search services, is combined with a geolocation widget connected to a context metadata service, and also to a usage data widget that highlights users with previous access to similar data sets. The described combination triggers services on the basis of different metadata repositories including usage metadata, contextual metadata and domain metadata. In this way, user will experience a richer information set than expected, increasing the possibility to link to other useful learning objects.

Under this perspective, services in the logic layer are used to encapsulate and hide complexity. They also greatly enhance technology reuse by providing a uniform interface to the presentation layer, which can be used by widgets as well as third party applications like plugins for e.g. Microsoft Office or AutoCAD. These applications can then connect to MACE and make use of the technical infrastructure to search for and retrieve contents and metadata.

It will be possible to physically distribute MACE services over several server systems that are connected through the Internet. Some parts like metadata stores, MACE user accounting and a registry for distributed services will have to be centralized, other services can run anywhere on the Internet. This allows a wide range of options to be used, from simple, single-server installations to a complex and distributed infrastructure.

To ensure full interoperability, all services will be based on open standards. As mentioned above, we use OAI-PMH for metadata harvesting and SOAP for remote web service connectivity. The search service is enabled through the Simple Query Interface [10] in order to be able for MACE to join LOR federations like Globe[2] and Ariadne[3]. SQI allows for the federation of queries and the collection of the query results. SQI can be combined with any query language, and is, for example, employed

---

[1] See following section : "Interface design strategy" for a deeper treatment of widgets.
[2] http://globe.edna.edu.au/
[3] http://www.ariadne-eu.org

in the GLOBE consortium to federate queries over the global network of learning repositories [11].

4   Interface Design Strategy

MACE builds on existing portals, bringing in their existing contents and metadata collections, as well as pre-existing facilities for search, access, navigation and browsing. Our goal is to connect these contents via metadata and make them jointly accessible, thus enabling multiple navigation paths and perspectives on the existing collections.

The vision of an experience multiplier is the leading idea for the interface design strategy in MACE. For the interface design, this means we need to:

- Provide convenient and effective ways to enrich the existing contents with metadata
- Make connections between contents accessible to the user, thus enabling inter-repository navigation paths
- Provide a search interface that allows users to benefit from multiple types of metadata for content retrieval.

As the main objective of the project is content enrichment, based on existing tools and the mentioned portals, we developed an interface design strategy taking both the project aims as well as the site owner interests into account, whilst maximizing the impact of our developed solutions.

4.1   Composing Widgets for Flexible Access

Based on these considerations, we developed an interface design strategy based on the notion of *"widgets"*, which are compact, specialized applications or application components. They can not only be combined to build more complex applications, but also be integrated into existing portals and content management solutions on their own. On the one hand, this provides immediate incentives for content providers and site owners to embed and use MACE service widgets, since they can enhance their existing sites with functionality, in a focused manner and with little effort. On the other hand, the MACE project benefits by having more contents available, generating more metadata, thus improving the findability of relevant resources and increasing inter–repository traffic.

The widget paradigm has been made popular in several domains over the last years: Apple's dashboard widgets[4] allow users to add mini-applications on a semi-transparent desktop layer, which can be activated by a hotkey. Also Yahoo widgets[5] or yourminis.com[6] provide widgets for use on a personalized web desktop, the OS desktop and embedded into other web pages. The range of available applications reaches from simple clock or weather forecast over dictionaries, games, content

---

[4] http://www.apple.com/macosx/features/dashboard/
[5] http://widgets.yahoo.com/
[6] http://yourminis.com

subscription up to planners, search engines or messaging services. Other online services such as del.icio.us[7], Technorati[8] or Plazes[9] provide HTML snippets to embed functional components into other web pages. There is a diversity of embeddable widgets available — displaying site statistics, allowing to search for contents, or displaying the site owner's latest bookmarks, music listened to or books read.

In MACE, all functionality for end users is made available in specialized widgets. For different metadata types or service functionality, a dedicated widget can be used to visualize metadata values, edit metadata, filter searches and navigate contents. The following MACE widget types can be distinguished:

- **Basic widgets** handle basic user management and navigation tasks. Examples are a login widget, a simple search box (triggering a search on the MACE portal) or a link list widget.
- **Content presentation widgets** can be used to display content collections from the repositories, such as related pictures for a given article, a list of search results or a single content item.
- **Metadata widgets** visualize metadata values and aggregations of metadata values (so-called metadata profiles). Additionally, they allow editing of metadata as well as meta-data based navigation, search and filtering.

We can further differentiate widgets by their **awareness and adaptation** with regard to context established by

- The host application or web site (e.g. currently presented contents)
- The user (e.g. log-in status, previously viewed pages, preferences). Here, we distinguish user *recognition* (e.g. via cookie) and user *login* (via authentification mechanism). Some personalized functionality might be available also for recognized, but not logged-in users.
- Other widgets (e.g. selections, navigation behavior)

To give a concrete example from our repositories: a map widget for displaying geo-location could be used to display the location of a building in a DYNAMO project (content-aware), the locations associated with the user's browsing history (user-aware) or related places for a selected keyword in a different widget (widget-aware).

The general goal is to make the "right" kind of information — fitting the user's current situation and preferences as well as the currently focussed contents — visually accessible and editable directly in place.

4.2 Embedding and Combining Widgets

The chosen technical and conceptual framework allows re-use and combination of widgets in many different usage scenarios: MACE widgets can be embedded into existing web portals, thus making MACE functionality and contents available directly to portal owners and their users (see Figure 3).

---

[7] http://del.icio.us
[8] http://technorati.com
[9] http://plazes.com

Furthermore, for example, a combination of widgets can be used for searching, browsing and filtering in a facetted search application (see Figure 4). Where applicable, the chosen technologies also allow an easy adaptation to desktop tools or browser extensions. MACE widgets are combinable and will be available for download and integration into web applications at the MACE portal.

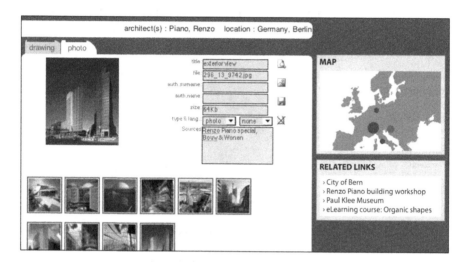

Fig. 3. Mockup of map widget and related links widget integration into the DYNAMO portal

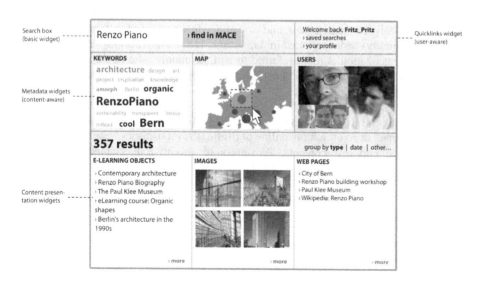

Fig. 4. Combining widgets for facetted search and browsing

4.3 Add and Edit in Place

Our approach relies on a multitude of available metadata. Whilst some of it is automatically generated, experts and other user can contribute meaningful information as well. For this reason, MACE widgets are used to edit metadata (see Figure 5). Where applicable, direct manipulation interfaces will enable visual, interactive access and manipulation, instead of tedious and error-prone form filling.

Fig. 5. Editing mode for widgets

We aim at making interaction with metadata not only as easy and natural as possible, but also open for all users. The recent success of collaborative tagging systems[10] has shown that providing users with a framework to tag publicly available resources in a "socially translucent" [12] manner can lead to rich and user-centered information architectures. A crucial component is making the users aware of both self-assigned tags as well as the tags and content that others contribute to the community: only immediate self and social feedback gives rise to the emergent, stable, community–wide patterns in tag usage [13]. The resulting multi–faceted, bottom–up organization is often referred to as folksonomy — a neologism based on the words "folk" and "taxonomy" [14]. We aim at generalizing this principle also for other metadata types.

Concerning incentives for actively contributing, we aim at win-win situations: if for the user, tagging contents is valuable for re–finding contents, helps succeeding in a "tagging game" or to enrich his online portfolio, the repositories benefit at the same time from the enriched contents. A variety of incentive mechanisms in online collaboration can be identified (see e.g. [15]). A further, promising perspective is the "undercover" creation of metadata from joyful activities such as gaming [16]. We are currently investigating, which of these techniques are best suited for our content partners and user groups.

4.4 Using Widgets for Browsing and Navigation

Additionally, our embedded widget approach fosters meaningful navigation and browsing across repositories: by presenting related metadata values and contents directly on the content pages, users can not only understand the nature and relevance

---

[10] Such as e.g. http://del.icio.us

of the presented contents, but also directly navigate to related items or query the MACE database for further contents based on metadata values. By presenting a variety of metadata fields, we enable multi-facetted navigation — not only on a semantic, but also a social and contextual level.

To enable meaningful, multiple navigation paths, value selection as well as weighting of the displayed values is crucial. This is especially important for inherently multi-valued metadata types (such as ratings and free-form keywords) as well as for accessing the whole content collections, such as a search result or the contents of a technology enhanced course.

For this purpose, our approach is based on weighting metadata values: if we define a context as a set of contents and their metadata values, a *metadata profile* will express the characteristics of this context in terms of its metadata distribution. In its simplest version, a metadata profile is represented as the set of occurring metadata values weighted by the number of occurrences.

The *global metadata profile* is the metadata profile for all available contents and hence represents the a priori distribution of metadata. A *local metadata profile* characterizes a subset of contents, such as a search result, the result of a filtering operation or a single content.

Mapping these profile values to visual attributes can create meaningful and immediately accessible insights. For example, the currently popular "tag clouds" employ this principle by mapping number of occurrences of term to font size. The established visual hierarchy allows quick skimming of many metadata values and at the same time indicating relative weights of values by visual salience. This allows users to quickly perceive the predominant metadata values and their relative proportions for e.g. a search result or a personal collection of contents. We will apply analogous principles to other types of data, places, time points or graphs, and their visualization.

Fig. 6. Weighted display of metadata; higher opacity indicates an unusually high weight in the current context compared to the global profile

An interesting extension of this principle is to highlight unusually high values compared to the a priori values, since these indicate what makes a data set special compared to the whole collection (see Figure 6). To give an example: If the proportion of articles tagged with "architecture" for a search for "Renzo Piano" is the same as for the whole collection, then we can conclude that the tag "architecture" is not especially characteristic for the search results. A high gain in proportion for values like "Bern", however, indicates that the search term and that metadata value are frequently co–occurring and thus related. Visually highlighting values can lead to interesting insights on the data and provide the user with good candidate values for further navigation and search. This principle has already been tested in a prototype [17] and is currently refined and evaluated.

We hypothesize that this navigation principle is especially suited for navigating multi-facetted and multivalent "long tail" [18] metadata structures, which typically arise from collaborative tagging activity [13], since this approach both allows quick and intuitive drill-down navigation as well as "context hopping". By successively selecting metadata values across facets, a "place" selection can provide an entry point for a concept space, where individual concepts might in turn be related to specific users and so on.

4.5 Outlook

Currently, we are in the process of defining a feasible and desirable set of widgets to implement in a user-centered, iterative design approach. First prototypes will be available on the MACE portal by autumn 2007. An overview of widgets considered up to now can be found in Figure 7.

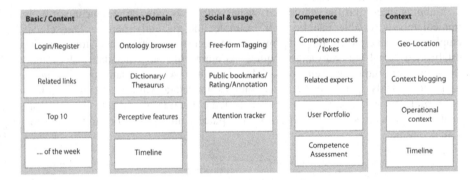

Fig. 7. Overview of considered basic, content and metadata widgets

5 Conclusion

By enriching and connecting existing portals and their contents, we provide a unique single access point for high quality content from the architectural domain. Enriching contents with various types of metadata, enables multiple perspectives and navigation paths, effectively leading to experience multiplication in technology enhanced learning about architecture and design.

Especially from an informal learning perspective, our interface and system design approach fosters experience multiplication via metadata on many levels:

- We create an open system and provide incentives for actively enriching and sharing knowledge. This opens doors to social navigation and online collaboration, which are both crucial constituents of an active learning experience.

- By linking complementary contents across repositories, we establish valuable connections to complementary knowledge for a given content.
- Displaying metadata values directly in place supports a better judgement of the relevance and context of a single piece of information. By making each metadata value a starting point for a potential query on the MACE portal, a rich web of contextual information is woven around each content component.
- Our facetted search approach creates an intuitively accessible model for navigating multi-dimensional data structures based on tailored, domain-specific tools. It enables directed search and browsing of contents with respect to features relevant for architectural knowledge in a unique combination. The underlying weighted activation model fosters understanding how metadata values and/or search terms relate to each other; revealing these relations can greatly contribute to learning experience.

Moreover, our service-oriented, distributed architecture allows reuse of both MACE contents as well as functionality in applications developed by third parties — by simply embedding ready-made MACE widgets or by connecting proprietary interfaces and applications to the MACE metadata service API. Interoperability is ensured by using open standards and protocols.

References

1. John, B.: Virtual Dimension: Architecture, Representation, and Crash Culture. Princeton Architectural Press, New York (1998)
2. Condotta, M., Del Ponte, I.: Digipolazione Architettonica, nuovi software convertiti, graduation thesis at Università IUAV di Venezia, Venezia (2002)
3. Vicario Giovanni Bruno: Psicologia Generale. CLUP editore. Padova (1991)
4. Lynn, G.: Animate Form. Priceton Architectural Press, New York (1999)
5. Pongratz, C., Perbellini, M.R.: Nati con il computer. Giovani architetti americani, Testo & Immagine, Italia (2000)
6. Beale, R.: Information fragments for a pervasive world. In: SIGDOC '05: Proceedings of the 23rd annual international conference on Design of communication, Coventry, United Kingdom, pp. 48–53. ACM Press, New York (2005)
7. Duval, E., (ed.): IEEE Standard for Learning Object Metadata 1484.12.1-2002. IEEE 2002 (2005)
8. OAI: 2002, Open Archives Initiative Protocol for Metadata Harvesting, Protocol Version 2.0 of 2002-06-14
9. Wolpers, M., Najjar, J., Verbert, K., Duval, E.: Tracking Actual Usage: the Attention Metadata Approach. International Journal Educational Technology and Society (ISSN: 1436-4522 (online) and 1176-3647 (print)), Special Issue on Advanced Technologies for Life-Long Learning (2007)
10. SQI: European Committee for Standardization (CEN) Workshop Agreement on A Simple Query Interface Specification for Learning Repositories (November 2005)
11. Ternier, S., Olmedilla, D., Duval, E.: Peer-to-Peer versus Federated Search: towards more Interoperable Learning Object Repositories. In: Kommers, P., Richards, G. (eds.) ED-Media 2005, pp. 1421–1428 (2005)

12. Erickson, T., Smith, D.N., Kellogg, W.A., Laff, M., Richards, J.T., Bradner, E.: Socially translucent systems: social proxies, persistent conversation. In: babble (ed.) CHI '99: Proceedings of the SIGCHI conference on Human factors in computing systems, Pittsburgh, Pennsylvania, United States: USA, ACM Press, New York (1999)
13. Golder, S., Huberman, B.A.: The Structure of Collaborative Tagging Systems. cs.DL/0508082 (2005), http://arxiv.org/abs/cs.DL/0508082
14. Quintarelli, E.: Folksonomies: power to the people. ISKO-Italy Uni-MIB meeting (2005), http://www-dimat.unipv.it/biblio/isko/doc/folksonomies.htm
15. Obreiter, P., Nimis, J.: A Taxonomy of Incentive Patterns - the Design Space of Incentives for Cooperation (eds.) In: Proceedings of the Second International Workshop on Agents and Peer-to-Peer Computing (AP2PC'03) Melbourne, Australia (2003)
16. von Ahn, L., Dabbish, L.: Labeling images with a computer game. In: CHI '04: Proceedings of the 2004 conference on Human factors in computing systems, pp. 319–326. ACM Press, New York (2004)
17. Stefaner, M., Müller, B.: Elastic lists for facet browsers. In: Proceedings of FIND07, International Workshop on Dynamic Taxonomies and Faceted Search (in conjunction with DEXA, IEEE, 2007 (forthcoming, 2007)
18. Anderson, C.: The Long Tail: Why the Future of Business Is Selling Less of More. Hyperion (2006)

ICT Supported Interorganizational Knowledge-Creation: Application of Change Laboratory

Seppo Toikka

University of Helsinki, Department of Psychology, P.O. Box 9 FIN-00014
University of Helsinki
seppo.toikka@helsinki.fi

Abstract. To answer the challenges of globally distributed organizations facing constant transformation of work, means of ICT supported interorganizational knowledge-creation is needed. First, concept of organizational knowledge-creation is studied and further enriched with concepts of practice and object of activity to conceptualize the social and transforming nature of knowledge. Second, Change Laboratory is introduced as a theory based method of implementing local organizational knowledge-creation. An empirical case of Change Laboratory in a global organization network is presented and the envisioned ICT tools to support the transition from local to networked knowledge-creation are introduced.

Keywords: Knowledge-creation, Learning, Organization Networks, Change Laboratory, ICT.

1 Introduction

The development of working life in the last years, especially due to the developments in information and communication technologies (ICTs), is radically changing the way people and organizations collaborate. Work in organization is increasingly becoming structured in groups supported by technology, characterized by distributed expertise and networked activities. This networked society is bringing new skill and competency requirements [1].

For organizations working in knowledge-intensive domains, ICT has removed the physical constraints of organizations bound to a single location and in the same time facilitates the emergence of global networks. These networks emerge due to organizational partnerships, but also due to a continuing trend for corporations to geographically distribute their units of operation.

In these networks, knowledge is a critical resource for development, and a fundamental challenge is to organize work with knowledge in a way that facilitates continuous knowledge advancement and supports the sharing of intellectual achievements among the members of the community. Therefore, a rising challenge is to bridge between informal learning strategies of individual experts and formal rules and routines of knowledge work in organizations [2].

E. Duval, R. Klamma, and M. Wolpers (Eds.): EC-TEL 2007, LNCS 4753, pp. 337–348, 2007.

2 Knowledge in Organizations

Nonaka and Takeuchi [3] propose a theory of knowledge-creation in organizations. In their model knowledge-creation is seen as interaction between tacit knowledge and explicit knowledge. In their model, the source of organizational knowledge-creation is tacit knowledge held by individuals, that they call the "rich, untapped source of new knowledge". A "knowledge spiral" (Figure 1) consists of four types of knowledge conversion: from tacit knowledge to tacit knowledge (socialization); from tacit to explicit knowledge (externalization); from explicit to explicit knowledge (combination) and from explicit to tacit knowledge (internalization).

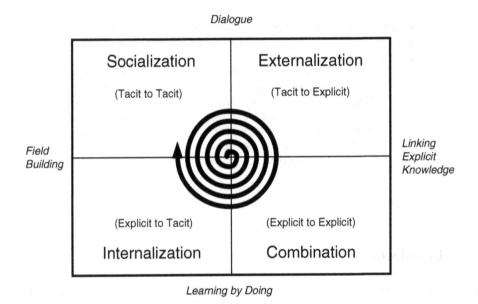

Fig. 1. Knowledge-creation Spiral

Iterative knowledge-creation spiral starts from socialization, phase where a common understanding about the task is created. The next phase, externalization, is the central one in knowledge-creation. In this phase tacit knowledge is explicated and conceptualized in dialogue by means of metaphors, analogies, and concepts. At the combination phase, units of already existing explicit knowledge are combined and exchanged. Finally, explicit knowledge of the organization must be internalized by individuals and transformed into tacit knowledge and into action through "learning by doing."

Holmqvist [4] points out that while knowledge in organizations is created by individuals, organizational knowledge cannot be reduced to knowledge of individuals. Holmqvist argues that e.g. documents, rules and routines are in fact forms of organizational knowledge. These organizational forms of knowledge are of central importance to organizations for two reasons. First, for individuals to be able to cooperate they need mutual knowledge. Second, mutual knowledge and shared artifacts are important in order to guarantee consistency in the organization, even if some individuals leave the organization. Following Nonaka and Takeuchi, Holmqvist proposes four modes of knowledge conversion in creating organizational knowledge (Figure 2).

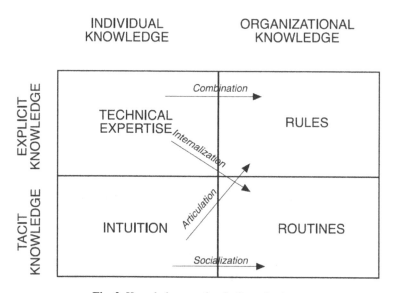

Fig. 2. Knowledge-creation in Organizations

Main distinction to Nonaka and Takeuchi's model is that Holmqvist makes a systematic distinction between individual and organizational knowledge. Organizational knowledge is created from individual knowledge through e.g. joint activities (socialization), collective reflection (articulation), creation of various databases (combination) or corporate bulletins (internalization).

2.1 Interorganizational Knowledge-Creation

For knowledge-creation in networks of organizations a new dimension of knowledge-creation is needed. Holmqvist [4] further presents an extension to the organizational knowledge-creation model. Holmqvist suggests that in networks of organizations not only knowledge conversions between individual knowledge and organizational know-ledge must be studied, but also transitions between the two and interorganizational knowledge (see Figure 3). To coordinate actions in interorganizational networks the knowledge of individuals and single organizations must be modified to support the collaboration of a network. Interorganizational knowledge consists of mutual knowledge, unique to the collaboration and independent of any single organization's knowledge.

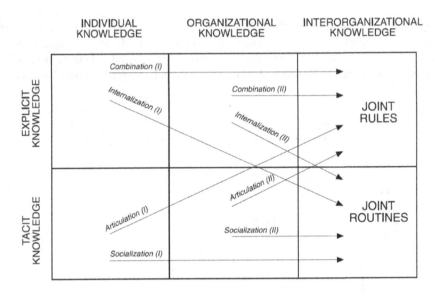

Fig. 3. Framework of Learning in Interorganizational Knowledge-creation

In Nonaka and Takeuchi's model the basic source of innovation is tacit knowledge, which needs to be socialized and then explicated in order to be transformed into knowledge that is useful at the levels of the group and the whole organization. Holmqvist [4] adds the dimension of interorganizational interactions to the knowledge spiral, arguing that in networks the source of innovation is twofold. First, collaboration of individuals of the network may come together and work closely on a project, having opportunities to create mutual tacit knowledge. In these situations they are also forced to articulate what they individually take for granted given the diverse backgrounds of involved actors. Second, knowledge related to an organization's rules and routines may be tacitly transferred between members of different organizational actors. The presensce of "outsiders" may also force reflection of organizational tacit routines and articulation of organizational tacit knowledge into interorganizational explicit knowledge.

2.2 Practice and Knowledge in Organizations

Other analogies for types of knowledge that follow the lines of tacit vs. explicit, are "stickiness" vs. "leakiness" and "know-how" vs "know-that". First analogy represents the challenge of moving knowledge inside organizations and, by contrast, undesirable flow or loss of knowledge. Second one represents the division between procedural, embodied knowledge and propositional or declarative knowledge. The basic assumption in all analogies is that the first type of knowledge is embodied in individuals while the second one is explicit, decontextualized knowledge. Several researchers, however, argue that in an attempt to conceptualize knowledge in organizations this kind of division is insufficient or even fundamentally flawed.

The problem is that it appears as the same knowledge can be both "sticky" and "leaky" [5]. The same knowledge that may be hard to pass inside an organization is easily leaked outside. The notion of tacit and explicit knowledge includes that there is always an irreducibly tacit aspect to any explicit knowledge [6]. This is often acknowledged, but no real effort to analyze the epistemological implications is made[1]. Brown and Duguid[5] propose the concept of practice as the "epistemic barrier" among the different communities inside a complex organization. "Stickiness" of knowledge or problems in creating explicit knowledge would be due to this barrier that rises from different practices inside an organization. In a complex organization practitioners most likely have more in common with their peers in other organizations than other employees in their own organization. Practice creates epistemic differences among the communities in a firm and the firm's advantage over the market lies in dynamically coordinating the knowledge produced by these communities despite such differences [6]. In other words, it seems as practice would be closely related to the utilization of knowledge.

2.3 Practice, Objects and Knowledge Creation

It seems that practice acts as a "gatekeeper" in knowledge conversion between tacit and explicit knowledge in same way as organizational structures and division of labor regulates knowledge conversion between individual and organizational (or interorganizational) level. This suggests that it would be fruitful to concentrate analysis of knowledge creation on the descriptions of the different actions of knowledge conversion.

While the concept of practice helps us to identify a possible weakness in the epistemological background of Nonaka and Takeuchi's model in pointing out that learning and understanding of knowledge is affected by boundaries of practice as well as boundaries of organizations, it does not help us further in explaining how new knowledge is created. Paavola and his colleagues [7] propose three metaphors of learning to emphasize processes of knowledge-creation. First metaphor is learning as knowledge acquisition, which views individual mind as a container of knowledge where learning is a process that fills the container. Knowledge is understood as a property of an individual mind. Second, participation metaphor sees learning as process of participation in various cultural practices. In participation metaphor knowledge is seen as inseparable from the practice where it is used. Third metaphor views learning as a process of knowledge-creation which concentrates on mediated processes where common objects of activity are developed collaboratively. Such processes include Nonaka and Takeuchi's model of organizational knowledge-creation as well as Engeström's theory of expansive learning [8],[9].

Theory of expansive learning is based on cultural-historical theory of activity that seeks to explain qualitative changes in human practices over time. Human cognition and behavior is considered to be embedded in collectively organized, artifact-mediated activity systems where activities are social practices oriented at objects [10]. The object of activity is constantly enacted and reconstructed in the social practice through temporally shorter actions. These short actions have clearly defined beginnings and ends while the object of activity is never fully reached or realized. Knowledge creation in cultural-historical theory of activity is closely related to this

---

[1] Both Nonaka & Takeuchi and Holmqvist write about "tacit component" in explicit knowledge.

process of object construction and redefinition [11]. Engeström points that Nonaka and Takeuchi's model starts with a relatively defined task and has no clear place for debate and analysis. However, he does suggest that Nonaka and Takeuchi's categories of knowledge conversion may be useful for analyzing different types of knowledge representation that are employed in the course of collaborative knowledge creation.

Despite their epistemological shortcomings Nonaka and Takeuchi's theory and Holmqvist's elaborations of levels of individual, organizational and interorganizational knowledge appear to be useful in the analysis of interorganizational knowledge creation, if the notion of social-practice perspective and process of object construction are taken into account.

3   ICT Supported Interorganizational Learning in KP-Lab Project

The empirical case presented is carried out in Knowledge Practices Laboratory – project [12], a 5 year IST project co-funded by the European Community. One of the main arguments of the project is that professional knowledge practices are still focused on the knowledge acquisition and participation metaphor of learning, while processes of knowledge-creation have been neglected.

A central aspect in approach on knowledge-creation is the interaction between different forms of knowledge (such as discursive knowledge, practice-related know how, tacit knowledge), organized in long-term processes. This has been a recurrent requirement put on information technologies during last years as far as knowledge management is concerned: how to facilitate the discovery and exploitation of tacit knowledge, how to be able to isolate, qualify and classify best practices through reflexive approaches, and how to appropriate distributed creativity. As such, one of the objectives of the project is to build ICT tools to enhance practices, retain and reuse knowledge and experience in new activities, and share informal knowledge and experience.

3.1   Pöyry Case: Networked Engineering Company

Research and development work described above is carried out in pilot sites, such as Pöyry plc. Pöyry is a client- and technology-oriented, globally operating consulting and engineering firm. Its core areas of expertise: energy, forest industry and infrastructure & environment. The Group's business concept is based on early involvement in its clients' business development. Pöyry offers services related to consulting, project development and implementation, and operations management and maintenance planning in all of its business sectors

Pöyry is facing a major challenge in transition from the locally managed Finnish company to a globally distributed network of business units. The new units are acquired mainly through corporate acquisitions. The traditionally held view of the corporate culture has been replaced by the variety of not-so-easily captured cultures and practices. At the same time, the entire concept of forest industry consulting and engineering is undergoing a profound change as proportion of bulk engineering is decreasing in the Western-European units and moving to developing countries either through corporate acquisitions or partnership contracts.

Design work is carried out in a network and the habitual way of working in the locally managed projects contradicts the project work being done in a global network. Pöyry is facing a challenge of how to reach shared practices and ways of running projects even when operating in a network and in the same time to ensure in a systematic way learning from one project to another over time.

The pilot aims at organizing the learning processes to support work at Pöyry by creating a new learning system for the company that will meet the concept-level changes of the core business activity.

3.2 Change Laboratory as a Facilitator of Interorganizational Knowledge-Creation

To reach its goals of creating shared knowledge practices in networks, the pilot utilizes the method of Change Laboratory (CL) which is an application based on the conceptual framework of Cultural-Historical Activity Theory and expansive learning [11][13]. The framework relies on theoretical tools that simultaneously address individual and social as well as material and organizational transformations. Its central tool is an activity system model (Figure 4), which points to cultural mediation, object-orientedness of human activity, and contradictions emerging between the elements of the system.

Interorganizational knowledge-creation and collaborative networks can be seen from the view point of interacting activity systems where each organizational unit constitutes a single activity system. Activities transform over lengthy periods of time and remediate their social basis, such as rules and division of labor, as well as material and symbolic tools, such as instruments and concepts. The contradictions generate dilemmas and problems in the activity, which may entail a crisis or, alternatively, a willingness to question normal work routines and carry out novel actions that may solve the dilemmas [14].

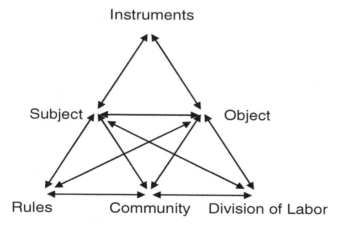

Fig. 4. Activity system model

Change Laboratory [15] is a specific intervention method which is used to systematically support the knowledge-creation process. The method enables ways of collaborative reflection of activities by structured combination of various qualitatively different representations of data. As a method of intervention, CL relies on a set of representational artifacts. Its core methodological principle is crystallized in the central tool of "a 3x3 set of surfaces for representing the work activity". The representational tool combines three surfaces of two dimensions: The vertical dimension of the surfaces represents movements in time, between the past, the present, and the future. The horizontal dimension displays the mirror surface reflecting the work at stake by videotaped episodes and interviews particularly on problem situations and disturbances, the surface reserved for ideas and tools articulated by the participants in the course of the CL sessions, and the model/vision surface of theoretical tools and conceptual analysis in which the triangle model is represented as a central tool for analyzing.

The process of CL is constituted according to the cycle of expansive learning, sequence of epistemic actions ascending from the abstract to the concrete (Figure 5). The process of expansive learning is seen as construction and resolution of successively evolving tensions or contradictions in a complex system that includes the object(s) of activity, mediating artifacts and the perspectives of the participants [11].

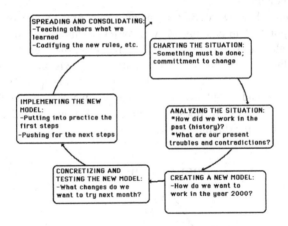

Fig. 5. Cycle of expansive learning

One of the main challenges in KP-Lab project is to develop ICT support for the Change Laboratory process. Traditional Change Laboratory setting consists of very few ICT tools, which presents a problem for implementing knowledge creation in organization networks which rely heavily on virtual communication. This sets a requisite to develop ICT to support implementation of Change Laboratory in organization networks.

3.3 Development of ICT Support for Change Laboratory Pilot

First Change Laboratory pilot in Pöyry has commenced in February 2007. Development of ICT solutions is carried out in close collaboration with the pilot participants and the CL user community in Finland. The first phase of the development work consisted of defining the use cases for ICT supported CL and defining the solutions and framework for software components. Envisioned solutions consist of:

Virtual learning environment to support activities specific in the context of CL. The environment consist of file management system for data gathered in the process, tools to manage and coordinate the collaborative CL process and synchronous communication tools to facilitate and capture virtual discussion. Further, it acts as a platform for the other functionalities.

Shared whiteboard for presentation of different modes of knowledge. The first developed software component is called "virtual whiteboard". It is an application that allows presenting multimedia content of actual working situations and linking this material with visual modeling of concepts and relations. The application is used to collaboratively identify and conceptualize practices within organizations or organization networks. The composition enables presentation of debate and multiple interpretations. First snapshot (Figure 6) shows the analysis phase of the Change Laboratory process considering a certain development object, in this case the use of Customer Relations Management (CRM) tool. Videotaped empirical data of working practices with the CRM tool is available for joint analysis of all users.

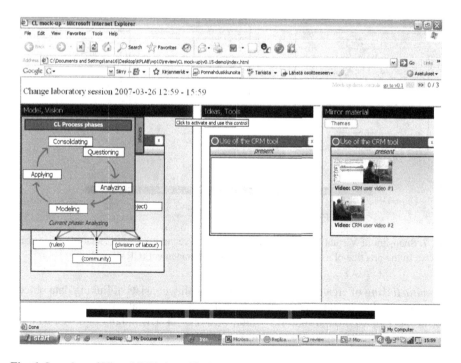

Fig. 6. Snapshot of Virtual Whiteboard in the beginning of collaborative reflection of practices

Presentation of previously selected short videotaped clips of problematic situations in an activity is used as a means to "force" reflection of ones own practices. Collaboration and communication tools allow the presentation different views on the practice while theoretical models are used to conceptualize the reflection. Presented views are recorded in an audio file of the discussion as well as in a shared memo.

Second snapshot (Figure 7) shows the representation of multiple "voices" while analyzing the concept of "customer". A potential problem in the activity is introduced by showing two video clips of practitioners in their work. While analyzing the Key Account Managers' practice, this has led to identification of a contradiction between the instrument (CRM tool) and defined object of activity (contact person). Several definitions of the closest concept in CRM tool (customer) have been presented by different practitioners in organization network and some of them are not compatible with the CRM tool.

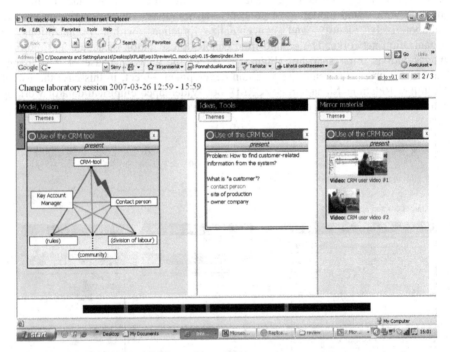

Fig. 7. Snapshot of Virtual Whiteboard with collaborative "multi-voiced" analysis of customer concept in the practice of using Customer Relations Management (CRM) tool

Semantic linking of created content. This functionality consists of linking data objects, timestamped log events of virtual whiteboard manipulation and recording of synchronous discussion around the whiteboard and further, linking of saved data and CL process (steps of expansive learning).

Toolkit for content analysis. The toolkit contains multimedia annotation tool for analyzing video, audio, graphical and textual data using ontology of activity theoretical framework to perform preliminary analysis of activity by marking and classifying and linking relevant segments of data. Analysis supporting functions such as profiling of activities, predictive analysis of CL process, or glossaries of theoretical concepts may be implemented as enough material has been collected.

From the viewpoint of interorganizational knowledge creation the CL tools will provide a platform for all types of knowledge conversion in individual, organizational and interorganizational level. The learning environment will facilitate the process of socialization via virtual communication tools. The virtual whiteboard combined with rich ethnographic data of work practices forces users to articulate their view on the practices collaboratively. For example, in the illustrated example (figure X) representatives from different organizations produced different meanings for customer. Produced new concepts can be semantically linked to concepts of the cultural historical theory of activity to provide a coherent set of organizational concepts allowing combination of explicit knowledge. Further in spreading and consolidating of the new practice the system provides explicit knowledge that may eventually lead into internalized routines.

4 Discussion

Interorganizational knowledge-creation can be seen as collaborative learning in organization networks that produces new solutions, procedures or systematic transformations in organizational or interorganizational practices. The pursuit of new knowledge seems to require transformations in individual, social, material and organizational level. With suitable conceptual tools that allow reflection, tacit knowledge concerning a practice may be articulated. Interestingly enough, interaction with an "informed outsider" has been reported to be useful in knowledge creation [3],[5],[6]. This would imply that practice is more of an epistemic boundary of knowledge creation than an active element. Further, it seems as the ICT solutions developed for Change Laboratory may act as this kind of "informed outsiders" that drive reflection and knowledge-creation.

In theory of organizational knowledge-creation the organizations rules and routines are produced and reproduced by individual's actions while in activity theory the "engine" of transformation is the reproduction of object of activity. Therefore, it appears that in order to support knowledge-creation ICT should be able to facilitate this kind of dialectic "motion". Definition of such requirements is a challenging venture where new innovative solutions are needed.

Acknowledgments. The presented work was conducted in Centre for Networked Learning and Knowledge Building. I thank Hanna Toiviainen, Mikko Höynälänmaa, Ali Rantakari and Anna Aminoff for their insights on the Pöyry case and Sami Paavola's for his insightful comments. I am in gratitude to Ritva Engeström for her invaluable comments on the first drafts of the paper. I also thank Liisa Ilomäki who persuaded me to write this paper.

References

1. Hakkarainen, K., Palonen, T., Paavola, S., Lehtinen, E.: Communities of Networked Expertise: Professional and Educational Perspectives. Elsevier, Amsterdam (2004)
2. Huysman, M., De Wit, D.: Knowledge Sharing in Practice. Kluwer, Boston (2002)
3. Nonaka, I., Takeuchi, H.: The knowledge-creating company: How Japanese companies create the dynamics of innovation. Oxford University Press, New York (1995)
4. Holmqvist, M.: Learning in imaginary organizations: creating interorganizational knowledge. Journal of Organizational Change Management. 5, 419–438 (1999)
5. Brown, J.S., Duguid, P.: Knowledge and Organization: A Social-Practice Perspective. Organization Science. 2, 198–213 (2001)
6. Gourlay, S.: Conceptualizing Knowledge Creation: A Critique of Nonaka's Theory. Journal of Management Studies. 7, 1415–1436 (2006)
7. Paavola, S., Hakkarainen, K.: The Knowledge Creation Metaphor - An Emergent Epistemological Approach to Learning. Science & Education 14, 535–557 (2005)
8. Paavola, S., Lipponen, L., Hakkarainen, K.: Models of Innovative Knowledge Communities and Three Metaphors of Learning. Review of Educational Research 4, 557–576 (2004)
9. Engeström, Y.: Learning by Expanding. Orienta-Konsultit, Helsinki (1987)
10. Leont'ev, A.: Activity, consciousness and personality. Prentice-Hall, Englewood Cliffs (1978)
11. Engeström, Y., Miettinen, R., Punamäki, R-L. (eds.): Perspectives on Activity Theory. Cambridge University Press, Cambridge (1999)
12. Hakkarainen, K., Ilomäki, L., Paavola, S., Muukkonen, H., Toiviainen, H., Markkanen, H., Richter, C.: Design Principles and Practices for the Knowledge Practices Laboratory (KP-Lab) project. In: Nejdl, W., Tochtermann, K. (eds.) EC-TEL 2006. LNCS, pp. 603–608. Springer, Heidelberg (2006)
13. Nardi, B.A. (ed.): Context and Consciousness: Activity Theory and Human-Computer Interaction. MIT Press, Cambridge, MA (1996)
14. Engeström, Y.: Expansive learning at work: toward an activity theoretical reconceptualization. Journal of Education and Work 1, 133–156 (2001)
15. Engeström, Y., Virkkunen, J., Helle, M., Pihlaja, J., Poikela, R.: Change Laboratory as a tool for transforming Work. Lifelong Learning in Europe. 2, 10–17 (1996)

Theoretical Framework of the iCampFolio – New Approach to Comparison and Selection of Systems and Tools for Learning Purposes

Terje Väljataga[1], Kai Pata[2], Mart Laanpere[2], and Mauri Kaipainen[2]

[1] Tampere University of Technology, Korkeakoulunkatu 10, FI-33720, Tampere, Finland
[2] Tallinn University, Narva road 25, 10120, Tallinn, Estonia
terje.valjataga@tut.fi, {kai.pata,mart.laanpere,
mauri.kaipainen}@tlu.ee

Abstract. We argue that current selection methods and comparison approaches of tools for learning purposes do not fit with the concept of e-learning 2.0 and Web 2.0 applications for creating personal learning environments. Available comparison methods being mainly as black-and-white check lists hinder to see the properties of various Web 2.0 applications. We propose a theoretical framework for designing a support tool for learners as well as for facilitators in order to facilitate the choice of learning/teaching tools from heterogeneous technological landscapes. Our theoretical framework is based on soft ontological approach enabling to compare systems and tools from multidimensional perspectives taking into account users best practices. We focus on elements of learning activities mediated by technology with respect to the concept of affordances and activity theory in combination of Alexander's pattern approach and IMS LD case descriptions.

Keywords: affordance, activity theory, activity pattern, social software.

1 Introduction

The digital culture, termed Web 2.0 coined by [23], starts to have a significant influence on e-learning and its mediating technology. The impact on e-learning is seen mainly in terms of paradigm change in learning and growing heterogeneity of technological landscape. Openness, personalization and decentralization in terms of learning content and tools are continuously replacing closed centralized approach to learning. So far e-learning has mainly been characterized as teacher-centered, where learning takes place around shared objectives and joint medium centrally controlled by facilitators. To the contrary, new epoch of e-learning leaves aside the centrality of facilitator and is based on the distributed control and coordinated actions between learners, where the locus of initiative changes from moment to moment. On the other hand in addition to institutionalized Course- and Learning Management Systems (LMS) technological landscape is enriched with tools called social software allowing everyone to publish resources on the Web and carry out social activities. The metaphor "landscape" refers to the heterogeneous space of software, tools and services. This new

E. Duval, R. Klamma, and M. Wolpers (Eds.): EC-TEL 2007, LNCS 4753, pp. 349–363, 2007.

generation of tools and systems enables building connections and networks within common interests, and allowing dispersed and partially improvised orchestration of collaborative performance between loosely connected learners using distributed tools.

Growing variety of choices regarding to tools and systems for learning purposes has put in danger institutional Learning Management Systems, Learning Object Repositories and other technology-enhanced learning tools used so far in education due to the new trend moving towards the use of social software. Continuously increasing domination of social software in e-learning is prognosed to reshape the e-learning landscapes towards dispersing learning environments. New e-learning landscapes mean the flexibility and freedom for learners to choose their favorite tools and software in order to create their personal learning spaces.

It is apparent, however, that disperse and personal learning environments, and growing information flow might create chaos in learning processes [10], where every learner faces new challenges. Various competencies will become important, such as the ability to find and choose the most appropriate learning tools and systems, to establish and maintain a viable learning environment and social network, to share knowledge and regulate one's learning with the remote others, and to be able to collaborate in distributed spaces. Therefore support and scaffolding are needed in terms of decision-making systems and reports of selection and comparison methods for facilitating the choice of tools according to personal needs.

This article provides a new theoretical framework for selection and comparison methods in order to support tool selection in iCamp project (http://www.icamp.eu). The main idea of the project is to gather various interoperable open source social software and institutionalized learning systems and tools into one common learning environment – iCamp Space. iCamp Space will not be developed as a single Web portal, a learning management system, or a Web-based service. Instead, iCamp Space can be defined as a Web-based activity space for Technology Enhanced Teaching and Learning projects (e.g. joint courses, portfolio-based accreditation of work experience). One of the outcomes of the project is to develop and design a decision support system iCampFolio for learners and facilitators in order to facilitate the tool selection for learning. The article also dissects the opportunities of pattern approach and IMS LD case descriptions in addition to soft ontology and activity theory with the concept of affordances as the aspects for our theoretical foundation in tool development.

2 Selection and Comparison Methods of Tools and Systems

2.1 Analysis of Current Selection Approaches for Learning Systems and Tools

Selecting the most appropriate technology for supporting learning activities becomes more and more complicated due to the growing heterogeneity of available software. In order to better understand the current situation regarding the selection of systems and tools for educational purposes in higher education, we analyzed current comparison approaches, as well as, tools for supporting decision-making regarding the selection of systems and tools (for example, the *Comparison of Online Course*

Delivery Software Products developed by Marshall University's Centre for Instructional Technology; the report *Comparative Features Analysis of Leading Course Management Systems* [28] and a collection of Web courseware comparisons and studies by the Ocotillo Group in Maricopa Community Colleges (available at http://www.mcli.dist.maricopa.edu/ocotillo/courseware/compare.html).

The extent and thoroughness of reports, studies and selection tools regarding the comparison of software for educational purposes varies a lot, ranging from a focus on some key features to the description of a comprehensive comparison between a set of tools. Some of them have taken into focus just a small selection of tools, while others have tried to capture as many tools as possible in order to provide a wide-ranging overview. The main purpose of the reports, studies and comparison tools is to assist in narrowing the selection and help academic institutions and individuals to make informed decisions according to their particular purposes and needs (see collection of comparison studies and reports collected by Ocotillo Group at Maricopa Community Colleges).

Decision-making tools (for example http://edutools.org created by B. Landon from Douglas College) mainly follow a similar approach, concentrating on the comparison of LMSs based on a set of functionalities, which are divided into different groups on the basis of technical specifications such as price, license and hardware requirements, media capabilities such as communication options, support tools for organizing and managing a course, and tools for learners to carry out different activities. In most of the cases a comparison method is based on a check-list of desired features enabling an indication whether each product offers a particular feature, or not.

2.2   Critical View on Current Selection Methods of Systems and Tools

Described comparison method embraces a rather "black and white" approach, where systems and tools are presented mainly from the narrow side of an economical and technical point of view. This kind of method focuses mainly on the comparison needs of institutions as being the main target group of LMS-s, and serves the individual educators' perspective only to a very limited extent. While we want to compensate the shortcomings and barriers that occur in the context of distance learning while carrying out various learning activities in collaborative settings or in the case of self-directed learning, current comparison and selection methods do not support decision-making with respect to learning medium. As the emphasis is on mainly technical description of tools rather than on learning functionalities, it does not help to choose a right tool according to individual learner's needs. The comparison would rather highlight an institutionalized point of view instead of taking into account individuals' learning requirements. Hence, from a pedagogical perspective this kind of checklist method for comparison fails to present the pedagogical value of a certain tool or its pedagogy driven design. Likewise, it hinders to bring forth the essence of the tool as a learning device and the holistic concept of the tool from designers', as well as, from learners' perspective. Furthermore, the provided features cannot be applied equally to all tools as we are facing a wide range of functionalities amongst the different tools. So far only one type of software systems, namely LMS-s, has been taken into account in the decision-making systems leaving totally aside the social software with its novel properties. This prevents comparing LMSs with other type of tools, which can support similar functionalities or even bring in those functionalities that LMS systems do not provide. Consequently, one-dimensional comparison approach does not give the required overview of the entire system or tool (especially from the pedagogical point of view), and does not allow comparing systems and tools from different perspectives. We propose that a multidimensional perspective of comparison tool, based on a soft ontological approach of pedagogical activity patterns and learning affordances, is more appropriate.

3   Theoretical Foundations of the iCampFolio Framework

3.1   Activity Theory as a Theory-Based Ontology

Before we could proceed with the development of the theoretical framework of iCampFolio – the ontology based decision-making tool for supporting learners' tool-selection and comparison for certain pedagogical activities – we have to build a theory-based ontology and conceptual model for describing learning activities, and validate it against the practice in authentic context that involves teaching and learning with social software. For defining the elements of online activities in social-software supported learning environments, at least two levels of the activity should be considered: the Activity System level [12], and the operation level [17]. The Activity System model [12] describes general information flows at the community level within or between the communities.

Model helps to explain how social artifacts and social organization mediate social action. In the system the subject refers to the individual or group engaged in the activities working towards the objectives (object) or target of the activity within the system. Tools refer to internal or external mediating artifacts, which help to accomplish the outcomes of the activity. Community defines the rules, as well as, the balance of activities among different people and artifacts in order to regulate actions and interactions within the system. According to [17] hierarchical conception, any shared activity can be defined through the shared motives that form the objectives of the activity; the activity consists of goal-directed actions conducted by the community members, which are realized by performing certain operations using the tools and artifacts as mediating devices. Kuuti's hierarchical elements of the activity enable to explain the functioning of the Activity System at each moment through activities, actions and operations. The internal sequence of the actions in the activity forms a specific activity pattern, indicating how subjects would realize their objectives. Important in describing an activity pattern is to consider how subjects perform the actions, which artifacts they might use, and which tool functionalities they might need for performing certain operations in each action. Some of these activity patterns can be described in great detail in sequential manner as workflows, the others are fuzzier, and contain a set of actions, which order is not predetermined to form the specified workflow. Activities, sequenced into more complex second level workflows and „criss-crossing" the Activity System enable the learners to establish, maintain and achieve their shared objectives.

Since now e-learning in Web 1.0 has exploited the activity patterns that form around shared objectives and joint medium in constrained group learning settings, in which facilitators centrally control learning. This has caused the over-exploitation of certain tutor-defined workflows as the basis of learning designs in LMS, which do not support connectivist paradigm of learning [24]. Connectivism presents a model of learning that acknowledges the tectonic shifts in society where learning is no longer an internal, individualistic activity but depends on how people work and function together when utilizing new tools. In e-learning with social software the centre of control changes from moment to moment between loosely connected learners using distributed tools. While performing a learning activity, learners have to decide, which actions must be undertaken, and with which functionalities of learning medium to put into operation in order to realize shared objectives. Workflows connect people, tasks, artifacts and tools at relatively short duration, and are continuously repeated and dynamically evolving because subjects have to come to the common ground on several aspects of the Activity System in the distributed settings. Following [5], the perception of Web 2.0 tools at the collective level is weakly structured, for each individual actor strongly structured. Tensions in regard to the meaning of tools are part of what actors have to take into account in their attempts to coordinate their different interests in elearning 2.0 with distributed tools. In these conditions predicting objectively the emergent learning functionalities of tools is impossible and needs the new approach based on affordances.

3.2 Pedagogical Activity Descriptions as Narratives

In developing the iCampFolio, activity patterns and workflows need to be described on the pedagogical basis. Our purpose is to collect different best practice learning activity cases in the social software settings as narratives, in order to present them in a coherent and accessible form for learners and facilitators. The importance of narrative descriptions of learning activities with social software is to show the sequence of activities that have to be accomplished by learners and tools used for performing the activity. From these descriptions the different functionalities of tools in activity settings would be extracted, which would be used as the building blocks of the soft ontology for iCampFolio. So far the structure of a course in LMS-s has been mostly based on the content, but we would like to concentrate on not only the content, but rather on activities, how to learn with different social software applications.

There are several attempts and various forms to write down best practices of learning activities. [15] has given an overview of various narrative patterns forms for describing a unit of learning. More or less these represent some kind of pattern or template approach on different level of granularity.

3.2.1 Pedagogical Patterns Based on Alexander's Concept

One option is to describe learning activities based on Alexander's concept of pattern language. The concept of pattern language gained its popularity in the field of architecture, first created and used by [2]. His idea was to organize implicit knowledge about the solutions of recurring problems in the context of architecture and collect this knowledge in the form of patterns. Patterns were based on fixed format problems and their solutions in the design context of architecture constituting a hierarchical system (pattern language) from high level design problems to low level design problems.

Due to the success of pattern approach in architecture, many other fields including education have adopted and modified the idea of Alexander's patterns. In pedagogy patterns have been used with an attempt to capture the essence of the practice and expert knowledge of teaching and learning in a compact form in order to pass them to novices and can be easily communicated [4]. Pedagogical pattern project (www. pedagogicalpatterns.org) is the biggest in this area, collecting successful experiences of learning and teaching [25]. Another considerable project in the field of pedagogy is E-LEN (http://www2.tisip.no/E-LEN/), which aimed to identify and gather best practices as a collection of patterns.

Although there are several attempts to adapt pattern approach into education, most existing pedagogical patterns were conceived for classroom situations, leaving aside the most important challenges for us: distance learning, cross-cultural collaboration, self-directed learning, social networking, heterogeneous set of tools, etc. Trials to implement Alexander's pattern approach directly into pedagogy for describing learning activities was accompanied by many drawbacks:

- Domain differences: architecture is about designing artifacts, but pedagogy is about designing a process;
- Absence of theoretical framework for detecting and implementing pedagogical patterns;
- Laborious and time-consuming process of pattern mining;
- Limited scope of language and unambiguous vocabulary (discrepancy between facilitators' pedagogical vocabulary and the language used in patterns);
- Different purpose: according to Alexander's approach patterns don't say how you do things, but why you do what you do. Inversely our purpose is to look for how to carry out certain learning activities with the use of social software applications.

On the other hand, pattern approach enables to describe and present best practices of learning activities in a consistent way. Narrative pattern descriptions provide also a record for monitoring and modifying an activity's progress, evaluating its effectiveness, and also they are basis for creating new activities. Pedagogical patterns can bring to the learning design a repository of well-documented best practices that can feed learning designers constructing units of learning with proven strategies [9] and means.

Recently, there has been a growing interest in activity patterns for designing activity-centered computing frameworks in the other domains like medical and business information systems [21]. The business activity management framework UAM [21] can serve as example of developing the similar framework for managing learning activity patterns in a distributed, personalized and heterogeneous virtual environment. Learning activity patterns are defined in UAM as re-usable learning activity structures that are represented as digital schemas, describing the properties of the learning activity and its relations to associated people, artifacts, tools and events. Therefore, generalized idea of Alexander's pattern approach can be used for describing pedagogical activity patterns if we look at the learning activity not just as a process and the sequence of actions, but rather as the whole Activity System with its components described above.

3.2.2 IMS LD for Describing a Unit of Learning

One of the considerable attempts for learning activity descriptions is an IMS Learning Design specification that provides a generic and flexible language to capture the specifics of the unit of learning, and to enable to express various pedagogies [16]. Learning design specifies a teaching-learning process trying to capture, under which conditions what activities have to be performed with the use of resources by learners and teachers, to enable learners to attain the desired learning objectives [18]. IMS LD pedagogical scenario is based on a stage-play metaphor, called a play, where a person gets a role (e.g. learner or staff) and works towards certain outcomes by performing activities within an environment that consists of the appropriate learning objects and services [18]. Activities can be assembled into activity structures by aggregating a set of related activities into a single structure. An activity-structure can model a sequence or a selection of activities [18].

A possible learning design process starts with the narrative description of some educational process in order to create more formal representation (sequence of activities, splitted roles, etc.) with the help of UML diagrams [26]. Generally IMS LD can be seen as a description of the learning activity, which is understood in our case as an activity pattern or workflow. Being more specific, in contrast with Alexander's approach, it helps to write down workflows of learning activities with detailed description, showing the roles, performed activities, as well as, artifacts and resources used while acting in the environment. Although as stated by [19] IMS LD lacks of information about the resources and services to specify the means for every learning activity, especially in collaborative settings and distributed learning environments. In our case IMS LD framework can be modified mainly in terms of vocabulary in relation to activity theory and specified description of means for carrying out a certain learning activity and affordance concept for describing the patterns of learning activities with social software.

3.3 Combined Learning Activity Descriptions

According to our vision IMS LD should be customized regarding to the vocabulary from Activity Theory and complemented with the modified version of Alexander's pattern approach. Patterns in Alexander's approach are abstractions describing a problem in pedagogy rather than a means to achieve learning objectives, while IMS LD describes a process at the unit of learning in a highly formalized manner [9]. Thus, Alexander's patterns with the three-rule part may form a learning design and serve as the first step in the creation of learning scenario, providing a context for a particular learning activity with the meaning how context caused the learners to act. Patterns help the facilitator to understand how the unit of learning could be used [15]. Unit of learning in IMS LD form a second order activity description, illustrating the solution for particular pattern and are the basis for more detailed diagrammed visualization of the workflows. Learning Design specifies a time ordered series of activities to be performed by learners and teachers (role), within the environment consisting of learning objects and services.

Our approach is based on the combination of Alexander's pattern concept and IMS LD narrative and diagrammed description. Description of the pattern elements is based on the Activity Theory vocabulary, where activity forms a flow of actions and operations performed by the subjects with certain tools and artifacts. Both approaches leave learning tools used for mediating learning activities, unattended. In the case of using social software applications in education, we find it necessary to highlight in these narrative and diagrammed descriptions the tools and their affordances for learning. This would give guidance to learners and facilitators of how software tools should be used in certain activity pattern circumstances.

3.4 Affordances Versus Functionalities of the Tools

How do the subjects perceive and operationalise the artefacts and tools in their learning processes could be described by the notion of „affordances" [14] defined affordances as the opportunities for action for the observer provided by an environment. However, as assumed by [13], affordances are primarily facts about action and interaction, not perception. This contrasts with the common impression that affordances refer to—approximately—situations in which one can see what to do [14]. The mainstream view to the affordances in educational technology settings considers them the objective properties of the tools, perceptible in the frames of some activities, suggesting that tools have concrete technological affordances for certain performances which can be brought into learner's perception with specific instructions [22,13]. Opposite to this objective view to the affordances, we assume that users actively participate in the interaction with the artefacts or tools; continuously interpret the situation, and construct or re-build meanings about them. Therefore, as stated by [8] and [27] affordances are context-dependent and dynamic. The ongoing interactions with the environment, tools and artefacts, where our previous knowledge applied during the activity in certain contexts helps us to evoke noticing of certain aspects, affordances, and knowing how these affordances could support the activity.

The ability to perceive affordances depends on the subject's ability to pick up the information provided by the context [20]. Hence understanding the properties of the context and the relationships between the subject and the mediating environment becomes important while perceiving what the environment can afford. At the same time context may function to highlight certain affordances and provide boundaries for perceiving them [1]. Contextual information can be used to guide the perception of affordances, while performing an activity. Here the important distinction between the concept of affordances, and functions of tools comes into play. While the affordances are always related to the subject's actions within the certain situation, then function refers to the tool-centric view focusing on "desired" role of the tool [6]. The main difference between the function and affordances is that functions are independent of activities, whereas affordances are dependent of them [6]. Functions are objectively describable properties of the tools.

3.5 Soft Ontology Approach

The LMS comparison frameworks like Edutools.net have established a fixed ontology for e-learning systems and tools that allows comparing the LMSs on „objective" basis. Openness and flexibility of personal learning environments (PLEs) based on social software tools calls for a different approach beyond the degrees of freedom allowed by standard hypermedia with fixed ontology. These aspects can be better implemented in terms of soft ontology. The current discussion concerns the level on which unstructured information domains are made sense of in terms of knowledge building, that is, the level of metadata, which, in turn is structured by ontologies. Soft ontology, first coined by [3], can be defined as explicit specifications of conceptualizations of information domains in a way that allows the weights given to its individual elements, as well as, its overall dimensionality to be flexible and negotiable. Ontology conceived of as being something "soft" or malleable, rather than something absolute, can be involved as a part of the interactive setting, and be made explicit and accessible to the user, who is also given the control over the ontology in terms of weighting, adding or deleting (equal to ignoring) descriptive properties of e-learning systems and tools. In this way, each user can form his or her personal perspective to a set of tools. The perspectives of different users can be then shared, negotiated and merged.

4 Theoretical Framework of the iCampFolio

4.1 Principles of the iCampFolio

iCampFolio, as one of the outcomes of iCamp project, is a multi-dimensional decision support system, facilitating the selection of technology enhanced learning (TEL) systems and tools. It is based on a soft-ontological approach enabling evaluation and comparison of different systems and tools along different dimensions. In addition to predefined list of perspectives as perceived affordances, users can rate to which extent the affordances are required in the activity, add their own perspectives and share these with other users.

In order to develop the iCampFolio, several steps need to be taken. The process starts with the collections of narrative descriptions of different learning activities with social software applications (see example 1), as well as, activities performed within the institutionalized learning management systems.

Example 1: *Forming the groups* (narrative description)
The learning activity started simultaneously at four separate universities: Tallinn University (Estonia), University of Science and Technology (Poland), Kaunas University of Technology (Lithuania), Isik University (Turkey). During the first week the activity took place in distributed spaces tagged together by the centralized demand from the trial facilitators. Learners at each site were instructed to create blog accounts in Wordpress.com to present themselves to the international participants. All the participants of the trial were supposed to create accounts in del.icio.us social bookmarking service by using the common tag „iCamp" for all the links related to the trial. Additional tag „blog" was to be used for indicating the blogs of participants and

collecting them in the common virtual space. They tagged their blogs with deli.icio.us, thus creating the common working space from where the participants from four countries could get in touch with each other's. Students were encouraged to visit each others' blogs and comment them for establishing the international teams with four members. This was realized as the learner-centered initiative. By the end of week several teams were formed and announced in individual blog spaces. From this point on, after one of the team members had created the shared blog for the team, the activity was shifted from the individual to the collaborative spaces.

Next step is to detect and describe activity patterns with the formalised language (activity diagram) from the collected narratives and finding and characterizing according to our theoretical framework the elements (learning activities, actions, operations) of different activity patterns. (see example 2).

Example 2: *Forming the groups* (activity pattern)
Create a blog. Introduce yourself and your interests in the blog. Create social visual artifact account (Flickr, Youtube etc.) and add visual artifacts with tags. Add artifacts to the blog. Create a social bookmarks account. Follow the tags or tags in tagcloud to analyze, which tags might be of interest, find the versions of the tags for your blog. Share your tags and social bookmarks. Receive blog entries and social visual artifacts with the tags of interest, analyze tag results, find and select key people with similar interests. Log in to RSS feed reader. Subscribe the feeds of these people. Make direct links between your own blog and their blog. Refer to the people of interest in your blog. Ask questions and respond to their contributions. Present your own interests in blog by using same tags as the people you feel closeness. Analyze information who are the visitors of your blog. Dashboard information may be used. Contact with interesting persons directly and ask to work together.

Learning activities written down in pattern format represent best practice of learning with heterogeneous set of tools accepted and evaluated by many users. With respect to soft ontology in our framework, activity patterns bring in the first level of „softness" as several users' experiences are recorded in these patterns. Each activity pattern gives us a general story and contextual information about the particular activity. Descriptions of activity patterns enable to construct diagrammed activity workflows in a more detailed level, whereby the vocabulary and the structure of the Activity System will be implemented. Workflows illustrate the sequence of actions within the activity, and the activity components and context for carrying out these actions. These workflows also help to define the affordances, which subjects perceive while performing certain activities within the environment complemented with various systems and tools, and analyze their actions in each activity as affordance based. Therefore, the third step is to evaluate the pedagogical affordances of social software and affordances evoked by actions of the described activities. The second level of „softness" is thereby manifested, as the perception of affordances is largely dependent on the subject, the nature of the activity, and the context surrounding the actor. The evaluation of activities in workflows by different learners brings forth a great variety of views towards available affordances of tools and systems. The data for iCampFolio, coming from detailed workflow descriptions given by many actors can be more or less calibrated and can be fed to the iCampFolio system.

The main principle in developing the user-friendly decision support system lies on the concept of affordances, as the iCampFolio enables to couple between the affordances the subjects plan to evoke when performing certain activities, and the possible affordances of tools and systems derived from the previous activities on soft ontology-basis. Thus, users can find suitable tools and systems for their actions in a workflow they need to carry out relaying on the set of evaluated pedagogical affordances of tools. The „softness" of the decision support system increases as users of the iCampFolio can rate the existing affordances of tools based on their learning and teaching experiences, and add affordances and tools to the iCampFolio for the others to evaluate and use. In this sense, the iCampFolio conveys the ideology of social software, becoming better in application. The possibility to evaluate existing affordances by users helps to calibrate the iCampFolio in terms of the affordance accuracy tied with the activities, and hereafter learners can use it for searching the tools for their own learning activities.

The iCampFolio tool uses the principle of coupling between the pedagogical affordances evoked by actions of the certain learning activity with the evaluated pedagogical affordances (instead of functionalities) of learning software in certain activity contexts (fig. 1). Activities are grouped according to general pedagogical aspects in order to enable the flexible construction of instructional designs from different groups of activities. In figure 1 on the left side is seen a list of possible activity patterns and on the right side a choice of social software applications. While performing an activity, as for example *forming a group* in distance cross-cultural collaborative setting, certain activities need to be performed such as establishing connections between learners and facilitators, getting to know co-learners etc., which consist of several sequences of actions conveying pedagogical meanings. For instance facilitators' actions of guiding learners how to form teams and use tools for it, sending /sharing this information with the learners via email blog, learner's actions of finding the teammates, creating the shared blog, making access to team-members, deciding (or not) the central leadership in team, publishing the team blog in shared area with tags, etc. While thinking of an action and choosing a tool for performing this action, affordances as properties that are relative and dependent of the subjects who perform some activities with the tools or artifacts that support them to realize their objects will be coupled by the affordances of tools, which indicate the possible ways how the tool can be used. Affordances combine action, actor and artifact, thus these can be used for helping the learners to select suitable tools for their learning process.

Based on the collected narratives and detected activity patterns the following affordances are represented in the iCampFolio as an open list: searching artifact, creating and editing artifact, group work with text-based artifact, group work with graph-based artifact, role distribution while editing artifact, listening and watching artifact, interacting with artifact, managing artifact, making notes related to the artifact, individual time management, group time management, self-analysis and reflection, modifying the learning environment, testing, self-testing, participating in questionnaire, giving and managing task, submiting individual assignment, submiting group work, assessing homeworks, creating group, finding group/learning partner, text-based group discussion, audio conversation, video conference, sending messages, role game, peer-evaluation, saving and montioring activities, asking help and feedback. Aforementioned list is the starting point to calibrate the iCampFolio in terms of evaluated pedagogical affordances evoked by the actions of certain learning activities.

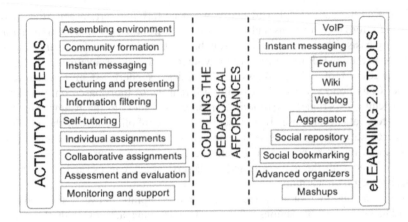

Fig. 1. Coupling affordances between activity patterns and tools

4.2   First Prototype of the iCampFolio

The first prototype of the iCamp portfolio of systems and tools for technology enhanced learning, or shortly iCampFolio (available at http://www.htk.tlu.ee/icamp) consists of three views: a *table of values view* (list of tool names), a *listing view* (full description of every tool) and an *ontology view* (shows the selection of tools). This view can be understood as an explorative decision support tool. The selector tool thus enables a user to investigate different TEL systems and tools, which have been added to the portfolio of tools beforehand according to different pre-selected perspectives with the respective numerical value. The values reflect the TEL systems and tools' capabilities to support different perspectives. To demonstrate the main principle of the first prototype of iCamp portfolio, didactical activities developed by [7] serve as an example of various ontological dimensions: learning material development, individual assignment, group assignment, self-study, c, guidance, presentation, and group discussion. Users of the iCampFolio can set the values to each pre-set ontological dimension or dismiss these dimensions completely and replace them with their own, self-defined properties of the e-learning systems and tools. In the second prototype of iCampFolio B. Collis didactical activities will be replaced by the list of pedagogical affordances extracted from workflow descriptions and previously described framework of tools' affordances will be implemented.

5   Participatory Design for Empirical Research

At this juncture empirical research of iCampFolio is work in progress. The usability and applicability of the iCampFolio in higher education will be evaluated using participatory design research. Participatory design traces its roots to Scandinavian work in the 60's and 70's being affected also by action research and sociotechnical design. Participatory design approach attempts to actively involve the real users in authentic context in the design process to increase the probability of a usable design [11]. The main idea lies in cooperation between potential end-users and researchers/

developers during the development process to find out if the product meets users' needs. It will help to analyze the applicability of a selector tool for facilitators as well as for learners in order to compare and evaluate various TEL systems and tools. In addition to software usability we are currently in the middle of gathering narrative descriptions of learning activities with the use of social software and analysing patterns occurred in institutionalised learning settings using LMS in order to evaluate the pedagogical expressiveness of activity descriptions according to the rules of the affordances.

In order to collect and describe the best practices of learning activities with social software tools, the recording of potential action and manipulation possibilities from the point of view of particular subjects or group of subjects is crucial. These would serve as the basis for soft ontology of learning affordances in iCampFolio. The design experiment involves 24 participants of the Web 2.0 learning design course of the Tallinn University (http://kaugkoolitus.wordpress.com). These learners will be introduced with the affordance-based principles of activity pattern descriptions. The open set of Web 2.0 tools is recommended for the learners. Their task is to compose self-directed and collaborative activity settings from these tools and test activity patterns individually and in groups. These activity patterns will be described by learners, using the framework explained in this study. The learners will explain the affordances of each activity-pattern in the seminars, and the affordances will be collaboratively evaluated by the group of learners. Next, each learner has to evaluate the affordances of their patterns from the following aspects: i) which affordances of their distributed sysem did they initially perceive and plan as part of their learning design; ii) which affordances they applied during the activity testing; and iii) which affordances they perceived as effective for their activity purposes. The individual evaluation of activity pattern affordances for collaborative activity patterns would also reveal the learner's different perception of the affordances of the same activity pattern. The dataset of affordances, collected from this design experiment, will be used as the basis for developing further the iCampFolio prototype. In the next phase of the development, the prototype will be used in the elearning 2.0 activity settings for selecting tools and evaluating their affordances in specific activity patterns.

6 Conclusions

Web 2.0 brings along new generation of systems and tools suitable for creating personal learning environments aside to the technical landscapes of tools provided by institutions. Great variety of new tools and systems expect also innovative approaches for their comparison and selection. Current comparison approaches focus on mainly LMS-s leaving social software applications unnoticed. This article introduces a new approach and first prototype of iCamp portfolio for selecting and comparing Web 2.0 technology as well as institutionalized learning systems. We propose an alternative way based on soft ontological approach for life-long learners within the context of e-learning 2.0, as well as, for teachers in order to facilitate the combination of abstracted didactical patterns with specific tools and systems and for creating their personal learning landscapes of suitable tools. With our theoretical framework we would like to show how this affordance-based approach could solve the drawbacks of current selection and comparison methods. Our purpose is to emphasize that every tool has emergent activity-based functionalities suitable best for carrying out certain learning and teaching patterns.

Acknowledgements. This study was a part of the activities within the iCamp project supported by Information Society's Technologies programmed under 6th Framework programme of European Commission.

References

1. Albrechtsen, H., Andersen, H.H.K., Bodker, S., Pejtersen, A.M.: Affordances in activity theory and cognitive systems engineering. Riso National Laboratory, Roskilde (2001)
2. Alexander, C., Ishikawa, S., Silverstein, M.: A Pattern Language: Towns, Buildings, Constructions. OUP (1977)
3. Aviles Collao, J., Diaz-Kommonen, L., Kaipainen, M., Pietarila, J.: Soft ontologies and similarity cluster tools to facilitate exploration and discovery of cultural heritage resources. In: IEEE Computer Society Digital Library. Prc. DEXA (2003)
4. Bergin, J.: A pattern language for initial course design. In: SIGCSE 2001, pp. 282–286 (2001)
5. Bowker, G.C., Star, S.L.: Sorting Things Out: Classification and Its Consequences. Parts II and III. MIT Press, Cambridge, MA (1999)
6. Brown, D., Blessing, L.: The relationship between function and affordance. In: Proceedings of IDETC/CIE: ASME 2005 International Design Engineering Technical Conferences Computers and Information in Engineering Conference. California, USA (2005)
7. Collis, B.: Pedagogical reengineering: a pedagogical approach to course enrichment and redesign with the www (1997) Available at, http://www.ub.es/forum/Conferencias/betty.htm
8. Cook, S.D.N., Brown, J.S.: Bridging epistomologies: the generative dance between organisatoral knowledge and knowing. Organisatoral Science 10(4), 381–400 (1999)
9. de Moura Filho, C.O., Derycke, A.: Pedagogical patterns and learning design: when two worlds cooperate (2005) Available at: dspace.ou.nl/bitstream/1820/474/9/09_DBU_review.pdf
10. Downes, S.: E-learning 2.0. eLearn Magazine, 10 (2005)
11. Ehn, P.: Scandinavian Design: On Participation and Skill. In: Adler, P.S., Winograd, T.A. (eds.) Usability: Turning technologies into tools, pp. 96–132. Oxford University Press, New York (1992)
12. Engeström, Y.: Learning by expanding. Helsinki: Orienta-konsultit (1987)
13. Gaver, W.W.: Affordances for interaction: the social is material for design. Ecological Psychology 8(2), 111–129 (1996), http://www.cs.ubc.ca/labs/spin/publications/related/gaver96.pdf
14. Gibson, J.J.: The ecological approach to visual perception. Boston, Houghton Mifflin (1979)
15. Griffiths, D.: From primitives to patterns: a discussion paper (2005)Available at http://iua.upf.es/ dgriffit/papers/primitives-patterns.pdf
16. IMSLD IMS Learning Design Best Practice and Implementation Guide. Version 1.0 final specification. IMS Global Learning Consortium, Inc. (2003)

17. Kuutti, K.: Activity Theory as a potential framework for human computer interaction research. In: Nardi, B. (ed.) Context and Consciousness: Activity Theory and Human Computer Interaction, pp. 17–44. MIT Press, Cambridge (1995)
18. Koper, R., Olivier, B.: Representing the Learning Design of Units of Learning. Educational Technology & Society 7(3), 97–111 (2004)
19. Leo, D.H., Asensio-Parez, J.I., Dimitriadis, Y.A.: IMS learning design support for the formalization of collaborative learning patterns. In: ICALT (2004)
20. McGrenere, J., Ho, W.: Affordances: clarifying and evolving a concept. In: Proceedings of Graphics Interface 2000, Montreal (2000)
21. Moody, P., Gruen, D., Muller, M.J., Tang, J., Moran, T.P.: Business activity patterns: A new model for collaborative business applications. IBM Systems Journal 45(4), 683–694 (2006)
22. Norman, D.O.: The Design of Everyday Things. New York: Basic Books (1988)
23. O'Reilly, T.: What is web 2.0. Design patterns and business models for the next generation of software (2005) Available at: http://www.oreillynet.com/pub/a/oreilly/tim/news/2005/09/30/what-is-web-20.html
24. Siemens, G.: Connectivism: A Learning Theory for the Digital Age (2004) Available at, http://www.elearnspace.org/Articles/connectivism.htm
25. Sharp, H., Manns, M.L., Eckstein, J.: The wider picture. In: OOPSLA 99 workshop (1999)
26. Tattrsall, C.: How does IMS learning design work? The Open University of the Netherlands and the UNFOLD project (2004) Available at, http://dsace.ou.nl
27. Vyas, D., Chisalita, C.M., der Veer, G.C.: Broadening affordances. In: Proceedings of CHI'07 (2007)
28. Whitmyer, C., Grimes, G.T.: Comparative Features Analysis of Leading Course management software. The University of the Future, LLC (1999) Available at, http://www.futureu.com/cmscomp/cms_comp.pdf

Evaluating the ALOCOM Approach for Scalable Content Repurposing

Katrien Verbert and Erik Duval

Dept. Computerwetenschappen, Katholieke Universiteit Leuven,
Celestijnenlaan 200A, B-3001 Leuven, Belgium
{Katrien.Verbert,Erik.Duval}@cs.kuleuven.be

Abstract. In this paper, an evaluation is presented of a framework that supports flexible content repurposing. Unlike the usual practice where content components, such as slides, images, definitions, text fragments, tables, or diagrams, are assembled manually through copy and paste, the framework enables on-the-fly access and repurposing. Retrieval of relevant components is enabled by automatic decomposition of legacy content and storage of individual components, enriched with metadata. Furthermore, the automatic assembly of these components in standard authoring tools is supported. The evaluation presented in this paper aims to assess the effectiveness and efficiency of such content reuse for presentations.

Keywords: content models, repurposing, metadata, repositories, evaluations.

1 Introduction

Learning objects (LOs) and their reusability are important current research topics within the learning technology community. In various publications, it is argued that reuse not only saves time and money [4][19], but also enhances the quality of digital learning experiences, resulting in efficient, economic and effective learning [5].

There is an inverse relationship between the size of a LO and its reusability [29]. As the LO's size decreases (lower granularity), its potential for reuse increases. Many shared LOs are, however, coarse-grained compositions and as such difficult to repurpose [12]. Paragraphs, images or diagrams are frequently assembled manually by copy-paste actions. However, it is possible to repurpose LOs effectively, if their components can be accessed on-the-fly. This requires innovative and flexible LO modeling [5].

In earlier work, we developed an abstract learning object content model (ALOCOM) that is a framework for LOs and their components [7]. The model defines both LO component types and relationships between components. As such, the model enables structuring of composite LOs and is a solid basis for the proposed dynamic approach. In [28], we presented a framework that supports the approach for presentations. The motivation for choosing presentations was based on their extensive use [8] and the fact that slides are often designed as self-contained pieces of content, representing a single topic or idea. The framework transforms (legacy) content into a representation compliant with the ALOCOM model. In this transformation process,

E. Duval, R. Klamma, and M. Wolpers (Eds.): EC-TEL 2007, LNCS 4753, pp. 364–377, 2007.

content is decomposed and components are individually stored in a LO repository, enriched with metadata. For scalability purposes, duplicate detection techniques are used to detect reuse for different component types in order to avoid duplicates. Furthermore, a ranking function is included that assigns a comparative value to a component based on its reuse, enabling ordering of result lists.

The fine-grained components stored in the repository are the necessary building blocks for supporting flexible content reuse. This requires a tight integration into standard authoring tools, as authors prefer to use authoring tools they are familiar with to create content. We developed a plug-in for Microsoft PowerPoint that enables users to search components, such as images, definitions, slides, text fragments, diagrams or tables, from within the application.

In this paper, we present an evaluation of the approach for presentation repurposing. A user evaluation has been performed that assessed the usability and utility of the plug-in for Microsoft PowerPoint. The goals of the evaluation were threefold: (i) to assess the efficiency and effectiveness of the approach for repurposing presentations; (ii) to assess the subjective acceptance of the ALOCOM interface; (iii) to determine to which level of granularity decomposition is relevant. A follow-up evaluation was necessary to confirm the results and assessed the quality of the created presentations.

In the next section, we briefly outline the ALOCOM architecture. The user evaluation and the quality evaluation are presented in section 3 and 4, followed by a discussion in section 5. Related work is presented in section 6. Conclusions and remarks on future work conclude this paper.

2 The ALOCOM Architecture

In the ALOCOM architecture, the server relies on the ARIADNE Knowledge Pool System [25] for storage of content components and their metadata. The architecture is depicted in Fig. 1 and consists of the following components:

- Client side applications that enable content uploading to and component retrieval from the repository from within authoring tools. We developed a plug-in that provides these functionalities for Microsoft PowerPoint.
- The Disaggregation module supports the actual decomposition. In the case of presentations, the presentation is decomposed into slides, and each slide is further decomposed into images, tables, diagrams, definitions and text fragments. The current implementation of this module supports the approach for PowerPoint presentations. Components are extracted, preview thumbnails are generated and results are stored through the AdvancedContentInserter.
- The AdvancedContentInserter provides support for storing not only complete LOs, but also components that are contained in the LO, for instance components stored in a SCORM content package or components that were extracted by the Disaggregation module. Reuse is detected using simple metrics that compute similarities between incoming and stored components, such as the cosine similarity measure for detecting overlaps between text fragments and hash functions for detecting identical images [20]. In the next step, LOM metadata is

generated for each component using the Automatic Metadata Generation framework (AMG) [1]. Relationship metadata are added that describe different relationships between parent and child components ("isPartOf", "hasPart") and between components ("ordering"). Finally, LO components are stored in the ALOCOM repository using the ARIADNE insert service [25].

- The ranking module assigns comparative values to components based on their reuse that enables ordering of result lists when a user searches for relevant objects, placing components with a high probability at the top of the list [16].

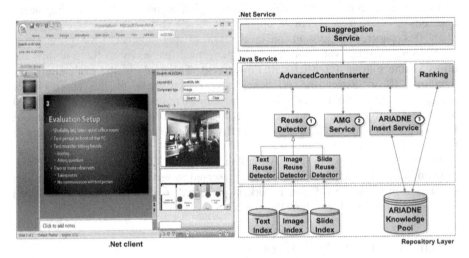

Fig. 1. The ALOCOM plug-in for PowerPoint (left) The ALOCOM Architecture (right)

The ALOCOM repository is currently filled with 62841 components that were extracted from 814 presentations. These components include 18149 slides, 7028 images, 226 tables, 30 diagrams and 35460 text fragments. We developed a plug-in for Microsoft PowerPoint that enables authors to automatically repurpose these components from within the application. As shown in Fig. 1, a custom Office Task Pane (on the right side) is used for integrating this functionality in Microsoft PowerPoint. This is accomplished with Visual Studio 2005 Tools for the Microsoft Office System [29].

The plug-in enables authors to search the repository for components they wish to repurpose in the presentation they are editing. An author can specify the component type, such as reference, definition, example, slide, image, or text fragment, and descriptive keywords. Thumbnails of components that satisfy the search criteria are shown in the Task Pane and the author can incorporate them into the current presentation by a single mouse-click. Metadata associated with the component is shown if the author hovers the mouse pointer over a component in the result list. Authors can add presentations to the repository by clicking the "Save into ALOCOM" button that we added to the standard PowerPoint menu.

3 User Evaluation

The user evaluation assessed the usability and utility of the ALOCOM plug-in for Microsoft PowerPoint. The goals of the evaluation were the following:

- to assess the efficiency and effectiveness of the approach for repurposing presentation components;
- to assess the subjective acceptance of the ALOCOM interface;
- to determine to which level of granularity decomposing presentations is useful.

3.1 Study Description

The study was conducted in October 2006 at K.U. Leuven. Each session involved one participant, who performed two tasks during a single session. There were 20 participants in the study, which typically results in a reasonably tight confidence interval [15]. Participants were mainly members of the junior staff of the Computer Science Department at K.U. Leuven.

Tasks. Each participant was asked to create two presentations: one on inheritance and one on exceptions in the programming language Java. The participants were divided in two groups. The first group created the presentation on exceptions in Java without ALOCOM support, and the presentation on inheritance in Java with ALOCOM support. They could use all information available on the World Wide Web for both presentations. The second group did the same, but in a different order. This group created the presentation on inheritance in Java without ALOCOM support, and the presentation on exceptions in Java with ALOCOM support.

We refer to the presentation created without ALOCOM support as *without-alocom presentation* and the presentation created with ALOCOM support as *with-alocom presentation* in the remainder of this paper.

78 presentations on both topics were gathered by a Google-search and uploaded to the repository: as described above, they were automatically decomposed and the components were automatically described. In total, 10281 components were made available for reuse, including 2964 slides, 933 images, 6367 text fragments, 12 tables and 5 diagrams.

Data Collection. Camtasia Studio[1] was used to record participant interactions, capturing the screen, voice and webcam video. Participants were also asked to complete a questionnaire after the tasks. The questionnaire was adopted from a usability evaluation of the ARIADNE search tool [13].

Measurements. The following characteristics were measured for the experiment:

- Time-on-task: represents the time needed to finish each task. The aim of the time comparison is to investigate whether the use of the ALOCOM plug-in can lead to savings in time. We are aware that time is influenced by other factors; however,

---

[1] http://www.techsmith.com/camtasia.asp

we included this comparison in order to obtain a first indication of improvements for time-on-task.

- Manual versus semi-automatic reuse: The distinction is made between manually reused components and semi-automatically reused components. Manually reused components are components that were added to the presentation by copy-pasting or reproducing existing content, typically found through Google. Semi-automatically reused components are those components that were found and inserted using the ALOCOM plug-in. By measuring and comparing both types of content reuse, we obtain a success rate indication of the ALOCOM approach for repurposing content, as authors typically tried the semi-automatic approach first and inserted content manually if no relevant components were found through the ALOCOM plug-in.
- Component granularity: the granularity of semi-automatically reused component types is measured in order to determine to which level of granularity decomposition of presentations is relevant.
- Satisfaction: user satisfaction was assessed through a questionnaire filled in by each participant after finishing the tasks. Questionnaire questions intended to measure the overall satisfaction on the usage of the plug-in.

3.2 Results

Time. Table 1 shows the average time participants spent on creating *without-alocom* and *with-alocom* presentations. At first sight, the difference is relatively limited: on average, 20.03 minutes were spent creating the *without-alocom* presentation and 17.79 minutes creating the *with-alocom* presentation. However, not all participants created presentations similar in length, covered sub-topics or quality in general.

Size normalizations were applied that were adopted from the software quality field [6]. A simple normalization that takes into account the number of slides in the presentation shows that on average 3.32 minutes were spent per slide in a *without-alocom* presentation, whereas 2.2 minutes were spent per slide created with ALOCOM support.

A second normalization was applied that takes into account the number of sub-topics. Some participants created presentations covering many sub-topics, such as polymorphism and dynamic binding for the presentation on inheritance, while others provided only a definition and an example. If we consider the number of sub-topics, we see that on average 4.5 minutes were spent on a sub-topic in a *without-alocom* presentation and 2.9 minutes on a *with-alocom* presentation sub-topic.

To statistically establish whether the difference between these average values is real or a by-product of natural variance, we applied a Paired-Samples T Test. The null hypothesis is that there is no difference between the required creation time for *with-alocom* and *without-alocom* presentations. Our alternative hypothesis is that there is indeed a difference. Results were obtained with a normal distribution.

We can reject the null hypothesis for normalized time values. Thus, taking into account the size of presentations, significant time savings are realized when creating presentations with support to automatically repurpose existing presentation

Table 1. Time (in minutes)

	without-alocom presentation	with-alocom	Sig.(2-tailed)
Total time	20.03	17.79	0.147
Time normalized by number of slides	3.32	2.2	0.001
Time normalized by number of subtopics	4.5	2.9	0.016

components. To validate these results, a second evaluation has been performed that assessed the quality of the created presentations. This evaluation is presented in section 4.

Reuse in With-Alocom Presentations. *With-alocom* presentations were further analyzed. The distinction is made between manual reuse, semi-automatic reuse and new components. Manually reused components are components that were added to the presentation by copy-pasting or reproducing existing content, found by a web search. Semi-automatically reused components are those components that were found and inserted using the ALOCOM plug-in. New components represent content the participant created from scratch, without using an existing resource.

Fig. 2(a) shows reuse patterns of individual participants. Some participants reused about the same amount of components manually as semi-automatically. Also, the amount of new components is high for some participants (more than 40%). Few participants created presentations without manual reuse.

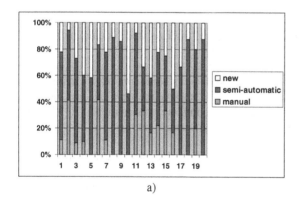

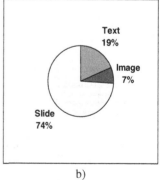

a)   b)

Fig. 2. Reuse patterns of individual participants (a); reuse/component type (b)

Table 2 shows that on average 57% of presentation components are semi-automatically reused using the ALOCOM plug-in. 18% of the components were reused manually, whereas 25% are new components. There is no significant difference if we compare this data for the presentation on exceptions in Java and the presentation on inheritance in Java, although more components were available covering topics on inheritance. The values were normally distributed and compared with a Paired-Samples T Test.

Comparing manual and semi-automatic reuse, we see that 76% of reused components were reused semi-automatically, whereas 24% were reused by copy-paste actions or reproduction of content. These values are a success rate indicator of the ALOCOM approach for reusing content, as participants typically tried the semi-automatic approach first and inserted content manually if no relevant components were found through the ALOCOM plug-in.

Table 2. Reuse in *with-alocom* presentations

	Manual	Semi-automatic	New
Overall	0.18	0.57	0.25
Presentation on inheritance (1)	0.19	0.58	0.23
Presentation on exceptions (2)	0.18	0.55	0.27
Comparing means (1) and (2) Sig. (2-tailed)	0.737	0.121	0.791

Granularity. Fig. 2(b) shows the reuse rate for semi-automatically reused component types. Complete slides are most often reused, probably because many slides represent a single idea or topic and are thus easy to reuse in a new context. Also the reuse of text fragments is significant. This is an interesting result, as it illustrates that breaking content down to the level of a single text fragment is useful. Images were not frequently reused; however, this result is probably influenced by the topic of the presentations.

Findings and Recommendation. In this section, findings and recommendations of the participants are discussed.

Lack of Context. Some participants remarked that more context is required for successful content reuse. They want to be able to retrieve the next and previous slide for a specific slide in the result list, or even the complete presentation(s) to which the slide belonged. Similar support is needed for other component types.

Behaviour Change. It was noted that this way of reusing content requires a behaviour change, as it is different from the usual practice of copy-pasting or reproducing content. It was reported that savings in time would be remarkable; however, a period of adaptation is required.

Drag and Drop Support. Many participants expected drag and drop support for inserting components. There is click-support for inserting a component: clicking a component in the result list will insert the component at the currently selected location. However, it is not possible to drag the component to a different location in the presentation due to limitations of the PowerPoint API [22].

Garbage Content. Not all components are reusable. As components are created by decomposing existing content automatically, it was expected that not all components are valuable for reuse. Results are ranked according to the number of times a component is reused. Hence, the impact of this issue will decrease over time.

Less Consistent Layout. Some participants noted that it is hard to keep the layout of different components consistent. The layout of slides is automatically adapted to the template the author is using. However, if the author changed for instance the font color of a text fragment in one particular slide, this modification is preserved when reusing the slide. Although desirable in some cases, this was reported as a difficulty.

More Valuable for Reuse of Own Content. Participants remarked that the use of the ALOCOM plug-in would be most valuable for reusing their own presentations.

Overall Satisfaction. Table 3 presents the responses of participants to questions concerning the overall use of the ALOCOM plug-in. The questionnaire was adopted from a usability evaluation of the ARIADNE search tool [13]. The popular attitude scale with seven points (ranging from 1 - poor to 7 - good) was used to measure the response of participants on the overall use of the plug-in.

Table 3. Satisfaction

	mean (ranging from 1–7)	Standard deviation
Ease of use	6.15	0.69
Information organization	5.23	0.93
Use of terminology	4.92	1.5
Navigation	6.07	1.04
Search and reuse of components	5.69	1.49
Result list easy to read	4.92	1.5

The mean for the level of ease-of-use was more than 6, meaning that the participants found the ALOCOM plug-in easy to use. The level of information organization and search and reuse of LO components was perceived as moderate (mean 5.23 and 5.69 respectively). We believe that this is related to the fact that there is a lack of context (it is not possible to automatically retrieve the original component to which a component belonged) and the fact that there is no drag and drop support.

Result lists were found rather difficult to read (mean 4.92). This result is a consequence of the fact that preview thumbnails of slides containing much content are difficult to read. We have worked on a solution that enables users to enlarge individual components. Each component in the result list has a context menu item that provides this functionality. This solution will resolve the issue if only few components are difficult to read.

4 Quality Evaluation

In a follow-up evaluation, the quality of *with-* and *without-alocom* presentations was assessed by a group of 19 participants. This evaluation was necessary for obtaining a more accurate estimation of the effectiveness and efficiency of the ALOCOM approach for repurposing presentations.

Following a common practice to reduce subjectivity in a quality evaluation, an evaluation framework was used. In [9], an overview is provided of the most common dimensions of Content Quality frameworks. Four dimensions that were relevant in the context of the experiment were used to evaluate the quality of the presentations: accuracy, completeness, relevancy and conciseness.

In an accurate presentation, the content contained in the presentation is correct, reliable and free of error. Completeness is defined as the extent to which information is not missing and is of sufficient breadth and depth for the task at hand. Relevancy measures whether the content contained in the presentation is applicable and helpful for the task at hand. Finally, in a concise presentation, content is broken up into smaller chunks that can be easily shared with an audience.

Participants in the experiment were requested to read the definition of each parameter before grading the presentations. The definitions were also available during the evaluation process.

The experiment was carried out online using a web application. After logging in, the system presented users with instructions. After reading the instructions, users were presented with a list of 20 randomly selected presentations. Once users had reviewed a presentation, they were asked to give grades on a 7-point scale, from "Extremely low quality" to "Extremely high quality", for each parameter. Only participants that graded all presentations were considered in the experiment.

The experiment was available for 2 weeks. During that period, 24 participants entered the system, but only 19 completed the evaluation. From those 19 participants, 13 were postgraduate students, 1 had a Ph.D. degree and 5 were active in software development. All participants had a degree in computer science.

4.1 Data Analysis

Because of the inherent subjectivity in measuring quality, the first step in the analysis of the data is to estimate the reliability of the evaluation [10]. In this kind of experiment, the evaluation is considered reliable if the variability between the grades given by different reviewers to a particular presentation is significantly smaller than the variability between the average grades given to different presentations. To estimate this difference, we use the Intra-Class Correlation (ICC) coefficient [21], which is commonly used to measure the inter-rater reliability. We calculate the average ICC measure using the two-way mixed model, given that all reviewers grade the same sample of presentations. In this configuration, the ICC is equivalent to another widely used reliability measure, the Cronbachs alpha [2]. The results for each quality parameter are reported in the Table 4.

Table 4. Intra-Class Correlation (ICC) coefficient for measuring the reliability

Parameter	ICC (average, two-way mixed)
Completeness	0.927
Accuracy	0.766
Conciseness	0.881
Relevancy	0.837

Generally, ICC values above 0.75 indicate good reliability between measures. None of the values fall below this cut-off value. Hence, the ICC suggests that reviewers provided similar values and further statistical analysis can be performed.

The second step is to assess whether there is a difference between the average grade given to *with-alocom* presentations and the average grade given to *without-alocom* presentations. These average values are presented in Fig. 3. To statistically establish whether the difference between average values is real or a by-product of natural variance, we applied a Paired-Samples T Test. Our null hypothesis is that there is no difference between the grades given to *with-alocom* and *without-alocom* presentations. Our alternative hypothesis is that there is indeed a difference. The results are presented in Table 5. Results were obtained with a normal distribution.

We can reject the null hypothesis for most of the parameters (completeness, conciseness and relevancy). The significant difference found in the completeness parameter indicates that users were able to create more complete presentations when provided with support to repurpose presentation components. The significant difference found in the conciseness parameter indicates that content extracted from existing presentations is more suitable for reuse as it is already presented in a form that can be shared with an audience. Furthermore, users were able to find more relevant content for *with-alocom* presentations. No significant difference was found in

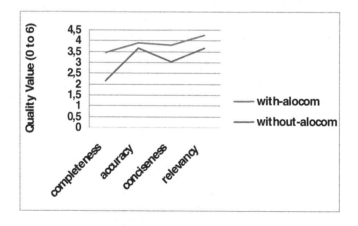

Fig. 3. Average quality grade for the different parameters

Table 5. Significance of the difference between the given grades

Parameter	T-value	Significance (2-tailed)
Completeness	-8.094	0.0
Accuracy	-1.412	0.160
Conciseness	-4.352	0.0
Relevancy	-2.981	0.003

the accuracy parameter. As the presentations were created by members of the junior staff of the Computer Science Department at K.U. Leuven, it was expected that no major mistakes would be made in creating presentations on inheritance and exceptions in Java.

5 Discussion

Although no direct improvement in savings in time was perceived, results of the quality evaluation indicate that providing on-the-fly access to presentation components in an authoring process enhances the quality of presentations. Presentations created with ALOCOM support are significantly more complete, concise and relevant. The results in completeness are consistent with the size normalizations applied to time values. Hence, we can conclude that there is also a significant improvement in time savings.

Results of the user evaluation indicate that the plug-in can be used in a successful way: 76% of reused components were reused semi-automatically. However, usability issues need to be resolved in order to make this kind of content reuse more efficient. Most important is the context issue. The user interface should be extended with the functionality to retrieve the component to which a component in the result list originally belonged. Furthermore, it is important to enable navigation in the original structure of presentations. For instance, support is needed to retrieve the next and previous slide for a specific slide in the result list. We will integrate these functionalities in the PowerPoint plug-in.

We cannot improve the consistent layout issue, as we use built-in copy and paste functions of the PowerPoint API for adding an existent slide to a presentation. If a user would manually copy-paste a slide, the same problem with consistency arises. Drag and drop support is also difficult to integrate. We will, however, investigate possibilities to improve the way a component can be inserted.

The method we used can be classified as a "discount usability engineering" approach [14] as it is definitely not "the perfect" method for evaluation and will not give absolute results. However, it enabled us to obtain a good indication of improvements towards savings in time or enhancements of quality and to highlight usability issues. A second evaluation will be performed after resolving the aforementioned issues with a group of participants from outside the computer science field.

6 Related Work

Reuse is considered to be an effective strategy for building high-quality content [26]. However, there is currently a lack of evaluation methods and metrics for measuring the impact of content reuse in terms of productivity and quality gains.

In the software engineering field, researchers have worked on metrics for measuring reuse benefits. Size, reuse rate and effort metrics are used for calculating these benefits. Furthermore, many frameworks have been presented that measure quality, in both software and information quality fields. In this paper, we have applied techniques and frameworks that are valid in our context.

In [11], an empirical evaluation is presented that assesses the impact of reuse on quality and productivity in object oriented systems. Similar to our evaluation, amount of reuse and total amount of hours spent on a system are measured. In [3], an analytical and empirical evaluation of software reuse metrics is presented. Software measures are categorized along orthogonal axes that measure attributes of the software product, such as quality of code, and attributes of the software process, such as cost of design review. In our case, the quality evaluation assessed product/content attributes, and time-on-task is an attribute of the process. Furthermore, reuse metrics that measure the amount of reuse, like our reuse measurements presented in section 4, are commonly used to estimate savings [3].

In the content management field, content reuse is reported to lead to savings in time and improvements of quality. Vasont [26] is a commercial content management system that enables organizations to create, manage and store their content for component-level reuse and delivery in multiple outputs. They report that substantial content reuse resulted in time savings in content creation, revisions, delivery, and translation. According to the study, content reuse varies by industry. Technology companies, such as software developers, have been found to achieve an average of 70% content reuse, while manufacturing companies achieve approximately 93% content reuse. Like many other commercial content management systems, the system supports reuse by manual transformation of content.

In contrast to Vasont, MagIR [8] is a system that supports automatic content transformations. Like our system, these transformations are supported for Microsoft PowerPoint presentations and include content decomposition. Decomposition is supported to the level of slides, while our system also extracts smaller components such as tables, diagrams, images and text fragments. Results of our user evaluation indicate that these fine-grained components are also often reused. MagIR is used for creation, administration and reutilization of PowerPoint slides in a corporate context and is aimed at reducing storage costs. The system has been evaluated in that context and results indicate that storage costs are significantly reduced.

Slide executive [23] is a commercial product that also supports reutilization of Microsoft PowerPoint slides. Individual slides can be retrieved in a browser. Like MagIR, decomposition is supported to the level of slides. Add-ins are provided to export PowerPoint slides to images in different formats and to import multiple images at once. However, no tight integration for component searching from within the application is provided. No information was found whether the system has been evaluated.

7 Conclusions

In this paper, an evaluation was presented of our framework that supports on-the-fly repurposing of presentation components, providing an indication of the effectiveness and efficiency of such content reuse. The analysis of the results indicates that there is a significant improvement of the quality of presentations and a significant time saving benefit.

We have extended the current implementation of the framework with support for (de-)composing SCORM Content Packages and Wikipedia pages. A plug-in has been developed for Microsoft Word that enables repurposing of components from Wikipedia pages and an equivalent plug-in has been developed for the RELOAD editor [18] that supports reuse of SCORM components. Evaluations have to be performed to assess whether these related approaches result in a similar impact on effective and efficient content reuse.

Acknowledgments. We gratefully acknowledge the financial support of the K.U.Leuven research council through the BALO project, the Interdisciplinary Institute for Broadband Technology (IBBT) through the Acknowledge project, and the European Commission through the ProLearn Network of Excellence on Professional Learning [17].

References

1. Cardinaels, K., Meire, M., Duval, E.: Automating Metadata Generation: the Simple Indexing Interface. In: International World Wide Web Conference, WWW 2005, Chiba, Japan, May 10-14, 2005, pp. 548–556 (2005)
2. Cronbach, L.J.: Coefficient alpha and the internal structure of tests. Psychometrika 16, 297–334 (1951)
3. Devanbu, P., Karstu, S., Melo, W., Thomas, W.: Analytical and Empirical Evaluation of Software Reuse Metrics. In: The 18th Internation Conference on Software Engineering, pp. 189–199 (1996)HYPERLINK, http://citeseer.ist.psu.edu/devanbu96analytical.html
4. Downes, S.: Learning Objects: resources for distance education worldwide. International Review of Research in Open and Distance Learning 2(1) (2001)
5. Duval, E., Hodgins, W.: A LOM research agenda. In: Proceedings of the 12th International World Wide Web Conference, Budapest, Hungary, pp. 1–9 (2003)
6. ISO/IEC 9126 -2 Software quality characteristics and metrics - External metrics (1998)
7. Jovanović, J., Gašević, D., Verbert, K., Duval, E.: Ontology of learning object content structure. In: Proc. of the 12th International Conference on Artificial Intelligence in Education, pp. 322–329. The Netherlands, Amsterdam (2005)
8. Kienreich, W., Sabol, V., Ley, T., Lindstaedt, S., Koronakis, P., Droschl, G.: MagIR: Distributed Creation, Administration and Reutilization of Multimedia Presentation Content. In: Althoff, K.-D., Dengel, A., Bergmann, R., Nick, M., Roth-Berghofer, T.R. (eds.) WM 2005. LNCS (LNAI), vol. 3782, pp. 481–486. Springer, Heidelberg (2005)
9. Knight, S.A., Burn, J.M.: Developing a Framework for Assessing Information Quality on the World Wide Web. Informing Science Journal 8, 159–172 (2005)

10. Meire, M., Duval, E., Ochoa, X.: SAmgI: Automatic Metadata Generation v2.0. In: Proceedings of ED-MEDIA 2007, World Conference on Educational Multimedia, Hypermedia & Telecommunications (to appear, 2007)

11. Melo, W.L., Briand, L.C., Basili, V.R.: Measuring the Impact of Reuse on Quality and Productivity on Object-Oriented Systems, Technical Report CS-TR-3395, University of Maryland, 1995, p. 16 (1995)

12. Motelet, O.: Enabling the Reuse of Learning Material in the Classroom. PhD Thesis (2004) HYPERLINK http://www.dcc.uchile.cl/ omotelet/papers/Thesis_Proposal_Motelet_ 2004,pdf

13. Najjar, J., Klerkx, J., Vuorikari, R., Duval, E.: Finding Appropriate Learning Objects: An Empirical Evaluation. In: Rauber, A., Christodoulakis, S., Tjoa, A.M. (eds.) ECDL 2005. LNCS, vol. 3652, pp. 323–335. Springer, Heidelberg (2005)

14. Nielsen, J.: Usability engineering at a discount. In: Salvendy, G., Smith, M.J. (eds.) Designing and Using Human-Computer Interfaces and Knowledge Based Systems, pp. 394–401. Elsevier Science Publishers, Amsterdam (1989)

15. Nielsen, J.: Quantitative Studies: How Many Users to Test? Alertbox, June 26, 2006, HYPERLINK http://www.useit.com/alertbox/quantitative_testing.html

16. Ochoa, X., Duval, E.: Use of contextualized attention metadata for ranking and recommending learning objects. In: Proceedings of the 1st international workshop on Contextualized attention metadata, Arlington, Virginia, USA, pp. 9–16 (2006)

17. ProLearn Network of Excellence on professional learning, HYPERLINK, http://www.prolearn-eu.org/

18. Reload Editor. HYPERLINK, http://www.reload.ac.uk/editor.html

19. Robson, R.: Context and the Role of Standards in Increasing the Value of Learning Objects. In: Online Education Using Learning Objects edited by R. McGreal, University of Athabasca,

20. Shivakumar, N., Garcia-Molina, H.: SCAM: A Copy Detection Mechanism for Digital Documents. In: Proceedings of the Second Annual Conference on the Theory and Practice of Digital Libraries, Austin, Texas, USA, June 11-13, 1995, pp. 11–13 (1995)

21. Shrout, P.E., Fleiss, J.L.: Intraclass Correlations: Uses in Assessing Rater Reliability. Psychological Bulletin (2), 420–428 (1979)

22. Khor, S.M., Leonard, A.: Installing and Using the Office 2003 Primary Interop Assemblies, Microsoft Office 2003 Technical Articles (2005)

23. Slide Executive - The PowerPoint Presentation Management Library HYPERLINK, http://www.slideexecutive.com/

24. Ternier, S., Duval, E.: 'Web services for the ARIADNE knowledge pool system. In: Duval, E. (ed.) Proceedings of the 3rd Annual ARIADNE Conference, pp. 1–9 (2003)

25. Vasont Systems, Vasont reuse case study (2007), http://www.vasont.com/vasont/literature/ contentreuse.asp

26. Verbert, K., Jovanovic, J., Gašević, D., Duval, E.: Repurposing Learning Object Components. In: Meersman, R., Tari, Z. (eds.) On the Move to Meaningful Internet Systems 2005: CoopIS, DOA, and ODBASE. LNCS, vol. 3760, pp. 1169–1178. Springer, Heidelberg (2005)

27. Visual Studio Tools for Office, HYPERLINK, http://msdn2.microsoft.com/en-us/library/ d2tx7z6d.aspx

28. Wiley, D.A.: Learning Objects: Difficulties and Opportunities (2003), http://wiley.ed.usu.edu/ docs/ lo_do.pdf

Community Tools for Repurposing Learning Objects

Chu Wang[2], Kate Dickens[1], Hugh C Davis[2], and Gary Wills[2]

[1] eLanguages, University of Southampton, UK
kate.dickens@soton.ac.uk
[2] School of Electronics and Computer Science, University of Southampton, UK
{cw2,hcd,gbw}@ecs.soton.ac.uk

Abstract. A critical success factor for the reuse of learning objects is the ease by which they may be repurposed in order to enable reusability in a different teaching context from which they were originally designed. The current generation of tools for creating, storing, describing and locating learning objects are best suited for users with technical expertise. Such tools are an obstacle to teachers who might wish to perform alterations to learning objects in order to make them suitable for their context. In this paper we describe a simple set of tools to enable practitioners to adapt the content of existing learning objects and to store and modify metadata describing the intended teaching context of these learning objects. We are deploying and evaluating these tools within the UK language teaching community.

Keywords: Learning objects, Community of Practice, repurposing, Wiki, contextual metadata.

1 Introduction

Widespread web-based learning has drawn educators' attentions to the concept of learning objects. Polsani [1] has defined a learning object as *"an independent and self-standing unit of learning content that is predisposed to reuse in multiple instructional contexts"*. This definition suggests several functional requirements which are essential for creating sensible learning objects. For example [1]:

- Accessibility (tagging with metadata so that it can be stored and referenced in a database);
- Reusability (functioning in different instructional contexts);
- Interoperability (should be independent of both the delivery media and knowledge management systems).

Of particular importance is sharing and reusing e-learning materials, which may lead to an improvement in the quality of teaching; the sharing of good practice; greater consistency and an enhanced sense of community [2]. Despite the various forms a learning object might take, digital or non-digital, in the scope of this paper we aim at tackling learning objects with HTML format. The community that we work with consists of language teachers and instructors who engage in producing pedagogically sound online learning objects but have limited technical expertise. In

E. Duval, R. Klamma, and M. Wolpers (Eds.): EC-TEL 2007, LNCS 4753, pp. 378–392, 2007.

this community, reusing online learning materials in different instructional contexts is a very common practice: it is traditional practitioners' experience in adapting teaching materials to suit different student groups.

When learning objects are reused in different educational scenarios, their context related information often changes. These contexts represent information about the intended target audience, the purpose of the teaching, instructional methods, pedagogic approach being used and so on. For example, teachers might take an existing learning object targeted at teaching nursing students study skills, to produce a different version of the same material targeted at engineering students; or teachers can constrain the size of certain materials to be viewed on different devices such as PDAs or mobile phones. With the change of context, learning objects have to be repurposed, generally, in terms of both their content and the metadata describing the nature of the learning objects. Metadata facilitates the identification, search and retrieval of learning objects and can be extended to represent different instructional contexts. IMS/GLC[1] has provided specifications and guidelines for metadata standards and extension rules. However, standard metadata is not sufficient to identify particular learning objects in our domain. Hence, extra context-rich metadata [3], in other words contextual metadata, plays an important role in promoting the reusability of a learning resource. Here context has been defined as "*A set of circumstances in which a learning object is used or may be used*" [4]. Particularly the context refers to the teaching and learning circumstances. Learning objects with such information attached are able to be identified by their context and then repurposed to suit different needs.

Inevitably challenges exist while reusing learning objects in differing contexts [5] especially in relation to issues about extensions on relevant standards, exchange formats for the contextualization of resources, and the creation of tools for development of contextualized learning resources. In particular, our community practitioners indicate that they find it problematic to repurpose learning objects in terms of both content and metadata. Current available tools such as Macromedia Dreamweaver™ could be used to edit learning object content; unfortunately, non-technical practitioners find this software complex and therefore difficult to use without proper training. Besides it is only available to licensed users and this means that not every practitioner has access to it. An open source tool, RELOAD[2], which was designed for editing learning object metadata and content packaging, has been used by community members. However, it is not particularly user-friendly, especially for users with limited technical capabilities. Such users often find it frustrating to use. Therefore a need has been identified for an easy-to-use and accessible tool. It is the authors' intention to address such a need by designing a novel toolkit to use with an existing repository of language learning objects in HTML format, and to test with an established Community of Practice.

The remainder of this paper is organized as follows: In section 2, we review issues of the contextual metadata and related work. Section 3 outlines the proposed toolkit with which users can repurpose learning content and metadata and discover relevant objects. In section 4 we illustrate how we developed an innovative Wiki-type editor for content repurposing; while section 5 and section 6 describe a metadata facilitator

---

[1] http://www.imsglobal.org/
[2] http://www.reload.ac.uk

in aiding users to modify learning object metadata easily, and a tool to help in the discovery of relevant learning objects to be repurposed. Section 7 reports the feedback from an initial evaluation. Finally the authors conclude the paper and explain the ongoing work in the project.

2 Contextual Metadata and Related Works

The last few years have seen a debate arise between the approaches to designing learning objects in contextualized and "de-contextualized" scenarios [4, 6, 7]. Some resources need to be designed to be context-neutral in order that learners from any subject area can easily engage with them. On the other hand, the contextualization of a learning object is beneficial to the learners, as the learning object can then be seen as more relevant to the subject being studied [6]. Learning objects are widely developed as free from the context of teaching and learning to facilitate interoperability, despite evidence that shows this to be contrary to teachers' needs (as from our community experience). It is our view that context is becoming increasingly important with the advent of IMS Learning Design and the use of other ontologies. We decided to extend the standard metadata with a set of contextualized metadata since the constrained taxonomy from international standards is not sufficient or accurate enough to describe our instructional context. Brooks and McCalla [8] has proposed an inspiring *ecological approach* to capture a larger set of end-use information as metadata in order to overcome the rigidities of standard approaches and assist software agents carry out automatic processing. Their work helped us form a better view of defining and collecting valuable contextual metadata, however we would still adopt standards by mapping our contextual metadata to LOM[3] to retain the interoperability of the learning objects amongst repositories.

Research carried out within the eLanguages group at Southampton[4] found that contextual metadata facilitates greater scope for reuse, and this was verified by tests conducted with our teacher/instructor communities. Indeed we are not alone, as several other projects have investigated the issues related to the application of contextualized metadata. For example, the RAFT project discovered that for mobile learning to be effective, standards and exchange formats need to be extended to include contextual data [5]. Providing subject specific information is another valuable usage for contextual metadata. One way to add context to learning objects, without limiting their usability and reusability, is by assigning metadata relevant to specific communities of practice. We discovered that it helps teachers to identify learning objects more effectively by attaching language specific metadata so that they can find the right learning material to reuse. Similar work has been carried out by the DocSouth digital library in considering the biographical and geographic metadata requirements of teachers [9]. Recent work has been undertaken to produce a repository query language, ProLearn Query Language (PLQL)[5]. The addition of a keyword-based search mechanism to extract learning objects that best match informal descriptions, would suit repositories that enable rich annotation of learning objects.

---

[3] http://ltsc.ieee.org/wg12/files/LOM_1484_12_1_v1_Final_Draft.pdf
[4] http://www.elanguages.ac.uk/research
[5] http://ariadne.cs.kuleuven.be/lomi/index.php/QueryLanguages

Such repositories can treat contextual metadata as informal descriptions, and including this information when preforming searches would enhance resource discovery. Our work draws on the experiences gained in these projects.

In the eLanguages L_2O project [3], Reusable Learning Objects (RLOs) contain extensions to UK LOM CORE[6] Metadata standards that directly address the needs of the Modern Languages Teaching Community of Practice. The learning objects are assembled in a content package with their associated pedagogic and technical assets and relevant metadata. The contextual metadata includes points of pedagogic information to guide a user, such as the "description for learners", "suggestions for further use" or "language specifics". Reuse is greatly enabled through this additional metadata, which describes the pedagogic nature of the learning objects.

3 Toolkit Overview

The MURLLO (Management, Use and Repurposing of Language Learning Objects) [10] project aims to tackle concerns surrounding the effective repurposing of RLOs. We have proposed a system with three components/tools to deal with these concerns in our community (as shown in Fig. 1):

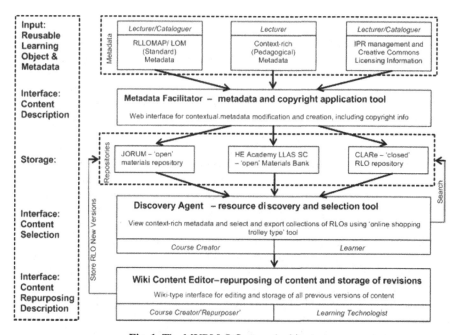

Fig. 1. The MURLLO System Architecture

- **The Wiki-Type Content Editor** allows repurposing of content, without the need for extra editing tools, and the storage of this content and its revisions.

---

[6] http://zope.cetis.ac.uk/profiles/uklomcore

- **The Metadata Facilitator** acts as an interface to allow a teacher-friendly application of customized context-rich metadata to RLOs and facilitates storage of resultant content packages in open and closed repositories.
- **The Discovery Agent** facilitates resource discovery by displaying contextual metadata and by allowing selection and export of collections of RLOs.

Learning objects produced in the community of language teachers with whom we are working are written in HTML, which appear as web pages. The Wiki style editor is a critical component which enables a non-technical user to adapt this type of learning objects. It directly affects how well users can achieve their repurposing targets. We will focus on the Wiki-type tool in this paper.

4   The Wiki-Type Content Editor

As pointed out in [11], the ease of collaboration in a Wiki can make it a powerful tool for project management and collaborative writing. In our case, the Wiki-type editing tool would provide the necessary facility to adapt and repurpose learning objects. First of all, the motivation for such a tool has been identified and is explained here.

4.1   The Need for Wiki Editing

There is research [6, 12] which focuses on design patterns or best practice for learning objects intended for reuse in other contexts. However, we have a different perspective in terms of reuse. The previous L_2O project has shown that it is easy to reuse pedagogic assets such as stand-alone audio files. However, it might be difficult for a non-technical educator to adapt HTML content within online learning objects for different target audiences. The need for an easy-to-use editing tool has been stressed many times by our community of users.

Our community comprises practitioners from four regional universities in UK Higher Education (HE) sector. They are mostly language teachers but also some learning technologists and researchers. Most of the practitioners did not have any previous experience of creating learning objects, and even though they have started to share and adapt learning materials stored in the community repository in L_2O, they still need technical support because of their limited knowledge of web related technologies. Therefore, demands for a tool to support the adaptation of online learning objects according to instructional contexts have emerged. This fits in with traditional practitioners' experience as previously mentioned (this finding was also supported by the attendees of an extended workshop[7]).

Furthermore, the concept of collaborative development of learning objects in the sense that different types of experts may need to cooperate to author or adapt an object has been suggested [1]. These experts can be programmers, graphic designers and subject experts/teachers. Similarly we discovered that, in a collaborative online environment, expertise can be shared, exchanged and viewed by the community in order to achieve adapting and editing goals. With these views in mind, a Wiki, a type

---

[7] e-Learning conference, http://www.llas.ac.uk/events/llaseventarchiveitem.aspx?resourceid= 2654#day2

of Web server that allows any reader of its pages to edit those pages, or create new ones using simple web forms [13], can provide an ideal collaborative editing environment. Meanwhile keeping different versions of adapted learning objects can help the community to track and view changes if needed. To rectify the current lack of relevant tools, the MURLLO project has proposed a Wiki-type editor to fill the gap. The requirements from the user community for such an editor are outlined in the next section.

4.2 The Wiki-Type Editor Requirements

A learning object produced within our Community of Practice usually comprises one or more HTML files defining the content; media files to be referred to by the HTML files; a set of metadata in XML format which needs to be attached to the learning object in order to comply with relevant learning object standards (IMS, IEEE LOM), together with corresponding schema definition files. All of these content resources are assembled in one package. Considering the structure of this type of package and the technical compentency of our user community, a Wiki-type editor specifically for adapting learning objects would require the following features:

- A WYSIWYG content editing environment suitable for non-technical users, as it is easy to use and has powerful formatting capabilities so that users do not need to worry about the underlying HTML syntax;
- A versioning system that creates a new version after a learning object is modified and stores all previous versions of learning objects;
- Viewing and rollback of earlier versions so that a version can be reverted if necessary;
- An edit summary showing the nature of the changes, to be used as a metadata field defining the relationships between different versions of the same learning object;
- The ability to handle embedded media objects and allow relatively easy editing of these components;
- An importing facility which allows users to upload learning objects (preferably as a content package) from local computers or external sources; and an exporting function by which users can select and download repurposed learning objects to local computers or external sources; these facilities will be linked with the metadata facilitator and discovery agent at a later stage.

4.3 The Design Choice for the Wiki-Type Editor

According to the requirements listed above, it was a natural inclination for our team to consider using or adapting an existing Wiki system as the learning object editor. In order to choose the most appropriate solution, we looked into a number of different Wiki environments, including Mediawiki, DokuWiki, Zwiki and many more; a Document Management System (DMS), TWiki; and Content Management Systems (CMSs), Silva and Plone. We compared some of the important features including user friendly WYSIWYG toolbars, versioning capability, and their ability to handle embedded media.

Although quite a few of them seemed to partially match with the above criteria, we were confronted with difficulties when importing the existing learning objects into the Wiki systems. The learning object content are basically web pages which are composed of standard HTML markup (with links to images, multimedia and embedded Shockwave Flash™ objects), whereas Wikis are created using their own markup language which is totally different from HTML. Therefore a learning object always needs to be converted into the format used by the Wiki before it can be used in the Wiki editor. It would also still need to be converted back to HTML before the learning object could be exported from the system. The underlying problem was that the "round-trip" conversion between HTML and Wiki markups causes a loss of information from the HTML web pages, especially embedded object tags and snippets defining page styles. For DMS/CMS (with built-in HTML editors), it was not necessary to convert between Wiki and HTML but the style information or embedded object tags did not display properly. If this information is not retained, both look-and-feel and functionality is affected. This would have a serious impact on users since they would be unable to repurpose materials if they could not see how the original learning objects had appeared. Furthermore, there were some other critical problems such as the lack of package importing functions for most Wikis and the unsuitable versioning facilities for the CMS systems.

As none of the above tools particularly fitted our requirements, we came to the conclusion that it would be more efficient to design our own system by integrating an HTML editor and to develop other essential functions like versioning and import/export facilities around it. The implementation of this solution is presented in the following section.

4.4   The Wiki-Type Editor Implementation and Usage

We decided to use a lightweight but powerful HTML editor, FCKeditor[8], to integrate a *Wiki-type* online editing workspace for our community. We labelled it "Wiki-type", since we have replicated a Wiki's collaborative authoring characteristics around a regular HTML editor. It is intended for peer-editing of existing learning objects but is not a "Wiki" in the more general sense of the term. As it was designed for teachers who have no web expertise, we have made the interface as intuitive as possible. The choice of HTML editor made the implementation process relatively smooth and with certain customisations it was turned into an effective editing tool for learning objects. A learning object can be uploaded as a standard IMS content package, and then the system handles de-packaging which separates the learning object content from metadata and other documents. The only step users need to take is to locate the learning object from an index page and click the title link which will lead to the learning object being displayed in their browser. The look-and-feel of a learning object is kept consistent even in the editing mode so that novice users can edit it without being confused by the underlying HTML syntax and can also edit the content as it appears to their students.

There are three possible types/levels of modifications a typical user might make to a learning object:

---

[8] http://www.fckeditor.net/

- Minor corrections which would not generally affect/change the nature of learning objects, including spelling, grammar, re-organization of sentences and so on. In this case, the metadata does not usually require amendments.
- More substantial modifications in terms of pedagogical design, which result in the possible re-ordering of content, alteration of activities or wording. In this case the relevant metadata would probably need to be modified accordingly.
- Complete repurposing of a learning object to be used in a very different instructional context, with dramatic changes in content, order, or style. For example, a new object might be made based on the template of an existing learning object but the theme and content diverge from the original. In this case, the learning object undergoes major changes and some or all of the metadata must be modified.

According to the above types of modifications, one issue in the development process was to decide whether to make new versions for each minor/major modification, or only associate each major change (changes affecting pedagogical design) with a new version. After careful consideration, the decision was made that versions should always be kept rather than overwriting existing copies no matter how many changes had been made. As some modifications to original learning objects could be controversial or subjective and may only reflect personal opinions, it is wise to keep a full version history with rollback facility, so that a faulty change can be reversed. Another decision we made was to consider versioning learning objects as whole packages, containing web pages, media attachments and metadata, not as in traditional Wikis, where versions are handled at page level (single document). Hence package level versioning was adopted to accommodate the nature of learning objects and to allow future extension on the toolkit to edit not only content but also metadata and other attachments in content packages. In this way, the learning objects are always treated as self-contained units of standard content packages. A user imports learning objects as stand-alone packages and similarly a package is generated automatically when a user creates a new version or exports an object. The packaging and disassembling are carried out behind the scenes so non-technical users do not need to get involved in the process.

The figures below show some scenarios using the Wiki-type editor. Fig. 2 and Fig. 3 show the same learning object in viewing mode (original look) and in editing mode. They look almost identical apart from the user-activated feedback mechanism (*Show answer/Hide answer* link in Fig. 2 and 3 below), which is expanded in the editing mode so that a user can easily change the text in the answer panel. A user can also make more complicated changes using the formatting toolbar near the top of the browser: from editing an image, adding a new multiple choice question, replacing an existing linked document with an updated version, to adding a new learning activity.

Scenario 1, illustrated by the figures below, presents that a learning object in the English language (Fig. 4) has been repurposed to be used by German students (see Fig. 5). Therefore they have the exact same content and subject but are represented in different languages in order to target different student groups. It can be easily adapted in the Wiki-type editor by simply replacing the English text with the equivalent German. Fig. 5 also shows how the text in the "Select your answer" box can be replaced straightforwardly by using the selection field toolbar.

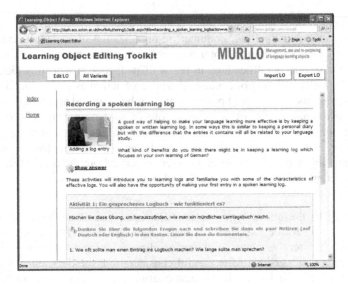

Fig. 2. A learning object in viewing mode

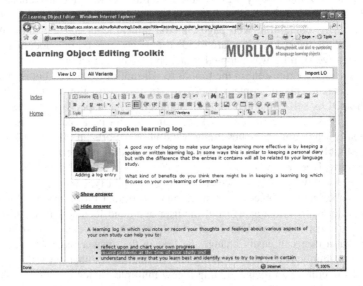

Fig. 3. A learning object in editing mode

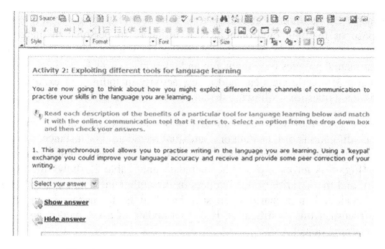

Fig. 4. A snapshot of learning object (English version)

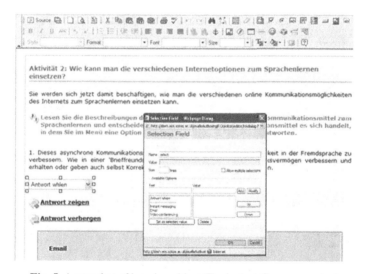

Fig. 5. A snapshot of learning object (Equivalent German version)

5   Metadata Facilitator

Repurposing learning objects not only requires content editing but also necessitates relevant modifications of metadata or contextual metadata in many cases. In the previous section, an example of repurposing a learning object was to switch the presentational language of the learning object from English to German (scenario 1). There can be many different ways of adapting learning objects using the editing tool. Here are some other possibilities:

- Scenario 2: practitioners can adapt aspects of learning objects to suit a particular purpose or learning environment. For instance, to personalize materials (e.g. images) for use in a particular course or institution, or to reflect different departmental policies on referencing and citation.
- Scenario 3: practitioners can add a new activity including, for example, a set of assessment questions following the current template and style.

Our experience indicates that both adaptations in scenario 1 and 2 would require relevant modifications of metadata or contextual metadata. For instance, in scenario 1 the metadata related to description, language and targeted audience need to be changed (Fig. 6 is an excerpt of the metadata and Table 1. shows the changes in metadata); and the description for learners or the author information would probably need to be altered in scenario 2. In scenario 3, it is not necessary to amend the metadata record if this modification is just an update of assessment questions in the existing learning object.

Title:	Im internet sprachen lernen (LO)
Native Language:	German/Deutsch
Description:	This German language resource reviews online communication tools for language learning, and includes links to different web-based communication tools for different languages.
Keywords:	Internet; language learning; online communication; German
Topic:	Using web-based communication tools for target language practice in written or spoken communication, and in asynchronous or synchronous mode.
Authors/Creators:	Watson, J. and Laxton, J.
Pedagogic Type:	Activity-based
Completion time:	20 mins
Task Purpose:	To explore the uses of different online communication tools for language learning.
Description for Learner:	In these activities you will consider different ways in which the internet can be exploited for language learning purposes and identify some useful web-based resources that allow you to practise your communication skills in the language that you are studying.
Language of Task Instructions:	German/Deutsch
Subject or Skill Area(s):	Language learning skills
Copyright Holder:	eLanguages, University of Southampton
Technical Assets:	None
Pedagogical Assets:	None
Associated Scaffolding:	Comment, answers, glossary, weblinks
Level of Task	Intermediate

Fig. 6. An excerpt of the metadata for the German version

According to our community experience, adding or changing metadata can be extremely difficult for non-technical users without the support of proper tools. The best available open source tool, RELOAD, is not particularly easy to use as the language teachers in our community found; moreover the metadata descriptions in RELOAD make use of LOM standard terms which might not be readily understandable by many teachers. These factors have contributed to the design of a metadata facilitator which is intuitive and accessible for language teachers. A web-form based metadata editing system is well suited in this case, in which certain LOM metadata fields are renamed with varied teacher-friendly terms along with optional hints for more detailed explanations so that it is more intuitive to use. In addition, the contextual metadata will be added or edited through the metadata facilitator as well, and this could be language teaching related information, such as "language specifics", "subject areas" and so on. Furthermore, the metadata facilitator will be integrated with the Wiki-type content editor so that both content and metadata can be modified from a single interface at the same time. A mechanism to allow users to create a standard content package from the repurposed materials and metadata has also been designed, which facilitates content packaging in the same system.

Since most practitioners are not experienced in using and attaching metadata, more features within the design have been provided to help them with the process. Firstly, a practitioner will be prompted to modify relevant metadata before a new version of learning object is saved; and he/she can get automated hints and suggestions while editing relevant metadata based on aspects of adaptation to the content. Meanwhile, the relationship between two revisions of the same learning object will be captured according to a user's selection. This relationship will be automatically recorded as a metadata field, for instance, a new revision *is based on* an earlier revision.

Table 1. Changes in metadata fields

metadata	**English Version**	**German Version**
Title	Using the internet for language learning	Im internet sprachen lernen
Native language	British English	German/Deutsch
Description	This English language resource reviews online communication tools for language learning and includes links to different web-based communication tools for different languages	This German language resource reviews online communication tools for language learning, and includes links to different web-based communication tools for different languages.
keywords	Internet, language, learning, online, communication, English	Internet; language learning; online communication; German
Authors/creators	Watson, Julie	Watson, J. and Laxton, J.

6 Discovery Agent

With the aim of further supporting our community practitioners in terms of sharing and reusing learning objects, a tool to assist the discovery and selection of relevant objects is being developed. Practitioners can use this discovery agent interface to search across different repositories holding collections of learning objects. The search will be based on the metadata fields such as title, description and keywords. Specifically the wealth of pedagogical and contextual metadata attached to the learning objects can offer great benefits to practitioners who want to find certain types of objects according to their learning and teaching context. Moreover this tool will use an "online shopping trolley" metaphor for the selection and export of the RLOs. From a list of searching results, practitioners can select one or more relevant RLOs and add them to the learning object "trolley". The learning objects in the "trolley" can be viewed as practitioners wish and those RLOs can be removed from the "trolley" at any time. The RLOs can be checked out which means they are to be exported, possibly to the Wiki-type editor so that they can be repurposed.

7 User Evaluation

In order to check and validate whether the Wiki-type editing tool is appropriate and useful for teachers, we undertook a qualitative evaluation during a workshop given to language teachers and learning technologists from within the UK. The workshop once again highlighted the strong desire from practitioners to share online learning materials, whilst the lack of skills and the need for supporting tools to develop and repurpose learning objects.

80% of the attendees were teachers who did not have much experience producing online learning materials or using a Wiki. They were asked to explore and use the tool to adapt a collection of existing learning objects. They were given a free choice as to the method they employed in order to evaluate the usability and effectiveness of the tool. Twenty one questionnaires were returned at the end of the session and during the session the development team observed the way the attendees interacted with the system. The general observation made was that most users managed to edit learning objects within a few minutes. They showed a great deal of enthusiasm towards the Wiki-type editor and were very keen to find out the possible modifications they could make to the learning objects. The observations provided valuable input for further improvements of the functionality of the editor.

The feedback we received from the questionnaires was positive. Some comments from the users are quoted here:

"...very easy to use and very effective..."
"...a good start, it could be more useful when more work has been done on it".
"...combines features of Dreamweaver, Word with Wiki tools. Nicely crafted tool with obvious utility".

The analysis shows 86% of the users had a very good impression of the tool; 90% of them found it easy to navigate and obtain the information they wanted; 75% regarded it an effective tool for adapting learning objects; and 70% considered it easy to become familiar with the tool. This indicated the editing tool is useful in repurposing learning objects and has the potential to be adopted in the current community. Many of the users can see how this tool could be used beyond its original scope. For example by including templates we could allow users to develop new and innovative learning objects from complicated components, something many find hard to do today.

8 Conclusion and Ongoing Work

Reuse and repurposing of learning objects has been much discussed but little practiced. Within the UK language teaching community there is a willingness and intent to reuse materials but the practitioners have identified their lack of technical expertise as a critical barrier. They have expressed their need for simple to use community tools. Furthermore, this trend can be observed throughout the World Wide Web where social and community approaches are embracing a whole new generation of computer users.

In this paper we have described our efforts to encourage and facilitate the reuse and repurposing of online learning objects within a Community of Practice by users with little technical expertise. The tools we created aim at this specific community to help discover, share and reuse HTML based learning objects. We have reasoned why a Wiki-type editing system could help such a community to adapt learning objects collaboratively via the Internet. We have explained the rationale for the design of an editing tool which reproduced the collaborative editing mechanisms of traditional Wikis for use by the community. The integration of a mature HTML editor has proved to be very effective in the case of adapting online learning materials for non-specialist users. The tool has been evaluated and received positive reactions within a group of community members.

We identified from our earlier work that the addition of extended forms of contextual metadata attached to the learning materials would provide a wealth of new information with which to enhance the discovery and reusability of learning objects. But adding or modifying metadata could be very difficult for non-technical users without support. This leads to the metadata facilitator being developed which will bridge this gap. Finally we are building a discovery agent to facilitate resource discovery and selection. Ultimately all three tools will be integrated to form a single toolkit to help the management and reuse of learning objects.

References

1. Polsani, P.R.: Use and Abuse of Reusable Learning Objects. Journal of Digital Information 3(4) Article No. 164 (2003)
2. Barker, E., James, H., Knight, G.: Long-Term Retention and Reuse of E-Learning Objects and Materials. Report commissioned by the JISC (2004)
3. JISC funded project Sharing Language Learning Objects (L$_2$O). Available at, http://www.elanguages.ac.uk/sharing
4. Johnston, P.: It's all in the context. eFoundations metadata, middleware, e-learning (2006) Last accessed February 23, 2007, http://efoundations.typepad.com/efoundations/2006/12/its_all_in_the_.html
5. Specht, M., Kravcik, M.: Authoring of learning objects in context. International Journal on E-Learning 5, 25–33 (2006)
6. Jones, R.: Designing Adaptable Learning Resources with Learning Object Patterns. Journal of Digital Information 6(1) Article No. 305 (2004)
7. Jeffery, A.: Context, metadata and e-learning: a literature review. Project report (2006) Last accessed February 23, 2007 http://dash.ecs.soton.ac.uk/dokuwiki/doku.php?id=documents:context_metadata_and_e-learning_a_literature_review
8. Brooks, C., McCalla, G.: Towards flexible learning object metadata. International Journal of Continuing Engineering Education and Lifelong Learning 16(1/2) (2006)

9. Pattuelli, M.C.: Context for content: Shaping learning objects and modeling a domain ontology. In: Blandford, A., Gow, J. (eds.) Digital Libraries in the Context of Users' Broader Activities. First International Workshop, DL-Cuba 2006, Chapel Hill, NC USA, DL-Cuba (2006)
10. Eduserv funded project MURLLO. Available at http://www.elanguages.ac.uk/murllo/
11. Wei, C., Maust, B., Barrick, J., Cuddihy, E., Spyridakis, J.H.: Wikis for Supporting Distributed Collaborative Writing. In: Wei, C., Maust, B., Barrick, J., Cuddihy, E., Spyridakis, J. (eds.) The Proceedings of the Society for Technical Communication 52nd Annual Conference, Seattle, WA, May 8-11 (2005)
12. Kravcik, M., Specht, M.: Authoring Adaptive Courses – ALE Approach. Advanced Technology for Learning 1(4), 215–220 (2004)
13. Leuf, B., Cunningham, W.: The Wiki way, quick collaboration on the Web. Addison-Wesley, Boston (2001)

Building Domain Ontologies from Text for Educational Purposes

Amal Zouaq[1], Roger Nkambou[2], and Claude Frasson[1]

[1] University of Montreal, CP 6128, Succ. Centre-Ville, Montreal, QC, H3C3J7
[2] UQAM, CP 8888, Succ. Centre-Ville, Montreal, QC, H3C3P8
{zouaq,frasson}@iro.umontreal.ca
nkambou.roger@uqam.ca

Abstract. In this paper, we present a (semi) automatic framework that aims to produce a domain concept map (DCM) from text and to derive a domain ontology from this concept map. This methodology targets particularly the educational field because of the need of such structures (Ontologies and CM) within the e-Learning and AIED communities to sustain the production of e-Learning resources tailored to learner's needs. This paper details the steps that transform textual resources (and particularly textual learning objects) into a domain concept map and explains how this abstract structure is transformed into a more formal domain ontology. The paper also shows how these structures make it possible to bridge the gap between e-learning standard learning objects and Intelligent Tutoring Systems.

Keywords: Knowledge extraction from text, domain ontology, domain concept map, e-Learning, Intelligent Tutoring Systems.

1 Introduction

The importance of automatic methods for enriching knowledge bases from free text is acknowledged within knowledge management and ontology communities. In fact, static knowledge bases are hard-to-maintain, time-consuming and expensive. This is especially true in the domain of online training. Learning object repositories represent rather static repositories and suffer from various shortcomings:

- First, learning objects are represented as "black-boxes". Metadata such as SCORM or LOM are used to describe various characteristics of the learning objects but do not model their inner content;
- Second, they suffer from their lack of adaptability to a learner model;
- Third, they do not obey to a computer-understandable pedagogical framework;
- Finally, they are restricted to the e-Learning community whereas they should offer a base for various kinds of training systems, such as intelligent tutoring systems.

In fact, there should be gains from integration and cooperation between the e-Learning and Intelligent Tutoring System (ITS) communities [3]. On one hand, eLearning-based environments focus on the reusability of learning resources, but they

E. Duval, R. Klamma, and M. Wolpers (Eds.): EC-TEL 2007, LNCS 4753, pp. 393–407, 2007.
© Springer-Verlag Berlin Heidelberg 2007

are not adaptable to suit learner needs, they do not really use instructional strategies and they do not have a rich knowledge representation. On the other hand, ITSs exploit rich knowledge structures, provide adaptive feedback and implement pedagogical strategies. However, their knowledge base is generally not reusable because it suffers from its dependence to the application domain and from proprietary programming. If we think about learning objects as resources to dynamically build an ITS Knowledge base, then it should be possible to benefit from both worlds.

We postulate that most conceptual and terminological domain structures are described in documents. Thus applying ontology generation from text seems to be an interesting issue. Creating ontology-based metadata that are both understandable by humans and machines is the vision of the Semantic Web and semantic languages, like RDF and OWL, allow to express semantic annotations in a standard way.

The paper is organized as follows: Firstly, we present the Knowledge Puzzle's philosophical foundations and provide some definitions. Secondly, we describe the (semi) automatic knowledge acquisition from text and the domain concept maps and ontology generation. Thirdly, we underline the interest of the approach to the educational community by explaining how the knowledge base can be used to generate Learning Knowledge Objects. Fourthly, we present a set of related works. Finally, an evaluation of various results is explained before a conclusion.

2   The Knowledge Puzzle Approach: Foundations

The semantic web vision relies on domain ontologies to describe web content and make it understandable by software agents. As such, the semantic web can be compared to a huge expert system knowledge base. Computer-based education and particularly e-Learning has realized the importance of this vision to sustain the production of reusable learning objects [8, 11]. In Intelligent Tutoring Systems, domain ontologies' importance has also grown and they are useful for modeling the expert and learner modules [25]. In general, new generation of robust ontology engineering environments such as Protégé [21] has fostered the creation of ontologies.

In such a context, the use of domain ontologies as a bridge between the e-Learning community and AIED and ITS communities appears as an interesting potential solution to a number of issues concerning domain knowledge acquisition and dissemination in computer-based education. These issues can be divided into content-related issues and competence and pedagogy related issues.

2.1   Content-Related Issues

There is a need of richer knowledge representations, concretized by ontology languages, to reflect learning object content [11]. We believe that concept maps represent an interesting and expressive knowledge model able to represent this content. Moreover, concept maps can be used to produce more formal domain ontologies through text mining and natural language processing. Both ITS and e-Learning systems can benefit from such formal representations.

2.2 Competence and Pedagogy Related Issues

The lack of adaptability to individual learners is one of the main shortcomings of traditional e-Learning approaches [22]. Better adaptability and suitability to a learner model should be adopted. A competence-based approach that exploits domain concept maps and ontologies allows the presentation of training sessions adapted to particular needs [30]. Ullrich [27] underlined that the pedagogical framework of learning objects is implicit and is left to the human expert, thus reducing the possibility to dynamically compose interesting resources. Therefore, an explicit representation of the instructional framework should be adopted to enhance reuse.

2.3 Some Definitions

This paper describes a semi-automatic methodology for building domain ontologies from concept maps generated through natural language processing. One of the specificities of the Knowledge Puzzle's approach lies in the use of intermediate knowledge models (concept maps) due to the dedication of this ontology to training.

Domain Ontology refers to a specific vocabulary used to describe a certain reality. It presupposes the identification of the *key concepts* and *relationships* in the domain of interest.

A *concept map* represents a semantic network showing the domain entities and their relationships. As such, it constitutes a skeleton on which to build more complete domain ontologies.

Human validation is essential at each step of the knowledge acquisition process. The design of a domain Ontology is not a linear process, it involves many revisions before a final consensual solution is developed. Moreover, because the Knowledge Puzzle Platform is designed with the final aim of training, it is very important to validate the results obtained at each step of the mining process. A human should confirm and complete the results to guarantee the quality of the ontology.

Figure1 shows the domain knowledge acquisition process.

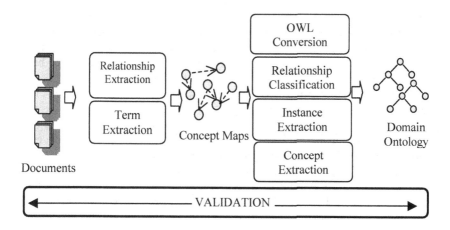

Fig. 1. The Domain Knowledge Acquisition Process

3   Domain Knowledge Acquisition in the Knowledge Puzzle

In computer-based education and particularly in intelligent tutoring systems, the domain knowledge is defined as the representation of the expert's knowledge. Domain knowledge is usually divided into two components: declarative and procedural. The Knowledge Puzzle focuses on mining declarative knowledge for the moment. It relies on natural language processing and machine learning.

The learning process in the Knowledge Puzzle's approach is based on a *syntactic* and *domain-independent* approach. The Knowledge Puzzle instantiates a set of extraction rules from a set of generic domain independent templates. Contrary to many ontology learning approaches, it does not guide this extraction and it does not rely on a supervised method that guides the learning process.

As shown in figure 1, the domain knowledge acquisition process relies on a number of steps: term extraction, relationship extraction, concept extraction, instance extraction, relationship classification and OWL conversion.

3.1   Terminological Extraction

Terminology extraction refers to discovery of terms that are good candidates for the concepts in an ontology. It can be facilitated by the exploitation of learning objects as the primary source of knowledge: learning objects are purely didactic documents, providing definitions and explanations about concepts to be learned. These concepts share the properties of low ambiguity and high specificity, due to their natural engagement in learning.

First, the Knowledge Puzzle needs to determine the content of each document. It works on plain text documents and partitions them into a set of paragraphs, containing a set of sentences. This is performed with annotators developed with the IBM's Unstructured Information Management Architecture (UIMA) [26].

Second, the Knowledge Puzzle uses a machine learning algorithm, Kea-3.0 [10], to extract representative n-grams from documents. We slightly modified the initial algorithm to process one document at a time, instead of working on a collection of documents. The extracted seed key expressions (one or more words) are then used to collect the sentences containing them. A natural language processing parser, *the Stanford Parser* [16], processes these sentences to output typed dependency representations: a set of grammatical relationships describing the links between different words. This process has been described elsewhere [9].

Each sentence is represented as a grammatical concept map, i.e. a set of terms linked by the Parser's typed dependencies.

We elaborated a set of rules that exploit the grammatical concept maps to retrieve particular predefined patterns. These patterns serve to extract a semantic concept map from the grammatical one (semantic terms + relationships).

In this work, a Pattern is represented by a set of input links and a set of output links. These links are represented by the various grammatical relationships that are output by the Stanford Parser [9]. Once a Pattern is identified, a method is fired to retrieve the semantic structure associated to this pattern. Table 1 shows some of the terminological patterns used to define semantic domain terms. Let t and u be terms:

Table 1. Some Terminology Extraction Patterns

Terminological Pattern	Input Links (t)	Output Links (t)	Method
Pattern 1	-	adjectival modifier (amod) with u as destination.	Create a new concept by aggregating t and u.
Pattern 2	-	noun compound modifier (nn) with u as destination.	Create a new concept by aggregating t and u.

Terminological patterns rely on modifiers such as adjectives or nouns to restrict the meaning of the modified noun, e.g. is-a (intelligent tutoring system, tutoring system). They constitute a very accurate heuristic for learning taxonomic relationships [17].

As an example, Figure 2 depicts a grammatical concept map that describes the different dependencies for the sentence:

"An asset can be described with asset metadata to allow for search and discovery within online repositories thereby enhancing opportunities of reuse."

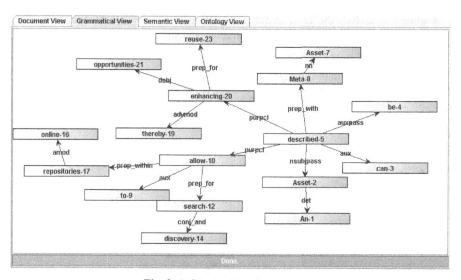

Fig. 2. A Grammatical Concept Map

The terminological extraction patterns allow to define the following domain terms: *Asset, Asset metadata, Opportunities, Reuse, Search, Discovery, Online repositories.* All these terms are candidate terms to express domain concepts.

3.2 Relationship Extraction

Domain terms must be related in some way. Relationship extraction refers to the identification of linguistic relationships among the discovered terms. Central to this extraction are verbs and their auxiliaries, which generally express also a domain knowledge. Again, grammatical pattern structures similar to the ones used in the previous step are exploited to extract relationships of interest. Table 2 shows examples of these Relational Patterns. Let t, u and v be terms:

Table 2. Some Relationship Extraction Patterns

Relational Pattern	Input Links (t)	Output Links(t)	Method
Pattern 1	-	NOMINAL_SUBJECT (nsubj) with u as destination, DIRECT_OBJECT(dobj) with v as destination.	Create a new relationship between u and v labelled with t.
Pattern 2	-	NOMINAL_SUBJECT (nsubj) with u as destination, COPULA (cop) with v as destination.	Create a new relationship between u and t labelled v.
Pattern 3	PURPOSE_ CLAUSE_ MODIFIER (Purpcl) with s as source	DIRECT_OBJECT (dobj) with u as destination	Create a new relationship between the object of v and u labelled with t.

Figure 3 describes the final terms and relationships for the sentence in figure 2. The following verbal relationships are extracted and shown in italic:

- Asset *can be described with* Asset Metadata
- Asset Metadata *to allow for* search
- Asset Metadata *thereby enhancing* opportunities

Other non-verbal relationships are extracted to complete the meaning of the previous tuples:

- Search *and* discovery
- Search *within* online repositories
- Opportunities *for* reuse

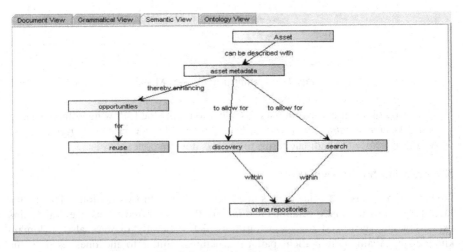

Fig. 3. A Semantic Concept Map

3.3 Domain Concept Maps Generation

The process described above is repeated over all the selected sentences. It is then possible to retrieve a term or a particular relationship and to be automatically directed to the source sentence, to the source paragraph or to the source document. This allows an enhanced retrieval of the appropriate knowledge. Indeed, one problem that faces online training is that there are not appropriate markers in the learning object content to identify relevant passages. For example, if a learning object x requires a prerequisite y, then the system loads the whole object y. This can be appropriate in some situations but not in others: the learner can be overloaded with non-pertinent information. A more fine-grained representation permits a more focused answer and retrieval of relevant document portions.

Each sentence is associated with its main subject (the term *Asset* in the previous example).

In the Knowledge Puzzle, a term is considered as a concept if:

1. It is the main subject of various sentences, thus being a frequent subject in the domain of interest;
2. It is linked to other domain terms through semantic relationships.

It is worth noting that a single concept may be expressed in different ways in the text. The Knowledge Puzzle is able to recognize the base form of a concept through stemming. The Knowledge Puzzle uses a java version of the *Porter Stemmer* [20] to produce the stem associated with each concept. For example, the words "stemmer", "stemming" and "stemmed" have the same root form: "stem". This allows particularly recognizing plural and singular forms. Another way of expressing a concept is through an abbreviation e.g.: Sharable Content Object = SCO. The Stanford Parser outputs abbreviation links as typed dependencies but they are not always correct. So, the Knowledge Puzzle implements an algorithm to identify if an indicated abbreviation is correct and if true, stores the abbreviation as an acronym of the current concept.

For the moment, the Knowledge Puzzle does not handle anaphora resolution and is not able to link two related words, such as reference model and the model in the sentence: "SCORM is a reference model …The model …".

3.4 Domain Ontology Generation

Domain ontology generation consists of instance and attribute extraction, and relationship classification. The domain concept maps constitute the knowledge base for this generation.

As aforementioned, concepts are domain terms that have multiple output semantic relationships. A threshold specifies the number of these relationships. The Knowledge Puzzle uses a linguistic approach to determine attributes, instances and relationship classification.

3.4.1 Instance and Attribute Extraction

Instance extraction enables to find objects that are instances of a particular concept. Hearst [14] was the first to talk about linguistic patterns for identifying hyponyms ("is a kind of"). Particularly, the pattern *"NP1 such as NP2, NP3 and NP4"* indicates a hyponymy relationship.

It seems sometimes a little bit difficult to differentiate linguistic expressions indicating an "instance-of" relationship from expressions indicating a sub-class relationship. Let's suppose that NP1 is a concept. The following rules were established:

- If NP2, NP3, or NP4 are also concepts, then they are considered as sub-classes of NP1.
- Otherwise, if NP2, NP3 and NP4 are not considered as concepts, they are stored as instances of NP1.
- Finally, if NP1 is not a domain concept as previously defined, then we leave the relationships "is a kind of" between these terms and the human evaluator is free to modify it to a sub-class, an instance or whatever.

Table 3 summarizes the Hearst's Patterns included in the Knowledge Puzzle.

Table 3. Lexicon-syntactic Patterns (Adapted from [14])

Lexicon-syntactic Pattern
NP1 such as NP2, NP3…and/or NPn
NP1, … , or/and other NPn
NP1, including NP2,…, or/and NPn
NP1, especially NP2, or/and NPn

As far as attributes are concerned, two kinds of relationships or properties can be extracted: inner and verbal attributes. **Inner Attributes** describe the concept itself. Term attributes can be extracted using contextual information or relies on nominal modifiers as expressing a potential property. **Verbal Relationships** describe the relationship of the concept with other ones. It relies on relational patterns as previously explained.

The Knowledge Puzzle uses the following patterns to extract **concept attributes**:

- *<attr> <C> <verb>* … where C is a concept and attr a modifier. An example of text matching this pattern is: … inline metadata is … where metadata is a concept.
- *<attr> of <C>* (e.g., "identifier of asset") or *<C>'s <attr>* ("asset's identifier").
- *<C> have/possess <attr>*

Similar techniques for identifying concept's attributes can be found in [1, 19]. If *<attr>* is a concept then the attribute is considered as an **OWL Object Property**, otherwise it is created as a **Data Type Property.**

Verbal relationships express more specialized relationships that are important in the domain. Basically, all verbal relationships between pairs of concepts are considered as potential ontological relationships.

3.4.2   Relationship Classification or Interpretation

Relationships between concepts should benefit from another level of abstraction to enable a program to reason more thoroughly over these structures by classifying semantic relationships according to an application domain or to more general categories. In fact, semantic relationships must be linked to a logical layer that acts as an interface between an application layer and the semantic layer.

A *Linguistic Editor* allows defining rules about semantic relationship categories hence constituting progressively a linguistic knowledge base. For the moment, we define the following generic categories:

- Taxonomical relationships (is-a, is-a-kind–of, appositions)
- Composition relationships (compose, contain, etc.)
- Description relationships (describes, is-described-by)
- Definition relationships (defines, is-defined-as, …)
- Explanation relationships (explains, is-explained-by)
- Causal relationships (causes, leads-to, is-caused-by, etc.)
- Reference relationships (refers-to, is-referenced-by, is-associated-with), etc.

The human expert is free to create new categories in the editor and to provide lexicon-semantic patterns denoting them or to enrich the available categories with new patterns. The same domain knowledge can then be "adapted" to fit particular needs. For example, in a training context, some kinds of links are usually represented such as composition links and aggregation links. A course about e-Learning norms would insist on the available objects and their relationship to each other's whereas other domains such as botany may focus on attributes and characteristics (plant colour, petal length, etc.).

3.5 The Interest of the Approach for the AIED and e-Learning Community

One of the more acute problem of knowledge-based systems is the famous "knowledge acquisition bottleneck". This is also an issue in training communities. Like we previously said, Intelligent Tutoring Systems have richer and more fine-grained knowledge representations than e-Learning systems.

Given the large amount of learning objects, it is possible to annotate their content semi-automatically through the generation of domain ontologies. From one side, this enables an accurate representation of learning objects and their contexts. It permits also a more focused answer to learners' needs and provides them with navigation facilities through the learning resources. From another side, this semantic annotation creates a common knowledge base representing a bridge between Intelligent Tutoring Systems and e-Learning systems: the automatic acquisition of a domain ontology enables to capture the semantics of the subject domain [3]. It can be used to retrieve the appropriate knowledge by:

- Intelligent Tutoring Systems in their teaching;
- Learning Management Systems when searching the most appropriate learning object;
- Teachers or course designers;
- Learners;

Moreover, the idea of generating a domain ontology from concept maps [13] is particularly useful for the educational field.

3.6 Context and Constructivism

Concept maps are not considered only as intermediary templates for building the domain ontology. In fact, concept maps alone have proved their usefulness for training within constructivist environments [18]. The Knowledge Puzzle defines a formal relationship between a concept and the generated concept map to enable its reuse in training sessions. This formal relationship represents the concept's context. This is very important within constructivist environments where prior knowledge is used as a framework for understanding and learning new knowledge.

Constructivist learning should allow exploration with learning material and related domain concepts. It should foster meaningful learning by relating previous knowledge with a new one. As previously shown, the Knowledge Puzzle offers such capabilities.

3.7 Learning Objects Types

We underlined the importance of more fine-grained retrieval of learning content. We believe that an ontology of instructional roles is essential to reach this goal [27]. In fact, learning objects can include various types of learning materials such as lectures, examples, exercises, etc. Due to its pedagogical natural aim, a learning object itself contains a set of instructional roles. In order to provide a standard model for binding knowledge and instructional roles to documents or parts of them, we propose to model an OWL ontology: The *instructional role ontology*. It defines instructional roles that can be found in documents and that can be used to provide a template to a learning material structure. This ontology can evolve according to expert's desires. We provide him with a tool to manually annotate the document according to instructional roles [29].

Thanks to the domain ontology, the links between the learning objects and the domain concepts are explicit. Thanks to the instructional role ontology, the links between instructional roles and learning objects are also explicit. Finally, instructional roles are applied on domain concepts, thus providing an inter-related meaningful structure (e.g.: an explanation about a concept X, a definition of concept Y, etc.)

4   Generating Learning Knowledge Objects

Because concept maps are extracted from domain learning objects, they constitute an interdependent structure of domain concepts and a library of learning materials. These learning objects must also be adapted to fit individual needs at various levels. The Knowledge Puzzle focuses on the definition of competencies as instructional objectives. It relies on a *Competence Ontology* that describes a competence as a set of skills on domain concepts. Skills are classified according to the Bloom taxonomy [2], which defines six levels of intellectual behavior important in learning and associates a set of verbs with each level. We also use action verbs to qualify the skills involved in a competence.

We adopt a *lazy aggregation* approach for learning knowledge objects generation: we push back the aggregation process until there is a need (just-in-time learning). This gives enough flexibility to the aggregation process and enables individual adaptation. This also means that learning knowledge objects are not stored, but automatically assembled on demand. A Competence Gap Analyzer compares the learner profile with the competence definition to detect training needs. Learner's instructional objectives are then indicated to the Instructional Plan Generator (IPG).

The IPG must follow an instructional strategy in order to provide efficient training through instructional theories. In fact, the authoring process of effective learning material must be supported by instructional design. The IPG can be configured to use various instructional theories. For the moment, we created a basic instructional theory editor that indicates the different steps of a theory and that map the aforementioned instructional roles to each step of the theory. For example, the theory can state that an introduction about a concept X must be presented first. Instructional theory steps are stored as instances of an *instructional theory ontology*.

A theory-aware learning knowledge object can then be generated according to the available theories. Being theory-aware does not mean that the Learning Knowledge Object has a fixed structure or is restricted to one theory. In fact, any instructional theory could be applied to constitute a Learning Knowledge Object. This brings the following advantage: the composition structure is known so a human or a program is able to understand it and to understand the instructional objective of the expert that provided the instructional rules.

Learning Knowledge Objects are then ready for presentation in a training environment. It is also possible to standardize their structure in order to make them compliant with an e-Learning standard such as SCORM and IMS-LD [28, 29].

5   Related Work

The Knowledge Puzzle is related to multiple disciplines such as ontology generation, concept map generation, competence-based learning and learning object composition. We refer the reader to [30] to gain more insight on the competence-based learning. We provide a brief state of the art about concept map and domain ontology generation and learning object composition.

5.1   Concept Map Generation

Some prior or concurrent works attempted to generate concept maps from documents [7, 21]. The main difference with the Knowledge Puzzle's approach is that these works do not try to convert the concept maps into domain ontologies. Moreover, Valerio and Leake [28] do not use prepositional forms as linking phrases whereas we do. Our approach is built on the progressive construction of concept maps around important domain concepts. Whole sentences are exploited in order to find as many semantic relationships as possible whereas other approaches only exploit verbal relationships.

For example, Valerio and Leake [28] present the sentence: "Paper is a thin, flat material produced by compressed fibers" and output the tuple <paper-is-a-thin,flat, material>. In addition, the Knowledge Puzzle extracts the relationship "thin,flat, material – produced by – compressed fibers".

5.2 Domain Ontology Generation

Ontology generation and population from text is a very active research field. Many projects were developed such as Text-2-Onto [12], OntoLT [6], and OntoLearn [17]. Some works tried to handle the whole process of knowledge acquisition and others only a part of it, using statistical analysis, linguistic parsing, web mining, clustering and so on. A good review about ontology learning from text could be found in [5].

The specificity of the proposed approach lies in the generation of concept maps and the extraction of a domain ontology from these maps. It also lies in the methodology adopted throughout the process and the final goal of the process, which is training.

5.3 Learning Object Generation and Composition

Among the works on learning object composition, The SeLeNe [15] project takes DocBook documents as input and transforms them into learning objects. SeLeNe generates learning structures called trails that are represented as RDF Sequences of learning objects forming the trail. The Trial-Solution [4] project aims to disaggregate existing electronic books into elementary learning resources, to edit these resources to refine the slicing and to annotate the resources with metadata. Finally, the aim of the IMAT project [8] is to reuse technical manuals as training material using automated document analysis (PDF documents) combined with ontology indexing techniques.
None of the projects handled the whole knowledge acquisition process or generated (semi) automatically a domain ontology.

6 Evaluation and First Results

In this paper, we evaluate two facets of the Knowledge Puzzle: the domain concept maps and the domain ontology (domain concepts and relationships).

We ran a small-scale evaluation on the Knowledge Puzzle's domain concept maps using a set of training manuals that present and explain the Sharable Content Object Reference Model [24]. Because SCORM manuals contain not only declarative knowledge in natural language, but also codes and algorithms, we extracted manually the declarative parts of the manuals into a set of 32 plain text documents.

After having run the structure annotators, we obtained a set of 157 paragraphs with an overall number of 1302 sentences. A set of 1354 domain terms was obtained after the concept maps generation as well as 2351 semantic relationships. A threshold **I** was specified to consider a domain term **X** as a domain concept. **I** is the number of semantic relationships where X is the source concept (the out-degree of X). Three thresholds were considered: 2, 5 and 8.

In the case of **threshold=2**, domain terms have been reduced to 477 domain concepts and 628 properties with specified domain and range.

In the case of **threshold=5**, we obtained 76 domain concepts and 228 properties.

In the case of **threshold=8**, we obtained 38 domain concepts and 156 properties.

Several questions arise to evaluate the domain ontology quality, which is a challenging issue:

- Estimating the pertinence of the domain concepts;
- Estimating the correctness of the relationships (label, arguments)
- Estimating the pertinence of the domain relationships;

Domain concepts and relationships were automatically exported to an OWL ontology.

Domain concepts were exported as classes of the new domain ontology. Only plausible relationships between pairs of domain concepts were considered as valid OWL object properties. For example, if we consider the tuple: *Assets can be described with Asset Metadata*, then the relationship *"can be described with"* is an OWL Object Property whose domain is the class *Assets* and whose range is the class *Asset Metadata*. Moreover, we exported the taxonomical links (is-a links) as subclasses, and instance links as OWL Individuals.

Note that the plausibility of the domain ontology is closely linked to the plausibility of the domain concept maps.

The authors of this paper inspected the domain ontologies in order to evaluate the correctness and plausibility of domain concepts. Moreover, because SCORM manuals include a glossary of important domain terms and acronyms, the authors were able to compare them to the extracted concepts.

The following table summarizes the author's evaluation of domain concepts and relationships' pertinence for each generated domain ontology.

Table 4. Human evaluation of concept and relationship pertinence

Thresholds	Domain Concepts Pertinence (%)	Domain Relationships pertinence (%)
2	86.79	70.7
5	92.10	77.19
8	97.36	87.82

We noted that the higher the threshold is, the lower is the generated noise. However, some pertinent knowledge is occulted. So a balanced value should be found, which takes into account the number of domain sentences that are available for processing. As far as relationships are concerned, each author judged if the domain concept map relationships were plausible. A relationship r between C1 and C2 is considered as plausible if it contains a plausible label and two plausible arguments. Plausible means that this relationship is true with respect to C1 and C2. For example: Asset *can be described with* Asset Metadata is a plausible relationship.

7   Conclusion and Further Work

Concept maps are a valuable resource whose rich structure can be exploited in information retrieval and in training. We presented a solution to semi-automatically generate concept maps from domain documents. These concept maps are useful to support meaningful learning and serve as 1) a knowledge base for building domain ontologies, 2) a skeleton for a more focused learning object composition. We based these extractions on lexicon-syntactic and semantic patterns.

In the knowledge acquisition side, our goal is now to tackle the issue of over-generation and of noise resulting from the overall process. The problem is to be able to automatically ignore non-domain knowledge. We also work to enhance the algorithm of the extraction patterns. It is not trivial to be able to interpret grammatical relationships semantically. Confidence rates should be attached to the extracted knowledge. Moreover, more thorough ontology and concept map evaluation techniques must be performed. The question of the pertinence of a threshold related to the out-degree of each domain concept remains opened and should be further investigated.

In the knowledge exploitation side, we would like to realize the generation of more complex learning objects that exploit the concept maps as well as available instructional theory ontologies [23] to fulfill a learning objective.

References

1. Almuhareb, A., Poesio, M.: Finding Concept Attributes in the Web Using a Parser. In: Proc. of the Corpus Linguistics Conference, Birmingham (2005)
2. Bloom, B.S.: Taxonomy of educational objectives: The classification of educational goals: Handbook I, cognitive domain. Longman, New York (1956)
3. Brooks, C., Greer, J., Melis, E., Ullrich, C.: Combining ITS and eLearning Technologies: Opportunities and Challenges. In: Ikeda, M., Ashley, K.D., Chan, T.-W. (eds.) ITS 2006. LNCS, vol. 4053, pp. 278–287. Springer, Heidelberg (2006)
4. Buffa, M., Dehors, S., Faron-Zucker, C., Sander, P.: Towards a Corporate Semantic Web Approach in Designing Learning Systems: Review of the trial solution Project. In: Proc. of International Workshop on Applications of Semantic Web Technologies for E-Learning, AIED, pp. 73–76. Amsterdam, Holland (2005)
5. Buitelaar, P., Cimiano, P., Magnini, B.: Ontology Learning from Text: An Overview. In: Buitelaar, P., Cimiano, P., Magnini, B. (eds.) Ontology Learning from Text: Methods, Evaluation and Applications. Frontiers in Artificial Intelligence and Applications, vol. 123, pp. 3–12. IOS Press, Amsterdam (2005)
6. Buitelaar, P., Olejnik, D., Sintek, M.: A protégé plug-in for ontology extraction from text based on linguistic analysis. In: Proc. of the 1st European Semantic Web Symposium, Heraklion, Greece, pp. 31–44 (2004)
7. Clariana, R.B., Koul, R.: A Computer-Based Approach for Translating Text into Concept Map-like Representations. In: Clariana, R.B., Koul, R. (eds.) Proc. of the First International Conference on Concept Mapping, Pamplona, Spain, vol. I, pp. 125–133 (2004)
8. De Hoog, R., Kabel, S., Barnard, Y., Boy, G., DeLuca, P., Desmoulins, C., Riemersma, J., Verstegen, D.: Re-using technical manuals for instruction: creating instructional material with the tools of the IMAT project. In: Cerri, S.A., Gouardéres, G., Paraguaçu, F. (eds.) ITS 2002. LNCS, vol. 2363, pp. 28–39. Springer, Heidelberg (2002)
9. De Marneffe, M-C., MacCartney, B., Manning, C.D.: Generating Typed Dependency Parses from Phrase Structure Parses. In: Proc. of 5th Conference on Language Resources and Evaluation, pp. 449–454, Genoa, Italy (2006)
10. Frank, E., Paynter, G.W., Witten, I.H., Gutwin, C., Nevill-Manning, C.G.: Domain-specific key phrase extraction. In: Proc. of the 16th International Joint Conference on Artificial Intelligence, pp. 668–673, San Francisco, USA (1999)

11. Gasevic, D., Jovanović, J., Devedzic, V.: Ontologies for Creating Learning Object Content. In: Proc. of the 8th International Conference on Knowledge-Based Intelligent Information & Engineering Systems, Wellington, New Zealand, pp. 284–291 (2004)
12. Haase, P., Volker, J.: Ontology learning and reasoning - Dealing with uncertainty and inconsistency. In: Proc. of the ISWC Workshop on Uncertainty Reasoning for the Semantic Web (URSW), Galway, Ireland, pp. 45–55 (2005)
13. Hayes, P., Eskridge, T., Saavedra, R., Reichherzer, T., Mehrotra, M., Bobrovnikoff, D.: Collaborative Knowledge Capture in Ontologies. In: Proc. of the 3rd International Conference on Knowledge Capture (K-CAP'2005), pp. 99–106. ACM Press, New York (2005)
14. Hearst, M.A.: Automatic acquisition of hyponyms from large text corpora. In: Proc. of the 14th International Conference on Computational Linguistics, Nantes, pp. 539–545 (1992)
15. Keenoy, K., Poulovassilis, A., Christophides, V., Rigaux, P., Papamarkos, G., Magkanaraki, A., Stratakis, M., Spyratos, N., Wood, P.T.: Personalisation Services for Self E-learning Networks. In: Koch, N., Fraternali, P., Wirsing, M. (eds.) ICWE 2004. LNCS, vol. 3140, pp. 215–219. Springer, Heidelberg (2004)
16. Klein, D., Manning, C.D.: Accurate unlexicalized parsing. In: Proc. of the 41st Meeting of the Association for Computational Linguistics, Sapporo, Japan, pp. 423–430 (2003)
17. Navigli, R., Velardi, P.: Learning Domain Ontologies from Document Warehouses and Dedicated Websites. Computational Linguistics 30(2), 151–179 (2004)
18. Novak, J.D.: Cañas, A. J, The Theory Underlying Concept Maps and How to Construct Them, Technical Report IHMC CmapTools 2006-01, Florida Institute for Human and Machine Cognition (2006)
19. Poesio, M., Almuhareb, A.: Identifying Concept Attributes Using A Classifier. In: Proc. of the ACL Workshop on Deep Lexical Acquisition, Ann Arbor, USA, pp. 18–27 (2005)
20. Porter, M.F.: An algorithm for suffix stripping. Program 14(3), 130–137 (1980)
21. The Protégé Ontology Editor. Retrieved From: http://protege.stanford.edu/
22. O'Keeffe, I., Brady, A., Conlan, O., Wade, V.: Just-in-time Generation of Pedagogically Sound, Context Sensitive Personalized Learning Experiences. International Journal on E-Learning (IJeL) 5(1), 113–127 (2006)
23. Psyché, V., Bourdeau, J., Nkambou, R., Mizoguchi, R.: Making Learning Design Standards Work with an Ontology of Educational Theories. In: Proc. of Artificial Intelligence in Education, pp. 725–731. IOS Press, Amsterdam (2005)
24. SCORM 2007, Retrieved April 13th, 2007 from, http://www.adlnet.gov/scorm/index.cfm
25. Suraweera, P., Mitrovic, A., Martin, B.: A Knowledge Acquisition System for Constraint-based Intelligent Tutoring Systems. In: Proc. of Artificial Intelligence in Education, pp. 638–645. IOS Press, Amsterdam (2005)
26. UIMA, Retrieved April 13th, 2007 from: http://uima-framework.sourceforge.net/
27. Ullrich, C.: Description of an instructional ontology and its application in web services for education. In: Proc. of Workshop on Applications of Semantic Web Technologies for E-learning, Hiroshima, Japan, pp. 17–23 (2004)
28. Valerio, A., Leake, D.: Jump-Starting Concept Map Construction with Knowledge Extracted From Documents. In: Proc. of the Second International Conference on Concept Mapping (CMC 2006), San José, Costa Rica, vol. 1, pp. 296–303 (2006)
29. Zouaq, A., Nkambou, R., Frasson, C.: Using a Competence Model to Aggregate Learning Knowledge Objects. In: Proc. of the 7th IEEE International Conference on Advanced Learning Technologies (ICALT 2007), Niigata, Japan (to appear, 2007)
30. Zouaq, A., Nkambou, R., Frasson, C.: An Integrated Approach for Automatic Aggregation of Learning Knowledge Objects. Interdisciplinary Journal of Knowledge and Learning Objects (IJKLO) 3, 135–162 (2007)

Organizational Learning at University

Marie-Hélène Abel, Dominique Lenne, and Adeline Leblanc

University of Technology of Compiègne, CNRS Heudiasyc
BP 20529, 60205 Compiègne CEDEX France
{Marie-Helene.Abel,Dominique.Lenne,Adeline.Leblanc}@utc.fr

Abstract. Information and Communication Technologies have transformed the way people work and have an increasing impact on the long life learning. Organizational Learning is an increasingly important area of research that concerns the way organizations learn and thus increase their competitive advantage, innovativeness, and effectiveness. Within the project MEMORAe2.0, our objective is to get ready students for their professional life, i.e. to learn to learn. To that end, we made the choice to consider a course as an organization and more precisely a learning organization. We developed the environment E-MEMORAe2.0 based on the model of an organizational memory to capitalize and to distribute knowledge and resources related to a course. By means of E-MEMORAe2.0, learners use, produce and exchange documents and knowledge. In this article, we present our approach of organizational learning in the project MEMORAe2.0 and we describe how we implemented it in the E-MEMORAe2.0 environment.

Keywords: Organizational Learning, Knowledge Management, Sharing and Learning, Group Learning Environment.

1 Introduction

Organizational Learning (OL) is an increasingly important area of research that concerns the way organizations learn and thus increase their competitive advantage, innovativeness, and effectiveness [1]. OL requires tools facilitating knowledge acquisition, information distribution, interpretation, and organization, in order to enhance learning at different levels: individual, group and organization.

Within the project MEMORAe2.0 [2], our objective is to get ready students for their professional life, i.e. to learn to learn. To that end, we made the choice to consider a course as an organization and more precisely a learning organization. A course unit is based on knowledge and competencies it should provide, on actors (learners, instructors, trainers, course designers, administrators, etc.) and on resources of different types (definitions, exercises with or without solution, case studies, etc.), and different forms (reports, books, web sites, etc.). In this sense, a course is an organization.

In order to support the learning within organization we developed the E-MEMORAe2.0 environment based on an organizational memory allowing the capitalization and the distribution of knowledge and resources. Thanks to this environment,

E. Duval, R. Klamma, and M. Wolpers (Eds.): EC-TEL 2007, LNCS 4753, pp. 408–413, 2007.

training actors can use, produce or exchange resources and knowledge. They have to access to the resources and to adapt them to their needs. An organizational memory enables to capitalize not only resources related to the pedagogical contents of the course but also those related to training actors themselves (specificities, background, profile, etc.). It enables also the course administrative management.

In this paper, we present the organizational learning approach and we stress the role of an organizational memory in this approach. Then we present the project MEMORAe2.0. Finally we describe how we implemented the organizational learning approach in the E-MEMORAe2.0 environment.

2 Organizational Learning

A learning organization (LO) is an organization in which processes are imbedded in the organizational culture that allows and encourages learning at the individual, group and organizational level [3]. Thus a LO must be skilled at creating, acquiring, and transferring knowledge, and at modifying its behaviour to reflect knew knowledge and insights [4]. According to [5], a LO is a firm that purposefully constructs structures and strategies so as to enhance and maximize organizational learning (OL).

OL includes personal learning of single members of an organization but goes beyond it. OL is more than the sum of individual learning results [6][7].

An organization cannot learn without continuous learning by its members. Individual learning is not organizational learning until it is converted into OL. The conversion process can take place through individual and organizational memory [8]. The results of individual learning are captured in individuals' memory. And, individual learning becomes organizational learning only when individual memory becomes part of organizational memory.

OL rarely occurs without access to organizational knowledge. In contrast to individual knowledge, organizational knowledge must be communicable, consensual, and integrated [9]. According to [8], being communicable means the knowledge must be explicitly represented in an easily distributed and understandable form. The consensual requirement stipulates that organizational knowledge is considered valid and useful by all members. Integrated knowledge represents the requirement of a consistent, accessible, well-maintained organizational memory.

3 Organizational Memory

According to [10], an organizational memory is defined as "the means by which knowledge from the past is brought to bear on present activities and may result in higher or lower levels of organizational effectiveness". It can be regarded as the explicit and persistent representation knowledge and information in an organization, in order to facilitate their access and their re-use by the adequate members of the organization for their tasks [11]. Thus, an organizational memory seems indispensable for organizational learning. An integrated organizational memory provides mechanism for compatible knowledge representation, as well as a common interface for sharing knowledge, resources and competencies.

4   The Project MEMORAe2.0

The project MEMORAe2.0 is an extension of the project MEMORAe [12]. Within the project MEMORAe, we were interested in the knowledge capitalization in the context of organizations and more precisely the capitalization of the resources related to this knowledge by means of a learning organizational memory. We particularly focused on the way organization actors could use this capitalization to get new knowledge. To that end, we developed the environment E-MEMORAe as support for e-learning. In such a system a learning content is indexed to knowledge organized by means of ontologies: domain and application. The domain ontology defines concepts shared by any organization; the application ontology defines concepts dedicated to a specific organization. Using these ontologies, actors can acquire knowledge by doing different tasks (solving problems or exercises, reading examples, definitions, reports…). We used Topic Maps [13] as a representation formalism facilitating navigation and access to the learning resources. The ontology structure is also used to navigate among the concepts as in a roadmap. The learner has to reach the learning resources that are appropriate for him. E-MEMORAe was positively evaluated [14] on the basis of a course on applied mathematics at the University of Picardy (France).

Within the project MEMORAe2.0 we are interested in using the MEMORAe approach in an organizational learning context. We particularly focused on the way learners attending a course could use this capitalization to get new knowledge and competencies. We designed the organizational learning memory around two types of sub-memory that constitute the final memory of the organization:

- Group memory: this kind of memory enables all the group members to access knowledge and resources shared by them. We distinguish three types of group memory (team, project, and organization) corresponding to different communities of practice.
- Individual memory: this kind of memory is private. Each member of the organization has its own memory in which he can organize, capitalize his/her knowledge and resources.

The MEMORAe model relies on two ontologies. The first one (domain ontology) describes the concepts of the « organization » domain (cf. figure 1). They can be people group (team, project, organization-wide), documents types (book, slides for oral presentation, web page, site, etc.), and media types (text, image, audio, and video). They can also be pedagogical characteristics (activity type) and they can refer to point of view (annotation).

The second ontology (application ontology) specifies notions which are used by members of a particular organization. All the memories share these ontologies. These ontologies define and structure the organizational memory. Each sub-memory can have its own resources and knowledge. This one is defined from the shared ontology. Resources, even if they are private – stored in a particular memory – are indexed by the concepts of the ontology.

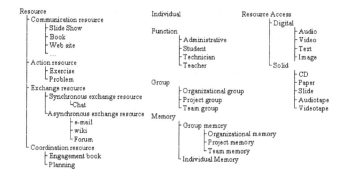

Fig. 1. Part of the domain ontology

5   The E-MEMORAe2.0 Environment

The purpose of the E-MEMORAe2.0 environment is to facilitate the organizational learning at university. It is an extension of the E-MEMORAe environment. This environment helps memory users to learn courses notions by facilitating exchanges, knowledge transfer within a community of learning (exchanges are implemented by means of Web2.0 technologies).

5.1   Knowledge Access

The environment enables to navigate in the application ontology dedicated to the selected formation and to find resources indexed by concepts. The general principle is to propose to the learner, at each step, either precise information on what he is searching for, or graphically displayed links that allow him to continue its navigation through the memory.

To be more precise, the user interface (Fig. 2) proposes: an access to the different memories (top left), entry points enabling to start the navigation with a given concept (left), a part of the ontology (center), a short definition of the current notion, a list of related resources (bottom) and an history of the navigation (right).

5.2   Knowledge Exchange

Ontologies enable the organization and capitalization exchanges. In order to facilitate the externalization and capitalization of tacit knowledge, we decided to associate exchange resources to each ontology concept. An exchange resource concerns one concept and can be asynchronous (forum, wiki) or synchronous (chat). It gives to group members the opportunity to exchange ideas, information about one subject; this subject is the concept which indexes the exchange resource. Currently, these informal exchanges are realized in a writing way. We plan to record oral exchanges via internet calls (for example skype).

In order to put into practice our approach, we used various tools in the E-MEMORAe2.0 environment. For example, we associated to each memory a forum

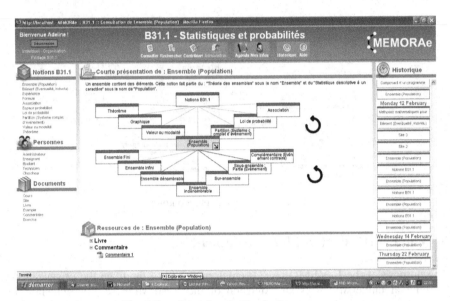

Fig. 2. Interface of navigation in the memory

whose fields correspond to the concepts of the application ontology. Exchanges are thus capitalized and accessible to actors according to their rights.

6 Conclusion

In this paper, we described the organizational learning approach and we showed how we implemented it in the E-MEMORAe2.0 environment for academic applications. The main component of this environment is an organizational memory which enables knowledge transfer at three levels: individual, group and organization. A first evaluation of this memory, that was restricted to the organization level, has given encouraging results. Students appreciated to have access to documents by the way of the course concepts.

In order to complete this evaluation, we plan now to experiment the two other levels through project-based activities. We also plan to examine to what extent teachers could benefit of this approach. The organizational memory could play a central role in knowledge transfer among teachers. Let us note however that software environments are not sufficient to promote organizational learning. It is also a question of culture, as well at university as in any other organization. If students acquire this culture at university, they should get better ready to their professional life.

References

1. McEvily, K.S., Chakravarthy, B.: The persistence of knowledge-based advantage: an empirical test for product performance and technological knowledge. Strategic Management Journal 23, 285–305 (2002)

2. Abel, M.-H., Barry, C., Benayache, A., Chaput, B., Lenne, D., Moulin, C.: Ontology-based Organizational Memory for e-learning. Educational Technology & Society Journal 7(4) (2004)
3. Sunassee, N., Haumant, V.: Organisational Learning versus the Learning Organisation. In: SAICSIT, pp. 264–268 (2004)
4. Garvin, D.: Building a learning organization. Bus. Cred. 96(1), 19–28 (1994)
5. Dodgson, M.: Organizational Learning: A review of some literatures. Organization studies 14, 175–194 (1993)
6. Nevis, E., DiBella, A., Gould, J.: Understanding Organizations as Learning Systems. Sloan Management Review, 73–85 (1995)
7. Paper, D., Johnson, J.: A Theoretical Framework Linking Creativity, Empowerment, and Organizational Memory. In: Lynn, M. (ed.) 29th Annual Hawaii International Conference on System Sciences, Los Alamitos, vol. IV, pp. 20–30 (1996)
8. Chen, J., Ted, E., Zhang, R., Zhang, Y.: Systems requirements for organizational learning. Communication of the ACM 46(12), 73–78 (2003)
9. Duncan, R., Weiss, A.: Organizational learning: Implications for organizational design. In: Staw, B. (ed.) Research in Organizational Behaviour, pp. 75–123. JAI Press, Greenwich, CT (1979)
10. Stein, E., Zwass, V.: Actualising organizational memory with information systems. Info. Syst. Res. 6(2), 85–117 (1995)
11. Dieng, R., Corby, O., Giboin, A., Ribière, M.: Methods and Tools for Corporate Knowledge Management. In: Eleventh Workshop on Knowledge Acquisition, Modelling and Management (KAW'98), Banff, Alberta, Canada (1998)
12. Abel, M.-H., Benayache, A., Lenne, D., Moulin, C.: E-MEMORAe: a content-oriented environment for e-learning. In: Pierre, S. (ed.) E-learning networked environments and Architectures: A Knowledge processing perspective. Springer Book Series: Advanced Information and Knowledge Processing (AI & KP), pp. 186–205 (2006)
13. XTM TopicMaps.org XTM Authoring Group. XML Topic Maps (XTM) 1.0: TopicMaps.org Specification (2001)
14. Benayache, A., Leblanc, A., Abel, M.-H.: Learning memory, evaluation and return on experience. In: Proceedings of Workshop of Knowledge Management and Organizational Memories, ECAI2006, Riva del Garda, Italy, August 28 – September 1, 2006, pp.14–18 (2006)

FAsTA: A Folksonomy-Based Automatic Metadata Generator

Hend S. Al-Khalifa and Hugh C. Davis

Learning Societies Lab
ECS, The University of Southampton
SO17 1BJ, Southampton, UK
hsak04r/hcd@ecs.soton.ac.uk

Abstract. Folksonomies provide a free source of keywords describing web resources, however, these keywords are free form and unstructured. In this paper, we describe a novel tool that converts folksonomy tags into semantic metadata, and present a case study consisting of a framework for evaluating the usefulness of this metadata within the context of a particular eLearning application. The evaluation shows the number of ways in which the generated semantic metadata adds value to the raw folksonomy tags.

1 Introduction

Folksonomy, a term coined by Thomas Vender Wal in 2005, is a mechanism to describe web resources using people's own vocabulary. As defined by an article in Wikipedia[1] folksonomy is "... *an Internet-based information retrieval methodology consisting of collaboratively generated, open-ended labels that categorize content such as Web pages, online photographs, and Web links.*"

Users have their own perspective when tagging a resource; they may add new contextual dimensions, for example to suggest its application or its relationship to neighboring domains. This effect has been witnessed in our domain of study (Web Design with Cascading Style Sheets 'CSS'), where people tag resources appearing in that domain with extra contextual dimensions such as the application of a web resource, its type and other parallel domains for instance 'PHP programming'.

Clearly, folksonomies are a potential source of useful metadata. As Peterson [1] said "*The overall usefulness of folksonomies is not called into question; just how they can be refined without losing the openness that makes them so popular*". In our work, rather than attempting to refine the tagging process we have taken the open vocabulary tags and mapped them against domain ontologies in order to derive structured semantic metadata from the folksonomies. This paper describes our tool, its evaluation and shows that folksonomies contain acceptable indexing words that can create semantic metadata with added value.

---

[1] http://en.wikipedia.org/wiki/Folksonomy (27thMarch 2007)

E. Duval, R. Klamma, and M. Wolpers (Eds.): EC-TEL 2007, LNCS 4753, pp. 414–419, 2007.
© Springer-Verlag Berlin Heidelberg 2007

2   Methodology

The semantic metadata elements used to describe CSS web recourses were constructed by mixing elements from the IEEE LOM standard and elements specific to the domain of CSS, in other words, creating a domain specific application profile from IEEE-LOM. The application profile consists of 15 elements, which include: *Title, Description, Keywords, Resource Type, Recommendation, Property, Selector, Unit, Attribute, Technique, Application, Subject, Layout, Difficulty level and Instructional level.*

In order to produce the CSS semantic metadata from folksonomy tags, we have implemented a tool that extracts tags form URLs talking about CSS in del.icio.us and utilizing these tags in the process of semantic metadata generation. Herein, we briefly present our tool, namely the FolksAnnotations Tool Architecture (FAsTA) and its components, however, for a full tool description the reader is referred to [2].

The main two processes used in FAsTA are: the Tags Extraction and Normalization pipeline and the Semantic Annotation pipeline.

The Tags Extraction and Normalization pipeline starts by fetching a bookmarked web resource from the del.icio.us bookmarking service, then the tag extraction process begins by extracting folksonomy tags from the web page of the bookmarked web resource. The extracted tags are then passed to the normalization process which performs a series of filters to clean the tags. The filters are preformed sequentially in the following order:

- **Lower-case filter:** Tags are converted to lower case,
- **Non-English filter:** Non-Roman Alphabet are dropped; this step is to insure that only English tags are present when doing the semantic annotation process,
- **Stemming filter:** stem tags using a modified version of the Porter Stemmer (http://www.tartarus.org/~martin/PorterStemmer/),
- **Tags sense Disambiguation filter:** stemmed tags are passed to this module to remove ambiguous tags, i.e. polysemy.
- **Grouping filter:** similar tags are grouped (e.g. inclusion of substrings),
- Finally, the **removal filter**, where the general concept tags in our domain of interest (e.g. programming, web, etc) and ambiguous tags are eliminated.

The process of normalization is done automatically and it is potentially useful to clean up the noise in people's tags. The normalized tags list is then passed to the semantic annotation process, where each normalized folksonomy tag is mapped to a corresponding ontological instance in one of the three ontologies, which are: the Web Design Ontology, the CSS Subject Ontology and the Resource Type Ontology [2]. This process will attach ontology instances as descriptors for a web resource.

3   Evaluations and Results

To evaluate the output of our prototype tool, many evaluation aspects need to be considered, including the usefulness, the quality and the representativeness of the generated metadata semantics.

Barritt and Alderman [3] determines the usefulness of metadata from two viewpoints: validity, i.e. creating valid metadata for every learning resource, and searchability, having the search tools in place to use that metadata. Guy et al. [4] defines metadata quality as "... *supports the functional requirements of the system it is designed to support.*" Thus, to stipulate the 'functional requirements' of the current work, we have considered that the semantic metadata needs to have no errors and the semantic descriptions need to correctly reflect the nature of the described web resource. Finally, the representativeness of a semantic metadata can be thought of as how well the metadata descriptors describe the semantics of the given domain, in this case the domain of Web design with CSS.

Therefore, to evaluate these different aspects, we have implemented an evaluation framework that consists of the following procedures:

- Metadata assignment evaluation, which consist of:
    o Metadata Representativeness.
    o Metadata Quality and Validity.
- Identifying niche tags in 'The Long Tail': this procedure investigates whether distinguishable values of the semantic metadata elements come from rare tags residing in 'The Long Tail'.

3.1 Metadata Assignment Evaluation

The metadata assignment evaluation stage is necessary to evaluate the quality, validity and representativeness of the generated semantic metadata record.

To verify these requirements, we used a blend of quantitative and qualitative evaluation techniques. Thus, to evaluate the previous requirements a set of questions need to be answered, which are:

- Are the semantics of the descriptors *clear* and *unambiguous*?
- How well does the metadata *describe* the resource?
- How accurate is the generated metadata *represents* the web resource?

To answer these questions, a questionnaire was designed and distributed to a group of subject domain experts to rate the appropriateness of the descriptors and the validity of the assigned metadata. The questionnaire also measured how well the respondent believes that the metadata predicts the actual contents of the web resource.

The questionnaire was distributed to two target populations (web designers and experts in the field of learning technologies and metadata, i.e. 'specialists'.). The web designers' community was reached using mailing lists that reside at Yahoo Groups or other focused groups such as css-discuss.org. The total response from the web designers group was 29 respondents. The specialist group was reached by distributing the questionnaire to the CETIS-Metadata mailing list and to colleagues from the Learning Societies Lab Research Group (LSL) at the University of Southampton, UK. The total number of respondents from the specialist group was 19.

3.1.1 Metadata Representativeness
Two questions in the questionnaire were designed to capture the respondents view on the representative-ness of the metadata elements. The first question handles the

descriptors of CSS web resources and the second question handles the required fields needed to search for CSS web resources. The respondents were asked to rate (based on a scale from 1 to 5 where 1 represents 'useless' and 5 represents 'very useful') how useful each metadata element was to describe and search for web resources in the domain of teaching web design with CSS.

For the question asking about '*how useful are the metadata descriptors used to describe a CSS web resource*'. The overall statistics for the web designers' group responses show that the mean of the metadata elements are all above average, except for one element which is slightly below midpoint. However, the standard deviation for all elements is quite high, which indicates the varied view between respondents.

On the other hand, the overall statistics for the specialist group responses show that the mean of the metadata elements are all above average with a quite high standard deviation for all elements, except for two elements which indicated an agreed view in their importance between respondents.

For the question asking about '*how useful are the metadata descriptors used to search for a CSS web resource*'. The overall statistics for the web designer's group responses show that the mean of the metadata elements are all above average, except for one element, again, which is slightly below midpoint. However, the standard deviation for most elements is quite high, which indicates the varied view between respondents, expect for two elements which indicates some consistency on the respondents rating towards these two elements. By comparing the means of all elements, it is apparent that most elements are equally likely useful descriptors for retrieving/searching for a CSS web resource.

In contrast, the overall statistics for the specialist group responses show that the mean of the metadata elements are all above average, except for three elements which were slightly below midpoint. However, the standard deviation for half of the elements was quite low, which indicates consistency in the respondents' view of these elements.

3.1.2 Metadata Quality and Validity

The questionnaire was also designed to include a question about the quality and validity of a random sample of three CSS web resources metadata records. These three automatically generated semantic metadata records were selected based on their coverage of the various aspects of the CSS metadata descriptors. Therefore, the three metadata records were exposed to both groups (web designers and specialist) to rate them based on a metric produced by Greenberg [5] to evaluate the quality and validity of metadata elements. The evaluation is based on a three-tier scale, which are: Good, Fair and Reject.

The results of the quality and validity for each metadata element of the three resources were assessed for each element. Thus, for the three annotated web resources both the web designers group and the specialist group agreed in giving the following metadata elements: *Title, Resource type, Subject, Application, Technique, Property, Attribute and Layout*; either a 'Good' or 'Fair' rate. However, the two groups diverge in their opinion of the rest of the metadata elements which are: *Description, Keywords* and *Selector*. In the specialist group they rate these elements as 'Fair', 'Good' and 'Fair' respectively; while, the web designers group has rated them as 'Reject'.

3.2 Exploring the Long Tail

As we were evaluating our generated semantic metadata, we observed that most fine grained semantics of the CSS domain came from minority tags. Thus, some niche folksonomy tags from the CSS ontology create a finer-grained indexing for a web resource. This observation helped us to form the following hypothesis: *"Fine-grained metadata values come from The Long Tail"*.

The Long Tail, as defined in Wikipedia[2]: "...The long tail is the colloquial name for a long-known feature of statistical distributions ... In these distributions a high-frequency or high-amplitude population is followed by a low-frequency or low-amplitude population which gradually "tails off." "

To verify our hypothesis we analyzed the distribution of the list of tags used to semantically annotate web resources in our data set. One observation we found when compiling the list of tags used to create the semantic metadata was that the distribution of all tags that are used for semantically annotating a web resource always yields a long tail shape, as shown in Fig. 1. Notice that the tags 'list' (1 time), 'menu' (2 times), 'button' (9 times) and 'rollover' (10 times), are niche instances from the CSS ontology and at the same time fall in 'The Long Tail' region.

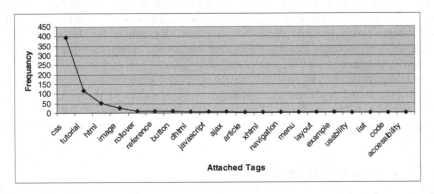

Fig. 1. The Long Tail shape for the tags used to semantically annotate the "What Are CSS Sprites? A Quick Example: Button Rollovers" web resource

Consequently, we examined the graph of each web resource tags list to determine the tags that fall within 'The Long Tail' portion and found that from the 100 annotated web resources 80% have one or more niche-tags. The average portion of niche-tags for all web resources was 16% with a standard deviation of 11.77%. This implies that on average 16% of the used tags for each resource will be a niche-tag. This finding verifies our claim about the source of the fine-grained metadata values.

4 Conclusion and Future Work

In this paper we have showed how we successfully managed to convert folksonomy tags into useful semantic metadata. In previous work [6] we have compared the

---

[2] http://en.wikipedia.org/wiki/The_Long_Tail (27th March 2007)

semantic metadata generated to the keywords extracted using context based keyword extraction technique, and demonstrated the improved value of the folksonomy tags.

In this work we have described a framework to evaluate and demonstrate the usefulness, the quality and the representativeness of the generated semantic metadata. Based on our evaluation framework, our findings can be summarized in three points:

1. Folksonomy tags demonstrated that they are 'good enough' source for creating semantic metadata. This might be attributed to the latent (implicit) semantics embedded in the tags used to describe web resources. The observed latent semantics helped us to build the appropriate ontologies that captured folksonomy semantics and converted folksonomy tags to semantic metadata.
2. Folksonomy tags showed the power of aggregating people's intelligence which helped in producing meaningful metadata. This was done without requiring their consensus in choosing the tags.
3. We have shown that useful fine grained metadata values in our case study came from The Long Tail. These values played a prominent role in distinguishing the metadata of a given web resource from other equivalent resources.

Finally, there are many potential extensions that could enhance the tool performance and output. The extensions could include: expanding the semantic metadata and ontologies, improving the normalization pipeline, and performing further evaluation procedures such as a comparative study to compare our tool performance against other automatic metadata generators.

References

[1] Peterson, E.: eneath the Metadata: Some Philosophical Problems with Folksonomy. D-Lib Magazine 12(11) (2006)
[2] Al-Khalifa, H.S., Davis, H.C.: Replacing the Monolithic LOM: A Folksonomic Approach. In: Proceedings of ICALT, Niigata, Japan (in press, 2007)
[3] Barritt, C., Alderman, F.: Creating a Reusable Learning Objects Strategy, San Diego: Pfeiffer (2004)
[4] Guy, M., Powell, A., Day, M.: Improving the Quality of Metadata in Eprint Archives. Ariadne (January 2004)
[5] Greenberg, J.: Metadata extraction and harvesting: A comparison of two automatic metadata generation applications. Journal of Internet Cataloging 6(4), 59–82 (2005)
[6] Al-Khalifa, H.S., Davis, H.C.: Exploring The Value Of Folksonomies For Creating Semantic Metadata. International Journal on Semantic Web and Information Systems (IJSWIS) 3(1), 13–39 (2007)

The Macro Design as an Own Task in WBT Production: Ideas, Concepts and a Tool

Abdelhak Aqqal, Christoph Rensing, and Ralf Steinmetz

[1] KOM - Multimedia Communications Lab, Technische Universität Darmstadt,
Merckstrasse 25, 64283 Darmstadt, Germany
{Abdelhak.Aqqal, Christoph.Rensing,
Ralf.Steinmetz}@kom.tu-darmstadt.de

Abstract. The conception and production of Web Based Training (WBT) is still too difficult for instructors. Semantic and didactic features are diluted during WBT development by teachers, due to the technical focus of the production task and the corresponding tools. Therefore, we claim a collaborative production as way to meet instructors' skills for an efficient WBT production. In addition to the content modeling and authoring, the proposed methodology points out so called "macro design" as an independent task to be supported. The macro design is innovative in two ways. First, it extends the existing way of content design by supporting instructors in expliciting their intentions and instructional design. Second, it demonstrates the possibility to use the Rhetorical Structure Theory (RST) as a communicative mechanism for the instructional design in order to give an explicit perception of the expected content.

1 Motivation and Scenario of Use

As we move into the third millennium, instructors (at schools, universities or in companies as well) are increasingly self-engaging in Web Based Training (WBT) practices as a way to author and deliver their educational materials. So far, WBT production is still too difficult. It integrates many interrelated processes, paradigms and disciplines and needs different technical skills that must be acquired and continuously updated. The problem is that an instructor is a domain expert first [5]. In addition he has knowledge about methodology of education but in general he is not trained in technical skills needed for WBT authoring and media creation. Therefore, we motivate a collaborative production as way to meet instructors' skills where authoring and media creation are done in a team so that the technical efforts spent by the instructor are reduced to a minimum. If so, such collaborative production will provide a natural way of working and a better investment of the instructor energy for a better WBT delivery [3]. Figure 1 shows the process-map of our authoring approach. We distinguish three different tasks as part of the production process: the so called "macro design", content modeling, authoring and media creation cycles with feedback loops under instructors supervision. In addition we define vertical to these processes a production management process in order to harmonize the collaboration between actors during the whole collaborative production.

E. Duval, R. Klamma, and M. Wolpers (Eds.): EC-TEL 2007, LNCS 4753, pp. 420–425, 2007.

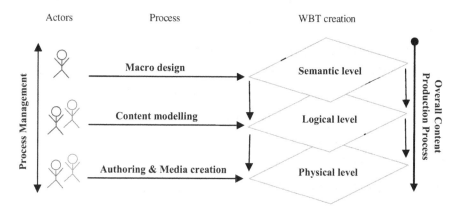

Fig. 1. The proposed approach for the overall content production process

The remainder of this paper is structured as follows: the following section will point out the "macro design" in detail. Section 3 will survey existing related work to discuss their shortcomings regarding our requirements. Then we will introduce in section 4 our approach and its components that we have implemented at the moment. Finally, the paper closes with the conclusion and gives an outlook on future work.

2 The Macro Design: Introduction and Requirements

In contrast to existing ways of WBT production, we postulate a phase in addition to content modelling, authoring and media creation which is often neglected or not fully taken into account. This phase, called temporary "the design thinking", covers instructor's ideas about what kind of WBT to produce, about a motif and reasons for a specific target group and about a list of themes that need to be taught. The instructor defines implicitly cognitive boundaries of main concepts of his WBT and semantic relations among these concepts according to both knowledge and learner domains. The "design thinking" is done in the mind of the instructor only. He could explain his ideas by speech or writing it down so far. Tool support starts in the content modelling phase nowadays. Most times WBT modelling is done using the table of content paradigm. Such a table of content records the main concepts which are used in content authoring only. The relationships between the main concepts as well as the instructional impact can not been expressed in such a simplified model. Being always only "in the instructor mind", most of the "design thinking" and parts of the modelling implicit data evaporates as soon as another person is consigned with the authoring and if the WBT is produced.

We introduce, the "macro design" as an explicit modelling phase corresponding to the "design thinking" in order to record what instructors have in mind and to forward instructors' ideas to all others involved in the WBT production, from the instructional level to the technical level (figure 2) in order to enhance their awareness and comprehension of the production context. As well, a possibility to express and to store the instructor intentions will increase consequently the chance to re-use parts of a produced WBT. Stated most simply, the macro design could be summarized into answering explicitly the following questions:

1. Why to produce a WBT and for which audience?
2. What to produce (in term of knowledge)?
3. In which form to produce this WBT and why in this form?

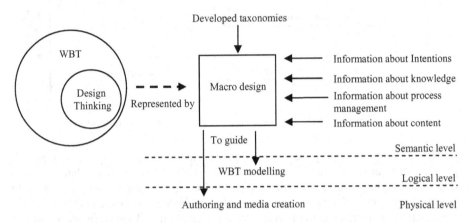

Fig. 2. Using the macro design to support the WBT production

Our goal is to build a tool to support the macro design without any overhead for the instructor. As requirements, first the proposed approach should not impose a certain pedagogical model for the instructor to avoid any semantic mismatch conflict between instructor intentions and the model mapping his intentions. Secondly, guidelines are needed to determine how the instructor should express his intentions, how to supervise and proceed the whole production process. This can be done by guiding him in a step-by-step manner. Taxonomies, as vocabulary for the representation of the WBT including "design thinking" data, are required to support such guidance.

3 Existing Support of CBT and WBT Production by Tools

Many approaches were purposed to support the WBT production by tools [7]. However, few suppose that the WBT production is done in a collaborative way supporting different roles and skills. Hence, using existing tools for a collaborative way of working will be quite fuzzy. In particular, these tools fail usually to support a macro design as stated in the previous section. For instance, web page editors (e.g. Macromedia Dreamweaver, FrontPage and Netscape Composer) and text editors (e.g. Microsoft Word, PowerPoint and Open Office) support the authoring phase only. Contrary, course composers (e.g. WebCT, TopClass or Blackboard) and some educational modelling languages (e.g. TeachML, LMML) support rather the content modelling phase [5]. WBT composers (e.g. Authorware, Toolbook, Mediator and Easy Prof) are professional WBT authoring tools and support both content modelling and authoring. Some academic approaches like GenDoc [1], ResourceCenter [4],

WB-Master [3] and SCENARI [1] could be listed in the same category too. But, generally, not all aspects of the macro design are considered in these approaches. Besides, the IMS-LD attempts to model the learning process in form of activities that contain content as black box or contain no content at all [5] [7]. IMS-LD by being so abstract, generic and constructivist oriented, it does not meet all the requirements of our projects.

4   Implementation and Work in Progress

4.1   Developing a Taxonomy of WBT Units for the Macro Design

In Macro Design both WBT domain and learner model have to be described by the instructor. So, he has to be supported to determine the elementary units of the WBT first. In addition, a general way to describe the relations among these units whether or not they are semantically interrelated have to be provided. Many related authoring approaches proposed hypotheses about what constitutes an elementary WBT unit. These hypotheses are based either on logical criteria (e.g. paragraph, section) or physical criteria (e.g. size, layout, image or page) [2]. For our scenario of use, we have developed an initial taxonomy where we distinguish 8 types of WBT Units and their instances to fit the macro design adequately. Our segmentation of WBT documents is rather grounded on semantic basis, where fragmentation and modularization of WBT units is determined by the existence of a certain meaning or didactic function in each unit. This unit, called "a semantic unit", should be a stand alone and didactically well-recognized. For instance, an illustration composed of an image and its description in paragraph format will be not considered as two units but only as one. This way of modelling does fulfil our requirements. It leads to a separation between the different production's levels (i.e. Semantic, Logical and Physical levels). The instructor has the ability to define the desired content in a complete abstract way in form of a set of semantic units.

4.2   Application of Rhetorical Structure Theory to Support the Macro Design

Our proposed mechanism to support the macro design is inspired from the Rhetorical Structure Theory (RST) [6]. RST is a framework for analyzing discourse structure and statements by positing hierarchical relations between spans of text in terms of what their intended effect on the reader is. RST has been chosen because it has many features which meet our requirements. First, RST is a natural and neutral mechanism for the semantic modelling that specifies a rigorous set of annotation guidelines without imposing any prior model for the conception. Secondly, RST respect perfectly our developed semantic taxonomy. A work to implement an RST based guidance in a tool is in progress. This tool will allow the instructor to express his macro design as well as to provide information to the technical team (authors) for the ongoing production process. To understand, we simplify briefly in the figure 3 an example of a passage via RST from a given learner and WBT modeling to a simple WBT semantic modeling as a part of the macro design.

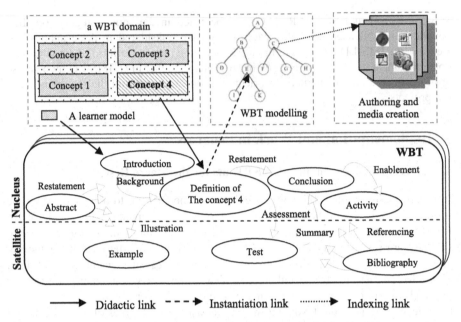

Fig. 3. Using RST and taxonomies to support the Macro Design

In this example, the WBT semantic modelling shows only WBT segmenting into semantic units and rhetorical relations among them to express some of the instructor's intentions. First, the instructor starts by the specification of concepts that the WBT domain of knowledge should include as well as the concepts known already by the learner. The second step is to map those concepts to certain semantic units which serve as abstracted containers of knowledge. All information which are needed about each semantic unit has to be defined explicitly such its mapping to given concepts, its semantic features, its intentional relations with other units and authoring properties if required. This specification is based on the RST framework and on our developed taxonomies. The resulting representation of the WBT when it is completed should be instantiated into a specific WBT model so that the last step to do is to enable this model by authoring and creating needed media. The modelling and authoring of the WBT must fulfil the representation and the requirements given by the instructor and should be done through an iteration controlled by the process management.

4.3 Building Blocks and Tool Concept

As proof of concept, we plan to implement an extension of ResourceCenter [4] to support the macro design by addition of a layer up on this tool and to support the processes management. ResourceCenter was chosen because it constitutes a browser based and instructor-friendly tool. Moreover, it supports separately the content modelling and authoring and implements already some required functionalities that we need for the collaborative production. The extension of ResourceCenter is currently in work.

5 Conclusion and Future Work

The conception and production of WBT is still technically complex for instructors. Consequently, the development of required technical skills became one of the top instructors' priorities for their professional policies. As a result today, technical concerns over WBT production have dominated teaching and pedagogical aspects. In order to develop a balanced management between the technical and pedagogical skills while producing WBTs, we motivated a collaborative production as way to meet instructors' skills for an efficient WBT production. The proposed methodology points out so called "macro design" as an independent task which has to be supported by a tool. The macro design is innovative in two ways. First, it extends the existing way of content design by supporting instructors in expliciting their intentions and instructional design. Second, it demonstrates the possibility to use the Rhetorical Structure Theory as a communicative mechanism for the instructional design in order to give an explicit perception of the expected content.

As future work, we will continue our semantic modelling and taxonomies development to adapt and to extend the RST framework in order to support completely all macro design requirements. The technical implementation of the macro design up on ResourceCenter will provide a "semantic enrichment" of this tool and evaluate, by the way, capabilities of our approach as compare as existing approaches.

References

1. Bachimont, B., Crozat, S., Mallard, R.: Managing learning content and digital formats. E-Learning for international markets: Development and use of eLearning in Europe (2004) (ISBN 3-7639-3115-5)
2. Duval, E., Hodgins, W.A.: LOM Research Agenda. In: proceedings of Twelfth International World Wide Web Conference WWW2003, Budapest, Hungary, pp. 659–667 (2003)
3. Helic, D., Maurer, H., Scerbakov, N.: Aspects of Collaborative Authoring in WBT Systems. In: Proceedings of International Conference on Advances in Infrastructure for Electronic Business, Education, Science, and Medicine on the Internet, January 2002 (2002) (ISBN 88-85280-62-5)
4. Hoermann, S., Hildebrandt, T., Rensing, C., Steinmetz, R.: ResourceCenter - A Digital Learning Object Repository with an Integrated Authoring Tool Set. In: Proceedings of World Conference on Educational Multimedia, Hypermedia and Telecommunications ED-MEDIA 2005, Montreal, pp. 3453–3460 (2005)
5. Lehmann, L., Aqqal, A., Rensing, C., Steinmetz, R.: A Content Modelling Language as Basis for the Support of the Overall Content Creation Process. In: Proceedings of ICALT 2006 conference: The 6th IEEE International Conference on Advanced Learning Technologies, Kerkrade, The Netherlands (2006)
6. Mann, W., Thompson, S.: Rhetorical Structure Theory: A theory of text organization. Technical Reports ISI/RS-87-190 (1987)
7. Pernin, J-P., Lejeune, A.: Learning design models for computers, for engineers or for teachers? In: Learning Networks for Lifelong Competence Development workshop, organized by the EU 6th Framework Integrated Project TENCompetence, Sofia, Bulgaria (April 2006)

Reasoning-Based Curriculum Sequencing and Validation: Integration in a Service-Oriented Architecture

Matteo Baldoni[1], Cristina Baroglio[1], Ingo Brunkhorst[2],
Elisa Marengo[1], and Viviana Patti[1]

[1] Dipartimento di Informatica, Università degli Studi di Torino
C.so Svizzera, 185 — I-10149 Torino, Italy
{baldoni,baroglio,patti}@di.unito.it, elisa.mrng@gmail.com
[2] L3S Research Center, University of Hannover, D-30539 Hannover, Germany
brunkhorst@l3s.de

Abstract. We present a service-oriented personalization system, set in an educational framework, based on a semantic annotation of courses including prerequisites and learning objectives. The system supports users in planning personalized curricula and in verifying the compliance of curricula against a model describing the designer goals. We have developed a prototype of the planning and validation services, by using SWI-Prolog and the SPIN model checker as reasoning engines. The services are supplied and combined in the Personal Reader framework.

1 Introduction

So far, reasoning in the Semantic Web is mostly reasoning about knowledge expressed in some ontology. However, personalization may involve also other kinds of reasoning and knowledge representation. Moreover, the next Web generation promises to deliver Semantic Web Services, that can be retrieved and *combined* in a way that satisfies the user. It opens the way to many forms of *service-oriented personalization*. Web services provide an ideal infrastructure for enabling *interoperability* among personalization applications and for constructing Plug&Play-like environments, where the user can select and combine the preferred kinds of services. Based on our previous work [2,3], our current goal is to implement such results in an organic system, where different reasoning-based personalization services can be combined for supporting the user in building a curriculum from a set of *learning resources* (courses). We achieve this by developing a Planner and a Validation Service within the Personal Reader(PR) Framework, where a service oriented approach to personalization is taken [12].

While in early times learning resources were simply considered as "contents", strictly tied to the platform used for accessing them, attention has been posed on the issue of *re-use* and of a *cross-platform* use of educational contents. The proposed solution is to adopt a *semantic annotation* of contents based on standard languages, e.g. RDF and LOM, and then to create learning resources formed by *educational contents* plus *semantic meta-data*, which supply information on the resources at a *knowledge level* (e.g. concepts from an ontology of the educational domain). Learning Resources are interpreted as *actions* [3,4], capturing the *learning objectives* and *pre-requisites*. Thus, we

E. Duval, R. Klamma, and M. Wolpers (Eds.): EC-TEL 2007, LNCS 4753, pp. 426–431, 2007.
© Springer-Verlag Berlin Heidelberg 2007

can rely on a classical theory of actions and apply different reasoning methods, like planning, for building personalized curricula. Our interpretation of learning resources also enables the use of model checking techniques for developing a validation service that detects if a curriculum is compliant w.r.t an abstract model, which encodes the *curricula-design goals*.

Motivating Scenario. Curriculum planning and validation offer useful support in many practical contexts for helping both students and teaching institutions. Since taking courses at different Universities is becoming more common in Europe, creating a personalized curriculum becomes a difficult task for students. Even if the students know what competency they would like to acquire, it's harder to find the courses that help to acquire it: an automatic system that can suggest a pathway through the course repository can be very helpful. The need for support in building personalized paths through learning resources has to be *combined* with the ability to ensure the compliance of the resulting curriculum with *curricula-design goals*, expressed by the teachers or by the *institution* offering the courses. Curricula models specify general rules for building learning paths, e.g. constraints designed by the University for guaranteeing the achievement of certain learning goals. These constraints are to be expressed in terms of knowledge elements, and maybe also on features that characterize the resources. For a provider or university, which needs to certify that a specific offered curricula for achieving a certain educational goal respects some European guidelines, we could define the guidelines as a set of constraints at an abstract level, i.e. as relations among a set of competencies which should be offered in a way that meets some given scheme. The automatic checking of compliance combined with curriculum planning could be used for implementing processes like cooperation among institutes in curricula design and integration, which are the focus of the *Bologna Process* [11], promoted by the EU.

2   Curricula Representation and Reasoning

All the different kinds of objects that we need to tackle (learning resources, curricula, and curricula models) are described on the basis of a set of *competencies*, i.e. terms identifying specific *knowledge elements*. Competencies can be thought of, and implemented, as concepts in a shared ontology. In our implementation, competencies have been semi-automatically extracted, and then stored in a RDF file (see the next section).

Learning Resources and Curricula. A *curriculum* is a sequence of *learning resources* that are homogeneous in their representation. Based on work in [3,4], we rely on an *action theory*, and take the abstraction of resources as *atomic actions*. A learning resource is modelled as an action for acquiring some competencies, called *effects*. For understanding the contents supplied by a learning resource, the user can be required to own other competencies, called *preconditions*. Both preconditions and effects can be expressed by means of a *semantic annotation* of the learning resource [4]. Since we will focus on university curricula, we will refer to learning resources as "courses". Given the above interpretation of learning resources, a *curriculum* is modelled as a *plan*, i.e. as a sequence of actions, whose execution causes transitions from a state to another, until some final state is reached. The *initial state* (possibly empty) contains all the competences that we suppose available before the curriculum is taken, e.g. the knowledge that the student already has. This set typically *grows* as the student studies and learns. Curricula are usually designed so to allow the achievement of a *learning goal*; in such cases the *final state* should contain specific knowledge elements, e.g. all those that compose the user's learning goal. A transition between two states is due to the application of the action corresponding to a learning resource. For an action to be applicable, its preconditions must hold in the state to which it should be applied. The application of the action consists in an *update* of the state. We assume that competences can only be added to states. The intuition behind this assumption is that the act of using a new resource will never erase from the students' memory the concepts acquired insofar.

Curricula Models. We would like to restrict the set of possible sequences of resources composing a curriculum, by imposing constraints on the *order* by which knowledge elements are added to the states, e.g. "a knowledge element α is to be acquired before a knowledge element β", or by specifying some *educational objective* to be achieved, in terms of knowledge that must be contained in the final state, e.g. "a knowledge element α must be acquired sooner or later". Therefore, we represent a *curricula model* as a set of temporal constraints building upon knowledge elements. A model is independent from the available resources and it can be reused in different contexts. A natural choice for representing temporal constraints on action paths is linear-time temporal logic (LTL) [10]. This kind of logic allows to verify if a property of interest is true for all the possible executions of a model (in our case the specific curriculum). This is often done by means of model checking techniques [8]. A curriculum as we represent it is, actually, a Kripke structure, that identifies a set of states with a transition relation for passing from a state to another. Since in our domain we assume that knowledge only grows, states will always contain *all* the competencies acquired up to that moment. The transition relation is given by the actions that are contained in the curriculum that is being checked. The LTL logic can be used to verify if a given formula holds starting from a state or if it holds for a set of states. For instance, in order to specify in the curricula model constraints on *what* to achieve, we can use the formula $\Diamond\alpha$ ($\Diamond$ is the *eventually* operator), meaning that a set of knowledge elements will be acquired sooner or later. Instead, constraints on *how* to achieve the educational objectives, such as "a knowledge element β cannot be acquired before the knowledge element α is acquired", can be expressed by the LTL formula $\neg\beta \, U \, \alpha$, where U is the *weak until* operator. Writing curricula models directly in LTL is not an easy task for the user. We are developing a graphical language, called DCML (Declarative Curricula Model Language) [5], inspired by DecSerFlow [15]. By means of DCML the user can easily write curricula models, maintaining a rigorous meaning due to the logic grounding of the language.

Curriculum Planning and Validation. Given a semantic annotation with preconditions and effects of the courses, classical planning techniques are exploited for creating *personalized curricula*, in the spirit of the work in [3,4]. Intuitively the idea is that, given a repository of annotated learning resources the user expresses a *learning goal* as a set of *knowledge elements* he/she would like to acquire, and possibly also a set of already owned competencies. Then, the system applies planning to build a sequence of learning resources that will allow him/her to achieve the goal. The planning methodology that we implemented (see Section 3) is a simple *depth-first forward planning* where actions cannot be applied more than once. An early prototype was presented in [1].

There are two main validation tasks that can be performed on curricula and curricula models. The simplest one consists in *checking the soundness* w.r.t. the learning dependencies and the learning goal of curricula which are built *by hand* by users themselves. Usually, soundness verification is performed manually by the learning designer, with hardly any guidelines or support [9]. Not all sequences which can be built starting from a set of learning resources are lawful. It is important to verify that all the *competencies*, that are necessary to fully understand the contents, offered by a learning resource, are introduced or available before that resource is accessed. In other words, a course can appear at a certain point in a sequence only there are no *competency gaps*. These implicit "applicability constraints" capture dependencies that are innate to the nature of the taught concepts. Given the interpretation of resources as actions, the verification of the *soundness of a curriculum*, w.r.t. the learning dependencies and the learning goal, can be interpreted as an *executability check* of the curriculum.

The other interesting verification task consists in checking if a curriculum (possibly automatically generated by a personalization service) is *compliant against the course design goals* [7]. A curriculum personalized w.r.t. the user desires, that is proved to be sound, cannot automatically be considered as being *valid* w.r.t. a particular *curricula model* describing some designer goal. The curricula model imposes further constraints on *what* to achieve and *how* achieving it. In our validation service (Section 3) the verification tasks are performed by using the SPIN model checker [13]. SPIN is used for verifying systems that can be represented by *finite state structures*, where the specification is given in an LTL logic. The verification algorithm is based on the exploration of the state space. This is exactly what we need for performing all the verification tests that we mentioned, provided that we can translate the curriculum in the internal representation used by the model checker (in SPIN such representation is given in Promela).

3   Implementation in the Personal Reader Framework

The Personal Reader Platform provides a framework for implementing personalization in the Semantic Web in a service-oriented approach, allowing to investigate how (semantic) web service technologies can provide a suitable infrastructure for building personalization applications. So called *Personalization Services* (PServices) [12] are the basic building blocks for implementing plug-and-play like personalization services in this architecture, they are semantic in the sense that they communicate solely on the basis of *RDF* documents. Besides PServices, the PR framework also includes other kinds of components, namely *Syndication Services*, *User Interfaces* and a *Connector*.

Corpus of Courses and Metadata Description. Despite some manual post-processing for fixing inconsistencies, we extracted a corpus of courses and the related meta-data by extracting real data from the Hannover University database via an automatic extraction with the Lixto [6] tool. We focussed only on a subset of the courses and manually post-processed the data, resulting in corpus with 65 courses, with 390 effects and 146 preconditions. Metadata contains also course names, semester, credit points, the type of course (e.g. laboratory, etc.), schedule and location.

Reasoners as PServices. We implemented two independent PServices for our system, the "Curriculum Planning PService", and the "Curriculum Validation PService" (Fig. 1), whic can be used by other applications as well.

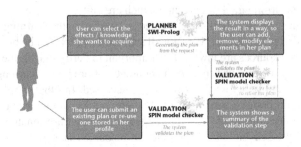

Fig. 1. The interaction with the system

The Curriculum Planning PService is basically divided in two parts: the core reasoner (the planner) and the wrapper (the web service implementation) interfacing with the PR framework. The reasoning engine that actually accomplish the curriculum planning task has been implemented in SWI Prolog by using a classical depth-first search algorithm. The initial state is set by using information about the user's context provided by the User Modelling module of the PR. SWI Prolog contains a semantic web library allowing to deal with RDF statements. Since all the inputs are sent to the reasoner in a *RDF request document*, it actually simplifies the process of interfacing the planner with the PR. The request document contains: a) links to the RDF document containing the database of courses, annotated with metadata, b) a reference to the user's context c) the user's actual learning goal, i.e. a set of knowledge concepts that the user would like to acquire, and that are part of the *domain ontology* used for the semantic annotation of the actual courses. The reasoner can also deal with information about credits provided by the courses, when the user sets a credit constraint together with the learning goal. The reasoner returns as output a *RDF response document*, which contains a list of plans that fulfill the user's learning goals and profile. Information stored in the user profile is used for *ranking higher* those plans that include the user's preferred topics.

An early prototype[1] of the Curriculum Validation PService based on the model checker SPIN has been designed and is currently being embedded in the PR. Model checking is the algorithmic verification of the fact that a finite state system complies to its specification. In our case the specification is given by the curricula model and consists of a set of temporal constraints, while the finite state system is the curriculum to be verified. The advantage of using a model checker like SPIN, rather than an ad hoc implementation is that it can handle any kind of LTL temporal formula. Moreover, we can also deal with the validation of *non-linear* curricula, i.e. curricula that contain branching points. This kind of curricula allow to account for *uncertainties* of the user. In fact a branching point corresponds to a possible choice among alternative resources.

---

[1] http://www.l3s.de/~brunkhor/semweb/curriculum/

4   Conclusion

In this work we have sketched the current state of the integration of semantic personalization web services for Curriculum Planning and Validation within the Personal Reader Framework. We are actually investigating how to extend the application with a module of geo-spatial reasoning working on meta-data like floor-plans and locations.

In [14] an analysis of pre- and post-requisite annotations of learning object is proposed with the aim of dealing with competency gap verification. In this approach, whenever an error will be detected by the validation phase, a correction engine will be activated, that produce suggestions on how to correct the wrong curriculum, by using reasoning-by-cases. The suggestions are presented to the course developer, who can decide which ones to adopt. Once a curriculum have been corrected, it must be validated again: the corrections might introduce errors. The proposal is inspired by the CocoA system [7], that allows to perform the consistency check of web-based courses.

References

1. Baldoni, M., Baroglio, C., Brunkhorst, I., Henze, N., Marengo, E., Patti, V.: A Personalization Service for Curriculum Planning. In: ABIS 2006. Proc. of the 14th Workshop on Adaptivity and User Modeling in Interactive Systems, Hildesheim, Germany, pp. 17–20 (2006)
2. Baldoni, M., Baroglio, C., Martelli, A., Patti, V., Torasso, L.: Verifying the compliance of personalized curricula to curricula models in the semantic web. In: Proc. of the Semantic Web Personalization Workshop, pp. 53–62, Budva, Montenegro (2006)
3. Baldoni, M., Baroglio, C., Patti, V.: Web-based adaptive tutoring: An approach based on logic agents and reasoning about actions. Artificial Intelligence Review 1(22), 3–39 (2004)
4. Baldoni, M., Baroglio, C., Patti, V., Torasso, L.: Reasoning about learning object metadata for adapting SCORM courseware. In: Proc. of EAW'04, pp. 4–13 (2004)
5. Baldoni, M., Marengo, E.: Curricula model checking: declarative representation and verification of properties. In: Duval, E., Klamma, R., Wolpers, M. (eds.) EC-TEL 2007. LNCS, vol. 4753, Springer, Heidelberg (2007)
6. Baumgartner, R., Flesca, S., Gottlob, G.: Visual web information extraction with Lixto. In: VLDB, pp. 119–128. Morgan Kaufmann, San Francisco (2001)
7. Brusilovsky, P., Vassileva, J.: Course sequencing techniques for large-scale web-based education. Int. J. Cont. Engineering Education and Lifelong learning 13(1/2), 75–94 (2003)
8. Clarke, O.E.M., Peled, D.: Model checking. MIT Press, Cambridge, MA, USA (2001)
9. De Coi, J.L., Herder, E., Koesling, A., Lofi, C., Olmedilla, D., Papapetrou, O., Sibershi, W.: A model for competence gap analysis. In: Proc. of WEBIST 2007 (2007)
10. Emerson, E.A.: Temporal and modal logic. Handbook of Theoretical Computer Science B, 997–1072 (1990)
11. European Commission, Education and Training. The Bologna process, http://europa.eu.int/comm/education/policies/educ/bologna/bologna_en.html
12. Henze, N., Krause, D.: Personalized access to web services in the semantic web. In: The 3rd Int. Semantic Web User Interaction Workshop, SWUI (November 2006)
13. Holzmann, G.J.: The SPIN Model Checker. Addison-Wesley, Reading (2003)
14. Melia, M., Pahl, C.: Automatic Validation of Learning Object Compositions. In: Information Technology and Telecommunications Conf. IT&T'2005: Doctoral Symposium (2006)
15. van der Aalst, W.M.P., Pesic, M.: DecSerFlow: Towards a Truly Declarative Service Flow Language. In: Bravetti, M., Núñez, M., Zavattaro, G. (eds.) WS-FM 2006. LNCS, vol. 4184, Springer, Heidelberg (2006)

Curriculum Model Checking: Declarative Representation and Verification of Properties

Matteo Baldoni and Elisa Marengo

Dipartimento di Informatica — Università degli Studi di Torino
C.so Svizzera, 185 — I-10149 Torino (Italy)
baldoni@di.unito.it,elisa.mrng@gmail.com

Abstract. When a curriculum is proposed, it is important to verify at least three aspects: that the curriculum allows the achievement of the user's learning goals, that the curriculum is compliant w.r.t. the course design goals, specified by the institution that offers it, and that the sequence of courses that defines the curriculum does not have competency gaps. In this work, we present a constrained-based representation for specifying the goals of "course design" and introduce a design graphical language, grounded into Linear Time Logic.

Keywords: formal model for curricula description, *model checking*, *verification of properties*, *competence gaps*.

1 Introduction and Motivations

As recently underlined by other authors, there is a strong relationship between the development of peer-to-peer, (web) service technologies and e-learning technologies [11,8]. The more learning resources are freely available through the Web, the more e-learning management systems (LMSs) should be able to take advantage from this richness: LMSs should offer the means for easily retrieving and assembling e-learning resources so to satisfy specific users' learning goals, similarly to how services are retrieved and composed [8]. As in a service composition it is necessary to verify that, at every point, all the information necessary to the subsequent invocations is available, in a learning domain, it is important to verify that all the *competencies*, i.e. the *knowledge*, necessary to fully understand a learning resource are introduced or available before that learning resource is accessed. The composition of learning resources, i.e. a *curriculum*, does not have to show any *competency gap*. Unfortunately, this verification, is usually performed *manually* by the designer, with hardly any guidelines or support [6].

In [11] an analysis of pre- and post-requisite annotations of the Learning Objects (LO), representing the learning resources, is proposed for automatizing the competency gap verification. A logic based validation engine can use these annotations to validate the LO composition. This proposal is inspired by the CocoA system [5], that allows to perform the analysis and the consistency check of static web-based courses. Competency gaps are checked by a prerequisite checker for *linear courses*, simulating the process of teaching with an overlay student model. Pre- and post-requisites are represented by concepts, elementary pieces of domain of knowledge.

Brusilovsky and Vassileva [5] sketch many other kinds of verification. In our opinion, two of them are particularly important: (a) verifying that the curriculum allows

E. Duval, R. Klamma, and M. Wolpers (Eds.): EC-TEL 2007, LNCS 4753, pp. 432–437, 2007.

to achieve the users' *learning goals*, and (b) verifying that the curriculum is compliant against the *course design goals*. Verifying (a) is fundamental to guarantee that users will acquire the desired knowledge. At the same time, manually or automatically supplied curricula, developed to reach that learning goal, should match the design document, a curricula model, specified by the institution. Curricula models specify general rules for designing sequences of learning resources (courses) and can be interpreted as *constraints*. These constraints are to be expressed in terms of *concepts* and, in general, it is not possible to associate them directly to a learning resource, as instead is done for pre-requisites, because they express constraints on the acquisition of concepts, independently from the resources that supply them.

This work differs from previous work [4], where the authors presented an adaptive tutoring system, that exploits *reasoning about actions and changes* to plan and verify curricula. That approach was based on abstract representations, capturing the *structure* of a curriculum, and implemented as prolog-like clauses. A procedure-driven planning was applied to build personalized curricula. The advantage of such planning techniques is that the only curricula that are tried are the possible executions of the procedure itself, and this restricts considerably the search space of the planning process. In this context, we proposed also forms of verification: of competency gaps, of learning goal achievement, and of whether a curriculum, given by a user, is compliant to the *course design* goals. The use of procedure clauses is, however, limiting because they, besides having a *prescriptive* nature, pose very strong constraints on the sequencing of learning resources. Clauses represent what is "legal" and whatever sequence is not foreseen by the clauses is "illegal". However, in an open environment where resources are extremely various, they are added/removed dynamically, this approach becomes unfeasible.

For this reason it is appropriate to take another perspective and represent only those constraints which are strictly necessary, in a way that is inspired by the so called *social approach* proposed by Singh for describing communication protocols for multi-agent systems and service oriented architecture [12]. In this approach only the *obligations* are represented. In our application context, obligations capture relations among the times at which different competencies are to be acquired. The advantage of this representation is that we do not have to represent all that is legal but only those *necessary conditions* that characterize a legal solution. To make an example, by means of constraints we can request that a certain knowledge is acquired before some other knowledge, without expressing what else is to be done in between.

In this paper we present a constraint-based representation of curricula models. Constraints are expressed as formulas in a temporal logic (LTL, linear-time logic [7]) represented by means of a simple graphical language that we call DCML (*Declarative Curricula Model Language*). This kind of logic allows the verification of some properties of interest for all the possible executions of a model, which in our case corresponds to the specific curriculum.

2 DCML: A Declarative Curricula Model Language

In this section we describe our Declarative Curricula Model Language (DCML), a graphical language to represent the relations that can occur among concepts supplied by attending courses. DCML is inspired by DecSerFlow, the Declarative Service Flow Language to specify, enact, and monitor web service flows [13]. As such, DCML is grounded in Linear Temporal Logic (LTL) [7] and it allows a curricula model to be described in an easy way, with a rigorous and precise meaning given by the logic representation. LTL includes temporal operators such as *next-time* ($\bigcirc\varphi$, the formula φ holds in the immediately following state of the run), *eventually* ($\Diamond\varphi$, φ is guaranteed to eventually become true), *always* ($\Box\varphi$, the formula φ remains invariably true throughout a run), *until* (α U β, the formula α remains true until β). The set of LTL formulas obtained for a curricula model are, then, used to verify whether a curriculum will respect it [3]. As an example, Fig. 1 shows a curricula model expressed in DCML. Every box

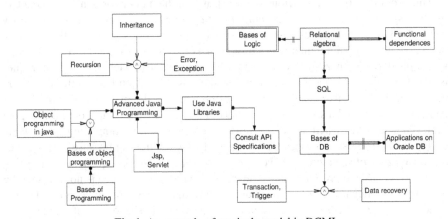

Fig. 1. An example of curricula model in DCML

contains at least one competency. Boxes/competencies are related by arrows, which represent (mainly) temporal constraints among the times at which they are to be acquired. Altogether the constraints describe a curricula model. Hereafter, we describe most of such elements.

The simplest kinds of constraint concern the *existence*, *absence*, or *possibility* of acquisition for a certain competency. The *existence constraint* imposes that a certain concept k must be acquired sooner or later. It captures the fact that a concept characterizes a curriculum, so a student cannot present a plan in which it does not appear. It is represented by the LTL formula $\Diamond k$, that is k must eventually become true. Similarly, a course designer can impose that a concept k must never appear in a curriculum. This is possible by means of the *absence constraint*. The LTL formula $\Box\neg k$ expresses this fact: it means that k cannot appear. On the diagram these two constraints are given by marking boxes with the "cardinality" of the concepts (1 for existence and 0 for absence). When both 0 and 1 appear on the same box, we have a *possibility constraint*. The corresponding LTL formula is $\Diamond k \vee \Box\neg k$. When no cardinality is expressed explicitly, possibility is assumed. The last constraint on concepts is represented by a double box, which means that a concept k must belong to the initial knowledge of the student. In other words, the simple logic formula k must hold in the initial state.

In DCML it is also possible to represent *Disjunctive Normal Form* (DNF) formulas as *conjunctions* and *disjunctions* of concepts. For lack of space, we do not describe the notation here, although an example can be seen in Fig. 1. The interested reader can find an extended version of this paper that is available in the home page of the authors.

Besides the representation of competencies and of constraints on competencies, DCML allows to represent *relations* among competencies. For simplicity, in the following presentation we will always relate simple competencies, although it is, of course, possible to connect DNF formulas.

Arrows ending with a little-ball, express the *before* temporal constraint between two concepts: a concept must be acquired *before* another one. This constraint can be used to express that, to understand a topic, some other knowledge is required. Notice that if the antecedent never becomes true, also the consequent must be invariably false. k_1 *before* k_2 corresponds to the LTL formula $\neg k_2 \cup k_1$.

One can express that a concept must be acquired *immediately before* some other by means of a triple line arrow that ends with a little-ball. The constraint "k_1 *immediate before* k_2" imposes that k_1 is acquired before k_2 and that either k_2 is true in the next state (w.r.t. when k_1 is acquired) or it is never acquired. Immediate before is stronger than before because it imposes that two concepts have to be acquired in strict sequence. The LTL formula for *immediate before* is $\neg k_2 \cup k_1 \wedge \Box(k_1 \supset (\bigcirc k_2 \vee \Box \neg k_2))$, that is k_1 *before* k_2 and whenever k_1 holds, either in the next state k_2 holds or k_2 never holds.

The *implication* relation specifies, instead, that if a certain concept holds, some other concept must be acquired sooner or later. The acquisition of the consequent is imposed by the truth value of the antecedent, but, in case this one is true, the implication does not specify when the consequent is to be achieved (it could be before, after or in the same state as the antecedent). k_1 *implies* k_2 is expressed by the LTL formula $\Diamond k_1 \supset \Diamond k_2$.

The *immediate implication* instead, specifies that the consequent must hold in the state right after the one in which the antecedent is acquired. This does not mean that it must be acquired in that state, but only that it cannot be acquired after. This is expressed by the LTL implication formula in conjunction with the constraint that whenever k_1 holds, k_2 holds in the next state: $\Diamond k_1 \supset \Diamond k_2 \wedge \Box(k_1 \supset \bigcirc k_2)$. *Implication* and *immediate implication* are graphically represented with an arrow that starts with a little-ball and with a triple line arrow that starts with a little-ball.

The last two kinds of temporal constraints are *succession* and *immediate succession* The *succession* relation specifies that if k_1 is acquired, afterwards k_2 is also achieved. Succession is expressed by the LTL formula $\Diamond k_1 \supset (\Diamond k_2 \wedge (\neg k_2 \cup k_1))$. While in the *before* relation, when the antecedent is never acquired also the consequent must be false, in the *succession* relation this is not relevant. This behaviour is due to the fact that the *succession* specifies a condition of the kind: *if k_1 then k_2*. The *before*, instead, represents a constraint without any conditional premise. The fact that the consequent must be acquired *after* the antecedent differentiates *implication* from *succession*.

The *immediate succession* imposes that the acquisition of the consequent must happen either in the same state the antecedent is acquired or in the state immediately after (not before nor later). The immediate succession is expressed by the LTL formula: $\Diamond k_1 \supset (\Diamond k_2 \wedge (\neg k_2 \cup k_1)) \wedge \Box(k_1 \supset \bigcirc k_2)$. The representation of (*immediate*) *succession*, see Fig. 1, is an (triple) arrow that starts and ends with a little-ball.

The graphical notations for "negative relations" is very intuitive: two vertical lines break the arrow that represents the constraint. Some examples are shown in Fig. 1.

k_1 *not before* k_2 specifies that the concept k_1 cannot be acquired before or in the same state of the concept k_2. The LTL formula is $\neg k_1 \ U \ (k_2 \wedge \neg k_1)$. Notice that this is not obtained by simply negating the before relation but it is weaker because the negation would impose the acquisition of the concepts specified as consequents, the *not before* does not. The *not immediate before* is translated exactly in the same way of the *not before*. Indeed, it is a special case of *not before*. This happens because the acquired knowledge cannot be forgotten.

By means of k_1 *not implies* k_2 we express that the acquisition of the concept k_1 implies that k_2 will never be acquired. We express this by the LTL formula $\Diamond k_1 \supset \Box \neg k_2$. Again, we choose to use a weaker formula than the natural negation of the implication relation, that is $\Diamond k_1 \wedge \Box \neg k_2$. k_1 *not immediate implies* k_2 constraint imposes that when the concept k_1 is acquired, in the immediately subsequent state, the concept k_2 must be false. Afterwards, the truth value of k_2 does not matter (it is weaker than $\neg(k_1$ *immediate implies* k_2)). The corresponding LTL formula is $\Diamond k_1 \supset (\Box \neg k_2 \vee \Diamond(k_1 \wedge \bigcirc \neg k_2))$.

The *not succession*, and the *not immediate succession* are weaker versions of, respectively, negation of succession and of immediate succession. The first one imposes that a concept cannot be acquired after another. This means that it could be acquired before, or it will always be false. The LTL formula is $\Diamond k_1 \supset (\Box \neg k_2 \vee k_1$ *not before* $k_2)$. The second imposes that if a concept is acquired in a certain state, in the state that follows another concept must be false: $\Diamond k_1 \supset (\Box \neg k_2 \vee k_1$ *not before* $k_2 \vee \Diamond(k_1 \wedge \bigcirc \neg k_2))$.

3   Conclusions

The presented work is an evolution of earlier works [2,4]. In those works, we semantically annotated learning objects with the aim of building compositions of new learning objects, based on the user's learning goals and by exploiting planning techniques. That proposal was based on a different approach, that relied on the experience of the authors in the use of techniques for reasoning about actions and changes. Of course, the new proposal, presented in this paper, can be applied also to learning objects, given a semantic annotation of theirs, as introduced in the cited works. In [1] we discuss the integration, into the Personal Reader Framework [9], of a verification web service that implements the explained techniques.

In particular, in this work we have introduced a graphical language to describe temporal constraints posed on the acquisition of competencies (supplied by courses). In the extended version, that is available on-line, we show how to use UML activity diagrams to specify sets of curricula, and we show how to translate them into Promela programs. Such programs can be used by the SPIN model checker [10] to verify whether the curriculum respects the DCML model. Model checking can also be applied for checking the achievement of the user's learning goals and the presence of competency gaps.

In [3] we extend the current proposal so as to include a representation of the *proficiency level* at which a competency is owned or supplied, as suggested in [6]. The key idea is to associate to each competency a variable, having the same name as the competency, which can be assigned natural numbers as values. The value denotes the proficiency level; zero means absence of knowledge. The next step will be to give a structure to competencies, e.g. by defining a proper ontology, for allowing more flexible forms of reasoning and verification.

We are currently working on an automatic translation from a textual representation of DCML curricula models into the corresponding set of LTL formulas and from a textual representation of an activity diagram, that describes a curriculum (comprehensive of the description of all courses involved with their preconditions and effects), into the corresponding Promela program. We are also going to realize a graphical tool to define curricula models by means of DCML.

Acknowledgements. The authors would like to thank Cristina Baroglio, and also Viviana Patti and Ingo Brunkhorst, for the helpful discussions. This research has partially been funded by the European Commission and by the Swiss Federal Office for Education and Science within the 6th Framework Programme project REWERSE number 506779 (cf. http://rewerse.net), and it has also been supported by MIUR PRIN 2005 "Specification and verification of agent interaction protocols" national project.

References

1. Baldoni, M., Baroglio, C., Brunkhorst, I., Marengo, E., Patti, V.: Curriculum Sequencing and Validation: Integration in a Service-Oriented Architecture. In: Duval, E., Klamma, R., Wolpers, M. (eds.) EC-TEL 2007. LNCS, vol. 4753, Springer, Heidelberg (2007)
2. Baldoni, M., Baroglio, C., Henze, N.: Personalization for the Semantic Web. In: Eisinger, N., Małuszyński, J. (eds.) Reasoning Web. LNCS, vol. 3564, pp. 173–212. Springer, Heidelberg (2005)
3. Baldoni, M., Baroglio, C., Marengo, E.: Curricula Modeling and Checking. In: Basili, R., Pazienza, M.T. (eds.) AI*IA 2007. LNCS (LNAI), vol. 4733, Springer, Heidelberg (2007)
4. Baldoni, M., Baroglio, C., Patti, V.: Web-based adaptive tutoring: an approach based on logic agents and reasoning about actions. Artificial Intelligence Review 22(1), 3–39 (2004)
5. Brusilovsky, P., Vassileva, J.: Course sequencing techniques for large-scale web-based education. Int. J. Cont. Engineering Education and Lifelong learning 13(1/2), 75–94 (2003)
6. De Coi, J.L., Herder, E., Koesling, A., Lofi, C., Olmedilla, D., Papapetrou, O., Sibershi, W.: A model for competence gap analysis. In: Proc. of WEBIST 2007, INSTICC Press (2007)
7. Emerson, E.A.: Temporal and model logic. Handbook of Theoretical Computer Science B, 997–1072 (1990)
8. Farrell, R., Liburd, S.D., Thomas, J.C.: Dynamic assebly of learning objects. In: Proc. of WWW 2004, New York, USA (2004)
9. Henze, N., Krause, D.: Personalized access to web services in the semantic web. In: Cruz, I., Decker, S., Allemang, D., Preist, C., Schwabe, D., Mika, P., Uschold, M., Aroyo, L. (eds.) ISWC 2006. LNCS, vol. 4273, Springer, Heidelberg (2006)
10. Holzmann, G.J.: The SPIN Model Checker. Addison-Wesley, Reading (2003)
11. Melia, M., Pahl, C.: Automatic Validation of Learning Object Compositions. In: Proc. of IT&T'2005: Doctoral Symposium, Carlow, Ireland (2006)
12. Singh, M.P.: Agent communication languages: Rethinking the principles. IEEE Computer 31(12), 40–47 (1998)
13. van der Aalst, W.M.P., Pesic, M.: DecSerFlow: Towards a Truly Declarative Service Flow Language. In: Bravetti, M., Núñez, M., Zavattaro, G. (eds.) WS-FM 2006. LNCS, vol. 4184, Springer, Heidelberg (2006)

Workplace Learning: How We Keep
Track of Relevant Information

Kerstin Bischoff, Eelco Herder, and Wolfgang Nejdl

L3S Research Center / University of Hannover
Appelstraße 9a
30167 Hannover, Germany
{bischoff,herder,nejdl}@l3s.de

Abstract. At the workplace, learning is often a by-product of working on complex projects, requiring self-steered, need-driven and goal-oriented retrieval of information just in time from documents or peers. The personal desktop provides a rich source for learning material and for adaptation of learning resources. Data within that personal information space enables learning from previous experience, sharing tacit and explicit knowledge, and allows for establishing context and context-aware delivery of learning materials and all relevant information. Results from personal desktop studies and the corresponding technologies thus have great potential to enhance TEL. Therefore, this paper (1) provides a short overview of desktop organization and search studies as well as applications and (2) suggests tighter incorporation of desktop research for innovative TEL infrastructures.

Keywords: workplace learning, desktop organization, desktop search, semantic desktop, desktop infrastructures, just-in-time information retrieval, task support.

1 Introduction

In our information-based society with its rapidly changing demands, knowledge gets outdated fast. As people often change jobs, the notions of lifelong learning and workplace learning have gained a lot of attention. To facilitate these types of learning, our perspective on learning has to be broadened [22]. Knowledge workers, who spend most of their time on retrieving, processing, creating and manipulating knowledge, rely on efficient access to data in different formats [22, 24]. Besides external (corporate) repositories, PC desktops – including possibly connected desktops of colleagues – provide a rich source of valuable material for informal learning.

This paper[1] is structured as follows. In the next section we motivate why personal (semantic) desktop environments are important for learning. In section three, we give a short overview on desktop organization and usage studies. The fourth section describes approaches toward supporting information access and delivery. Finally, we discuss how innovative learning scenarios can effectively employ such techniques.

---

[1] A longer version of this paper is available as technical report: http://www.l3s.de/~bischoff/DesktopLearning.pdf.

E. Duval, R. Klamma, and M. Wolpers (Eds.): EC-TEL 2007, LNCS 4753, pp. 438–443, 2007.

2 Learning in Context

The PC desktop provides a lot of learning resources in various formats. Personal information - including documents, emails, web cache, notes, calendars, links, instant messaging, all connected to the users and their peers – provides a rich source of prior working experiences [4, 22]. Some may be well-structured learning objects, but most resources are just documents, emails and visited websites. The desktop can provide rich data about user activities and interests to enable context-aware delivery of information. These personal resources encourage *learning from experience*: learning at the workplace less based on instruction than on collaboration with peers and learning in action and by reflection [1, 11]. Technological support to raise awareness of relevant knowledge and solutions from the past enables the integration of continuous experiential learning into work processes. It offers a great opportunity to connect new information to prior knowledge and experience in a meaningful way and to make us aware of what we know and of potential gaps we have. These rich, personal repositories are likely to be more effective for disseminating highly context-specific – often *tacit* - knowledge [11]. Moreover, as learning takes place at the workplace itself, no or only minor transfer of *context* is necessary.

3 How Do We Keep Track of Relevant Information?

Several studies have examined organizational behaviour on the personal desktop. In this section we review research and studies that focus on the strategies that people employ to refind their documents, emails and information encountered on the Web.

Documents typically contain frequently used information closely related to current tasks, which later becomes *archived* [2]. Some users systematically order their documents, others just *pile* them [18]. Users may pile because they can't properly classify the information [16] or anticipate future usage and retrieval. On the other hand, piles may serve as *reminders* [18]. Barreau and Nardi [2] found that electronic documents are usually organized into thematic folders. A proper folder structure provides means for relocating documents and timely reminders. Users tend to place items that need to be paid attention to on the desktop or some other place where they likely will notice them. However, archiving old information is often not considered worth the effort [2].

For refinding documents, users often engage in 'orienteering behavior': instead of providing an exact query, they navigate to the target document in smaller steps [25]. As defining a query is often as hard as efficiently organizing the data [2, 16], location-based orienteering – skimming through a list of folders – is often preferred to keyword search. According to [2], users only employ search tools after other unsuccessful trials. A possible explanation is that current text search tools do not support the rich associations that people use as retrieval cues [7, 16].

Due to its interpersonal nature, **email**, and the ways users handle it, differs much from other information items. Email predominantly carries *ephemeral* information [2] that is only needed for a short time, such as memos, to-do-lists, and mail messages. Email plays an important role in everyday life, supporting activities as contact management, personal archiving and document exchange [9, 26, 27].

Many users keep almost all of their emails in the Inbox, as archiving costs time and effort. Besides, the Inbox serves as a list of reminders [27]. As far as archiving is concerned, users may be classified as *no filers*, *frequent filers* and *spring cleaners* [27]. Only frequent filing provides effectiveness and the chance of being reminded, but it does not always compensate for the archiving time. [9] found shallow file hierarchies – organized by sender, organization, project – to be common to have immediate access. Location-based search and sorting of mails by sender or date with subsequent browsing were popular strategies employed when looking for a message. Search tools and automatic filters were less frequently used.

Bruce et al. [4] empirically collected a list of common keeping methods for important **information encountered on Web sites**. Among them: sending an email with the URL to self, printing out a Web page, bookmarking, saving it to a file, pasting the URL into a document, writing the URL down. These methods are not heavily used; though. Although browsers provide several means for relocating information found earlier on the Web – including the back button, bookmarks, URL auto-completion and the history toolbar – these tools do not provide the functionality needed for refinding information. In a study on revisitation [19], we found that users particularly had problems in relocating a page visited weeks or months before, as the Web address mostly did not reside in the browser's memory – and not in the user's memory either. This left users with little more choice than a *repeated search*, which often turned out to be unsuccessful, due to the user's inability to replicate the original query, or due to the fact that the original query did not directly led to the desired page. The results showed the need for better support for *orienteering* behaviour [25].

Concluding, users face many problems in managing their data. While location-based browsing is often successfully used to find personal files, classification and structuring is time-consuming and cognitively hard. Even less effort is commonly spent on archiving emails. Search tools are not frequently used, because they lack important features. **Fragmentation of information access** exacerbates these problems: resources are spread over the PC and bound to specific applications [26]. Thus, assistance in (multiple, flexible) filing, search facilities offering enhanced attributes, and reminding, integrated desktop infrastructures as well as task management are critical.

4   Systems Supporting Information Access on the Desktop

The next sections present some innovative approaches and applications for organizing and searching our personal information space more naturally and more efficiently.

4.1   Integrated Search Infrastructures

Beagle++ [6] is a desktop search system that indexes all personal documents and generates additional metadata that describes these documents, other resources, as well as their relationships. Triggered by modification events, Beagle++ annotates the material that the user has read, used, written or commented upon. *Haystack* [15] generates annotations and provides dynamic collection views and focuses on agents exploiting user specific and predefined ontologies. It supports search, as well as associative browsing or 'orienteering'. *Stuff I've seen* (SIS) [10] uses rich contextual cues such as time, people, thumbnails and previews to support retrieval and presentation. SIS was extended to comprise timeline visualization, where important personal and public landmarks (photographs, calendar or news events, holidays) were displayed together with results of a keyword search [21]. *Phlat* [8] is a follow-up, enhanced to allow tagging information with multiple meaningful, personal annotations. Similarly, the integrated platform *MyLifeBits* [12] was developed around *annotations* and *links*. As an alternative to filing, manual annotations (or tags) serve for organizing information, and for meaningful, intuitive search or browsing by content. Linking enables associative browsing and serendipitous encounters.

4.2 Recommending Personal Information

While the former approaches enhance the refinding of information, users may often be *unaware* of information related to their current work already existing on their desktops – or they do not have the time to search for it. Just-in-time Information Retrieval (JITIR) Agents [20] *proactively recommend* relevant resources, by modelling the user's preferences and tasks from the user's current activities and interactions like Web navigation, saving, or printing.

Rhodes and Maes [20] describe the implementation of three different agents. The *Remembrance Agent* monitors the user and continuously searches the desktop or databases for related items matching the current task. Suggestions are displayed in a side window. *Margin Notes* links Web pages to personal files by rewriting the source code on-the-fly. *Jimminy* bases his suggestions on various environment-aware sensors contained in a shoulder-mounted wearable computer. The results are shown on a head-mounted display. *Watson* [5] additionally uses a simple and explicit task model to interpret user actions in order to anticipate a user's information need.

4.3 Supporting Tasks and Processes

Tasks are central in working. The value of resources is mainly determined by their relation to the current context. *TaskMaster* [3] organizes emails, attached documents or sent URLs around tasks. These communication threads – or 'thrasks' – are built by analyzing message data. Task specific meta-information – deadlines, appointments, to-dos – can also be added and visualized. A similar approach is followed in *UMEA* [14], which uses *projects* as organizational units and provides interaction history as context. By contrast, the *TaskTracer* project [24] employs machine learning to learn and predict user tasks from traced interactions with the operating system/applications. Based on learned correlations between tasks and folders, a Folder Predictor suggests a folder for saving or opening resources, thus saving interaction costs.

We will now illustrate how TEL scenarios can benefit from such techniques.

5 Information Finding in Innovative Learning Scenarios

Authors of e-Learning content may be supported in creating learning material by their own desktop resources, for instance by semi-automatically *enriching* a course with available publications, in order to adapt to different knowledge levels [13]. Systems in the Sidewalk Project [17] allow for manually marking and linking one's own resources to concepts of a lesson; these links could be created automatically to provide a personalized, enriched concept map that promotes elaboration and motivation.

The benefit of establishing context and providing easy access to already existing resources seems even more important in workplace settings. In these situations, advanced features – like recommendation of experts and reuse of previous experience – as well as techniques for context sharing seem promising. In addition to providing elaborate, semantically enriched and flexible browsing and search facilities, JITIR agents can continuously recommend relevant resources from the repository, in which similar prior problems and solutions are described. Delivery can be personalized and contextualized by compiling a profile that is built from keywords from the desktop or the current task. As an example, the LIP system supports the situation-aware retrieval of resources adapted to the current context [23]. Created context information can also be reused as metadata for learning resources and information fragments.

6 Conclusion and Outlook

Workplace learning requires advanced information finding functionalities to retrieve relevant knowledge. This paper provides a short overview over relevant research, motivating learning in context, and discusses information finding and organizing strategies, approaches and systems. We describe state-of-the-art systems supporting information access on the desktop, which provide advanced search, recommendation or task support functionalities. Future research on advanced technology enhanced learning solutions will have to take such techniques into account, enabling innovative learning solutions at the workplace and in knowledge rich environments.

Acknowledgements. the research reported in this paper has taken place in the contexts of the PROLEARN Network of Excellence and the European IST Ten Competence. Both projects are member of the Professional Learning Cluster.

References

[1] Agyris, C., Schön, D.A.: Organizational Learning: A Theory of Action Perspective. Addison-Wesley, Reading, MA (1978)
[2] Barreau, D., Nardi, B.A.: Finding and Reminding. File Organization from the Desktop. SIGCHI Bulletin 27(3), 39–43 (1995)
[3] Bellotti, V., Ducheneaut, N., Howard, M., Smith, M.I.: Taking Email to Task: The Design and Evaluation of a Task Management Centered Email Tool. In: Proc. CHI 2003, pp. 345–352 (2003)
[4] Bruce, H., Jones, W., Dumais, S.: Information behavior that keeps found things found. Information Research 10(1) (2004)
[5] Budznik, J., Hammond, K.: Anticipating and Contextualizing Information Needs. In: Proc. of the 62nd Annual Meeting of the American Society for Information Science (1999)
[6] Chirita, P.-A., Gavriloaie, R., Costache, S., Nejdl, W., Paiu, R.: Beagle++: Semantically Enhanced Searching and Ranking on the Desktop. In: Sure, Y., Domingue, J. (eds.) ESWC 2006. LNCS, vol. 4011, pp. 348–362. Springer, Heidelberg (2006)

[7] Cutrell, E., Dumais, S.T., Teevan, J.: Searching to Eliminate Personal Information Management. Communications of the ACM 49(1), 58–64 (2006)

[8] Cutrell, E., Robbins, D.C., Dumais, S.T., Sarin, R.: Fast, flexible filtering with Phlat - Personal search and organization made easy. In: Proc. CHI 2006, pp. 261–270 (2006)

[9] Duchenaut, N., Bellotti, V.: E-mail as Habitat. An Exploration of Embedded Personal Information Management. Interactions 8(5) (2001)

[10] Dumais, S., Cutrell, E., Cadiz, J.J., Jancke, G., Sarin, R., Robbins, D.C.: Stuff I've Seen: A System for Personal Information Retrieval and Re-Use. Proc. SIGIR'03, 72–79 (2003)

[11] Eraut, M.: Informal learning in the workplace. Studies in Continuing Education 26(2), 247–273 (2004)

[12] Gemell, J., Bell, G., Lueder, R.: MyLifeBits: A Personal Database for Everything. Communications of the ACM 49(1), 88–95 (2006)

[13] Hendrix, M., Cristea, A.I., Nejdl, W.: Authoring Adaptive Learning Material on the Semantic Desktop. In: Proc. A3H@AH 2006 (2006)

[14] Kaptelinin, V.: UMEA: Translating Interaction Histories into Project Contexts. In: Proc. CHI 2003, pp. 353–360 (2003)

[15] Karger, D.R., Bakshi, K., Huynh, D., Quan, D., Sinha, V.: Haystack: A Customizable General-Purpose Information Management Tool for End Users of Semistructured Data. In: Proc. CIDR 2005, pp. 13–26 (2005)

[16] Landsdale, M.W.: The psychology of personal information management. Applied Ergonomics 19(1), 55–66 (1988)

[17] Maier, D., Archner, D., Delcambre, L., Murthy, S., Annareddy, T.J., Cassel, L.N., Gangula, D., Teng, G.B., Fox, E.A., Murthy, U.: Personal Information Enhancement for Education. In: Proc. PIM 2006, pp. 86–89 (2006)

[18] Malone, T.W.: How Do People Organize Their Desks? Implications for the Design of Office Information Systems. ACM Transactions on Office Information Systems 1(1), 99–112 (1983)

[19] Obendorf, H., Weinreich, H., Herder, E., Mayer, M.: Web Page Revisitation Revisited: Implications of a Long-term Click-stream Study of Browser Usage. In: Proc. CHI 2007 (2007)

[20] Rhodes, B.J., Maes, P.: Just in time information retrieval agents. IBM Systems Journal 39(3/4), 685–704 (2000)

[21] Ringel, M., Cutrell, E., Dumais, S., Horvitz, E.: Milestones in Time: The Value of Landmarks in Retrieving Information from Personal Stores. In: Proc. Interact'03, pp. 184–191 (2003)

[22] Rosenberg, M.J.: E-Learning. Strategies for Delivering Knowledge in the Digital Age. McGraw-Hill, New York (2001)

[23] Schmidt, A., Braun, S.: Context-Aware Workplace Learning Support: Concept, Experiences, and Remaining Challenges. In: Nejdl, W., Tochtermann, K. (eds.) EC-TEL 2006. LNCS, vol. 4227, pp. 518–524. Springer, Heidelberg (2006)

[24] Stumpf, S., Bao, X., Dragunov, A., Dietterich, T.G., Herlocker, J., Johnsrude, K., Li, L., Shen, J.: Predicting User Tasks: I Know What You're Doing! In: Proc. AAAI-05 (2005)

[25] Teevan, J., Alvarado, C., Ackerman, M.S., Karger, D.R.: The Perfect Search Engine Is Not Enough: A Study of Orienteering Behavior in Directed Search. In: Proc. CHI 2004, pp. 415–422 (2004)

[26] Whittaker, S., Bellotti, V., Gwizda, J.: Email in Personal Information Management. Communications of the ACM 49(1), 68–73 (2006)

[27] Whittaker, S., Sidner, C.: Email Overload: exploring personal information management of email. In: Proc. CHI 1996, pp. 276–283 (1996)

A Digital Library Framework for Reusing e-Learning Video Documents*

Paolo Bolettieri, Fabrizio Falchi, Claudio Gennaro,
and Fausto Rabitti

ISTI-CNR, via G. Moruzzi 1, 56124 Pisa, Italy
paolo.bolettieri,fabrizio.falchi,claudio.gennaro,
fausto.rabitti@isti.cnr.it

Abstract. The objective of this paper is to demonstrate the reuse of digital content, as video documents or PowerPoint presentations, by exploiting existing technologies for automatic extraction of metadata (OCR, speech recognition, cut detection, MPEG-7 visual descriptors, etc.). The multimedia documents and the extracted metadata are then indexed and managed by the Multimedia Content Management System (MCMS) MILOS, specifically developed to support design and effective implementation of digital library applications. As a result, the indexed digital material can be retrieved by means of content based retrieval on the text extracted and on the MPEG-7 visual descriptors (via similarity search), assisting the user of the e-Learning Library (student or teacher) to retrieve the items not only on the basic bibliographic metadata (title, author, etc.).

Keywords: MPEG-7, LOM, Metadata, Automatic Extraction, Multimedia Content Management System, Similarity Search, User Interface.

1   Introduction

In this paper we present the architecture of a Digital Library for enabling the reuse of learning documents. The Digital Library is based on MILOS, a general purpose Multimedia Content Management System created to support design and effective implementation of digital library applications. MILOS supports the storage and content based retrieval of any multimedia documents whose descriptions are provided by using arbitrary metadata models represented in XML. We present the architecture and the functions of MILOS, a Repository System intended to efficiently support the distributed storage and retrieval of Multimedia Learning Objects, developed by the ISTI-CNR laboratory in the context of the VICE italian project.

VICE is a three-year project, started in 2003, financed by the Italian Ministry of Education, University and Research (MIUR). The objective of the project is

---

* This work was partially supported by the VICE project (Virtual Communities for Education), funded by the Italian government.

E. Duval, R. Klamma, and M. Wolpers (Eds.): EC-TEL 2007, LNCS 4753, pp. 444–449, 2007.

to enable high quality and effective distance learning in a cost-effective manner, supporting, in an integrated fashion, teaching/learning activities organized by an authority (e.g., be an academic institution, an enterprise, an education provider, etc.) and self-learning (based on self-identified needs and goals), in the context of working activities. In this research we try to apply digital library techniques to support the management, retrieval and reuse of Learning Objects, i.e. collection of content/activities, that can be composed according to different needs and different goals.

The activity carried out from ISTI concerns the implementation of the prototype of repository system for multimedia LOs making advantage of the Multimedia Content Management System MILOS discussed below.

The main contribution of this paper is to show how the combination of the MILOS system and of state of the art tools for automatically extracting metadata from digital content is useful in enabling the reusing of digital material (such as videos, PowerPoint® presentations, etc.) in the domain e-Learning.

In this experimentation we have used LOM and MPEG-7 as metadata standards for the repository, and have proposed the specific use of a XML database combined with an access structure for similarity search for searching and retrieving the stored LOs. In particular our we have concentrated on the generation of "video-centric" LOs based on the analysis of some university lessons of the *Nettuno* [1] consortium, and of some PowerPoint documents taken from the web. To each digital items is associated a LOM descriptors created by hand (in XML), and an MPEG-7 description extracted automatically.

This paper is organized as follows: Section 2 presents the architecture of the MILOS MCMS. Then in Section 3 we present the metadata management by showing the model adopted and the tools exploited. Section 4 gives an overview of the search and browsing Web interface provided with reposting of the VICE project. Finally, Section 5 summarizes our contribution.

2   Repository System Architecture

In this section, we shortly describe the architecture of MILOS, the Repository System for Learning Objects which constitutes the main contribution of the ISTI-CNR Unit within the VICE project. MILOS is designed to support the storage and retrieval of multimedia Learning Objects (LO).

MILOS is a Multimedia Content Management System with a number of characteristics that make it particularly suitable for the development of Digital Library applications. MILOS is based on powerful multimedia database, able to guarantee advanced features for the persistence, search, and retrieval of Learning Objects written as XML documents and described using W3C XML schema [5]. Since the managed document are in XML format, it is possible to integrate heterogeneous XML descriptions such as LOM (The IEEE Learning Object Metadata (LOM) standard [4]) and MPEG-7 [2] metadata standards, since they are fully supported by the XML schemas. In particular, in the context of project VICE, LOM has be used to describe LOs, and MPEG-7 has be exploited for enriching multimedia components of the LOs. Multimedia components of LOs can be images, videos, PowerPoint presentation, etc. MILOS is based on a three-tier architecture (see Section 2), and the search functionality exported by the services of business logic can be easily adapted on the basis of the XML–Schema of the managed documents.

The system is based on a three–tier architecture and composed of five main logical components: *Interface Logic, Automatic Metadata Integrator, Repository Service Logic, LO Database, and Metadata Database*. The Interface Logic includes components that allow users to interact with the system on the web, via normal browsers. The Automatic Metadata Integrator analyzes multimedia part of the LOs, to automatically extract metadata, integrating it to the metadata produced during the authoring phase. The Repository Service Logic manages accesses to data stored in the LO repository and metadata database, on behalf of the other two components. All the components communicate by means of protocols for distributed systems integration (e.g. SOAP). Further details about MILOS can be found in [3].

3   Metadata Management

As explained earlier Multimedia Metadata can be automatically generated using specific processors (e.g., OCR, speech recognizer, cut detector, etc.). The typical LO ingestion workflow is the following (see Figure 1):

1. When a new Raw Media Element is inserted, the phase of Automatic Metadata Integration starts. It extracts some multimedia features (such as scenes, OCR, etc) and transform them in MPEG-7 format.
2. The Raw Media Element is stored in the Large Object DB including its keyframes in case of audiovisual content.
3. The LOM description is created by editing the LOM metadata using a standard Metadata Editor.
4. The LOM description and the MPEG-7 description are associated and stored by means of the Repository Service Logic.

Metadata Representation and Extraction. The metadata generated by the Automatic Metadata Integrator component are represented in MPEG-7. For each Raw Media Element we generate exactly one MPEG-7 description in XML format. The Automatic Metadata Integrator is organized in plug-ins each of devoted to the automatic extraction of metadata of a specific type of Raw Media Element. In this way we guarantee the maximal flexibility and extensibility of the repository. In our implementation we have incorporated plug-ins for the metadata generation from video and PowerPoint documents. Each LO of the repository is composed of a LOM description that contains the educational metadata and a MPEG-7 description that describes the content of the raw media element associated. The two descriptions are integrated using URI link from the LOM description to the MPEG-7 description.

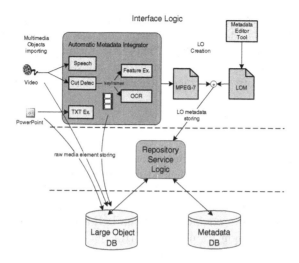

Fig. 1. Learning Obect ingestion workflow

Automatic Metadata Integration of Videos. The MPEG-7 description for e-Learning Video Documents is composed of several MPEG-7 descriptors. We have used the *CreationInformation* descriptor for expressing the common bibliographic metadata (such as, Title, Abstract, Location, Creation Data, etc.), and the *MediaDecomposition* descriptor for expressing the Video Transcript (by means of the AudioSegment descriptor) and the video decomposition in scenes and key–frames (by means of the VideoSegment descriptor). Inside the VideoSegment descriptor we have included the text extracted by the Video OCR component and the Visual Descriptors related to the key-frames. *MetaExtractor* is the tool that includes a set of modules for automatically generating MPEG-7 metadata from video lessons in MPEG-1/2 format. The tool provides the following functionalities:

Scene Detection: This component is used for segmenting video sequences by automatically locating boundaries of shots scene transition effects.
Visual Feature Extraction: This component extracts five MPEG-7 Visual Descriptors (SC, CL, CS, EH, and HT) from each key–frame of the scene detected by the *Scene Detection* component.
Video OCR: It detects, extracts and recognizes the texts contained in the video to enable text-based retrieval from spoken language documents.
Video Transcript: It generates transcript to enable text-based retrieval from spoken language documents.

Automatic Metadata Integration of PowerPoint Presentations. The extraction of metadata from the PowerPoint presentations is performed by extracting the title and the text contained in the slides. This content is organized by means of the MPEG-7, which is able to describe the decomposition of the presentation in slides. We use a free Java tool for automatic extracting the text content from the PowerPoint slides. The text content is the used for creating the MPEG-7 output.

Automatic Image Processing. Feature extraction techniques and automatic generation of MPEG-7 data Feature extraction was performed employing an application we built upon the MPEG-7 experimentation model of MPEG-7 Part 6: Reference Software. The software can extract all MPEG-7 VisualDescriptors. For the VICE repository we extract 5 MPEG-7 descriptors.in an image).

4   Web Search and Browsing Interface

The whole retrieval interface layout consists of four parts: (i) a *query frame*, in which the user can formulate fielded and full–text queries (top-left frame), (ii) an *hitlist frame*, in which the ranked list of matching items with some basic metadata (title, type, etc.) is displayed (bottom-left frame), a (iii) *LOM view frame*, where the whole metadata set of the LOM description for the selected item is displayed (top-right frame), and a (iv) *raw media element frame*, where the details of the raw media element associated with LOM are displayed (bottom-right frame). Through the menu "metadata" the fielded search form allows us to select which metadata model (LOM or MPEG-7) we have to use for the query search (Figure 2, left side). Selecting a specific model, the fields of the form on which to perform the search are automatically restored on the basis the metadata model selected. In particular, selecting the MPEG-7 model we can make searches on the OCR of the keyframes of the videos, on the transcripts of the spoken of the videos and on the textual content of the PowerPoint presentations slides.

The full–text interface contains only a simple input box, allowing us to submit queries at the same time on the entire metadata database independently from the model type. The two frames on the right side allow us to visualize an item of the list returned by the query (in the hitlist frame). By selecting an item from the hitlist the top frame show the content of its LOM metadata and the bottom frame the content of the raw media element. In particular, if the retrieved MPEG-7 is associated with a video, the raw media element frame displays the keyframes of the scene identified in the video and the complete transcription of speech (see

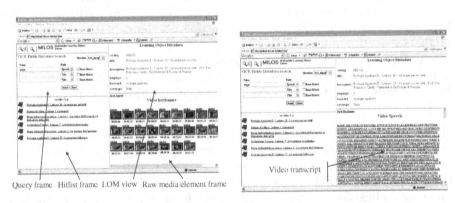

Query frame Hitlist frame LOM view Raw media element frame

Fig. 2. Visualization of the video keyframes (left) and of the video transcript (right)

Figures 2, right side). From here, by making click on a keyframe or a phrase of the transcription, it is possible to play the video from the time corresponding to the scene or spoken phrase. By selecting the link "similar", present on top of each keyframe, it is possible to perform a search for similarity over all the keyframes of all the videos of the repository If the MPEG-7 description is associated to a PowerPoint document, the raw media element frame executes the presentation starting from the slide that matched the search.

5   Conclusions

Although from the theoretical point of view the idea of using automatic tools for the extraction and the enhancement of metadata in the field of the digital libraries is not at all new, it finds it hard to be used in the real world. The reason may be due both to the high cost of these tools or simply to the fact that people do not give sufficient confidence in their results. Moreover, sometimes digital libraries and metadata are seen by the user with suspicious eyes. We argue that the use of automatic tools is the only way to convince people of the importance of metadata and indexing techniques. This is demonstrated by the success of tools as *Desktop Search*: nobody is willing to install a digital library on his or her own personal computer for searching personal documents manually filled with metadata.

With this article we want to demonstrate, instead, that these technologies are truly useful. Also because some of them are available free of charge. We propose the use of a content management system based on a XML search engine and we experimented it on a dataset of documents belonging to the domain of the e–Learning. We showed that with a minimal cost in terms of time spent by the cataloguers (who have just to add the LOM descriptions) it is possible to reuse audiovisual and PowerPoint documents facilitating their utilization. We believe that the proposed approach can also be applied to other domains of digital library beyond the one of the e–Learning. To see a demo of the web search interface of VICE, go to the Web site http://milos2.isti.cnr.it/milos/vice/.

References

1. Nettuno, http://www.uninettuno.it
2. Mpeg requirements group, mpeg-7 overview,
   Doc. ISO/IEC JTC1/SC29/WG11N5525 (2003)
3. Amato, G., Gennaro, C., Savino, P., Rabitti, F.: Milos: a multimedia content management system for digital library applications. In: Heery, R., Lyon, L. (eds.) ECDL 2004. LNCS, vol. 3232, pp. 14–25. Springer, Heidelberg (2004)
4. Committee, I.L.T.S.: Ieee 1484.12.1-2002, draft standard for learning object metadata (2002), http://ltsc.ieee.org/wg12/index.html
5. Consortium, W.W.W.: XML path language (XPath), version 1.0, W3C. Recommendation (November 1999)

A Situation-Based Delivery of Learning Resources in Pervasive Learning

Amel Bouzeghoub, Kien Ngoc Do, and Claire Lecocq

GET/INT, CNRS UMR SAMOVAR 9, rue Charles Fourier 91011 Évry France
{firstName.lastName}@int-edu.eu

Abstract. Pervasive learning systems must define new mechanism to deliver the right resource, at the right time, at the right place to the right learner. This means that rich context information has to be considered: time, place, user knowledge, user activity, user environment and device capacity. As context is based on numerous information which may change frequently (coming from a collection of captors), a more aggregate view is defined to work on more abstract objects: the situations. Context information and situation information have to be widespread into all the models of learning systems: context preferences have to be handled in the learner model, well-adapted situation and situation scenarios have to be memorized in learning resource model. The adaptation process is enriched too.

Keywords: Pervasive learning, context, learning resources, user profile, adaptation.

1 Introduction

Pervasive learning systems are characterized by non predictable situations and are subject to even more unpredictable environments and user requirements. Modeling the context is thus needed to better understand user's activities and to adapt the content to these activities. This leads to the design of systems that deliver more appropriate learning content and services to satisfy learner requirement and to be aware of situation changes by automatically adapt themselves to such changes. This means that a pervasive learning system must take into account at least two dimensions. Firstly, it provides the learner with exactly the material he needs, and appropriate to his knowledge level and which makes sense in the special learning situation. Secondly, it introduces many different constraints (e.g., device processing power, display ability, network bandwidth, connectivity options, intermittent connections, location and time).

In order to support situation-aware adaptation, it is necessary to model and specify context and situation. Like in [15], we consider that a situation is a set of contexts over a period of time that affects system behavior. A context is any instantaneous, detectable and relevant property of the environment, system or users. Besides modeling the situation, it is important to contextualize learning resources (LR) by associating information about the device, the display dimension, etc. In other words, a LR should be related to a specific situation which is characterized by all the resource constraints. For example, in the RAFT project [13], additional metadata (e.g., location, time) are used

E. Duval, R. Klamma, and M. Wolpers (Eds.): EC-TEL 2007, LNCS 4753, pp. 450–456, 2007.

for contextualized LRs . Our objective is to enrich our model by associating one (or more) situation(s) to each LR with the purpose of facilitating the delivering of LRs.

In this paper we describe the evolution of the SIMBAD system [3] to consider learner's environment. This evolution is based on the introduction of context and situation models as well as the definition of an associated resources adaptation process. The definition of these models constitutes the main contribution of the paper[1]. The organization of the paper is as follows. In section 2, we enrich our SIMBAD system with contextual information. In section 3, we present the semi-dynamic adaptation process allowing the deployment of context-sensitive resources. Section 4 compares our propositions to related works. Finally, we conclude in section 5.

2   Context Modeling in SIMBAD

This presentation of SIMBAD is an extension to the logical architecture presented in details in [3]. This system is proposed for three categories of users: learners, authors of resources and experts of the system. The learner may follow a particular course or enhance his/her knowledge relative to a set of concepts. The author can search for resources, compose resources in order to generate new ones or create new resources and annotate them. The expert is in charge of the management of the domain ontology. To provide these functions, our system is based on different ontologies (domain ontology and several context ontologies) and models: domain, learner, resource, context, situation and event models.

2.1   Ontologies Used in SIMBAD

We distinguish the domain ontology from the set of context ontologies:

Domain Ontology. The domain ontology is shared between all the users of the system. It is an organization of the knowledge domain concepts linked with hierarchical and rhetoric relations (e.g., "is synonym of"). This ontology is essential for the indexation of either learners or resources.

Context Ontologies. Considering the literature, it appears clearly that there is not just one and single definition for the concept of context [12]. We consider that a typical mobile user is involved in a number of different overlapping contexts, thus any activity is influenced by the interactions between these contexts. The definition of an overlapping context is not new, though it has generally not been highlighted in IS research. The contextual model used by [5] implies that overlapping contexts contribute to and influence the interactions and experiences that people have when performing certain activities. Our suggestion is that the context is a multi dimensional space where each dimension is represented by one ontology: learner (knowledge and preferences model), learning activity (learning and normal activities), environment (which includes technical computing context and physical context), device, location and time. The contextual information is thus organized in a multidimensional space

---

[1] This work is partially supported by P-LearNet (ANR) and Ad-Context (CAPES-COFECUB) projects.

where each ontology represents a dimension which should be handled separately (as shown in Figure 1).

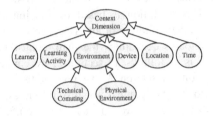

Fig. 1. Context modelling

2.2 Context, Situation and Event Models

Context Model. We define a context as a view on one or many dimensions of the space made of the context ontologies. It is a set of binary semantic relations between concepts and instances belonging to the same ontology or different ontologies (O_i).

Context={Relation$_1$(O_i.Concept,O_j.Instance), Relation$_2$(O_j.Instance, O_k.Instance)}

For example, John uses his PDA at INT School to access to a course for revising his exam:

C_j={in($O_{Learner}$.John,$O_{Location}$.INT),do($O_{Learner}$.John,$O_{Activity}$.revise),use($O_{Learner}$.John, O_{Device}. PDA)}

Situation Model. A situation is the complete state of the universe at an instant or at an interval of time. It is formed by a sequence of contexts with invariant characteristic through the time interval. A situation can consider and combine many dimensions at the same time and a user may be in several situations at the same time (one can be both walking in the street and on the phone). A situation is a projection of the context on an ontology describing temporal properties.

Situation={ {Relations}; intervalStabilization; startTime; endTime}

Event Model. The information generated after each change of situation is important for the adaptation phase. Indeed, it is a trigger for activating adaptation rules. We have called this information an event. For example, the fact that the learner changes the use of his device from laptop to PDA. An event will be generated to adapt the presentation of the resource from laptop to PDA. Thus, we assume that an event is either a change between situations (it occurs at the beginning and the end of a situation) or an internal change of the situation (it occurs during the situation under certain conditions). An event can be formalized as:

Event = {EventName; Situation; Conditions; OccurrenceTime}

3   Contextual Adaptation

We distinguish two learning styles. The *push* mode corresponds to a course-based learning strategy: a learner selects a course; the system adapts the corresponding resource to the learner knowledge level, preferences and presents only useful information. The *pull* mode corresponds to a goals-based learning strategy: a learner formulates a query over concepts of the domain model and specifies the knowledge level he/she wants to achieve for a specific role (e.g., *"introduction"*, *"definition"*). The system composes then "on the fly" one resource satisfying theses goals. An adaptation process is proposed for the two styles. This process is extended in order to take into account the learner's situation. We add a new filter (situation filter) to this process.

3.1 Static Adaptation Process

Situation Filter. The resource adaptation to the situation consists in the definition of mechanisms to compare situations. Thus, situations are dynamically gathered with hierarchical relation to facilitate their use and their comparison. We need to compare learner situation with resource intentional situation in order to know if the resource context is adapted to the learner current context. A situation may be described with one or more dimensions (context ontologies). We can compare two situations if there exists at least one common dimension. We define two functions: **sim()** which calculates the similarity degree between two situations and **contains()** which tests if one situation is included in another one. These functions not only use the similarity between the dimensions but also the relations between these dimensions.

Preference Filter and Personalized Presentation. Learner preferences are described in the learner model. They are used in the adaptation process to filter resources that correspond to his/her preferences in terms of colors, language, media. The template of presentation is defined according to the situation which allows constructing dynamically user interfaces.

3.2 Semi-dynamic Adaptation Process

The adaptation process has to be reactive for each new situation. For example Alice is using her PDA for revising her lecture in the train. When she arrives at her office, she wants to use her laptop and carry on with the same activity. This event has triggered a new situation and activates the corresponding adaptation strategy. The scenario will be modeled formally as:

AliceInTrainSituation{in($O_{Learner}$.Alice, $O_{Location}$.Train), use($O_{Learner}$.Alice, O_{Device}.PDA), do($O_{Learner}$.Alice, $O_{Activity}$.revise)}
AliceInOfficeSituation{in($O_{Learner}$.Alice, $O_{Location}$.Office), in(O_{Device}.Laptop, $O_{Location}$.Office)}

Adaptation can be applied at different dimensions (learner, device or environment) with different manners (static or semi-dynamic). Indeed, each element of situation can present any character of context and the similarity between two situations is calculated independently to learner characteristics. The semi-dynamic adaptation is more reactive than the static one as it is based on captured events which are raised by the change of situations.

3.3 Implementation

We present our architecture which is an extension of the system SIMBAD. The new architecture of SIMBAD is proposed by integrating the situation-awareness mechanisms. As shown in figure 2, our architecture is made of three major blocks: Learning Resource Delivery (LRD), Context Manager (CM) and Inference Engine (IE). LRD receives learner query and asks CM to get the current learner situation which will be compared with the intentional situation in each LR. LRD gives learners the most situational adequate resource. CM is in charge of collecting, analyzing and abstracting the contextual information which consists in 4 modules: Collection Manager collects the values captured from sensors by mobile agent. Situation Analyzer/Event Recognition deduces high level contextual information using the IE and the situation/event model. Context Manager Interface plays the role of entry for all the modules which want to interact with the CM in order to have the ability of context sensitive.

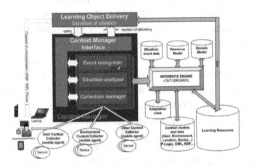

Fig. 2. SIMBAD extended architecture

4   Related Work

Pervasive learning is an emerging learning method which provides the capacity for identifying the right contents, right services in the right place at the right time and in the right form based on the current situation of learner. An interesting reference [11] proposes a theory of learning for a mobile society. Our work is closely related to other pervasive learning and computing researches like [2, 7, 10, 15, 17]. We share with [2] the idea of pervasive learning is attractive but it is not easily implemented. Indeed, the authors in [10] have tried to determine thirteen principles grouped in four key components considered during the creation of Pervasive Learning environments: community, autonomy, locationality and relationality. Our system also is able to assure these principles based on our general models (i.e.., context, situation, event). In terms of architecture, distributed and central systems with different models (learner, context, environment) are proposed like GlobalEdu   [2, 10]. We developed a distributed system with ontology-based models which is more detailed and flexible.

Our work is also connected to the context, situation aware computing. Many context and situation models have been proposed. In CoBra [4], an agent-oriented infrastructure for context representation is presented. In [9], the authors used first order logic to represent context. Krisch and al. in [6] applied object-oriented models for describing the user's organizational context for awareness purposes. In relation to situation, the authors in [1, 8, 16] proposed context modeling through ontology based situation-aware. In comparison with these works, our model of situation is more detailed, more generic which allow easily creating, detecting, comparing situations and enhancing the process of delivering LRs (what, when and how to deliver LRs). MobiLearn [17] is an European project about mobile learning which is an adaptation of the e-learning systems to access through wireless networks. It advanced a hierarchical description of context as a dynamic process with historical dependencies. Our description of context is more abstract and general.

5 Conclusion

In this paper we have described our on-going development of a situation-based framework which is an evolution of the system SIMBAD to support pervasive learning environment. This evolution is based on the introduction of context and situation models as well as the definition of an associated resources adaptation process. The context is an ontology-based model in which different type of information are considered: time, place, user knowledge, user activity, user environment and device capacity. The situation model is a view on the context model describing temporal properties. By means of operators, this model provides abilities to design, to compare or to infer new situations. Furthermore, it supplies an enhanced adaptation process which takes into account the dynamic change of situations. Finally, we have presented our initial prototype which is an extension of the system SIMBAD.

References

[1] Anagnostopoulos, C.B., Ntarladimas, Y., Hadjiefthymiades, S.: Situation Awareness: Dealing with Vague Context. In: ACS/IEEE International Conference on Pervasive Services (2006)

[2] Barbosa, D.N.F., Augustin, I., Barbosa, J.L.V., Yamim, A.C., da Silva, L.C., Fernando, C., Geyer, R.: Learning in a large-scale pervasive environment. In: Pervasive Computing and Communications Workshops (2006)

[3] Bouzeghoub, A., Defude, B., Duitama, F., Lecocq, C.: A Knowledge-Based Approach to Describe and Adapt Learning Objects. InternationalJournal on E. Learning 5(1), 95–102 (2006) Special Issue: LearningObjectsin Context, pp. 95-102. Chesapeake,VA : AACE(ISSN1537- 2456)

[4] Chen, H., Finin, T., Joshi, A.: An Ontology for Context-Aware Pervasive Computing Environments. Special Issue on Ontologies for Distributed Systems, Knowledge Engineering Review 18, 197–207 (2004)

[5] Falk, J.H., Dierking, L.D.: Lessons without Limit: How free-choice learning is transforming education. AltaMira Press, Walnut Creek, California (2002)

[6] Kirsch-Pinheiro, M., Gensel, J., Martin, H.: Representing Context for an Adaptative Awareness Mechanism. In: de Vreede, G.-J., Guerrero, L.A., Marín Raventós, G. (eds.) CRIWG 2004. LNCS, vol. 3198, pp. 339–348. Springer, Heidelberg (2004)

[7] Lemlouma, T., Layaïda, N.: Context-Aware Adaptation for Mobile Devices. In: IEEE International Conference on Mobile Data Management, Berkeley, CA, USA, pp. 106–111 (2004)

[8] Weißenberg, N., Gartmann, R., Voisard, A.: An Ontology-Based Approach to Personalized Situation-Aware Mobile Service Supply'. Geoinformatica Journal, 55–90 (2006)

[9] Ranganathan, A., Campbell, R.H.: An infrastructure for context-awareness based on first-order logic. Personal and Ubiquitous Computing 7, 353–364 (2003)

[10] Rosa, G.P.J., Ogata, H., Yano, Y.: A multi-Model Approach for Supporting the Personalization of Ubiquitous Learning Applications. In: IEEE International Workshop on Wireless and Mobile Technologies in Education, pp. 40–44 (2005)

[11] Sharples, M., Taylor, J., Vavoula, G.: A Theory of Learning for the Mobile Age. In: Andrews, R., Haythornthwaite, C. (eds.) The Sage Handbook of Elearning Research, pp. 221–247. Sage, London (2007)

[12] Schilit, B., Adams, N., Want, R.: Context-Aware Computing Applications. In: Proc. Workshop on Mobile Computing Systems and Applications, Santa Cruz, CA, U.S,

[13] Specht, M., Kravcik, M.: Authoring of Learning Objects in Context. International Journal on E-Learning 5(1), 25–33 (2006)

[14] Thomas, S.: Pervasive, persuasive eLearning: modeling the pervasive learning space. In: Proceedings of the 3rd Int'l Conf. on Pervasive Computing and Communications Workshops (2005)

[15] Yang, S.J.H., Huang, A.F.M., Chen, H.R., Tseng, S.-S., Shen, Y.-S.: Context Model and Context Acquisition for Ubiquitous Content Access in ULearning Environments. In: Proc. of the IEEE International Conference on Sensor Networks, Ubiquitous, and Trustworthy Computing, vol. 2, pp. 78–83 (2006)

[16] Yau, S., Liu, S.: J.: Hierarchical Situation Modeling and Reasoning for Pervasive Computing. SEUS-WCCIA, pp. 5–10 (2006)

[17] MobiLearn final report (version 2003), http://www.mobilearn.org/

Web Services Plug-in to Implement *"Dispositives"* on Web 2.0 Applications

Pierre-André Caron

Team NOCE, Trigone/LIFL laboratory,
University of Sciences and Technology, Lille, France
`pa.caron@ed.univ-lille1.fr`

Abstract. This paper presents an engineering process in order to build pedagogical *"dispositives"* on Web 2.0 applications. This engineering process relies on three tasks: modeling the *"dispositive"*, defining its context and building it. The main feature of our process is to wrap the building functionalities of a Web Application by Web Services. To consume these services, we use the Model Driven Engineering approach. This approach guarantees the easy implementation of every specific Web application modeler and constructor considered. Experimental results have already been obtained on the WikiniMST platform.

Keywords: e-Learning, Web 2.0, Model Driven Engineering, Web Services.

1 Introduction

An essential part of Web 2.0 is harnessing collective intelligence, turning the web into a kind of global brain. [1]. New applications like Blogs, Wikis, Social networks, Collaborative Map of Tags, Forum, Search engines, are examples of new uses set up by active users. These users build their environment collaboratively and the way to use it. E-Learning 2.0 is about the pedagogical use of theses applications [2]. The use of such applications in the field of education brings about a change of paradigm for E-Learning. This document aims to clarify this new paradigm. The pedagogical uses of Web 2.0 applications challenges the type of community of practice teachers build, the type of creativity they use, the type of learning they implement, the learning object they agree with. The aim of our paper is also to offer the tools and objects which may assist teachers in their preparatory work with Web 2.0 applications. For the specific case of a small team of teachers using pedagogical *"bricolage"*, we will show that it is possible to define an infrastructure allowing *"dispositives"* building on Web 2.0 application. This paper is organised as follows. In the next section we present a new paradigm for E-Learning 2.0. This paradigm uses new concepts as *"Dispositives"* and *"Bricolage"*, presented in section 2. Section 3 will present our conceptual approach, addressing platforms as services describing its functionalities, and then call these services via the model driven engineering. Section 4 will detail our experimentation's. Finally, section 5 will present related work and Section 6 our conclusions and future work.

E. Duval, R. Klamma, and M. Wolpers (Eds.): EC-TEL 2007, LNCS 4753, pp. 457–462, 2007.
© Springer-Verlag Berlin Heidelberg 2007

2   *"Bricolage"* and *"Dispositive"*

To describe a pedagogical use of Web 2.0 application, a new paradigm is necessary. Its users are small scale teaching teams who do not have access to an Instructional Designer. The software they have to choose from does not match their pedagogical purpose. This *"make do"* process resembles more *"Bricolage"* than an engineering process.

"The bricoleur is adept at performing a large number of diverse tasks; but, unlike the engineer, he does not subordinate each of them to the availability of raw materials and tools conceived and procured for the purpose of the project.[...]. The bricoleur may not ever complete his purpose but he always puts something of himself into it" [3]. This parallelism between teachers and craftsmen has been used for years to describe pedagogical design, since teachers are always on the lookout for a middle way between craftsmanship and engineering. It can be applied to E-Learning in so far as "Bricolage" is not defined by its output but by the way it has been achieved: using several times -and if necessary diverting them from their original use- texts, activities, and materials [4].

For teachers, making the choice of a Web 2.0 application, because it is available and offers some of the functionalities they wish to use can be considered as sheer *"pedagogical bricolage"*. To facilitate this *"pedagogical bricolage"* on Web 2.0 applications, teachers have to be provided with Learning Objects that are sufficiently weak to be handled within the frame of controlled improvisation of his teaching. We believe that such objects –that can be manipulated and constructed- can be technically implemented in a Web 2.0 application thanks to a pre structuring device, which represents the technical aspect of a more complex entity the *"pedagogical dispositive"*.

The word *"dispositive"* is used in French to describe a system set up for a specific purpose. According to Michel Foucault a *"dispositive"* is a*" decidedly heterogeneous ensemble "*, *"a resolutely heterogeneous assemblage, containing discourses, institutions, architectural buildings, reglementary decisions, scientific statements, philosophical, moral, philanthropic propositions, in one word: said as well as non-said, those are the dispositif's elements. The dispositif in itself is the network that we can establish between those elements."* [5]. This definition underline the twofold nature of a *"dispositive"*: organizing.../ ...with a special intent. A *"dispositive"* is a cluster of elements organized with a special intent. *"Dispositive"* is an open object, that teachers and learner can interpret in its usage. It can be seen as possibility space as opposed to a scenario that is a planning space. For that reason *"Dispositive"* notion is particularly suited to pedagogical *"Bricolage"*. *"Dispositive"* provides a conceptual framework for teacher, it leverages meaning making by the part of learners. *"Dispositive"*, from engineering point of view, is a computational object; it can be modeled, manipulated and built in a Web application. Finally its open feature makes a *"Dispositive"* an excellent support for *"teaching bricolage"*. This triple adequacy between *"dispositives"* and teachers is the reason we propose to provide an infrastructure to assist teachers when designing a *"dispositive"*. *"An infrastructure can be defined as a social and technical substrate that stabilize and permit creating instrumental and intentional activities in a given area"* [6]. We propose to define a computing infrastructure to model, to contextualize and to build *"dispositives"* in Web 2.0 Applications.

3   Our Proposition

The use of generic web applications implies the acceptance of the fact that there are not completely adapted to the teaching project the teacher wants to carry out. We propose to plug on these applications a pre-structuring model facilitating their use in an educational context.

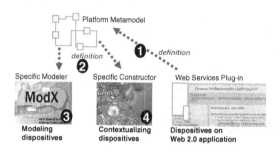

Fig. 1. From modeling to building

Our approach is founded on the definition of an infrastructure that allows building pedagogical *"dispositives"* on a Web 2.0 application via the Web Service call. To achieve our goal, we will define a pluggable web services module for every application. This Plug-in is inspired from IMS enterprise standard [7] and is a wrapper for Web 2.0 application. From this plug-in, we will define the metamodel of the application (1). This metamodel, expressed in Meta Object Facilities [8] language, enables us to parameter a specific modeler of the application, and to build a *"dispositive"* constructor (2). Then, it is possible to express a specific *"dispositive"* model of the application (3). The engineering process, we want to set up, is able to structure an application in order to promote its pedagogical use. Web 2.0 applications single out emerging structuring mechanisms; witch is why our infrastructure identifies a context defining phase. This phase allows a dialog between "dispositive" models and the emerging structures (4).

4   Evaluation and Experimental Results

The experiment was conducted as part of *"collaborative distributed practice for learning using the Internet"* project. This project aims to enable more active forms of learning over the Internet. This experiment has been carried out as a part of the task: Collaborative-construction and evolution of an infrastructure, deployment and realization. It intends to be used by undergraduate students and concerns the remote collaborative trainees' tutorships and the production of a professional master thesis.

The first phase of the project was described previously in [9]. To carry out this tutorship, the teacher designs a set defined by the name "Personal and Collective Actions Browser" (PCAB). In the whole potential workspace of the PCAB, each student should be allowed to create his own personal workspace. This personal workspace has to be singled out (automatically) by the identity of the student (name, surname and year). To use PCAB, this personal workspace must be pre-structured in 5 "tasks": investigate, build the tutorship, formalize the mission, conduct conceptual investigations and gather references. On the basis of these "task workspaces", a student will be allowed creating all the pages he wishes.

For the second phase of the experimentation, we have defined a new metamodel from fusion of metamodels previously made, in order to simplify modeler uses. It is now possible to refine and contextualize a pedagogical model. The expected "dispositive" has been modified: personal workspace is already in use, some group space and management aspects have been defined. The figure 7 summarizes our engineering process in order to build specific infrastructure and the use of this infrastructure in order to model, contextualize and build a "dispositive".

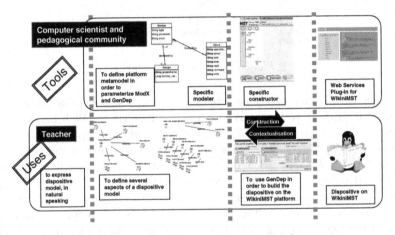

Fig. 2. Engineering process and use of a specific infrastructure

Transformations are now automatic. They generate the operational model without the intervention of the user. Finally, we have introduced the possibility for a model to call web services in order to take into account the emerging structuring mechanisms in Web 2.0 applications. This possibility not only defines the context of a "dispositive" with an emerging use but also allows the composing of the "dispositives", while separating the different aspects of a global "dispositive".

5 Related Work

Many standards permit to construct objects automatically on the Learning Management System. The Sharable Content Object Reference Model [10] allows to design Learning Object sequencing and to deploy it on platforms. The deployment tool is often provided by the e-learning platforms. However it's not possible to match package SCORM with elements (person, group, service) already present on the platform. The IMS Learning Design [11] permits to express under multiple sequencing process, various activities that pupils and teachers can lead in an educational script. However, in spite of many works achieved to simplify understanding of this standard, its complexity makes it difficult to use [12]. In a general way, besides the fact that these standards are destined to be used in e-Learning platform and not in Web 2.0 application, they don't offer a possibility to match their elements with the elements or services already defined on the platforms.

Our approach is less ambitious because it only handles *"dispositives"* and not activities. Besides the advantages of the *"dispositive"* approach (previously explained), our proposition permits to define the context for a modeled *"dispositive"*. A specific constructor permits to match model with existing elements and services, and with other *"dispositives"* (already deployed). It's up to a specific feature of our modeling environment to provide this possibility. It permits to divide a global *"dispositive"* in interdependent *"sub-dispositives"*.

6 Conclusion and Future Work

Our approach allows building pedagogical *"dispositives"* on web applications. It's set on a three steps process: modeling, defining context and building the *"dispositive"*. To make these steps operational, we propose to develop a web service plug-in for each application. This plug-in builds the *"dispositive"*, in the context of the application, via its services. To implement it, we make use of the IMS-ES specification; we define for each application a specific modeler and a specific constructor. Our proposal is to easily build these tools with an MDE approach. In this way, we offer a method for defining the interaction model of the platform. This model is the base of conformity for our modeler. For a classic web application, the simple interpretation of the web services and the model generates nearly 6000 code lines automatically; only 300 lines are left to be implemented (statistics from WikiniMST project).

We think that, web services plug-ins will be easier to implement when Web application will be based on the SOA architecture. In the future, we aim to factorize our work and propose a coherent framework of service permitting educational *"dispositives"* construction on web applications. The experimentations we conducted, allowed us to evolve our approach from explicit transformation mechanism used in the first phase to fusion of models. We are entering now into a new phase of experimentation on the Claroline and Moodle platforms, and e-Portfolio Web applications [13]. These various experimentations aim to study the use of our engineering processes, as well as to explore new ways with the possibility to express methodologies and to bind these methodologies to the generated models.

Acknowledgements

The author wished to thank "la Direction de la Technologie du Ministère de l'Education Nationale" and "l'Agence Nationale pour le Recherche" for their partial financial support.

References

1. O'Reilly, T.: What Is Web 2.0, Design Patterns and Business Models for the Next Generation of Software, [cited march 2007] (2005) Available from, http://www.oreillynet.com/pub/a/oreilly/tim/news/2005/09/30/what-is-web-20.html.
2. Downes, S.: E-learning 2.0, in National Research Council of Canada ACM - Association for Computing Machinery. Elearn magazine (2005)
3. Levi Strauss, C.: The Savage Mind. University of Chicago Press, Chicago, IL (1962)
4. Rees, M.: a better word for mashup? Words and Phrases, January 22, 2006 [cited] Available from, http://blog.mrees.biz/myblog/?p=9
5. Foucault, M.: Discipline and Punish: the Birth of the Prison. Random House, New York (1975)
6. Derycke, A., et al.: Chapitre 8, in Environnement Informatiques pour l'apprentissage Humain sous la direction de Jean-Marc Labat et Monique Grandbastien, Lavoisier, Editor, Hermès Sciences Publication. p. 181 (2006)
7. IMS-ES. IMS-ES. [cited; Available from: http://www.imsglobal.org/es/
8. OMG, Meta Object Facility (MOF) Specification, O.D. AD/97-08-14, Editor (1997)
9. Caron, P.-A., Le Pallec, X., Sockeel, S.: Configuring a web based tool through pedagogical scenarios. In: IADIS Virtual Multi Conference on Computer Science and Information Systems (MCCSIS 2006) (2006)
10. SCORM_2004. SCORM 2004 3rd edn. 2006 [cited March 2007] Available from: http://www.adlnet.gov/scorm
11. IMS-LD. IMS LD. [cited; Available from: http://www.imsproject.org/learningdesign/
12. De la Teja, I., Lundgren-Cayrol, K., Paquette, G.: Transposing MISA Learning Scenarios into IMS Units of Learning. Journal of Educational technology and Society ET&S (2006) (Special issue on Learning Design)
13. Kaddouci, S., Vantroys, T., Chevrin, V.: From Task Model to Multi-Channel Access: Services Integration in the Ubi-Learn Platform. In: Web-based Education, Chamonix France (2007)

Flexible Processes in Project-Centred Learning

Stefano Ceri[1], Maristella Matera[1], Alessandro Raffio[1],
and Howard Spoelstra[2]

[1] DEI – Politecnico di Milano
P.zza L. da Vinci, 32 - 20133 – Milano - Italy
{ceri,matera,raffio}@elet.polimi.it
[2] OUNL – Open University of the Netherlands
Valkenburgerweg 177 - 6419 AT Heerlen - The Netherlands
howard.spoelstra@ou.nl

Abstract. Project-centred learning is increasingly used both in academia and in companies; universities train students to master complex tasks, often suggested by real-life situations, while companies train users to learn about new products, methods, technologies. This paper introduces a model-driven, extensible environ-ent, delivered on the Web, which is able to support long-distance collaboration of teams working on complex projects. The main merit of this proposal is the ability to self-organize processes, by using a simple Web interface and a library of activities and templates which cover most of the needs of this well-defined class of applications. This paradigm for dynamic workflow management is very general and can be applied to other application contexts, after understanding and modelling the relevant collaboration activities and templates.

Keywords: Flexible Processes, E-learning, Web Application Design.

1 Introduction

Project-centred learning provides environments where learners' teams cooperate on complex projects, collaborating by means of computer-mediated services. Increasingly, such environments are adopted in the context of workplace learning, to support scientific and technical studies, where teams work on a given project, and where teachers' support is substituted by interaction with a small group of advisors and tutors.

In this context, learning environments are organized so that to enhance team collaboration. Team members therefore can i) act individually, by producing separate results later combined to achieve a group result; ii) cooperate, by sharing and discuss ideas; iii) jointly collaborate, following planned procedures to reach a team result.

Collaboration requires some form of coordination ([4][6]), which often relies on the definition of processes guiding the learners' activities. Process-oriented collaboration is an important challenge today. Workflow management systems might appear suitable for modelling collaboration processes. However, while workflow-based applications are characterized by well-defined, predictable and repetitive

E. Duval, R. Klamma, and M. Wolpers (Eds.): EC-TEL 2007, LNCS 4753, pp. 463–468, 2007.

procedures, collaboration processes are difficult to plan completely in advance. Such processes indeed need the consensus of the involved actors. Also, they are *flexible* [4], since they might need to be adapted, even during their execution, to the preferences of team members, as well as to the team members' evolution of background knowledge and competencies due to learning.

So far, several frameworks and tools have been developed to support e-learning teamwork activities (see for example the IMS-LD Design initiative, and also tools like IBM LearningSpace, WebCT, Blackboard, etc.). Such proposals offer facilities for resource sharing, synchronous and asynchronous communication, course planning and help desk. However, they are still "task-oriented", not "process-oriented" [5]. Very often they are designed to support individual activities, while they do not sustain the schedule and organization of collaborative processes. Some recent proposals also address the management of dynamic and flexible processes in teamwork collaboration ([4][5][6][7]), and introduce environments where team collaboration is driven by flexible, yet controlled, means of progressing through processes ([5][6][7]). Based on workflow technologies, on one hand such approaches ensure flexibility; however, on the other hand they often require users to learn concepts and primitives related to process design.

Our approach tries to overcome the limitations exposed by the previous approaches, and introduces an environment, delivered on the Web, which is able to support collaboration in virtual teams. A salient goal of our research is to propose a reference model for teamwork collaboration processes, enabling the management of *flexible* processes that can be defined and modified by end-users at runtime to accommodate their collaboration needs. As described in this paper, the model has guided the development of a Web-based platform, supporting flexible learning processes with pedagogical scenarios and tools enabling cooperation [1].

The paper is organized as follows: Sections 2 and 3 illustrate the main ingredients of our approach, namely a library of collaboration activities, and a Web-based interface for flexible process composition and modification. Section 4 then gives an overview of the architecture of our collaborative platform. Section 5 finally draws our conclusion.

2 Collaboration Activity Libraries

The most salient feature of our collaborative environment is that it allows team members working on a project to:

- *Dynamically define collaborative processes*, to organize and structure collaboration, on the basis of the team's preferred procedures.
- *Easily modify the planned processes*, to cope with the evolution of individuals as well as of the whole team.

Giving the end-users the possibility to define and modify their processes requires the system to offer easy-to-use definition interfaces, based on mechanisms that can guide the team members in the composition of processes, without requiring any specific knowledge and expertise on process design. Guiding inexperienced users requires that the system be "aware" of the semantics of the domain where processes must be executed. Such awareness can be achieved by means of libraries of pre-defined activity types, able to reflect the semantics of the possible tasks that users might need to coordinate and execute in a given context. Starting from this library, the system then guides the composition of "well-structured" processes [2].

Our framework is therefore based on the notion of *atomic activities*, i.e. small pieces of processes that are regularly performed by users to collaborate, and that therefore can be used for the definition of collaborative processes. Due to their fine granularity, they are reusable in several process definitions.

Some atomic activities have a general nature (e.g., those related to the management of documents), and can therefore be adopted in several domains where collaborative processes are required. Some other activities may however be particular for specific contexts and their identification requires an investigation of the addressed domain. In the context of the Cooper EU project [1], we have investigated *virtual company* scenarios [8], which situate learning in a virtual business environment, enabling learning-while-working. We have also analysed the domain of project-based education at two academic institutions (ALaRI[1], and ASP[2]), and project-based training at the CoWare company[3]. As a consequence, we developed a library that includes some forty atomic activities, classified according to the main cooperation goals they are related to:

- *Teamwork planning activities* support the scheduling of the team activities, such as the assignment of roles and tasks, the definition of milestones, etc.
- *Resource management activities* refer to the publication, access and also recommendation of resources (i.e., documents, forum messages, wikies, etc.).
- *Communication activities* enable the invocation of synchronous communication services (e.g., video conferences), and asynchronous communication tools (e.g., forum).
- *Reviewing and assessing activities* refer to the review of artefacts produced by the team, and to the assessment of team members, both individually and in the context of the team.

In our framework, which aims to deliver cooperative processes on the Web, atomic activities are realized as Web pages, expressing the interface through which users can execute them. A particular feature is that such pages are developed by means of a conceptual modelling approach, based on the WebML visual model [3]. The model-driven approach facilitates the extension of the library with new atomic activities, which just requires modelling new pages at a high level of abstraction.

Atomic activities constitute basic pieces of processes. Besides them, our framework also provides *templates*, i.e., pre-defined process models that can be the basis for the definition of new processes. Templates generally correspond to typical "patterns of collaboration". In some cases, they can be pre-defined by the institution where teams operate, and are therefore used to suggest teams some "certified procedures". Examples of built-in templates are: "Team Formation", "Voting", or "Delivery of Project Results". Team members are also allowed to create their own templates and build a personal library, to be used for process composition.

---

[1] Advanced Learning and Research Institute - http://www.alari.org
[2] Alta Scuola Politecnica – http://www.asp-poli.it
[3] http://www.coware.com

3 Web-Based Definition and Execution of Processes

Our collaborative platform is deployed on the Web, and makes use of standard Web technologies and of a hypertext-based interface to provide users with easy-to-use interfaces for the definition and execution of their collaboration processes. Process definition by end users requires the selection of atomic activities and/or templates from the library, and the definition of some constraints controlling the activity assignment to users and resources and the activity transition during process execution.

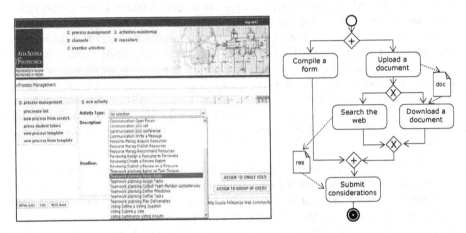

Fig. 1. A web page for activity selection   **Fig. 2.** Example of structured process

An example of Web page for process definition is shown in Fig. 1: the user selects the type of activity (e.g., "Assign Roles") from the library, and enters a short activity description. S/He is then required to assign the activity to one or more members of her/his team. In case of multiple actors executing an activity, the user also needs to indicate the kind of parallelism governing the activity execution. Depending on the type of activity, the user might also associate the activity to some resources to manage possible documental flows. By means of a guided visit to subsequent form-based pages, users are allowed to compose processes and templates of any kind of complexity (as the one in Fig. 2), selecting and configuring one activity at a time. (Nested) blocks of parallel activities are created by means of a depth-first composition of each parallel branch. Users can also modify the definition of existing processes and templates at run-time.

Once the process has been defined, its execution consists in providing the users with the Web pages associated to the process activities. Process execution therefore implies guiding the users through the "right" sequence of Web pages, in accordance with the defined activity flow.

4 System Overview

Fig. 3 illustrates the architecture of our framework. Our approach in particular addresses flexible processes delivered on the Web. Therefore, in line with the

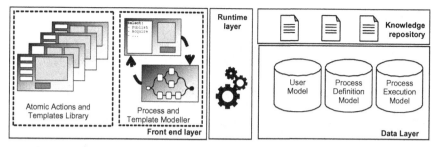

Fig. 3. The architecture of the framework supporting the definition and execution of flexible processes

classical architecture of Web applications, our proposal is characterized by a *data layer*, a *runtime layer* and a *front-end layer*.

The data layer stores some *process metadata*, representing the actors involved into the process (*User Model*), the process model (*Process Definition Model*) as defined by end-users, as well as some process execution data to control the process execution and also monitor users' activities (*Process Execution Model*). The hypertext layer then provides the front-end through which end-users dynamically compose processes and templates and feed the process model metadata (*Process and Template Modeller*). Such layer also includes the pages to execute the process activities (*Atomic Activity Library*). The runtime layer finally offers support for: *i)* computing the hypertext pages through which end-users define processes; *ii)* governing the execution of processes, according to the user-defined process model; *iii)* computing the pages supporting the execution of atomic activities.

In addition to the previous layers, the architecture relies on the availability of a knowledge repository that stores the resources needed by team members for developing projects, and that therefore can be the object of the activities composing a process.

5 Conclusions

In this paper we have presented a solution enabling the run-time user-driven definition of flexible collaborative processes. This solution has been implemented in educational scenarios for academic learning and industrial training, which rely on collaboration in project-based learning. Some first experiments with users in three different institutions have demonstrated the usefulness of the proposed environment in the academic and industrial domains where project-based learning is crucial. We nevertheless believe that the conceived solution and the proposed framework architecture have a general value for the management of dynamic flexible process, and can be replicated as well in other domains requiring process flexibility.

Acknowledgments

This work is founded by the FP6 EU Project COOPER (IST – 027073). We are really grateful to Dr. Jan van Bruggen and to Drs. Ellen Rusman for the help offered in the identification of atomic activities.

References

[1] Bongio, A., et al.: Towards a Collaborative Open Environment of Project-Centred Learning. In: Nejdl, W., Tochtermann, K. (eds.) EC-TEL 2006. LNCS, vol. 4227, pp. 561–566. Springer, Heidelberg (2006)

[2] Ceri, S., Daniel, F., Matera, M., Raffio, A.: Providing Flexible Workflow Support to Porject-Centered Learning. Technical Report, DEI-Politecnico di Milano (June 2007)

[3] Ceri, S., Fraternali, P., Bongio, A., Brambilla, M., Comai, S., Matera, M.: Designing Data Intensive Web Applications. Morgan Kaufmann, San Francisco (2002)

[4] Charoy, F., Guabtni, A., Valdes, M.: Faura. A Dynamic Workflow Management System for Coordination of Cooperative Activities. In: Proc. of the First Int. DPM '06 Workshop (2006)

[5] Lin, J., Ho, C., Sadiq, W., Orlowska, M.W.: Using Workflow Technology to Manage Flexible e-Learning Services. Educational Technology & Society 5(4) (2002)

[6] Nodenot, T., Marquesuzaa, C., Laforcade, P., Sallaberry, C.: Model-based Engineering of Learning Situation for Adaptive Web Based Educational Systems. In: Proc. of WWW 2004, pp. 94–103. ACM Press, New York (2004)

[7] Sadiq, S., Sadiq, W., Orlowska, M.: Pockets of Flexibility in Workflow Specifications. In: Kunii, H.S., Jajodia, S., Sølvberg, A. (eds.) ER 2001. LNCS, vol. 2224, pp. 513–526. Springer, Heidelberg (2001)

[8] Westera, W., Sloep, P.B., Gerrissen, J.: The Design of the Virtual Company; Synergism of Learning and Working in a Networked Environment. Innovations in Education and Training International 37(1), 24–33 (2000)

A p2p Framework for Interacting with Learning Objects

Andrea Clematis, Paola Forcheri, and Alfonso Quarati

Istituto di Matematica Applicata e Tecnologie Informatiche del CNR
Genova, Italy
{Clematis,Forcheri,Quarati}@ge.imati.cnr.it

Abstract. In this paper we propose a distributed scenario in which users may express their comments about Learning Objects (LO), and point out relationships among them. Considering comments we associate ranks to each LO. The relationships allow users to evolve from a local view, based on the analysis of a single LO, to an enlarged perspective of a network of them. The implementation of such environment in a Super Peer Network is outlined.

Keywords: Learning objects, Distributed systems, Super peer networks.

1 Introduction

The experience gained in the work on learning object repositories (LORs) highlighted the difficulty of creating a critical mass of high quality material easily accessible from a number of communities [1].

To overcome this difficulty, efforts have then been oriented towards the issue of efficiently interrelating distributed and heterogeneous repositories. An example is constituted by the Global Learning Objects Brokered Exchange (GLOBE) alliance [2], that aims to create a network of linked and interoperable repositories. Another example is the eduSource project, a joint venture of Canadian partners aimed to create the prototype for a network of interoperable LORs [3]. Methods for realising a Distributed Learning Object Repository Network, aimed to limit the barriers to the access to LOs, are also proposed [4].

To create a critical mass of high quality material, in our view, LORs should moreover be endowed with features that support motivation for users/teachers to put their time and effort in usage, implementation and diffusion of LOs. As already noted, in fact, sharing didactical materials is no straightforward task for teachers, but requires of them a good amount of labour both to integrate in their own lessons other people's productions and to prepare new contributions in a form that can be easily re-used and adapted by their colleagues [5]. On this basis, we suggest to regard at LORs as a foundation for developing a network of communities of practice, that produces and shares valuable ideas and new artefact as a result of the experience gained dealing with LOs [6]. To this end, a network of distributed and inter-related user-defined comments is established to explore the content of LORs.

The above depicted scenario is a typically distributed one in which stakeholders and LOs are spread across different physical locations, as a consequence networked

E. Duval, R. Klamma, and M. Wolpers (Eds.): EC-TEL 2007, LNCS 4753, pp. 469–474, 2007.

computer access becomes the basic technology to support it. Our implementation relies on peer to peer (p2p) technology, and more specifically on the design and realisation of a Super Peer Network [7]. As shown in the following sections, this solution seems to be particularly suitable to realise the proposed model.

2   Interacting with Learning Objects

To realise a network of these kinds of communities, LOs should be enriched with the expressive power deriving from the interactions with both the users and other LOs. Accordingly, we introduce two levels of interaction between a user and a LO.

A *reflection level,* represented by the variety of users' opinions about the LO. These opinions may further refined as:

- User opinion (u), a non-qualified comment of a generic user;
- Peer review (p), the opinion of an expert officially entrusted with the task;
- Results of the experience (e), the description of a realm where the object has been used and the students' reaction;

An *interconnection level,* represented by the conceptual network of LOs, including the LO at hand, dynamically created by users during the search and the interaction process. The kinds of relationships defined by users may be classified as:

- Specialisation (s), a learning object LO_j is indicated by a user as a specialisation of another, say LO_i if, for example, the user thinks that LO_j could be used to go in deep or to show an example of a concept which is tackled by LO_i;
- Complementary (c), learning object LO_j is indicated by a user as a complement of LO_i if, for example, the user thinks the two LOs can be coupled in the same context or he experienced this use;
- Affinity (a), learning object LO_j is indicated by a user as similar to LO_i if the user thinks that LO_j and LO_i could be used indifferently.

This view leads us to interpret each LO as an annotated graph of both the connections between users' reflections on it and the interconnections, as seen by the users, between the LO at hand and other LOs in the network (See Fig. 1). LOs are identified by nodes. Interactions between user and LOs are identified by means of *interaction arcs,* labelled by tuples of the form *<User, Relation, Comment>,* where:

- *User* is any suitable reference to identify the user annotating the object;
- *Relation* is the identifier of the relation being established for the object, where *Relation* pertains to the set (u, p, e, s, c a);
- *Comment* is the annotation associated to the relation. The comment can be expressed in textual, audio-visual or mixed form.

In the labelled graph of Fig. 1 five relationships are represented for learning object LO_p: two opinions and a peer-review, created by users U_k, U_j and U_i respectively; a specialisation suggested by user U_i about learning object LO_q w.r.t. LO_i; and a complementarity with learning object LO_t individuated by user U_j. For the sake of simplicity the *Comment* elements aren't shown on Fig. 1.

The interconnection arcs (the dashed ones) linking the LOs establish a *graph of comments* and relationships that enforces, with new meta-knowledge, the LORs provided by the participants to the network.

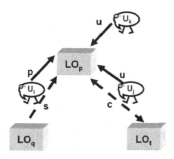

Fig. 1. Graph of comments for learning object *LOp*

As result of the comment activities, each LO can be associated to a set of weights, namely *ranks* (possibly one for each type of comment related to the LO at hand) accounting for the number of comments it received by users. Similarly to PageRank™ used by Google to evaluate search-results on the Web, these weights measure the degree of popularity of a fixed LO among the learning communities, and supplies users with a useful quantitative index. Ranks along with comments (qualitative index) establish a new, and more exhaustive user-centric view of LOs and of their dynamic interrelations.

For learning object LO_p of Fig. 1, we have the ranks depicted in Table 1, where the last column (rank) is the number of all comments expressed on LO_p.by users.

Table 1. Popularity measures for learning object *LOp*

	u-rank	p-rank	e-rank	s-rank	c-rank	a-rank	rank
LO_p	2	1	-	1	1	-	5

The per-object view of interconnections among LOs can be combined in three different graphs that summarize at the community level the network of relationships among objects. The *specialization* graph is a direct graph that allows to identify objects that constitute a specialization process from some general content to a set of specific information. Thus, it defines a learning path in a knowledge domain. The *complementary* and *affinity* relations generate undirected graphs, since comple-mentary and affinity interconnections identify symmetric relations between two objects. By means of the complementary relation it is possible to get an help in order to identify a set of LOs that represent available resources on a given domain. One of the possible uses of the affinity graph is to set up a catalogue of learning objects that have a similar content and approach in addressing a selected topic.

3   A Super Peer Network for Interacting with LOs

The inherently distributed and collaborative nature of the above depicted application suggests us to model the graph of comments on LOs, by means of peer to peer technology.

The advance of research on this field has led to the proposal of Super Peer Networks (SPN) [7]. Super Peer Networks try to combine the better aspects of pure and centralized p2p architectures by introducing specific nodes, namely *super peers node* (SPs) that act as a query server with respect to a set of clients (normal peers) and as peers with respect to the other super peer nodes. Each client node is connected exactly to one SP node. This means that, to post a query, each client has to interact only with its super peer node, which in turn interacts with other super peers. Peer-to-peer attracted the attention of researchers involved in e-learning and different proposals and research projects where developed in the recent past [1], [8], [9]. One of the key issues addressed by these studies is the definition of a suitable metadata organization in order to provide interoperability of heterogeneous learning objects. Here we do not consider this aspect, but we look at SPN as a way to improve availability of information about comments on LOs.

To reflect the graph structure of Fig. 1, each comment is stored in a file on a peer node, while the information labelling the interaction arcs relating to the comment, namely a *comment-tuple*, is maintained on the SP node.

We observe that, in our application, a limited number of individuals provide their own specific contributions that vary from those of the other users. Differently, usual p2p applications are characterized by the fact that a huge amount of possibly redundant files is shared by a wide community of users. Consequently, by following the baseline pattern, a rather reduced set of information (comments) shall be returned to a querying user.

To overcome this limitation, a SP node has to hold further and more detailed meta-information about the comments located on its client nodes. When a peer leaves the system, meta-information about its comments will be returned, if it is the case, in response of user searches. Accordingly, comment-tuples are of the form<*User, Relation,Object1,Object2,FileName,ExtraInfo*>.

Relation is an identifier denoting one of the six relationships defined in Section 2, *Object1* and *Object2* are the URIs of the learning objects involved in the relationship (the same URI in the case of the "Reflection" three relationships) commented by *User* and stored on the peer location expressed by *FileName*. The *ExtraInfo* field extends the comment-tuple with further meta-information (e.g. user properties, comment properties, keywords, ...), that allows to maintain at users' disposal some kind of "asynchronous view" of the overall graph of comments and relationships built upon LOs by all peers of the SP node. To realize this asynchronicity, furthermore, appropriate changes to the standard behaviour of *join* and *leave* operations are necessary. In this way users will be supplied with a paramount, though not exhaustive, view of the resources potentially at disposal.

3.1 Deploying Comments with JXTA

Project JXTA is a p2p framework developed by Sun Microsystems in 2001 and released to the public under an open source licence (www.jxta.org). JXTA consists of a set of protocols and APIs that establish a virtual network (*overlay network*) on top of the Internet, in which peer nodes can directly interact with one another regardless of the underlying network topology.

Different proposals in the e-learning field are based on JXTA. For example, the already mentioned Edutella. Edutella services complement the JXTA services adapting then to a p2p-based e-learning scenario. In [10] JXTA is used to implement an ubiquitous learning environment. JEF [11] is an extensible educational framework, providing tools for instructors to easily integrate collaborative functionalities into a virtual classroom space.

We chose JXTA for a number of reasons: firstly JXTA guarantees interoperability, thus enabling cooperation of heterogeneous entities. Secondly, its capability of firewall and NAT (network address translator) traversal is necessary in normally secured educational environments. A third consideration regards JXTA's ability to quickly adapt to changes in network topology, as it happens in collaborative applications, where users frequently join and leave the environment. Moreover, JXTA core tools and mechanisms to structure and query a p2p network smoothly fit our comments network.

Let us examine our choices for implementing the graph of comments and some user scenario, according to the main JXTA features.

Users creating or querying for comments about LOs reside on JXTA *edge peers,* that is peers that act by exchanging (enquiring or answering) messages with others. The sharing of comments information is granted by the setting of a number of *rendezvous* peers (that is peers that forward discovery requests to help other peers to discover resources) acting as SP nodes. *Relay* peers (maintaining information about the routes to other peers and routing messages between peers) are activated to trespass barriers (e.g. NAT or firewall protected environments) between different organizations involved in the community, bridging different physical and/or logical networks.

Our design choices leverage on two key issues of JXTA 1) *advertisements* (i.e. XML documents) used by each peer in a JXTA network to announce its existence and available resources. Advertisements enable other peers on the network to learn how to connect to, and interact with, a peer; 2) SRDI (shared resource distributed index) service, running on *rendezvous* peers, that manages indexes of advertisements published by edge peers.

When a user wants to create a new comment, the Creation service of the peer is invoked. After the editing, the comment is saved on the user file system, and an Advertisement object for the associated comment-tuple is created then published both locally and remotely (on the *rendezvous* node related to the peer). Note that the advertisement is stored and indexed in the peer's local cache, while only the index for the advertisement is sent to the *rendezvous* peer which stores it on the SRDI index.

When a user browses the network for comments, the Browse service, relying on the Rendezvous Service, issues a discovery query that is propagated to all the other SPs in the community SP nodes supply the complete comments for the connected peers and, by using the *ExtraInfo*, some useful hints about the comments produced by disconnected peers. Thus, a better view of the whole collection of comments is provided.

4 Concluding Remarks

We propose to employ SPN technology as architectural basis to support the development of a distributed network oriented to e-learning and centred on LOs. In our case, the technological structure supporting the network has to guarantee, at every moment, availability of the overall graph of comments and relationships built upon LOs by all peers, including contributions of peers which are not connected.

Learning Objects are gaining an increasing interest in the e-learning community. Their availability in a distributed Web-based environment represents an opportunity for further developments generated by a richer context of interaction that permits to different stakeholders to use, comment and evolve available objects, thus providing each other with suggestions and insights.

References

1. Ternier, S., Duval, E., Neven, F.: Using a p2p architecture to provide interoperability between LearningObjects. In: Proceedings of World Conference on Educational Multimedia, Hypermedia and Telecommunications, pp. 148–151 (2003)
2. MacLoad, D.: Learning Object Repositories: Deployment and Diffusion, CANARIE discussion paper, CANARIE inc. (2005)
3. McGreal, R., Anderson, T., Babin, G., Downes, S., Friesen, N., Harrigan, K., Hatala, M., MacLeod, D., Mattson, M., Paquette, G., Richards, G., Roberts, T., Schafer, S.: EduSource: Canada's Learning Object Repository Network. Int. J. of Instructional Technology and Distant Learning 1(3) (2004)
4. Downes, S.: Design and reusability of learning objects in an academic context. USDLA Journal, 17 (1) (2003), http://www.usdla.org/html/journal/JAN03_Issue/article01.html
5. Busetti, E., Dettori, G., Forcheri, P., Ierardi, M.G.: Guidelines towards effectively sharable LOs. In: Liu, W., Shi, Y., Li, Q. (eds.) ICWL 2004. LNCS, vol. 3143, pp. 416–423. Springer, Heidelberg (2004)
6. Busetti, E., Dettori, G., Forcheri, P., Ierardi, M.G., Molfino, M.T.: Repositories of Learning Objects as Learning Environments for Teachers. In: Proceedings of ICALT 2004, pp. 450–454. IEEE Comp. Soc. Press, Los Alamitos (2004)
7. Yang, B., Garcia-Molina, H.: Designing a super-peer network (2002) http://dbpubs.stanford.edu: 8090/pub/2002-13
8. Nejdl, W., Wolf, B., Qu, C., Decker, S., Sintek, M., Naeve, A., Nilsson, M., Palmer, M., Risch, T., Edutella, A.: p2p Networking Infrastructure Based on RDF. In: Proceedings of the 11th international conference on World Wide Web, pp. 604–615 (2002)
9. Neidl, W., Wolpers, M., Siberski, W., Schmitz, C., Schlosser, M., Brunkhorst, I., Loser, A.: Super-peer-based routing strategies for RDF-based peer-to-peer networks. Journal of Web Semantics , 177–186 (2004)
10. Zhang, G., Jin, Q., Shih, T.K.: Peer-to-Peer Based Social Interaction Tools in Ubiquitous. ICPADS (1), 230–236 (2005)
11. Leighton, G., Müldner, T.: Applying Peer-To-Peer Technology to the Building of Distributed Educational Systems. Journal of Interactive Learning Research. 16(3), 295–315 (2005)

A Framework for the Automatic Generation of Algorithm Animations Based on Design Techniques

Luis Fernández-Muñoz[1], Antonio Pérez-Carrasco[2], J. Ángel Velázquez-Iturbide[2], and Jaime Urquiza-Fuentes[2]

[1] Departamento de Lenguajes, Proyectos y Sistemas Informáticos,
Escuela Universitaria de Informática, Universidad Politécnica de Madrid,
Ctra. Valencia km 7, 28031 Madrid, Spain
setillo@eui.upm.es
[2] Departamento de Lenguajes y Sistemas Informáticos,
Universidad Rey Juan Carlos,
C/ Tulipán s/n, 28933 Móstoles, Madrid, Spain
{angel.velazquez,jaime.urquiza}@urjc.es

Abstract. A novel approach to algorithm animation consists in displaying algorithms based on their design technique. In this paper, we describe a framework to generate these animations without effort from the instructor. We describe a preprocessing phase that modifies the source code of the algorithm to visualize. When the transformed code is executed, a trace is stored and then used to generate an animation. We also describe the architecture of the animation subsystem. Finally, we outline the main features of SRec, a system that we have built to illustrate the feasibility of this approach. It is aimed at visualizing multiple views of recursion, namely traces, the control stack and activation trees.

Keywords: Computer science education, recursion, program visualization, program animation, automation.

1 Introduction

Algorithm animations have been used in education for the last 25 years. However, they are not in the mainstream of educational software because of two main reasons:

- Lack of evidence of educational effectiveness [1], and
- Heavy workload posed on animation constructors (typically, educators) [2].

Several approaches have been adopted to reduce construction effort [3]. One of them consists in automatically generating visualizations tightly coupled to source code (i.e. program visualizations). When an algorithm is executed, visualizations of its successive states are generated as a side effect by associating graphical operations to selected operations in the code. An animation consists in playing the visualizations gathered using interaction controls. We have applied a variant of this approach to the functional programming paradigm [4], and there is evidence of its educational effectiveness [5].

E. Duval, R. Klamma, and M. Wolpers (Eds.): EC-TEL 2007, LNCS 4753, pp. 475–480, 2007.

In this paper, we present an implementation framework of this approach to animate algorithm design techniques [6]. In the second section, we describe several phases of processing and translation of the algorithm source code. In section 3 we describe the architecture of the animation subsystem. Section 4 introduces SRec, a system developed to check the feasibility of our approach. It is aimed at visualizing recursion, which is often used in algorithm design techniques. The fifth section explains the transformations performed on the source code to visualize recursion. In section 6 we discuss related work. Finally, we summarize our conclusions and future work.

2 Preprocessing of Source Code

A key decision for an automatic animation system is to identify those changes in the program state that must produce a change in the visualization. In the WinHIPE programming environment [4], we selected every expression generated during an evaluation. We then modified the interpreter to graphically visualize them.

We propose here a different approach. Instead of modifying the language processor and not modifying the source code to visualize, we modify the source code so that the language processor remains unchanged. Consequently, we need a preprocessing phase to modify the original source code at selected events with visualization actions.

The preprocessing phase is performed using XML as an intermediate language. It is summarized in Fig. 1 and is as follows. Firstly, the Java code of the algorithm is transformed into its equivalent representation in XML. Secondly, the XML representation is converted into a DOM hierarchical structure. Thirdly, the resulting representation of the algorithm is further transformed by inserting new nodes in the DOM representation. These nodes are statements that report changes of state that must produce a change of visualization. A fourth step transforms the manipulated hierarchical structure back into a modified Java code, containing the inserted statements embedded into the algorithm. Finally, the Java code is compiled. The resulting file will be executed by the Java virtual machine once the user has entered its arguments. As a result of its execution, a trace will be created. The animation subsystem, described in Section 3, uses the trace to create the visualizations that will form the animation.

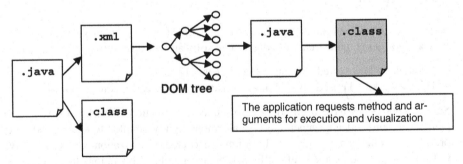

Fig. 1. Preprocessing phase of the algorithm source code written in Java

3   Architecture of the Animation Subsystem

The architecture of the animation subsystem is generic and reusable. Its structure is independent from any specific algorithm design technique. However, some parts will be implemented differently for each design technique. It is shown in Fig. 2.

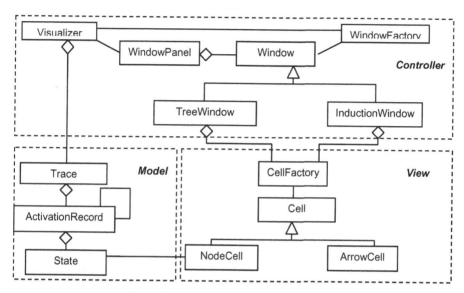

Fig. 2. Diagram of the animation architecture

The application is based on the Model-View-Controller architecture [7]. The model contains the data to visualize. For the recursion system described below, a composite pattern is used. Execution data are stored as a trace of activation records. Each record consists of two states, respectively storing the values of arguments and the result. The view is a panel to display a particular visualization. The controller consists in a factory pattern that supports different kinds of visualizations. All of the visualizations are handled from the main window panel of the application.

4   SRec, a System with Multiple Views for Recursion Animation

The framework we have described should be put into practice in order to check its feasibility. Therefore, we developed SRec, a system to animate recursion using multiple views: traces, the control stack, and activation trees.

Fig. 3 shows a snapshot of SRec for the 6th number of the Fibonacci series. The file source code is displayed in the left top panel. The other panels display the three views: traces at the left bottom panel, the control stack at the central panel, and an activation tree at the rightmost panel. Animation controls are placed at the right top corner of the main window. They are similar to VCR controls, allowing forward/backward, automatic/manual animation.

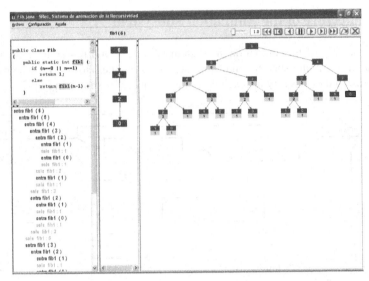

Fig. 3. A snapshot of SRec animating Fibonacci numbers

The user generates an animation from a Java file. After entering the file and the method names, the source code is preprocessed, as explained in section 2. On entering parameter values, the algorithm is executed and the trace is generated. Animations may also be stored in or loaded from disk for convenience of the instructor.

Most graphical features can be customized. More importantly, each node of the activation tree may contain either one or several of the arguments, the result, or both. Furthermore, historic information (i.e. finished calls) may be colored in the same way, attenuated or omitted.

5 Modification of Source Code of Recursive Algorithms

We describe in this section the preprocessing necessary to visualize recursion. Statements are inserted to record the state changes that must have a visible effect over the display, i.e. a recursive call entry or exit.

For instance, consider a class containing an algorithm to compute the Fibonacci series. The Java class generated follows, where the statements inserted are bolded. The first block of statements inserts the arguments of the method invocation into the trace. The second block of statements does similarly for the result of any call. All of this information is stored in a lineal data structure, implemented in the *Trace* class. The *Singleton* static method assures that a single instance of the *Trace* class exists during the execution of an algorithm. Every set of arguments or every result is inserted in the trace as a new state (i.e. a variable-length array of values). The ugly identifiers for variables *pppppp01* and *rrrrrr01* refer respectively to 'parameters' and 'result', so that it is unlikely that a programmer will use the same identifier in his/her algorithm.

```
class Fibbonaci {
    public static int fib (int n) {
```

```
      Object ppppp01[] = new Object[1];
      ppppp01[0]=n;
      Trace.singleton().addInput(new State(ppppp01));
      int result = 0;
      if (n==1)
         result = 1;
      else if (n==2)
         result = 1;
      else
         result = fib(n-1)+fib(n-2);
      Object rrrrr01[] = new Object[1];
      rrrrr01[0] = result;
      Trace.singleton().addOutput(new State(rrrrr01));
      return result;
   }
}
```

6   Related Work

There are few descriptions of the architecture of animation systems based on design patterns. A design pattern has been proposed for visualizing objects of arbitrary complexity [8]. It also uses the factory pattern to represent visualization elements. An observer architecture has been proposed [9] that mirrors the syntactic structure of program elements with a parallel structure of visualization elements. Both works address the architecture of object visualization, but not the application architecture.

Several systems have been designed to assist in the learning of recursion via visualization: Recursion Animator [10], EROSI [11], ETV [12], the Java Function Visualizer [13] and SimRECUR [14]. Some systems support multiple views of recursion, but none supports activation trees.

7   Conclusions and Future Work

We have described a framework to generate, without effort from the instructor, program animations. We described a preprocessing phase that extends the Java source code of the algorithm to visualize by inserting statements. When this transformed Java code is executed, these inserted statements report relevant changes of the display to a trace. The animation of the algorithm is generated by interpreting the trace. We have also described the architecture of the animation subsystem in terms of design patterns.

We have introduced SRec, a system that we have built to illustrate the feasibility of this approach. It is aimed at visualizing recursion, by means of multiple views: traces, the control stack and activation trees. We described its main features and the particular statements that SRec inserts in the algorithm code during preprocessing.

We plan to continue this work in several ways. In the near future, a release of SRec will be delivered. We will evaluate it in the classroom to check its educational effectiveness. Finally, work to visualize algorithm design techniques will be resumed. In particular, divide-and-conquer should be available after minor changes [8].

Acknowledgments. This work was supported by projects TIN2004-07568 of the Spanish Ministry of Education and Science and S-0505/DPI/0235 of the Autonomous Region of Madrid.

References

1. Naps, T., et al.: Exploring the role of visualization and engagement in computer science education. ACM SIGCSE Bulletin 35(2), 131–152 (2003)
2. Naps, T., et al.: Evaluating the educational impact of visualization. ACM SIGCSE Bulletin 35(4), 124–136 (2003)
3. Ihantola, P., Karavirta, V., Korhonen, A., Nikander, J.: Taxonomy of effortless creation of algorithm visualization. In: Proc. 2005 International Workshop on Computing Education Research, pp. 123–133. ACM Press, New York (2005)
4. Velázquez-Iturbide, J.Á., Pareja-Flores, C., Urquiza-Fuentes, J.: An approach to effortless construction of program animations. Computers & Education (in press)
5. Urquiza-Fuentes, J., Velázquez Iturbide, J.Á.: An evaluation of the effortless approach to build algorithm animations with WinHIPE. In: Proc. Fourth Program Visualization Workshop, University of Florence, Italy, pp. 29–33 (2006)
6. Fernández-Muñoz, L., Velázquez-Iturbide, J.Á.: A study of visualizations for algorithm design techniques. In: Proc. VII International Conf. Human-Computer Interaction, Universidad de Castilla-La Mancha, Spain, pp. 315–324 (In Spanish) (2006)
7. Gamma, E., Helm, R., Johnson, R., Vlissides, J.: Design Patterns, Elements of Reusable Object-Oriented Software. Addison-Wesley, Reading (1995)
8. Korhonen, A., Malmi, L., Saikkonen, R.: Design pattern for algorithm animation and simulation. In: Proc. First Program Visualization Workshop, pp. 89–100. University of Joensuu, Finland (2000)
9. Kumar, A.N., Kasabov, S.: Observer architecture of program visualization. In: Proc. Fourth Program Visualization Workshop, pp. 17–22. University of Florence, Italy (2006)
10. Wilcocks, D., Sanders, I.: Animating recursion as an aid to instruction. Computers & Education 23(3), 221–226 (1994)
11. Dershem, H.L., Parker, D.E., Weinhold, R.: A Java function visualizer. Journal of Computing in Small Colleges 15(1), 220–230 (1999)
12. George, C.E.: EROSI – Visualizing recursion and discovering new errors. In: Proc. 31st SIGCSE Technical Symp. on Computer Science Education, pp. 305–309. ACM Press, New York (2000)
13. Terada, M.: ETV: A program trace player for students. In: Proc. 10th Annual Conference on Innovation and Technology in Computer Science Education, pp. 118–122. ACM Press, New York (2005)
14. Wu, C.-C., Lin, J.M.-C., Hsu, I.Y-W.: Closed laboratories using SimLIST and SimRECUR. Computers & Education 28(1), 55–64 (1997)

The Development of TE-Cap: An Assistance Environment for Online Tutors

Elise Garrot, Sébastien George, and Patrick Prévôt

LIESP Laboratory, INSA-Lyon, F-69621, France
{elise.garrot,sebastien.george;patrick.prevot}@insa-lyon.fr

Abstract. Our research is based on the hypothesis that the most important problem that has to be solved, so as to help tutors, is the gap between required competencies of distance tutoring and the lack of training and recommendations given to them on the role they have to play in the learning process. In this article, we detail the development of the assistance environment for tutors named TE-Cap (Tutoring Experience Capitalization). We first present results of interviews conducted with tutors to define their explicit and implicit needs. We then detail functionalities of the TE-Cap (Tutoring Experience Capitalization) platform we developed and first results of an experiment, in terms of computing functionalities and interface design. Finally, we present some future directions of our research.

Keywords: Assistance Environment for Tutor, Community of Practice, Experiences sharing, Knowledge Management.

1 Research Issues

Nowadays, there is an obvious need of assistance for tutors that we define as those who monitor students' activities at distance. Our research is based on the hypothesis that the most important problem that has to be solved, so as to help tutors, is the gap between required competencies of distance tutoring [1] (matter expertise, technical, pedagogical, information and communication skills) and the lack of training and the recommendations given to them on the role they have to play in the learning process. Formation methods remain specific to each campus, and therefore quite isolated and rather ad-hoc [2]. This hypothesis is illustrated by the fact that for several years, we can notice the creation of several communities of practice of tutors, like t@d (http://jacques.rodet.free.fr/), that highlight the need to provide some help to these actors, beyond the frontiers defined by institutions. In fact, in most educational institutions, tutors have an environment which proposes forums, chat or blog in order to incite them to interact together and with students. In some cases, these environments propose an assistant tool to help tutors to monitor students' activities and to retrieve traces of their work. We think that these environments and tools can be useful, when they are adopted by tutors [3], but are not sufficient. Firstly, tutors cannot interact with tutors of other institutions. Secondly, assistance tools depend on the environment, so it is quite difficult to use a same tool in various contexts. Furthermore, it seems useless to provide information about students to tutors if they do not know the

E. Duval, R. Klamma, and M. Wolpers (Eds.): EC-TEL 2007, LNCS 4753, pp. 481–486, 2007.
© Springer-Verlag Berlin Heidelberg 2007

theme of their work. Basing on this hypothesis, our research aims at developing an innovative assistance environment for tutors going over existing frontiers (e.g. institution, training program, teaching subject), which takes into account and values all tutors' skills, to improve their efficiency and the way they work.

One of the difficulties of our research is to find or create relations between actors from different institutions. Indeed, within the context of one institution, there are many subjects that can form the basis of interactions: common courses, common goals, common learners to monitor, etc. But, when we pass beyond the borders of the institution, which subject will create interactions between tutors? The environment that we develop must be itself the catalyst of the interactions, in order to lead tutors to help each other. Another important difficulty to overcome is the determination of tutors' needs in terms of help or assistance, independently of the institution to which they belong. It implies the development of an environment which responds to needs which are not precisely identified or not expressed by these actors. Since tasks assigned to tutors vary according to institutions, our objective is not to develop an environment that would optimize some tasks, to which correspond recognizable needs. The finality of the system we develop is to support an emerging helping process between tutors that could not be well defined *a priori*. The development of the assistance system TE-Cap (Tutoring Experience Capitalization) relies on a participative and iterative design process based on the framework proposed by Mackay and Fayard [4]. The aim is to give birth gradually to needs and expectations of tutors, so as to make evolve the system functionalities at the same time as the needs are expressed.

2   Definition of Explicit and Implicit Needs

The first development life-cycle aimed at knowing tutors activities and practices and identifying their needs and expectations by interviewing them. We conducted seven interviews with tutors of different institutions, with different backgrounds and from different disciplines (educational sciences, computer science, training to set-up blended learning, use of ICT in education and training). These interviews were based on a literature survey on tutor roles in distance learning [5]. Several questions guided these interviews: What are the experiences and the initial skills of tutors? What training was given to them? How do they build their practices? Do they exchange them? What is the nature of the interactions between them?

As a result, we determined tutors' needs and expectations and, moreover, a model of the factors in relation with a practice of tutoring. This model summarizes the vocabulary used by tutors in their day-to-day practice. So, a tutoring practice can be bound to the institutional context, to the teaching situation or to the tutor's profile. We give more details in [6]. By analysing interviews retranscription, we highlighted some lacks for tutors:

- Lack of training to become a tutor, so they develop their own practices, which is very difficult for a novice.
- Lack of interactions between tutors of an institution and of various institutions.
- Lack of professional identity, so tutors do not know of what their work consists in.
- Lack of practices sharing between tutors.

We also raised several points important to exploit in tutors' practice and profile:

- The variety of the careers and training of the tutors: it implies a variety of skills (e.g. educational, technical, expertise of the subject) that can be exploited to facilitate the sharing and the development of tutors' skills.
- The adoption of practices of capitalization by building a repository to hold their role with more efficiency. A shared capitalization would be a source of inspiration for many tutors, in particular for the novices.
- Numerous interests for sharing practices.

With regards to the literature, we decided to base our work on the concept of Community of Practice (CoP) developed by Wenger [7]. We detail this concept and the reasons of our choice in [6]. We consider that in the framework of a CoP, tutors will be able to share and develop their experiences, competencies and practices. We also base the development of our experiment prototype on the concept of knowledge management, in order to store and retrieve the explicit and tacit knowledge produced by the CoP of tutors [8]. The environment has to support the following needs:

- To facilitate the perception of the community members.
- To facilitate interactions, experiences sharing and mutual aid between tutors.
- To encourage the reflexivity of tutors on their practices.
- To use a vocabulary common to the CoP (in our case adapted to tutoring).
- To capitalize the exchanges between tutors in a contextual way.
- To register the present expertise in the community.
- To adopt an effective classification of knowledge (messages, documents …).
- To make the members participate in the evolution of the platform.

3 TE-Cap Development and Experiment Results

This second cycle leads to the development of the assistance environment TE-Cap (Tutoring Experience Capitalization) based on the requirements previously identified. The conception of the platform relies on the CMS (Content Management System) opensource Joomla!. We opted for this CMS according to some criteria and among a consequent list of existing CMS (http://cmsmatrix.org/). The main reasons of this choice are, on the one hand, that it proposes basic functionalities which thus do not need to be developed again (such as articles, documents and users management) and, on the other hand, that its functionalities are based on independent components, so the evolution capacities and the modularity of TE-Cap is largely facilitated. We modified some components and developed some others so as to answer needs identified.

3.1 TE-Cap Functionalities

1. Perception and sharing among community members: the environment displays the list of tutors who belong to the community. For each member, it is possible to consult its profile and to send to another a personal e-mail directly from the interface. In this way, a tutor novice in a domain of skill (technical or educational skills or skills concerning contents) can ask directly for help a more expert tutor in this

domain. The visualization of members' profiles brings conviviality to the site, in-citing to participate in the community life.

2. Personal space within the community portal: by connecting to the platform, the tu-tor can display messages, documents and Web links which s/he proposed to the community, with as indication the number of times they were viewed by other tu-tors (Fig. 1). S/he can also consult the comments made on a message. Tutors have the choice to diffuse or not the messages they write. This functionality plays the role of a log book which can contain private and public parts. Furthermore, before validating a message, the tutor has to precise his intention: testimony, discussion or ask for help. This constrains him/her to have a reflection on its intention and cre-ates a first classification of messages. Before sending a message, the tutor has to classify it with a dedicated interface which is presented in the next section.

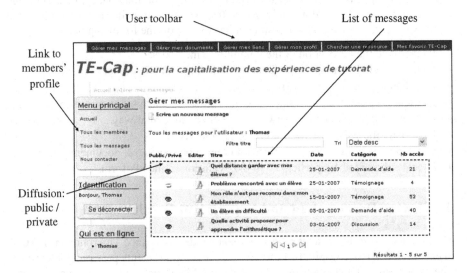

Fig. 1. The personal space of messages publication

3. Knowledge capitalization: with the need of management of the knowledge pro-duced by the community, we developed a component of knowledge classification, integrated in the CMS. The classification is based on the model developed in the first cycle and uses a vocabulary adapted to the community. The classification ap-pears in the form of a dynamic arborescence. This component offers two main functionalities:

- When a tutor sends a message, a document or a Web link, he has to choose the corresponding subjects in the dynamic arborescence. For example, if a tutor asks for help because s/he does not know how to react in front of a learner in trouble within a workgroup, s/he can check the box "In trouble" in the subject "Position inside the group " in the part "Concerned learners".
- The tutor can look for all the types of resources relating to one or several sub-jects in relation with tutoring. If s/he finds an interesting resource, s/he can

consult it and add it to his/her favourites. Furthermore, s/he can choose to react to a message, to bring assistance or to pursue a discussion for instance.

The classification tool is in the heart of the participative design of the environment. Tutors can make evolve the initial classification, by proposing new categories. These are proposed to the moderator of the community who decides to add the proposed category or not. Furthermore, the categories used by tutors are recorded, which allows for example to highlight useless ones. This approach offers the possibility to tutors to really adopt the environment, that is essential if we want them to use it.

3.2 First Results of the Experiment

The experiment of the prototype involved the participation of twelve tutors from six countries: Costa Rica, Senegal, Algeria, France, Tunisia and Canada. We have chosen tutors from different institutions and disciplines (e.g. educational science, computer science, mathematics, pedagogy, project management). They used the prototype TE-Cap during two months and tried to integrate it into their practice.

The experiment has just finished. We have defined criteria to observe the response of this prototype to tutors' needs. These criteria are based on the theories that we have chosen to develop (communities of practice and knowledge management). Hence the three categories of criteria are: usability and sociability of the environment [9], measure of the creating and sharing knowledge activities [10] and adoption of the environment by users [3]. These criteria are measured by retrieving and analyzing traces of use and by a questionnaire addressed to tutors.

By observing the day-to-day environment use, we can already notice that tutors did not interact a lot. Some messages have been posted but there were not many answers to them. We also notice that there were only two documents proposed and no Web link. Is it because they do not have documents to exchange? Or is it because the environment is not convenient for them to exchange resources? The analysis of use traces is not finished yet and we will have more results with the return of questionnaires sent to tutors. We make three first hypotheses to explain these observations:

- There were not enough members in the community (12 tutors) to generate high interactions between tutors. It implies that there is a minimal size for the community to observe the emergence of rich interactions.
- Tutors prefer to receive information rather than to have to connect to the environment to see new messages, new comments or new documents. So, we propose to add notification of information by integrating the technology of syndication feed.
- The usability of the interface we have developed to classify and search resources is not well adapted to tutors. The presentation of the classification in the form of a dynamic arborescence has to be modified and improved.

4 Conclusion and Futures Directions

In this article, we developed a participative and iterative process adopted to develop the of the assistance environment for tutors named TE-Cap. Tutors interviews gave information on their explicit and implicit needs. We then referred to theory to suppose global implicit needs, so as to develop a first prototype. The experiment of this prototype was not as successful as we supposed, because tutors did not interact a lot inside the environment. So we will not have enough quantitative information by the way of traces of use of the environment. That is why it is necessary to address a questionnaire to tutors to have more qualitative information.

Concerning the development of TE-Cap, we will base the future cycle on the results of the experiment. It consists in offering to actors, on the one hand, the tools to manage all the knowledge produced by the members' participation in the community, and on the other hand, the tools to create interactions in regards to these knowledge. The development of TE-Cap will be also centered on an adapted interface, which will be more attractive, intuitive and efficient for tutors in their practice. In the end of the third cycle, we will determine the adequacy of the final environment tutors' needs and expectations.

References

1. McPherson, M., Nunes, M.B.: The role of tutors as an integral part of online learning support. European Journal of Open, Distance and E-Learning (EURODL I (2004) retrieved March 28, 2007 from /www.eurodl.org/materials/contrib/2004/Maggie_MsP.html
2. Class, B., Schneider, D.: Tutorat, socio-constructivisme et capitalisation des connaissances dans un portail communautaire utilisé en éducation à distance. Colloque Eifad (École d'Ingénierie de la Formation à Distance). Poitiers (2004) retrieved March 28, 2007 from http://www.cned.fr/colloqueeifad/Documents/Class_Schneider.pdf
3. West, R.E., Waddoups, G., Graham, C.R.: Understanding the experiences of instructors as they adopt a course management system. Educational Technology Research and Development 55, 1–26 (2007)
4. Mackay, W.E., Fayard, A-L.: HCI, Natural Science and Design: A Framework for Triangulation Across Disciplines. In: Proceedings of ACM DIS'97: Designing Interactive Systems. Amsterdam, pp. 223–234. ACM Press, New York (1997)
5. Garrot, E., George, S., Prévôt, P.: A Platform to Support a Virtual Community of Tutors in Experience Capitalizing. In: proceedings of Web Based Communities Conference (WBC 2007) Salamanca, Spain pp. 103–110 (2007)
6. Garrot, E., George, S., Prévôt, P.: TE-Cap: une plate-forme support au partage et à la capitalisation d'expériences entre tuteurs. In: Proceedings of EIAH 2007 Conference. Lausanne (to be published, 2007)
7. Wenger, E.: Communities of practice: Learning, meaning, and identity. Cambridge University Press, Cambridge, U.K., New York (1998)
8. Nonaka, I., Takeuchi, H.: The knowledge creating company. Oxford Press, New York, USA (1995)
9. Preece, J.: Online Communities: Designing Usability, Supporting Sociability. John Wiley & Sons, Chichester, UK (2000)
10. Koh, J., Kim, Y.G.: Knowledge sharing in virtual communities: an e-business perspective. Expert Systems with Applications 26(2), 155–166 (2004)

KnowledgeBus – An Architecture to Support Intelligent and Flexible Knowledge Management

Knut Hinkelmann[1], Johannes Magenheim[2], Wolfgang Reinhardt[2],
Tobias Nelkner[2], Kai Holzweißig[2], and Michael Mlynarski[2]

[1] University of Applied Sciences Northwestern Switzerland, Riggenbachstrasse 16,
4600 Olten, Switzerland
knut.hinkelmann@fhnw.ch
[2] University of Paderborn, Institute of Computer Science, Working Group Didactics of
Informatics, Fürstenallee 11, 33102 Paderborn, Germany
{jsm,wolle,tobin,kwh,funky}@uni-paderborn.de

Abstract. MoKEx (Mobile Knowledge Experience) is an international project series focusing on actual challenges in knowledge management and e-learning. The project series is in cooperation with universities and industrial partners in Germany and Switzerland and links communities of practice with the innovative approaches of learning communities. As a result of the recent execution of the project, an architecture was developed that supports the flexible connection of various independent knowledge systems via the so-called KnowledgeBus. This paper introduces the concept of Single Point of Information (SPI) and the KnowledgeBus itself.

Keywords: Information Integration, Knowledge Management, E-Learning.

1 Introduction

Knowledge is a core asset in today's information society. Digitalized information, as a special kind of explicit knowledge, is of major value to businesses and public institutions and functions as a critical business factor. In order to make this knowledge easily accessible, it would be optimal to have integrated or unified systems of knowledge storage and retrieval. Unfortunately, many corporate system architectures are characterized by a rich heterogeneity of IT-systems, creating information silos within organizational units. This leads to a serious problem because information is stored in various independent applications that often do not interface with each other for the purposes of information exchange. To enable information access and sharing it is necessary to integrate the isolated applications. A naive way of integration would be to create direct links between the systems, resulting in a large number of point-to-point connections that are difficult to maintain if applications are changing or additional applications are added to the architecture. Enterprise Application Integration (EAI) tries to avoid these problems by using middleware technologies or service-oriented architectures [1]. While EAI tends to be data-centric, our main goal is to design a content-oriented knowledge management architecture that transparently integrates disparate, knowledge-rich applications and systems. This is achieved by a single point of

E. Duval, R. Klamma, and M. Wolpers (Eds.): EC-TEL 2007, LNCS 4753, pp. 487–492, 2007.

information and by using cross-application metadata which support services for information storage and retrieval across systems boundaries.

MoKEx (Mobile Knowledge Experience) is an international project series with universities and industrial partners from Germany and Switzerland. The MoKEx II project analyzed training and information management scenarios in three companies and obviously the companies' problem is the consistent and efficient handling of different sources of information. Common to all companies was the co-existence of various knowledge sources that often led to time-consuming searches and redundant data. A first step towards avoiding inconsistencies and to support informal learning at the workplace would be to have a single point of access to all available knowledge sources. Our vision of such a point is explained in the following chapter.

2 The Vision

If information is stored redundantly in different sources, not only the search is complicated but also inconsistencies may arise. A workspace set-up that supports the user's easy access to the right information quickly and reliably would gain added value for the user and the organization. In the context of actual e-learning and blended learning scenarios, the authoring process can profit from a single point of information (SPI) where several disjoint knowledge bases in various disparate knowledge intense subsystems can be accessed. Our vision attempts to create such a SPI in order to provide the user with simple and fast access to relevant information without the user concerning him or herself about where specific data is stored and how he or she can access it.

2.1 Single Point of Information

The productivity of each organisation depends on how fast knowledge can be shared. When we think of the increasing number of enterprise applications, different communication standards and several information access methods, it is obvious that both the productivity and efficiency of the staff is decreasing because nobody knows where to consistently store information. As an implication of this, information cannot be found with any regularity. One would wish to have a single accesspoint, where documents can be created and stored and where any information can be found. The bulk of separate working applications could be connected to a larger virtual application, which is accessible via this single access point. The vision of a SPI strongly depends on intelligent strategies for information storage and retrieval. Only the connection of data objects with good metadata paves the way to intelligent information retrieval techniques. The consequent use and reuse of metadata strongly improves the quality of our approach. In the context of e-learning scenarios, metadata mining is the key requirement of the (semi-)automatically creation of new learning objects and the connection of learning and data objects.

We identified three basic user operations that represent the core of any information-based work: the creation and storage of knowledge objects as well as the search for them. These three aspects are closely related; we cannot consider finding information without taking into account the creation or storage process.

2.2 Create, Store, Search

In the context of knowledge management every user action can be reduced to the creation, storage and retrieval of knowledge objects. Typically, users are trying to organize their local file structure according to specific criteria like creation date, topic, context and name files or directories accordingly. Following this naming approach, a user has to have explicit knowledge on how he named a specific knowledge object and where he or she placed it in order to retrieve it. Research studies have shown that users spent a lot of time assigning objects according to their own rules of object naming and storage structure (cf. [2,3,4]) and nevertheless are overtaxed by their own rules [5]. Transformed to a larger organizational context, it is obvious that this problem becomes even more complex. Our SPI approach liberates the user from knowing about specific taxonomies and the back-pedalling of arbitrary naming and storages rules by supporting him with transparent storage and intelligent information retrieval techniques. By offering a single interface for storing knowledge objects, the user does not have to worry where his or her objects are saved. The main software application decides in which subsystem a specific object should be stored, based on data- and user-taxonomies. Problems of inconsistent naming of different knowledge objects of the same type are eliminated since the user is no longer in direct charge of the main application. The process of storing a knowledge object does not base itself on specific naming criteria or positions in a file tree; storage is based on object type, particular subsystem and other object-inherent metadata. This abstraction does support the user in finding knowledge instead of searching file trees or complex system-specific user interfaces. By providing the user with a single search interface, which abstracts from actual application borders, the user is given the possibility to perform information-oriented instead of document-oriented searches. Through a transparent search over various distributed applications, the user can easily access the explicit knowledge objects stored in single applications. In the context of e-learning and blended learning scenarios, the concept of a single point of information yields several advantages.

3 Architecture and Prototype

According to our vision, the system should be able to create simple semantic connections between different objects like files and learning objects in order to rather support the user's creation and retrieval of data. All the information that is centrally stored in the data pool should be seamlessly available from every integrated subsystem. The resulting concept is a server that connects several subsystems and manages the data flow and object-specific metadata for each connected subsystem. The graphical user interface is connected to the server via Java RMI while the subsystems are connected via RMI and SOAP interfaces, depending on the specific connection possibilities of the subsystem. The design of our architectural approach, as well as the final prototype itself, was mainly influenced by the requirements and expectations of our partners. The integration of a reduced sign on (RSO) concept and the prevention of data corruption through concurrent write operations were core technical requirements of all companies. To keep track of the different versions of the knowledge objects, we implemented a multi-dimensional version management process that assures that every version of a knowledge object can be restored at any time. Another requirement was that all knowledge objects should be accessible via a simple-to-use search interface. This is achieved by a common metadata database that stores the metadata of every single knowledge object of all connected subsystems. With the combination of integrated metadata and reduced sign on, we achieved the mapping of the system-specific rights management to a transparent cross-system information access.

3.1 Architecture of the KnowledgeBus

The KnowledgeBus (KNB) serves as a central integration interface between all coupled subsystems and operates in the middle tier being responsible for the overall communication and data exchange between the tiers. The KNB contains connectors to communicate with and execute processes on systems of the EIS tier.

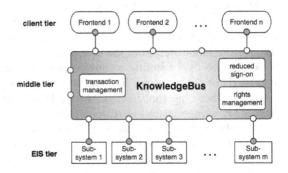

Fig. 1. General architecture of the KnowledgeBus

It uses a metadata database as essential part of the architecture, which contains the relevant metadata that describe the content of the subsystems as well as user specific access rights. The metadata database represents the knowledge base in the system, which keeps track of all knowledge objects available in the different systems. As soon as a new knowledge object is added to on of the integrated systems the KNB starts a transaction that stores manually entered and automatically generated metadata in the metadata database and the object in the according subsystem. Searching for an object is performed only in the metadata database, which contains descriptions of all knowledge objects. This results in a very efficient search because no access to the connected subsystems is needed. Only when the user requests to read or edit an object does the KNB fetch it from the subsystem. As the subsystems themselves can be very different with respect to their functionality and connectivity it is necessary to have a flexible interface concept. The use of standardised protocols like SOAP and RPC achieves this design goal on the technical level. To integrate a new subsystem with the KNB, a server interface has to be written that can establish the connection to the subsystem and be dynamically loaded by the KNB.

3.2 Metadata for Storage and Retrieval

The convergence of the knowledge-intense systems described above strongly fosters the global reuse, continuous maturing, classification and archiving of knowledge objects. The realization of these features within the KNB is strongly dependent on the underlying metadata approach. We developed and employed a multi-dimensional metadata approach, which is basically a customized and extended set of the LOM standard that accommodates our specific requirements. Every knowledge object indexed in the metadata database is associated with the metadata set of its author. Associated author information is valuable since personal background information of the owner, such as department membership, current project and individual skills, yield additional information regarding the business context of the required knowledge object. Every knowledge object receives a classification according to the company's specific taxonomy, which reflects the structural organization of the company. Another dimension of the metadata model consists of metadata that has to be entered manually during the creation or alteration of a knowledge object. This metadata contains all data that is not extractable via contextual and/or automatic generation (e.g. learning time, level of difficulty, relations to other knowledge objects, etc.). In the last dimension, automatically generated metadata is used. We have taken a close look at the possibilities of automatic generation of metadata, such as keyword extraction, automatic text summary, file information extraction etc. However, due to technical and feasibility reasons, only one automatic generation feature has been implemented so far.

3.3 The First Prototype

To demonstrate the generality and flexibility of our approach, our first prototype – the *"intelligent flexible Knowledge Management System"* (ifKMS) – is connected to three different kinds of subsystems: a document management system (DMS), a learning management system (LMS) and a problem solving support system. While every application with an outside controlling interface can be connected to the KNB, the degree of integration may vary. Because the purpose of the document management system is closely related to the objectives of the KNB they both can be fully integrated. Every storage and retrieval function of the DMS can be triggered from outside the system. This results in full transparency for the user and allows seamless interoperability between the DMS and the other subsystems. The learning management system is only partially integrated because some LMS functionalities cannot be mapped to the ifKMS functionalities. Therefore the user needs direct access to the LMS, for example for some of its functionality and application. On the one hand, this is useful in order to keep the interface of the ifKMS general and simple with respect to its objective, i.e., the integration of various information sources. On the other hand, there is a disadvantage in that the user has to switch between user interfaces and applications. But since the system can use only one single knowledge base, this aspect can be neglected. The problem solving support system (solver) is not integrated in this sense because the whole administration is done in the system's own dialogues. However, the generated metadata is imported into the global metadata database of the ifKMS system. Thus, it is possible to access the problem solvers knowledge base from the central ifKMS system.

On the one hand, the ifKMS enables a unique access to different applications and thereby supports the system-wide unique storage of documents. On the other hand, this middleware fosters the efficient retrieval and delivery of data and learning materials by using metadata, which are related to personal and collaborative contexts of employees and business processes.

4 Conclusions and Further Work

In MoKEx II, we developed a middleware concept that enables and combines intelligent knowledge management and technology enhanced methods of e-learning. We identified several surpluses as outcomes of our approach, which enhance traditional standalone solutions such as the seamless integration of our software in present desktop workflows by employment of the conventionalized create-store-search paradigm and the global indexation and retrieval of knowledge objects. Our convergence approach via the KNB yields pervasive knowledge management software that fosters the global use and reuse, continuous maturing taxonomy-related classification of knowledge objects for purposes of knowledge management and e-learning. The ifKMS prototype underwent singular tests but extended empirical tests in real-life scenarios are still missing. In the meantime, we enhanced the basic architecture of the KnowledgeBus to a new level that allows an even more flexible connection of different knowledge-intense subsystems. We added additional metadata extractors and semantic analyzers to the architecture to improve the quality of the automatically-extracted metadata. This improved approach is currently under development and will comprise the core of another publication due in 2008.

References

1. Hasselbrink, W.: Information System Integration. Communications of the ACM 43(6), 32–38 (2000)
2. Barreau, D.K., Nardi, B.A.: Finding and reminding: file organization from the desktop. SIGCHI Bulletin 27(3), 39–43 (1995)
3. Sellen, A.J., Harper, R.H.R.: The myth of the paperless office. MIT Press, Cambridge, MA (2002)
4. Bruce, H., Jones, W., Dumais, S.: Information behaviour that keeps found things found. Information Research, 10(1) (2004)
5. Tauscher, L.M., Greenberg, S.: How people revisit web pages: empirical findings and implications for the design of history systems. International Journal of Human-Computer Studies 47(1), 97–137 (1997)

IKASYS: Using Mobile Devices for Memorization and Training Activities

Naiara Maya[1,2], Ana Urrutia[1,2], Oihan Odriozola[1], Josune Gereka[1],
Ana Arruarte[2], and Jon Ander Elorriaga[2]

[1] Gipuzkoako Ikastolen Elkartea, 5186 P.K., E-20018
[2] University of the Basque Country, 649 P.K., E-20080
{a.arruarte,jon.elorriaga}@ehu.es

Abstract. Mobile learning *(m-learning)* integrates the current mobile computing technology with educational aspects to enhance the effectiveness of the traditional learning process. This paper describes IKASYS, an m-learning management tool that provides support for the whole cycle of memorization and training activities in a wide range of domains. The tool has been developed for being used in school-wide environments. This paper focuses mainly on IKASYS Trainer, the application for the mobile device.

1 Introduction

M-learning is increasingly recognized as a strategic tool that has the potential to enable global access to educational materials and improve the quality of education [1]. The small size and portability of mobile devices (PDAs, mobile phones, etc.) make learning location-independent; it is possible to study anywhere and anytime. Although in the context of m-learning most researchers assume that mobile devices are always connected to the Net, this doesn't happen always. Mobile devices can be disconnected, either intentionally or not (connection is too expensive or the adequate infrastructure is not provided [2]).

Regarding hardware, some common characteristics of the current mobile devices are: small screen size, small phone-style keyboard or touch screen, small memory size and limited processing power. Effective m-learning software must be developed trying to overcome technology limits. Even more, it is necessary to follow some guidelines for the design of m-learning software [3]: first design good contents, fit the learning to the learner and then to the device, keep learning efficient, make the learning experience reliable, and accomplish worthy goals. Although the incorporation of mobile devices into learning processes is still at its beginning some attempts are already in development [4][5][6][7].

In educational contexts memorization is conceived as a skill that allows an individual to recall important information verbatim. Although memorization draws upon one of the most fundamental human faculties, it is one of the least exercised techniques in contemporary education, due mainly to the progressive establishment of the constructivist education approach. In order to train this skill several memorization exercises must be carried out. Those exercises involve working with numbers, letters, syllables,

E. Duval, R. Klamma, and M. Wolpers (Eds.): EC-TEL 2007, LNCS 4753, pp. 493–498, 2007.

words, signs, drawings, sentences and texts. Solving these activities demands a great effort of attention and concentration.

Along this paper the project called IKASYS is presented. IKASYS is a multilingual system that provides support for the whole cycle of memorization and exercitation activities in a wide range of domains. First, it allows instructional designer to author those activities using a web application. Second, IKASYS includes software for students to perform the activities in a mobile device. Third, it provides teachers with a web application for both configuring the student training and inspecting the progress of individual students and groups. The paper starts describing IKASYS System architecture and basis. Then, the paper focuses on the application that runs in the mobile device. Finally, some conclusions and future work are drawn.

2 IKASYS System Architecture and Basis

The architecture of IKASYS framework is shown in Figure 1. It is composed of the next three modules:

IKASYS Designer [8] is a web application that provides the instructional designers with an environment for the creation of different types of memorization and exercitation activities. As output this application produces the Didactic Units (DUs).

IKASYS Trainer is an application that allows students to solve the memorization and exercitation activities of a DU in a mobile device. As output it creates a Student Data (SD).

IKASYS Inspector is a web application to evaluate the learning process of each student. The IKASYS Inspector must be initialised with the DUs that are going to be used. It takes the SDs as input and visualizes graphically the information about the students´ learning progress as well as student groups' progress. It also allows teachers to change certain parameters of the system to personalize the students training. This way, the next time IKASYS Trainer is executed it will take into account the changes carried out.

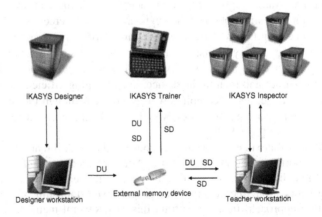

Fig. 1. IKASYS architecture and dataflow

Physically there is one IKASYS Designer server and several IKASYS Inspector servers, one for each school. Data is transferred from one module to another using an external memory device. So, IKASYS based training does not need internet connection. The exchanged information is organized in Didactic Units (DUs) and Student Data (SD). A DU represents a collection of exercises for a domain organized in a pedagogic way. A SD represents the information about the evolution and results of the learner and more general information.

The three components of the systems share the same view of the **learning domain**. It is hierarchically organized in six levels: Knowledge area, Content block, Module, Multilevel package, Level and Exercise. Each learning domain is joined to a specific Area that will be the root of the unit (for example, geography). Each Knowledge area (e.g. Geography) is made up of Content Blocks (e.g. rivers). The content blocks are formed with different Modules (e.g. rivers of Europe). Each module contains Multilevel Packages (e.g. test exercises), those are composed of difficulty based organised Levels in which, finally, are the Exercises without any order.

IKASYS offers several **exercise types** to complete DUs. They are classified into two different groups of exercises: static exercises and generative exercises. In static exercises the content designer specifies the whole exercise definition parameters meanwhile in generative exercises only some exercise creation conditions are defined. In other words, the program that runs in the mobile device is able to generate exercises in real time taking into account the conditions that are defined by IKASYS Designer. Among others exercise types IKASYS includes: multiple choices, fill-in-table, word completion, ordering exercises, crosswords, wordsearch puzzle, sudoku, matching columns and classification exercises.

3 IKASYS Trainer

IKASYS Trainer is the application for training memorization and exercitation activities in mobile devices. IKASYS Trainer allows teachers to adapt the exercise sequencing depending on the learner characteristics and necessity.

Amongst other capabilities, IKASYS Trainer is able to read, present and manage the content of the DU that the teacher assigns to the learner. The information, such as, the DU, the learner's details and the information about student's performance in the training sessions are stored in an external memory device, personal for each user. So, IKASYS Trainer has to read all the necessary information from the external memory device. In the same way, once the user decides to finish the session, IKASYS Trainer updates the SD with the learners´ current level of knowledge, the number of exercises performed and, for each exercise, the result and time that s/he needed to answer. The system also stores some information for the next session, given that the next session will resume the training in the same point.

Upon successful authentication, the program will dispatch exercises to the learner. In Figure 2 the application shows a generative exercise, concretely, a product between two numbers. The values of the variables are calculated in execution time taking into account that those values must satisfy exercise specifications. In this way, the same exercise offers lots of different activities.

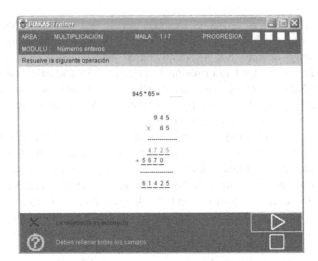

Fig. 2. Product exercise in IKASYS Trainer

3.1 Exercise Sequencing

To achieve a personalized learning IKASYS Trainer takes into account the initial difficulty grade that the teacher has assigned to the learner. In addition, exercise sequencing is controlled using several parameters that the teacher can change. Those parameters are: the percentage of exercises the student has to do at least at each level and the percentage of exercise solved correctly per level to allow the student to start the following level. The parameters can be defined and changed by the teacher by means of IKASYS Inspector and are stored in the file which stores student data and exchanged with IKASYS Trainer. Thus, the teacher can define different learning rhythm for each student. During the session exercises are sequenced with an appropriate level of difficulty taking into account the learner progress and the learner will not pass the current level if s/he does not fulfil the demanded requirements.

When learners start a new session, IKASYS Trainer creates four groups of exercises: group of exercises of the current level, group of exercises of the previous level solved correctly, group of exercises of the previous level solved incorrectly and group of exercises that have not done in the previous level.

The exercise sequencing algorithm chooses a number of exercises from each group. This percentage is configurable. In addition, in order to avoid repetitive executions of the same exercises the algorithm includes a random factor.

3.2 Other Pedagogical Issues

Regarding other pedagogical issues, feedback relies on correct requirements defined for each type of exercise. Furthermore, it has been probed that visual memory plays an important role in learning. Due to it, IKASYS Trainer will always show the correct answer, although the learner answer is incorrect. Finally, in order to keep the learners engaged and improve the motivation, the training session should be entertaining. The application attempts to achieve this goal visualizing recreational exercises once in a while, for example Sudokus. This type of exercises is a good way to practice mathematics because it increases children's interest in the subject.

3.3 Technical Issues

The implementation of IKASYS Trainer was written in Java due to its multi-platform nature. Regarding the operating system, Linux has been chosen because of processor support, reliability, cost, widespread use and its promising future.

Furthermore, this application has been designed taking into account internationalization and localization issues. The current application is localized for Basque, Spanish, Catalan and English.

IKASYS Trainer has been already tested on two different mobile devices; Sharp Zaurus SL-3100 which is shown in figure 3, and in a device designed exclusively for the IKASYS project, shown in the figure 4. Both devices have similar characteristics. They use Linux as operating system. However, Java virtual machines are different: meanwhile Zaurus uses Blackdown 1.3.1 the specialized device uses JVM 1.4.2. Taking into account that Java is multi-platform there is not much difficulty in the migration from one version to another one. Both devices have a screen with 320x240 pixels and a mini-keyboard. In a near future IKASYS Trainer will be tested with more devices in order to finally choose the most appropriate one for real use in a classroom context. The main factors for the final decision are: the cost of the device, the application speed and the ergonomic characteristics of the device, taking into account that it is going to be used mainly with children.

Fig. 3. Mobile device   **Fig. 4.** Ikasys Trainer

4   Conclusions

IKASYS is an m-learning system that is able to author memorization and training activities, to dispatch them in a mobile device, and to evaluate the student progress. IKASYS is composed of three applications that work together but have an independent logical functionality: IKASYS Designer, IKASYS Trainer and IKASYS Inspector.

IKASYS Designer provides instructional designer with an environment for authoring memorization and training exercises organized in Didactic Units. IKASYS Trainer is the application for students to work with memorization and training activities in mobile devices. IKASYS Trainer adapts the exercise sequencing depending on the parameters set by the teacher. IKASYS Inspector allows teachers to visualize the knowledge state of both individual students and group of students and to establish the appropriate parameters taking into account the learner characteristics and evolution.

Concerning IKASYS Designer a team of specialized instructional designers from the *Gipuzkoako Ikastolen Elkartea (GIE)* has already created several real DUs in two domains: Basque language orthography and mathematics. The first one is composed of more than 1,400 exercises and the second one with around 1000 exercises. Regarding IKASYS Trainer it has been already tested on two different mobile devices. Finally, with respect to IKASYS Inspector it has been evaluated by teachers at different educational levels.

IKASYS is SCORM compliant. It provides a follow-up system for supervising the learning process of each individual student or students groups. In addition IKASYS is able to adapt the exercises sequencing to the student behaviour and the capacity to support internalization for which is possible to create content in four different languages sharing the same interface: Basque, Spanish, Catalan and English.

Acknowledgments. This work has been partially supported by the University of the Basque Country (UE06/19), the Spanish Ministry of Education and Science (TIN2006-14968-C02-0), and the Gipuzkoa Council in collaboration with the European Union

References

1. Mobile Learning for Expanding Educational Opportunities: Workshop Report ICT in Education Unit, UNESCO Bangkok (2005), http://firgoa.usc.es/drupal/node/30629
2. Trifonova, A., Ronchetti, M.: A General Architecture to Support Mobility in Learning. In: Proceedings of ICALT 2004, pp. 26–30 (2004)
3. Horton, W.: Mobile Learning for Expanding Educational Opportunities: Workshop Report ICT in Education Unit, UNESCO Bangkok (2005), http://firgoa.usc.es/drupal/node/30629
4. Trifonova, A., Knapp, J., Ronchetti, M., Gamper, J.: Mobile ELDIT: Transition from an e-Learning to an m-Learning System. In: Proceedings of ED-MEDIA 2004, Lugano, Switzerland, pp. 188–193 (2004)
5. Bull, S., Reid, E.: Individualised revision materiak for use on a handheld computer. In: Learning with mobile devices. Proceedings of MLEARN 2004, pp. 35–42 (2004)
6. Martín, E., Carro, R.M., Rodríguez, P.: A Mechanism to Support Context-Based Adaptation in M-Learning. In: Nejdl, W., Tochtermann, K. (eds.) EC-TEL 2006. LNCS, vol. 4227, pp. 302–315. Springer, Heidelberg (2006)
7. Collei, J., Stead, G.: Take a bite: producing accessible learning materials for mobile devices. Learning with mobile devices. In: Proceedings of MLEARN 2004, pp. 43–46 (2004)
8. Urrutia, A., Maya, N., Gereka, J., Odriozola, O., Elorriaga, J.A., Arruarte, A.: Memorization and training activities in mobile devices. In: Proceedings of ICALT 2007 (in press)

Pedagogical Validation of Courseware

Mark Melia and Claus Pahl

School of Computing, Dublin City University, Dublin 9, Ireland
mmelia@computing.dcu.ie

Abstract. A lack of pedagogy in courseware can lead to its rejection by learners. It is therefore vital that pedagogy is a central concern in courseware construction. Courseware validation allows the course creator ensure courseware adheres to a specific pedagogy. In this paper we investigate the information needed to automate courseware validation and propose an information model to be used as a basis for validation. We then demonstrate an approach to courseware validation using this information model.

1 Introduction

To produce quality courseware, course creators aim to apply specific pedagogical principles to courseware they create. This can be difficult, especially when there are seemingly more pressing issues for courseware delivery, such as standards compliance and deadlines. Unfortunately, the neglection of pedagogy can lead to a course which confuses, demotivates and/or isolates the learner, ultimately leading to the rejection of the course [8].

Due to the importance of pedagogy in courseware, we must therefore ensure that a course creator's pedagogical principles are always adhered to in the courseware he or she produces. To do this, we propose automated post-construction courseware validation. The literature notes the importance of post-construction course validation or course auditing as an essential part of a holistic course construction methodology [7,6]. Automated validation of courseware, with regard to some specified pedagogy, safeguards courseware from the possible implications of pedagogical neglect, mentioned above. Automated validation is now possible due to courseware packaging specifications formally separating learning design from content and the annotation of learning objects (LOs) with metadata.

In this paper we identify the information that is required for courseware validation and how this information can be explicitly represented using a layered information model. After this, we outline how the information model is used to validate courseware, we do this using a case-study databases course. The paper concludes with a discussion on the presented and related work.

2 Layered Model for Courseware Validation

The "courseware aspects" is the implicit information which defines the scope, the content, and the pedagogy of courseware. By making the courseware aspects

E. Duval, R. Klamma, and M. Wolpers (Eds.): EC-TEL 2007, LNCS 4753, pp. 499–504, 2007.

available and explicit post-construction, these aspects can be used to validate the course. In Fig. 1, we have cataloged the courseware aspects which come together to create the courseware. The information shown in Fig. 1 is available but is implicit. By modeling this information, we can use it to validate courseware before delivering it to the learner.

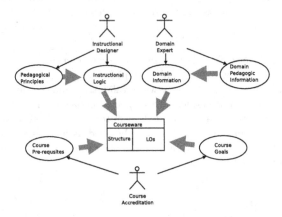

Fig. 1. Course Construction Elements

The Courseware Authoring Validation Model (CAVaM), allows courseware aspects and the courseware created to be explicitly represented in a layered model. CAVaM is an extension to the LAOS model [3] used to author Adaptive Educational Hypermedia (AEH). Each layer is developed in the context of the lower layers, for example a goal and constraint model is based on a domain model. We use layering to keep the domain model free of pedagogical information, and also due to the implicit layering found in the course aspects. Fig. 1 specifies two such implicit layering - domain pedagogic information is layered on domain information and pedagogical principles is used to formulate instructional logic.

Validation Model
Course Model
Learner Model
Goal and Constraint Model
Domain model

Fig. 2. Courseware Authoring Validation Model (CAVaM)

Each courseware construction aspect is captured at some layer of the CAVaM. The domain model captures the domain to be taught to the learner, and is pedagogy neutral. The goal and constraint layer allows the course creator to specify the goal of the courseware and domain pedagogic information, such as pre-requisite constraints between concepts in the domain model. The learner model captures the learner assumed knowledge on initiating the courseware.

The courseware itself is represented as a Directed Cyclical Graph (DCG), where each node is a LO and each edge is a potential learner path. Each LO node in the courseware is associated with at least one concept in the domain model. This annotation allows for the the formation of concept groupings, grouping LOs according to the concepts they teach. We demonstrate this in Fig. 3. Concept groupings allows us to discriminate courseware validation between inter-conceptual pedagogy and intra-conceptual pedagogy.

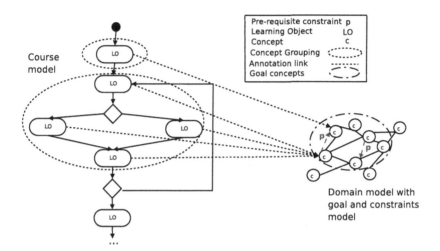

Fig. 3. Grouping LOs according to the concept they cover

The top layer, the validation model layer, allows the course creator to express pedagogical rules that the course must adhere to.

3   Courseware Validation Strategy

CAVaM splits pedagogical validation into two parts, validating pedagogical strategy and validating pedagogical rules. Pedagogical strategy is defined by the domain and constraint model. Pedagogical rules are expressed in the validation model.

3.1   Validating Course Pre-requisites

In this section we demonstrate our approach to one type of pedagogical strategy validation, pre-requisite constraint validation, as specified in the goal and constraint model. Pre-requisite validation aims to verify that the learner has any needed pre-requisite knowledge needed for a course element. In validating courseware pre-requisites, we classify the pre-requisite constraints into categories. These categories are "Pre-requisite verified", "Minor ordering error" - simple sequencing

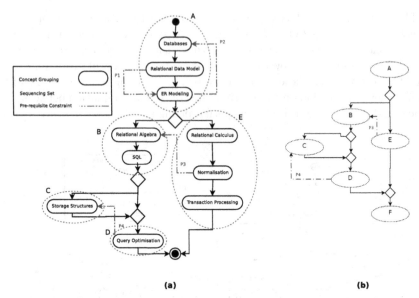

Fig. 4. (a) Database course model with pre-requisites (b) Course divided into sequencing sets

fix required, "Warning" - possible for the learner to miss some needed course material, "Error" - learner cannot view pre-requisite material due to the sequencing constraints or the pre-requisite material covered in the course.

To demonstrate how pre-requisite constraint validation will work and to demonstrate its value we will use a case study course.

Fig. 4(a) outlines the databases course model we will use for our case study. The databases course model has been divided into concept groupings, the name of each concept group indicates the name of the concept that the concept grouping refers to in the domain model. The dashed arrows, labeled Pχ, indicate pre-requisite constraints between concept groupings, which are derived from pre-requisite constraints between concepts in the goal and constraint model.

Fig. 4(a) specifies four pre-requisites for the database course. The directional pre-requisite arrow points to the concept grouping which teaches a pre-requisite concept, therefore according to P1 "ER modelling" must be understood before the "Relation Data Model".

Concept groupings in the course are further grouped into "sequencing sets" - sets of concept groups which are not linear (i.e. contain no choices in learner paths). We use letters to denote each sequencing set.

The algorithm firstly locates any pre-requisite constraint where the pre-requisite's source and target are in the same sequencing set. In this case P2 and P1 are identified as such constraints (source and target are in set A). The order of the concept groupings are checked where the target of the pre-requisite must be encountered before its source. P2 is satisfied, but P1 is not valid as the source of the pre-requisite is encountered before the target. The P1 constraint violation is classified as causing a "Minor ordering error", while P2 is classified as "Pre-requisite verified".

Pre-requisite constraints can be represented at the sequencing set level, where pre-requisites between concept groupings in different sequencing sets are represented as pre-requisites between sequencing sets. Fig. 4(b) depicts the sequencing sets derived from the database course outlined in Fig. 4(a). We also show two pre-requisites from the database course which are concerned with concept groupings from two different sequencing sets, P4 and P3. Pre-requisites, which have not been classified at this stage either fall into the "Warning" category (when there is a possibility through learner choice that pre-requisite concept LOs will be by-passed) or "Error" category (where it is not possible for the learner to encounter the sequencing set which contains LOs that teach the pre-requisite concept before the learner reaches the sequencing set which requires it).

When the algorithm checks P4, the target sequencing set is first located (set C). The potential learner paths from set C are then traversed in order to find the pre-requisite source sequencing set, set D. In this case set D is found, this means that the pre-requisite constraint could be respected, although there is a possibility that the learner may violate this pre-requisite, depending on the learner's individual path through the courseware. P4 is classified in the "Warning" category as it is possible for the constraint to be satisfied but is subject to learner path choice. If the source of the pre-requisite is not found, which is the case for P3 we can conclude that if the learner has navigated to the pre-requisite source he or she will not have seen the target of the pre-requisite, this is classified as causing a sequencing "Error".

3.2 Pedagogical Rule Validation

Pedagogical rules allow the course creator to express desirable or undesirable small-grained pedagogical traits, such as the suitability of LOs at a particular point in a courseware design [4]. Pedagogical rules are expressed in the validation model layer of the CAVaM.

The implementation of the validation rules in the validation model can be captured using a logics-based rule language. In our investigation we have implemented a validation model using the JESS rule language [5]. When validation rules are expressed in JESS, a JESS rule engine can be used to validate a given courseware against the validation rules.

4 Discussion

In our investigation, we have found the literature does not address the diversity of information available for courseware validation. The CoCoA tool developed at Carnegie Technology Education maps a course to a concept map so to reason about learning material in the context of the concept map [2]. Baldoni et. al. have investigated using of logics for courseware representation and then reason about possible problems [1]. In our research we look to further this research by addressing the diversity of information available for courseware validation. In this paper we introduce an information model which allows for the explicit representation of the information needed for courseware validation.

Using CAVaM we were able to develop an approach to courseware validation, which addresses the validation of pedagogical strategy and pedagogical rules. Pedagogical strategy looks at issues such as conceptual sequencing, while pedagogical rules allows the course creator to specify rules which must hold for a course to be deemed valid.

References

1. Baldoni, M., Baroglio, C., Patti, V., Torasso, L.: Reasoning about learning object metadata for adapting SCORM courseware. In: Proceeding of the International Workshop on Engineering the Adaptive Web: Methods and Technologies for personalization adn adaptation in the Semantic Web (EAW204). LNCS, Springer, Heidelberg (2004)
2. Brusilovsky, P., Vassileva, J.: Course sequencing techniques for large-scale web-based education. International Journal Continuing Engineering Education adn Lifelong Learning 13(1/2), 75–94 (2003)
3. Cristea, A.I., de Mooij, A.: LAOS: Layered WWW AHS Authoring Model and their corresponding Algebraic Operators. In: Proceedings of The Twelfth International World Wide Web Conference (WWW03), Alternate Track on Education, ACM Press, New York (2003)
4. Dagger, D.: Personalised eLearning Development Environments. PhD thesis, University of Dublin (2006)
5. Friedman-Hill, E.: JESS in Action: Java Rule-Based Systems. Manning Publications, Greenwich, Connecticut (2003)
6. Persico, D.: Courseware validation: a case study. Journal of Computer Assisted Learning 12, 232–244 (1996)
7. Rosmalen, P.V., Vogten, H., Es, R.V., Passier, H., Poelmans, P., Koper, R.: Authoring a full life cycle model in standards-based, adaptive e-learning. Journal of Educational Technology and Society 9(1), 72–83 (2006)
8. Samples, J.W.: The pedagogy of technology - our next frontier? Connexions 14(2), 4–5 (2002)

Improving Authoring-by-Aggregation and Using Aggregation Context for Query Expansion

Marek Meyer[1,2], Christoph Rensing[2], and Ralf Steinmetz[2]

[1] SAP AG, SAP Research CEC Darmstadt, Bleichstr. 8, 64283, Germany
marek.meyer@sap.com
[2] KOM Multimedia Communications Lab, Darmstadt University of Technology,
Merckstr. 25, 64832 Darmstadt, Germany
{rensing,steinmetz}@kom.tu-darmstadt.de

Abstract. Authoring-by-Aggregation is an authoring paradigm for creating new Learning Resources by composing several smaller ones. However finding suitable Learning Resources that can be reused in a particular course is a time-consuming task. The user has to query a repository and review the resulting list of Learning Resources whether they are applicable. In this paper we present a new method for narrowing the result set by taking the aggregation context into account. Context features are used as additional query attributes, leading to more precise query results. This paper also presents an improved Authoring-by-Aggregation process and a corresponding implementation, which facilitates the creation of new Learning Resources.

1 Introduction

The use of E-Learning for education and advanced training has grown over the past years. Many E-Learning technologies are based on digital materials, also called Learning Resources. Some of these materials are produced based on didactic guidelines, following best practices. Especially large content producers rely on content models as blueprints for didactically well-structured courses. There are different kinds of authoring process; one of them is the Authoring-by Aggregation (AbA) paradigm. This paper is mainly based on the AbA reference process introduced by Hoermann [1].

Learning Resources that are supposed to be reused have to be made accessible to other users. Learning Object Repositories (LOR) are storage systems for Learning Resources. A LOR typically offers retrieval interfaces, which can be used to search for and obtain Learning Resources. Recent initiatives work towards standardization of these interfaces, for instance the Simple Query Interface (SQI) [2] that is based on web service technology. However, most known implementations of SQI use a very limited query language, which allows to search for plain text search terms only, but not for specific metadata fields.

Authoring-by-Aggregation systems are currently designed only to work on a single - primarily local - repository. Access to different remote repositories is not yet supported. Thus, a user who wants to reuse Learning Resources from other

E. Duval, R. Klamma, and M. Wolpers (Eds.): EC-TEL 2007, LNCS 4753, pp. 505–510, 2007.

repositories has to search for them manually, download them and afterwards load them into his authoring tool. However, it would be more intuitive if the retrieval of Learning Resources were integrated into the authoring tool.

Current authoring tools and repositories have shortcomings regarding efficiency of AbA. It is time consuming to search a repository for many different small contents, which might be reusable for authoring a new Learning Resource.

In order to improve efficiency of Authoring-by-Aggregation, this paper proposes the use of aggregation context information for rewriting queries. Furthermore, an improved AbA process has been developed, which enables more intuitive and efficient retrieval and integration of existing Learning Resources.

The structure of this paper is as follows. Section 2 presents a definition of aggregation context and explains how it can be determined and used. An improved AbA process, which will be used as foundation of our prototype is shown in section 3. An implementation of the approach is presented in section 4. Finally, some conclusions and an outlook are given.

2   Context in Authoring Environments

As mentioned in the previous section retrieval methods for Learning Object Repositories still lack some functionality. This section focusses on how the aggregation context of an authoring process can be used for query refinement.

Search results of LOM queries may become quite large. Especially if a user searches for multiple Learning Resources one after another, the required time adds to the production costs and may make reuse of Learning Resources inefficient. Query expansion - rewriting a query based on additional knowledge - could improve the quality of retrieval results and thereby reestablish the economical benefit of reuse.

Context information from authoring environments and relevance feedback mechanisms are promising candidates for query expansion. Context is defined here as any information that is known about the author, his authoring environment and the tasks he is performing. Different types of context information are imaginable, particularly system context, explicit project context and aggregation context (see Fig. 1).

As system context we subsume all information about the user, the tools and systems he uses and what he has generally done in the past. Exemplary context information is for instance technological restrictions of his authoring system. Explicit project context is all information, which has been explicitly specified by the author about the project he is currently working on. Project here typically refers to a particular Learning Resource the author is working on. Examples for project context are the intended course language, target document formats, target group (age, role, difficulty level, interaction level, etc.). Also, limits for the total amount of learning time or acquisition costs may have an impact on which Learning Resources are suitable for aggregation. Aggregation context is implicit information about the current project, which is deduced from the contents already existing in the project. Aggregation context information may be deduced

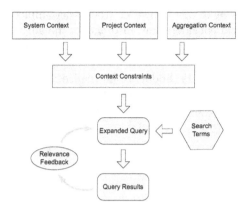

Fig. 1. Usage of context information as input for query expansion

either from the contents itself or their metadata records; in practice, metadata is easier to use. The more Learning Resources are aggregated in a project over time, the better the aggregation context may automatically be determined.

A similar approach has already been proposed by Sanchez and Sicilia [3]. They apply the design-by-contract paradigm from object oriented software construction to the composition of Learning Resources. Their goal is to automatically select and aggregate Learning Resources for a given learning target. However, because of the design-by-contract paradigm the approach supports only a binary matching: either a Learning Resource fits or it does not. Furthermore, a formal contract has to be specified for each Learning Resource; thus, the method is not applicable to plain LOM metadata. In practice, Learning Resources - and their metadata records - are rarely perfectly fitting. But Learning Resources can be adapted to fit into the new course [4]. Therefore, fuzzy queries, which produce a ranked result set, are better suited than strict matching.

3   Improved Authoring-by-Aggregation Process

Authoring-by-Aggregation is a lightweight rapid authoring approach, which is based on recursive aggregation of modular contents. One shortcoming of existing AbA tools is the missing support of didactic design and more general the non-existing separation of different authoring phases.

Therefore, this section presents an improved authoring process, which supports multi-phase authoring. The process is based on Hoermann's process [1]. It is assumed that a Learning Resource is created by a single author at a time. Existing Learning Resources are supposed to be stored in a repository and specified by adequate metadata.

In total the new process consists of five authoring phases: the didactic design phase, the retrieval and replacement phase, the adaptation phase, the content authoring phase and the publishing phase. These phases may be arranged in a strictly sequential way. Each phase has to be completed before the author may proceed to the next one. However, the strict implementation is mainly thought for theoretical consideration. In practice, the author will not always be able to finish the phases one after another. Imagine an author has designed a course structure, replaced most placeholders, adapted the contents and is now creating the missing contents. Suddenly he realizes that an exercise is missing in his structure. The strict process would not allow to go back and change the structure. Therefore we define a relaxed process, which allows iterations of authoring phases.

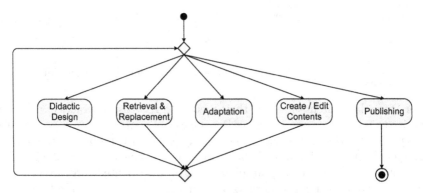

Fig. 2. Relaxed Authoring-by-Aggregation process

In the relaxed process, the first four phases may be repeated in any order. The author may choose at any time to either edit the course structure, to replace placeholder items with existing Learning Resources, to adapt a Learning Resource or to create own contents. When the author has decided that the Learning Resource is finished he invokes the publishing phase and thereby ends the process. The relaxed process is shown in Fig. 2.

4   Implementation

Having presented theoretical approaches in the previous sections, this section shows an actual implementation. The Authoring-by-Aggregation process, combined with context-based query expansion, has been implemented in the Content Sharing project [5]. It has been integrated into the Content Sharing Module Editor, which is an re-authoring tool for SCORM-based Learning Resources. In the following, the term *module* is used for SCORM-based Learning Resources, which comply to the Content Sharing specification. Particularly, the specification extends SCORM by enabling aggregation of SCORM packages by reference [6]. Besides aggregation, the tool also supports adaptation of Learning Resources to new contexts [4].

The AbA process has been realized by extending the SCORM editor of the re-authoring tool. Didactic design is supported by creating empty placeholder items in the SCORM manifest of a module. Thus, the structure of a module is

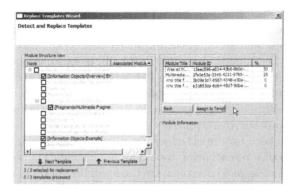

Fig. 3. Retrieval and replacement of Learning Resources

first created as a skeleton SCORM manifest without linked content files. Each placeholder element has three attributes, which may be specified by the author: keywords, granularity and didactic type. Keywords describe the topic of an element. Granularity and didactic type specify its didactic function. Didactic types can be chosen from Meder's didactic ontologies [7]. Granularity and didactic type may be selected graphically by drag&drop from a template collection.

The placeholder attributes are utilized for the retrieval of existing modules. A replacement wizard presents a list of all placeholders to the user and lets him assign existing modules to them (Fig. 3). Whenever a placeholder is selected, the connected repository is searched for suitable modules. The placeholders are then replaced by references to the chosen modules. For those placeholder elements that could not be replaced by existing modules, new content files may be created.

The retrieval of Learning Resources is based on the attributes of placeholder elements, which have been explicitly specified by the author. However, with a growing amount of modules, which have already been aggregated, there are more and more implicit constraints that impact the suitability of other modules. For instance, if most existing modules are known to be specifically designed for schoolchildren, a module from adult education will less likely fit in. Many other metadata can be used similarly to judge the suitability of further modules, such as language, format or difficulty level.

For the current implementation the four LOM fields language, end user role, typical age range and difficulty have been chosen to be determined as aggregation context. As a method for formally determining the aggregation context, a selection of metadata fields of present modules is analyzed for frequent values. A threshold of 75% is applied for considering a repeatedly occurring metadata value as context constraint.

5   Conclusion and Outlook

This paper has introduced a number of contributions to the idea of reuse of e-Learning contents. The intention of the presented approaches is to improve the usability of reuse processes for authors in semi-professional environments. Based on a critical study of existing approaches for Authoring-by-Aggregation and Learning Resource retrieval an improved authoring process for AbA has been developed. Learning Resource retrieval still lacks some features which are common in (Multimedia) Information Retrieval. One of these features is query expansion - modifying queries for improving the performance. This paper has shown how context information can be used for query expansion.

Both, the improved AbA approach and query expansion based on context information have been implemented within the Content Sharing project as integral components of a re-authoring tool. The implementation is only considered as a first proof of concept to demonstrate the feasibility of the approach. Further usability studies of the re-authoring tool are planned for the future.

However, still a lot of research has to be done in the area of Learning Resource retrieval. In particular, transferring methods from Multimedia Information Retrieval to the area of e-Learning may lead to further improvements.

Acknowledgments

This work is supported by the German Federal Ministry of Economics and Technology in the context of the Content Sharing project.

References

1. Hoermann, S.: Wiederverwendung von digitalen Lernobjekten in einem auf Aggregation basierenden Autorenprozess. PhD thesis, TU Darmstadt (2005)
2. Simon, B., Massart, D., van Assche, F., Ternier, S., Duval, E., Brantner, S., Olmedilla, D., Miklos, Z.: A simple query interface for interoperable learning repositories. In: Proceedings of the 1st Workshop on Interoperability of Web-based Educational Systems, Chiba, Japan, CEUR, pp. 11–18 (2005)
3. Sanchez, S., Sicilia, M.A.: On the semantics of aggregation and generalization in learning object contracts. In: Proceedings of the 4th IEEE International Conference on Advanced Learning Technologies (ICALT '04), IEEE Computer Society Press, Los Alamitos (2004)
4. Zimmermann, B., Rensing, C., Steinmetz, R.: Format-übergreifende Anpassungen von elektronischen Lerninhalten. In: Proceedings of the Deutsche e-Learning Fachtagung Informatik (DeLFI) 2006 (2006)
5. Content Sharing project: [last accessed, 2007-03-21] Project website http://www.contentsharing.com
6. Meyer, M., Rensing, C., Steinmetz, R.: Supporting Modularization and Aggregation of Learning Resources in a SCORM Compliance Mode. In: Proceedings of the 6th IEEE International Conference on Advanced Learning Technologies (ICALT '06), pp. 933–935. IEEE Computer Society Press, Los Alamitos (2006)
7. Meder, N.: Didaktische Ontologien. Globalisierung und Wissensorganisation: Neue Aspekte für Wissen, Wissenschaft und Informationssysteme 6, 401–416 (2000)

Questioning Usability of Visual Instructional Design Languages: The Case of CPM

Nodenot Thierry

LIUPPA Laboratory, IUT de Bayonne
3, avenue Jean Darrigrand, 64115 Bayonne Cedex, France
Thierry.Nodenot@iutbayonne.univ-pau.fr

Abstract. CPM is a visual instructional design language which provides the designers with a set of concepts allowing to semi formally describe Problem-Based learning scenarios and to document them. CPM is thus a language which is both useful for designers and for developers of Technology-Enhanced Learning systems while implementing all or part of such learning scenarios. This article reports a few lessons that we learned from CPM language; we question CPM usability from different case-studies in the 'real-world' and we draw conclusions that go beyond the scope of CPM language.

Keywords: Instructional Design, Visual languages, UML profiles, Model-Driven Engineering.

1 Introduction

Visual instructional design languages currently provide notations for representing the intermediate and final results of a knowledge engineering process. As some languages particularly focus on the formal representation of a learning design that can be transformed into machine interpretable code, others have been developed to support the creativity of designers while exploring their problem-spaces and solutions.

CPM (**C**ooperative **P**roblem-based learning **M**etamodel) is a visual instructional language that belongs to the latter category. On the one hand, the CPM sketches of a Problem-Based Learning situation (PBL) can improve communication within multidisciplinary ID teams; on the other hand, CPM blueprints can describe the functional components that a Technology-Enhanced Learning (TEL) system should offer to support such a PBL situation.

Several articles and reports have been already published about the CPM language. The CPM metamodel (abstract syntax) and the CPM profile (concrete syntax) were described in [1] and [2]. Different case-studies in the 'real world' were presented in [3] and [4]. From an analysis of the CPM diagrams produced in the course of these case-studies, this paper will present a few results about the CPM usability. Sections 2 and 3 will respectively present and comment the following lessons:

- Lesson U1: Though CPM adopts the jargon that many pedagogues and educational designers already use, producing a set of coherent CPM models for a given case-study is still a complex activity.

E. Duval, R. Klamma, and M. Wolpers (Eds.): EC-TEL 2007, LNCS 4753, pp. 511–516, 2007.

- Lesson U2: Even though most pedagogues are not able to produce a set of CPM coherent models by themselves, both pedagogues and developers can contribute to and benefit from such design models.

2   Lesson U1

Real world case studies that we specified with the CPM language had in common that they could not be mastered by a single designer. All the modelling elements could not be represented in the same UML class diagram: learner, tutor roles, learning goals and success criteria had to be contextualized according to the steps of the learning process; both dynamics and structure of resources and activities had to be specified, *etc.* Relying on our experience in designing such case-studies, we argue that in most cases, we need an approach that structures the design of complex learning scenarios at different levels with dedicated packages. We also observed that among available CPM diagrams, designers had to adequately choose those that could help them to produce some simple yet coherent perspectives of the relevant model elements. Indeed, choosing a specialisation of UML to describe learning scenarios requires to rethink current uses / to elicit new uses of the UML diagrams for dealing with the complexity of learning scenarios. Table 1 provides a synthesis of the practices that we noticed during our case-studies.

Table 1. Best practices for CPM diagrams

	Use
Activity Diagram	- External analysis of the learning Scenario - Description of collaborative activities - Internal analysis of activities and activity-structures
Use Case Diagram	- Activity cut-out - Role identification
Class Diagram	- Learning goal description - Role and resources description - External analysis of activities and activity-structures - Description of the concepts from the domain model
State Machine Diagram	- Description of active classes (resources, learning goals, activities, roles)
Object Diagram	- instances from the domain model (concepts being studied, knowledge and know-hows that learners must acquire)

During the course of our experiments, we noticed that designers (educators and computer-scientists) encountered two types of difficulties when trying to map their design intents with available CPM notations (those provided by the different types of diagrams available). First, most designers were inclined to start from a visual notation (e.g. the notation for class diagrams) and then tried using this specific notation to represent all perspectives of the model being studied, even if such a notation was not convenient for all aspects of the model. Second, we noticed that designers had questions about the notation they would be advised to use, particularly at the beginning of a learning scenario design process. We also noticed that designers were first surprised (and a bit confused) because they were constrained by both the rules of the UML notations and of the CPM metamodel.

The observations presented in this section show that designers need time to gain the necessary experience required to relevantly exploit the CPM language. Our study also showed that educators can understand the meaning of a set of CPM diagrams but that the (semi) formal nature of the CPM language could hinder some educators' commitment in producing such visual designs. They ask for cognitive assistance during the design process: since CPM editors do not allow free drawing, designers require some feedback enabling them to do some opportunistic productions: to-do lists, checklists, wizards, *etc*. The first cognitive tools that we have developed were contextual menus that could infer the metaclass to be used from the knowledge of both the diagram type and the stereotype chosen by the designer. In the framework of our latest project [5], we also provided designers (educators and computer-scientists) with the best-practices of CPM diagrams and with a set of sample CPM diagrams for each design intent listed in Table 1. Best practices for CPM diagrams.

But it is already clear that our toolset is still a research prototype that proved expressive capabilities but cannot be distributed to an interdisciplinary team without care and minimal human guidance. Even though the current state of research presented in this section can provide substantial support in understanding PBL scenarios, in designing and documenting new scenarios, it is clear that a lot of work is still necessary to transform educators into CPM autonomous designers.

3 Lesson U2

Though educational expressivity of CPM diagrams, Lesson U1 pinpointed some difficulties encountered by designers who used the CPM toolset. In the course of the conducted case-studies, we firstly observed that, at any level of the learning scenario analysis (conceptual design, functional design), designers might produce simple yet expressive CPM diagrams (*cf.* Lesson U2 - *Observation 1*): it is a matter of focusing on one and only one perspective at a time. We also noticed that a correct stratification of the learning scenario is important (*cf. Lesson U2 – Observation 2*) to ensure a smooth transition between the perspectives drawn during learning scenario conceptual design and those drawn to address the functional design of a TEL system that could manage such a learning scenario at runtime.

3.1 Lesson U2 - Observation 1

Our experience is that most pedagogues can concretely draw various CPM diagrams if they keep in mind that each diagram should focus on one perspective that remains simple and expressive. We consider that educators relying on CPM for conceptual design with CPM should strive for an 80% solution: at this stage, visual design should be used to represent the intermediate and then the final results of the design, thus providing means of communication between educators and developers.

CPM activity diagrams are other important perspectives to consider because they are a (natural) bridge between the use-case diagrams (which are useful to represent educational roles, goals and activities) and the class-diagrams (that developers need to implement required functionality on a learning platform). During our experiments, such diagrams represented an interesting communication trade off between our business logic experts (educators and interaction designers) and Information Technology experts (software designers, learning platform specialists, *etc.*).

We noticed that educators encountered various difficulties to draw some CPM activity diagrams by themselves. Actually, these diagrams are not simple to create but they allow to efficiently represent complex system/interaction processing. In order to get round this obstacle, we advised educators to produce a use-case diagram for identifying the activities of interest and their relationships; Information Technology designers then discussed with them from such sketches; and they produced together the final 80% solution. Interestingly enough, once this deadlock broken, educators were able to go further in the conceptual design process.

From this set of observations, we learnt that when using CPM diagrams for modelling a learning/tutoring scenario, it is important to capture the requirements at a high level of abstraction. Whatever the diagram, the perspective must remain simple; such an approach allows designers to emphasize important model elements while hiding low-level processing details; such details can indeed obscure the model's true purpose that consists a/ in identifying key activities and dependencies, and b/ in promoting exchanges and communication in the Instructional Design team.

This is particularly true when drawing activity diagrams; in our experiments, some of them proved to be potential deadlocks that frustrated most educators during the design process. Dedicated cognitive tools (wizards, to-do-lists, *etc.*) could probably make them more confident; but we consider that the correct answer relies on an efficient communication in the Instructional Design team: CPM sketches (even when they represent intermediate design results) can thus play a central role.

3.2 Lesson U2 - Observation 2

UML is a widely accepted language to describe software systems. With the different perspectives of a TEL system that CPM offers, our profile adopts the same fundamentals (UML notation, UML semantics that we specialized with the CPM metamodel semantics) to also describe the educational context. At conceptual level, the language addresses the need to manage educational requirements effectively. At functional level, the language addresses the need to describe the required functionality of a TEL System in tune with such educational requirements.

Whatever the design level (conceptual *vs.* functional), it is thus very important to communicate design decisions (and understanding) in an unambiguous form to all the partners involved in the Instructional Design Team. In the previous subsections, we showed that CPM enables designers to produce multiple perspectives for a learning scenario: these perspectives favour coherent, unambiguous (within the limit of the UML semantics) but intelligible design decisions. Our case-studies have yet demonstrated that to reach such a goal, these multiple perspectives of a learning scenario should be correctly stratified. We noticed in [5] that, from the very beginning of the design process, some geographers were trying to map some educational goals with functionalities of the Geographical Information System viewer that they used to work with. Such design decisions were problematic because on the one hand, educational goals had still to be further detailed and on the other hand, such a detailed analysis failed because the designers mixed conceptual and functional model elements. The main gains of a correct stratification are modularity and design simplicity (*cf.* Lesson U2 Observation 1). Modularity allows easier adaptability of changing requirements; it also allows clear separation of the domains of trust. By starting with the most fundamental educational factors (conceptual design) and designing them to be contextually appropriate, we were able to build successive layers design and eventually reach functional design.

4 Discussion

In this paper, we have presented a few lessons that we learned about CPM language usability. Both lessons lead us to the following conclusions. UML is a language; so is CPM. Current object-oriented methods focus on the specification of the static structure of software objects. A noticeable deficiency of these methods is that they do not provide any help on how requirements are refined, how class diagrams can be derived from scenarios, how to specify the active/dynamic parts of a system, how such a specification may be transformed into an implementation. During conceptual design, the analysis of the different case-studies that we have conducted promotes the idea of bridging the gap between educational needs elicitation (including requirements elicitation, requirements refinement using a combination of use-case diagrams, of activity diagrams, *etc.*), and the more formal specification of class diagrams which are required to prepare the implementation of a TEL System [1]. The way we used CPM language is as follows. The specification process starts from the definition of use-cases. Each use-case diagram is refined either by other use-case diagrams or by one ore more activity diagrams (representing teaching/learning scenarios). All model elements used in these diagrams are not unrelated parts; they are attributes, messages, *etc.* that are finally declared in the class diagrams. The behaviour of each class is represented by a set of scenarios (activity diagrams / state machine diagrams) covering the events declared in the specification part of the class.

The lessons that we learned go beyond the scope of CPM language since our results can benefit to all Instructional Design practitioners that choose dedicated languages relying on specializations of the UML language: *cf.* the *coUML* profile [6], the recent *LD* profile [7], *etc.* Yet, our study of CPM language usability demonstrates that modelling learning situations with a specialisation of UML is not an easy and usual task for practitioners. Among the several reasons that account for this fact, we can mention two obvious ones. First, practitioners are used to adapt their courses to learners *in situ,* as events occur happen (opportunistic approach) and they prefer to think in terms of content and coarse-grained activities. Second, in educational sciences, models are driven by learning events to detect and to react upon, rather than by a mere sequence of activities – typical of the computer world (*cf.* workflow sub-domain). So practitioners are not used to indulge in highly structured course modelling in their everyday work. Because we are aware of that, we have already proposed guidelines related to CPM through 'best-practices' and a design process in order to help practitioners. As we intend to go further in that direction, we are developing cognitive tools dedicated to promoting good practices for CPM language.

References

1. Nodenot, T., et al.: Model based Engineering of Learning Situations for Adaptive Web Based Educational Systems. In: ACM Thirteenth International World Wide Web Conference (IW3C2 Conference), ACM, New York (2004)
2. Laforcade, P.: Towards an UML-based Educational Language. In: The 5th IEEE International Conference on Advanced Learning Technologies (ICALT), Kaohsiung (Taiwan) (2005)
3. Laforcade, P.: Méta-modélisation UML pour la mise en oeuvre de situations problèmes coopératives, in LIUPPA 2004: Doctorat en informatique de l'Université de Pau et des Pays de l'Adour (2004)
4. Nodenot, T.: Contribution à l'Ingénierie Dirigée par les modèles en EIAH: le cas des situations-problèmes coopératives, Habilitation à diriger les recherches en informatique de l'Université de Pau et des Pays de l'Adour: Bayonne (2005)
5. Nodenot, T., et al.: From Electronic Documents to Problem-based Learning Environments: an ongoing Challenge for Educational Modeling Languages. In: 7th International Conference on Information Technology Based Higher Education and Training (ITHET 2006) Sydney (Australia) (2006)
6. Derntl, M., Motschnig-Pitrik, R.: coUML – A Visual Modeling Language for Cooperative Environments. In: Botturi, L., Stubbs, T. (eds.) Handbook of Visual Languages in Instructional Design; Theories and Practice (in Press), IDEA Group, Hershey, PA (2007)
7. TELCERT, Learning Design UML Profile 2006, TELCERT Project: Technology Enhanced Learning: Conformance - European Requirements & Testing (2006) cf dspace.ou.nl/ bitstream/1820/657/1/AD39_Learning_Design_UML_Profile_v1.0.doc

Author Index

Abel, Fabian 143
Abel, Marie-Hélène 408
Al-Khalifa, Hend S. 414
Apelt, Stefan 322
Aqqal, Abdelhak 420
Arruarte, Ana 493

Baldoni, Matteo 426, 432
Baptista-Nunes Miguel 232
Baroglio, Cristina 426
Bischoff, Kerstin 438
Bolettieri, Paolo 444
Bouzeghoub, Amel 450
Broisin, Julien 1
Brooks, Christopher 112
Brunkhorst, Ingo 426
Burgos, Daniel 247

Cao, Yiwei 307
Caron, Pierre-André 457
Ceri, Stefano 463
Clematis, Andrea 469
Cocea, Mihaela 14
Condotta, Massimiliano 322
Cristea, Alexandra 71
Cristea, Dan 202

Dalla Vecchia, Elisa 322
Davis, Hugh C. 378, 414
De Bra, Paul 292
De Coi, Juri L. 26
de Hoog, Robert 158
Delgado, Jose Antonio 292
Després, Christophe 41
Devedžić, Vladan 112
Dickens, Kate 378
Do, Kien Ngoc 450
Dobrzański, Jarosław 172
Duval, Erik 262, 322, 364

El-Kechaï, Naïma 41
Elorriaga, Jon Ander 493
Evans, Diane 202

Faatz, Andreas 217
Falchi, Fabrizio 444

Fernández-Manjón, Baltasar 247
Fernández-Muñoz, Luis 475
Forcheri, Paola 469
Frasson, Claude 393

Garrot, Elise 481
Gašević, Dragan 112
Gennaro, Claudio 444
George, Sébastien 481
Gereka, Josune 493
Glahn, Christian 56
Godehardt, Eicke 217
Goertz, Manuel 217
Gzella, Adam 172

Hatala, Marek 112
Hendrix, Maurice 71
Herder, Eelco 143, 438
Heyer, Susanne 86
Hildebrandt, Tomas 187
Hinkelmann, Knut 487
Holzweißig, Kai 487
Hurley, Teresa 101

Jovanović, Jelena 112

Kaipainen, Mauri 349
Karacapilidis, Nikos 127
Kärger, Philipp 26, 143
Kienle, Andrea 217
Killing, Alex 202
Klamma, Ralf 307
Koesling, Arne W. 26
Kooken, Jose 158
Koper, Rob 56
Kruk, Sebastian Ryszard 172

Laanpere, Mart 349
Leblanc, Adeline 408
Lecocq, Claire 450
Lehmann, Lasse 187
Lemnitzer, Lothar 202
Lenne, Dominique 408
Ley, Tobias 158
Lokaiczyk, Robert 217

Magenheim, Johannes   487
Marengo, Elisa   426, 432
Matera, Maristella   463
Maya, Naiara   493
McDaniel, Bill   172
McPherson, Maggie   232
Melia, Mark   499
Meyer, Marek   505
Mlynarski, Michael   487
Monachesi, Paola   202
Moreno-Ger, Pablo   247

Nabeth, Thierry   277
Nejdl, Wolfgang   438
Nelkner, Tobias   487
Nkambou, Roger   393

Oberhuemer, Petra   86
Ochoa, Xavier   262
Odriozola, Oihan   493
Olmedilla, Daniel   26, 143

Pahl, Claus   499
Pata, Kai   349
Patti, Viviana   426
Pérez-Carrasco, Antonio   475
Prenner, Philipp   86
Prévôt, Patrick   481

Quarati, Alfonso   469

Rabitti, Fausto   444
Raffio, Alessandro   463
Reinhardt, Wolfgang   487
Rensing, Christoph   187, 420, 505

Roda, Claudia   277
Romero, Cristóbal   292

Siberski, Wolf   143
Sierra, José Luis   247
Simov, Kiril   202
Spaniol, Marc   307
Specht, Marcus   56, 322
Spoelstra, Howard   463
Stefaner, Moritz   322
Steinmetz, Ralf   187, 420, 505

Thierry, Nodenot   511
Toikka, Seppo   337
Tzagarakis, Manolis   127

Ulbrich, Armin   217
Urquiza-Fuentes, Jaime   475
Urrutia, Ana   493

Väljataga, Terje   349
Velázquez-Iturbide, J. Ángel   475
Ventura, Sebastián   292
Verbert, Katrien   364
Vertan, Cristina   202
Vidal, Philippe   1

Wang, Chu   378
Weibelzahl, Stephan   14, 101
Wessner, Martin   217
Wills, Gary   378
Wolpers, Martin   322
Woroniecki, Tomasz   172

Zander, Stefan   86
Zouaq, Amal   393

Lecture Notes in Computer Science

Sublibrary 2: Programming and Software Engineering

For information about Vols. 1– 4053
please contact your bookseller or Springer

Vol. 4753: E. Duval, R. Klamma, M. Wolpers (Eds.), Creating New Learning Experiences on a Global Scale. XII, 518 pages. 2007.

Vol. 4749: B.J. Krämer, K.-J. Lin, P. Narasimhan (Eds.), Service-Oriented Computing – ICSOC 2007. XIX, 629 pages. 2007.

Vol. 4741: C. Bessière (Ed.), Principles and Practice of Constraint Programming – CP 2007. XV, 890 pages. 2007.

Vol. 4680: F. Saglietti, N. Oster (Eds.), Computer Safety, Reliability, and Security. XV, 548 pages. 2007.

Vol. 4670: V. Dahl, I. Niemelä (Eds.), Logic Programming. XII, 470 pages. 2007.

Vol. 4634: H. Riis Nielson, G. Filé (Eds.), Static Analysis. XI, 469 pages. 2007.

Vol. 4615: R. de Lemos, C. Gacek, A. Romanovsky (Eds.), Architecting Dependable Systems IV. XIV, 435 pages. 2007.

Vol. 4610: B. Xiao, L.T. Yang, J. Ma, C. Muller-Schloer, Y. Hua (Eds.), Autonomic and Trusted Computing. XVIII, 571 pages. 2007.

Vol. 4609: E. Ernst (Ed.), ECOOP 2007 – Object-Oriented Programming. XIII, 625 pages. 2007.

Vol. 4608: H.W. Schmidt, I. Crnković, G.T. Heineman, J.A. Stafford (Eds.), Component-Based Software Engineering. XII, 283 pages. 2007.

Vol. 4591: J. Davies, J. Gibbons (Eds.), Integrated Formal Methods. IX, 660 pages. 2007.

Vol. 4589: J. Münch, P. Abrahamsson (Eds.), Product-Focused Software Process Improvement. XII, 414 pages. 2007.

Vol. 4574: J. Derrick, J. Vain (Eds.), Formal Techniques for Networked and Distributed Systems – FORTE 2007. XI, 375 pages. 2007.

Vol. 4556: C. Stephanidis (Ed.), Universal Access in Human-Computer Interaction, Part III. XXII, 1020 pages. 2007.

Vol. 4555: C. Stephanidis (Ed.), Universal Access in Human-Computer Interaction, Part II. XXII, 1066 pages. 2007.

Vol. 4554: C. Stephanidis (Ed.), Universal Acess in Human Computer Interaction, Part I. XXII, 1054 pages. 2007.

Vol. 4553: J.A. Jacko (Ed.), Human-Computer Interaction, Part IV. XXIV, 1225 pages. 2007.

Vol. 4552: J.A. Jacko (Ed.), Human-Computer Interaction, Part III. XXI, 1038 pages. 2007.

Vol. 4551: J.A. Jacko (Ed.), Human-Computer Interaction, Part II. XXIII, 1253 pages. 2007.

Vol. 4550: J.A. Jacko (Ed.), Human-Computer Interaction, Part I. XXIII, 1240 pages. 2007.

Vol. 4542: P. Sawyer, B. Paech, P. Heymans (Eds.), Requirements Engineering: Foundation for Software Quality. IX, 384 pages. 2007.

Vol. 4536: G. Concas, E. Damiani, M. Scotto, G. Succi (Eds.), Agile Processes in Software Engineering and Extreme Programming. XV, 276 pages. 2007.

Vol. 4530: D.H. Akehurst, R. Vogel, R.F. Paige (Eds.), Model Driven Architecture - Foundations and Applications. X, 219 pages. 2007.

Vol. 4523: Y.-H. Lee, H.-N. Kim, J. Kim, Y.W. Park, L.T. Yang, S.W. Kim (Eds.), Embedded Software and Systems. XIX, 829 pages. 2007.

Vol. 4498: N. Abdennahder, F. Kordon (Eds.), Reliable Software Technologies - Ada-Europe 2007. XII, 247 pages. 2007.

Vol. 4486: M. Bernardo, J. Hillston (Eds.), Formal Methods for Performance Evaluation. VII, 469 pages. 2007.

Vol. 4470: Q. Wang, D. Pfahl, D.M. Raffo (Eds.), Software Process Dynamics and Agility. XI, 346 pages. 2007.

Vol. 4468: M.M. Bonsangue, E.B. Johnsen (Eds.), Formal Methods for Open Object-Based Distributed Systems. X, 317 pages. 2007.

Vol. 4467: A.L. Murphy, J. Vitek (Eds.), Coordination Models and Languages. X, 325 pages. 2007.

Vol. 4454: Y. Gurevich, B. Meyer (Eds.), Tests and Proofs. IX, 217 pages. 2007.

Vol. 4444: T. Reps, M. Sagiv, J. Bauer (Eds.), Program Analysis and Compilation, Theory and Practice. X, 361 pages. 2007.

Vol. 4440: B. Liblit, Cooperative Bug Isolation. XV, 101 pages. 2007.

Vol. 4408: R. Choren, A. Garcia, H. Giese, H.-f. Leung, C. Lucena, A. Romanovsky (Eds.), Software Engineering for Multi-Agent Systems V. XII, 233 pages. 2007.

Vol. 4406: W. De Meuter (Ed.), Advances in Smalltalk. VII, 157 pages. 2007.

Vol. 4405: L. Padgham, F. Zambonelli (Eds.), Agent-Oriented Software Engineering VII. XII, 225 pages. 2007.

Vol. 4401: N. Guelfi, D. Buchs (Eds.), Rapid Integration of Software Engineering Techniques. IX, 177 pages. 2007.

Vol. 4385: K. Coninx, K. Luyten, K.A. Schneider (Eds.), Task Models and Diagrams for Users Interface Design. XI, 355 pages. 2007.

Vol. 4383: E. Bin, A. Ziv, S. Ur (Eds.), Hardware and Software, Verification and Testing. XII, 235 pages. 2007.

Vol. 4379: M. Südholt, C. Consel (Eds.), Object-Oriented Technology. VIII, 157 pages. 2007.

Vol. 4364: T. Kühne (Ed.), Models in Software Engineering. XI, 332 pages. 2007.

Vol. 4355: J. Julliand, O. Kouchnarenko (Eds.), B 2007: Formal Specification and Development in B. XIII, 293 pages. 2006.

Vol. 4354: M. Hanus (Ed.), Practical Aspects of Declarative Languages. X, 335 pages. 2006.

Vol. 4350: M. Clavel, F. Durán, S. Eker, P. Lincoln, N. Martí-Oliet, J. Meseguer, C. Talcott, All About Maude - A High-Performance Logical Framework. XXII, 797 pages. 2007.

Vol. 4348: S. Tucker Taft, R.A. Duff, R.L. Brukardt, E. Plödereder, P. Leroy, Ada 2005 Reference Manual. XXII, 765 pages. 2006.

Vol. 4346: L. Brim, B. Haverkort, M. Leucker, J. van de Pol (Eds.), Formal Methods: Applications and Technology. X, 363 pages. 2007.

Vol. 4344: V. Gruhn, F. Oquendo (Eds.), Software Architecture. X, 245 pages. 2006.

Vol. 4340: R. Prodan, T. Fahringer, Grid Computing. XXIII, 317 pages. 2007.

Vol. 4336: V.R. Basili, D. Rombach, K. Schneider, B. Kitchenham, D. Pfahl, R.W. Selby (Eds.), Empirical Software Engineering Issues. XVII, 193 pages. 2007.

Vol. 4326: S. Göbel, R. Malkewitz, I. Iurgel (Eds.), Technologies for Interactive Digital Storytelling and Entertainment. X, 384 pages. 2006.

Vol. 4323: G. Doherty, A. Blandford (Eds.), Interactive Systems. XI, 269 pages. 2007.

Vol. 4322: F. Kordon, J. Sztipanovits (Eds.), Reliable Systems on Unreliable Networked Platforms. XIV, 317 pages. 2007.

Vol. 4309: P. Inverardi, M. Jazayeri (Eds.), Software Engineering Education in the Modern Age. VIII, 207 pages. 2006.

Vol. 4294: A. Dan, W. Lamersdorf (Eds.), Service-Oriented Computing - ICSOC 2006. XIX, 653 pages. 2006.

Vol. 4290: M. van Steen, M. Henning (Eds.), Middleware 2006. XIII, 425 pages. 2006.

Vol. 4279: N. Kobayashi (Ed.), Programming Languages and Systems. XI, 423 pages. 2006.

Vol. 4262: K. Havelund, M. Núñez, G. Roşu, B. Wolff (Eds.), Formal Approaches to Software Testing and Runtime Verification. VIII, 255 pages. 2006.

Vol. 4260: Z. Liu, J. He (Eds.), Formal Methods and Software Engineering. XII, 778 pages. 2006.

Vol. 4257: I. Richardson, P. Runeson, R. Messnarz (Eds.), Software Process Improvement. XI, 219 pages. 2006.

Vol. 4242: A. Rashid, M. Aksit (Eds.), Transactions on Aspect-Oriented Software Development II. IX, 289 pages. 2006.

Vol. 4229: E. Najm, J.-F. Pradat-Peyre, V.V. Donzeau-Gouge (Eds.), Formal Techniques for Networked and Distributed Systems - FORTE 2006. X, 486 pages. 2006.

Vol. 4227: W. Nejdl, K. Tochtermann (Eds.), Innovative Approaches for Learning and Knowledge Sharing. XVII, 721 pages. 2006.

Vol. 4218: S. Graf, W. Zhang (Eds.), Automated Technology for Verification and Analysis. XIV, 540 pages. 2006.

Vol. 4214: C. Hofmeister, I. Crnković, R. Reussner (Eds.), Quality of Software Architectures. X, 215 pages. 2006.

Vol. 4204: F. Benhamou (Ed.), Principles and Practice of Constraint Programming - CP 2006. XVIII, 774 pages. 2006.

Vol. 4199: O. Nierstrasz, J. Whittle, D. Harel, G. Reggio (Eds.), Model Driven Engineering Languages and Systems. XVI, 798 pages. 2006.

Vol. 4192: B. Mohr, J.L. Träff, J. Worringen, J.J. Dongarra (Eds.), Recent Advances in Parallel Virtual Machine and Message Passing Interface. XVI, 414 pages. 2006.

Vol. 4184: M. Bravetti, M. Núñez, G. Zavattaro (Eds.), Web Services and Formal Methods. X, 289 pages. 2006.

Vol. 4166: J. Górski (Ed.), Computer Safety, Reliability, and Security. XIV, 440 pages. 2006.

Vol. 4158: L.T. Yang, H. Jin, J. Ma, T. Ungerer (Eds.), Autonomic and Trusted Computing. XIV, 613 pages. 2006.

Vol. 4157: M. Butler, C. Jones, A. Romanovsky, E. Troubitsyna (Eds.), Rigorous Development of Complex Fault-Tolerant Systems. X, 403 pages. 2006.

Vol. 4143: R. Lämmel, J. Saraiva, J. Visser (Eds.), Generative and Transformational Techniques in Software Engineering. X, 471 pages. 2006.

Vol. 4134: K. Yi (Ed.), Static Analysis. XIII, 443 pages. 2006.

Vol. 4119: C. Dony, J.L. Knudsen, A. Romanovsky, A.R. Tripathi (Eds.), Advanced Topics in Exception Handling Techniques. X, 302 pages. 2006.

Vol. 4111: F.S. de Boer, M.M. Bonsangue, S. Graf, W.-P. de Roever (Eds.), Formal Methods for Components and Objects. VIII, 447 pages. 2006.

Vol. 4089: W. Löwe, M. Südholt (Eds.), Software Composition. X, 339 pages. 2006.

Vol. 4085: J. Misra, T. Nipkow, E. Sekerinski (Eds.), FM 2006: Formal Methods. XV, 620 pages. 2006.

Vol. 4079: S. Etalle, M. Truszczyński (Eds.), Logic Programming. XIV, 474 pages. 2006.

Vol. 4067: D. Thomas (Ed.), ECOOP 2006 - Object-Oriented Programming. XIV, 527 pages. 2006.

Vol. 4066: A. Rensink, J. Warmer (Eds.), Model Driven Architecture - Foundations and Applications. XII, 392 pages. 2006.

Vol. 4063: I. Gorton, G.T. Heineman, I. Crnković, H.W. Schmidt, J.A. Stafford, C.A. Szyperski, K. Wallnau (Eds.), Component-Based Software Engineering. XI, 394 pages. 2006.

Vol. 4054: A. Horváth, M. Telek (Eds.), Formal Methods and Stochastic Models for Performance Evaluation. VIII, 239 pages. 2006.